Elmira Prison Camp Roster

Volume III

Elmira Prison Camp Roster

Volume III, O-Z

By

Richard H. Triebe

First published by Coastal Books

ISBN—13: 978-0-9798965-9-0

ISBN—10: 0-9798965-9-2

Cover photograph:
 This photograph was taken from the observatory and shows Confederate prisoners outside their barracks.

Other books by this author:

Confederate Fort Fisher, ISBN 1484032497

Elmira Prisoner of War Camp, ISBN 1539496791

Fort Fisher to Elmira, ISBN 1530023238

Point Lookout Prison Camp and Hospital, ISBN 1495310140

On A Rising Tide, ISBN 1-4208-7849-2

Port Royal, ISBN 0-9798-9650-9

Printed in the United States of America

This book is printed on acid-free paper.

Coastal Books

Acknowledgements

I owe a debt of gratitude to these people and institutions. I wish to thank Tom Fagart for his help in furnishing important Elmira Prison documents. Also, I want to thank Joe Beasley for helping me with the Excel Spreadsheet regarding the prisoners. I also wish to commend the Federal Army for its meticulous record keeping. Without the prisoners records this book would not have been possible. I also owe a debt of gratitude to the National Archives for storing these records in such an organized manner.

Table of Contents

Roster of Prisoners Volume III, O-Z
July 6, 1864-July 5, 1865

All prisoners who died are buried in Woodlawn National Cemetery,
Elmira, New York, unless otherwise noted.

Name & Rank	Age	Enlisted	Regiment and State	Where Captured	Prison	Remarks
Oakley, Asa D. Sergeant	Unk	December 9, 1861, Camp Trousdale, Tennessee	Co. D, 44th Tennessee Infantry	June 17, 1864, Petersburg, Virginia	Point Lookout, Maryland, transferred to Elmira Prison, NY, July 23, 1864	Oath of Allegiance May 12, 1865
Oakley, John D. Private	28	August 30, 1863, Camp Holmes, Near Raleigh, North Carolina	Co. J, 4th North Carolina Infantry	May 20, 1864, Spotsylvania Court House, Virginia	Point Lookout, Maryland, transferred to Elmira Prison, NY, July 12,1864	Oath of Allegiance June 22, 1865
Oakley, Moses L. Private	Unk	July 21, 1862, Camp Holmes, Raleigh, North Carolina	Co. E, 35th North Carolina Infantry	June 17, 1864, Petersburg, Virginia	Point Lookout, Maryland, transferred to Elmira Prison, NY, July 30, 1864	Oath of Allegiance June 12, 1865
Oaks, James Private	Unk	January 22, 1864, Bristol, Tennessee	Co. I, 14th Tennessee Infantry	May 24, 1864, Hanover Junction, Virginia	Point Lookout, Maryland, transferred to Elmira Prison, NY, July 12, 1864	Died November 9, 1864 of Angeioleucitis, Grave 782
Oaks, Robert M. Private	38	January 27, 1863, Rockingham County, Virginia	Captain J. W. Carter's Co., Stewart's Horse Artillery, Virginia	September 14, 1863, Near Culpepper Court House, Virginia	Point Lookout, Maryland, transferred to Elmira Prison, NY, August 18, 1864	Exchanged February 25, 1865 at Boulware's or Cox Wharf on the James River, Virginia
Oats, J. P. Private	19	December 23, 1861, Georgetown, South Carolina	Co. B, 21st South Carolina Infantry	January 15, 1865, Fort Fisher, North Carolina	February 1, 1865, Elmira Prison Camp, New York	Oath of Allegiance July 7, 1865
Oats, John C. Private	Unk	Unknown	Co. G, 36th Regiment, 2nd North Carolina Artillery	January 15, 1865, Fort Fisher, North Carolina	February 1, 1865, Elmira Prison Camp, New York	Oath of Allegiance June 23, 1865

Name & Rank	Age	Enlisted	Regiment and State	Where Captured	Prison	Remarks
Oberst, Christian Sergeant	21	May 27, 1861, Memphis, Tennessee	Co. B, 1st Tennessee Heavy Artillery	August 23, 1864, Fort Morgan, Alabama	Fort Columbus, NY Harbor. Transferred February 4, 1865 Elmira, Prison Camp, NY	Exchanged March 10, 1865 at Boulware's Wharf on the James River, Virginia
Oberst, S. W. Private	24	May 27, 1861, Memphis, Tennessee	Co. L, 1st Jackson's Tennessee Heavy Artillery	August 23, 1864, Fort Morgan, Alabama.	New Orleans, Louisiana transferred to Elmira Prison, NY, December 4, 1864.	Exchanged February 25, 1865 at Boulware's or Cox Wharf on the James River, Virginia
Oberst, William Private	24	September 23, 1862, Vicksburg, Mississippi	Co. L, 1st Jackson's Tennessee Heavy Artillery	August 23, 1864, Fort Morgan, Alabama.	New Orleans, Louisiana transferred to Elmira Prison, NY, December 4, 1864.	Exchanged February 25, 1865 at Boulware's or Cox Wharf on the James River, Virginia
O'Brian, Edward Sergeant	Unk	August 7, 1861, Wilmington, North Carolina	Co. H, 8th North Carolina Infantry	June 3, 1864, Gaines Farm Cold Harbor, Virginia	Point Lookout, Maryland, transferred to Elmira Prison, NY, July 12, 1864	Died October 2, 1864 of Pneumonia Grave No. 621
O'Brian, John Private	Unk	August 1, 1861, Brunswick, Georgia	Co. A, 26th Georgia Infantry	July 12, 1864, Near Washington, DC	Old Capital Prison, Washington DC. Transferred to Elmira Prison Camp, New York, July 25, 1864.	Oath of Allegiance May 15, 1865
O'Briant, William Private	26	March 17, 1862, Murfreesboro, North Carolina	Co. A, 24th North Carolina Infantry	June 17, 1864, Petersburg, Virginia	Point Lookout, Maryland, transferred to Elmira Prison, NY, July 30, 1864	Died March 8, 1865 of Typhoid Fever, Grave No. 2366
O'Brien, John Sailor	Unk	Unknown	Confederate States Navy	January 15, 1865, Fort Fisher, North Carolina	February 1, 1865, Elmira Prison Camp, New York	Oath of Allegiance May 14, 1865
O'Brien, John Civilian	Unk	Unknown	Citizen of Louisiana	July 27, 1864, New Orleans, Louisiana	New Orleans, Louisiana, Transferred to Elmira Prison, New York, November 19, 1864	Exchanged March 10, 1865 at Boulware's Wharf on the James River, Virginia

Name & Rank	Age	Enlisted	Regiment and State	Where Captured	Prison	Remarks
O'Brien, M. J. Private	Unk	April 30, 1861, Camp Moore, New Orleans, Louisiana	Co. H, 5th Louisiana Infantry	November 7, 1863, Rappahan-nock, Virginia	Point Lookout, Maryland, transferred to Elmira Prison, NY, July 12,1864	Died Month and Date Unknown 1865 of Unknown Disease. No Grave Found in Woodlawn Cemetery, Elmira NY.
O'Brien, William Private	50	June 24, 1861, Camp Moore, Louisiana	Co. F, 6th Louisiana Infantry	May 5, 1864, Wilderness, Virginia	Point Lookout, Maryland, transferred to Elmira Prison, NY, August 17, 1864	Oath of Allegiance May 15, 1865
O'Brien, William Private	Unk	July 27, 1861, New Orleans, Louisiana	Co. A, 14th Louisiana Infantry	May 12, 1864, Spotsylvania Court House, Virginia	Point Lookout, Maryland, transferred to Elmira Prison, NY, July 25, 1864	Exchanged February 13, 1865 at Boulware's wharf on the James River, Virginia
O'Bryan, R. S. Private	Unk	April 3, 1862, Bryan County, Georgia	Co. H, 7th Georgia Cavalry	June 11, 1864, Trevilian Station, Louisa Court House, Virginia	Point Lookout, Maryland, transferred to Elmira Prison, NY, July 25, 1864	Exchanged October 29, 1864, at Venus Point, Savannah River, GA.
O'Connor, Daniel Private	27	August 15, 1861, Athens, Georgia	Co. C, Cobb's Legion Georgia	September 23, 1863, Madison County, Virginia. Gunshot Wound Left Leg, Amp-utated Leg.	Old Capital Prison, Washington, DC transferred to Elmira Prison, NY, August 27, 1864	Exchanged February 13, 1865 at Boulware's or Cox Wharf on the James River, Virginia
O'Connor, John A. Private	25	May 10, 1861, New Orleans, Louisiana	Co. E, 5th Louisiana Infantry	May 12, 1864, Spotsylvania Court House, Virginia	Point Lookout, Maryland, transferred to Elmira Prison, NY, August 17, 1864	Oath of Allegiance May 17, 1865
Odam, J. J. Sergeant	Unk	September 2, 1862, Butler County, Alabama	Co. A, 1st Alabama Artillery	August 23, 1864, Fort Morgan, Alabama.	New Orleans, Louisiana transferred to Elmira Prison, NY, December 4, 1864.	Died February 25, 1865 of Chronic Diarrhea, Grave No. 2276

Name & Rank	Age	Enlisted	Regiment and State	Where Captured	Prison	Remarks
Odell, Joel R. Private	19	December 28, 1861, Springfield, Missouri	Co. F, 1st Missouri Cavalry	May 17, 1863, Big Black Bridge, Champion Hill, Mississippi	Point Lookout, Maryland, transferred to Elmira Prison, NY, August 18, 1864	Exchanged February 13, 1865 at Boulware's wharf on the James River, Virginia
Odell, John Private	Unk	June 25, 1861, Wytheville, Virginia	Co. I, 50th Virginia Infantry	May 12, 1864, Spotsylvania Court House, Virginia	Point Lookout, Maryland, transferred to Elmira Prison, NY, August 2, 1864	Oath of Allegiance June 23, 1865
Odell, Levi Private	45	February 22, 1864, Dublin, Virginia	Co. C, 4th Virginia Infantry	May 13, 1864, Spotsylvania Court House, Virginia. Gunshot Wound Hip.	Old Capital Prison, Washington DC. Transferred to Elmira Prison Camp, New York, July 25, 1864.	Exchanged October 29, 1864, at Venus Point, Savannah River, GA.
Odell, Robert Private	Unk	June 25, 1861, Wytheville, Virginia	Co. I, 50th Virginia Infantry	May 12, 1864, Spotsylvania Court House, Virginia	Point Lookout, Maryland, transferred to Elmira Prison, NY, August 2, 1864	Exchanged October 29, 1864, at Venus Point, Savannah River, GA.
Oden, William W. W. Private	Unk	March 9, 1861, Wetumpka, Alabama	Co. E, 1st Battalion Alabama Artillery	August 23, 1864, Fort Morgan, Alabama	Steam Press No. 4, New Orleans, Louisiana transferred to Elmira October 8, 1864.	Died January 30, 1865 of Pneumonia, Grave No. 1799
Odle, Andrew J. Private	Unk	September 13, 1862, Kinston, North Carolina	Co. D, 5th North Carolina Cavalry	May 12, 1864, Spotsylvania Court House, Virginia	Point Lookout, Maryland, transferred to Elmira Prison, NY, July 25, 1864	Oath of Allegiance May 13, 1865
Odom, A. J. Private	Unk	August 11, 1861, Gwinnett, Georgia	Co. H, 16th Georgia Infantry	June 1, 1864, Cold Harbor, Virginia	Point Lookout, Maryland, transferred to Elmira Prison, NY, July 12, 1864	Oath of Allegiance June 16, 1865
Odom, Alfred Private	Unk	March 10, 1864, Camp Holmes, North Carolina	Co. F, 32nd North Carolina Infantry	May 10, 1864, Wilderness, Virginia	Point Lookout, Maryland, transferred to Elmira Prison, NY, August 6, 1864	Died November 20, 1864 of Chronic Diarrhea, Grave No. 949

Name & Rank	Age	Enlisted	Regiment and State	Where Captured	Prison	Remarks
Odom, Arnold Private	24	November 28, 1862, Fort Fisher, North Carolina	Co. J, 36th Regiment, 2nd North Carolina Artillery	January 15, 1865, Fort Fisher, North Carolina	February 1, 1865, Elmira Prison Camp, New York	Exchanged March 14, 1865 at Boulware's Wharf on the James River, Virginia
Odom, Daniel Private	Unk	May 9, 1862, Reidsville, Georgia	Co. H, 61st Georgia Infantry	May 20, 1864, Spotsylvania Court House, Virginia	Point Lookout, Maryland, transferred to Elmira Prison, NY, July 3, 1864	Exchanged March 10, 1865 at Boulware's Wharf on the James River, Virginia
Odom, Hansford A. Private	Unk	January 18, 1864, Butler County, Alabama	Co. G, 12th Alabama Infantry	July 16, 1864, Frederick, Maryland	Old Capital Prison, Washington DC. Transferred to Elmira Prison Camp, NY, July 25, 1864.	Died October 24, 1864 of Chronic Diarrhea, Grave No. 862
Odom, J. H. Corporal	Unk	September 2, 1862, Butler County, Alabama	Co. A, 1st Alabama Artillery	August 23, 1864, Fort Morgan, Alabama.	New Orleans, Louisiana transferred to Elmira Prison, NY, December 4, 1864.	Died January 4, 1865 of Chronic Diarrhea, Grave No. 1251
Odom, John H. Private	Unk	August 21, 1861, Conyers, Georgia	Co. B, 35th Georgia Infantry	May 5, 1864, Wilderness, Virginia	Point Lookout, Maryland, transferred to Elmira Prison, NY, August 17, 1864	Died October 11, 1864 of Phthisis Pulmonalis, Grave No. 577
Odom, Ruffin Private	Unk	March 15, 1864, Orange County Court House, North Carolina	Co. G, 3rd North Carolina Infantry	May 12, 1864, Near Spotsylvania County Court House, Virginia	Point Lookout, Maryland, transferred to Elmira Prison, NY, August 14, 1864	Exchanged October 29, 1864, at Venus Point, Savannah River, GA.
Odom, William B. Sergeant	21	December 25, 1861, Bennettsville, South Carolina	Co. F, 21st South Carolina Infantry	January 15, 1865, Fort Fisher, North Carolina	February 1, 1865, Elmira Prison Camp, New York	Oath of Allegiance July 26, 1865
O'Donnell, Phillip Private	18	March 13, 1862, Danville, Virginia	Co. C, 5th Virginia Cavalry	June 11, 1864, Louisa Court House, Trevilian Station, Virginia	Point Lookout, Maryland, transferred to Elmira Prison, NY, July 30, 1864	Oath of Allegiance June 19, 1865

Name & Rank	Age	Enlisted	Regiment and State	Where Captured	Prison	Remarks
Odum, Ferdinand G. Sergeant	22	May 18, 1861, Lumberton, North Carolina	Co. D, 18th North Carolina Infantry	May 12, 1865, Spotsylvania Court House, Virginia. Gunshot Left Foot.	Old Capital Prison, Washington D. C. Transferred to Elmira Prison, NY, August 12, 1864	Oath of Allegiance June 23, 1865
O'Farrell, John Private	Unk	February 15, 1864, Lafayette, Louisiana	Co. G, Ogden's Louisiana Cavalry	September 29, 1864, Natchez, Mississippi	New Orleans, Louisiana transferred to Elmira November 19, 1864.	Exchanged February 13, 1865 at Boulware's wharf on the James River, Virginia
Offlighter, George W. Private	Unk	May 27, 1861, Staunton, Virginia	Co. D, 25th Virginia Infantry	May 12, 1864, Spotsylvania Court House, Virginia	Point Lookout, Maryland, transferred to Elmira Prison, NY, August 2, 1864	Exchanged October 29, 1864 at Venus Point, Savannah River, GA.
Ogburn, Joseph P. Sergeant	23	October 4, 1861, Wake County, North Carolina	Co. C, 31st North Carolina Infantry	June 1, 1864, Cold Harbor, Virginia	Point Lookout, Maryland, transferred to Elmira Prison, NY, July 12, 1864	Oath of Allegiance June 14, 1865
Oglesby, Benjamin F. Private	Unk	February 19, 1862, Burton's Farm, Virginia	Co. C, 26th Virginia Infantry	June 17, 1864, Petersburg, Virginia	Point Lookout, Maryland, transferred to Elmira Prison, NY, July 30,1864	Died March 28, 1865 of Variola (Smallpox), Grave No. 2495
Oglesby, George W. Private	Unk	March 8, 1863, Burton's Farm, Virginia	Co. G, 26th Virginia Infantry	June 15, 1864, Near Petersburg, Virginia	Point Lookout, Maryland, transferred to Elmira Prison, NY, July 12, 1864	Exchanged 10/29/64. Died 1/?/65 of Chronic Diarrhea at CSA Hospital, Danville, VA.
Oglesby, Richard A. Private	26	June 2, 1861, Little Plymouth, Virginia	Co. G, 26th Virginia Infantry	June 15, 1864, Petersburg, Virginia	Point Lookout, Maryland, transferred to Elmira Prison, NY, July 30, 1864	Died September 19, 1864 of Chronic Diarrhea, Grave No. 503
Oglesby, Thomas L. Private	Unk	September 10, 1861, Covington, Georgia	Co. D, 3rd Battalion Georgia Sharp Shooters	August 16, 1864, Front Royal, Virginia	Old Capital Prison, Washington, DC transferred to Elmira Prison, NY, August 29, 1864	Oath of Allegiance June 16, 1865

Name & Rank	Age	Enlisted	Regiment and State	Where Captured	Prison	Remarks
Oglesby, William H. Private	Unk	March 22, 1864, Decatur, Georgia	Co. A, 12th Georgia Infantry	May 6, 1864, Wilderness, Virginia	Point Lookout, Maryland, transferred to Elmira Prison, NY, July 23, 1864	Oath of Allegiance December 9, 1864. Early Release per Lincoln's Proclamation, 12/8/1863.
O'Hara, Henry Sergeant	Unk	March 9, 1861, Selma, Alabama	Co. C, 1st Battalion Alabama Artillery	August 23, 1864, Fort Morgan, Alabama	New Orleans, Louisiana transferred to Elmira Prison, NY, December 4, 1864.	Oath of Allegiance May 17, 1865
Oiler, George W. Private	Unk	Monroe Draft Conscript, Virginia	Co. A, 26th Battalion, Virginia Infantry	May 31, 1864, Cold Harbor, Virginia	Point Lookout, Maryland, transferred to Elmira Prison, NY, July 12, 1864	Oath of Allegiance July 11, 1865
O'Keefe, Michael Sergeant	Unk	April 25, 1861, New Orleans, Louisiana	Co. E, 1st Louisiana Infantry	May 12, 1864, Spotsylvania Court House, Virginia	Point Lookout, Maryland, transferred to Elmira Prison, NY, July 11, 1864	Oath of Allegiance May 15, 1865
O'Kennon, John Private	Unk	Unknown	Co. B, Hood's Battalion, Virginia Reserves	June 15, 1864, Petersburg, Virginia	Point Lookout, Maryland, transferred to Elmira Prison, NY, July 30, 1864	Exchanged October 29, 1864 at Venus Point, Savannah River, GA.
O'Leary, Michael Private	Unk	April 4, 1861, Vicksburg, Mississippi	Co. G, 48th Mississippi Infantry	June 13, 1864, White Oak Swamp, Gaines Mill, Virginia	Point Lookout, Maryland, transferred to Elmira Prison, NY, July 30, 1864	Oath of Allegiance May 15, 1865
Oliff, Henry J. Private	Unk	September 1, 1861, Eden Station, Georgia	Co. D, 61st Georgia Infantry	May 12, 1864, Spotsylvania Court House, Virginia	Point Lookout, Maryland, transferred to Elmira Prison, NY, July 30, 1864	Transferred for Exchange 10/11/64. Died 10/17/64 of Unknown Causes at US Army Hospital Baltimore, MD
Oliff, Richard A. Private	Unk	March 5, 1862, Fort Lowry, Virginia	Co. E, 55th Virginia Infantry	May 6, 1864, Wilderness, Virginia	Point Lookout, Maryland, transferred to Elmira Prison, NY, August 14, 1864	Exchanged October 29, 1864, at Venus Point, Savannah River, GA.

Name & Rank	Age	Enlisted	Regiment and State	Where Captured	Prison	Remarks
Olive, D. H. Private	31	July 15, 1862, Raleigh, North Carolina	Co. G, 1st North Carolina Infantry	May 12, 1864, Wilderness, Spotsylvania Court House, Virginia	Point Lookout, Maryland, transferred to Elmira Prison, NY, August 6, 1864	Oath of Allegiance June 21, 1865
Olive, James H. Private	28	February 12, 1862, Raleigh, North Carolina	Co. J, 3rd North Carolina Cavalry	May 27, 1864, Hanover, Virginia	Point Lookout, Maryland, transferred to Elmira Prison, NY, July 12, 1864	Died March 1, 1865 of Chronic Diarrhea, Grave No. 2106. Name Oliver on Headstone.
Oliver, Franklin Private	Unk	October 25, 1862, Chaffin's Farm, Virginia	Co. C, 26th North Carolina Infantry	June 17, 1864, Near Petersburg, Virginia	Point Lookout, Maryland, transferred to Elmira Prison, NY, July 30, 1864	Transferred for Exchange 10/11/64. Died 10/26/64 of Diarrhea and Scurvy at US Army Hospital, Baltimore, MD.
Oliver, James C. Private	Unk	April 22, 1862, Athens, Georgia	Co. C, Cobb's Legion Georgia	May 12, 1864, Spotsylvania, Virginia	Point Lookout, Maryland, transferred to Elmira Prison, NY, July 12, 1864	Oath of Allegiance June 16, 1865
Oliver, James D. Private	24	June 3, 1861, Newbern, North Carolina	Co. K, 2nd North Carolina Infantry	May 8, 1864, Wilderness, Virginia	Point Lookout, Maryland, transferred to Elmira Prison, NY, August 14, 1864	Oath of Allegiance June 14, 1865
Oliver, John Private	24	May 18, 1861, Edenton, North Carolina	Co. A, 1st North Carolina Infantry	May 12, 1864, Wilderness, Spotsylvania Court House, Virginia	Point Lookout, Maryland, transferred to Elmira Prison, NY, August 6, 1864	Oath of Allegiance June 21, 1865
Oliver, John L. Private	Unk	April 25, 1864, Carlton's Store, Virginia	Co. C, 26th North Carolina Infantry	June 17, 1864, Near Petersburg, Virginia	Point Lookout, Maryland, transferred to Elmira Prison, NY, July 30, 1864	Exchanged October 29, 1864, at Venus Point, Savannah River, GA.
Oliver, Laughlin J. Private	23	July 1, 1862, Raleigh, North Carolina	Co. D, 33rd North Carolina Infantry	July 14, 1863, Falling Waters, Maryland	Point Lookout, Maryland, transferred to Elmira Prison, NY, August 18, 1864	Exchanged March 10, 1865 at Boulware's Wharf on the James River, Virginia

Name & Rank	Age	Enlisted	Regiment and State	Where Captured	Prison	Remarks
Oliver, P. Private	30	Unknown	No Co., 4th Louisiana Cavalry	October 13, 1864, Lavinia, Louisiana	New Orleans, Louisiana transferred to Elmira November 19, 1864.	Orders for Elmira Prison Camp but Died in Transit December 12, 1864 of Chronic Diarrhea at General Hospital Fort Columbus, NY.
Oliver, Peter Private	29	March 11, 1862, Spring Garden, North Carolina	Co. D, 45th North Carolina Infantry	May 10, 1864, Spotsylvania Court House, Virginia	Point Lookout, Maryland, transferred to Elmira Prison, NY, August 6, 1864	Died March 19, 1865 of Chronic Diarrhea, Grave No. 1729
Oliver, William Private	Unk	June 11, 1861, Drayton, Georgia	Co. F, 12th Georgia Infantry	May 10, 1864, Spotsylvania Court House, Virginia	Point Lookout, Maryland, transferred to Elmira Prison, NY, July 25, 1864	Oath of Allegiance June 19, 1865
Ollie, Alexander Private	Unk	June 17, 1861, Alamance County, North Carolina	Co. E, 6th North Carolina Infantry	July 4, 1864, Gettysburg, Pennsylvania	Old Capital Prison, Washington DC. Transferred to Elmira Prison Camp, New York, July 25, 1864.	Exchanged February 20, 1865 at Boulware's or Cox Wharf on the James River, Virginia
Omear, Washington Private	Unk	Unknown	Co. B, Mosby's Virginia Cavalry	September 6, 1863, Aldie, Virginia	Point Lookout, Maryland, transferred to Elmira Prison, NY, August 18, 1864	Exchanged March 10, 1865 at Boulware's Wharf on the James River, Virginia
O'Nails, W. David Private	Unk	March 22, 1863, Darlington, South Carolina	Co. G, 21st South Carolina Infantry	January 15, 1865, Fort Fisher, North Carolina	February 1, 1865, Elmira Prison Camp, New York	Oath of Allegiance July 11, 1865
O'Nails, Wiley Private	Unk	March 22, 1863, Darlington, South Carolina	Co. G, 21st South Carolina Infantry	January 15, 1865, Fort Fisher, North Carolina	February 1, 1865, Elmira Prison Camp, New York	Exchanged February 20, 1865 at Boulware's or Cox Wharf on the James River, Virginia

Name & Rank	Age	Enlisted	Regiment and State	Where Captured	Prison	Remarks
O'Neal, James Private	Unk	August 1, 1863, Staunton, Virginia	Co. D, 2nd Maryland Cavalry	May 7, 1864, Harpers Ferry, Virginia	Old Capital Prison, Washington DC. Transferred to Elmira Prison Camp, New York, July 25, 1864.	Transferred July 13, 1865 to Elmira Post Hospital. No Further Information Found.
O'Neall, R. E. Private	Unk	August 27, 1862, Lagrange, Georgia	Co. F, 14th Alabama Infantry	May 6, 1864, Wilderness, Virginia	Point Lookout, Maryland, transferred to Elmira Prison, NY, August 17, 1864	Exchanged March 2, 1865 at Akins Landing on the James River, Virginia
O'Neal, William Private	25	May 5, 1862, Salisburry, North Carolina	Co. D, 42nd North Carolina Infantry	June 3, 1864, Gaines Farm Cold Harbor, Virginia	Point Lookout, Maryland, transferred to Elmira Prison, NY, July 12, 1864	Oath of Allegiance July 3, 1865
O'Neill, James Private	Unk	Unknown	Captain Norwood's Home Guard, Florida	September 27, 1864, Marianna, Florida	New Orleans, Louisiana transferred to Elmira November 19, 1864.	Died March 5, 1865 of Pneumonia, Grave No. 2418
Oringer, J. E. Private	Unk	Unknown	Co. K, 10th Louisiana Infantry	May 6, 1864, Spotsylvania Court House, Virginia	Point Lookout, Maryland, transferred to Elmira Prison, NY, July 12, 1864	Exchanged February 25, 1865 at Boulware's or Cox Wharf on the James River, Virginia
Orndorff, Simon Private	Unk	January 1, 1863, Camp Skinker, Virginia	Co. A, 10th Virginia Infantry	May 12, 1864, Spotsylvania Court House, Virginia	Point Lookout, Maryland, transferred to Elmira Prison, NY, August 2, 1864	Oath of Allegiance June 19, 1865
O'Rourk, John Private	Unk	February 3, 1863, Salem, Virginia	Co. I, 26th Battalion, Virginia Infantry	June 2, 1864, Gaines Farm Cold Harbor, Virginia	Point Lookout, Maryland, transferred to Elmira Prison, NY, July 17, 1864	Died December 14, 1864 of Chronic Diarrhea, Grave No. 1120
O'Rourke, Owen E. Private	Unk	July 20, 1861, Wytheville, Virginia	Co. C, 51st Virginia Infantry	July 14, 1864, Rockville, Virginia	Old Capital Prison, Washington DC. Transferred to Elmira Prison Camp, New York, July 25, 1864.	Oath of Allegiance June 14, 1865

Name & Rank	Age	Enlisted	Regiment and State	Where Captured	Prison	Remarks
Orr, Alexander G. Corporal	Unk	November 1, 1862, Lebanon, Tennessee	Co. A, Jackson's 1st Regiment, Tennessee Heavy Artillery	August 23, 1864, Fort Morgan, Alabama	New Orleans, Louisiana transferred to Elmira Prison, NY, December 4, 1864.	Exchanged February 13, 1865 at Boulware's wharf on the James River, Virginia
Orr, Timothy C. Private	23	May 1, 1862, Wilmington, North Carolina	Co. G, 61st North Carolina Infantry	August 27, 1863, Battery Wagner, Morris Island, South Carolina	Point Lookout, Maryland, transferred to Elmira Prison, NY, August 18, 1864	Exchanged March 10, 1865 at Boulware's Wharf on the James River, Virginia
Orr, William H. Private	27	August 23, 1861, Camp Trousdale, Tennessee	Co. D, 23rd Tennessee Infantry	June 17, 1864, Petersburg, Virginia	Point Lookout, Maryland, transferred to Elmira Prison, NY, July 30, 1864	Oath of Allegiance March 15, 1865. Early Release per Lincoln's Proclamation, 12/8/1863.
Orrison, George W. Private	Unk	October 1, 1862, Snickersville, Virginia	Co. C, 35th Virginia Cavalry	July 18, 1863, Hillsboro, Virginia	Point Lookout, Maryland, transferred to Elmira Prison, NY, August 18, 1864	Oath of Allegiance June 16, 1865
Orrison, Jonah L. Private	Unk	July 15, 1861, Leesburg, Virginia	Co. K, 6th Virginia Cavalry	June 9, 1863, Beverly Ford, Brandy Station, Virginia	Point Lookout, Maryland, transferred to Elmira Prison, NY, August 18, 1864	Died October 4, 1864 of Chronic Diarrhea, Grave No. 599. Headstone has Orison.
Osban, J. W. Private	Unk	December 4, 1862, Mount Pleasant, South Carolina	Co. H, 22nd South Carolina Infantry	July 30, 1864, Petersburg, Virginia	Point Lookout, Maryland, transferred to Elmira Prison, NY, August 12, 1864	Oath of Allegiance May 13, 1865
Osborn, Enoch Private	27	August 15, 1862, Statesville, North Carolina	Co. A, 37th North Carolina Infantry	May 12, 1864, Spotsylvania Court House, Virginia	Point Lookout, Maryland, transferred to Elmira Prison, NY, August 12, 1864	Oath of Allegiance May 19, 1865
Osbornd, Hiram Private	25	May 6, 1861, Grove Hill, Alabama	Co. J, 5th Alabama Infantry	July 24, 1863, Manassas Gap, Virginia	Point Lookout, Maryland, transferred to Elmira Prison, NY, August 18, 1864	Exchanged October 29, 1864 at Venus Point, Savannah River, GA.

Name & Rank	Age	Enlisted	Regiment and State	Where Captured	Prison	Remarks
Osborne, Hampden Private	Unk	January 3, 1864, Orange County Court House, North Carolina	Co. B, 53rd North Carolina Infantry	May 8, 1864, Wilderness, Virginia	Point Lookout, Maryland, transferred to Elmira Prison, NY, August 14, 1864	Exchanged October 29, 1864, at Venus Point, Savannah River, GA.
Osborne, Herbert Private	22	July 24, 1861, Union, Virginia	Co. A, 6th Virginia Cavalry	September 14, 1863, Near Culpepper Court House, Virginia	Point Lookout, Maryland, transferred to Elmira Prison, NY, August 18, 1864	Exchanged March 10, 1865 at Boulware's Wharf on the James River, Virginia
Osborne, Joseph Private	Unk	March 21, 1861, Tallapoosa, Alabama	Co. E, 1st Battalion Alabama Artillery	August 23, 1864, Fort Morgan, Alabama	New Orleans, Louisiana transferred to Elmira Prison, NY, December 4, 1864.	Oath of Allegiance May 19, 1865
Osborne, Michael Private	Unk	July 22, 1861, Camp Moore, Louisiana	Co. B, 10th Louisiana Infantry	May 12, 1864, Spotsylvania Court House, Virginia	Point Lookout, Maryland, transferred to Elmira Prison, NY, July 25, 1864	Exchanged March 2, 1865 at Akins Landing on the James River, Virginia
Osboure, William L. Private	Unk	July 2, 1861, Wytheville, Virginia	Co. I, 50th Virginia Infantry	May 12, 1864, Spotsylvania Court House, Virginia	Point Lookout, Maryland, transferred to Elmira Prison, NY, August 2, 1864	Transferred for Exchange 10/11/64. Nothing Further.
O'Shields, John Private	Unk	August 14, 1863, Spartanburg, South Carolina	Co. G, 27th South Carolina Infantry	June 24, 1864, Near Petersburg, Virginia	Point Lookout, Maryland, transferred to Elmira Prison, NY, August 18, 1864	Exchanged October 29, 1864, at Venus Point, Savannah River, GA.
Otey, Jesse Private	Unk	May 25, 1862, Floyd Court House, Virginia	Co. B, 42nd Virginia Infantry	May 12, 1864, Spotsylvania Court House, Virginia	Point Lookout, Maryland, transferred to Elmira Prison, NY, August 2, 1864	Oath of Allegiance June 19, 1865
Ott, Elmore Private	Unk	March 10, 1864, Secessionville, James Island, South Carolina	Co. F, 25th South Carolina Infantry	January 15, 1865, Fort Fisher, North Carolina	February 1, 1865, Elmira Prison Camp, New York	Died March 5, 1865 of Pneumonia, Grave No. 1981. Headstone has William E. Ott.

Name & Rank	Age	Enlisted	Regiment and State	Where Captured	Prison	Remarks
Ott, John D. Private	22	April 21, 1862, Orangeburg, South Carolina	Co. G, 25th South Carolina Infantry	August 21, 1864, Weldon Railroad, Near Petersburg, Virginia. Gunshot Wound Left Thigh, Above Knee.	Old Capital Prison, Washington, DC transferred to Elmira Prison, NY, August 27, 1864	Exchanged February 20, 1865 at Boulware's or Cox Wharf on the James River, Virginia
Ott, Samuel H. Private	Unk	May 9, 1862, Secessionville, James Island, South Carolina	Co. F, 25th South Carolina Infantry	January 15, 1865, Fort Fisher, North Carolina	February 1, 1865, Elmira Prison Camp, New York	Oath of Allegiance July 11, 1865
Ottaway, Robert M. Private	17	February 25, 1864, Fort Fisher, New Hanover County, North Carolina	Co. G, 36th Regiment, 2nd North Carolina Artillery	January 15, 1865, Fort Fisher, North Carolina	February 1, 1865, Elmira Prison Camp, New York	Died May 5, 1865 of Variola (Smallpox), Grave No. 2762
Otters, Cooney Private	25	April 14, 1862, Charlotte, Mecklenburg County, North Carolina	Co. B, 53rd North Carolina Infantry	July 12, 1864, Near Washington, DC	Old Capital Prison, Washington DC. Transferred to Elmira Prison Camp, New York, July 25, 1864.	Died January 24, 1865 of Variola (Smallpox), Grave No. 1611
Otwell, Jesse R. Private	Unk	July 8, 1862, Greensboro, North Carolina	Co. H, 1st North Carolina Infantry	May 12, 1864, Spotsylvania Court House, Virginia	Point Lookout, Maryland, transferred to Elmira Prison, NY, August 6, 1864	Died October 4, 1864 of Intermittent Fever, Grave No. 638
Outlaw, Jackson K. Private	Unk	April 26, 1864, Fort Holmes, Near Raleigh, North Carolina	Co. G, 40th Regiment, 3rd North Carolina Artillery	January 15, 1865, Fort Fisher, North Carolina	February 1, 1865, Elmira Prison Camp, New York	Exchanged February 20, 1865 at Boulware's or Cox Wharf on the James River, Virginia
Outlaw, John Lewis Private	26	February 5, 1862, Winton, Hertford County, North Carolina	Co. C, 3rd Battalion North Carolina Light Artillery	January 15, 1865, Fort Fisher, North Carolina	February 1, 1865, Elmira Prison Camp, New York	Died March 28, 1865 of Pneumonia, Grave No. 2511
Outlaw, R. Private	Unk	Unknown	Co. G, 7th Battalion South Carolina Infantry	May 16, 1864, Near Drury's Bluff, Virginia	Point Lookout, Maryland, transferred to Elmira Prison, NY, August 17, 1864	Exchanged October 29, 1864, at Venus Point, Savannah River, GA.

Name & Rank	Age	Enlisted	Regiment and State	Where Captured	Prison	Remarks
Outlaw, Rufus A. Private	Unk	June 11, 1862, Dublin, Georgia	Co. H, 14th Georgia Infantry	May 12, 1864, Spotsylvania Court House, Virginia. Gunshot Wound Right Leg.	Old Capital Prison, Washington DC. Transferred to Elmira Prison Camp, New York, July 25, 1864.	Oath of Allegiance June 14, 1865
Outten, Edgar A. Sergeant	Unk	July 12, 1861, Norfolk County, Virginia	Co. F, 15th Virginia Cavalry	June 19, 1864, Norfolk County, Virginia	Point Lookout, Maryland, transferred to Elmira Prison, NY, July 25, 1864	Exchanged February 25, 1865 at Boulware's or Cox Wharf on the James River, Virginia
Ouzts, John Private	Unk	July 13, 1861, Hartwell, Georgia	Co. C, 16th Georgia Infantry	June 1, 1864, Gaines Farm Cold Harbor, Virginia	Point Lookout, Maryland, transferred to Elmira Prison, NY, July 12, 1864	Oath of Allegiance June 16, 1865
Overback, Henry Private	Unk	June 15, 1864, Camp Holmes, Near Raleigh, North Carolina	Co. K, 22nd North Carolina Infantry	July 1, 1864, Petersburg, Virginia. Came Into Enemy Lines and Surrendered.	Point Lookout, Maryland, transferred to Elmira Prison, NY, July 26,1864	Oath of Allegiance May 15, 1865
Overcash, L. A. Private	25	July 4, 1862, Salisbury, North Carolina	Co. A, 57th North Carolina Infantry	July 12, 1864, Near Washington, DC	Old Capital Prison, Washington DC. Transferred to Elmira Prison Camp, New York, July 25, 1864.	Exchanged October 29, 1864, at Venus Point, Savannah River, GA.
Overstreet, John D. Private	Unk	March 16, 1862, Grove Hill, Alabama	Co. J, 5th Alabama Infantry	May 5, 1864, Wilderness, Virginia	Point Lookout, Maryland, transferred to Elmira Prison, NY, August 17, 1864	Oath of Allegiance June 23, 1865
Overstreet, John W. Private	Unk	April 7, 1862, Gloucester Point, Virginia	Co. H, 34th Virginia Infantry	June 15, 1864, Near Petersburg, Virginia	Point Lookout, Maryland, transferred to Elmira Prison, NY, July 12, 1864	Died June 6, 1865 of Chronic Diarrhea, Grave No. 2893

Name & Rank	Age	Enlisted	Regiment and State	Where Captured	Prison	Remarks
Overstreet, Joseph W. Private	Unk	August 12, 1862, Staunton, Virginia	Co. H, 34th Virginia Infantry	June 15, 1864, Near Petersburg, Virginia	Point Lookout, Maryland, transferred to Elmira Prison, NY, July 12, 1864	Exchanged February 13, 1865 at Boulware's wharf on the James River, Virginia
Overstreet, Samuel S. Private	Unk	August 12, 1862, Staunton, Virginia	Co. H, 34th Virginia Infantry	June 15, 1864, Near Petersburg, Virginia	Point Lookout, Maryland, transferred to Elmira Prison, NY, July 12, 1864	Oath of Allegiance July 3, 1865
Overton, Andrew Corporal	18	July 12, 1861, Halifax County, North Carolina	Co. F, 5th North Carolina Infantry	May 20, 1864, Spotsylvania Court House, Virginia	Point Lookout, Maryland, transferred to Elmira Prison, NY, July 3, 1864	Oath of Allegiance June 14, 1865
Overton, James W. Private	18	April 18, 1861, Jefferson Court House, Virginia	Co. A, 2nd Virginia Infantry	May 12, 1864, Near Spotsylvania Court House, Virginia	Point Lookout, Maryland, transferred to Elmira Prison, NY, August 6, 1864	Oath of Allegiance May 17, 1865
Owen, Amos E. Private	Unk	March 25, 1861, Montgomery, Alabama	Co. F, 1st Battalion Alabama Artillery	August 23, 1864, Fort Morgan, Alabama	Steam Press No. 4 New Orleans, Louisiana transferred to Elmira Prison, NY, October 8, 1864.	Oath of Allegiance May 14, 1865
Owen, Daniel H. Private	Unk	April 3, 1864, Camp Holmes, North Carolina	Co. H, 13th North Carolina Infantry	May 6, 1864, Wilderness, Virginia	Point Lookout, Maryland, transferred to Elmira Prison, NY, July 25, 1864	Exchanged March 2, 1865 at Akins Landing on the James River, Virginia
Owen, George P. Private	Unk	Unknown	Co. E, 37th Virginia Infantry	May 6, 1864, Wilderness, Virginia	Point Lookout, Maryland, transferred to Elmira Prison, NY, July 23, 1864	Oath of Allegiance May 29, 1865
Owen, Harbin Private	Unk	Unknown	Co. J, 3rd North Carolina Infantry	May 6, 1864, Wilderness, Virginia	Point Lookout, Maryland, transferred to Elmira Prison, NY, July 25, 1864	Died October 10, 1864 of Chronic Diarrhea, Grave No. 683

Name & Rank	Age	Enlisted	Regiment and State	Where Captured	Prison	Remarks
Owen, James A. Private	Unk	February 13, 1863, Corbin's Neck, Virginia	Co. E, 42nd Virginia Infantry	May 12, 1864, Near Spotsylvania Court House, Virginia	Point Lookout, Maryland, transferred to Elmira Prison, NY, August 6, 1864	Exchanged March 2, 1865 at Akins Landing on the James River, Virginia
Owen, Jeremiah B. Private	24	August 23, 1861, Camp Trousdale, Tennessee	Co. H, 23rd Tennessee Infantry	June 17, 1864, Petersburg, Virginia	Point Lookout, Maryland, transferred to Elmira Prison, NY, July 30, 1864	Oath of Allegiance May 2, 1865
Owen, John A. Private	Unk	December 18, 1863, Surry County, North Carolina	Co. E, 53rd North Carolina Infantry	May 24, 1864, Hanover Junction, Virginia	Point Lookout, Maryland, transferred to Elmira Prison, NY, July 11, 1864	Died February 16, 1865 of Chronic Diarrhea, Grave No. 2209
Owen, John A. Private	33	July 18, 1861, Urbana, Virginia	Co. C, 55th Virginia Infantry	May 6, 1864, Wilderness, Virginia. Gunshot Wound Knee.	Old Capital Prison, Washington DC. Transferred to Elmira Prison Camp, New York, July 25, 1864.	Exchanged March 2, 1865 at Akins Landing on the James River, Virginia
Owen, John C. Private	24	May 29, 1861, Holly Springs, Mississippi	Co. D, 17th Mississippi Infantry	May 8, 1864, Spotsylvania Court House, Virginia. Gunshot Wound Left Forearm.	Old Capital Prison, Washington, DC transferred to Elmira Prison, NY, August 27, 1864	Oath of Allegiance June 19, 1865
Owen, Joseph Private	Unk	April 3, 1864, Camp Holmes, North Carolina	Co. J, 22nd North Carolina Infantry	May 6, 1864, Wilderness, Virginia	Point Lookout, Maryland, transferred to Elmira Prison, NY, July 25, 1864	Died August 28, 1864 of Chronic Diarrhea, Grave No. 46
Owen, Michael S. Private	19	October 19, 1861, Elizabethtown, Bladen County, North Carolina	Co. J, 36th Regiment, 2nd North Carolina Artillery	January 15, 1865, Fort Fisher, North Carolina	February 1, 1865, Elmira Prison Camp, New York	Died April 19, 1865 of Chronic Diarrhea, Grave No. 1367. Headstone has L. H. Owens.
Owen, Newsom A. Private	Unk	March 4, 1862, Forsyth, Georgia	Co. B, 45th Georgia Infantry	May 20, 1864, Spotsylvania Court House, Virginia	Point Lookout, Maryland, transferred to Elmira Prison, NY, July 3, 1864	Exchanged March 10, 1865 at Boulware's Wharf on the James River, Virginia

Name & Rank	Age	Enlisted	Regiment and State	Where Captured	Prison	Remarks
Owen, Thomas Love Private	18	July 9, 1861, Fort Johnson, Brunswick County, North Carolina	Co. F, 20th North Carolina Infantry	July 4, 1864, Harpers Ferry, Virginia	Old Capital Prison, Washington DC. Transferred to Elmira Prison Camp, New York, July 25, 1864.	Oath of Allegiance June 16, 1865
Owen, Thomas S. Private	25	March 7, 1862, Fort Fisher, North Carolina	Co. J, 36th Regiment, 2nd North Carolina Artillery	January 15, 1865, Fort Fisher, North Carolina	February 1, 1865, Elmira Prison Camp, New York	Oath of Allegiance June 21, 1865
Owen, William R. Private	Unk	August 21, 1861, Conyers, Georgia	Co. B, 35th Georgia Infantry	May 5, 1864, Wilderness, Virginia	Point Lookout, Maryland, transferred to Elmira Prison, NY, August 17, 1864	Oath of Allegiance May 19, 1865
Owens, Dempsey Private	Unk	December 1, 1862, C. C. Parish, South Carolina	Co. E, 5th South Carolina Infantry	July 29, 1864, Petersburg, Virginia	Point Lookout, Maryland, transferred to Elmira Prison, NY, August 12, 1864	Died September 12, 1864 of Chronic Diarrhea, Grave No. 178
Owens, Ed B. Sergeant	Unk	February 3, 1862, Georgetown, South Carolina	Co. F, 4th South Carolina Cavalry	June 11, 1864, Trevilian Station, Louisa Court House, Virginia	Point Lookout, Maryland, transferred to Elmira Prison, NY, July 25, 1864	Exchanged October 29, 1864, at Venus Point, Savannah River, GA.
Owens, George P. Private	Unk	Unknown	Co. E, 37th Virginia Infantry	May 12, 1864, Spotsylvania Court House, Virginia	Point Lookout, Maryland, transferred to Elmira Prison, NY, July 25, 1864	Oath of Allegiance May 29, 1865
Owens, George R. Private	21	May 8, 1862, Wilson, North Carolina	Co. F, 61st North Carolina Infantry	June 16, 1864, Petersburg, Virginia	Point Lookout, Maryland, transferred to Elmira Prison, NY, July 25, 1864	Exchanged March 10, 1865 at Boulware's Wharf on the James River, Virginia
Owens, H. Private	Unk	Unknown	Co. E, 37th Virginia Infantry	May 6, 1864, Wilderness, Virginia	Point Lookout, Maryland, transferred to Elmira Prison, NY, July 23, 1864	Oath of Allegiance May 29, 1865

Name & Rank	Age	Enlisted	Regiment and State	Where Captured	Prison	Remarks
Owens, Henry Private	Unk	January 10, 1862, Columbia, South Carolina	Co. C, 22nd South Carolina Infantry	July 30, 1864, Petersburg, Virginia	Point Lookout, Maryland, transferred to Elmira Prison, NY, August 12, 1864	Died January 7, 1865 of Typhoid Fever, Grave No. 1500
Owens, Henry H. Private	Unk	August 23, 1861, Camp Trousdale, Tennessee	Co. H, 23rd Tennessee Infantry	June 17, 1864, Petersburg, Virginia	Point Lookout, Maryland, transferred to Elmira Prison, NY, July 30, 1864	Exchanged February 25, 1865 at Boulware's or Cox Wharf on the James River, Virginia
Owens, J. A. Private	Unk	May 22, 1863, Pickens, South Carolina	Co. E, 27th South Carolina Infantry	June 24, 1864, Near Petersburg, Virginia	Point Lookout, Maryland, transferred to Elmira Prison, NY, August 18, 1864	Exchanged March 2, 1865 at Akins Landing on the James River, Virginia
Owens, J. C. Corporal	Unk	Unknown	Co. C, 14th Virginia Infantry	April 6, 1865, Sailor's Creek, Virginia	Old Capital Prison, Washington D. C. Transferred to Elmira Prison, NY, May 12, 1865.	Oath of Allegiance July 7, 1865
Owens, J. L. Private	Unk	January 25, 1862, Charleston, South Carolina	Co. E, 27th South Carolina Infantry	June 24, 1864, Near Petersburg, Virginia	Point Lookout, Maryland, transferred to Elmira Prison, NY, August 18, 1864	Oath of Allegiance July 11, 1865
Owens, J. R. B. Private	24	July 13, 1861, Jacksonville, Florida	Co. E, 2nd Florida Infantry	June 25, 1864, Near Petersburg, Florida	Point Lookout, Maryland, transferred to Elmira Prison, NY, July 25, 1864	Oath of Allegiance May 21, 1865
Owens, James A. Private	Unk	February 13, 1863, Corbin's Neck, Virginia	Co. E, 42nd Virginia Infantry	May 12, 1864, Near Spotsylvania Court House, Virginia	Point Lookout, Maryland, transferred to Elmira Prison, NY, August 6, 1864	Exchanged March 2, 1865 at Akins Landing on the James River, Virginia
Owens, Jesse P. Private	20	October 13, 1861, Dawson, Forsyth County, Georgia	Co. N, 38th Georgia Infantry	May 22, 1864, Milford Station, Hanover Junction, Virginia	Point Lookout, Maryland, transferred to Elmira Prison, NY, July 23, 1864	Died August 22, 1864 of Chronic Diarrhea, Grave No. 34, Has Ga Artillery on Headstone.

Name & Rank	Age	Enlisted	Regiment and State	Where Captured	Prison	Remarks
Owens, John R. Private	Unk	Unknown	Co. H, 50th Virginia Infantry	May 12, 1864, Spotsylvania Court House, Virginia	Point Lookout, Maryland, transferred to Elmira Prison, NY, August 2, 1864	Died February 26, 1865 of Variola (Smallpox), Grave No. 2283
Owens, Robert D. Private	21	June 13, 1861, Clarkson, Virginia	Co. J, 26th North Carolina Infantry	June 17, 1864, Near Petersburg, Virginia	Point Lookout, Maryland, transferred to Elmira Prison, NY, July 30, 1864	Oath of Allegiance July 3, 1865
Owens, Samuel Private	Unk	February 20, 1862, Charleston, South Carolina	Co. A, 21st South Carolina Infantry	January 15, 1865, Fort Fisher, North Carolina	February 1, 1865, Elmira Prison Camp, New York	Died February 21, 1865 of Long Fever, Grave No. 2301
Owens, Thomas A. Private	Unk	April 27, 1862, Charleston, South Carolina	Co. C, 22nd South Carolina Infantry	July 30, 1864, Petersburg, Virginia	Point Lookout, Maryland, transferred to Elmira Prison, NY, August 12, 1864	Died October 10, 1864 of Chronic Diarrhea, Grave No. 669
Owens, Thomas S. Private	18	June 7, 1861, Middle Sound, New Hanover County, North Carolina	Co. E, 1st North Carolina Infantry	May 12, 1864, Near Spotsylvania Court House, Virginia	Point Lookout Prison, Maryland. Transferred to Elmira Prison Camp New York August 6, 1864.	Exchanged March 2, 1865. Died April 19, 1865 of Typhoid Fever at Jackson Hospital, Richmond, VA.
Owens, William Private	Unk	January 10, 1862, Columbia, South Carolina	Co. C, 22nd South Carolina Infantry	July 30, 1864, Petersburg, Virginia	Point Lookout, Maryland, transferred to Elmira Prison, NY, August 12, 1864	Died November 29, 1864 of Chronic Diarrhea, Grave No. 987
Owens, William C. Private	19	February 24, 1862, Charleston, South Carolina	Co. K, 25th South Carolina Infantry	January 15, 1865, Fort Fisher, North Carolina	February 1, 1865, Elmira Prison Camp, New York	Died March 21, 1865 of Catarrh, Grave No. 1537
Owens, William Jr. Private	Unk	February 11, 1862, Camp Harlee, Georgetown, South Carolina	Co. A, 21st South Carolina Infantry	January 15, 1865, Fort Fisher, North Carolina	February 1, 1865, Elmira Prison Camp, New York	Died April 26, 1865 of Chronic Diarrhea, Grave No. 1424. Headstone has 22nd SC.
Owins, John C. Private	16	April 9, 1862, Morganton, North Carolina	Co. B, 54th North Carolina Infantry	November 7, 1863, Rappahannock, Virginia	Old Capital Prison, Washington, DC. Transferred to Elmira Prison Camp, NY, Date Unknown.	Died March 30, 1865 of Variola (Smallpox), Grave No. 2540

Name & Rank	Age	Enlisted	Regiment and State	Where Captured	Prison	Remarks
Owry, Alfred S. Sergeant	Unk	April 1, 1863, Wythe County, Virginia	Co. J, 37 Battalion Virginia Cavalry	July 17, 1864, Near Harpers Ferry, Loudoun County, Virginia	Old Capital Prison, Washington DC. Transferred to Elmira Prison Camp, New York, July 25, 1864.	Exchanged February 20, 1865 at Boulware's or Cox Wharf on the James River, Virginia
Ozburn, C. R. Private	Unk	March 2, 1864, Covington, Georgia	Co. H, 13th Georgia Infantry	May 23, 1864, Hanover Junction, Virginia	Point Lookout, Maryland, transferred to Elmira Prison, NY, July 11, 1864	Exchanged March 14, 1865 at Boulware's Wharf on the James River, Virginia
Ozler, T. B. Private	44	August 20, 1862, Camp Near Richmond, Drury's Bluff, Virginia	Co. H, 32nd North Carolina Infantry	May 10, 1864, Spotsylvania, Virginia	Point Lookout, Maryland, transferred to Elmira Prison, NY, August 6, 1864	Died January 23, 1865 of Pneumonia, Grave No. 1606. Name Oyler on Headstone.
Ozment, Charles M. Private	Unk	February 28, 1864, Camp Terrel, Virginia	Co. B, 5th North Carolina Infantry	May 12, 1864, Spotsylvania Court House, Virginia	Point Lookout, Maryland, transferred to Elmira Prison, NY, August 6, 1864	Exchanged February 20, 1865 at Boulware's or Cox Wharf on the James River, Virginia

Name & Rank	Age	Enlisted	Regiment and State	Where Captured	Prison	Remarks
Pace, Henry C. Sergeant	Unk	June 22, 1861, Henry County, Virginia	Co. F, 42nd Virginia Infantry	May 12, 1864, Near Spotsylvania Court House, Virginia	Point Lookout, Maryland, transferred to Elmira Prison, NY, August 6, 1864	Exchanged March 14, 1865 at Boulware's Wharf on the James River, Virginia
Pace, Henry V. Sergeant	23	January 21, 1862, Rolesville, North Carolina	Co. J, 1st North Carolina Infantry	May 12, 1864, Spotsylvania Court House, Virginia	Point Lookout, Maryland, transferred to Elmira Prison, NY, August 6, 1864	Oath of Allegiance June 12, 1865
Pace, John B. F. Corporal	23	October 5, 1861, Hendersonville, North Carolina	Co. G, 35th North Carolina Infantry	June 17, 1864, Near Petersburg, Virginia	Point Lookout, Maryland, transferred to Elmira Prison, NY, July 30, 1864	Oath of Allegiance June 12, 1865

Name & Rank	Age	Enlisted	Regiment and State	Where Captured	Prison	Remarks
Pace, John W. Private	Unk	July 14, 1861, Norfolk, Virginia	Co. E, 3rd Alabama Infantry	May 12, 1864, Spotsylvania Court House, Virginia	Point Lookout, Maryland, transferred to Elmira Prison, NY, August 12, 1864	Exchanged February 25, 1865 at Boulware's or Cox Wharf on the James River, Virginia
Pace, Samuel S. Private	Unk	July 24, 1863, Miller County, Georgia	Co. D, 51st Georgia Infantry	June 3, 1864, Gaines Farm Cold Harbor, Virginia	Point Lookout, Maryland, transferred to Elmira Prison, NY, July 12, 1864	Died August 20, 1864, Rubeola (Measles), Grave No. 109
Pace, W. T. Private	Unk	December 28, 1861, Camp Hampton Legion, South Carolina	Co. F, Holcombe Legion, South Carolina	May 8, 1864, Jarrett's Depot, Virginia	Point Lookout, Maryland, transferred to Elmira Prison, NY, August 17, 1864	Oath of Allegiance June 21, 1865
Pack, Robert S. Private	Unk	August 30, 1862, Camp Hill, Virginia	Co. C, 26th Battalion, Virginia Infantry	June 3, 1864, Gaines Farm Cold Harbor, Virginia	Point Lookout, Maryland, transferred to Elmira Prison, NY, July 17, 1864	Died October 3, 1864 of Chronic Diarrhea, Grave No. 630
Pack, William N. Private	28	August 30, 1862, Camp Hill, Virginia	Co. C, 26th Battalion, Virginia Infantry	June 3, 1864, Gaines Farm Cold Harbor, Virginia	Point Lookout, Maryland, transferred to Elmira Prison, NY, July 17,1864	Exchanged October 29, 1864, at Venus Point, Savannah River, GA.
Paddock, Robert L. Private	Unk	June 1, 1863, Brandon, Tennessee	Co. A, Jackson's 1st Regiment, Tennessee Heavy Artillery	August 23, 1864, Fort Morgan, Alabama	New Orleans, Louisiana transferred to Elmira Prison, NY, December 4, 1864.	Oath of Allegiance January 16, 1865 per Commissary General of Prisoners.
Paden, Andrew W. Private	20	August 1, 1861, Decatur, Georgia	Co. C, Cobb's Georgia Legion	June 1, 1864, Gaines Mill Cold Harbor, Virginia	Point Lookout, Maryland, transferred to Elmira Prison, NY, July 17, 1864	Died April 8, 1865 of Hospital Gangrene, Grave No. 2569
Padgett, Asa J. Private	21	May 10, 1861, Washington, North Carolina	Co. J, 3rd North Carolina Infantry	May 12, 1864, Near Spotsylvania County Court House, Virginia	Point Lookout, Maryland, transferred to Elmira Prison, NY, August 14, 1864	Died September 12, 1864 of Typhoid Fever, Grave No. 180

Name & Rank	Age	Enlisted	Regiment and State	Where Captured	Prison	Remarks
Padgett, F. L. Private	Unk	April 20, 1862, Camp Finnegan, Florida	Co. K, 10th Florida Infantry	July 29, 1864, Petersburg, Virginia	Point Lookout, Maryland, transferred to Elmira Prison, NY, August 12, 1864	Died November 2, 1864 of Pneumonia, Grave No. 751
Padgett, Martin Private	18	March 21, 1861, Baldwin, Florida	Co. F, 11th South Carolina Infantry	August 21, 1864, Weldon Railroad, Near Petersburg, VA. Gunshot Wound Left Hand. Amputation of Four Fingers.	Old Capital Prison, Washington, DC transferred to Elmira Prison, NY, August 27, 1864	Exchanged March 10, 1865 at Boulware's Wharf on the James River, Virginia
Padgett, Timothy D. Private	22	April 22, 1861, City of Norfolk, Virginia	Co. C, 6th Virginia Infantry	July 30, 1864, Petersburg, Virginia	Fort Columbus, N Y Harbor, transferred to Elmira December 4, 1864.	Oath of Allegiance June 21, 1865
Pagard, Thaddeus Private	Unk	September 29, 1863, Petersburg, Virginia	Captain B. H. Smith Company, Virginia Artillery	June 15, 1864, Petersburg, Virginia	Point Lookout, Maryland, transferred to Elmira Prison, NY, July 12, 1864	Exchanged February 25, 1865 at Boulware's or Cox Wharf on the James River, Virginia
Page, Bennett Private	37	February 24, 1863, Fort Caswell, Brunswick County, North Carolina	Co. G, 36th Regiment, 2nd North Carolina Artillery	January 15, 1865, Fort Fisher, North Carolina	February 1, 1865, Elmira Prison Camp, New York	Died March 7, 1865 of Dramatic Pericardis, Grave No. 2400
Page, Henry C. Sergeant	19	September 7, 1861, Albemarle, North Carolina	Co. K, 28th North Carolina Infantry	May 12, 1864, Spotsylvania Court House, Virginia	Point Lookout, Maryland, transferred to Elmira Prison, NY, August 12, 1864	Oath of Allegiance May 17, 1865
Page, J. R. Private	Unk	March 4, 1862, Hartwell, Georgia	Co. C, 16th Georgia Infantry	June 1, 1864, Gaines Farm Cold Harbor, Virginia	Point Lookout, Maryland, transferred to Elmira Prison, NY, July 12, 1864	Died April 1, 1865 of Diarrhea, Grave No. 2584
Page, William Private	Unk	March 7, 1862, Magnolia, Duplin County, North Carolina	Co. B, 3rd North Carolina Infantry	May 12, 1864, Near Spotsylvania Court House, Virginia	Point Lookout, Maryland, transferred to Elmira Prison, NY, August 14, 1864	Oath of Allegiance June 23, 1865

Name & Rank	Age	Enlisted	Regiment and State	Where Captured	Prison	Remarks
Paige, Benjamin G. Private	Unk	May 27, 1861, New Orleans, Louisiana	Co. F, 15th Louisiana Infantry	May 12, 1864, Spotsylvania Court House, Virginia	Point Lookout, Maryland, transferred to Elmira Prison, NY, July 25, 1864	Oath of Allegiance May 15, 1865
Paine, William R. Private	Unk	Unknown	Co. A, 12th Virginia Infantry	July 25, 1864, Winchester, Virginia	Old Capital Prison, Washington D. C. Transferred to Elmira Prison, NY, August 12, 1864	Oath of Allegiance May 29, 1865
Painter, George M. Private	15	March 12, 1864, Bristol, Tennessee	Co. A, 14th Tennessee Infantry	May 6, 1864, Wilderness, Virginia	Point Lookout, Maryland, transferred to Elmira Prison, NY, July 23, 1864	Oath of Allegiance May 19, 1865
Painter, James H. Private	22	May 14, 1861, Orange County Court House, Tennessee	Co. A, 14th Tennessee Infantry	May 12, 1864, Spotsylvania Court House, Virginia	Point Lookout, Maryland, transferred to Elmira Prison, NY, July 3, 1864	Oath of Allegiance and Enlisted in US Army
Painter, M. A. Private	Unk	September 19, 1861, Dalton, Georgia	Co. F, 60th Georgia Infantry	May 6, 1864, Wilderness, Virginia	Old Capital Prison, Washington D. C. Transferred to Elmira Prison, NY, July 14, 1864	Oath of Allegiance June 21, 1865
Pair, J. L. Private	25	April 25, 1864, Halifax County, North Carolina	Co. G, 12th North Carolina Infantry	May 12, 1864, Near Spotsylvania, Virginia	Point Lookout, Maryland, transferred to Elmira Prison, NY, August 14, 1864	Oath of Allegiance July 11, 1865
Palmer, Charles Private	21	March 25, 1861, Luka, Mississippi	Co. C, Jeff Davis Legion, Mississippi Cavalry	June 11, 1864, Louisa Court House, Trevilian Station, Virginia	Point Lookout, Maryland, transferred to Elmira Prison, NY, July 28, 1864	Oath of Allegiance July 3, 1865
Palmer, Edward V. Sergeant	21	April 23, 1861, Gloucester Court House, Virginia	Co. B, 26th Virginia Infantry	June 15, 1864, Near Petersburg, Virginia	Point Lookout, Maryland, transferred to Elmira Prison, NY, July 12, 1864	Exchanged March 10, 1865 at Boulware's Wharf on the James River, Virginia

Name & Rank	Age	Enlisted	Regiment and State	Where Captured	Prison	Remarks
Palmer, Erastus Corporal	23	August 1, 1861, Waynesboro, Georgia	Co. E, Cobb's Legion Georgia	August 16, 1864, Front Royal, Virginia	Old Capital Prison, Washington, DC transferred to Elmira Prison, NY, August 29, 1864	Oath of Allegiance June 19, 1865
Palmer, F. N. Private	Unk	April 25, 1864, Newton, Alabama	Co. K, 6th Alabama Infantry	May 20, 1864, Spotsylvania Court House, Virginia	Point Lookout, Maryland, transferred to Elmira Prison, NY, July 3, 1864	Died August 22, 1864 of Chronic Diarrhea and Rubeola (Measles) Grave No. 491
Palmer, Francis H. Private	27	September 29, 1861, Camp Trousdale, Tennessee	Co. D, 44th Tennessee Infantry	May 16, 1864, Fort Darling, Virginia	Point Lookout, Maryland, transferred to Elmira Prison, NY, July 23, 1864	Oath of Allegiance March 31, 1865
Palmer, Harrison Private	Unk	Unknown	Co. K, 6th North Carolina Infantry	July 10, 1864, Frederick, Middletown, Maryland	Old Capital Prison, Washington DC. Transferred to Elmira Prison Camp New York July 25, 1864.	Oath of Allegiance May 15, 1865
Palmer, John T. Sergeant	Unk	July 30, 1861, Marion, Virginia	Co. D, 4th Virginia Infantry	May 12, 1864 Spotsylvania Court House, Virginia	Point Lookout, Maryland, transferred to Elmira Prison, NY, August 2, 1864. Ward No. 4.	Exchanged February 25, 1865 at Boulware's or Cox Wharf on the James River, Virginia
Palmer, Lewis F. Private	Unk	July 15, 1861, Leesburg, Virginia	Co. K, 6th Virginia Cavalry	August 20, 1864, Near Leesburg, Virginia	Old Capital Prison, Washington, DC transferred to Elmira Prison, NY, August 29, 1864	Exchanged March 14, 1865 at Boulware's Wharf on the James River, Virginia
Palmer, Tiberius Private	Unk	June 22, 1861, Wytheville, Virginia	Co. K, 50th Virginia Infantry	July 16, 1864, Loudoun County, Virginia	Old Capital Prison, Washington DC. Transferred to Elmira Prison Camp New York July 25, 1864.	Oath of Allegiance October 15, 1864 by Orders of Commissary General of Prisoners.

Name & Rank	Age	Enlisted	Regiment and State	Where Captured	Prison	Remarks
Paragoy, John Private	Unk	Unknown	Co. F, 2nd Maryland Infantry	July 23, 1864, Point of Rocks, Maryland	Old Capital Prison, Washington D. C. Transferred to Elmira Prison, NY, August 12, 1864	Exchanged October 29, 1864, at Venus Point, Savannah River, GA.
Parberry, Henry E. Private	Unk	January 15, 1862, Springfield, Missouri	Co. F, 3rd Battalion Missouri Cavalry	May 17, 1863, Big Black Bridge, Champion Hill, Mississippi	Point Lookout, Maryland, transferred to Elmira Prison, NY, August 18, 1864	Exchanged February 25, 1865 at Boulware's wharf on the James River, Virginia
Pardew, William Martin Sergeant	19	October 4, 1861, Raleigh, North Carolina	Co. B, 33rd North Carolina Infantry	July 29, 1864, Petersburg, Virginia	Point Lookout, Maryland, transferred to Elmira Prison, NY, August 12, 1864	Oath of Allegiance July 7, 1865
Pardue, George W. Private	Unk	January 25, 1862, Columbia, South Carolina	Co. A, 22nd South Carolina Infantry	June 15, 1864, Petersburg, Virginia	Point Lookout, Maryland, transferred to Elmira Prison, NY, July 12, 1864	Oath of Allegiance May 29, 1865
Paris, Dickerson Private	Unk	May 10, 1862, Cartersville, Georgia	Co. K, 60th Georgia Infantry	May 20, 1864, Spotsylvania Court House, Virginia	Point Lookout, Maryland, transferred to Elmira Prison, NY, July 3, 1864	Oath of Allegiance June 19, 1865
Parish, William M. Private	18	March 1, 1862, Greensboro, North Carolina	Co. B, 45th North Carolina Infantry	May 10, 1864, Spotsylvania Court House, Virginia	Point Lookout, Maryland, transferred to Elmira Prison, NY, August 6, 1864	Transferred for Exchange 2/20/65. Became Ill on the Route. Oath of Allegiance 3/20/65 at Fort McHenry.
Park, A. Private	19	October 28, 1864, Near Hempstead, Texas	Co. A, 12th Texas Cavalry	August 25, 1864, Bullitt's Bayou, Concordia Parish, Louisiana	New Orleans, Louisiana, Transferred to Elmira Prison, New York, November 19, 1864	Exchanged March 2, 1865. Died March 11, 1865 of Chronic Diarrhea at Wayside Hospital No. 9, Richmond, Virginia

Name & Rank	Age	Enlisted	Regiment and State	Where Captured	Prison	Remarks
Parker, Abner P. Private	Unk	July 15, 1863, Mount Tabor, Forsyth County, North Carolina	Co. C, 3rd Battalion North Carolina Light Artillery	January 15, 1865, Fort Fisher, North Carolina	February 1, 1865, Elmira Prison Camp, New York	Oath of Allegiance June 12, 1865
Parker, Badgegood B. Sergeant	32	December 20, 1861, Chesterfield, South Carolina	Co. E, 21st South Carolina Infantry	January 15, 1865, Fort Fisher, North Carolina	February 1, 1865, Elmira Prison Camp, New York	Died July 11, 1865 of Chronic Diarrhea, Grave No. 2847
Parker, Benjamin Private	18	May 6, 1861, Jacksonville, North Carolina	Co. B, 24th North Carolina Infantry	June 17, 1864, Petersburg, Virginia	Point Lookout, Maryland, transferred to Elmira Prison, NY, July 30, 1864	Died December 5, 1864 of Chronic Diarrhea, Grave No. 1020
Parker, C. H. Private	Unk	Unknown	Captain Chisholm's Co., Alabama Cavalry	September 23, 1864, Euchee Anna, Louisiana	New Orleans, Louisiana transferred to Elmira November 19, 1864.	Exchanged February 20, 1865 at Boulware's wharf on the James River, Virginia
Parker, Edwin Private	Unk	Unknown	Co. D, 4th South Carolina Infantry	Unknown	Point Lookout Prison Camp, Maryland. Transferred to Elmira Prison Camp, NY August 25, 1864	Died October 4, 1864 of Unknown Disease, Grave No. 606
Parker, Ervin M. Private	Unk	February 3, 1862, Georgetown, South Carolina	Co. F, 4th South Carolina Cavalry	June 11, 1864, Trevilian Station, Louisa Court House, Virginia	Point Lookout, Maryland, transferred to Elmira Prison, NY, July 25, 1864	Died February 21, 1865 of Pneumonia, Grave No. 2310. Name Irwin M. Parker on Headstone.
Parker, Everett Private	Unk	June 2, 1863, Wilmington, North Carolina	Co. E, 51st North Carolina Infantry	June 1, 1864, Cold Harbor, Virginia	Point Lookout, Maryland, transferred to Elmira Prison, NY, July 12, 1864	Exchanged October 29, 1864, at Venus Point, Savannah River, GA.
Parker, G. M. Sergeant	Unk	March 4, 1862, Starkville, Lee County, Georgia	Co. B, 51st Georgia Infantry	June 3, 1864, Gaines Farm Cold Harbor, Virginia	Point Lookout, Maryland, transferred to Elmira Prison, NY, July 12, 1864	Oath of Allegiance July 11, 1865

Name & Rank	Age	Enlisted	Regiment and State	Where Captured	Prison	Remarks
Parker, George F. Private	Unk	September 20, 1863, Kinston, North Carolina	Co. F, 10th Regiment, 1st North Carolina Artillery	January 15, 1865, Fort Fisher, North Carolina	February 1, 1865, Elmira Prison Camp, New York	Oath of Allegiance July 11, 1865
Parker, George R. Private	36	July 15, 1862, Fort Caswell, Brunswick County, North Carolina	Co. A, 36th Regiment, 2nd North Carolina Artillery	January 15, 1865, Fort Fisher, North Carolina	February 1, 1865, Elmira Prison Camp, New York	Died June 18, 1865 of Chronic Diarrhea, Grave No. 2808
Parker, J. A. Private	Unk	May 5, 1862, Zebulon, Georgia	Co. H, 53rd Georgia Infantry	June 1, 1864, Gaines Mill Cold Harbor, Virginia	Point Lookout, Maryland, transferred to Elmira Prison, NY, July 17,1864	Exchanged March 2, 1865 at Akins Landing on the James River, Virginia
Parker, J. M. Private	Unk	Unknown	Co. J, 12th Alabama Infantry	May 12, 1864, Spotsylvania Court House, Virginia	Point Lookout, Maryland, transferred to Elmira Prison, NY, August 6, 1864	Exchanged February 20, 1865 at Boulware's or Cox Wharf on the James River, Virginia
Parker, Jackson Private	Unk	March 11, 1863, Macon County, North Carolina	Co. D, 13th Battalion North Carolina Light Artillery	January 15, 1865, Fort Fisher, North Carolina	February 1, 1865, Elmira Prison Camp, New York	Exchanged March 2, 1865 at Akins Landing on the James River, Virginia
Parker, Jacob L. Private	Unk	May 6, 1862, Tuscaloosa, Alabama	Co. A, 41st Alabama Infantry	May 16, 1864, Near Drury's Bluff, Virginia	Point Lookout, Maryland, transferred to Elmira Prison, NY, August 17, 1864	Oath of Allegiance June 23, 1865
Parker, Jacob W. Private	25	March 3, 1862, Wilmington, North Carolina	Co. E, 30th North Carolina Infantry	May 20, 1864, Spotsylvania Court House, Virginia	Point Lookout, Maryland, transferred to Elmira Prison, NY, July 3, 1864	Exchanged March 2, 1865 at Akins Landing on the James River, Virginia
Parker, James F. Private	Unk	September 6, 1862, Statesville, North Carolina	Co. A, 23rd North Carolina Infantry	May 12, 1864, Near Spotsylvania Court House, Virginia	Point Lookout Prison, Maryland. Transferred to Elmira Prison Camp New York August 14, 1864.	Died September 18, 1864 of Chronic Bronchitis, Grave No. 156

Name & Rank	Age	Enlisted	Regiment and State	Where Captured	Prison	Remarks
Parker, John Private	19	December 15, 1864, New Hanover County, North Carolina	Co. D, 13th Battalion North Carolina Light Artillery	January 15, 1865, Fort Fisher, North Carolina	February 1, 1865, Elmira Prison Camp, New York	Exchanged February 20, 1865 at Boulware's or Cox Wharf on the James River, Virginia
Parker, John E. Private	Unk	April 27, 1861, Wetumpka, Alabama	Co. J, 3rd Alabama Infantry	May 12, 1864, Spotsylvania Court House, Virginia	Point Lookout, Maryland, transferred to Elmira Prison, NY, August 12, 1864	Oath of Allegiance June 14, 1865
Parker, John W. Private	24	April 22, 1861, Leesburg, Virginia	Co. C, 17th Virginia Infantry	July 16, 1864, Loudoun County, Virginia	Old Capital Prison, Washington DC. Transferred to Elmira Prison Camp, New York, July 25, 1864.	Exchanged at Venus Point, Savannah River, GA, 11/15/1864
Parker, Joseph Private	Unk	March 1, 1862, Dallas County, Texas	Co. J, 18th Texas Cavalry	July 19, 1864, Rodney, Mississippi	New Orleans, Louisiana, Transferred to Elmira Prison, New York, November 19, 1864	Oath of Allegiance June 19, 1865
Parker, Joseph Private	Unk	June 28, 1862, Poplar Springs, Hall County, Georgia	Co. J, 24th Georgia Infantry	June 1, 1864, Cold Harbor, Virginia	Point Lookout, Maryland, transferred to Elmira Prison, NY, July 12, 1864	Exchanged 2/13/65. Died 3/8/65 of Rheumatism at Jackson Hospital, Richmond, VA.
Parker, Mumford S. Private	19	September 15, 1862, Raleigh, North Carolina	Co. B, 31st North Carolina Infantry	June 1, 1864, Cold Harbor, Virginia	Point Lookout, Maryland, transferred to Elmira Prison, NY, July 12, 1864	Exchanged March 14, 1865 at Boulware's Wharf on the James River, Virginia
Parker, Myrick N. Private	23	September 15, 1862, Camp Mangum, Raleigh	Co. B, 31st North Carolina Infantry	June 1, 1864, Cold Harbor, Virginia	Point Lookout, Maryland, transferred to Elmira Prison, NY, July 12, 1864	Died April 11, 1865 of Pneumonia, Grave No. 2691
Parker, Nathaniel W. Private	Unk	June 15, 1861, Buena Vista, Georgia	Co. K, 12th Georgia Infantry	May 10, 1864, Spotsylvania Court House, Virginia	Point Lookout Prison Camp, Maryland. Transferred to Elmira Prison, NY, July 28, 1864	Died February 5, 1865 of Pneumonia, Grave No. 1900

Name & Rank	Age	Enlisted	Regiment and State	Where Captured	Prison	Remarks
Parker, Pinkney D. Private	Unk	May 16, 1861, Alisona, Tennessee	Co. A, 17th Tennessee Infantry	June 17, 1864, Petersburg, Virginia	Point Lookout, Maryland, transferred to Elmira Prison, NY, July 30, 1864	Exchanged February 25, 1865 at Boulware's or Cox Wharf on the James River, Virginia
Parker, Robert Private	Unk	May 1, 1862, Augusta, Georgia	Co. F, 12th Battalion Georgia Light Artillery	July 15, 1864, Leesburg, Virginia	Old Capital Prison, Washington D. C. Transferred to Elmira Prison, NY, August 12, 1864	Oath of Allegiance May 29, 1865
Parker, T. F. Sergeant	27	January 13, 1862, Darlington District, South Carolina	Co. G, 21st South Carolina Infantry	June 17, 1864, Petersburg, Virginia	Point Lookout, Maryland, transferred to Elmira Prison, NY, July 30, 1864	Oath of Allegiance July 3, 1865
Parker, Thomas J. Private	Unk	March 8, 1862, Rapides Parish, Louisiana	Co. H, 8th Louisiana Infantry	May 12, 1864, Spotsylvania Court House, Virginia	Point Lookout, Maryland, transferred to Elmira Prison, NY, August 17, 1864	Exchanged October 29, 1864, at Venus Point, Savannah River, GA.
Parker, William H. Private	Unk	Unknown	Co. H, 13th Georgia Infantry	July 7, 1864, Near Maryland Heights, Maryland	Old Capital Prison, Washington DC. Transferred to Elmira Prison Camp, New York, July 25, 1864.	Exchanged March 10, 1865 at Boulware's Wharf on the James River, Virginia
Parker, William H. Private	26	July 9, 1861, Antioch, Georgia	Co. F, 21st Georgia Infantry	July 9, 1864, Frederick, Maryland	Old Capital Prison, Washington DC. Transferred to Elmira Prison Camp, New York, July 25, 1864.	Oath of Allegiance May 29, 1865
Parkins, J. A. Private	19	October 12, 1862, Charleston, Virginia	Co. E, 4th Virginia Infantry	May 12, 1864, Near Spotsylvania Court House, Virginia	Point Lookout, Maryland, transferred to Elmira Prison, NY, July 23, 1864	Oath of Allegiance May 15, 1865
Parkman, John B. Private	Unk	August 8, 1861, Pike County, Alabama	Co. F, 5th Alabama Infantry	May 5, 1864, Wilderness, Virginia	Point Lookout, Maryland, transferred to Elmira Prison, NY, August 17, 1864	Exchanged October 29, 1864, at Venus Point, Savannah River, GA.

Name & Rank	Age	Enlisted	Regiment and State	Where Captured	Prison	Remarks
Parks, B. W. Private	Unk	August 15, 1862, Kanawha Court House, Virginia	Co. H, 22nd Virginia Infantry	June 3, 1864, Gaines Farm Cold Harbor, Virginia	Point Lookout, Maryland, transferred to Elmira Prison, NY, July 12, 1864	Oath of Allegiance June 16, 1865
Parks, Britton Private	30	September 7, 1861, Albemarle, North Carolina	Co. K, 28th North Carolina Infantry	May 12, 1864, Near Spotsylvania Court House, Virginia	Point Lookout, Maryland, transferred to Elmira Prison, NY, August 14, 1864	Died April 1, 1865 of Chronic Valve Disease of Heart, Grave No. 2573
Parks, Creed J. Private	Unk	May 8, 1861, Kanawha Court House, Virginia	Co. H, 22nd Virginia Infantry	June 3, 1864, Gaines Farm Cold Harbor, Virginia	Transferred From Point Lookout Prison, MD, July 12, 1864. Train Never Arrived at Elmira Prison Camp, NY.	Died July 15, 1864 in Train Wreck at Shohola, Pennsylvania.
Parks, G. W. Private	Unk	Unknown	Co. G, 34th, North Carolina Infantry	May 24, 1864, Hanover Junction, Virginia	Point Lookout, Maryland, transferred to Elmira Prison, NY, July 12, 1864	Oath of Allegiance May 17, 1865
Parks, Henry D. Private	Unk	September 4, 1862, Butler County, Alabama	Co. A, 1st Battalion Alabama Artillery	August 23, 1864, Fort Morgan, Alabama	New Orleans, Louisiana transferred to Elmira Prison, NY, December 4, 1864.	Died January 18, 1865 of Variola (Smallpox), Grave No. 1433
Parks, Samuel S. Private	Unk	September 6, 1862, Calhoun, Georgia	Co. C, Cobb's Legion Georgia Infantry	June 11, 1864, Trevilian Station, Louisa Court House, Virginia	Point Lookout, Maryland, transferred to Elmira Prison, NY, July 25, 1864	Died January 4, 1865 of Pneumonia, Grave No. 1252
Parks, William Private	Unk	March 18, 1862, Mocksville, Davie County, North Carolina	Co. E, 42nd North Carolina Infantry	June 1, 1864, Gaines Farm Cold Harbor, Virginia	Point Lookout, Maryland, transferred to Elmira Prison, NY, July 12, 1864	Died September 27, 1864 of Chronic Diarrhea, Grave No. 381
Parks, William A. Corporal	Unk	March 10, 1863, Montrose, Virginia	Co. A, 15th Virginia Cavalry	September 14, 1863, Near Culpepper Court House, Virginia	Point Lookout, Maryland, transferred to Elmira Prison, NY, August 18, 1864	Oath of Allegiance June 14, 1865

Name & Rank	Age	Enlisted	Regiment and State	Where Captured	Prison	Remarks
Parks, William L. Private	Unk	March 7, 1862, Abingdon, Virginia	Co. H, 37th Virginia Infantry	May 20, 1864, Spotsylvania Court House, Virginia	Point Lookout, Maryland, transferred to Elmira Prison, NY, July 3, 1864	Oath of Allegiance May 29, 1865
Parks, William M. Private	Unk	Unknown	Co. C, 2nd Texas Infantry	April 23, 1864, Cane River, Louisiana	New Orleans, Louisiana, Transferred to Elmira Prison, New York, November 19, 1864	Oath of Allegiance May 15, 1865
Parler, Edwin Private	Unk	October 30, 1862, South Santee, South Carolina	Co. D, 4th South Carolina Cavalry	June 11, 1864, Trevilian Station, Louisa Court House, Virginia	Point Lookout, Maryland, transferred to Elmira Prison, NY, July 25, 1864	Died October 5, 1864 of Chronic Diarrhea, Grave No. 2310
Parley, Charles H. Sergeant	34	June 21, 1861, New Orleans, Louisiana	Co. F, 15th Louisiana Infantry	May 5, 1864, Wilderness, Virginia	Point Lookout, Maryland, transferred to Elmira Prison, NY, July 25, 1864	Oath of Allegiance April 1, 1865
Parmer, John N. Private	Unk	May 21, 1863, Montgomery, Alabama	Co. A, 61st Alabama Infantry	May 12, 1864, Spotsylvania Court House, Virginia	Point Lookout, Maryland, transferred to Elmira Prison, NY, July 30, 1864	Died March 16, 1865 of Diarrhea. No Grave in Woodlawn Cemetery.
Parmer, William R. Private	Unk	November 1, 1861, Pickens, South Carolina	Co. C, 2nd South Carolina Infantry	June 2, 1864, Harbor, Virginia	Point Lookout, Maryland, transferred to Elmira Prison, NY, July 17,1864	Oath of Allegiance May 29, 1865
Parmore, L. B. Private	Unk	August 27, 1862, Henry County, Alabama	Co. A, 1st Battalion Alabama Artillery	August 23, 1864, Fort Morgan, Alabama	New Orleans, Louisiana transferred to Elmira Prison, NY, December 4, 1864.	Died March 18, 1865 of Diarrhea Grave No. 1708. Headstone Has Perymore.
Parnell, Joshua Private	Unk	June 10, 1863, Morris Island, South Carolina	Co. E, 21st South Carolina Infantry	January 15, 1865, Fort Fisher, North Carolina	February 1, 1865, Elmira Prison Camp, New York	Oath of Allegiance June 14, 1865
Parnell, R. N. Private	25	January 1, 1862, Darlington District, South Carolina	Co. B, 21st South Carolina Infantry	June 24, 1864, Near Petersburg, Virginia	Point Lookout, Maryland, transferred to Elmira Prison, NY, August 18, 1864	Exchanged March 2, 1865 at Boulware's Wharf on the James River, Virginia

Name & Rank	Age	Enlisted	Regiment and State	Where Captured	Prison	Remarks
Parnell, T. N. Private	22	December 23, 1861, Georgetown, South Carolina	Co. B, 21st South Carolina Infantry	January 15, 1865, Fort Fisher, North Carolina	February 1, 1865, Elmira Prison Camp, New York	Exchanged March 14, 1865 at Boulware's Wharf on the James River, Virginia
Parnell, Thomas H. Private	Unk	Unknown	Co. H, 2nd North Carolina Infantry	July 13, 1864, Near Washington, DC	Old Capital Prison, Washington DC. Transferred to Elmira Prison Camp, New York, July 25, 1864.	Exchanged October 29, 1864, at Venus Point, Savannah River, GA.
Parnell, William D. Private	18	July 15, 1861, Selma, Alabama	Jeff Davis Alabama Artillery	May 5, 1864, Wilderness, Virginia	Point Lookout, Maryland, transferred to Elmira Prison, NY, August 17, 1864	Transferred For Exchange October 11, 1864 to Point Lookout Prison Camp, MD. Died October 25, 1864.
Parr, John L. Private	Unk	January 30, 1864, Richmond, Virginia	Co. F, 3rd Virginia Cavalry	August 16, 1864, Front Royal, Virginia	Old Capital Prison, Washington, DC transferred to Elmira Prison, NY, August 29, 1864	Oath of Allegiance June 10, 1865
Parram, Joseph Private	Unk	July 8, 1861, Griffin, Georgia	Co. C, 13th Georgia Infantry	May 20, 1864, Spotsylvania Court House, Virginia	Point Lookout, Maryland, transferred to Elmira Prison, NY, July 3, 1864	Exchanged March 10, 1865 at Boulware's Wharf on the James River, Virginia
Parramore, W. T. Private	Unk	July 8, 1861, Griffin, Georgia	Co. C, 13th Georgia Infantry	May 20, 1864, Spotsylvania Court House, Virginia	Point Lookout, Maryland, transferred to Elmira Prison, NY, July 3, 1864	Oath of Allegiance June 30, 1865
Parrett, Hiram Private	Unk	December 9, 1861, Camp Trousdale, Tennessee	Co. J, 44th Tennessee Infantry	May 16, 1864, Near Drury's Bluff, Virginia	Point Lookout, Maryland, transferred to Elmira Prison, NY, August 17, 1864	Exchanged February 25, 1865 at Boulware's or Cox Wharf on the James River, Virginia

Name & Rank	Age	Enlisted	Regiment and State	Where Captured	Prison	Remarks
Parrill, James A. Private	25	June 1, 1861, Romney, Virginia	Co. F, 7th Virginia Cavalry	September 14, 1863, Near Culpepper Court House, Virginia	Point Lookout, Maryland, transferred to Elmira Prison, NY, August 18, 1864	Exchanged February 20, 1865 at Boulware's or Cox Wharf on the James River, Virginia
Parris, Johnson Private	Unk	July 15, 1862, Raleigh, North Carolina	Co. E, 1st North Carolina Infantry	May 12, 1864, Wilderness, Spotsylvania Court House, Virginia	Point Lookout, Maryland, transferred to Elmira Prison, NY, August 6, 1864	Oath of Allegiance May 29, 1865
Parris, W. B. Private	Unk	July 1, 1863, Spartanburg, South Carolina	Co. J, 27th South Carolina Infantry	June 24, 1864, Near Petersburg, Virginia	Point Lookout, Maryland, transferred to Elmira Prison, NY, August 18, 1864	Exchanged October 29, 1864, at Venus Point, Savannah River, GA.
Parrish, A. J. Private	Unk	Unknown	Co. B, 44th Virginia Infantry	May 12, 1864, Spotsylvania Court House, Virginia	Point Lookout, Maryland, transferred to Elmira Prison, NY, August 2, 1864	Died March 21, 1865 of Erysipelas, Grave No. 1543
Parrish, Francis M. Private	Unk	February 1, 1863, Choctaw Bluff, Alabama	Co. A, 21st Alabama Infantry	August 23, 1864 Fort Morgan, Alabama	New Orleans, Louisiana. Transferred to Elmira Prison Camp October 8, 1864	Died June 17, 1865 of Pneumonia, Grave No. 2877. Headstone has T. M.
Parrish, Jackson Private	28	September 3, 1862, Dale County, Alabama	Co. A, 1st Battalion Alabama Artillery	August 23, 1864, Fort Morgan, Alabama	New Orleans, Louisiana transferred to Elmira Prison, NY, December 4, 1864.	Exchanged February 25, 1865 at Boulware's or Cox Wharf on the James River, Virginia
Parrish, John D. Private	22	July 6, 1861, Fort Mason, Texas	Co. H, Yeager's 1st Texas Cavalry	August 26, 1864, Near Morganza, Louisiana	New Orleans, Louisiana, Transferred to Elmira Prison, New York, November 19, 1864	Oath of Allegiance June 16, 1865
Parrish, John F. Private	23	September 15, 1862, Auburn, North Carolina	Co. D, 31st North Carolina Infantry	May 31, 1864, Cold Harbor, Virginia	Point Lookout, Maryland, transferred to Elmira Prison, NY, July 12, 1864	Exchanged March 2, 1865 at Akins Landing on the James River, Virginia

Name & Rank	Age	Enlisted	Regiment and State	Where Captured	Prison	Remarks
Parrish, John W. Private	Unk	February 8, 1863, Camp Ashley, Virginia	Co. E, 6th Virginia Cavalry	May 11, 1864, Henrico County, Virginia	Point Lookout, Maryland, transferred to Elmira Prison, NY, August 17, 1864	Oath of Allegiance June 16, 1865
Parrish, Johnson H. Private	Unk	July 15, 1862, Raleigh, North Carolina	Co. C, 5th North Carolina Infantry	May 12, 1864, Spotsylvania Court House, Virginia	Point Lookout, Maryland, transferred to Elmira Prison, NY, August 6, 1864	Oath of Allegiance May 29, 1865
Parrish, Joseph M. Sergeant	Unk	February 16, 1862, Camp Allegheny, Virginia	Co. E, 6th Virginia Cavalry	May 11, 1864, Henrico County, Virginia	Point Lookout, Maryland, transferred to Elmira Prison, NY, August 17, 1864	Oath of Allegiance June 16, 1865
Parrish, Joseph W. Private	Unk	June 8, 1861, Isbell's Store, Virginia	Co. D, 44th Virginia Infantry	May 12, 1864, Spotsylvania Court House, Virginia	Point Lookout, Maryland, transferred to Elmira Prison, NY, August 2, 1864	Died September 22, 1864 of Chronic Diarrhea, Grave No. 493
Parrish, Matt Private	Unk	Unknown	Co. F, 12th Georgia Infantry	August 19, 1864, Weldon Railroad, Virginia	Old Capital Prison, Washington D. C. Transferred to Elmira Prison, NY, May 2, 1865.	Oath of Allegiance July 3, 1865
Parrish, Paschal Private	18	September 15, 1861, Auburn, Wake County, North Carolina	Co. D, 31st North Carolina Infantry	June 1, 1864, Gaines Farm Cold Harbor, Virginia	Point Lookout, Maryland, transferred to Elmira Prison, NY, July 12, 1864	Exchanged March 14, 1865 at Boulware's Wharf on the James River, Virginia
Parrish, Pascal B. Private	Unk	July 15, 1862, Raleigh, North Carolina	Co. C, 5th North Carolina Infantry	May 12, 1864, Spotsylvania Court House, Virginia	Point Lookout, Maryland, transferred to Elmira Prison, NY, August 6, 1864	Oath of Allegiance May 15, 1865
Parrish, Troy Private	33	July 15, 1862, Smithfield, North Carolina	Co. J, 24th North Carolina Infantry	June 17, 1864, Petersburg, Virginia	Point Lookout, Maryland, transferred to Elmira Prison, NY, July 30, 1864	Oath of Allegiance May 29, 1865

Name & Rank	Age	Enlisted	Regiment and State	Where Captured	Prison	Remarks
Parrott, Henry C. Private	Unk	April 11, 1862, Washington County, Virginia	Co. J, 48th Virginia Infantry	May 12, 1864, Spotsylvania Court House, Virginia	Point Lookout, Maryland, transferred to Elmira Prison, NY, August 2, 1864	Exchanged October 29, 1864 at Venus Point, Savannah River, GA.
Parrott, Joseph M. Sergeant	Unk	May 12, 1862, Darlington, South Carolina	Co. B, 21st South Carolina Infantry	January 15, 1865, Fort Fisher, North Carolina	February 1, 1865, Elmira Prison Camp, New York	Died July 16, 1865 of Unknown Disease, Grave No. 2873
Parrott, Orange Private	Unk	May 13, 1862, Petersburg, Virginia	Co. C, 22nd Georgia Infantry	May 26, 1864, North Anna, Virginia	Point Lookout, Maryland, transferred to Elmira Prison, NY, July 11, 1864	Oath of Allegiance June 14, 1865
Parsons, George W. Private	Unk	July 20, 1863, Ashe County, North Carolina	Co. L, 58th North Carolina Infantry	July 1, 1864, Currituck County, North Carolina	Point Lookout, Maryland, transferred to Elmira Prison, NY, August 6, 1864	Transferred August 14, 1864 to Norfolk, VA, to Report to Brigadier General George F. Shipley.
Partain, Henry H. Corporal	50	October 15, 1861, Haley's Store, Georgia	Co. F, 38th Georgia Infantry	May 20, 1864, Spotsylvania Court House, Virginia	Point Lookout, Maryland, transferred to Elmira Prison, NY, July 3, 1864	Exchanged October 29, 1864, at Venus Point, Savannah River, GA.
Partain, John Private	Unk	September 19, 1861, Dalton, Georgia	Co. C, 60th Georgia Infantry	July 25, 1864, Sharpsburg, Maryland	Old Capital Prison, Washington D. C. Transferred to Elmira Prison, NY, August 12, 1864	Oath of Allegiance June 23, 1865
Partin, John Private	44	August 18, 1863, Wake County, North Carolina	Co. D, 36th Regiment, 2nd North Carolina Artillery	January 15, 1865, Fort Fisher, North Carolina	February 1, 1865, Elmira Prison Camp, New York	Died March 10, 1865 of Chronic Diarrhea, Grave No. 1865. Headstone has John Paiting.
Partin, John W. Private	Unk	December 7, 1861, Spring Hill, South Carolina	Co. G, 20th South Carolina Infantry	June 1, 1864, Cold Harbor, Virginia	Point Lookout, Maryland, transferred to Elmira Prison, NY, July 12, 1864	Exchanged February 20, 1865 at Boulware's or Cox Wharf on the James River, Virginia

Name & Rank	Age	Enlisted	Regiment and State	Where Captured	Prison	Remarks
Paschal, Micajah B. Private	23	April 1, 1862, Coosa, Alabama	Co. K, 59th Alabama Infantry	March 29, 1865, Hatchers Run, Virginia. Gunshot Wound Left Chest.	Old Capital Prison, Washington D. C. Transferred to Elmira Prison, NY, May 2, 1865.	Oath of Allegiance June 17, 1865
Paschall, Richard H. C. Private	Unk	March 4, 1862, Eatonton, Georgia	Co. C, 44th Georgia Infantry	May 20, 1864, Spotsylvania Court House, Virginia	Point Lookout, Maryland, transferred to Elmira Prison, NY, July 3, 1864	Oath of Allegiance June 19, 1865
Paschall, Robert W. Corporal	37	February 12, 1862, Warrenton, North Carolina	Co. G, 43rd North Carolina Infantry	May 30, 1864, Old Church, Cold Harbor, Virginia	Old Capital Prison, Washington DC. Transferred to Elmira Prison Camp, New York, July 25, 1864.	Oath of Allegiance June 30, 1865
Pasten, Fielding Private	Unk	January 24, 1863, Wytheville, Virginia	Co. D, 30th Battalion Virginia Sharp Shooters	July 13, 1864, Near Washington, DC	Old Capital Prison, Washington, DC. Transferred to Elmira Prison, New York July 25, 1864	Died April 20, 1865 of Pneumonia, Grave No. 1425. Headstone has F. Posting.
Pate, Abel Private	28	Unknown	Co. K, 19th Georgia Infantry	August 19, 1864, Weldon Railroad, Near Petersburg, VA. Gunshot Wound Left Thigh.	DeCamp General Hospital, David's Island New York Harbor.	Died March 5, 1865 of Chronic Diarrhea, Grave No. 2421
Pate, Asa Private	Unk	February 5, 1864, Fort Holmes, Near Raleigh, North Carolina	Co. G, 40th Regiment, 3rd North Carolina Artillery	January 15, 1865, Fort Fisher, North Carolina	February 1, 1865, Elmira Prison Camp, New York	Died April 2, 1865 of Pneumonia, Grave No. 2580
Pate, Charles Private	Unk	August 1, 1863, Goldsboro, North Carolina	Co. C, 66th North Carolina Infantry	June 3, 1864, Gaines Mill Cold Harbor, Virginia	Point Lookout, Maryland, transferred to Elmira Prison, NY, July 12, 1864	Oath of Allegiance July 3, 1865
Pate, Daniel Private	Unk	December 8, 1863, Goldsboro, North Carolina	Co. F, 10th Regiment, 1st North Carolina Artillery	January 15, 1865, Fort Fisher, North Carolina	February 1, 1865, Elmira Prison Camp, New York	Oath of Allegiance July 3, 1865

Name & Rank	Age	Enlisted	Regiment and State	Where Captured	Prison	Remarks
Pate, Daniel Private	24	May 6, 1862, Bladen County, North Carolina	Co. K, 40th 3rd Regiment North Carolina Artillery	January 15, 1865, Fort Fisher, North Carolina	February 1, 1865, Elmira Prison Camp, New York	Died May 9, 1865 of Chronic Diarrhea, Grave No. 2782
Pate, Drury Private	Unk	September 18, 1862, Coffee County, Alabama	Co. K, 5th Alabama Infantry	May 5, 1864, Wilderness, Virginia	Point Lookout, Maryland, transferred to Elmira Prison, NY, August 17, 1864	Died October 31, 1864 of Pneumonia, Grave No. 744
Pate, Edwin A. Private	54	May 15, 1862, Columbus County, North Carolina	Co. C, 1st Battalion North Carolina Heavy Artillery	January 15, 1865, Fort Fisher, North Carolina	February 1, 1865, Elmira Prison Camp, New York	Oath of Allegiance July 3, 1865
Pate, Jackson Private	24	July 6, 1861, Beaufort, North Carolina	Co. F, 10th Regiment, 1st North Carolina Artillery	January 15, 1865, Fort Fisher, North Carolina	February 1, 1865, Elmira Prison Camp, New York	Oath of Allegiance May 29, 1865
Pate, John C. Private	18	March 20, 1864, Bladen County, North Carolina	Co. K, 40th 3rd Regiment North Carolina Artillery	January 15, 1865, Fort Fisher, North Carolina	February 1, 1865, Elmira Prison Camp, New York	Died March 26, 1865 of Remittent Fever, Grave No. 2466
Pate, John L. Private	19	July 2, 1861, Goldsboro, North Carolina	Co. F, 10th Regiment, 1st North Carolina Artillery	January 15, 1865, Fort Fisher, North Carolina	February 1, 1865, Elmira Prison Camp, New York	Oath of Allegiance July 26, 1865
Pate, Richard W. Private	20	July 2, 1861, Goldsboro, North Carolina	Co. F, 10th Regiment, 1st North Carolina Artillery	January 15, 1865, Fort Fisher, North Carolina	February 1, 1865, Elmira Prison Camp, New York	Oath of Allegiance July 7, 1865
Pate, Stephen Private	27	September 23, 1863, Brunswick County, North Carolina	Co. K, 40th 3rd Regiment North Carolina Artillery	January 15, 1865, Fort Fisher, North Carolina	February 1, 1865, Elmira Prison Camp, New York	Exchanged March 2, 1865 at Akins Landing on the James River, Virginia
Pate, Stephen W. Private	22	June 1, 1861, Richmond County, North Carolina	Co. F, 18th North Carolina Infantry	May 12, 1864, Spotsylvania Court House, Virginia	Point Lookout, Maryland, transferred to Elmira Prison, NY, August 6, 1864	Oath of Allegiance June 12, 1865

Name & Rank	Age	Enlisted	Regiment and State	Where Captured	Prison	Remarks
Paterson, John E. Private	20	March 9, 1863, Fayetteville, North Carolina	Co. E, 8th, North Carolina Infantry	May 31, 1864, Cold Harbor, Virginia	Point Lookout, Maryland, transferred to Elmira Prison, NY, July 12,1864	Exchanged October 29, 1864, at Venus Point, Savannah River, GA.
Patman, Thomas H. Private	Unk	June 14, 1861, Camp McDonald, Georgia	Co. C, 18 Georgia Infantry	June 1, 1864, Cold Harbor, Virginia	Point Lookout, Maryland, transferred to Elmira Prison, NY, July 17,1864	Exchanged October 29, 1864, at Venus Point, Savannah River, GA.
Patram, William Private	Unk	May 5, 1864, Petersburg, Virginia	Co. D, 3rd Battalion Virginia Reserves	June 9, 1864, Near Petersburg, Virginia	Point Lookout, Maryland, transferred to Elmira Prison, NY, July 23, 1864	Oath of Allegiance May 29, 1865
Patrick, James Private	Unk	Unknown	Co. D, 50th Virginia Infantry	May 12, 1864, Spotsylvania Court House, Virginia	Point Lookout, Maryland, transferred to Elmira Prison, NY, August 2, 1864	Died January 6, 1865 of Chronic Diarrhea, Grave No. 1240
Patrick, James M. Private	18	June 3, 1861, Washington, North Carolina	Co. E, 4th North Carolina Infantry	July 13, 1864, Near Washington, DC	Old Capital Prison, Washington DC. Transferred to Elmira Prison Camp, New York, July 25, 1864.	Oath of Allegiance January 30, 1865 by Orders of Commissary General of Prisoners.
Patrick, James W. Private	18	August 15, 1862, Pitt County, North Carolina	Co. G, 8th, North Carolina Infantry	May 31, 1864, Cold Harbor, Virginia	Point Lookout, Maryland, transferred to Elmira Prison, NY, July 11, 1864	Exchanged February 20, 1865 at Boulware's or Cox Wharf on the James River, Virginia
Patrick, Jasper G. Private	18	March 24, 1862, Charleston, South Carolina	Co. F, 18th South Carolina Infantry	July 30, 1864, Petersburg, Virginia	Point Lookout, Maryland, transferred to Elmira Prison, NY, August 12, 1864	Oath of Allegiance June 21, 1865
Patrick, John M. Private	Unk	July 10, 1862, Kanawha, Virginia	Co. H, 22nd Virginia Infantry	June 3, 1864, Gaines Farm, Cold Harbor, Virginia	Transferred From Point Lookout Prison, MD, July 12, 1864. Train Never Arrived at Elmira Prison Camp, NY.	Died July 15, 1864 in Train Wreck at Shohola, Pennsylvania.

Name & Rank	Age	Enlisted	Regiment and State	Where Captured	Prison	Remarks
Patrick, Robert C. Private	23	December 28, 1861, Camp Hampton, Tennessee	Co. F, 18th South Carolina Infantry	July 30, 1864, Petersburg, Virginia	Fort Columbus, N Y Harbor, transferred to Elmira December 4, 1864.	Died February 5, 1865 of Chronic Diarrhea, Grave No. 1918
Patrick, Thomas C. Private	21	March 4, 1862, Fort Gaines, Georgia	Co. J, 51st Georgia Infantry	May 6, 1864, Wilderness, Virginia	Old Capital Prison, Washington D. C. Transferred to Elmira Prison, NY, July 14, 1864	Oath of Allegiance June 23, 1865
Patten, James W. Private	Unk	July 6, 1863, Richmond, Virginia	Co. F, 1st Maryland Cavalry	July 16, 1864, Loudoun County, Virginia	Old Capital Prison, Washington DC. Transferred to Elmira Prison Camp, New York, July 25, 1864.	Died November 10, 1864 of Pneumonia, Grave No. 829. Headstone has Patton.
Patterson, Alexander Sergeant	29	April 26, 1861, Elizabethtown, North Carolina	Co. K, 18th North Carolina Infantry	May 12, 1864, Spotsylvania Court House, Virginia	Point Lookout, Maryland, transferred to Elmira Prison, NY, August 6, 1864	Exchanged February 13, 1865 at Boulware's wharf on the James River, Virginia
Patterson, Henry R. Private	21	March 11, 1862, Winchester, Virginia	Co. C, 12 Virginia Cavalry	July 13, 1864, Near Washington, DC	Old Capital Prison, Washington DC. Transferred to Elmira Prison Camp, New York, July 25, 1864.	Exchanged March 10, 1865 at Boulware's Wharf on the James River, Virginia
Patterson, John E. Private	20	March 9, 1863, Fayetteville, North Carolina	Co. E, 8th North Carolina Infantry	May 31, 1864, Cold Harbor, Virginia	Point Lookout, Maryland, transferred to Elmira Prison, NY, July 12,1864	Transferred for Exchange October 11, 1864. Died October 30, 1864 of Unknown Disease at Fort Monroe, VA.
Patterson, John T. Private	Unk	October 3, 1862, Bunker Hill, Virginia	Co. F, 2nd Virginia Infantry	May 10, 1864, Spotsylvania, Virginia	Old Capital Prison, Washington, DC, transferred to Elmira Prison, NY, December 17, 1864	Oath of Allegiance June 14, 1865

Name & Rank	Age	Enlisted	Regiment and State	Where Captured	Prison	Remarks
Patterson, John W. Private	Unk	September 17, 1861, Atlanta, Georgia	Co. C, 35th Georgia Infantry	May 5, 1864, Wilderness, Virginia	Point Lookout, Maryland, transferred to Elmira Prison, NY, July 23, 1864	Died, December 30, 1864 of Chronic Diarrhea, Grave No. 1312
Patterson, R. Private	Unk	Unknown	Co. D, 35th Virginia Cavalry	August 10, 1864, Rockville, Maryland	Old Capital Prison, Washington, DC transferred to Elmira Prison, NY, August 29, 1864	Oath of Allegiance June 16, 1865
Patterson, Turner Private	26	May 28, 1861, Raleigh, North Carolina	Co. G, 22nd North Carolina Infantry	May 31, 1864, Chickahominy, Cold Harbor, Virginia	Point Lookout, Maryland, transferred to Elmira Prison, NY, July 12, 1864	Oath of Allegiance June 16, 1865
Patterson, William B. Private	17	January 20, 1862, Dallas County, Texas	Co. E, 18th Texas Infantry	October 22, 1864, Pointe Coupee, Louisiana	New Orleans, Louisiana transferred to Elmira November 19, 1864.	Oath of Allegiance June 14, 1865
Patterson, William H. Private	26	July 29, 1861, Taylorsville, North Carolina	Co. K, 7th North Carolina Infantry	May 6, 1864, Wilderness, Virginia	Point Lookout, Maryland, transferred to Elmira Prison, NY, August 14, 1864	Died September 26, 1864 of Chronic Diarrhea, Grave No. 454
Patterson, William H. Private	Unk	Unknown	Co. K, 48th Virginia Infantry	May 5, 1864, Wilderness, Virginia	Point Lookout, Maryland, transferred to Elmira Prison, NY, July 17,1864	Oath of Allegiance May 21, 1865
Patterson, William T. Private	Unk	July 24, 1861, Hackneyville, Alabama	Co. J, 14th Alabama Infantry	May 31, 1864 Mechanicsville, Virginia	Point Lookout, Maryland, transferred to Elmira Prison, NY, July 12, 1864	Oath of Allegiance June 14, 1865
Patterson, William Thompson Private	25	October 10, 1862, North East, Alexander County, North Carolina	Co. H, 56th North Carolina Infantry	May 13, 1864, Drury's Bluff, Near Fort Darling, Virginia	Point Lookout, Maryland, transferred to Elmira Prison, NY, July 23, 1864	Died May 10, 1865 of Pneumonia, Grave No. 2789

Name & Rank	Age	Enlisted	Regiment and State	Where Captured	Prison	Remarks
Patteshall, William R. Corporal	24	August 31, 1861, Green Mountain, North Carolina	Co. E, 8th, North Carolina Infantry	June 1, 1864, Gaines Mill Cold Harbor, Virginia	Point Lookout, Maryland, transferred to Elmira Prison, NY, July 17,1864	Exchanged October 29, 1864, at Venus Point, Savannah River, GA.
Pattishall, Z. G. Private	36	April 6, 1863, Chatham County, North Carolina	Co. E, 8th North Carolina Infantry	June 1, 1864, Gaines Mill, Cold Harbor, Virginia	Point Lookout, Maryland, transferred to Elmira Prison, NY, July 17, 1864	Exchanged March 2, 1865. Died March 15, 1865 of Unknown Disease at Jackson Hospital, Richmond, VA.
Patton, A. H. Private	Unk	November 3, 1862, Selma, Alabama	Jeff Davis Alabama Artillery	May 5, 1864, Wilderness, Virginia	Point Lookout, Maryland, transferred to Elmira Prison, NY, August 17, 1864	Transferred For Exchange October 11, 1864 to Point Lookout Prison Camp, MD. Died October 31, 1864 of Chronic Diarrhea at US Army Hospital Baltimore, MD.
Patton, Augustus B. Private	20	June 10, 1861, Selma, Alabama	Jeff Davis Alabama Artillery	May 5, 1864, Wilderness, Virginia	Point Lookout, Maryland, transferred to Elmira Prison, NY, August 17, 1864	Oath of Allegiance June 14, 1865
Patton, G. W. Private	Unk	July 20, 1861, Jefferson, Georgia	Co. G, 16th Georgia Infantry	June 1, 1864, Gaines Mill Cold Harbor, Virginia	Point Lookout, Maryland, transferred to Elmira Prison, NY, July 12, 1864	Exchanged October 29, 1864, at Venus Point, Savannah River, GA.
Patton, George W. Private	28	Unknown	Co. C, 7th Georgia Infantry	May 8, 1863, Narrow Passage, Shenandoah County, Virginia	Point Lookout, Maryland, transferred to Elmira, New York, July 23, 1864.	Oath of Allegiance December 23, 1864. Early Release per Lincoln's Proclamation, 12/8/1863.
Patton, Hardy P. Private	Unk	Unknown	Co. A, 50th Virginia Infantry	May 12, 1864, Spotsylvania Court House, Virginia	Point Lookout, Maryland, transferred to Elmira Prison, NY, August 2, 1864	Died January 27, 1865 of Variola (Smallpox), Grave No. 1649

Name & Rank	Age	Enlisted	Regiment and State	Where Captured	Prison	Remarks
Patton, William W. Private	19	August 13, 1861, Rock Hill, South Carolina	Co. H, 12th South Carolina Infantry	July 29, 1864, Petersburg, Virginia	Point Lookout, Maryland, transferred to Elmira Prison, NY, August 12, 1864	Oath of Allegiance June 21, 1865
Paugh, Jeremiah Private	18	May 27, 1861, Buckhannon, Virginia	Co. B, 25th Virginia Infantry	May 12, 1864, Spotsylvania Court House, Virginia	Point Lookout, Maryland, transferred to Elmira Prison, NY, July 30, 1864	Oath of Allegiance June 23, 1865
Paugh, Joseph Private	Unk	May 27, 1861, Buckhannon, Virginia	Co. B, 25th Virginia Infantry	May 12, 1864, Spotsylvania Court House, Virginia	Point Lookout, Maryland, transferred to Elmira Prison, NY, August 12, 1864	Exchanged October 29, 1864, at Venus Point, Savannah River, GA.
Paul, Columbus W. Private	Unk	May 25, 1862, Floyd Court House, Virginia	Co. B, 42nd Virginia Infantry	May 12, 1864, Spotsylvania Court House, Virginia	Point Lookout, Maryland, transferred to Elmira Prison, NY, August 2, 1864	Oath of Allegiance June 19, 1865
Paul, Micajah J. Private	Unk	March 21, 1862, Floyd Court House, Virginia	Co. B, 42nd Virginia Infantry	May 12, 1864, Spotsylvania Court House, Virginia	Point Lookout, Maryland, transferred to Elmira Prison, NY, August 2, 1864	Oath of Allegiance June 19, 1865
Paul, Thomas W. Private	Unk	May 25, 1862, Floyd Court House, Virginia	Co. B, 42nd Virginia Infantry	May 12, 1864, Spotsylvania Court House, Virginia	Point Lookout, Maryland, transferred to Elmira Prison, NY, August 2, 1864	Oath of Allegiance June 16, 1865
Paulk, George R. Private	Unk	March 4, 1862, Irwinville, Georgia	Co. F, 49th Georgia Infantry	May 6, 1864, Wilderness, Virginia	Old Capital Prison, Washington D. C. Transferred to Elmira Prison, NY, July 14, 1864	Exchanged March 2, 1865 at Akins Landing on the James River, Virginia
Payne, Archibald Private	Unk	December 10, 1863, Fort Morgan, Alabama	Co. F, 1st Battalion Alabama Artillery	August 23, 1864, Fort Morgan, Alabama	Steam Press No. 4 New Orleans, Louisiana transferred to Elmira Prison, NY, October 8, 1864.	Died December 4, 1864 of Pleuro-Pneumonia, Grave No. 883

Name & Rank	Age	Enlisted	Regiment and State	Where Captured	Prison	Remarks
Payne, Asbury J. Private	Unk	April 18, 1861, Harrisonburg, Virginia	Co. B, 10th Virginia Infantry	May 12, 1864, Spotsylvania Court House, Virginia	Point Lookout, Maryland, transferred to Elmira Prison, NY, August 2, 1864	Oath of Allegiance June 27, 1865
Payne, Cary J. Private	Unk	May 15, 1861, Edneyville, North Carolina	Co. A, 25th North Carolina Infantry	June 17, 1864, Petersburg, Virginia	Point Lookout, Maryland, transferred to Elmira Prison, NY, July 30, 1864	Died February 2, 1865 of Pneumonia, Grave No. 1754
Payne, J. W. Private	Unk	July 13, 1862, White County, Georgia	Co. C, 24th Georgia Infantry	August 16, 1864, Front Royal, Virginia	Old Capital Prison, Washington, DC transferred to Elmira Prison, NY, August 29, 1864	Oath of Allegiance June 16, 1865
Payne, James C. Private	21	August 23, 1861, Camp Trousdale, Tennessee	Co. D, 23rd Tennessee Infantry	June 17, 1864, Petersburg, Virginia	Point Lookout, Maryland, transferred to Elmira Prison, NY, July 30, 1864	Exchanged February 25, 1865 at Boulware's or Cox Wharf on the James River, Virginia
Payne, John Foster Private	Unk	April 22, 1862, Gordonville, Virginia	Co. H, 13th Virginia Infantry	May 20, 1864, Spotsylvania Court House, Virginia	Point Lookout, Maryland, transferred to Elmira Prison, NY, July 3, 1864	Exchanged March 2, 1865 at Akins Landing on the James River, Virginia
Payne, Martin D. Private	Unk	December 10, 1861, Bowling Green, Kentucky	Co. D, 23rd Tennessee Infantry	June 17, 1864, Petersburg, Virginia	Point Lookout, Maryland, transferred to Elmira Prison, NY, July 30, 1864	Exchanged February 25, 1865 at Boulware's or Cox Wharf on the James River, Virginia
Payne, Robert E. Private	Unk	July 24, 1861, John Papley's, Franklin County, Virginia	Co. E, 58th Virginia Infantry	May 20, 1864, Spotsylvania Court House, Virginia	Point Lookout, Maryland, transferred to Elmira Prison, NY, July 3, 1864	Exchanged March 10, 1865 at Boulware's Wharf on the James River, Virginia
Paysour, Caleb Private	26	August 15, 1862, Iredell County, North Carolina	Co. J, 37th North Carolina Infantry	May 12, 1864, Spotsylvania Court House, Virginia	Point Lookout, Maryland, transferred to Elmira Prison, NY, August 12, 1864	Exchanged October 29, 1864, at Venus Point, Savannah River, GA.

Name & Rank	Age	Enlisted	Regiment and State	Where Captured	Prison	Remarks
Payton, John H. Private	Unk	August 24, 1861, Hamer, Banks County Georgia	Co. A, 24th Georgia Infantry	June 1, 1864, Cold Harbor, Virginia	Point Lookout, Maryland, transferred to Elmira Prison, NY, July 12, 1864	Died January 21, 1865 of Pneumonia, Grave No. 1584
Peabody, Charles H. Corporal	20	June 23, 1861, Camp Moore, Louisiana	Co. B, 8th Louisiana Infantry	May 12, 1864, Spotsylvania Court House, Virginia	Point Lookout, Maryland, transferred to Elmira Prison, NY, August 14, 1864	Oath of Allegiance May 29, 1865
Peacock, Ansel Private	Unk	March 8, 1862, Abbeville, Alabama	Co. B, 6th Alabama Infantry	May 11, 1864, Spotsylvania Court House, Virginia. Gunshot Wound of Shoulder.	Old Capital Prison, Washington DC. Transferred to Elmira Prison Camp, New York, July 25, 1864.	Oath of Allegiance June 30, 1865
Peacock, Benajah T. Private	Unk	April 10, 1864, Augusta, Georgia	Co. K, 12th Georgia Infantry	May 10, 1864, Spotsylvania Court House, Virginia	Point Lookout, Maryland, transferred to Elmira Prison, NY, July 25, 1864	Oath of Allegiance June 16, 1865
Peacock, George W. Private	Unk	September 3, 1862, Mocksville, North Carolina	Co. G, 7th Confederate Cavalry	June 4, 1864, Petersburg, Virginia	Point Lookout, Maryland, transferred to Elmira Prison, NY, July 25, 1864	Died January 8, 1865 of Chronic Diarrhea, Grave No. 1229
Peacock, Jacob Private	Unk	April 26, 1864, Raleigh, Wake County, North Carolina	Co. G, 2nd North Carolina Infantry	July 18, 1864, Frederick, Maryland	Old Capital Prison, Washington DC. Transferred to Elmira Prison Camp, New York, July 25, 1864.	Died September 4, 1864 of Chronic Diarrhea, Grave No. 232
Peacock, Rufus Private	22	August 13, 1862, Camp Hill, North Carolina	Co. G, 5th North Carolina Infantry	May 12, 1864, Spotsylvania Court House, Virginia	Point Lookout, Maryland, transferred to Elmira Prison, NY, August 6, 1864	Oath of Allegiance June 14, 1865
Peacock, Samuel H. Private	Unk	July 3, 1861, Glennville, Alabama	Co. H, 15th Alabama Infantry	May 6, 1864, Wilderness, Virginia	Point Lookout, Maryland, transferred to Elmira Prison, NY, August 17, 1864	Exchanged March 14, 1865 at Boulware's Wharf on the James River, Virginia

Name & Rank	Age	Enlisted	Regiment and State	Where Captured	Prison	Remarks
Peagler, Jacob W. Private	16	August 21, 1863, Ashepoo, South Carolina	Co. C, 11th South Carolina Infantry	June 16, 1864, Petersburg, Virginia	Point Lookout, Maryland, transferred to Elmira Prison, NY, July 25, 1864	Oath of Allegiance May 14, 1865.
Peak, Joseph Private	Unk	Unknown	Co. J, 50th Virginia Infantry	May 12, 1864, Spotsylvania Court House, Virginia	Point Lookout, Maryland, transferred to Elmira Prison, NY, July 25, 1864	Oath of Allegiance May 29, 1865
Peak, Noah Sergeant	Unk	June 4, 1861, Fork of Wilson, Virginia	Co. D, 50th Virginia Infantry	May 12, 1864, Spotsylvania Court House, Virginia	Point Lookout, Maryland, transferred to Elmira Prison, NY, July 3, 1864	Oath of Allegiance June 19, 1865
Peal, A. D. Private	Unk	July 1, 1861, Columbia, South Carolina	Co. D, 5th South Carolina Infantry	May 22, 1864, North Anna, Virginia	Point Lookout, Maryland, transferred to Elmira Prison, NY, July 23, 1864	Died September 29, 1864 of Chronic Diarrhea and Rubeola (Measles), Grave No. 344.
Peal, John Abner Private	18	July 21, 1861, Yatesville, North Carolina	Co. B, 5th North Carolina Infantry	May 12, 1864, Spotsylvania Court House, Virginia	Point Lookout, Maryland, transferred to Elmira Prison, NY, August 6, 1864	Oath of Allegiance May 19, 1865
Pearce, Marscellus E. Private	24	August 1, 1861, Forestville, North Carolina	Co. J, 1st North Carolina Infantry	May 12, 1864, Spotsylvania Court House, Virginia	Point Lookout, Maryland, transferred to Elmira Prison, NY, August 6, 1864	Oath of Allegiance June 27, 1865
Pearson, A. J. Private	Unk	February 17, 1864, Columbia, South Carolina	Co. C, 22nd South Carolina Infantry	July 30, 1864, Petersburg, Virginia	Point Lookout, Maryland, transferred to Elmira Prison, NY, August 12, 1864	Died October 16, 1864 of Chronic Diarrhea, Grave No. 552
Pearson, David Private	Unk	May 18, 1864, Louisville, Mississippi	Co. C, 22nd South Carolina Infantry	June 18, 1864, Petersburg, Virginia	Point Lookout, Maryland, transferred to Elmira Prison, NY, July 25, 1864	Oath of Allegiance May 29, 1865

Name & Rank	Age	Enlisted	Regiment and State	Where Captured	Prison	Remarks
Pearson, E. W. Private	Unk	May 16, 1861, Alisona, Tennessee	Co. A, 17th Tennessee Infantry	June 17, 1864, Petersburg, Virginia	Point Lookout, Maryland, transferred to Elmira Prison, NY, July 30, 1864	Exchanged March 2, 1865 at Akins Landing on the James River, Virginia
Pearson, G. L. Private	Unk	October 17, 1863, Spartanburg, South Carolina	Co. K, 27th South Carolina Infantry	June 24, 1864, Near Petersburg, Virginia	Point Lookout, Maryland, transferred to Elmira Prison, NY, August 18, 1864	Exchanged October 29, 1864, at Venus Point, Savannah River, GA.
Pearson, G. M. Private	Unk	February 19, 1864, Coosa County, Alabama	Co. G, 12th Alabama Infantry	May 8, 1864, Wilderness, Virginia	Point Lookout, Maryland, transferred to Elmira Prison, NY, August 17, 1864	Oath of Allegiance June 21, 1865
Pearson, J. W. Private	Unk	December 20, 1862, Orangeburg, South Carolina	Co. H, 25th South Carolina Infantry	January 15, 1865, Fort Fisher, North Carolina	February 1, 1865, Elmira Prison Camp, New York	Oath of Allegiance July 11, 1865
Pearson, John E. Private	Unk	May 16, 1862, Alisona, Tennessee	Co. A, 17th Tennessee Infantry	June 17, 1864, Petersburg, Virginia	Point Lookout, Maryland, transferred to Elmira Prison, NY, July 30, 1864	Exchanged February 25, 1865 at Boulware's or Cox Wharf on the James River, Virginia
Pearson, Rufus Private	26	June 20, 1861, Abingdon, Virginia	Co. B, 48th Virginia Infantry	May 12, 1864, Spotsylvania Court House, Virginia	Point Lookout, Maryland, transferred to Elmira Prison, NY, August 2, 1864	Oath of Allegiance, June 23, 1865
Pearson, S. Jefferson Private	Unk	January 10, 1862, Columbia, South Carolina	Co. C, 22nd South Carolina Infantry	July 30, 1864, Petersburg, Virginia	Point Lookout, Maryland, transferred to Elmira Prison, NY, August 12, 1864	Died September 24, 1864 of Hospital Gangrene, Grave No. 461
Pearson, Stanford Private	20	April 15, 1861, Pittsboro, North Carolina	Co. I, 32nd North Carolina Infantry	May 10, 1864, Wilderness, Virginia	Point Lookout, Maryland, transferred to Elmira Prison, NY, August 6, 1864	Died November 2, 1864 of Disease of the Heart, Grave No. 846
Pearson, W. G. Private	Unk	February 13, 1864, Dublin, Virginia	Co. B, 4th Virginia Infantry	May 12, 1864, Spotsylvania Court House, Virginia	Point Lookout, Maryland, transferred to Elmira Prison, NY, August 2, 1864	Oath of Allegiance June 27, 1865

Name & Rank	Age	Enlisted	Regiment and State	Where Captured	Prison	Remarks
Peay, Samuel H. Private	Unk	June 22, 1861, Henry County, Virginia	Co. F, 42nd Virginia Infantry	May 12, 1864, Near Spotsylvania Court House, Virginia	Point Lookout, Maryland, transferred to Elmira Prison, NY, August 6, 1864	Died March 30, 1865 of Chronic Diarrhea, Grave No. 2542. Name Pedy on Headstone.
Peay, Turner C. Private	18	March 20, 1862, Reidsville, Rockingham County, North Carolina	Co. G, 45th North Carolina Infantry	May 10, 1864, Spotsylvania Court House, Virginia	Point Lookout, Maryland, transferred to Elmira Prison, NY, August 6, 1864	Exchanged October 29, 1864, at Venus Point, Savannah River, GA.
Peck, Eli Private	38	August 6, 1861, Mount Pleasant, North Carolina	Co. H, 8th North Carolina Infantry	June 1, 1864, Gaines Mill Cold Harbor, Virginia	Point Lookout, Maryland, transferred to Elmira Prison, NY, July 12, 1864	Died October 7, 1864 of Chronic Diarrhea, Grave No. 594
Peck, H. Private	Unk	Unknown	Nelligan's Regiment, Co. K, 1st Louisiana Infantry	June 2, 1864, Mechanicsville, Virginia	Point Lookout, Maryland, transferred to Elmira Prison, NY, July 12, 1864	Oath of Allegiance May 13, 1865
Peck, John E. Private	Unk	April 1, 1861, Blacksburg, Virginia	Co. E, 4th Virginia Infantry	May 12, 1864, Near Spotsylvania Court House, Virginia	Point Lookout, Maryland, transferred to Elmira Prison, NY, August 2, 1864	Exchanged March 14, 1865 at Boulware's Wharf on the James River, Virginia
Peck, John L. Corporal	19	September 7, 1861, Mount Pleasant, North Carolina	Co. H, 8th, North Carolina Infantry	May 31, 1864, Cold Harbor, Virginia	Point Lookout, Maryland, transferred to Elmira Prison, NY, July 12, 1864	Exchanged February 13, 1865 at Boulware's wharf on the James River, Virginia
Peck, William H. Corporal	Unk	April 6, 1862, Lewisburg, Virginia	Co. D, 26th Battalion Virginia Infantry	June 3, 1864, Gaines Farm Cold Harbor, Virginia	Point Lookout, Maryland, transferred to Elmira Prison, NY, July 17, 1864	Died December 31, 1864 of Variola (Smallpox), Grave No. 1321
Peddicord, George Private	24	March 1, 1863, Salem, Burke County, North Carolina	Co. G, 2nd Battalion North Carolina Infantry	July 13, 1864, Near Washington, DC	Old Capital Prison, Washington DC. Transferred to Elmira Prison Camp, New York, July 25, 1864.	Died December 7, 1864 of Your, Grave No. 1177. Headstone has Petticord.

Name & Rank	Age	Enlisted	Regiment and State	Where Captured	Prison	Remarks
Peebles, John D. Private	18	October 13, 1861, Camp Mangum, Raleigh, North Carolina	Co. H, 31st North Carolina Infantry	June 1, 1864, Gaines Mill Cold Harbor, Virginia	Point Lookout, Maryland, transferred to Elmira Prison, NY, July 12, 1864	Oath of Allegiance July 19, 1865
Peebles, Selburn H. Private	Unk	October 29, 1863, Forsyth County, North Carolina	Co. F, 3rd North Carolina Infantry	May 12, 1864, Near Spotsylvania Court House, Virginia	Point Lookout, Maryland, transferred to Elmira Prison, NY, July 23, 1864	Oath of Allegiance May 29, 1865
Peek, Robert Private	22	July 30, 1861, Livingston, Tennessee	Co. G, 25th Tennessee Infantry	May 16, 1864, Near Drury's Bluff, Virginia	Point Lookout, Maryland, transferred to Elmira Prison, NY, August 17, 1864	Exchanged February 25, 1865 at Boulware's or Cox Wharf on the James River, Virginia
Peel, James Private	Unk	October 31, 1864, Fort Holmes, Near Raleigh, North Carolina	Co. G, 40th Regiment, 3rd North Carolina Artillery	January 15, 1865, Fort Fisher, North Carolina	February 1, 1865, Elmira Prison Camp, New York	Died April 4, 1865 of Hepatatic Disease (Disease Affecting the Liver), Grave No. 2554
Peel, R. H. Private	25	July 1, 1862, Bertie County, North Carolina	Co. K, 33rd North Carolina Infantry	May 6, 1864, Wilderness, Virginia	Old Capital Prison, Washington D. C. Transferred to Elmira Prison, NY, July 14, 1864	Died October 13, 1864 of Chronic Diarrhea, Grave No. 568
Pegg, Edward Private	Unk	May 8, 1861, Bowling Green, Virginia	Co. F, 30th Virginia Infantry	July 7, 1864, Howlett's Farm, Virginia	Point Lookout, Maryland, transferred to Elmira Prison, NY, August 6, 1864	Oath of Allegiance May 13, 1865
Pelletier, L. L. Private	Unk	February 1, 1863, Chesterfield, South Carolina	Co. D, 21st South Carolina Infantry	January 15, 1865, Fort Fisher, North Carolina	February 1, 1865, Elmira Prison Camp, New York	Oath of Allegiance July 7, 1865
Pence, Harrison Private	Unk	April 16, 1862, Rudes Hill, Virginia	Co. F, 2nd Virginia Infantry	May 12, 1864, Spotsylvania Court House, Virginia	Point Lookout, Maryland, transferred to Elmira Prison, NY, August 2, 1864. Ward No. 41	Died August 12, 1864 of Chronic Diarrhea, Grave No. 18. Headstone has 2nd SC.

Name & Rank	Age	Enlisted	Regiment and State	Where Captured	Prison	Remarks
Pender, James T. Private	Unk	April 28, 1862, Marietta, Georgia	Co. M, Phillips Legion, Georgia	June 2, 1864, Gaines Farm Cold Harbor, Virginia	Point Lookout, Maryland, transferred to Elmira Prison, NY, July 12, 1864	Oath of Allegiance July 7, 1865
Pendergrass, Nathaniel Private	21	September 2, 1861, Orange County, North Carolina	Co. G, 28th North Carolina Infantry	May 12, 1864, Near Spotsylvania Court House, Virginia	Point Lookout, Maryland, transferred to Elmira Prison, NY, August 14, 1864	Exchanged February 20, 1865 at Boulware's or Cox Wharf on the James River, Virginia
Pendleton, James French Private	27	December 20, 1861, Saint Claire County, Missouri	Co. E, 1st Missouri Cavalry	May 17, 1863, Big Black Bridge, Champion Hill, Mississippi	Point Lookout, Maryland, transferred to Elmira Prison, NY, August 18, 1864	Exchanged February 13, 1865 at Boulware's wharf on the James River, Virginia
Pendleton, William Private	21	July 4, 1862, Lincolnton, North Carolina	Co. G, 57th North Carolina Infantry	May 24, 1864, Hanover Junction, Virginia	Point Lookout, Maryland, transferred to Elmira Prison, NY, July 11, 1864	Oath of Allegiance June 16, 1865
Pengra, Marshall M. Private	Unk	August 1, 1861, Camp Clark, Harrisburg, Texas	Co. F, 4th Texas Infantry	June 3, 1864, Old Church, Cold Harbor, Virginia	Point Lookout, Maryland, transferred to Elmira Prison, NY, July 11,1864	Exchanged October 29, 1864, at Venus Point, Savannah River, GA.
Penninger, Henry Private	Unk	April 20, 1864, Concord, North Carolina	Co. H, 8th North Carolina Infantry	June 1, 1864, Gaines Mill Cold Harbor, Virginia	Point Lookout, Maryland, transferred to Elmira Prison, NY, July 12, 1864	Died September 2, 1864 of Chronic Diarrhea, Grave No. 79. Name Hy Perringer on Headstone.
Pennington, E. Private	Unk	Unknown	Co. B, 30th Georgia Infantry	July 8, 1864, Near Maryland Heights, Maryland	Old Capital Prison, Washington DC. Transferred to Elmira Prison Camp, New York, July 25, 1864.	Oath of Allegiance June 23, 1865
Pennington, John B. Sergeant	Unk	Unknown	Co. K, 25th Virginia Infantry	May 5, 1864, Wilderness, Virginia	Point Lookout, Maryland, transferred to Elmira Prison, NY, August 2, 1864	Oath of Allegiance May 17, 1865

Name & Rank	Age	Enlisted	Regiment and State	Where Captured	Prison	Remarks
Pennington, Solomon Sergeant	Unk	May 18, 1861, Franklin, Virginia	Co. K, 25th Virginia Infantry	May 5, 1864, Wilderness, Virginia	Point Lookout, Maryland, transferred to Elmira Prison, NY, August 14, 1864	Exchanged March 14, 1865 at Boulware's Wharf on the James River, Virginia
Pennington, T. E. Private	Unk	September 29, 1862, Calhoun, Georgia	Co. I, 51st Georgia Infantry	June 3, 1864, Gaines Farm Cold Harbor, Virginia	Point Lookout, Maryland, transferred to Elmira Prison, NY, July 12, 1864	Exchanged October 29, 1864 at Venus Point, Savannah River, GA.
Penny, James M. Sergeant	Unk	June 11, 1861, Drayton, Georgia	Co. F, 12th Georgia Infantry	May 6, 1864, Wilderness, Virginia	Point Lookout, Maryland, transferred to Elmira Prison, NY, August 14, 1864	Oath of Allegiance June 23, 1865
Penny, William J. Private	21	March 7, 1862, Wilmington, North Carolina	Co. H, 51st North Carolina Infantry	June 3, 1864, Gaines Mill, Cold Harbor, Virginia	Point Lookout Prison Camp, Maryland. Transferred to Elmira Prison, August 14, 1864	Died January 22, 1865 of Pneumonia, Grave No. 1605
Peoples, Martin V. Private	24	July 10, 1861, Edgecombe County, North Carolina	Co. C, 8th North Carolina Infantry	June 1, 1864, Cold Harbor, Virginia	Point Lookout, Maryland, transferred to Elmira Prison, NY, July 12, 1864	Died October 10, 1864 of Chronic Diarrhea, Grave No. 668
Peppard, Oliver Private	18	December 25, 1861, Springfield, Missouri	Co. F, 3rd Battalion Missouri Cavalry	May 17, 1863, Big Black Bridge, Champion Hill, Mississippi	Point Lookout, Maryland, transferred to Elmira Prison, NY, August 18, 1864	Exchanged October 29, 1864, at Venus Point, Savannah River, GA.
Pepper, Patrick Private	Unk	April 27, 1861, Vicksburg, Mississippi	Co. G, 48th Mississippi Infantry	July 31, 1864, Deserted from Picket Post, Petersburg, Virginia	Point Lookout, Maryland, transferred to Elmira Prison, NY, August 12, 1864	Oath of Allegiance February 3, 1865. Early Release per Lincoln's Proclamation, 12/8/1863.
Perdue, Andrew G. Sergeant	28	February 12, 1863, Washington County, Virginia	Co. J, 26th Virginia Infantry	June 3, 1864, Gaines Mill, Cold Harbor, Virginia. Gunshot Wound Breast.	Old Capital Prison, Washington, DC transferred to Elmira Prison, NY, August 29, 1864	Exchanged October 29, 1864, at Venus Point, Savannah River, GA.

Name & Rank	Age	Enlisted	Regiment and State	Where Captured	Prison	Remarks
Perdue, B. J. Private	Unk	Unknown	Co. B, Hood's Battalion, Virginia Reserves	June 15, 1864, Petersburg, Virginia	Point Lookout, Maryland, transferred to Elmira Prison, NY, July 30, 1864	Oath of Allegiance June 21, 1865
Perdue, Charles Private	30	October 16, 1861, Lenoir County, North Carolina	Co. G, 40th Regiment, 3rd North Carolina Artillery	January 15, 1865, Fort Fisher, North Carolina	January 30, 1865, Elmira Prison Camp, New York.	Died March 22, 1865 of Continued Fever, Grave No. 1539
Perdue, Charles Private	17	May 1, 1862, Chesterfield, South Carolina	Co. E, 21st South Carolina Infantry	January 15, 1865, Fort Fisher, North Carolina	February 1, 1865, Elmira Prison Camp, New York	Died June 21, 1865 of Pneumonia, Grave No. 2812. Headstone has C. Perdieux.
Perdue, Henry H. Private	18	October 20, 1862, Asheboro, North Carolina	Co. F, 2nd Battalion North Carolina Infantry	July 10, 1864, Harpers Ferry, Virginia	Old Capital Prison, Washington DC. Transferred to Elmira Prison Camp, New York, July 25, 1864.	Oath of Allegiance May 29, 1865
Perdue, William Private	49	April 22, 1863, Fort Johnson, Smithville, North Carolina	Co. G, 40th Regiment, 3rd North Carolina Artillery	January 15, 1865, Fort Fisher, North Carolina	February 1, 1865, Elmira Prison Camp, New York	Exchanged March 2, 1865. Died April 5, 1865 of Chronic Diarrhea at Pettigrew Hospital, No. 13, Raleigh, North Carolina.
Perkins, E. Private	Unk	Unknown	Co. C, 31st Georgia Infantry	May 20, 1864, Spotsylvania Court House, Virginia	Point Lookout, Maryland, transferred to Elmira Prison, NY, July 3, 1864	Exchanged March 10, 1865 at Boulware's Wharf on the James River, Virginia
Perkins, George Private	21	July 22, 1861, Camp Moore, Louisiana	Co. E, 10th Louisiana Infantry	May 12, 1864, Spotsylvania Court House, Virginia	Point Lookout, Maryland, transferred to Elmira Prison, NY, July 25, 1864	Exchanged February 25, 1865 at Boulware's or Cox Wharf on the James River, Virginia
Perkins, James A. Private	Unk	June 8, 1861, Isbell's Store, Virginia	Co. D, 44th Virginia Infantry	May 12, 1864, Spotsylvania Court House, Virginia	Point Lookout, Maryland, transferred to Elmira Prison, NY, August 2, 1864	Exchanged March 10, 1865 at Boulware's Wharf on the James River, Virginia

Name & Rank	Age	Enlisted	Regiment and State	Where Captured	Prison	Remarks
Perkins, John A. Sergeant	Unk	July 5, 1861, Buffalo Gap, Virginia	Co. D, 44th Virginia Infantry	May 12, 1864, Spotsylvania Court House, Virginia	Point Lookout, Maryland, transferred to Elmira Prison, NY, August 2, 1864	Exchanged March 10, 1865 at Boulware's Wharf on the James River, Virginia
Perkins, John B. Private	Unk	March 4, 1862, Monroe, Georgia	Co. C, 9th Georgia Infantry	July 4, 1863, Gettysburg, Pennsylvania	Point Lookout, Maryland, transferred to Elmira Prison, NY, July 11, 1864	Oath of Allegiance June 14, 1865
Perkins, John E. Corporal	Unk	August 18, 1861, Camp Harmon, Virginia	Co. A, 4th Virginia Infantry	May 12, 1864, Spotsylvania Court House, Virginia	Point Lookout, Maryland, transferred to Elmira Prison, NY, August 2, 1864	Oath of Allegiance July 7, 1865
Perkins, John Wesley Sergeant	Unk	May 20, 1861, Palmyra, Virginia	Co. F, 44th Virginia Infantry	May 12, 1864, Spotsylvania Court House, Virginia	Point Lookout, Maryland, transferred to Elmira Prison, NY, August 2, 1864	Exchanged March 2, 1865 at Akins Landing on the James River, Virginia
Perkins, John William Private	Unk	May 20, 1861, Palmyra, Virginia	Co. F, 44th Virginia Infantry	May 12, 1864, Spotsylvania Court House, Virginia	Point Lookout, Maryland, transferred to Elmira Prison, NY, August 2, 1864	Oath of Allegiance June 14, 1865
Perkins, Richard J. Private	18	May 10, 1861, Lynchburg, Virginia	Captain Shoemaker's Co., Stewart's Horse Artillery, Virginia	September 13, 1863, Near Culpepper Court House, Virginia	Point Lookout, Maryland, transferred to Elmira Prison, NY, August 18, 1864	Exchanged March 10, 1865 at Boulware's Wharf on the James River, Virginia
Perkins, William Private	Unk	July 2, 1861, Camp McDonald, Georgia	Co. E, 18th Georgia Infantry	June 1, 1864, Cold Harbor, Virginia	Point Lookout, Maryland, transferred to Elmira Prison, NY, July 17, 1864	Exchanged February 2, 1865 on the James River, Virginia
Perkins, William T. Sergeant	Unk	June 4, 1861, Fork of Wilson, Virginia	Co. D, 50th Virginia Infantry	May 12, 1864, Spotsylvania Court House, Virginia	Point Lookout, Maryland, transferred to Elmira Prison, NY, August 2, 1864	Oath of Allegiance June 19, 1865

Name & Rank	Age	Enlisted	Regiment and State	Where Captured	Prison	Remarks
Perkins, Wyatt L. Private	32	March 16, 1863, Skinkers Neck, Virginia	Co. B, 1st North Carolina Infantry	May 12, 1864, Spotsylvania Court House, Virginia	Point Lookout Prison Camp, Maryland. Transferred to Elmira Prison, August 6, 1864	Died March 28, 1865 of Pneumonia, Grave No. 2507
Perkinson, Robert H. Corporal	Unk	Unknown	Co. B, Hood's Battalion Virginia Reserves	June 15, 1864, Petersburg, Virginia	Point Lookout, Maryland, transferred to Elmira Prison, NY, July 12, 1864	Transferred for Exchange 10/11/64. Died October 13, 1864 of Chronic Diarrhea at US Army Hospital, Baltimore, MD
Perks, John L. Private	Unk	June 21, 1861, Port Royal, Virginia	Co. E, 47th Virginia Infantry	May 28, 1864, Central Point Virginia	Transferred From Point Lookout Prison, MD, July 12, 1864. Train Never Arrived at Elmira Prison Camp, NY.	Died July 15, 1864 in Train Wreck at Shohola, Pennsylvania.
Pernell, Wiley Private	37	March 6, 1862, Milton, North Carolina	Co. I, 45th North Carolina Infantry	May 10, 1864, Spotsylvania Court House, Virginia	Point Lookout, Maryland, transferred to Elmira Prison, NY, August 6, 1864	Exchanged October 29, 1864, at Venus Point, Savannah River, GA.
Perrey, Lewis H. Private	Unk	October 20, 1864, Wilmington, North Carolina	Co. K, 10th Regiment, 1st North Carolina Artillery	January 15, 1865, Fort Fisher, North Carolina	February 1, 1865, Elmira Prison Camp, New York	Oath of Allegiance July 19, 1865
Perrin, John C. Private	Unk	February 1, 1863, Augusta, Georgia	Co. A, 7th Georgia Cavalry	June 11, 1864, Trevilian Station, Louisa Court House, Virginia	Point Lookout, Maryland, transferred to Elmira Prison, NY, July 25, 1864	Oath of Allegiance June 21, 1865
Perrine, David Private	16	April 23, 1863, Randolph, Virginia	Co. G, 25th Virginia Infantry	May 15, 1864, Spotsylvania Court House, Virginia	Point Lookout, Maryland, transferred to Elmira Prison, NY, August 14, 1864	Transferred for Exchange 10/11/1864. Transported to Venus Point, Savannah River, GA, 11/15/1864.
Perrine, Noah R. Private	Unk	February 11, 1864, Orange County, Virginia	Co. G, 25th Virginia Infantry	May 15, 1864, Spotsylvania Court House, Virginia	Point Lookout, Maryland, transferred to Elmira Prison, NY, August 14, 1864	Exchanged October 29, 1864 at Venus Point, Savannah River, GA.

Name & Rank	Age	Enlisted	Regiment and State	Where Captured	Prison	Remarks
Perrine, Shadrach C. Private	23	April 23, 1863, Randolph, Virginia	Co. G, 25th Virginia Infantry	May 15, 1864, Spotsylvania Court House, Virginia	Point Lookout, Maryland, transferred to Elmira Prison, NY, August 14, 1864	Exchanged October 29, 1864 at Venus Point, Savannah River, GA.
Perry, B. P. Private	Unk	May 16, 1861, Radfordsville, Perry County, Alabama	Co. K, 8th Alabama Infantry	July 4, 1863, Gettysburg, Pennsylvania	Point Lookout, Maryland, transferred to Elmira Prison, NY, August 17, 1864	Oath of Allegiance June 19, 1865
Perry, Daniel A. Private	23	August 22, 1862, Statesville, North Carolina	Co. J, 7th North Carolina Infantry	May 6, 1864, Wilderness, Virginia	Point Lookout, Maryland, transferred to Elmira Prison, NY, August 14, 1864	Oath of Allegiance June 12, 1865
Perry, David Private	Unk	September 6, 1862, Statesville, North Carolina	Co. A, 23rd North Carolina Infantry	July 13, 1864, Near Washington, DC	Old Capital Prison, Washington DC. Transferred to Elmira Prison Camp, NY, July 25, 1864.	Oath of Allegiance May 29, 1865
Perry, Erasmus L. Sergeant	27	May 21, 1861, Brownsburg, Virginia	Co. H, 25th Virginia Infantry	May 5, 1864, Wilderness, Virginia	Point Lookout, Maryland, transferred to Elmira Prison, NY, August 14, 1864	Exchanged October 29, 1864 at Venus Point, Savannah River, GA.
Perry, H. M. Private	Unk	Unknown	Co. D, 61st North Carolina Infantry	July 10, 1863, Morris Island, South Carolina	Point Lookout, Maryland, transferred to Elmira Prison, NY, August 18, 1864	Exchanged March 10, 1865 at Boulware's Wharf on the James River, Virginia
Perry, Hiram N. Private	Unk	Unknown	Co. G, 40th Regiment, 3rd North Carolina Artillery	January 15, 1865, Fort Fisher, North Carolina	February 1, 1865, Elmira Prison Camp, New York	Died April 2, 1865 of Diarrhea, Grave No. 2578
Perry, John C. Private	18	March 20, 1864, Brunswick County, North Carolina	Co. B, 36th Regiment, 2nd North Carolina Artillery	January 15, 1865, Fort Fisher, North Carolina	February 1, 1865, Elmira Prison Camp, New York	Died March 20, 1865 of Variola (Smallpox), Grave No. 1562
Perry, John R. Sergeant	Unk	May 21, 1863, Macon County, Alabama	Co. A, 61st Alabama Infantry	May 12, 1864, Spotsylvania Court House, Virginia	Point Lookout, Maryland, transferred to Elmira Prison, NY, July 30, 1864	Oath of Allegiance June 19, 1865

Name & Rank	Age	Enlisted	Regiment and State	Where Captured	Prison	Remarks
Perry, L. H. Corporal	Unk	December 15, 1864, New Hanover County, North Carolina	Co. B, 13th Battalion North Carolina Light Artillery	January 15, 1865, Fort Fisher, North Carolina	February 1, 1865, Elmira Prison Camp, New York	Died July 6, 1865 of Chronic Diarrhea, Grave No. 2838
Perry, Presley Private	Unk	January 9, 1862, Columbia, South Carolina	Co. E, 22nd South Carolina Infantry	June 17, 1864, Petersburg, Virginia	Point Lookout, Maryland, transferred to Elmira Prison, NY, July 30, 1864	Died August 9, 1864 of Chronic Diarrhea, Grave No. 138
Perry, Montague Private	25	June 17, 1861, Lewisburg, North Carolina	Co. K, 24th North Carolina Infantry	June 17, 1864, Near Petersburg, Virginia	Point Lookout, Maryland, transferred to Elmira Prison, NY, July 30, 1864	Exchanged February 20, 1865 at Boulware's or Cox Wharf on the James River, Virginia
Perry, Samuel A. Private	19	July 2, 1861, Nicholsville, Scott County, Virginia	Co. E, 48th Virginia Infantry	May 12, 1864, Spotsylvania Court House, Virginia	Point Lookout, Maryland, transferred to Elmira Prison, NY, July 30, 1864	Exchanged February 13, 1865 at Boulware's wharf on the James River, Virginia
Perry, Samuel J. Private	Unk	May 8, 1862, Augusta, Georgia	Co. A, 7th Georgia Cavalry	June 11, 1864, Trevilian Station, Louisa Court House, Virginia	Point Lookout, Maryland, transferred to Elmira Prison, NY, July 25, 1864	Exchanged March 14, 1865 at Boulware's Wharf on the James River, Virginia
Perry, Wiley N. Private	19	January 28, 1862, Bladen County, North Carolina	Co. B, 36th Regiment, 2nd North Carolina Artillery	January 15, 1865, Fort Fisher, North Carolina	February 1, 1865, Elmira Prison Camp, New York	Exchanged March 2, 1865. Died March 15, 1865 of Typhoid Fever at Moore Hospital, Richmond, VA.
Perryman, J. L. Private	Unk	May 25, 1862, Camp Moore, Louisiana	Co. E, 3rd Wingfield's Louisiana Cavalry	October 6, 1864, Clinton, Louisiana	New Orleans, Louisiana transferred to Elmira November 19, 1864.	Exchanged February 13, 1865 at Boulware's wharf on the James River, Virginia
Persinger, Charles O. Private	25	May 1, 1862, White Sulfur Springs, Virginia	Co. D, 22nd Virginia Infantry	May 31, 1864, Gaines Mill Cold Harbor, Virginia	Point Lookout, Maryland, transferred to Elmira Prison, NY, July 12, 1864	Oath of Allegiance June 30, 1865

Name & Rank	Age	Enlisted	Regiment and State	Where Captured	Prison	Remarks
Pescay, Charles W. Private	Unk	February 12, 1864, Shreveport, Louisiana	Co. E, Harrison's 3rd Louisiana Cavalry	October 6, 1864, Near Hampton's Ferry, Louisiana	New Orleans, Louisiana transferred to Elmira November 19, 1864.	Exchanged February 13, 1865 at Boulware's wharf on the James River, Virginia
Peters, Joseph B. Sergeant	23	May 13, 1861, Fetterman, Virginia	Co. A, 25th Virginia Infantry	May 12, 1864, Spotsylvania Court House, Virginia	Point Lookout, Maryland, transferred to Elmira Prison, NY, August 2,1864	Died December 22, 1864 of Chronic Diarrhea, Grave No. 1086
Peters, Wales W. W. Private	20	July 2, 1861, Nickelsville, Scott County, Virginia	Co. E, 48th Virginia Infantry	May 12, 1864, Spotsylvania Court House, Virginia	Point Lookout, Maryland, transferred to Elmira Prison, NY, August 2, 1864	Oath of Allegiance, June 27, 1865
Peterson, Haywood L. Corporal	18	May 17, 1861, Lower Black River District, North Carolina	Co. E, 18th North Carolina Infantry	May 12, 1864, Spotsylvania Court House, Virginia	Point Lookout, Maryland, transferred to Elmira Prison, NY, August 6, 1864	Died November 8, 1864 of Chronic Diarrhea, Grave No. 780
Peterson, John Private	Unk	March 18, 1861, Mobile, Alabama	Co. F, 1st Battalion Alabama Artillery	August 23, 1864, Fort Morgan, Alabama	Steam Press No. 4 New Orleans, Louisiana transferred to Elmira Prison, NY, October 8, 1864.	Oath of Allegiance May 17, 1865
Peterson, John Private	Unk	February 28, 1862, Lumberton, North Carolina	Co. E, 51st North Carolina Infantry	June 1, 1864, Cold Harbor, Virginia	Point Lookout, Maryland, transferred to Elmira Prison, NY, July 12, 1864	Died February 14, 1865 of Chronic Diarrhea, Grave No. 2034
Peterson, Oclious Private	Unk	March 4, 1862, Fort Gaines, Georgia	Co. I, 51st Georgia Infantry	June 3, 1864, Gaines Farm Cold Harbor, Virginia	Point Lookout, Maryland, transferred to Elmira Prison, NY, July 12, 1864	Oath of Allegiance June 21, 1865
Petree, Pink C. Sergeant	23	September 3, 1861, Spartanburg District, South Carolina	Co. J, 13th South Carolina Infantry	July 14, 1863, Falling Waters, Maryland	Point Lookout, Maryland, transferred to Elmira Prison, NY, August 18, 1864	Exchanged March 10, 1865 at Boulware's Wharf on the James River, Virginia

Name & Rank	Age	Enlisted	Regiment and State	Where Captured	Prison	Remarks
Petry, Henderson F. Private	Unk	August 22, 1862, Mercer County, Virginia	Co. D, 17th Virginia Cavalry	July 16, 1864, Loudoun County, Virginia	Old Capital Prison, Washington DC. Transferred to Elmira Prison Camp, NY, July 25, 1864.	Died September 4, 1864 of Chronic Dysentery, Grave No. 72. Headstone has Petsey.
Pettet, James H. Civilian	Unk	Unknown	Citizen of Fairfax County, Virginia	December 1, 1863, Fairfax County, Virginia	Point Lookout, Maryland, transferred to Elmira Prison, NY, July 25, 1864	Transferred For Exchange October 11, 1864 to Point Lookout Prison Camp, MD. Nothing Further.
Petteway, Lewis S. Sergeant	21	May 6, 1861, Jacksonville, North Carolina	Co. B, 24th North Carolina Infantry	June 17, 1864, Petersburg, Virginia	Point Lookout, Maryland, transferred to Elmira Prison, NY, July 30, 1864	Exchanged March 14, 1865 at Boulware's Wharf on the James River, Virginia
Petty, William S. Private	Unk	October 28, 1861, Fort Henry, Tennessee	Co. B, 1st Jackson's Tennessee Heavy Artillery	August 23, 1864, Fort Morgan, Alabama.	New Orleans, Louisiana transferred to Elmira Prison, NY, December 4, 1864.	Orders for Elmira, New York. Died in Transit December 20, 1864 of Variola at US Army Hospital Fort Columbus, New York Harbor.
Petway, Seth Private	Unk	February 1, 1864, Virginia	Co. D, 2nd North Carolina Infantry	May 12, 1864, Spotsylvania Court House, Virginia	Point Lookout, Maryland, transferred to Elmira Prison, NY, August 14, 1864	Exchanged October 29, 1864, at Venus Point, Savannah River, GA.
Pewett, Archibald Private	16	March 6, 1862, Morganton, Burke County, North Carolina	Co. K, 35th North Carolina Infantry	June 17, 1864, Petersburg, Virginia	Point Lookout, Maryland, transferred to Elmira Prison, NY, July 30, 1864	Exchanged October 29, 1864, at Venus Point, Savannah River, GA.
Peyton, Even B. Private	Unk	August 24, 1862, Harrisonburg, Virginia	Co. F, 1st Virginia Cavalry	August 19, 1864, Strider's Mill, Waterford, Virginia	Old Capital Prison, Washington, DC transferred to Elmira Prison, NY, August 29, 1864	Oath of Allegiance July 7, 1865

Name & Rank	Age	Enlisted	Regiment and State	Where Captured	Prison	Remarks
Peyton, Franklin Private	Unk	September 21, 1863, Rappahannock County, Virginia	Co. B, 7th Virginia Infantry	May 11, 1864, Spotsylvania Court House, Virginia	Point Lookout, Maryland, transferred to Elmira Prison, NY, July 25, 1864. Ward No. 31	Died September 11, 1864 of Chronic Diarrhea, Grave No. 15
Pfifer, William Sergeant	20	November 16, 1862, McMinnville, Tennessee	Co. K, 25th Tennessee Infantry	May 16, 1864, Near Drury's Bluff, Virginia	Point Lookout, Maryland, transferred to Elmira Prison, NY, August 17, 1864	Exchanged March 10, 1865 at Boulware's Wharf on the James River, Virginia
Phalen, Michael Private	Unk	May 7, 1861, New Orleans, Louisiana	Co. K, 5th Louisiana Infantry	May 12, 1864, Spotsylvania Court House, Virginia	Point Lookout, Maryland, transferred to Elmira Prison, NY, August 17, 1864	Exchanged March 10, 1865 at Boulware's Wharf on the James River, Virginia
Phelps, Britton Private	19	September 3, 1862, Mocksville, North Carolina	Co. G, 7th Confederate Cavalry	May 7, 1864, Congress Bridge, Virginia	Point Lookout, Maryland, transferred to Elmira Prison, NY, August 17, 1864	Transferred For Exchange October 11, 1864 to Point Lookout Prison Camp, MD. Died October 25, 1864 of Chronic Diarrhea.
Phelps, Elisha Private	30	May 23, 1861, Garysburg, North Carolina	Co. A, 15th North Carolina Infantry	June 2, 1864, Near Talapatomoy Creek, Hanover, Virginia	Point Lookout, Maryland, transferred to Elmira Prison, NY, July 12, 1864	Died September 4, 1864 of Chronic Diarrhea & Scurvy, Grave No. 228
Phelps, William Thomas Private	21	January 23, 1862, Windsor, Bertie County, North Carolina	Co. C, 3rd Battalion North Carolina Light Artillery	January 15, 1865, Fort Fisher, North Carolina	February 1, 1865, Elmira Prison Camp, New York	Oath of Allegiance June 12, 1865
Phibbs, Robert J. Private	30	July 15, 1862, Guilford County, North Carolina	Co. A, 1st North Carolina Infantry	May 12, 1864, Wilderness, Spotsylvania Court House, Virginia	Point Lookout, Maryland, transferred to Elmira Prison, NY, August 6, 1864	Died February 3, 1865 of Chronic Diarrhea, Grave No. 1751. Name Fibbs on Headstone.

Name & Rank	Age	Enlisted	Regiment and State	Where Captured	Prison	Remarks
Philen, Robert D. Sergeant	Unk	May 29, 1863, Montgomery County, Alabama	Co. B, 61st Alabama Infantry	May 12, 1864, Spotsylvania Court House, Virginia	Point Lookout, Maryland, transferred to Elmira Prison, NY, July 30, 1864	Died November 12, 1864 of Pneumonia, Grave No. 821
Philips, John Private	Unk	January 7, 1862, Memphis, Tennessee	Co. F, 1st Battalion Confederate States Infantry	May 5, 1864, Wilderness, Virginia	Point Lookout, Maryland, transferred to Elmira Prison, NY, August 17, 1864	Exchanged March 10, 1865 at Boulware's Wharf on the James River, Virginia
Philips, Wyley Private	Unk	August 1, 1863, Macon, Georgia	Co. H, 7th Georgia Cavalry	June 11, 1864, Trevilian Station, Louisa Court House, Virginia	Point Lookout, Maryland, transferred to Elmira Prison, NY, July 25, 1864	Died March 15, 1865 of Diarrhea. Grave No. 1689
Phillips, Benjamin W. Private	17	February 26, 1862, Camp Leon, Madison, Florida	Co. D, 5th Florida Infantry	May 12, 1864, Spotsylvania Court House, Virginia	Point Lookout, Maryland, transferred to Elmira Prison, NY, July 30, 1864	Transferred for Exchange 10/11/64. Died 11/3/64 at US Army General Hospital, Baltimore, MD.
Phillips, Bryant Private	18	March 26, 1863, Chatham County, North Carolina	Co. G, 40th Regiment, 3rd North Carolina Artillery	January 15, 1865, Fort Fisher, North Carolina	February 1, 1865, Elmira Prison Camp, New York	Died April 8, 1865 of Chronic Diarrhea, Grave No. 2633. Headstone Has Bryan Phillips.
Phillips, Eli Private	Unk	November 29, 1862, Georgetown, South Carolina	Co. A, 21st South Carolina Infantry	January 15, 1865, Fort Fisher, North Carolina	February 1, 1865, Elmira Prison Camp, New York	Died February 20, 1865 of Diarrhea, Grave No. 2328
Phillips, George W. Sergeant	Unk	April 20, 1862, Webster, North Carolina	Co. B, 25th North Carolina Infantry	June 17, 1864, Petersburg, Virginia	Point Lookout, Maryland, transferred to Elmira Prison, NY, July 30, 1864	Oath of Allegiance August 7, 1865 at US Army Hospital, Elmira, NY.
Phillips, George W. Private	Unk	Unknown	Co. F, 50th Virginia Infantry	May 12, 1864, Spotsylvania Court House, Virginia	Point Lookout, Maryland, transferred to Elmira Prison, NY, July 30, 1864	Oath of Allegiance May 17, 1865

Name & Rank	Age	Enlisted	Regiment and State	Where Captured	Prison	Remarks
Phillips, Hugh L. Private	Unk	December 30, 1861, Nashville, Tennessee	Co. J, 25th Tennessee Infantry	May 16, 1864, Near Drury's Bluff, Virginia	Point Lookout, Maryland, transferred to Elmira Prison, NY, August 17, 1864	Exchanged February 25, 1865 at Boulware's or Cox Wharf on the James River, Virginia
Phillips, J. R. Corporal	Unk	April 13, 1862, Timmonsville, South Carolina	Co. E, 8th South Carolina Infantry	May 30, 1864, Chickahominy, Cold Harbor, Virginia	Point Lookout, Maryland, transferred to Elmira Prison, NY, July 12, 1864	Oath of Allegiance June 19, 1865
Phillips, James Private	Unk	Unknown	Co. H, 50th Virginia Infantry	May 12, 1864, Spotsylvania Court House, Virginia	Point Lookout, Maryland, transferred to Elmira Prison, NY, August 2, 1864	Died April 10, 1865 of Chronic Diarrhea, Grave No. 2608
Phillips, James B. Private	Unk	Unknown	Co. F, 3rd North Carolina Infantry	May 6, 1864, Wilderness, Virginia	Point Lookout, Maryland, transferred to Elmira Prison, NY, July 25, 1864	Oath of Allegiance May 29, 1865
Phillips, Jeremiah Private	27	May 14, 1862, Saltillo, Mississippi	Co. K, 42nd Mississippi Infantry	August 18, 1864, Petersburg, Virginia. Gunshot Wound Left Five.	Old Capital Prison, Washington, DC, transferred to Elmira, NY December 17, 1864	Died March 1, 1865 of Diarrhea, Grave No. 2102
Phillips, Joel M. Private	Unk	May 20, 1862, Camp Parish, Louisiana	Co. I, 2nd Louisiana Infantry	May 12, 1864, Spotsylvania Court House, Virginia	Point Lookout, Maryland, transferred to Elmira Prison, NY, August 17, 1864	Exchanged February 13, 1865 at Boulware's wharf on the James River, Virginia
Phillips, John Private	17	March 18, 1862, Dobson, North Carolina	Co. A, 28th North Carolina Infantry	May 12, 1864, Near Spotsylvania Court House, Virginia	Point Lookout, Maryland, transferred to Elmira Prison, NY, August 14, 1864	Oath of Allegiance June 19, 1865
Phillips, John Private	Unk	December 9, 1861, Camp Hampton, South Carolina	Co. H, 17th South Carolina Infantry	July 30, 1864, Petersburg, Virginia	Point Lookout, Maryland, transferred to Elmira Prison, NY, August 12, 1864	Oath of Allegiance May 13, 1865

Name & Rank	Age	Enlisted	Regiment and State	Where Captured	Prison	Remarks
Phillips, John Private	30	December 20, 1861, Georgetown, South Carolina	Co. A, 21st South Carolina Infantry	January 15, 1865, Fort Fisher, North Carolina	February 1, 1865, Elmira Prison Camp, New York	Died February 6, 1865 of Chronic Diarrhea, Grave No. 1916
Phillips, John R. Private	20	June 6, 1861, Campbellton, Georgia	Co. A, 21st Georgia Infantry	May 22, 1864, North Anna, Virginia	Point Lookout, Maryland, transferred to Elmira Prison, NY, July 25, 1864	Oath of Allegiance May 17, 1865
Phillips, John R. Private	Unk	March 4, 1863, Blackshear, Georgia	Co. A, 50th Georgia Infantry	June 1, 1864, Gaines Mill, Cold Harbor, Virginia	Point Lookout, Maryland, transferred to Elmira Prison, NY, July 17,1864	Oath of Allegiance July 7, 1865
Phillips, Joseph N. Private	Unk	June 7, 1861, New Market, Virginia	Co. F, 49th Virginia Infantry	May 30, 1864, Gaines Mill Cold Harbor, Virginia	Point Lookout, Maryland, transferred to Elmira Prison, NY, July 11, 1864	Oath of Allegiance June 30, 1865
Phillips, Joseph W. Corporal	Unk	April 30, 1862, Louisville, Alabama	Co. E, 59th Alabama Infantry	June 17, 1864, Near Petersburg, Virginia	Point Lookout, Maryland, transferred to Elmira Prison, NY, July 30, 1864	Oath of Allegiance June 23, 1865
Phillips, Levi Private	18	August 27, 1861, Jacksonville, Onslow County, North Carolina	Co. G, 3rd North Carolina Infantry	May 12, 1864, Near Spotsylvania County Court House, Virginia	Point Lookout, Maryland, transferred to Elmira Prison, NY, August 14, 1864	Oath of Allegiance June 27, 1865
Phillips, Levi W. Private	Unk	September 16, 1861, Meriwether County, Georgia	Co. A, 60th Georgia Infantry	May 20, 1864, Spotsylvania Court House, Virginia	Point Lookout, Maryland, transferred to Elmira Prison, NY, July 3, 1864	Transferred for Exchange 10/11/64. Died 10/22/64 at Point Lookout, MD.
Phillips, Nelson Private	Unk	Unknown	Co. D, 7th Tennessee Infantry	May 14, 1864, Spotsylvania Court House, Virginia	Point Lookout, Maryland, transferred to Elmira Prison, NY, July 23, 1864	Died December 21, 1864 of Unknown Disease, Grave No. 1083
Phillips, Robert L. Private	Unk	May 15, 1862, Camp Harris, Tennessee	Co. C, 17th Tennessee Infantry	June 17, 1864, Petersburg, Virginia	Point Lookout, Maryland, transferred to Elmira Prison, NY, July 30, 1864	Exchanged February 25, 1865 at Boulware's or Cox Wharf on the James River, Virginia

Name & Rank	Age	Enlisted	Regiment and State	Where Captured	Prison	Remarks
Phillips, Rodney E. Sergeant	29	June 19, 1861, Camp Moore, Louisiana	Co. J, 8th Louisiana Infantry	May 12, 1864, Spotsylvania Court House, Virginia	Point Lookout, Maryland, transferred to Elmira Prison, NY, August 17, 1864	Exchanged February 13, 1865 at Boulware's Wharf on the James River, Virginia
Phillips, Rolley P. Private	Unk	March 9, 1862, Coosa County, Alabama	Co. H, 13th Alabama Infantry	May 12, 1864, Spotsylvania Court House, Virginia	Point Lookout, Maryland, transferred to Elmira Prison, NY, July 30, 1864	Oath of Allegiance June 19, 1865
Phillips, Samuel Y. Private	Unk	January 14, 1862, Camp Hampton, South Carolina	Co. D, 17th South Carolina Infantry	July 30, 1864, Petersburg, Virginia	Point Lookout, Maryland, transferred to Elmira Prison, NY, August 12, 1864	Exchanged October 29, 1864, at Venus Point, Savannah River, GA.
Phillips, W. A. Sergeant	20	July 1, 1862, Pointe Coupee, Louisiana	Co. H, Consolidated Crescent, Louisiana Infantry	September 22, 1864, Bayou Alabama, Louisiana	New Orleans, Louisiana transferred to Elmira November 19, 1864.	Exchanged February 13, 1865 at Boulware's wharf on the James River, Virginia
Phillips, W. F. Private	Unk	March 17, 1864, Greenville, East Tennessee	Co. C, 3rd Battalion Georgia Sharp Shooters	August 16, 1864, Front Royal, Virginia	Old Capital Prison, Washington, DC transferred to Elmira Prison, NY, August 29, 1864	Exchanged October 29, 1864, at Venus Point, Savannah River, GA.
Philyan, A. H. Private	Unk	March 20, 1864, Demoholis, Alabama	Co. E, 5th Alabama Infantry	May 8, 1864, Wilderness, Virginia	Point Lookout Prison Camp, Maryland. Transferred to Elmira Prison, August 17, 1864	Died the 26th 1865 of Pneumonia, Grave No. 1421
Phipps, David Private	28	August 15, 1862, Statesville, North Carolina	Co. K, 37th North Carolina Infantry	May 12, 1864, Spotsylvania Court House, Virginia	Point Lookout, Maryland, transferred to Elmira Prison, NY, August 12, 1864	Died September 3, 1864 of Chronic Diarrhea, Grave No. 68
Phipps, George W. Private	19	April 8, 1862, Camp Mangum, North Carolina	Co. B, 45th North Carolina Infantry	May 10, 1864, Spotsylvania Court House, Virginia	Point Lookout, Maryland, transferred to Elmira Prison, NY, August 6, 1864	Exchanged February 20, 1865 at Boulware's or Cox Wharf on the James River, Virginia

Name & Rank	Age	Enlisted	Regiment and State	Where Captured	Prison	Remarks
Phipps, James C. Private	21	March 3, 1862, Greensboro, North Carolina	Co. B, 45th North Carolina Infantry	May 10, 1864, Spotsylvania Court House, Virginia	Point Lookout, Maryland, transferred to Elmira Prison, NY, August 6, 1864	Died May 7, 1865 of Chronic Diarrhea, Grave No. 2768
Phipps, Richard Private	22	October 25, 1861, Columbus County, North Carolina	Co. A, 36th Regiment, 2nd North Carolina Artillery	January 15, 1865, Fort Fisher, North Carolina	February 1, 1865, Elmira Prison Camp, New York	Oath of Allegiance July 13, 1865
Phipps, W. H. Seaman	Unk	Unknown	Confederate States Navy assigned to CSS Steamer Bombshell	May 5, 1864, Albemarle Sound, North Carolina	Point Lookout, Maryland, transferred to Elmira Prison, NY, July 25, 1864	Oath of Allegiance March 6, 1865
Pickard, John Sergeant	32	March 22, 1862, Yadkin County, North Carolina	Co. D, 53rd North Carolina Infantry	May 20, 1864, Spotsylvania Court House, Virginia	Point Lookout, Maryland, transferred to Elmira Prison, NY, July 3, 1864	Died April 24, 1865 of Variola (Smallpox), Grave No. 1411
Pickering, Houston W. Private	Unk	May 25, 1862, Little Rock, Texas	Co. F, 12th Texas Cavalry	August 25, 1864, Bullitt's Bayou, Concordia Parish, Louisiana	New Orleans, Louisiana, Transferred to Elmira Prison, New York, November 19, 1864	Died December 2, 1864 of Remittent Fever, Grave No. 1011. Headstone has Wesley H. Pickering, 3rd Tennessee.
Pickett, Charles Private	22	May 10, 1862, Quincy, Florida	Co. B, 8th Florida Infantry	May 6, 1864, Wilderness, Virginia	Point Lookout, Maryland, transferred to Elmira Prison, NY, July 30, 1864	Oath of Allegiance July 11, 1865
Pickett, E. Private	Unk	January 13, 1862, Charleston, South Carolina	Co. G, 18th South Carolina Infantry	July 30, 1864, Petersburg, Virginia	Point Lookout, Maryland, transferred to Elmira Prison, NY, August 12, 1864	Oath of Allegiance July 3, 1865
Pickett, James Private	Unk	March 12, 1862, Shelby County, Alabama	Co. H, 44th Alabama Infantry	June 3, 1864, Gaines Farm Cold Harbor, Virginia	Point Lookout, Maryland, transferred to Elmira Prison, NY, July 12, 1864	Died September 2, 1864 of Chronic Diarrhea, Grave No. 86

Name & Rank	Age	Enlisted	Regiment and State	Where Captured	Prison	Remarks
Pickett, N. M. Private	Unk	Unknown	Co. C, Virginia Legion Infantry	June 4, 1864, Gaines Farm Cold Harbor, Virginia	Point Lookout, Maryland, transferred to Elmira Prison, NY, July 12, 1864	Oath of Allegiance June 21, 1865
Pickett, William H. Private	23	June 4, 1861, Duplin County, North Carolina	Co. B, 3rd North Carolina Infantry	May 12, 1864, Near Spotsylvania Court House, Virginia	Point Lookout, Maryland, transferred to Elmira Prison, NY, August 14, 1864	Oath of Allegiance June 21, 1865
Pickler, John W. Private	28	March 25, 1862, Albemarle, North Carolina	Co. J, 52nd North Carolina Infantry	July 14, 1863, Falling Waters, Maryland	Point Lookout, Maryland, transferred to Elmira Prison, NY, August 18, 1864	Exchanged March 14, 1865 at Boulware's Wharf on the James River, Virginia
Pierce, Daniel G. Corporal	Unk	April 30, 1862, Wilmington, North Carolina	Co. G, 51st North Carolina Infantry	May 31, 1864, Cold Harbor, Virginia	Point Lookout, Maryland, transferred to Elmira Prison, NY, July 12, 1864	Oath of Allegiance June 30, 1865
Pierce, Lodowick Private	Unk	July 1, 1861, Colerain, North Carolina	Co. F, 5th North Carolina Infantry	May 12, 1864, Spotsylvania Court House, Virginia	Point Lookout, Maryland, transferred to Elmira Prison, NY, August 6, 1864	Oath of Allegiance May 29, 1865
Pierce, Nixon Corporal	40	March 3, 1862, Wilmington, North Carolina	Co. E, 30th North Carolina Infantry	May 12, 1864, Near Spotsylvania Court House, Virginia	Point Lookout, Maryland, transferred to Elmira Prison, NY, August 14, 1864	Oath of Allegiance June 23, 1865
Pierce, Richard C. Corporal	Unk	June 10, 1861, Morgan, Georgia	Co. D, 12th Georgia Infantry	July 16, 1864, Snickers Gap, Virginia	Old Capital Prison, Washington DC. Transferred to Elmira Prison Camp, New York, July 25, 1864.	Exchanged October 29, 1864, at Venus Point, Savannah River, GA.
Pierce, Taylor Private	20	August 2, 1861, New Orleans, Louisiana	Co. B, 1st Louisiana Infantry	May 5, 1864, Wilderness, Virginia	Point Lookout, Maryland, transferred to Elmira Prison, NY, August 17, 1864	Died February 8, 1865 of Chronic Diarrhea, Grave No. 1928

Name & Rank	Age	Enlisted	Regiment and State	Where Captured	Prison	Remarks
Pierce, Timothy B. Private	20	June 2, 1861, Gloucester Point, Virginia	Co. B, 26th Virginia Infantry	June 15, 1864, Near Petersburg, Virginia	Point Lookout, Maryland, transferred to Elmira Prison, NY, July 12,1864	Oath of Allegiance July 3, 1865
Pierce, W. J. Corporal	Unk	June 31, 1861, Camp McDonald, Georgia	Co. D, 18th Georgia Infantry	July 3, 1863, Gettysburg, Virginia	Point Lookout, Maryland, transferred to Elmira Prison, NY, July 17, 1864	Died August 1, 1864 of Remittent Fever, Grave No. 143. Headstone has 18th LA.
Pierce, William Private	Unk	Unknown	Co. A, 12th Georgia Infantry	May 12, 1864, Spotsylvania, Virginia	Old Capital Prison, Washington, DC, transferred to Elmira Prison, NY, December 17, 1864	Exchanged March 2, 1865 at Boulware's Wharf on the James River, Virginia
Pierce, William A. Private	Unk	July 27, 1862, Boone, North Carolina	Co. H, 6th North Carolina Cavalry	June 22, 1864, Jackson's Mills, Near Kinston, North Carolina	Point Lookout, Maryland, transferred to Elmira Prison, NY, July 25, 1864	Oath of Allegiance May 29, 1865
Pigford, Jacob L. Private	20	May 17, 1861, Lower Black River District, North Carolina	Co. E, 18th North Carolina Infantry	May 12, 1864, Spotsylvania Court House, Virginia	Point Lookout, Maryland, transferred to Elmira Prison, NY, August 6, 1864	Exchanged March 14, 1865 at Boulware's Wharf on the James River, Virginia
Piland, Joseph Private	26	May 1, 1862, South Mills, North Carolina	Co. D, 32nd North Carolina Infantry	May 10, 1864, Spotsylvania, Virginia	Point Lookout, Maryland, transferred to Elmira Prison, NY, August 6, 1864	Died January 28, 1865 of Pneumonia, Grave No. 1643. Name Philand on Headstone.
Pilkenton, Murphy Private	30	February 4, 1864, Orange County Court House, North Carolina	Co. J, 26th North Carolina Infantry	May 12, 1864, Spotsylvania Court House, Virginia	Point Lookout, Maryland, transferred to Elmira Prison, NY, July 30, 1864	Exchanged October 29, 1864, at Venus Point, Savannah River, GA.
Pilson, William L. Private	Unk	March 7, 1864, Raleigh, Wake County, North Carolina	Co. J, 57th North Carolina Infantry	July 13, 1864, Near Washington, DC	Old Capital Prison, Washington DC. Transferred to Elmira Prison Camp, NY, July 25, 1864.	Oath of Allegiance May 15, 1865

Name & Rank	Age	Enlisted	Regiment and State	Where Captured	Prison	Remarks
Piner, James M. Private	23	May 13, 1861, Golden Place, Onslow County, North Carolina	Co. E, 3rd North Carolina Infantry	May 20, 1864, Spotsylvania Court House, Virginia	Point Lookout, Maryland, transferred to Elmira Prison, NY, July 3, 1864	Exchanged February 20, 1865 at Boulware's or Cox Wharf on the James River, Virginia
Pines, J. J. Private	27	August 2, 1863, Wilmington, North Carolina	Co. E, 30th North Carolina Infantry	May 20, 1864, Spotsylvania Court House, Virginia	Point Lookout, Maryland, transferred to Elmira Prison, NY, July 3, 1864	Died March 4, 1865 of Variola (Smallpox), Grave No. 1964
Piney, Robert Private	Unk	Unknown	Co. B, 5th Virginia Cavalry	June 30, 1864, Near Petersburg, Virginia	Point Lookout, Maryland, transferred to Elmira Prison, NY, July 23, 1864	Oath of Allegiance May 17, 1865
Pinkard, John M. Private	25	June 23, 1861, Camp Moore, Louisiana	Co. G, 8th Louisiana Infantry	August 8, 1864, Simsport, Louisiana	New Orleans, Louisiana transferred to Elmira November 19, 1864.	Died December 13, 1864 of Pneumonia, Grave No. 1128
Pinson, William Civilian	Unk	Louisiana	Co. A, 3rd Louisiana Cavalry	September 19, 1864, Tensan Parish, Louisiana	New Orleans, Louisiana, Transferred to Elmira Prison, New York, November 19, 1864	Died December 17, 1864 of Pneumonia, Grave No. 1271. Headstone has 1st Louisiana Cavalry.
Piper, William Private	Unk	March 3, 1863, Tullahoma, Tennessee	Co. A, 23rd Tennessee Infantry	June 17, 1864, Petersburg, Virginia	Point Lookout, Maryland, transferred to Elmira Prison, NY, July 30, 1864	Exchanged February 25, 1865 at Boulware's or Cox Wharf on the James River, Virginia
Pitchford, Robert D. Private	22	August 8, 1862, Camp Beauregard, North Carolina	Co. E, 1st North Carolina Cavalry	June 1, 1864, Near Talapatomy Creek, Cold Harbor, Virginia	Transferred From Point Lookout Prison, MD, July 12, 1864. Train Never Arrived at Elmira Prison Camp, NY.	Died July 15, 1864 in Train Wreck at Shohola, Pennsylvania.

Name & Rank	Age	Enlisted	Regiment and State	Where Captured	Prison	Remarks
Pitman, Isham Private	Unk	May 5, 1862, Camp Holmes, New Hanover, North Carolina	Co. E, 51st North Carolina Infantry	June 1, 1864, Cold Harbor, Virginia	Point Lookout, Maryland, transferred to Elmira Prison, NY, July 12, 1864	Transferred for Exchange October 29, 1864. Died November 2, 1864 at Fort Monroe, VA.
Pitman, Noah Private	Unk	March 1, 1862, Heathsville, Virginia	Co. F, 40th Virginia Infantry	July 14, 1863, Falling Waters, Maryland	Point Lookout, Maryland, transferred to Elmira Prison, NY, August 18, 1864	Exchanged October 29, 1864 at Venus Point, Savannah River, GA.
Pitman, W. T. Private	Unk	May 21, 1862, Richmond, Virginia	Co. I, 16th Georgia Infantry	June 1, 1864, Gaines Mill Cold Harbor, Virginia	Point Lookout, Maryland, transferred to Elmira Prison, NY, July 12, 1864	Oath of Allegiance July 7, 1865
Pitre, C. C. Private	Unk	October 10, 1862, Camp Pratt, Louisiana	Co. B, Consolidated Crescent Infantry	September 19, 1864, Tensan Parish, Louisiana	New Orleans, Louisiana, Transferred to Elmira Prison, New York, November 19, 1864	Exchanged February 25, 1865 at Boulware's or Cox Wharf on the James River, Virginia
Pittman, F. R. Private	Unk	Unknown	Co. A, Captain Norwood's Home Guard Florida	September 27, 1864, Marianna, Florida	New Orleans, Louisiana transferred to Elmira November 19, 1864.	Oath of Allegiance December 12, 1864 Due to Debility. Early Release Granted by Commissary General of Prisoners.
Pittman, H. R. Private	29	Unknown	Captain Chisholm's Co., Alabama Cavalry	September 27, 1864, Marianna, Louisiana	New Orleans, Louisiana transferred to Elmira November 19, 1864.	Oath of Allegiance May 29, 1865
Pittman, Hillary C. Private	Unk	May 15, 1861, Montgomery, Alabama	Co. C, 6th Alabama Infantry	May 8, 1864, Ely's Ford, Wilderness, Virginia	Point Lookout, Maryland, transferred to Elmira Prison, NY, August 17, 1864	Exchanged March 14, 1865 at Boulware's Wharf on the James River, Virginia
Pittman, Oliver E. Private	30	May 6, 1861, Jacksonville, North Carolina	Co. B, 24th North Carolina Infantry	June 17, 1864, Petersburg, Virginia	Point Lookout, Maryland, transferred to Elmira Prison, NY, July 30, 1864	Oath of Allegiance July 3, 1865

Name & Rank	Age	Enlisted	Regiment and State	Where Captured	Prison	Remarks
Pitts, Creed T. Private	Unk	September 6, 1862, Butler, Alabama	Co. F, 1st Battalion Alabama Artillery	August 23, 1864, Fort Morgan, Alabama	Steam Press No. 4 New Orleans, Louisiana transferred to Elmira Prison, NY, October 8, 1864.	Exchanged February 20, 1865 at Boulware's or Cox Wharf on the James River, Virginia
Pitts, D. W. Private	Unk	June 25, 1863, Mobile, Alabama	Co. F, 1st Battalion Alabama Artillery	August 23, 1864, Fort Morgan, Alabama	Steam Press No. 4 New Orleans, Louisiana transferred to Elmira Prison, NY, October 8, 1864.	Died November 15, 1864 of Chronic Diarrhea, Grave No. 799
Pitts, D. Y. Private	26	May 4, 1862, Laurence District, South Carolina	Co. A, 6th South Carolina Cavalry	June 11, 1864, Trevilian Station, Louisa Court House, Virginia	Point Lookout, Maryland, transferred to Elmira Prison, NY, July 11, 1864	Oath of Allegiance May 29, 1865
Pitts, Isaac Private	Unk	August 24, 1861, Clarksville, Georgia	Co. K, 24th Georgia Infantry	June 1, 1864, Cold Harbor, Virginia	Point Lookout, Maryland, transferred to Elmira Prison, NY, July 12, 1864	Oath of Allegiance July 7, 1865
Pitts, J. Y. Private	Unk	February 28, 1863, Charleston, South Carolina	Co. D, 27th South Carolina Infantry	June 24, 1864, Near Petersburg, Virginia	Point Lookout, Maryland, transferred to Elmira Prison, NY, August 18, 1864	Oath of Allegiance June 14, 1865
Pitts, John D. Private	27	June 4, 1861, Corinth, Mississippi	Co. H, 18th Mississippi Infantry	February 1, 1864, Port Hudson, Louisiana	New Orleans, Louisiana, Transferred to Elmira Prison, New York, November 19, 1864	Oath of Allegiance June 19, 1865
Placide, Robert E. Private	Unk	April 1, 1863, Lacy Spring, Maryland	Co. D, 1st Maryland Cavalry	May 27, 1864, Hanover Junction, Virginia	Point Lookout, Maryland, transferred to Elmira Prison, NY, July 12, 1864	Exchanged March 10, 1865 at Boulware's Wharf on the James River, Virginia
Plasters, Creed W. Private	Unk	May 1, 1862, G. Bridge, Virginia	Co. E, 6th Virginia Infantry	May 12, 1864, Near Spotsylvania Court House, Virginia	Point Lookout, Maryland, transferred to Elmira Prison, NY, August 6, 1864	Exchanged October 29, 1864 at Venus Point, Savannah River, GA.

Name & Rank	Age	Enlisted	Regiment and State	Where Captured	Prison	Remarks
Platt, Charles H. Corporal	Unk	May 8, 1862, Augusta, Georgia	Co. A, 7th Georgia Cavalry	June 11, 1864, Trevilian Station, Louisa Court House, Virginia	Point Lookout, Maryland, transferred to Elmira Prison, NY, July 25, 1864	Oath of Allegiance June 14, 1865
Player, Richard L. Sergeant	27	July 4, 1861, Rocky Point, North Carolina	Co. G, 3rd North Carolina Infantry	May 12, 1864, Near Spotsylvania County Court House, Virginia	Point Lookout, Maryland, transferred to Elmira Prison, NY, August 14, 1864	Exchanged October 29, 1864, at Venus Point, Savannah River, GA.
Plemmons, Z. T. Private	17	September 19, 1861, Dalton, Georgia	Co. E, 60th Georgia Infantry	November 27, 1863, Locust Grove, Mine Run, Virginia. Gunshot Wound Left Thigh, Amputated.	Point Lookout, Maryland, transferred to Elmira Prison, NY, July 12,1864	Exchanged October 29, 1864, at Venus Point, Savannah River, GA.
Plott, John Private	40	April 7, 1862, Salisbury, North Carolina	Co. D, 42nd North Carolina Infantry	June 2, 1864, Cold Harbor, Virginia	Point Lookout, Maryland, transferred to Elmira Prison, NY, July 12, 1864	Exchanged March 14, 1865 at Boulware's Wharf on the James River, Virginia,
Plowden, John Covert Private	36	March 18, 1862, Camp Manigault, Georgetown, South Carolina	Co. J, 25th South Carolina Infantry	January 15, 1865, Fort Fisher, North Carolina	February 1, 1865, Elmira Prison Camp, New York	Died May 2, 1865 of Chronic Diarrhea, Grave No. 2754
Plowman, William Private	Unk	November 30, 1863, Camp Holmes, North Carolina	Co. I, 28th North Carolina Infantry	July 29, 1864, Petersburg, Virginia	Point Lookout, Maryland, transferred to Elmira Prison, NY, August 12, 1864	Oath of Allegiance May 9, 1865
Plummer, F. E. Private	Unk	July 4, 1862, Salisbury, North Carolina	Co. K, 8th, North Carolina Infantry	May 31, 1864, Cold Harbor, Virginia	Point Lookout, Maryland, transferred to Elmira Prison, NY, July 12, 1864	Oath of Allegiance June 12, 1865
Plunkett, Lysander H. Private	18	April 18, 1861, Greenville, Virginia	Co. E, 5th Virginia Infantry	July 12, 1864, Rockville, Maryland	Old Capital Prison, Washington DC. Transferred to Elmira Prison Camp, NY, July 25, 1864.	Exchanged March 10, 1865 at Boulware's Wharf on the James River, Virginia

Name & Rank	Age	Enlisted	Regiment and State	Where Captured	Prison	Remarks
Poague, Allen M. Private	18	March 10, 1862, Hold County, Missouri	Co. C, 1st Missouri Cavalry	May 17, 1863, Big Black Bridge, Champion Hill, Mississippi	Point Lookout, Maryland, transferred to Elmira Prison, NY, August 18, 1864	Exchanged February 13, 1865 at Boulware's wharf on the James River, Virginia
Poe, C. D. Private	Unk	March 1, 1864, Chatham County, North Carolina	Co. D, 35th North Carolina Infantry	June 7, 1864, Petersburg, Virginia. Gunshot Wound Right Hip and Scrotum, Penis and Testicles.	Old Capital Prison, Washington, DC transferred to Elmira Prison, NY, August 27, 1864	Oath of Allegiance June 19, 1865
Poe, David Private	Unk	Unknown	Co. D, 61st North Carolina Infantry	August 27, 1863, Battery Wagner, Morris Island, South Carolina	Point Lookout, Maryland, transferred to Elmira Prison, NY, August 18, 1864	Exchanged October 29, 1864, at Venus Point, Savannah River, GA.
Poe, Rueben P. Private	25	December 20, 1861, Orange County, North Carolina	Co. G, 28th North Carolina Infantry	May 12, 1864, Near Spotsylvania Court House, Virginia	Point Lookout, Maryland, transferred to Elmira Prison, NY, August 14, 1864	Exchanged October 29, 1864, at Venus Point, Savannah River, GA.
Poellnitz, Sidney C. Private	20	June 26, 1862, Tupelo, Mississippi	Co. C, 21st Alabama Infantry	August 23, 1864, Fort Morgan, Alabama	New Orleans, Louisiana, Transferred to Elmira Prison, New York, October 8, 1864	Died December 21, 1864 of Pneumonia, Grave No. 1085
Poff, Samuel Private	Unk	February 13, 1864, Dublin, Virginia	Co. B, 4th Virginia Infantry	May 12, 1864, Spotsylvania Court House, Virginia	Point Lookout, Maryland, transferred to Elmira Prison, NY, August 2, 1864	Transferred for Exchange 10/11/64. Died 10/13/64, buried at Port Royal, SC.
Poff, Thomas W. Private	Unk	February 13, 1864, Dublin, Virginia	Co. B, 4th Virginia Infantry	May 12, 1864, Near Spotsylvania Court House, Virginia	Point Lookout, Maryland, transferred to Elmira Prison, NY, August 6, 1864	Died December 2, 1864 of Chronic Diarrhea, Grave No. 895
Pofford, James W. Sergeant	19	June 20, 1861, Abingdon, Virginia	Co. B, 48th Virginia Infantry	May 12, 1864, Spotsylvania Court House, Virginia	Point Lookout, Maryland, transferred to Elmira Prison, NY, August 12, 1864	Oath of Allegiance June 19, 1865

Name & Rank	Age	Enlisted	Regiment and State	Where Captured	Prison	Remarks
Pohley, Samuel Private	Unk	June 8, 1861, New Orleans, Louisiana	Co. K, 15th Louisiana Infantry	May 12, 1864, Spotsylvania Court House, Virginia	Point Lookout, Maryland, transferred to Elmira Prison, NY, July 25, 1864	Oath of Allegiance May 17, 1865
Poindexter, Isaac C. Private	23	June 18, 1861, East Bend, North Carolina	Co. F, 28th North Carolina Infantry	May 12, 1864, Spotsylvania Court House, Virginia	Point Lookout, Maryland, transferred to Elmira Prison, NY, August 17, 1864	Exchanged March 14, 1865 at Boulware's Wharf on the James River, Virginia
Poindexter, Thomas L. Pivate	Unk	May 18, 1862, Camp Harris, Tennessee	Co. F, 17th Tennessee Infantry	June 17, 1864, Petersburg, Virginia	Point Lookout, Maryland, transferred to Elmira Prison, NY, July 30, 1864	Oath of Allegiance April 14, 1865
Pointer, John F. Private	21	April 20, 1861, Belle Roi., Virginia	Co. A, 26th Virginia Infantry	June 15, 1864, Near Petersburg, Virginia	Point Lookout, Maryland, transferred to Elmira Prison, NY, July 12,1864	Oath of Allegiance July 3, 1865
Polk, Joel Private	Unk	May 20, 1864, Petersburg, Virginia	Co. K, 21st South Carolina Infantry	January 15, 1865, Fort Fisher, North Carolina	February 1, 1865, Elmira Prison Camp, New York	Oath of Allegiance July 7, 1865
Polk, Levi M. Private	Unk	August 6, 1863, Poplar Springs, Hall County, Georgia	Co. J, 24th Georgia Infantry	August 16, 1864, Front Royal, Virginia	Point Lookout, Maryland, transferred to Elmira Prison, NY, August 29, 1864	Died February 15, 1865 of Chronic Diarrhea, Grave No. 2166
Pollard, Daniel W. Private	Unk	February 6, 1863, Skinker's Neck, Virginia	Co. D, 10th Virginia Infantry	May 12, 1864, Spotsylvania Court House, Virginia	Point Lookout, Maryland, transferred to Elmira Prison, NY, August 2, 1864	Oath of Allegiance June 23, 1865
Pollard, John T. Private	20	June 9, 1861, Quitman, Georgia	Co. H, 9th Georgia Infantry	May 6, 1864, Wilderness, Virginia	Old Capital Prison, Washington D. C. Transferred to Elmira Prison, NY, July 14, 1864	Exchanged October 29, 1864 at Venus Point, Savannah River, GA.
Pollard, Samuel Private	Unk	September 8, 1862, Statesville, North Carolina	Co. A, 18th North Carolina Infantry	May 12, 1864, Spotsylvania Court House, Virginia	Point Lookout, Maryland, transferred to Elmira Prison, NY, July 17, 1864	Oath of Allegiance May 19, 1865

Name & Rank	Age	Enlisted	Regiment and State	Where Captured	Prison	Remarks
Polsen, James Douglas Private	26	June 19, 1861, Camp Moore, Louisiana	Co. A, 8th Louisiana Infantry	May 20, 1864, Spotsylvania Court House, Virginia	Point Lookout, Maryland, transferred to Elmira Prison, NY, July 3, 1864	Exchanged October 29, 1864, at Venus Point, Savannah River, GA.
Polson, James Private	Unk	Unknown	Co. B, 1st Alabama Artillery	August 23, 1864, Fort Morgan, Alabama	New Orleans, Louisiana transferred to Elmira November 19, 1864.	Died April 19, 1865 of Unknown Causes, Grave No. 1374
Pond, Joseph J. Private	Unk	April 26, 1861, Livingston, Sumpter County, Alabama	Co. E, 5th Alabama Infantry	May 5, 1864, wilderness, Virginia	Point Lookout, Maryland, transferred to Elmira Prison, New York, August 17, 1864.	Exchanged March 10, 1865 at Boulware's Wharf on the James River, Virginia
Ponder, Benjamin F. Private	Unk	May 8, 1862, Madison, Florida	Co. E, 5th Florida Infantry	May 12, 1864, Spotsylvania Court House, Virginia	Point Lookout, Maryland, transferred to Elmira Prison, NY, July 30, 1864	Exchanged October 29, 1864, at Venus Point, Savannah River, GA.
Ponder, George R. Private	Unk	February 1, 1863, Greenville, South Carolina	Co. H, 6th South Carolina Cavalry	June 21, 1864, Near White House, Virginia	Point Lookout, Maryland, transferred to Elmira Prison, NY, August 18, 1864	Oath of Allegiance July 3, 1865
Ponder, James T. Private	Unk	April 28, 1862, Marietta, Cobb County, Georgia	Co., Phillips Legion Georgia Infantry	June 3, 1864, Gaines Farm, Cold Harbor, Virginia	Point Lookout, Maryland, transferred to Elmira Prison, NY, July 17,1864	Oath of Allegiance July 7, 1865
Pool, Albert J. Private	20	March 12, 1862, Lincolnton, North Carolina	Co. I, 11th North Carolina Cavalry	May 27, 1864, Hanover, Virginia	Point Lookout, Maryland, transferred to Elmira Prison, NY, July 12, 1864	Oath of Allegiance May 19, 1865
Pool, George Private	Unk	August 20, 1863, Henderson, North Carolina	Co. K, 3rd North Carolina Infantry	November 28, 1863, Locust Grove, Mine Run, Virginia.	Old Capital Prison, Washington DC. Transferred to Elmira Prison Camp, NY, July 25, 1864.	Died October 14, 1864 of Scorbutis (Scurvy), Grave No. 706. Headstone has 3rd NC Cavalry.

Name & Rank	Age	Enlisted	Regiment and State	Where Captured	Prison	Remarks
Pool, Henson Civilian	Unk	Unknown	Citizen of Fairfax County, Virginia	January 13, 1864, Loudoun County, Virginia	Point Lookout, Maryland, transferred to Elmira Prison, NY, July 25, 1864	Died March 27, 1865 of Diarrhea, Grave No. 2513
Pool, James N. Private	Unk	March 10, 1862, Wytheville, Virginia	Co. A, 4th Virginia Infantry	May 12, 1864, Spotsylvania Court House, Virginia	Point Lookout, Maryland, transferred to Elmira Prison, NY, August 2, 1864	Oath of Allegiance June 27, 1865
Pool, James T. Private	Unk	Unknown	Co. J, 53rd North Carolina Infantry	June 11, 1864, Cold Harbor, Virginia	Old Capital Prison, Washington DC. Transferred to Elmira Prison Camp, NY, July 25, 1864.	Died December 7, 1864 of Pneumonia, Grave No. 1193
Pool, John F. Private	29	July 15, 1862, Raleigh, North Carolina	Co. C, 5th North Carolina Infantry	May 12, 1864, Spotsylvania Court House, Virginia	Point Lookout, Maryland, transferred to Elmira Prison, NY, August 6, 1864	Oath of Allegiance July 11, 1865
Pool, John R. Private	Unk	April 25, 1862, Glade Spring, Virginia	Co. F, 37 Virginia Infantry	July 10, 1864, Near Frederick, Maryland	Old Capital Prison, Washington DC. Transferred to Elmira Prison Camp, NY, July 25, 1864.	Oath of Allegiance July 7, 1865
Pool, Randolph Private	23	August 6, 1861, Mocksville, North Carolina	Co. F, 13th North Carolina Infantry	July 14, 1863, Falling Waters, Maryland	Point Lookout, Maryland, transferred to Elmira Prison, NY, August 18, 1864	Exchanged March 10, 1865 at Boulware's Wharf on the James River, Virginia
Pool, William R. Private	32	July 16, 1862, Raleigh, Wake County, North Carolina	Co. G, 14th North Carolina Infantry	July 13, 1864, Near Washington, DC	Old Capital Prison, Washington DC. Transferred to Elmira Prison Camp, NY, July 25, 1864.	Exchanged March 10, 1865 at Boulware's Wharf on the James River, Virginia
Poole, B. S. Private	Unk	July 27, 1861, New Orleans, Louisiana	Co. A, 14th Louisiana Infantry	May 12, 1864, Spotsylvania Court House, Virginia	Point Lookout, Maryland, transferred to Elmira Prison, NY, July 25, 1864	Exchanged February 25, 1865 at Boulware's or Cox Wharf on the James River, Virginia

Name & Rank	Age	Enlisted	Regiment and State	Where Captured	Prison	Remarks
Poole, James L. Private	18	June 6, 1861, Newton, North Carolina	Co. F, 23rd North Carolina Infantry	May 12, 1864, Near Spotsylvania Court House, Virginia	Point Lookout Prison, Maryland. Transferred to Elmira Prison Camp New York August 14, 1864.	Exchanged October 29, 1864, at Venus Point, Savannah River, GA.
Poole, Quenton R. Private	23	July 1, 1863, Camp Davis, North Carolina	Co. D, 31st North Carolina Infantry	May 31, 1864, Cold Harbor, Virginia	Point Lookout, Maryland, transferred to Elmira Prison, NY, July 12, 1864	Died October 3, 1864 of Typhoid Fever, Grave No. 625
Poole, Thomas G. Private	37	May 16, 1861, Columbia, North Carolina	Co. H, 32nd North Carolina Infantry	May 10, 1864, Near Spotsylvania Court House, Virginia	Point Lookout, Maryland, transferred to Elmira Prison, NY, August 6, 1864	Exchanged October 29, 1864, at Venus Point, Savannah River, GA.
Poovey, John S. Private	32	August 20, 1862, Camp Hill, North Carolina	Co. C, 18th North Carolina Infantry	May 12, 1864, Spotsylvania Court House, Virginia	Point Lookout, Maryland, transferred to Elmira Prison, NY, July 17, 1864	Oath of Allegiance May 19, 1865
Pope, Alexander C. Private	18	July 17, 1862, Randolph County, North Carolina	Co. H, 3rd North Carolina Infantry	May 12, 1864, Near Spotsylvania Court House, Virginia	Point Lookout, Maryland, transferred to Elmira Prison, NY, August 14, 1864	Oath of Allegiance June 23, 1865
Pope, C. T. Private	Unk	June 20, 1863, Greene County, Alabama	Co. B, 7th Alabama Cavalry	July 22, 1864, Mobile Point, Louisiana	New Orleans, Louisiana, Transferred to Elmira Prison, New York, November 19, 1864	Died December 6, 1864 of Pneumonia, Grave No. 1190
Pope, David E. Corporal	Unk	January 14, 1862, Camp Walsh, South Carolina	Co. J, Holcombe Legion, South Carolina	May 7, 1864, Stony Creek, Virginia	Point Lookout, Maryland, transferred to Elmira Prison, NY, August 17, 1864	Transferred For Exchange 10/11/64. Died 10/13/64 of Unknown Causes. Brought to US Army Hospital, Baltimore, MD, Dead.

Name & Rank	Age	Enlisted	Regiment and State	Where Captured	Prison	Remarks
Pope, Doctor W. Private	Unk	April 26, 1862, Cumberland County, North Carolina	Co. J, 51st North Carolina Infantry	June 1, 1864, Cold Harbor, Virginia	Transferred From Point Lookout Prison, MD, July 12, 1864. Train Never Arrived at Elmira Prison Camp, NY.	Died July 15, 1864 in Train Wreck at Shohola, Pennsylvania.
Pope, J. W. Private	24	April 8, 1861, New Orleans, Louisiana	Co. G, 1st Louisiana Infantry	May 20, 1864, Spotsylvania Court House, Virginia	Point Lookout, Maryland, transferred to Elmira Prison, NY, July 3, 1864	Exchanged February 13, 1865 at Boulware's wharf on the James River, Virginia
Pope, James D. Private	30	March 27, 1862, Cumberland County, North Carolina	Co. J, 51st North Carolina Infantry	June 1, 1864, Cold Harbor, Virginia	Point Lookout, Maryland, transferred to Elmira Prison, NY, July 12, 1864	Exchanged March 2, 1865 at Akins Landing on the James River, Virginia
Pope, John N. Corporal	20	May 15, 1861, Hawkinsville, Georgia	Co. G, 8th Georgia Infantry	May 6, 1864, Wilderness, Virginia	Old Capital Prison, Washington D. C. Transferred to Elmira Prison, NY, July 14, 1864	Died June 5, 1865 of Pneumonia, Grave No. 2894
Pope, Stephen Private	41	September 23, 1863, Brunswick County, North Carolina	Co. G, 40th 3rd Regiment North Carolina Artillery	January 15, 1865, Fort Fisher, North Carolina	February 1, 1865, Elmira Prison Camp, New York	Oath of Allegiance June 12, 1865
Pope, William A. Private	20	July 15, 1862, Raleigh, North Carolina	Co. K, 1st North Carolina Infantry	May 12, 1864, Spotsylvania Court House, Virginia	Point Lookout, Maryland, transferred to Elmira Prison, NY, August 6, 1864	Died January 22, 1865 of Chronic Diarrhea, Grave No. 1604
Pope, William H. Private	20	June 2, 1861, Jefferson Court House, Virginia	Co. A, 2nd Virginia Infantry	May 12, 1864, Near Spotsylvania Court House, Virginia	Point Lookout, Maryland, transferred to Elmira Prison, NY, August 6, 1864	Oath of Allegiance June 27, 1865
Pope, William Streety Corporal	28	October 19, 1861, Elizabethtown, Bladen County, North Carolina	Co. J, 36th Regiment, 2nd North Carolina Artillery	January 15, 1865, Fort Fisher, North Carolina	February 1, 1865, Elmira Prison Camp, New York	Oath of Allegiance June 12, 1865

Name & Rank	Age	Enlisted	Regiment and State	Where Captured	Prison	Remarks
Poplin, Richard Private	35	March 24, 1862, Salisbury, North Carolina	Co. C, 42nd North Carolina Infantry	June 3, 1864, Cold Harbor, Virginia	Point Lookout, Maryland, transferred to Elmira Prison, NY, July 12, 1864	Oath of Allegiance July 3, 1865
Porter, George W. D. Sergeant	Unk	December 7, 1861, Camp Trousdale, Tennessee	Co. E, 44th Tennessee Infantry	June 17, 1864, Petersburg, Virginia	Point Lookout, Maryland, transferred to Elmira Prison, NY, July 30, 1864	Exchanged February 25, 1865 at Boulware's or Cox Wharf on the James River, Virginia
Porter, James T. Private	19	October 3, 1861, Anson County, North Carolina	Co. B, 31st North Carolina Infantry	June 1, 1864, Cold Harbor, Virginia	Point Lookout, Maryland, transferred to Elmira Prison, NY, July 17,1864	Exchanged October 29, 1864, at Venus Point, Savannah River, GA.
Porter, Jesse Private	22	August 10, 1861, Gatesville, Gates County, North Carolina	Co. E, 33rd North Carolina Infantry	May 6, 1864, Wilderness, Virginia	Point Lookout, Maryland, transferred to Elmira Prison, NY, August 14, 1864	Exchanged February 13, 1865 at Boulware's wharf on the James River, Virginia
Porter, Josiah F. Private	Unk	June 15, 1861, Eatonton, Georgia	Co. G, 12th Georgia Infantry	May 10, 1864, Spotsylvania Court House, Virginia	Point Lookout, Maryland, transferred to Elmira Prison, NY, July 30, 1864	Oath of Allegiance May 12, 1865
Porter, Samuel B. A. Corporal	Unk	July 24, 1861, Tappahannock, Virginia	Co. E, 55th Virginia Infantry	July 14, 1863, Falling Waters, Maryland	Point Lookout, Maryland, transferred to Elmira Prison, NY, August 18, 1864	Exchanged March 10, 1865 at Boulware's Wharf on the James River, Virginia
Porter, Samuel P. Private	17	March 17, 1862, Charleston, South Carolina	Co. F, 18th South Carolina Infantry	July 30, 1864, Petersburg, Virginia	Point Lookout, Maryland, transferred to Elmira Prison, NY, August 12, 1864	Oath of Allegiance July 3, 1865
Porter, Wiley B. Private	28	March 27, 1862, Cumberland County, North Carolina	Co. J, 51st North Carolina Infantry	May 16, 1864, Near Drury's Bluff, Virginia	Point Lookout, Maryland, transferred to Elmira Prison, NY, August 18, 1864	Oath of Allegiance May 29, 1865

Name & Rank	Age	Enlisted	Regiment and State	Where Captured	Prison	Remarks
Porter, William Alex Private	32	Unknown	Co. D, 1st Virginia Cavalry	July 27, 1864, Loudoun County, Virginia. Deserted to Union Lines.	Old Capital Prison, Washington D. C. Transferred to Elmira Prison, NY, August 12, 1864	Oath of Allegiance April 4, 1865. Early Release per Lincoln's Proclamation, 12/8/1863.
Portlock, William J. Private	24	March 27, 1862, Lynn Beach, Virginia	Co. C, 15th Virginia Cavalry	May 11, 1864, Near Ashland, Virginia	Point Lookout, Maryland, transferred to Elmira Prison, NY, August 17, 1864	Exchanged October 29, 1864, at Venus Point, Savannah River, GA.
Posey, James J. Private	Unk	May 14, 1862, Sandersville, Georgia	Co. F, 49th Georgia Infantry	May 6, 1864, Wilderness, Virginia	Point Lookout, Maryland, transferred to Elmira Prison, NY, August 14, 1864	Oath of Allegiance June 14, 1865
Posey, William A. Private	21	May 5, 1861, Hendersonville, North Carolina	Co. J, 16th North Carolina Infantry	May 5, 1864, Wilderness, Virginia	Point Lookout, Maryland, transferred to Elmira Prison, NY, August 14, 1864	Oath of Allegiance June 27, 1865
Potter, Benjamin W. Private	19	March 8, 1862, Brunswick County, North Carolina	Co. G, 51st North Carolina Infantry	May 31, 1864, Cold Harbor, Virginia	Point Lookout, Maryland, transferred to Elmira Prison, NY, July 12,1864	Exchanged October 29, 1864, at Venus Point, Savannah River, GA.
Potter, Franklin L. Private	Unk	October 9, 1861, Savannah, Georgia	Co. C, 31st Georgia Infantry	May 20, 1864, Spotsylvania Court House, Virginia	Point Lookout, Maryland, transferred to Elmira Prison, NY, July 3, 1864	Exchanged October 29, 1864, at Venus Point, Savannah River, GA.
Potter, John B. Private	Unk	May 26, 1861, Heathsville, Virginia	Co. C, 40th Virginia Infantry	July 14, 1863, Falling Waters, Maryland	Point Lookout, Maryland, transferred to Elmira Prison, NY, August 18, 1864	Exchanged March 10, 1865 at Boulware's Wharf on the James River, Virginia
Potter, Rufus H. Private	17	December 4, 1861, Bladen County, North Carolina	Co. B, 36th Regiment, 2nd North Carolina Artillery	January 15, 1865, Fort Fisher, North Carolina	February 1, 1865, Elmira Prison Camp, New York	Died April 9, 1865 of Chronic Diarrhea, Grave No. 2613
Potter, Samuel Private	35	May 10, 1861, Washington, North Carolina	Co. J, 3rd North Carolina Infantry	May 12, 1864, Near Spotsylvania County Court House, Virginia	Point Lookout, Maryland, transferred to Elmira Prison, NY, August 14, 1864	Oath of Allegiance June 27, 1865

Name & Rank	Age	Enlisted	Regiment and State	Where Captured	Prison	Remarks
Potter, Thomas N. Corporal	Unk	July 20, 1861, Jefferson, Georgia	Co. G, 16th Georgia Infantry	June 1, 1864, Gaines Farm Cold Harbor, Virginia	Point Lookout, Maryland, transferred to Elmira Prison, NY, July 12, 1864	Died September 13, 1864 of Pneumonia, Grave No. 269
Potter, William M. Private	18	December 5, 1861, Sac River, St. Clair County, Missouri	Co. G, 1st Missouri Cavalry	May 17, 1863, Big Black Bridge, Champion Hill, Mississippi	Point Lookout, Maryland, transferred to Elmira Prison, NY, August 18, 1864	Exchanged February 25, 1865 at Boulware's wharf on the James River, Virginia
Potts, Calvin J. Corporal	27	February 5, 1862, Salisbury, North Carolina	Co. B, 46th North Carolina Infantry	July 29, 1864, Petersburg, Virginia	Point Lookout, Maryland, transferred to Elmira Prison, NY, August 12, 1864	Died January 5, 1865 of Chronic Diarrhea, Grave No. 1261
Potts, James W. Private	Unk	September 5, 1862, Clark County, Alabama	Co. K, 3rd Alabama Infantry	May 12, 1864, Spotsylvania Court House, Virginia	Point Lookout, Maryland, transferred to Elmira Prison, NY, August 12, 1864	Died April 6, 1865 of Pneumonia, Grave No. 2658
Potts, Jefferson L. Private	Unk	June 11, 1861, Camp McDonald, Georgia	Co. G, 18th Georgia Infantry	June 1, 1864, Cold Harbor, Virginia	Point Lookout, Maryland, transferred to Elmira Prison, NY, July 17, 1864	Oath of Allegiance June 21, 1865
Potts, L. G. Private	22	January 1, 1863, Williamsville, Virginia	Co. G, 18th Virginia Cavalry	June 29, 1864, McConnersburg Pennsylvania	Point Lookout, Maryland, transferred to Elmira Prison, NY, July 25, 1864	Oath of Allegiance June 23, 1865
Potts, Montraville P. Private	Unk	Unknown	Co. J, 30th Georgia Infantry	June 1, 1864, Bowling Green, Kentucky	Point Lookout, Maryland, transferred to Elmira Prison, NY, July 17, 1864	Died April 10, 1865 of Unknown Disease, Grave No. 2615 Headstone has Patts.
Pounds, William T. Private	Unk	March 7, 1861, Randolph, Alabama	Co. C, 1st Battalion Alabama Artillery	August 23, 1864, Fort Morgan, Alabama	New Orleans, Louisiana transferred to Elmira Prison, NY, December 4, 1864.	Oath of Allegiance May 17, 1865

Name & Rank	Age	Enlisted	Regiment and State	Where Captured	Prison	Remarks
Pouns, Jacob A. Sergeant	22	April 23, 1862, Old Brunswick Town, North Carolina	Co. G, 36th Regiment, 2nd North Carolina Artillery	January 15, 1865, Fort Fisher, North Carolina	February 1, 1865, Elmira Prison Camp, New York	Died February 13, 1865 of Pneumonia, Grave No. 2051
Pouns, Samuel J. Private	17	Fort Fisher, New Hanover County, NC, 4/19/1864	Co. G, 36th Regiment, 2nd North Carolina Artillery	January 15, 1865, Fort Fisher, North Carolina	February 1, 1865, Elmira Prison Camp, New York	Transferred for Exchange February 20, 1865. No Further Information.
Powe, Ellerbe F. Private	40	December 20, 1861, Cheraw, South Carolina	Co. D, 21st South Carolina Infantry	January 15, 1865, Fort Fisher, North Carolina	February 1, 1865, Elmira Prison Camp, New York	Oath of Allegiance July 7, 1865
Powe, James F. Corporal	Unk	April 3, 1862, Camp Manigault, Chesterfield, South Carolina	Co. D, 21st South Carolina Infantry	January 15, 1865, Fort Fisher, North Carolina	February 1, 1865, Elmira Prison Camp, New York	Died May 5, 1865 of Pneumonia, Grave No. 2764
Powe, Joseph E. Corporal	Unk	April 3, 1862, Camp Manigault, Chesterfield, South Carolina	Co. D, 21st South Carolina Infantry	January 15, 1865, Fort Fisher, North Carolina	February 1, 1865, Elmira Prison Camp, New York	Died March 8, 1865 of Pneumonia, Grave No. 2364
Powell, Abraham Private	Unk	September 12, 1861, Reidsville, Tattnall County, Georgia	Co. H, 61st Georgia Infantry	May 12, 1864, Spotsylvania Court House, Virginia	Point Lookout, Maryland, transferred to Elmira Prison, NY, July 30, 1864. Ward No. 33	Oath of Allegiance June 30, 1865
Powell, C. Thomas Private	Unk	August 21, 1863, Ashepoo, South Carolina	Co. C, 11th South Carolina Infantry	June 16, 1864, Petersburg, Virginia	Point Lookout, Maryland, transferred to Elmira Prison, NY, July 12, 1864	Exchanged March 10, 1865 at Boulware's Wharf on the James River, Virginia
Powell, Charles Private	Unk	May 13, 1862, Myersville, South Carolina	Co. H, 25th South Carolina Infantry	January 15, 1865, Fort Fisher, North Carolina	February 1, 1865, Elmira Prison Camp, New York	Exchanged March 2, 1865 at Akins Landing on the James River, Virginia
Powell, Charles W. Private	Unk	July 2, 1861, Richmond, Virginia	Co. G, 21st Virginia Infantry	May 12, 1864, Spotsylvania Court House, Virginia	Point Lookout, Maryland, transferred to Elmira Prison, NY, August 12, 1864	Exchanged February 20, 1865 at Boulware's or Cox Wharf on the James River, Virginia

Name & Rank	Age	Enlisted	Regiment and State	Where Captured	Prison	Remarks
Powell, David, Private	Unk	May 13, 1862, Myersville, South Carolina	Co. F, 25th South Carolina Infantry	January 15, 1865, Fort Fisher, North Carolina	February 1, 1865, Elmira Prison Camp, New York	Exchanged March 2, 1865 at Akins Landing on the James River, Virginia
Powell, E., Private	Unk	May 7, 1862, Myersville, South Carolina	Co. H, 25th South Carolina Infantry	January 15, 1865, Fort Fisher, North Carolina	February 1, 1865, Elmira Prison Camp, New York	Died June 23, 1865 of Inflammation of Liver, Grave No. 2815
Powell, F., Private	Unk	Unknown	Whitford's Artillery, State Unknown	August 18, 1863, Big Black, Mississippi	Point Lookout, Maryland, transferred to Elmira Prison, NY, August 18, 1864	Exchanged February 13, 1865 at Boulware's wharf on the James River, Virginia
Powell, G. W., Private	Unk	May 1, 1862, Augusta, Georgia	Co. A, 7th Georgia Cavalry	June 11, 1864, Trevilian Station, Louisa Court House, Virginia	Point Lookout, Maryland, transferred to Elmira Prison, NY, July 25, 1864	Exchanged March 2, 1865 at Akins Landing on the James River, Virginia
Powell, George L., Private	24	October 1862, Morganton, North Carolina	Co. F, 3rd North Carolina Cavalry	May 27, 1864, Hanover, Virginia	Point Lookout, Maryland, transferred to Elmira Prison, NY, July 12, 1864	Died November 28, 1864 of Typhoid Fever, Grave No. 993
Powell, George W., Private	25	March 1, 1861, Nashville, North Carolina	Co. H, 32nd North Carolina Infantry	May 10, 1864, Near Spotsylvania Court House, Virginia	Point Lookout, Maryland, transferred to Elmira Prison, NY, August 6, 1864	Exchanged March 14, 1865 at Boulware's Wharf on the James River, Virginia
Powell, George W., Private	20	July 23, 1861, Matthews Court House, Virginia	Co. F, 5th Virginia Cavalry	May 11, 1864, Yellow Tavern, Hanover County, Virginia	Point Lookout, Maryland, transferred to Elmira Prison, NY, August 17, 1864	Oath of Allegiance June 21, 1865
Powell, Henry J., Private	20	June 7, 1861, Camp Moore, Louisiana	Co. K, 7th Louisiana Infantry	May 11, 1864, Spotsylvania Court House, Virginia	Point Lookout, Maryland, transferred to Elmira Prison, NY, August 17, 1864	Exchanged February 25, 1865 at Boulware's or Cox Wharf on the James River, Virginia

Name & Rank	Age	Enlisted	Regiment and State	Where Captured	Prison	Remarks
Powell, James B. Private	35	January 30, 1862, Lillington, North Carolina	Co. C, 1st North Carolina Infantry	May 12, 1864, Spotsylvania Court House, Virginia	Point Lookout, Maryland, transferred to Elmira Prison, NY, August 6, 1864	Exchanged March 2, 1865 at Akins Landing on the James River, Virginia
Powell, James E. Private	Unk	Unknown	Co. A, 3rd Louisiana Cavalry	September 19, 1864, Tensan Parish, Louisiana	New Orleans, Louisiana, Transferred to Elmira Prison, New York, November 19, 1864	Died January 11, 1865 of Pneumonia, Grave No. 1493
Powell, James H. Private	25	May 1, 1862, South Mills, North Carolina	Co. C, 32nd North Carolina Infantry	May 10, 1864, Near Spotsylvania Court House, Virginia	Point Lookout, Maryland, transferred to Elmira Prison, NY, August 6, 1864	Exchanged March 2, 1865 at Akins Landing on the James River, Virginia
Powell, James M. Private	22	July 19, 1861, Selma, Alabama	Jeff Davis Alabama Artillery	July 5, 1863, Gettysburg, Pennsylvania	Point Lookout, Maryland, transferred to Elmira Prison, NY, July 25, 1864	Died February 22, 1865, Variola (Smallpox), Grave No. 2251
Powell, James T. Private	24	May 16, 1862, Clinton, North Carolina	Co. C, 5th North Carolina Cavalry	September 22, 1863, Near Madison Court House, Virginia	Point Lookout, Maryland, transferred to Elmira Prison, NY, August 18, 1864	Exchanged March 10, 1865 at Boulware's Wharf on the James River, Virginia
Powell, Jeremiah Private	Unk	April 15, 1861, Buena Vista, Georgia	Co. K, 12th Georgia Infantry	May 10, 1864, Spotsylvania Court House, Virginia	Point Lookout, Maryland, transferred to Elmira Prison, NY, July 25, 1864	Died November 6, 1864 of Chronic Diarrhea, Grave No. 767
Powell, John Private	Unk	April 1, 1862, Fredericksburg, Virginia	Co. A, 60th Virginia Infantry	August 17, 1864, Winchester, Virginia	Old Capital Prison, Washington, DC transferred to Elmira Prison, NY, August 29, 1864	Died January 31, 1865 of Variola (Smallpox), Grave No. 1788.
Powell, John F. Private	Unk	Unknown	Co. K, 19th Virginia Cavalry	July 15, 1864, Near Harpers Ferry, Loudoun County, Virginia	Old Capital Prison, Washington DC. Transferred to Elmira Prison Camp, NY, July 25, 1864.	Oath of Allegiance May 15, 1865

Name & Rank	Age	Enlisted	Regiment and State	Where Captured	Prison	Remarks
Powell, John J. Civilian	Unk	Louisiana	Citizen of Louisiana	September 19, 1864, Tensan Parish, Louisiana	New Orleans, Louisiana, Transferred to Elmira Prison, New York, November 19, 1864	Died February 19, 1865 of Pneumonia, Grave No. 2338
Powell, John L. Private	Unk	May 9, 1861, New Orleans, Louisiana	Co. B, 2nd Louisiana Infantry	May 20, 1864, Spotsylvania Court House, Virginia	Point Lookout, Maryland, transferred to Elmira Prison, NY, July 3, 1864	Exchanged February 13, 1865 at Boulware's wharf on the James River, Virginia
Powell, John W. Private	25	March 1, 1861, Nashville, North Carolina	Co. H, 32nd North Carolina Infantry	May 10, 1864, Near Spotsylvania Court House, Virginia	Point Lookout, Maryland, transferred to Elmira Prison, NY, August 6, 1864	Died September 9, 1864 of Chronic Diarrhea, Grave No. 206
Powell, Joseph Private	Unk	Unknown	Florida Home Guard	October 7, 1864, Moore, Louisiana	Old Capital Prison, Washington, DC, transferred to Elmira, NY December 4, 1864	Exchanged February 20, 1865 at Boulware's or Cox Wharf on the James River, Virginia
Powell, Lewis A. Private	Unk	October 15, 1863, Columbia, South Carolina	Co. C, 22nd South Carolina Infantry	July 30, 1864, Petersburg, Virginia	Point Lookout, Maryland, transferred to Elmira Prison, NY, August 12, 1864	Died September 14, 1864 of Pneumonia, Grave No. 127
Powell, Richard O. Private	Unk	July 26, 1861, Montgomery, Alabama	Co. E, 13th Alabama Infantry	May 12, 1864, Spotsylvania Court House, Virginia	Point Lookout, Maryland, transferred to Elmira Prison, NY, August 2, 1864	Exchanged October 29, 1864 on the James River, Virginia
Powell, Warren T. Private	20	September 24, 1861, Roberson County, North Carolina	Co. E, 40th 3rd Regiment North Carolina Artillery	January 15, 1865, Fort Fisher, North Carolina	February 1, 1865, Elmira Prison Camp, New York	Exchanged March 2, 1865. Died April 24, 1865 of Chronic Diarrhea at Jackson Hospital, Richmond, VA.
Powell, William B. Private	Unk	July 20, 1861, Richmond, Virginia	Co. E, 59th Virginia Infantry	May 7, 1864, Nottoway Bridge, Virginia	Point Lookout, Maryland, transferred to Elmira Prison, NY, August 17, 1864	Died February 25, 1865 of Chronic Diarrhea, Grave No. 2288. Headstone has N. P. Powell.

Name & Rank	Age	Enlisted	Regiment and State	Where Captured	Prison	Remarks
Powell, William F. Private	35	March 22, 1862, Porter's Precinct, Virginia	Co. B, 15th Virginia Cavalry	May 11, 1864, Near Ashland, Virginia	Point Lookout, Maryland, transferred to Elmira Prison, NY, August 17, 1864	Exchanged October 29, 1864, at Venus Point, Savannah River, GA.
Powell, William W. Private	32	April 17, 1862, Northampton County, North Carolina	Co. D, 32nd North Carolina Infantry	May 10, 1864, Near Spotsylvania Court House, Virginia	Point Lookout, Maryland, transferred to Elmira Prison, NY, August 6, 1864	Died March 17, 1865 of Variola (Smallpox), Grave No. 1704
Powell, Wilson Private	Unk	September 1, 1862, Troy, Alabama	Co. J, 15th Alabama Infantry	May 6, 1864, Wilderness, Virginia	Point Lookout, Maryland, transferred to Elmira Prison, NY, August 17, 1864	Oath of Allegiance June 23, 1865
Powell, Wyatt H. Private	33	October 4, 1861, Wake County, North Carolina	Co. C, 31st North Carolina Infantry	May 31, 1864, Gaines Farm Cold Harbor, Virginia	Point Lookout, Maryland, transferred to Elmira Prison, NY, July 12, 1864	Oath of Allegiance June 19, 1865
Power, John W. Private	18	May 25, 1861, Marshall County, Mississippi	Co. J, 19th Mississippi Infantry	July 24, 1864, Frederick, Maryland	Old Capital Prison, Washington D. C. Transferred to Elmira Prison, NY, August 12, 1864	Oath of Allegiance May 17, 1865
Powers, Barfield Private	18	January 1, 1862, Georgetown, South Carolina	Co. A, 21st South Carolina Infantry	June 24, 1864, Near Petersburg, Virginia	Point Lookout, Maryland, transferred to Elmira Prison, NY, August 18, 1864	Oath of Allegiance July 11, 1865
Powers, E. C. Corporal	19	May 3, 1862, Macon, Georgia	Captain Slayton's Battery Macon Light Artillery, Georgia Artillery	June 17, 1864, Near Petersburg, Virginia	Point Lookout, Maryland, transferred to Elmira Prison, NY, July 30, 1864	Oath of Allegiance June 14, 1865
Powers, George Private	Unk	April 11, 1862, Coles Island, South Carolina	Co. G, 27th South Carolina Infantry	June 24, 1864, Near Petersburg, Virginia	Point Lookout, Maryland, transferred to Elmira Prison, NY, August 18, 1864	Died April 12, 1865 of Chronic Diarrhea, Grave No. 2677

Name & Rank	Age	Enlisted	Regiment and State	Where Captured	Prison	Remarks
Powers, James R. Private	22	April 15, 1862, Asheville, Swannanoa, North Carolina	Co. K, 11th North Carolina Infantry	July 14, 1863, Falling Waters, Maryland	Point Lookout, Maryland, transferred to Elmira Prison, NY, August 18, 1864	Exchanged March 10, 1865 at Boulware's Wharf on the James River, Virginia
Powers, Lawrence Private	Unk	August 21, 1863, Church Flats, South Carolina	Co. B, 7th Battalion South Carolina Infantry	May 16, 1864, Near Drury's Bluff, Virginia	Point Lookout, Maryland, transferred to Elmira Prison, NY, August 17, 1864	Exchanged February 20, 1865 at Boulware's or Cox Wharf on the James River, Virginia
Powers, Levi Private	18	January 1, 1862, Georgetown, South Carolina	Co. A, 21st South Carolina Infantry	June 24, 1864, Near Petersburg, Virginia	Point Lookout, Maryland, transferred to Elmira Prison, NY, August 18, 1864	Oath of Allegiance July 11, 1865
Powers, William Private	25	June 25, 1861, Russell, Virginia	Co. K, 48th Virginia Infantry	May 12, 1864, Spotsylvania Court House, Virginia	Point Lookout, Maryland, transferred to Elmira Prison, NY, August 12, 1864	Died January 23, 1865 of Pneumonia, Grave No. 1614
Powers, William E. Private	23	May 10, 1861, Jackson County, Florida	Co. F, 2nd Florida Infantry	May 12, 1864, Spotsylvania Court House, Virginia	Point Lookout, Maryland, transferred to Elmira Prison, NY, August 12, 1864	Oath of Allegiance November 16, 1864. Early Release per Lincoln's Proclamation, 12/8/1863.
Prader, Presley M. Private	19	August 10, 1861, Camp Butler, South Carolina	Co. D, 14th South Carolina Infantry	July 29, 1864, Petersburg, Virginia	Point Lookout, Maryland, transferred to Elmira Prison, NY, August 12, 1864	Died December 18, 1864 of Typhoid-Pneumonia, Grave No. 1067
Prather, George F. Private	Unk	August 24, 1862, Jefferson, Virginia	Co. A, 14th Alabama Infantry	May 24, 1864, Hanover Junction, Virginia	Point Lookout, Maryland, transferred to Elmira Prison, NY, July 11, 1864	Oath of Allegiance June 14, 1865
Pratt, S. M. Private	Unk	March 13, 1864, Anson County, North Carolina	Co. B, 31st North Carolina Infantry	June 1, 1864, Cold Harbor, Virginia	Point Lookout, Maryland, transferred to Elmira Prison, NY, July 12, 1864	Exchanged October 29, 1864, at Venus Point, Savannah River, GA.

Name & Rank	Age	Enlisted	Regiment and State	Where Captured	Prison	Remarks
Pratt, Thomas A. Private	Unk	May 28, 1861, Matthews Court House, Virginia	Co. D, 26th Virginia Infantry	May 8, 1864, Nottaway Bridge, Virginia	Point Lookout, Maryland, transferred to Elmira Prison, NY, August 17, 1864	Died January 15, 1865 of Pneumonia. Grave No. 1453
Pratt, William Sailor	Unk	Unknown	Confederate States Navy	January 15, 1865, Fort Fisher, North Carolina	February 1, 1865, Elmira Prison Camp, New York	Oath of Allegiance July 21, 1865
Presgrave, Thomas L. Private	Unk	October 1, 1862, Snickersville, Virginia	Co. K, 7th Virginia Cavalry	September 14, 1863, Near Culpepper Court House, Virginia	Point Lookout, Maryland, transferred to Elmira Prison, NY, August 18, 1864	Exchanged February 20, 1865 at Boulware's or Cox Wharf on the James River, Virginia
Presley, E. B. Private	Unk	September 11, 1862, Greenville, Alabama	Co. A, 1st Battalion Alabama Artillery	August 23, 1864, Fort Morgan, Alabama	New Orleans, Louisiana transferred to Elmira Prison, NY, December 4, 1864.	Died February 28, 1865 of Diarrhea, Grave No. 2131
Presley, J. A. Private	Unk	September 1, 1862, Greenville, Alabama	Co. A, 1st Battalion Alabama Artillery	August 23, 1864, Fort Morgan, Alabama	New Orleans, Louisiana transferred to Elmira Prison, NY, December 4, 1864.	Died February 10, 1865 of Chronic Diarrhea, Grave No. 2088
Pressley, H. M. Private	Unk	April 9, 1863, James Island, South Carolina	Co. C, 25th South Carolina Infantry	January 15, 1865, Fort Fisher, North Carolina	February 1, 1865, Elmira Prison Camp, New York	Exchanged March 2, 1865 at Akins Landing on the James River, Virginia
Presson, John E. Private	Unk	Unknown	Co. B, Hood's Battalion, Virginia Reserves	June 15, 1864, Petersburg, Virginia	Point Lookout, Maryland, transferred to Elmira Prison, NY, July 30, 1864	Died February 19, 1865 of Pneumonia, Grave No. 2336
Prestgraves, Richard Civilian	Unk	Unknown	Citizen of Loudoun County, Virginia	December 26, 1864, Loudoun County, Virginia	Point Lookout, Maryland, transferred to Elmira Prison, NY, July 25, 1864	Died January 19, 1865 of Chronic Diarrhea, Grave No. 1207

Name & Rank	Age	Enlisted	Regiment and State	Where Captured	Prison	Remarks
Preston, Walter C. Private	23	March 15, 1862, Charlottesville, Virginia	Captain Carrington's Battery Virginia Light Artillery	May 12, 1864, Spotsylvania Court House, Virginia. Gunshot Fracture of Left Humerus. Amputation at Left Shoulder.	Old Capital Prison, Washington D. C. Transferred to Elmira Prison, NY, August 12, 1864	Exchanged October 29, 1864, at Venus Point, Savannah River, GA.
Prevatt, Elias Private	19	February 28, 1862, Lumberton, North Carolina	Co. E, 51st North Carolina Infantry	June 1, 1864, Cold Harbor, Virginia	Point Lookout, Maryland, transferred to Elmira Prison, NY, July 12, 1864	Died December 13, 1864 of Chronic Diarrhea, Grave No. 1141
Prevatt, Forney Private	20	May 18, 1861, Lumberton, North Carolina	Co. D, 18th North Carolina Infantry	May 6, 1864, Wilderness, Virginia	Point Lookout, Maryland, transferred to Elmira Prison, NY, August 6, 1864	Oath of Allegiance June 12, 1865
Prevatt, Henry C. Private	Unk	May 1, 1862, Camp Holmes, New Hanover, North Carolina	Co. E, 51st North Carolina Infantry	June 1, 1864, Cold Harbor, Virginia	Point Lookout, Maryland, transferred to Elmira Prison, NY, July 12, 1864	Exchanged 2/20/65. Died 3/27/65 at Howard's Grove Hospital, Richmond, VA.
Prevatt, James P. Corporal	26	February 24, 1862, Lumberton, North Carolina	Co. F, 3rd North Carolina Infantry	May 12, 1864, Near Spotsylvania Court House, Virginia	Point Lookout, Maryland, transferred to Elmira Prison, NY, August 14, 1864	Oath of Allegiance June 19, 1865
Prevatt, Joseph Corporal	20	May 18, 1861, Lumberton, North Carolina	Co. D, 18th North Carolina Infantry	May 12, 1864, Spotsylvania Court House, Virginia	Point Lookout, Maryland, transferred to Elmira Prison, NY, August 6, 1864	Oath of Allegiance June 14, 1865
Prevett, Wesley Private	Unk	October 15, 1862, Raleigh, North Carolina	Co. K, 42nd North Carolina Infantry	June 3, 1864, Cold Harbor, Virginia	Point Lookout, Maryland, transferred to Elmira Prison, NY, July 12, 1864	Oath of Allegiance June 21, 1865
Prevette, Abner Private	39	September 21, 1863, Camp Vance, North Carolina	Co. J, 4th North Carolina Infantry	May 20, 1864, Spotsylvania Court House, Virginia	Point Lookout Prison Camp, Maryland. Transferred to Elmira Prison Camp, NY, July 6, 1864	Died July 5, 1864 of Unknown Disease, Grave No. 2855. Died on Passage from Point Lookout MD.

Name & Rank	Age	Enlisted	Regiment and State	Where Captured	Prison	Remarks
Prewett, Calvin Private	Unk	February 27, 1862, Milton County, Georgia	Co. B, 38th Georgia Infantry	May 20, 1864, Spotsylvania Court House, Virginia	Point Lookout, Maryland, transferred to Elmira Prison, NY, July 3, 1864	Exchanged October 29, 1864, at Venus Point, Savannah River, GA.
Price, Alexander Private	Unk	May 16, 1861, Montgomery, Alabama	Co. K, 6th Alabama Infantry	May 16, 1864, Spotsylvania Court House, Virginia	Point Lookout, Maryland, transferred to Elmira Prison, NY, August 16, 1864	Died October 10, 1864 of Pneumonia, Grave No. 686
Price, Eli P. Private	36	July 5, 1861, Halifax County, North Carolina	Co. J, 8th North Carolina Infantry	June 1, 1864, Cold Harbor, Virginia	Point Lookout, Maryland, transferred to Elmira Prison, NY, July 12, 1864	Exchanged 2/13/65. Died 3/3/65 at Howard's Grove Hospital, Richmond, VA
Price, Erastus Private	Unk	April 12, 1862, Camp Success, Virginia	Co. E, 4th Virginia Infantry	May 2, 1864, Ely's Ford, Virginia	Point Lookout, Maryland, transferred to Elmira Prison, NY, July 23, 1864	Oath of Allegiance May 29, 1865
Price, F. M. Private	Unk	Unknown	Co. B, 50th Virginia Infantry	May 12, 1864, Spotsylvania Court House, Virginia	Point Lookout, Maryland, transferred to Elmira Prison, NY, August 2, 1864	Oath of Allegiance June 19, 1865
Price, Floyd W. Sergeant	Unk	July 16, 1861, Blacksburg, Virginia	Co. L, 4th Virginia Infantry	May 12, 1864, Near Spotsylvania Court House, Virginia	Point Lookout, Maryland, transferred to Elmira Prison, NY, August 2, 1864	Oath of Allegiance June 19, 1865
Price, Irvin Private	19	April 12, 1864, Raleigh, North Carolina	Co. E, 7th North Carolina Infantry	May 6, 1864, Wilderness, Virginia	Point Lookout, Maryland, transferred to Elmira Prison, NY, August 14, 1864	Died October 12, 1864 of Chronic Diarrhea. No Grave in Woodlawn Cemetery.
Price, J. Private	Unk	Unknown	Louisiana Reserve Corps.	October 6, 1864, Clinton, Louisiana	New Orleans, Louisiana transferred to Elmira November 19, 1864.	Oath of Allegiance January 24, 1865 Per Orders Commanding General of Prisoners.

Name & Rank	Age	Enlisted	Regiment and State	Where Captured	Prison	Remarks
Price, Jackson Private	23	May 1, 1861, Nashville, North Carolina	Co. H, 32nd North Carolina Infantry	May 10, 1864, Near Spotsylvania Court House, Virginia	Point Lookout, Maryland, transferred to Elmira Prison, NY, August 6, 1864	Died September 25, 1864 of Chronic Diarrhea, Grave No. 359
Price, James C. Corporal	20	April 17, 1861, Christiansburg, Virginia	Co. G, 4th Virginia Infantry	May 12, 1864, Near Spotsylvania Court House, Virginia	Point Lookout, Maryland, transferred to Elmira Prison, NY, August 2, 1864	Died January 3, 1865 of Variola (Smallpox), Grave No. 1334
Price, James H. Private	Unk	August 1, 1861, Manassas, Alabama	Co. D, 6th Alabama Infantry	May 20, 1864, Spotsylvania Court House, Virginia	Point Lookout, Maryland, transferred to Elmira Prison, NY, July 3, 1864	Oath of Allegiance May 29, 1865
Price, James W. Private	42	February 14, 1862, Camp Price, Virginia	Co. A, 3rd North Carolina Infantry	May 12, 1864, Near Spotsylvania Court House, Virginia	Point Lookout, Maryland, transferred to Elmira Prison, NY, August 14, 1864	Oath of Allegiance June 19, 1865
Price, John Private	Unk	Unknown	Co. E, 37th North Carolina Infantry	May 12, 1864, Spotsylvania Court House, Virginia	Point Lookout Prison Camp, Maryland. Transferred to Elmira Prison Camp, New York July 17, 1864	Died November 2, 1864 of Chronic Diarrhea, Grave No. 575
Price, John Private	Unk	January 8, 1862, Camp Hampton, Spartanburg, South Carolina	Co. K, 18th South Carolina Infantry	July 30, 1864, Petersburg, Virginia	Point Lookout, Maryland, transferred to Elmira Prison, NY, August 12, 1864	Died September 18, 1864 of Chronic Diarrhea, Grave No. 314
Price, John D. Private	Unk	Unknown	Co. B, Prince's Battalion Louisiana	October 3, 1864, West Baton Rouge, Louisiana	New Orleans, Louisiana transferred to Elmira November 19, 1864.	Exchanged February 25, 1865 at Boulware's or Cox Wharf on the James River, Virginia
Price, John M. Sergeant Major	Unk	March 29, 1862, Lewisburg, Virginia	Co. D, 26th Battalion, Virginia Infantry	June 3, 1864, Gaines Mill Cold Harbor, Virginia	Point Lookout, Maryland, transferred to Elmira Prison, NY, July 17, 1864	Exchanged February 25, 1865 at Boulware's or Cox Wharf on the James River, Virginia

Name & Rank	Age	Enlisted	Regiment and State	Where Captured	Prison	Remarks
Price, Levan B. Private	23	May 10, 1862, Wayne County, North Carolina	Co. G, 55th North Carolina Infantry	May 12, 1864, Spotsylvania Court House, Virginia	Point Lookout, Maryland, transferred to Elmira Prison, NY, August 12, 1864	Oath of Allegiance June 12, 1865
Price, Michael M. Private	Unk	August 1, 1863, N. R. B., Virginia	Co. D, 21st Virginia Cavalry	July 16, 1864, Loudoun County, Virginia	Old Capital Prison, Washington DC. Transferred to Elmira Prison Camp, NY, July 25, 1864.	Exchanged March 2, 1865 at Akins Landing on the James River, Virginia
Price, Robert T. Private	18	August 19, 1863, Wayne County, North Carolina	Co. G, 40th 3rd Regiment North Carolina Artillery	January 15, 1865, Fort Fisher, North Carolina	February 1, 1865, Elmira Prison Camp, New York	Died February 13, 1865 of Pneumonia, Grave No. 2066
Price, Smith Private	26	March 14, 1862, Wilkesboro, North Carolina	Co. F, 52nd North Carolina Infantry	May 12, 1864, Spotsylvania Court House, Virginia	Point Lookout, Maryland, transferred to Elmira Prison, NY, August 12, 1864	Exchanged March 2, 1865 at Akins Landing on the James River, Virginia
Price, Thomas Private	Unk	February 1, 1864, Liberty Mills, Virginia	Co. E, 37th North Carolina Infantry	May 12, 1864, Near Spotsylvania Court House, Virginia	Point Lookout, Maryland, transferred to Elmira Prison, NY, August 14, 1864	Exchanged October 29, 1864, at Venus Point, Savannah River, GA.
Price, Thomas A. Private	20	March 28, 1862, Union County, North Carolina	Co. D, 37th North Carolina Infantry	July 29, 1864, Gravel Hill, Near Petersburg, Virginia	Point Lookout, Maryland, transferred to Elmira Prison, NY, August 12, 1864	Oath of Allegiance May 29, 1865
Price, Thomas L. Private	Unk	June 2, 1862, Luray, Virginia	Co. K, 10th Virginia Infantry	May 12, 1864, Spotsylvania Court House, Virginia	Point Lookout, Maryland, transferred to Elmira Prison, NY, August 2, 1864	Oath of Allegiance May 19, 1865
Prickett, Joseph H. Sergeant	Unk	April 11, 1862, Coles Island, South Carolina	Co. F, 25th South Carolina Infantry	January 15, 1865, Fort Fisher, North Carolina	February 1, 1865, Elmira Prison Camp, New York	Died June 15, 1865 of Chronic Diarrhea, Grave No. 2880. Headstone has Brickett, J. H.

Name & Rank	Age	Enlisted	Regiment and State	Where Captured	Prison	Remarks
Pridemore, J. W. Private	Unk	November 12, 1863, Place Unknown	Co. E, 37th Virginia Infantry	May 20, 1864, Spotsylvania, Virginia	Point Lookout, Maryland, transferred to Elmira Prison, NY, July 23, 1864	Oath of Allegiance May 19, 1865
Pridgen, Charles J. Private	28	August 15, 1861, Camp Wyatt, North Carolina	Co. E, 18th North Carolina Infantry	May 12, 1864, Spotsylvania Court House, Virginia	Point Lookout, Maryland, transferred to Elmira Prison, NY, August 6, 1864	Oath of Allegiance June 12, 1865
Pridgen, Edwin S. Private	16	July 23, 1863, Fort Branch, Martin County, Hamilton, North Carolina	Co. G, 40th Regiment, 3rd North Carolina Artillery	January 15, 1865, Fort Fisher, North Carolina	February 1, 1865, Elmira Prison Camp, New York	Oath of Allegiance June 12, 1865
Pridgen, Henry R. Corporal	23	April 23, 1861, Snow Hill, North Carolina	Co. A, 3rd North Carolina Infantry	May 12, 1864, Near Spotsylvania County Court House, Virginia	Point Lookout, Maryland, transferred to Elmira Prison, NY, August 14, 1864	Exchanged February 20, 1865 at Boulware's or Cox Wharf on the James River, Virginia
Pridgen, Melvin Private	22	March 3, 1862, Wilmington, New Hanover County, North Carolina	Co. D, 36th Regiment, 2nd North Carolina Artillery	January 15, 1865, Fort Fisher, North Carolina	February 1, 1865, Elmira Prison Camp, New York	Died April 15, 1865 of Chronic Diarrhea, Grave No. 2713. Headstone has M. Pidgeon.
Pridgen, Thomas J. Sergeant	28	February 16, 1863, Fort Caswell, Brunswick County, North Carolina	Co. D, 36th Regiment, 2nd North Carolina Artillery	January 15, 1865, Fort Fisher, North Carolina	February 1, 1865, Elmira Prison Camp, New York	Oath of Allegiance June 16, 1865
Pridgen, William A. Private	19	April 27, 1861, Friars' Point, Mississippi	Co. B, 11th Mississippi Infantry	May 5, 1864, Wilderness, Virginia	Point Lookout, Maryland, transferred to Elmira Prison, NY, August 17, 1864	Exchanged October 29, 1864, at Venus Point, Savannah River, GA.
Pridgen, William Lafayette Private	20	May 16, 1862, Wilmington, New Hanover County, North Carolina	Co. D, 36th Regiment, 2nd North Carolina Artillery	January 15, 1865, Fort Fisher, North Carolina	February 1, 1865, Elmira Prison Camp, New York	Oath of Allegiance June 16, 1865
Priest, George F. Private	Unk	March 1, 1862, Goldsborough, Georgia	Co. G, 24th Georgia Infantry	June 1, 1864, Cold Harbor, Virginia	Point Lookout, Maryland, transferred to Elmira Prison, NY, July 17,1864	Oath of Allegiance July 11, 1865

Name & Rank	Age	Enlisted	Regiment and State	Where Captured	Prison	Remarks
Priest, John A. Private	18	November 12, 1861, Wilmington, New Hanover County, North Carolina	Co. B, 36th Regiment, 2nd North Carolina Artillery	January 15, 1865, Fort Fisher, North Carolina	February 1, 1865, Elmira Prison Camp, New York	Oath of Allegiance June 7, 1865
Prim, William R. Private	Unk	March 14, 1863, Carroll County, Virginia	Co. C, 29th, Virginia Infantry	June 1, 1864, Gaines Mill Cold Harbor, Virginia	Point Lookout, Maryland, transferred to Elmira Prison, NY, July 12, 1864	Oath of Allegiance May 29, 1865
Primm, John Private	Unk	February 12, 1863, Camp of Instruction, Virginia	Co. A, 4th Virginia Infantry	May 5, 1864, Wilderness, Virginia	Point Lookout, Maryland, transferred to Elmira Prison, NY, July 25, 1864	Oath of Allegiance May 29, 1865
Prince, Berryman Private	Unk	October 30, 1861, Pickens District, South Carolina	Co. B, 2nd South Carolina Infantry	June 3, 1864, Mechanicsville, Virginia	Point Lookout, Maryland, transferred to Elmira Prison, NY, July 17, 1864	Died April 25, 1865 of Chronic Diarrhea, Grave No. 1413
Prince, Daniel F. Private	18	April 2, 1862, Wilmington, North Carolina	Co. H, 51st North Carolina Infantry	June 1, 1864, Cold Harbor, Virginia. Gunshot Wound Head and Right Finger.	DeCamp General Hospital, David's Island New York Harbor.	Exchanged February 13, 1865 at Boulware's wharf on the James River, Virginia
Prince, Jefferson Private	Unk	December 13, 1861, Columbia, South Carolina	Co. C, 18th South Carolina Infantry	July 30, 1864, Petersburg, Virginia	Point Lookout, Maryland, transferred to Elmira Prison, NY, August 12, 1864	Oath of Allegiance July 3, 1865
Prince, William A. Private	Unk	May 2, 1861, Crawford, Alabama	Co. F, 6th Alabama Infantry	July 14, 1864, Poolesville, Virginia	Old Capital Prison, Washington DC. Transferred to Elmira Prison Camp, NY July 25, 1864.	Oath of Allegiance June 14, 1865
Printup, Daniel S. Major	Unk	May 17, 1862, Griffin, Georgia	Staff, 55th Georgia Infantry	September 9, 1863, Cumberland Gap, Virginia	Johnson's Island, Ohio. Transferred February 7, 1865 Elmira, Prison Camp, NY	Oath of Allegiance February 7, 1865

Name & Rank	Age	Enlisted	Regiment and State	Where Captured	Prison	Remarks
Printz, Martin G. Private	Unk	March 7, 1862, Luray, Virginia	Co. K, 10th Virginia Infantry	May 12, 1864, Spotsylvania Court House, Virginia	Point Lookout, Maryland, transferred to Elmira Prison, NY, August 2, 1864	Exchanged October 29, 1864 at Venus Point, Savannah River, GA.
Printz, Philip M. Private	Unk	June 2, 1862, Luray, Virginia	Co. K, 10th Virginia Infantry	May 12, 1864, Spotsylvania Court House, Virginia	Point Lookout, Maryland, transferred to Elmira Prison, NY, August 2, 1864	Oath of Allegiance June 19, 1865
Pritchard, Henderson Sergeant	23	April 1, 1862, Windsor, North Carolina	Co. G, 32nd North Carolina Infantry	May 10, 1864, Wilderness, Virginia	Point Lookout, Maryland, transferred to Elmira Prison, NY, August 6, 1864	Exchanged February 20, 1865 at Boulware's or Cox Wharf on the James River, Virginia
Privett, Thomas H. Private	19	May 18, 1861, Edenton, North Carolina	Co. A, 1st North Carolina Infantry	August 19, 1863, Big Black, Mississippi	Point Lookout, Maryland, transferred to Elmira Prison, NY, August 18, 1864	Exchanged March 14, 1865 at Boulware's Wharf on the James River, Virginia
Privitt, Sampson C. Private	Unk	February 15, 1864, Jefferson County, North Carolina	Co. B, 37th North Carolina Infantry	May 12, 1864, Near Spotsylvania Court House, Virginia	Point Lookout, Maryland, transferred to Elmira Prison, NY, August 14, 1864	Died January 1, 1865 of Chronic Diarrhea, Grave No. 1330
Proctor, James A. Private	33	August 31, 1861, Lincolnton, North Carolina	Co. G, 34th North Carolina Infantry	July 14, 1863, Falling Waters, Maryland	Point Lookout, Maryland, transferred to Elmira Prison, NY, August 18, 1864	Exchanged February 13, 1865 at Boulware's wharf on the James River, Virginia
Proctor, Thomas F. Private	Unk	March 4, 1862, Fredericksburg, Virginia	Co. A, 24th Virginia Cavalry	June 3, 1864, Near Talapatomoy Creek, Cold Harbor, Virginia	Point Lookout, Maryland, transferred to Elmira Prison, NY, July 12, 1864	Oath of Allegiance June 19, 1865
Proffit, Andrew J. Private	28	August 22, 1862, Wilkes County, North Carolina	Co. D, 18th North Carolina Infantry	May 12, 1864, Spotsylvania Court House, Virginia	Point Lookout, Maryland, transferred to Elmira Prison, NY, July 17, 1864	Exchanged February 20, 1865 at Boulware's or Cox Wharf on the James River, Virginia.

Name & Rank	Age	Enlisted	Regiment and State	Where Captured	Prison	Remarks
Propst, Daniel F. Private	20	June 9, 1861, Highland County Court House, Virginia	Co. E, 25th Virginia Infantry	May 5, 1864, Wilderness, Virginia	Point Lookout, Maryland, transferred to Elmira Prison, NY, August 2, 1864	Oath of Allegiance July 19, 1865
Propst, Henry M. Private	31	September 14, 1862, Camp Holmes, North Carolina	Co. E, 8th North Carolina Infantry	May 31, 1864, Cold Harbor, Virginia	Point Lookout, Maryland, transferred to Elmira Prison, NY, July 12, 1864	Oath of Allegiance June 12, 1865
Prothro, Joseph L. Private	Unk	August 13, 1861, Camp Moore, Louisiana	Co. C, 12th Louisiana Infantry	May 16, 1863, Baker's Creek, Champion Hill, Mississippi	Point Lookout, Maryland, transferred to Elmira Prison, NY, August 18, 1864	Exchanged February 25, 1865 at Boulware's Wharf on the James River, Virginia
Province, Thomas Private	Unk	June 4, 1861, Camp Moore, Louisiana	Co. A, 6th Louisiana Infantry	May 5, 1864, Wilderness, Virginia	Point Lookout, Maryland, transferred to Elmira Prison, NY, August 17, 1864	Exchanged February 13, 1865 at Boulware's Wharf on the James River, Virginia
Provost, Clarence Private	28	February 24, 1862, Charleston, South Carolina	Co. A, 25th South Carolina Infantry	January 15, 1865, Fort Fisher, North Carolina	February 1, 1865, Elmira Prison Camp, New York	Oath of Allegiance June 19, 1865
Prowell, Andrew M. Private	Unk	January 30, 1862, Nashville, Tennessee	Co. E, 44th Tennessee Infantry	June 17, 1864, Petersburg, Virginia	Point Lookout, Maryland, transferred to Elmira Prison, NY, July 23, 1864	Oath of Allegiance May 29, 1865
Pruden, John W. Private	Unk	August 24, 1861, Beaver Dam, Isle of Wight County, Virginia	Co. F, 61st Virginia Infantry	July 30, 1864, Petersburg, Virginia	Point Lookout, Maryland, transferred to Elmira Prison, NY, August 12, 1864	Died December 26, 1864 of Typhoid Fever, Grave No. 1270
Pruett, Joshua A. Private	Unk	March 28, 1862, Suffolk, Virginia	Co. E, 3rd Battalion Georgia Sharp Shooters	August 16, 1864, Front Royal, Virginia	Old Capital Prison, Washington, DC transferred to Elmira Prison, NY, August 29, 1864	Oath of Allegiance July 7, 1865

Name & Rank	Age	Enlisted	Regiment and State	Where Captured	Prison	Remarks
Pruitt, Alonzo Private	Unk	August 24, 1861, Hartwell, Georgia	Co. B, 24th Georgia Infantry	June 1, 1864, Cold Harbor, Virginia	Point Lookout, Maryland, transferred to Elmira Prison, NY, July 12, 1864	Exchanged October 29, 1864, at Venus Point, Savannah River, GA.
Pruitt, E. B. Private	Unk	September 2, 1862, Camp Randolph, Georgia	Co. E, Phillips Legion, Georgia	June 2, 1864, Gaines Farm Cold Harbor, Virginia	Point Lookout, Maryland, transferred to Elmira Prison, NY, July 12, 1864	Oath of Allegiance July 7, 1865
Pryor, Columbus M. Private	19	February 28, 1863, Wilkes County, North Carolina	Co. K, 33rd North Carolina Infantry	May 12, 1864, Spotsylvania Court House, Virginia	Point Lookout, Maryland, transferred to Elmira Prison, NY, July 3, 1864	Oath of Allegiance May 15, 1865
Puckett, F. M. Private	17	September 23, 1861, Camp Meyers, Livingston, Tennessee	Co. F, 25th Tennessee Infantry	May 16, 1864, Near Drury's Bluff, Virginia	Point Lookout, Maryland, transferred to Elmira Prison, NY, August 17, 1864	Exchanged February 25, 1865 at Boulware's or Cox Wharf on the James River, Virginia
Pugh, Robert Sergeant	Unk	June 4, 1861, Fork of Wilson, Virginia	Co. D, 50th Virginia Infantry	May 12, 1864, Spotsylvania Court House, Virginia	Point Lookout, Maryland, transferred to Elmira Prison, NY, August 2, 1864	Oath of Allegiance June 19, 1865
Pugh, William W. Private	19	April 22, 1861, Washington, North Carolina	Co. K, 10th Regiment, 1st North Carolina Artillery	January 15, 1865, Fort Fisher, North Carolina	February 1, 1865, Elmira Prison Camp, New York	Exchanged February 20, 1865 at Boulware's or Cox Wharf on the James River, Virginia
Pugh, Willis J. Private	Unk	October 27, 1861, Hawkinsville, Georgia	Co. F, 31st Georgia Infantry	July 16, 1864, Snickers Gap, Virginia	Old Capital Prison, Washington DC. Transferred to Elmira Prison Camp, NY, July 25, 1864.	Oath of Allegiance June 16, 1865
Pullen, James H. Sergeant	20	August 23, 1861, Camp Trousdale, Tennessee	Co. D, 23rd Tennessee Infantry	June 17, 1864, Petersburg, Virginia	Point Lookout, Maryland, transferred to Elmira Prison, NY, July 30, 1864	Exchanged February 25, 1865 at Boulware's or Cox Wharf on the James River, Virginia

Name & Rank	Age	Enlisted	Regiment and State	Where Captured	Prison	Remarks
Pulliam, James Private	28	May 3, 1862, Person County, North Carolina	Co. I, 45th North Carolina Infantry	May 10, 1864, Spotsylvania Court House, Virginia	Point Lookout, Maryland, transferred to Elmira Prison, NY, August 6, 1864	Exchanged October 29, 1864, at Venus Point, Savannah River, GA.
Pullins, Jesse H. Private	Unk	June 11, 1861, Hevener's Store, Virginia	Co. E, 31st Virginia Infantry	May 30, 1864, Old Church, Cold Harbor, Virginia	Point Lookout, Maryland, transferred to Elmira Prison, NY, July 12, 1864	Oath of Allegiance May 13, 1865
Purcell, Duncan Private	35	March 12, 1862, Fort Fisher, North Carolina	Co. C, 36th Regiment, 2nd North Carolina Artillery	January 15, 1865, Fort Fisher, North Carolina	February 1, 1865, Elmira Prison Camp, New York	Died April 10, 1865 of Chronic Diarrhea, Grave No. 2668
Purcell, James R. Private	Unk	January 15, 1862, Lynchburg, Virginia	Co. A, 42nd Virginia Infantry	May 12, 1864, Spotsylvania Court House, Virginia	Point Lookout, Maryland, transferred to Elmira Prison, NY, August 2, 1864	Oath of Allegiance July 3, 1865
Purcell, Thomas Private	Unk	August 16, 1862, Montgomery, Alabama	Co. F, 1st Battalion Alabama Artillery	August 23, 1864, Fort Morgan, Alabama	Steam Press No. 4 New Orleans, Louisiana transferred to Elmira Prison, NY, October 8, 1864.	Died April 11, 1865 of Remittent Fever, Grave No. 2688
Purcer, Benjamin Private	Unk	December 20, 1862, Geneva, Alabama	Co. F, 1st Battalion Alabama Artillery	August 23, 1864, Fort Morgan, Alabama	Steam Press No. 4 New Orleans, Louisiana transferred to Elmira Prison, NY, October 8, 1864.	Died April 5, 1865 of Chronic Diarrhea, Grave No. 2544
Purdum, Lewis Corporal	Unk	July 29, 1861, Satilla, Georgia	Co. D, 26th Georgia Infantry	May 20, 1864, Spotsylvania Court House, Virginia	Point Lookout, Maryland, transferred to Elmira Prison, NY, July 3, 1864	Oath of Allegiance June 30, 1865
Purdy, Samuel A. Private	19	July 20, 1861, Camp Pickens, Anderson District, South Carolina	Co. G, 1st South Carolina Infantry	July 14, 1863, Falling Waters, Maryland	Point Lookout, Maryland, transferred to Elmira Prison, NY, August 18, 1864	Exchanged February 13, 1865 at Boulware's wharf on the James River, Virginia

Name & Rank	Age	Enlisted	Regiment and State	Where Captured	Prison	Remarks
Purkel, Antoine Sergeant	42	July 22, 1861, Camp Moore, Louisiana	Co. J, 10th Louisiana Infantry	May 20, 1864, Spotsylvania, Virginia	Point Lookout, Maryland, transferred to Elmira Prison, NY, July 23, 1864	Oath of Allegiance May 19, 1865
Purnell, Calvin Private	30	September 24, 1861, Red Springs, Roberson County, North Carolina	Co. E, 40th 3rd Regiment North Carolina Artillery	January 15, 1865, Fort Fisher, North Carolina	February 1, 1865, Elmira Prison Camp, New York	Died March 15, 1865 of Chronic Diarrhea, Grave No. 1664
Pursley, Pinkney L. Private	26	March 19, 1862, Charleston, South Carolina	Co. G, 18th South Carolina Infantry	July 30, 1864, Petersburg, Virginia	Point Lookout, Maryland, transferred to Elmira Prison, NY, August 12, 1864	Oath of Allegiance July 3, 1865
Pursley, Samuel M. Private	37	March 5, 1863, Gaston County, North Carolina	Co. C, 38th North Carolina Infantry	July 14, 1863, Falling Waters, Maryland	Point Lookout, Maryland, transferred to Elmira Prison, NY, August 18, 1864	Exchanged March 2, 1862. Died March 29, 1865 of Delilitas.
Purviance, D. H. Private	Unk	Unknown	Co. F, 12th Battalion North Carolina Cavalry	September 14, 1863, Near Culpepper Court House, Virginia	Point Lookout, Maryland, transferred to Elmira Prison, NY, August 18, 1864	Exchanged March 10, 1865 at Boulware's Wharf on the James River, Virginia
Purvis, J. Henry Private	Unk	December 28, 1861, Georgetown, South Carolina	Co. K, 21st South Carolina Infantry	January 15, 1865, Fort Fisher, North Carolina	February 1, 1865, Elmira Prison Camp, New York	Died February 12, 1865 of Chronic Diarrhea, Grave No. 2057. Headstone has Henry Pervis.
Purvis, James L. Private	28	June 10, 1861, Matthews, North Carolina	Co. G, 26th North Carolina Infantry	May 12, 1864, Spotsylvania Court House, Virginia	Point Lookout, Maryland, transferred to Elmira Prison, NY, July 30, 1864	Oath of Allegiance May 2, 1865
Purvis, Joseph Private	Unk	September 13, 1861, Whitesville, Georgia	Co. E, 61st Georgia Infantry	May 12, 1864, Spotsylvania Court House, Virginia	Point Lookout, Maryland, transferred to Elmira Prison, NY, July 30, 1864	Exchanged March 2, 1865 at Akins Landing on the James River, Virginia

Name & Rank	Age	Enlisted	Regiment and State	Where Captured	Prison	Remarks
Putignat, John P. Private	Unk	July 1, 1861, Selma, Alabama	Jeff Davis Alabama Artillery	May 5, 1864, Wilderness, Virginia	Point Lookout, Maryland, transferred to Elmira Prison, NY, August 17, 1864	Escaped October 7, 1864 by Tunneling Under Fence.
Putman, James Private	Unk	August 1, 1863, N. R. B., Virginia	Co. D, 21st Virginia Cavalry	July 16, 1864, Loudoun County, Virginia	Old Capital Prison, Washington DC. Transferred to Elmira Prison Camp, NY July 25, 1864.	Oath of Allegiance May 29, 1865
Putnam, John L. Private	19	October 1, 1861, Shelby, North Carolina	Co. H, 34th North Carolina Infantry	July 14, 1863, Falling Waters, Hagerstown, Maryland	Point Lookout, Maryland, transferred to Elmira Prison, NY, August 18, 1864	Exchanged October 29, 1864 at Venus Point, Savannah River, GA.
Putney, Richard Private	Unk	June 6, 1861, New Canton, Virginia	Co. C, 44th Virginia Infantry	May 12, 1864, Spotsylvania Court House, Virginia	Point Lookout, Maryland, transferred to Elmira Prison, NY, August 2, 1864	Oath of Allegiance June 16, 1865
Pyle, Augustus J. Sergeant	Unk	June 10, 1861, Richmond, Virginia	Co. E, 44th Virginia Infantry	May 12, 1864, Spotsylvania Court House, Virginia	Point Lookout, Maryland, transferred to Elmira Prison, NY, August 12, 1864	Oath of Allegiance May 19, 1865

Name	Age	Enlisted	Regiment and State	Where Captured	Prison	Remarks
Quakenbush, Frederic S. Private	24	March 5, 1862, Orange County, North Carolina	Co. G, 28th North Carolina Infantry	May 12, 1864, Near Spotsylvania Court House, Virginia	Point Lookout, Maryland, transferred to Elmira Prison, NY, August 14, 1864	Oath of Allegiance June 27, 1865
Quarles, David W. Private	Unk	June 10, 1863, Brandy Station, Virginia	Co. E, 6th Virginia Cavalry	May 11, 1864, Henrico County, Virginia	Point Lookout, Maryland, transferred to Elmira Prison, NY, August 17, 1864	Exchanged October 29, 1864, at Venus Point, Savannah River, GA.
Quarles, William O. Private	Unk	March 29, 1862, Lowdesbon, Alabama	Co. H, 3rd Alabama Infantry	May 3, 1864, Wilderness, Virginia. Gunshot Wound of Right Shoulder and Chest.	Old Capital Prison, Washington, DC transferred to Elmira Prison, NY, August 29, 1864	Died October 1, 1864 of Chronic Diarrhea, Grave No. 414
Queen, John Private	Unk	March 17, 1862, Dallas, North Carolina	Co. M, 16th North Carolina Infantry	July 14, 1863, Hagerstown, falling Waters, Maryland	Point Lookout, Maryland, transferred to Elmira Prison, NY, August 18, 1864	Exchanged March 10, 1865 at Boulware's Wharf on the James River, Virginia
Quesenberry, James M. Private	Unk	Unknown	Co. D, 50th Virginia Infantry	May 12, 1864, Spotsylvania Court House, Virginia	Point Lookout, Maryland, transferred to Elmira Prison, NY, August 2, 1864	Exchanged October 29, 1864, at Venus Point, Savannah River, GA.
Quesenberry, John Private	Unk	Unknown	Co. C, 50th Virginia Infantry	May 12, 1864, Spotsylvania Court House, Virginia	Point Lookout, Maryland, transferred to Elmira Prison, NY, August 2, 1864	Died February 13, 1865 of Chronic Diarrhea. No Grave Found in Woodlawn Cemetery.
Quick, Angus Private	32	December 25, 1861, Bennettsville, South Carolina	Co. F, 21st South Carolina Infantry	January 15, 1865, Fort Fisher, North Carolina	February 1, 1865, Elmira Prison Camp, New York	Exchanged March 2, 1865 at Akins Landing on the James River, Virginia
Quick, Henry S. Sergeant	Unk	Unknown	Co. C, 12th Virginia Cavalry	October 19, 1864, Waterford, Virginia	Old Capital Prison, Washington, DC transferred to Elmira Prison, NY, August 29, 1864	Oath of Allegiance June 27, 1865

Quick, James E. Private	28	May 16, 1861, Columbia, North Carolina	Co. H, 32nd North Carolina Infantry	May 10, 1864, Near Spotsylvania Court House, Virginia	Point Lookout, Maryland, transferred to Elmira Prison, NY, August 6, 1864	Died March 4, 1865 of Variola (Smallpox), Grave No. 1967
Quick, Leggett Private	Unk	January 12, 1862, Bennettsville, South Carolina	Co. E, 4th South Carolina Cavalry	June 11, 1864, Trevilian Station, Louisa Court House, Virginia	Point Lookout, Maryland, transferred to Elmira Prison, NY, July 25, 1864	Exchanged February 16, 1865 at Akins Landing on the James River, Virginia
Quigley, J. Private	Unk	September 4, 1862, Drainsville, Virginia	Co. F, 4th Virginia Cavalry	June 11, 1864, Trevilian Station, Louisa Court House, Virginia	Point Lookout, Maryland, transferred to Elmira Prison, NY, July 25, 1864	Oath of Allegiance May 13, 1865
Quilin, George W. Private	Unk	June 4, 1861, Fork of Wilson, Virginia	Co. D, 50th Virginia Infantry	May 12, 1864, Spotsylvania Court House, Virginia	Point Lookout, Maryland, transferred to Elmira Prison, NY, August 2, 1864	Died September 23, 1864 of Scorbutus (Scurvy), Grave No. 473. Name Guillen on Headstone.
Quinn, A. W. Private	33	April 22, 1861, Shelby, Cleveland County, North Carolina	Co. E, 12th North Carolina Infantry	July 12, 1864, Near Washington, DC	Old Capital Prison, Washington DC. Transferred to Elmira Prison Camp, NY July 25, 1864.	Exchanged February 20, 1865 at Boulware's or Cox Wharf on the James River, Virginia
Quinn, Jesse Private	32	August 1, 1861, Wilmington, North Carolina	Co. I, 18th North Carolina Infantry	July 14, 1863, Falling Waters, Maryland	Old Capital Prison, Washington, DC. Transferred to Elmira Prison, NY August 18, 1864	Died April 17, 1865 of Variola (Smallpox), Grave No. 1350
Quinn, John T. Private	23	April 26, 1862, Wilmington, New Hanover County, North Carolina	Co. D, 1st Battalion North Carolina Heavy Artillery	January 15, 1865, Fort Fisher, North Carolina	January 30, 1865, Elmira Prison Camp, New York	Exchanged March 2, 1865 at Akins Landing on the James River, Virginia
Quinn, Owen Private	38	July 27, 1861, New Orleans, Louisiana	Co. K, 14th Louisiana Infantry	May 12, 1864, Spotsylvania Court House, Virginia	Point Lookout, Maryland, transferred to Elmira Prison, NY, July 25, 1864	Exchanged February 20, 1865 at Boulware's or Cox Wharf on the James River, Virginia

Quinn, Sylonus Private	47	Unknown	Co. D, 40th 3rd Regiment North Carolina Artillery	January 15, 1865, Fort Fisher, North Carolina	February 1, 1865, Elmira Prison Camp, New York	Exchanged March 2, 1865 at Akins Landing on the James River, Virginia
Quintin, James Private	31	April 1, 1863, Charleston, South Carolina	Co. G, 5th South Carolina Cavalry	June 11, 1864, Trevilian Station, Louisa Court House, Virginia	Point Lookout, Maryland, transferred to Elmira Prison, NY, July 25, 1864	Exchanged March 10, 1865 at Boulware's Wharf on the James River, Virginia
Quisenberry, L. Private	Unk	Unknown	Co. H, 5th Virginia Infantry	May 12, 1864 Spotsylvania Court House, Virginia	Point Lookout, Maryland, transferred to Elmira Prison, NY, August 2, 1864	Oath of Allegiance June 27, 1865

Name & Rank	Age	Enlisted	Regiment and State	Where Captured	Prison	Remarks
Rabeck, William M. Private	44	March 10, 1864, Hancock County, Tennessee	Co. D, 7th Tennessee Infantry	May 12, 1864, Spotsylvania Court House, Virginia	Point Lookout, Maryland, transferred to Elmira Prison, NY, July 23, 1864	Oath of Allegiance April 1, 1865
Rabon, George W. Private	33	April 16, 1862, Old Brunswick Town, North Carolina	Co. G, 36th Regiment 2nd North Carolina Artillery	January 15, 1865, Fort Fisher, North Carolina	February 1, 1865, Elmira Prison Camp, New York	Oath of Allegiance July 19, 1865
Rabon, William P. Private	18	September 11, 1863, Fort Caswell, Brunswick County, North Carolina	Co. G, 36th Regiment 2nd North Carolina Artillery	January 15, 1865, Fort Fisher, North Carolina	February 1, 1865, Elmira Prison Camp, New York	Oath of Allegiance July 3, 1865
Rachels, William Private	21	May 6, 1862, Old Hundred, North Carolina	Co. D, 46th North Carolina Infantry	May 12, 1864, Spotsylvania Court House, Virginia	Point Lookout, Maryland, transferred to Elmira Prison, NY, July 30, 1864	Oath of Allegiance June 19, 1865
Rackley, Benjamin F. Private	22	September 1, 1862, Choctaw County, Alabama	Co. E, 1st Battalion Alabama Artillery	August 23, 1864, Fort Morgan, Alabama	Steam Press No. 4, New Orleans, Louisiana transferred to Elmira October 8, 1864.	Oath of Allegiance to July 7, 1865

Name & Rank	Age	Enlisted	Regiment and State	Where Captured	Prison	Remarks
Rackley, George W. Sergeant	22	April 20, 1861, Sampson County, North Carolina	Co. A, 30th North Carolina Infantry	May 12, 1864, Near Spotsylvania Court House, Virginia	Point Lookout, Maryland, transferred to Elmira Prison, NY, August 14, 1864	Oath of Allegiance June 19, 1865
Radcliff, Dennis Private	23	May 22, 1861, Wadesboro, North Carolina	Co. A, 23rd North Carolina Infantry	May 20, 1864, Spotsylvania Court House, Virginia	Point Lookout, Maryland, transferred to Elmira Prison, NY, July 3, 1864	Oath of Allegiance June 12, 1865
Radcliffe, William Private	Unk	Unknown	Co. B, Hood's Battalion, Virginia Reserves	June 15, 1864, Petersburg, Virginia	Point Lookout, Maryland, transferred to Elmira Prison, NY, July 30, 1864	Oath of Allegiance July 3, 1865
Radford, Z. T. Private	Unk	February 23, 1863, Macon, Georgia	Co. B, 64th Georgia Infantry	June 17, 1864, Petersburg, Virginia	Point Lookout, Maryland, transferred to Elmira Prison, NY, July 30, 1864	Oath of Allegiance June 16, 1865
Rafferty, Patrick Sergeant	Unk	April 17, 1862, Petersburg, Virginia	Co. A, 12th Virginia Infantry	June 6, 1864, Cold Harbor, Virginia	Point Lookout, Maryland, transferred to Elmira Prison, NY, July 23, 1864	Oath of Allegiance May 17, 1865
Ragin, John H. Private	Unk	January 11, 1864, James Island, South Carolina	Co. C, 25th South Carolina Infantry	May 14, 1864, Near Fort Darling, Virginia	Point Lookout, Maryland, transferred to Elmira Prison, NY, August 17, 1864	Exchanged March 14, 1865 at Boulware's Wharf on the James River, Virginia
Ragland, Beverly B. Sergeant	Unk	April 1, 1861, Lacy's Store, Virginia	Co. B, 44th Virginia Infantry	May 12, 1864, Spotsylvania Court House, Virginia	Point Lookout, Maryland, transferred to Elmira Prison, NY, August 2, 1864	Oath of Allegiance June 21, 1865
Ragland, Hugh D. Sergeant	Unk	April 1, 1861, Lacy's Store, Virginia	Co. B, 44th Virginia Infantry	May 12, 1864, Spotsylvania Court House, Virginia	Point Lookout, Maryland, transferred to Elmira Prison, NY, August 2, 1864	Exchanged March 10, 1865 at Boulware's Wharf on the James River, Virginia
Ragland, Thaddeus Private	Unk	Unknown	Richmond Howitzer's Artillery	June 15, 1864, Near Petersburg, Virginia	Point Lookout, Maryland, transferred to Elmira Prison, NY, July 12, 1864	Exchanged February 25, 1865 at Boulware's or Cox Wharf on the James River, Virginia

Name & Rank	Age	Enlisted	Regiment and State	Where Captured	Prison	Remarks
Ragland, Thomas B. Private	25	September 1, 1862, Rockingham County, North Carolina	Co. F, 45th North Carolina Infantry	May 20, 1864, Spotsylvania Court House, Virginia	Point Lookout, Maryland, transferred to Elmira Prison, NY, July 3, 1864	Oath of Allegiance May 17, 1865
Rahn, Thomas L. Private	Unk	March 31, 1864, Savannah, Georgia	Co. E, 7th Georgia Cavalry	June 11, 1864, Trevilian Station, Louisa Court House, Virginia	Point Lookout, Maryland, transferred to Elmira Prison, NY, July 12,1864	Exchanged October 29, 1864, at Venus Point, Savannah River, GA.
Raiden, James M. Private	Unk	April 28, 1862, Lexington, Georgia	Co. E, 38th Georgia Infantry	May 6, 1864, Wilderness, Virginia	Point Lookout, Maryland, transferred to Elmira Prison, NY, August 17, 1864	Oath of Allegiance June 23, 1865
Railey, Riddick Private	20	April 24, 1861, Camden, South Carolina	Co. G, 2nd South Carolina Infantry	July 29, 1864, Petersburg, Virginia	Point Lookout, Maryland, transferred to Elmira Prison, NY, August 12, 1864	Oath of Allegiance July 3, 1865
Rainer, G. C. Private	Unk	May 25, 1862, Camp Moore, Louisiana	Co. E, 3rd Louisiana Cavalry	October 6, 1864, Clinton, Louisiana	New Orleans, Louisiana transferred to Elmira November 19, 1864.	Exchanged February 25, 1865 at Boulware's or Cox Wharf on the James River, Virginia
Raines, Caleb Private	Unk	July 3, 1861, Peterstown, Virginia	Co. D, 26th Battalion, Virginia Infantry	June 1, 1864, Gaines Mill Cold Harbor, Virginia	Point Lookout, Maryland, transferred to Elmira Prison, NY, July 17, 1864	Oath of Allegiance May 29, 1865
Raines, Henry A. Private	Unk	May 6, 1862, Fort Powhatan, Virginia	Co. D, 53rd Virginia Infantry	July 1, 1864, Petersburg, Virginia	Point Lookout, Maryland, transferred to Elmira Prison, NY, July 23, 1864	Died April 17, 1865 of Chronic Diarrhea, Grave No. 1354
Rainey, George W. Private	Unk	July 20, 1861, Arkadelphia, Clark County, Arkansas	Co. E, 12th Arkansas Infantry	July 5, 1864, Port Hudson, Louisiana	New Orleans, Louisiana, Transferred to Elmira Prison, New York, November 19, 1864	Exchanged February 13, 1865 at Boulware's wharf on the James River, Virginia

Name & Rank	Age	Enlisted	Regiment and State	Where Captured	Prison	Remarks
Rainey, William Private	Unk	October 11, 1861, Salisbury, North Carolina	Co. B, 4th North Carolina Infantry	May 12, 1865, Spotsylvania Court House, Virginia	Point Lookout, Maryland, transferred to Elmira Prison, NY, August 14, 1864	Oath of Allegiance June 12, 1865
Rainwaters, Joshua W. Private	Unk	January 12, 1862, Bennettsville, South Carolina	Co. E, 4th South Carolina Cavalry	June 11, 1864, Trevilian Station, Louisa Court House, Virginia	Point Lookout, Maryland, transferred to Elmira Prison, NY, July 23, 1864	Died October 21, 1864 of Chronic Diarrhea, Grave No. 526
Ramage, James H. Private	28	August 6, 1861, Martins Point, Lawreus District, South Carolina	Co. A, 13th South Carolina Infantry	May 12, 1864, Spotsylvania Court House, Virginia. Gunshot Wound Left Shoulder and Arm.	Old Capital Prison, Washington DC. Transferred to Elmira Prison Camp, New York, July 25, 1864.	Oath of Allegiance June 27, 1865
Ramey, James W. Private	Unk	April 1, 1862, Salem, Virginia	Co. H, 6th Virginia Cavalry	August 18, 1863, Markham Station, Virginia	Point Lookout, Maryland, transferred to Elmira Prison, NY, August 18, 1864	Exchanged March 10, 1865 at Boulware's Wharf on the James River, Virginia
Ramey, William M. Private	Unk	April 1, 1862, Salem, Virginia	Co. H, 6th Virginia Cavalry	August 2, 1862, Rappahannock County, Virginia	Point Lookout, Maryland, transferred to Elmira Prison, NY, July 25, 1864	Died September 8, 1864 of Chronic Diarrhea, Grave No. 210. Last Name Raymond on Headstone.
Ramsey, Benjamin T. Private	Unk	September 26, 1862, Gloucester Point, Virginia	Co. E, 34th Virginia Infantry	June 15, 1864, Petersburg, Virginia	Point Lookout, Maryland, transferred to Elmira Prison, NY, July 30, 1864	Died March 28, 1865 of Pneumonia, Grave No. 2365
Ramsey, James A. Private	Unk	July 6, 1861, Rich Mountain, Virginia	Co. H, 25th Virginia Infantry	May 15, 1864, Spotsylvania, Virginia	Point Lookout, Maryland, transferred to Elmira Prison, NY, August 14, 1864	Oath of Allegiance June 27, 1865
Ramsey, L. R. Private	Unk	September 5, 1862, Tallapoosa, Alabama	Co. G, 5th Alabama Infantry	May 20, 1864, Spotsylvania Court House, Virginia	Point Lookout, Maryland, transferred to Elmira Prison, NY, July 3, 1864	Oath of Allegiance June 19, 1865

Name & Rank	Age	Enlisted	Regiment and State	Where Captured	Prison	Remarks
Ramsey, Reuben W. Private	Unk	December 3, 1863, C. Bailey, Virginia	Co. G, 26th Virginia Infantry	June 3, 1864, Gaines Farm Cold Harbor, Virginia	Point Lookout, Maryland, transferred to Elmira Prison, NY, July 12, 1864	Oath of Allegiance May 29, 1865
Ramsey, Richard T. Sergeant	22	May 5, 1861, Roxboro, North Carolina	Co. A, 24th North Carolina Infantry	June 17, 1864, Petersburg, Virginia	Point Lookout, Maryland, transferred to Elmira Prison, NY, July 30, 1864	Oath of Allegiance May 19, 1865
Ramsey, William G. Private	Unk	July 6, 1861, Rich Mountain, Virginia	Co. H, 25th Virginia Infantry	May 15, 1864, Wilderness, Virginia	Point Lookout, Maryland, transferred to Elmira Prison, NY, August 14, 1864	Oath of Allegiance June 14, 1865
Ramsey, William J. Private	Unk	April 3, 1862, Tuscaloosa, Alabama	Co. G, 41st Alabama Infantry	May 10, 1864, Richmond Turnpike, Petersburg, Virginia	Point Lookout, Maryland, transferred to Elmira Prison, NY, July 25, 1864	Died November 9, 1864 of Pneumonia, Grave No. 789
Ramsey, William T. Private	23	May 1, 1862, White Sulfur Springs, Virginia	Co. C, 26th Battalion, Virginia Infantry	June 2, 1864, Cold Harbor, Virginia	Point Lookout, Maryland, transferred to Elmira Prison, NY, July 12, 1864	Exchanged March 10, 1865 at Boulware's Wharf on the James River, Virginia
Randal, Robert D. Private	Unk	May 1, 1862, Griffin, Georgia	Co. D, 2nd Battalion Georgia Infantry	May 3, 1864, Near Petersburg, Virginia	Old Capital Prison, Washington, DC. Transferred to Elmira, Prison, NY, July 25, 1864	Died February 12, 1865 of Variola (Smallpox), Grave No. 2071
Randit, Henry J. Private	Unk	June 15, 1861, Americus, Sumter County, Georgia	Co. A, 12th Georgia Infantry	May 10, 1864, Spotsylvania Court House, Virginia	Point Lookout, Maryland, transferred to Elmira Prison, NY, July 30, 1864	Oath of Allegiance June 27, 1865
Randolph, Charles Civilian	Unk	Unknown	Citizen of North Carolina	January 15, 1865, Fort Fisher, North Carolina	February 1, 1865, Elmira Prison Camp, New York	Exchanged March 14, 1865 at Boulware's Wharf on the James River, Virginia

Name & Rank	Age	Enlisted	Regiment and State	Where Captured	Prison	Remarks
Randolph, John T. Private	30	May 13, 1862, Goldsboro, North Carolina	Co. A, 3rd North Carolina Infantry	May 12, 1864, Near Spotsylvania Court House, Virginia	Point Lookout, Maryland, transferred to Elmira Prison, NY, August 14, 1864	Oath of Allegiance June 27, 1865
Randolph, John T. W. Private	Unk	July 20, 1863, Jefferson, Georgia	Co. G, 16th Georgia Infantry	June 3, 1864, Gaines Mill Cold Harbor, Virginia	Point Lookout, Maryland, transferred to Elmira Prison, NY, July 12, 1864	Exchanged February 20, 1865 at Boulware's or Cox Wharf on the James River, Virginia
Randolph, William M. Private	35	July 17, 1862, Richmond, Virginia	Co. A, 3rd North Carolina Infantry	May 6, 1864, Wilderness, Virginia	Point Lookout, Maryland, transferred to Elmira Prison, NY, August 17, 1864	Exchanged October 29, 1864, at Venus Point, Savannah River, GA.
Randolph, William T. Private	17	May 22, 1861, Norfolk County, Virginia	Co. F, 6th Virginia Infantry	May 12, 1864, Near Spotsylvania Court House, Virginia	Point Lookout, Maryland, transferred to Elmira Prison, NY, August 6, 1864	Died January 13, 1865 of Variola (Smallpox), Grave No. 1457
Raney, Isaac A. Private	34	March 18, 1862, Salisbury, North Carolina	Co. D, 42nd North Carolina Infantry	June 3, 1864, Cold Harbor, Virginia	Point Lookout, Maryland, transferred to Elmira Prison, NY, July 12, 1864	Died September 6, 1864 of Chronic Diarrhea and Scurvy, Grave No. 220
Raney, James W. Private	Unk	June 19, 1861, Camp Moore, Louisiana	Co. E, 2nd Louisiana Infantry	May 12, 1864, Spotsylvania Court House, Virginia	Point Lookout, Maryland, transferred to Elmira Prison, NY, August 17, 1864	Exchanged February 25, 1865 at Boulware's or Cox Wharf on the James River, Virginia
Raney, James W. Private	15	June 19, 1861, Camp Moore, Louisiana	Co. E, 8th Louisiana Infantry	May 12, 1864, Wilderness, Virginia	Point Lookout, Maryland, transferred to Elmira Prison, NY, August 15, 1864	Exchanged February 25, 1865 at Boulware's or Cox Wharf on the James River, Virginia
Raney, Mark Private	Unk	December 22, 1863, Camp Ward, Florida	Co. D, 64th Georgia Infantry	June 17, 1864, Petersburg, Virginia	Point Lookout, Maryland, transferred to Elmira Prison, NY, July 30, 1864	Died September 14, 1864 of Chronic Diarrhea, Grave No. 292

Name & Rank	Age	Enlisted	Regiment and State	Where Captured	Prison	Remarks
Rank, Permain A. Private	Unk	February 14, 1864, Raleigh, North Carolina	Co. K, 21st North Carolina Infantry	July 12, 1864, Middletown, Near Harper's Ferry, Maryland	Old Capital Prison, Washington, DC, transferred to Elmira, NY December 17, 1864	Died April 3, 1865 of Diarrhea, Grave No. 2564. Headstone has Permain Rook, 21st South Carolina.
Rankin, Alfred F. Private	18	February 27, 1862, Reidsville, North Carolina	Co. E, 45th North Carolina Infantry	May 10, 1864, Spotsylvania Court House, Virginia	Point Lookout, Maryland, transferred to Elmira Prison, New York, August 6, 1864	Exchanged March 14, 1865 at Boulware's Wharf on the James River, Virginia
Rankin, Anthony Private	23	December 1, 1861, Fort Gaines, Alabama	Co. F, 1st Battalion Alabama Artillery	August 23, 1864, Fort Morgan, Alabama	Steam Press No. 4 New Orleans, Louisiana transferred to Elmira Prison, NY, October 8, 1864.	Died April 18, 1865 of Chronic Diarrhea, Grave No. 1362
Rankin, John H. Sergeant	18	February 28, 1863, Greensboro, North Carolina	Co. B, 45th North Carolina Infantry	May 10, 1864, Spotsylvania Court House, Virginia	Point Lookout, Maryland, transferred to Elmira Prison, NY, August 6, 1864	Oath of Allegiance June 12, 1865
Rankin, Thomas Private	Unk	August 2, 1861, Staunton, Virginia	Co. G, 52nd Virginia Infantry	May 30, 1864 Mechanicsville, Virginia	Point Lookout, Maryland, transferred to Elmira Prison, NY, July 9, 1864	Oath of Allegiance June 30, 1865
Rankin, William Private	Unk	September 2, 1863, Camp of Instruction, South Carolina	Co. E, 1st South Carolina Rifles	July 29, 1864, Petersburg, Virginia	Point Lookout, Maryland, transferred to Elmira Prison, NY, August 12, 1864	Died January 30, 1865 of Remittent Fever, Grave No. 1785
Ransom, John C. Private	Unk	March 1, 1864, Columbia, South Carolina	Co. C, Orr's Rifles, 1st South Carolina Infantry	May 24, 1864 Charlesburg, Virginia	Point Lookout, Maryland, transferred to Elmira Prison, NY, July 12, 1864	Oath of Allegiance June 21, 1865
Ransom, Washington Private	Unk	March 22, 1864, Decatur, Georgia	Co. A, 12th Georgia Infantry	May 20, 1864, Spotsylvania Court House, Virginia	Point Lookout, Maryland, transferred to Elmira Prison, NY, July 3, 1864	Oath of Allegiance December 12, 1864. Early Release per Lincoln's Proclamation, 12/8/1863.

Name & Rank	Age	Enlisted	Regiment and State	Where Captured	Prison	Remarks
Ransom, William N. Private	17	July 20, 1861, Camp Pickens, South Carolina	Co. C, Orr's Rifles, 1st South Carolina Infantry	May 24, 1864 Charlesburg, Virginia	Point Lookout, Maryland, transferred to Elmira Prison, NY, July 12, 1864	Oath of Allegiance June 21, 1865
Raper, William C. Private	19	March 5, 1862, Greensboro, North Carolina	Co. B, 45th, North Carolina Infantry	June 2, 1864, Old Church, Cold Harbor, Virginia	Point Lookout, Maryland, transferred to Elmira Prison, NY, July 17, 1864	Died September 2, 1864 of Chronic Diarrhea, Grave No. 65
Rascoe, Alexander H. Private	24	December 25, 1861, Bennettsville, South Carolina	Co. F, 21st South Carolina Infantry	January 15, 1865, Fort Fisher, North Carolina	February 1, 1865, Elmira Prison Camp, New York	Exchanged March 14, 1865 at Boulware's Wharf on the James River, Virginia
Rash, Noah Private	Unk	September 25, 1863, Camp Vance, North Carolina	Co. B, 23rd North Carolina Infantry	May 10, 1864, Spotsylvania Court House, VA. Gunshot Wound Fracture of Left Clavicle and Shoulder Blade.	Old Capital Prison, Washington, DC transferred to Elmira Prison, NY, August 29, 1864	Exchanged October 29, 1864, at Venus Point, Savannah River, GA.
Ratley, Hinant Private	50	March 19, 1863, Fort Fisher, New Hanover County, North Carolina	Co. K, 40th 3rd Regiment North Carolina Artillery	January 15, 1865, Fort Fisher, North Carolina	February 1, 1865, Elmira Prison Camp, New York	Died February 10, 1865 of Chronic Diarrhea, Grave No. 2087. Headstone has Kenyon Rautley.
Ratliff, Charles H. Private	19	September 15, 1862, Camp Mangum, Raleigh, North Carolina	Co. B, 31st North Carolina Infantry	June 1, 1864, Cold Harbor, Virginia	Point Lookout, Maryland, transferred to Elmira Prison, NY, July 12, 1864	Oath of Allegiance May 29, 1865
Raulerson, David Private	Unk	September 22, 1862, Waynesville, Georgia	Co. G, 7th Georgia Cavalry	June 11, 1864, Trevilian Station, Louisa Court House, Virginia	Point Lookout, Maryland, transferred to Elmira Prison, NY, July 25, 1864	Oath of Allegiance July 7, 1865
Rauls, James L. Private	Unk	December 20, 1861, Georgetown, South Carolina	Co. A, 21st South Carolina Infantry	January 15, 1865, Fort Fisher, North Carolina	February 1, 1865, Elmira Prison Camp, New York	Died April 5, 1865 of Chronic Diarrhea, Grave No. 2548. Headstone has James Rawls.

Name & Rank	Age	Enlisted	Regiment and State	Where Captured	Prison	Remarks
Raum, Robert H. Private	28	April 23, 1861, New Orleans, Louisiana	Co. J, 1st Louisiana Infantry	July 10, 1864, Frederick, Maryland	Old Capital Prison, Washington DC. Transferred to Elmira Prison Camp, New York, July 25, 1864.	Exchanged February 25, 1865 at Boulware's or Cox Wharf on the James River, Virginia
Rawles, J. Private	Unk	Unknown	Co. K, 21st South Carolina Infantry	January 15, 1865, Fort Fisher, North Carolina	February 1, 1865, Elmira Prison Camp, New York	Exchanged March 14, 1865 at Boulware's Wharf on the James River, Virginia
Rawlings, John J. Private	44	September 26, 1863, Camp Wappoo, South Carolina	Co. J, 59th Virginia Infantry	May 8, 1864, Nottoway Bridge, Virginia	Point Lookout, Maryland, transferred to Elmira Prison, NY, August 17, 1864	Died September 27, 1864 of Typhoid Fever, Grave No. 383
Rawls, Alfred D. Private	18	May 29, 1861, Newbern, North Carolina	Co. D, 2nd North Carolina Infantry	May 12, 1864, Near Spotsylvania, Virginia	Point Lookout, Maryland, transferred to Elmira Prison, NY, August 14, 1864	Oath of Allegiance June 14, 1865
Rawls, Hosey Private	26	July 27, 1864, St. Johns, Hartford County, North Carolina	Co. C, 3rd Battalion North Carolina Light Artillery	January 15, 1865, Fort Fisher, North Carolina	February 1, 1865, Elmira Prison Camp, New York	Died May 27, 1865 of Debility, Grave No. 2915
Rawls, Joseph A. Private	Unk	August 3, 1864 at St. Johns, North Carolina	Co. C, 3rd Battalion North Carolina Light Artillery	January 15, 1865, Fort Fisher, North Carolina	February 1, 1865, Elmira Prison Camp, New York	Exchanged March 14, 1865. Died March 31, 1865 at Jackson Hospital, Richmond, VA
Rawls, Joseph J. Private	Unk	May 14, 1862, Greenville, North Carolina	Co. K, 10th Regiment, 1st North Carolina Artillery	January 15, 1865, Fort Fisher, North Carolina	February 1, 1865, Elmira Prison Camp, New York	Oath of Allegiance July 26, 1865
Rawls, William R. Private	Unk	July 28, 1864, St. Johns, Hartford County, North Carolina	Co. C, 3rd Battalion North Carolina Light Artillery	January 15, 1865, Fort Fisher, North Carolina	February 1, 1865, Elmira Prison Camp, New York	Exchanged March 14, 1865 at Boulware's Wharf on the James River, Virginia

Name & Rank	Age	Enlisted	Regiment and State	Where Captured	Prison	Remarks
Ray, Angus J. Private	Unk	July 20, 1862, Moore County, North Carolina	Co. C, 3rd North Carolina Infantry	May 12, 1864, Near Spotsylvania County Court House, Virginia	Point Lookout, Maryland, transferred to Elmira Prison, NY, August 14, 1864	Died July 10, 1865 of Chronic Diarrhea, Grave No. 2845
Ray, Archibald A. Corporal	25	May 1, 1862, Kinston, North Carolina	Co. C, 35th North Carolina Infantry	June 17, 1864, Petersburg, Virginia	Point Lookout, Maryland, transferred to Elmira Prison, NY, July 30, 1864	Oath of Allegiance June 12, 1865
Ray, Brace A. Private	28	November 19, 1863, Alamance County, North Carolina	Co. F, 53rd North Carolina Infantry	July 12, 1864, Near Washington, DC	Old Capital Prison, Washington, DC. Transferred to Elmira Prison Camp, NY, July 25, 1864.	Died March 27, 1865 Diarrhea, Grave No. 2484
Ray, Charles K. Private	Unk	June 15, 1861, Columbia, South Carolina	Hart's Battalion, South Carolina, Horse Artillery	May 9, 1864, Spotsylvania Court House, Virginia	Point Lookout, Maryland, transferred to Elmira Prison, NY, August 17, 1864	Exchanged March 2, 1865 at Akins Landing on the James River, Virginia
Ray, Chesley Private	22	March 18, 1864, Monroe Draft, Virginia	Co. K, 22nd Virginia Infantry	June 3, 1864, Gaines Farm Cold Harbor, Virginia	Point Lookout, Maryland, transferred to Elmira Prison, NY, July 12, 1864. Ward No. 18	Died September 4, 1864 of Chronic Diarrhea Grave No. 7
Ray, George W. Private	Unk	Unknown	Co. B, 59th Alabama Infantry	June 18, 1864, Petersburg, Virginia	Point Lookout, Maryland, transferred to Elmira Prison, NY, July 25, 1864	Oath of Allegiance May 29, 1865
Ray, John P. Private	Unk	April 8, 1864, Madison, Florida	Co. 8th Florida Infantry	May 25, 1864, North Anna River, Virginia	Point Lookout, Maryland, transferred to Elmira Prison, NY, July 12, 1864	Transferred for Exchange 10/11/64. Died 10/13/64 at US Army Hospital, Baltimore, MD
Ray, S. L. Private	26	July 13, 1861, Unionville, Tennessee	Co. F, 23rd Tennessee Infantry	June 17, 1864, Petersburg, Virginia	Point Lookout, Maryland, transferred to Elmira Prison, NY, July 30, 1864	Died September 2, 1864 of Typhoid Fever, Grave No. 82

Name & Rank	Age	Enlisted	Regiment and State	Where Captured	Prison	Remarks
Ray, Thomas J. Private	Unk	July 13, 1861, Unionville, Tennessee	Co. C, 23rd Tennessee Infantry	June 17, 1864, Petersburg, Virginia	Point Lookout, Maryland, transferred to Elmira Prison, NY, July 30, 1864	Died January 3, 1865 of Chronic Diarrhea, Grave No. 1335
Ray, William B. Private	Unk	August 27, 1862, LaGrange, Georgia	Co. F, 14th Alabama Infantry	May 6, 1864, Wilderness, Virginia	Point Lookout, Maryland, transferred to Elmira Prison, NY, July 23, 1864	Died November 1, 1864 of Chronic Diarrhea, Grave No. 753.
Rayborn, Henry Private	28	July 16, 1861, Forestville, North Carolina	Co. J, 1st North Carolina Infantry	May 12, 1864, Spotsylvania Court House, Virginia	Point Lookout, Maryland, transferred to Elmira Prison, NY, August 6, 1864	Oath of Allegiance June 12, 1865
Rayford, Henry B. Private	Unk	June 15, 1861, Americus, Sumter County, Georgia	Co. A, 12th Georgia Infantry	May 10, 1864, Spotsylvania Court House, Virginia	Point Lookout, Maryland, transferred to Elmira Prison, NY, July 30, 1864	Exchanged October 29, 1864, at Venus Point, Savannah River, GA.
Raymond, Joseph S. Sergeant	27	June 8, 1861, Lexington, Virginia	Co. I, 4th Virginia Infantry	May 12, 1864, Spotsylvania Court House, Virginia	Point Lookout, Maryland, transferred to Elmira Prison, NY, August 6, 1864	Exchanged March 10, 1865 at Boulware's Wharf on the James River, Virginia
Raymond, William M. Private	23	May 25, 1861, Camp Howard, Brunswick County, North Carolina	Co. G, 3rd North Carolina Infantry	May 12, 1864, Near Spotsylvania Court House, Virginia	Point Lookout, Maryland, transferred to Elmira Prison, NY, August 14, 1864	Died October 22, 1864 of Pneumonia, Grave No. 868
Rayner, Henry M. Private	24	July 23, 1861, Cameron, North Carolina	Co. E, 8th, North Carolina Infantry	June 1, 1864, Gaines Mill Cold Harbor, Virginia	Point Lookout, Maryland, transferred to Elmira Prison, NY, July 12, 1864	Died January 27, 1865 of Chronic Diarrhea, Grave No. 1653
Rea, D. A. Private	Unk	July 9, 1861, Jonesboro, Georgia	Co. E, 10th Georgia Infantry	May 6, 1864, Wilderness, Virginia	Old Capital Prison, Washington D. C. Transferred to Elmira Prison, NY, July 14, 1864	Oath of Allegiance June 21, 1865

Name & Rank	Age	Enlisted	Regiment and State	Where Captured	Prison	Remarks
Rea, John W. Private	Unk	Fedruary 1, 1862, Tullahoma, Tennessee	Co. H, 17th Tennessee Infantry	June 17, 1864, Petersburg, Virginia	Point Lookout, Maryland, transferred to Elmira Prison, NY, July 30, 1864	Died March 21, 1865 of Diarrhea, Grave No. 1526, Last Name Ray on Headstone.
Rea, William F. Private	36	February 26, 1862, Monroe, North Carolina	Co. B, 43rd North Carolina Infantry	July 12, 1864, Near Washington, DC	Old Capital Prison, Washington DC. Transferred to Elmira Prison Camp, New York, July 25, 1864.	Oath of Allegiance May 29, 1865
Read, Abner A. Private	Unk	April 27, 1861, Tuskegee, Alabama	Co. C, 3rd Alabama Infantry	May 12, 1864, Spotsylvania Court House, Virginia	Point Lookout, Maryland, transferred to Elmira Prison, NY, August 12, 1864	Exchanged October 29, 1864, at Venus Point, Savannah River, GA.
Reade, Edward B. Private	18	May 5, 1861, Roxboro, North Carolina	Co. A, 24th North Carolina Infantry	June 17, 1864, Petersburg, Virginia	Point Lookout, Maryland, transferred to Elmira Prison, NY, July 30, 1864	Oath of Allegiance May 13, 1865
Reader, James B. Private	Unk	February 2, 1863, Chesterfield District, South Carolina	Co. F, 26th South Carolina Infantry	July 30, 1864, Petersburg, Virginia	Point Lookout, Maryland, transferred to Elmira Prison, NY, August 12, 1864	Exchanged March 14, 1865 at Boulware's Wharf on the James River, Virginia
Ready, Henry Private	Unk	July 1, 1861, New Orleans, Louisiana	Co. H, 14th Louisiana Infantry	May 20, 1864, Spotsylvania Court House, Virginia	Point Lookout, Maryland, transferred to Elmira Prison, NY, July 3, 1864	Exchanged February 25, 1865 at Boulware's or Cox Wharf on the James River, Virginia
Reagin, Thomas E. Private	26	May 1, 1862, Cat Island, South Carolina	Co. J, 4th South Carolina Cavalry	May 28, 1864, Hawes Shop, Hanover, VA. Gunshot Wound Abdomen, Severe.	Old Capital Prison, Washington, DC transferred to Elmira Prison, NY, August 27, 1864	Exchanged February 13, 1865 at Boulware's Wharf on the James River, Virginia
Reap, Ephraim Private	17	February 28, 1862, Salisbury, North Carolina	Co. C, 42nd North Carolina Infantry	June 3, 1864, Cold Harbor, Virginia	Point Lookout, Maryland, transferred to Elmira Prison, NY, July 12, 1864	Exchanged March 14, 1865 at Boulware's Wharf on the James River, Virginia

Name & Rank	Age	Enlisted	Regiment and State	Where Captured	Prison	Remarks
Reardan, John E. Private	19	April 25, 1861, Harper's Ferry, Virginia	Co. C, 2nd Virginia Infantry	May 12, 1864, Spotsylvania Court House, Virginia	Point Lookout, Maryland, transferred to Elmira Prison, NY, August 6, 1864	Died September 13, 1864 of Chronic Diarrhea, Grave No. 276
Reaser, James Private	23	March 29, 1862, Lewisburg, Virginia	Co. D, 26th Battalion Virginia Infantry	June 3, 1864, Cold Harbor, Virginia	Point Lookout, Maryland, transferred to Elmira Prison, NY, July 12, 1864	Exchanged October 29, 1864, at Venus Point, Savannah River, GA.
Reaser, Philip Private	Unk	March 29, 1862, Lewisburg, Virginia	Co. D, 26th Battalion Virginia Infantry	June 3, 1864, Cold Harbor, Virginia	Transferred From Point Lookout Prison, MD, July 12, 1864. Train Never Arrived at Elmira Prison Camp, NY.	Died July 15, 1864 in Train Wreck at Shohola, Pennsylvania.
Reasons, Cotton Private	24	June 24, 1861, Williamston, North Carolina	Co. G, 1st North Carolina Infantry	May 12, 1864, Spotsylvania Court House, Virginia	Point Lookout, Maryland, transferred to Elmira Prison, NY, August 6, 1864	Oath of Allegiance June 12, 1865
Reaves, Jerry P. Private	18	May 10, 1863, Fort Fisher, New Hanover County, North Carolina	Co. G, 36th Regiment 2nd North Carolina Artillery	January 15, 1865, Fort Fisher, North Carolina	February 1, 1865, Elmira Prison Camp, New York	Exchanged February 20, 1865 at Boulware's or Cox Wharf on the James River, Virginia
Reaves, John W. Private	33	October 7, 1863, Fort Caswell, Brunswick County, North Carolina	Co. D, 36th Regiment 2nd North Carolina Artillery	January 15, 1865, Fort Fisher, North Carolina	February 1, 1865, Elmira Prison Camp, New York	Died March 26, 1865 of Bronchitis, Grave No. 2477. Headstone has J. W. Reeves.
Reaves, Joseph T. Private	22	April 24,1861, Bug Hill, North Carolina	Co. C, 18th North Carolina Infantry	May 12, 1864, Spotsylvania Court House, Virginia	Point Lookout, Maryland, transferred to Elmira Prison, NY, August 6, 1864	Exchanged 3/2/64. Died 3/24/65 of Chronic Diarrhea at General Hospital No. 9, Richmond, VA
Reaves, Samuel Private	35	April 16, 1862, Old Brunswick, Brunswick County, North Carolina	Co. G, 36th Regiment 2nd North Carolina Artillery	January 15, 1865, Fort Fisher, North Carolina	February 1, 1865, Elmira Prison Camp, New York	Died April 13, 1865 of Variola (Smallpox), Grave No. 2701. Headstone has S. F. Reebe.

Name & Rank	Age	Enlisted	Regiment and State	Where Captured	Prison	Remarks
Reaves, Samuel Private	18	April 27, 1863, Fort Anderson, Brunswick County, North Carolina	Co. E, 36th Regiment 2nd North Carolina Artillery	January 15, 1865, Fort Fisher, North Carolina	February 1, 1865, Elmira Prison Camp, New York	Exchanged March 2, 1865 at Akins Landing on the James River, Virginia
Reaves, William H. Private	18	June 29, 1861, Goldsboro, North Carolina	Co. C, 2nd North Carolina Infantry	August 10, 1864, White's Ford, Virginia	Old Capital Prison, Washington, DC transferred to Elmira Prison, NY, August 29, 1864	Died January 29, 1865 of Variola (Smallpox), Grave No. 1798. Headstone has Reeves.
Reaves, William L. Private	Unk	January 18, 1862, Camp Hampton, Columbia, South Carolina	Co. F, 22nd South Carolina Infantry	June 17, 1864, Petersburg, Virginia	Point Lookout, Maryland, transferred to Elmira Prison, NY, July 30, 1864	Died December 13, 1864 of Pneumonia, Grave No. 1124
Rectleff, J. R. Civilian	Unk	Louisiana	Citizen of Louisiana	July 27, 1864, New Orleans, Louisiana	New Orleans, Louisiana transferred to Elmira November 19, 1864.	Exchanged February 20, 1865 at Boulware's wharf on the James River, Virginia
Rector, A. B. Private	27	August 20, 1862, Statesville, North Carolina	Co. B, 18th North Carolina Infantry	May 12, 1864, Spotsylvania Court House, Virginia	Point Lookout, Maryland, transferred to Elmira Prison, NY, August 6, 1864	Oath of Allegiance May 29, 1865
Rector, Amos J. Private	Unk	April 25, 1862, Fayette, Alabama	Co. J, 43rd Alabama Infantry	May 16, 1864, Near Drury's Bluff, Virginia	Point Lookout, Maryland, transferred to Elmira Prison, NY, August 17, 1864	Oath of Allegiance June 21, 1865
Rector, Elihu W. Private	Unk	October 9, 1861, Alexandria County, North Carolina	Co. D, 18th North Carolina Infantry	May 12, 1864, Spotsylvania Court House, Virginia	Point Lookout, Maryland, transferred to Elmira Prison, NY, August 6, 1864	Oath of Allegiance May 29, 1865
Redding, Alfred Private	40	March 31, 1863, Asheboro, North Carolina	Co. F, 2nd Battalion North Carolina Infantry	July 12, 1864, Near Washington, DC	Old Capital Prison, Washington, DC. Transferred to Elmira Prison Camp New York July 25, 1864	Died August 24, 1864 of Chronic Diarrhea, Grave No. 48

Name & Rank	Age	Enlisted	Regiment and State	Where Captured	Prison	Remarks
Redick, Epinetus Private	17	August 31, 1861, Crab Tree, Raleigh, North Carolina	Co. F, 30th North Carolina Infantry	July 13, 1864, Silver Springs, VA. Gunshot Wound Ear Extending to Left Eye, Fracture Maxillary Bone	Old Capital Prison, Washington, DC transferred to Elmira Prison, NY, August 29, 1864	Died February 7, 1865 of Pneumonia Grave No. 1921
Redman, Willford Private	Unk	October 8, 1862, Paris, Virginia	Co. A, 6th Virginia Cavalry	July 25, 1864, Berlin, Virginia. Deserted to Union Lines.	Old Capital Prison, Washington D. C. Transferred to Elmira Prison, NY, August 12, 1864	Oath of Allegiance December 2, 1864. Early Release per Lincoln's Proclamation, 12/8/1863.
Redmond, Albert J. Private	21	April 22, 1861, Shelby, North Carolina	Co. E, 12th North Carolina Infantry	July 5, 1863, Hagerstown, Maryland	Point Lookout, Maryland, transferred to Elmira Prison, NY, August 14, 1864	Exchanged February 20, 1865 at Boulware's or Cox Wharf on the James River, Virginia
Reece, Alfred C. Private	Unk	October 6, 1861, Milton County, Georgia	Co. D, 38th Georgia Infantry	May 20, 1864, Spotsylvania Court House, Virginia	Point Lookout, Maryland, transferred to Elmira Prison, NY, July 3, 1864	Exchanged 3/2/65. Died 3/11/65 of Chronic Diarrhea at Wayside Hospital No. 9, Richmond, VA
Reece, John E. Private	24	April 15, 1863, Harrisonburg, Virginia	Co. H, 12th Virginia Cavalry	May 22, 1864, Hanover Junction, Virginia	Point Lookout, Maryland, transferred to Elmira Prison, NY, July 25, 1864	Oath of Allegiance June 21, 1865
Reed, D. B. R. Private	Unk	August 29, 1861, Pensacola, Florida	Co. A, 2nd Florida Infantry	May 12, 1864, Spotsylvania Court House, Virginia	Point Lookout, Maryland, transferred to Elmira Prison, NY, August 12, 1864	Exchanged March 14, 1865 at Boulware's Wharf on the James River, Virginia
Reed, James Private	27	June 5, 1861, Dobson, North Carolina	Co. H, 25th South Carolina Infantry	May 16, 1864, Near Drury's Bluff, Virginia	Point Lookout, Maryland, transferred to Elmira Prison, NY, August 17, 1864	Died February 13, 1865 of Variola (Smallpox), Grave No. 2192
Reed, James Private	Unk	Unknown	Co. H, 25th South Carolina Infantry	January 15, 1865, Fort Fisher, North Carolina	February 1, 1865, Elmira Prison Camp, New York	Died March 13, 1865 of Variola (Smallpox), Grave No. 2436. Headstone has Reid

Name & Rank	Age	Enlisted	Regiment and State	Where Captured	Prison	Remarks
Reed, John Private	24	March 18, 1862, Dobson, North Carolina	Co. A, 28th North Carolina Infantry	May 12, 1864, Near Spotsylvania Court House, Virginia	Point Lookout, Maryland, transferred to Elmira Prison, NY, August 14, 1864	Oath of Allegiance May 29, 1865
Reed, Lawrence Firemen	Unk	Unknown	CSS Steamer Arrow, Confederate States Navy	July 28, 1864, Bennett's Creek, North Carolina	Point Lookout, Maryland, transferred to Elmira Prison, NY, August 18, 1864	Exchanged March 10, 1865 at Boulware's Wharf on the James River, Virginia
Reed, Thomas B. Private	Unk	March 12, 1862, Serenata, Mississippi	Co. K, 17th Mississippi Infantry	May 22, 1864, Mott's Tavern, Spotsylvania, Virginia	Point Lookout, Maryland, transferred to Elmira Prison, NY, July 23, 1864	Exchanged March 10, 1865 at Boulware's Wharf on the James River, Virginia
Reed, William F. Corporal	Unk	June 18, 1861, New Orleans, Louisiana	Co. B, 21st Louisiana Infantry	July 4, 1863, Vicksburg, Mississippi	New Orleans, Louisiana transferred to Elmira November 19, 1864.	Oath of Allegiance May 15, 1865
Reed, Z. T. Civilian	Unk	Unknown	Citizen of Loudoun County, Virginia	October 21, 1863, Leesburg, Virginia	Point Lookout, Maryland, transferred to Elmira Prison, NY, July 25, 1864	Exchanged March 10, 1865 at Boulware's Wharf on the James River, Virginia
Reedy, Andrew J. Private	Unk	June 4, 1861, Fork of Wilson, Virginia	Co. D, 58th Virginia Infantry	May 12, 1864, Spotsylvania, Virginia	Point Lookout Prison Camp, Maryland. Transferred to Elmira Prison Camp, NY, July 6, 1864	Died May 7, 1865 of Pneumonia, Grave No. 2771
Reedy, Andrew J. Private	Unk	June 4, 1861, Fork of Wilson, Virginia	Co. D, 50th Virginia Infantry	May 12, 1864, Spotsylvania Court House, Virginia	Point Lookout, Maryland, transferred to Elmira Prison, NY, July 3, 1864	Oath of Allegiance June 19, 1865
Reedy, Samuel Private	Unk	July 30, 1861, Marion, Virginia	Co. D, 4th Virginia Infantry	May 12, 1864 Spotsylvania Court House, Virginia	Point Lookout, Maryland, transferred to Elmira Prison, NY, August 2, 1864	Oath of Allegiance June 19, 1865
Reep, Albert M. Private	Unk	March 11, 1864, Newton, North Carolina	Co. E, 32nd North Carolina Infantry	May 10, 1864, Wilderness, Virginia	Point Lookout, Maryland, transferred to Elmira Prison, NY, August 6, 1864	Oath of Allegiance June 27, 1865

Name & Rank	Age	Enlisted	Regiment and State	Where Captured	Prison	Remarks
Reep, Daniel A. Private	26	August 14, 1861, Newton, North Carolina	Co. E, 32nd North Carolina Infantry	May 10, 1864, Wilderness, Virginia	Point Lookout, Maryland, transferred to Elmira Prison, NY, August 6, 1864	Oath of Allegiance June 27, 1865
Rees, James Private	20	May 15, 1861, Edneyville, North Carolina	Co. A, 25th North Carolina Infantry	June 17, 1864, Petersburg, Virginia	Point Lookout, Maryland, transferred to Elmira Prison, NY, July 30, 1864	Oath of Allegiance July 3, 1865
Rees, Robert M. Sergeant	Unk	January 22, 1862, Columbia, South Carolina	Co. B, 22nd South Carolina Infantry	July 30, 1864, Petersburg, Virginia	Point Lookout, Maryland, transferred to Elmira Prison, NY, August 12, 1864	Transferred for Exchange 10/11/64. Died 11/14/64 of Unknown Causes at Port Royal, SC.
Reese, Matthew A. Private	Unk	January 20, 1862, Lombardy Grove, Virginia	Co. D, 22nd Battalion Virginia Infantry	May 6, 1864, Wilderness, Virginia	Point Lookout, Maryland, transferred to Elmira Prison, NY, August 14, 1864	Died September 23, 1864 of Remittent Fever, Grave No. 354
Reese, Newton R. Private	Unk	February 15, 1861, Montgomery, Alabama	Co. E, 1st Battalion Alabama Artillery	August 23, 1864, Fort Morgan, Alabama	Steam Press No. 4, New Orleans, Louisiana transferred to Elmira October 8, 1864.	Oath of Allegiance to June 14, 1865
Reese, Pleasant H. Private	Unk	July 8, 1861, Griffin, Georgia	Co. J, 13th Georgia Infantry	May 12, 1864, Spotsylvania Court House, Virginia	Washington DC. Transferred to Elmira Prison Camp New York July 25, 1864.	Oath of Allegiance June 21, 1865
Reese, William M. Private	Unk	October 1, 1863, Selma, Alabama	Jeff Davis Alabama Artillery	May 5, 1864, Wilderness, Virginia	Point Lookout, Maryland, transferred to Elmira Prison, NY, August 17, 1864	Exchanged March 2, 1865 at Akins Landing on the James River, Virginia
Reeves, Edward Private	31	February 26, 1862, Chapel Hill, North Carolina	Co. G, 11th North Carolina Infantry	July 14, 1863, Falling Waters, Maryland	Point Lookout, Maryland, transferred to Elmira Prison, NY, August 18, 1864	Died September 24, 1864 of Chronic Diarrhea, Grave No. 468. Headstone has Reaves.

Name & Rank	Age	Enlisted	Regiment and State	Where Captured	Prison	Remarks
Reeves, Franklin J. Sergeant	21	July 8, 1861, Griffin, Georgia	Co. D, 13th Georgia Infantry	May 12, 1864, Spotsylvania Court House, Virginia. Gunshot Wound of Left Shoulder and Right Thigh.	Old Capital Prison, Washington D. C. Transferred to Elmira Prison, NY, August 12, 1864	Oath of Allegiance June 19, 1865
Reeves, Jacob Private	Unk	March 4, 1862, Jonesboro, Georgia	Co. D, 44th Georgia Infantry	May 20, 1864, Spotsylvania Court House, Virginia	Point Lookout, Maryland, transferred to Elmira Prison, NY, July 3, 1864	Exchanged October 29, 1864, at Venus Point, Savannah River, GA.
Reeves, James B. Private	34	July 15, 1862, Raleigh, North Carolina	Co. C, 1st North Carolina Infantry	May 12, 1864, Near Spotsylvania Court House, Virginia	Point Lookout Prison, Maryland. Transferred to Elmira Prison Camp New York August 6, 1864.	Oath of Allegiance June 27, 1865
Regan, Addison Private	17	June 28, 1863, Fort Fisher, New Hanover County, North Carolina	Co. J, 36th Regiment 2nd North Carolina Artillery	January 15, 1865, Fort Fisher, North Carolina	February 1, 1865, Elmira Prison Camp, New York	Exchanged March 14, 1865 at Boulware's Wharf on the James River, Virginia
Regan, Neill Private	17	March 4, 1864, Fort Fisher, New Hanover County, North Carolina	Co. J, 36th Regiment 2nd North Carolina Artillery	January 15, 1865, Fort Fisher, North Carolina	February 1, 1865, Elmira Prison Camp, New York	Died May 23, 1865 of Pneumonia, Grave No. 2929
Reger, John H. Private	Unk	May 1, 1862, West View, Virginia	Co. B, 25th Virginia Infantry	May 12, 1864, Spotsylvania Court House, Virginia	Point Lookout, Maryland, transferred to Elmira Prison, NY, July 30, 1864	Oath of Allegiance June 14, 1865
Register, Chester A. Private	Unk	March 14, 1862, Jasper, Florida	Co. F, 5th Florida Infantry	May 12, 1864, Spotsylvania Court House, Virginia	Point Lookout, Maryland, transferred to Elmira Prison, NY, July 30, 1864	Oath of Allegiance July 7, 1865
Register, George R. Private	34	March 1, 1862, Magnolia, North Carolina	Co. B, 51st North Carolina Infantry	June 1, 1864, Cold Harbor, Virginia	Point Lookout, Maryland, transferred to Elmira Prison, NY, July 12, 1864	Exchanged March 14, 1865 at Boulware's Wharf on the James River, Virginia
Register, Guiford Private	Unk	August 23, 1861, Brunswick, Georgia	Co. D, 26th Georgia Infantry	May 20, 1864, Spotsylvania Court House, Virginia	Point Lookout, Maryland, transferred to Elmira Prison, NY, July 3, 1864	Oath of Allegiance June 30, 1865

Name & Rank	Age	Enlisted	Regiment and State	Where Captured	Prison	Remarks
Register, James Private	24	January 1, 1862, Darlington District, South Carolina	Co. B, 21st South Carolina Infantry	June 24, 1864, Near Petersburg, Virginia	Point Lookout, Maryland, transferred to Elmira Prison, NY, August 18, 1864	Oath of Allegiance July 3, 1865
Register, W. O. Private	20	March 4, 1862, Shepherdsville, North Carolina	Co. C, 7th North Carolina Infantry	May 6, 1864, Wilderness, Virginia	Point Lookout, Maryland, transferred to Elmira Prison, NY, August 14, 1864	Oath of Allegiance June 12, 1865
Rehberg, Charles Corporal	Unk	May 3, 1862, Bainbridge, Georgia	Co. A, 59th Georgia Infantry	May 6, 1864, Wilderness, Virginia	Point Lookout, Maryland, transferred to Elmira Prison, NY, August 14, 1864	Oath of Allegiance June 14, 1865
Reich, Rueben V. Private	Unk	March 12, 1864, Camp Holmes, Raleigh, North Carolina	Co. A, 57th North Carolina Infantry	May 23, 1864, North Anna, Hanover Junction, Virginia	Point Lookout, Maryland, transferred to Elmira Prison, NY, July 23, 1864	Died 11/8/64 of Chronic Diarrhea, Grave No. 830. Last Name Rich on Headstone.
Reid, Alfred Private	Unk	Unknown	Co. K, 59th Alabama Infantry	April 2, 1865, Five Forks, Virginia	Old Capital Prison, Washington D. C. Transferred to Elmira Prison, NY, May 2, 1865.	Oath of Allegiance July 7, 1865
Reid, H. C. Sergeant	Unk	April 24, 1861, Madison Court House, Virginia	Co. C, 4th Virginia Cavalry	August 16, 1864, Front Royal, Virginia	Old Capital Prison, Washington, DC transferred to Elmira Prison, NY, August 29, 1864	Oath of Allegiance June 23, 1865
Reid, J. J. Private	Unk	February 26, 1863, Pendleton, South Carolina	Co. C, 4th South Carolina Cavalry	June 11, 1864, Trevilian Station, Louisa Court House, Virginia	Point Lookout, Maryland, transferred to Elmira Prison, NY, July 25, 1864	Died August 30, 1864 of Pneumonia, Grave No. 95. Name Reed on Headstone.
Reid, James R. Private	Unk	April 4, 1862, Hardeeville, South Carolina	Co. E, 11th South Carolina Infantry	June 24, 1864, Near Petersburg, Virginia	Point Lookout, Maryland, transferred to Elmira Prison, NY, August 18, 1864	Oath of Allegiance June 30, 1865

Name & Rank	Age	Enlisted	Regiment and State	Where Captured	Prison	Remarks
Reid, Lewis H. Sergeant Major	Unk	September 23, 1861, Washington, North Carolina	Co. D, 13th Battalion North Carolina Light Artillery	January 15, 1865, Fort Fisher, North Carolina	February 1, 1865, Elmira Prison Camp, New York	Oath of Allegiance June 14, 1865
Reid, Martin V. B. Private	20	June 17, 1861, Lewisburg, North Carolina	Co. K, 24th North Carolina Infantry	June 18, 1864, Petersburg, Virginia	Point Lookout, Maryland, transferred to Elmira Prison, NY, July 30, 1864	Exchanged March 14, 1865 at Boulware's Wharf on the James River, Virginia
Reighley, D. H. Private	Unk	March 6, 1862, Camp Gregg, Grahamville, South Carolina	Co. B, 4th South Carolina Cavalry	June 11, 1864, Trevilian Station, Louisa Court House, Virginia	Point Lookout, Maryland, transferred to Elmira Prison, NY, July 25, 1864	Oath of Allegiance June 19, 1865
Reinhartz, Fred Private	Unk	September 1, 1862, New Braunfels, Texas	Co. B, 7th Texas Cavalry	November 20, 1863, Camp Pratt, Cross Bayou, Louisiana	New Orleans, Louisiana, Transferred to Elmira Prison, New York, November 19, 1864	Oath of Allegiance May 19, 1865
Remshart, Robert Bruce Private	Unk	May 13, 1862, Savannah, Georgia	Co. G, 7th Georgia Cavalry	June 11, 1864, Trevilian Station, Louisa Court House, Virginia	Point Lookout, Maryland, transferred to Elmira Prison, NY, July 25, 1864	Exchanged October 29, 1864, at Venus Point, Savannah River, GA.
Rendleman, John L. Private	20	July 4, 1862, Salisbury, North Carolina	Co. C, 57th North Carolina Infantry	August 22, 1864, Charlestown, Virginia	Old Capital Prison, Washington, DC transferred to Elmira Prison, NY, August 29, 1864	Oath of Allegiance June 21, 1865
Rendleman, Pinkney L. Private	26	June 22, 1862, Garysburg, North Carolina	Co. K, 23rd North Carolina Infantry	May 12, 1864, Near Spotsylvania Court House, Virginia	Point Lookout Prison, Maryland. Transferred to Elmira Prison Camp New York August 14, 1864.	Exchanged October 29, 1864, at Venus Point, Savannah River, GA.
Rendon, Andrew Sergeant	Unk	May 9, 1861, New Orleans, Louisiana	Co. B, 2nd Louisiana Infantry	May 12, 1864, Spotsylvania Court House, Virginia	Point Lookout, Maryland, transferred to Elmira Prison, NY, August 17, 1864	Exchanged February 25, 1865 at Boulware's or Cox Wharf on the James River, Virginia

Name & Rank	Age	Enlisted	Regiment and State	Where Captured	Prison	Remarks
Renew, Anderson Private	17	February 26, 1862, Madison, Florida	Co. E, 5th Florida Infantry	July 3, 1864, Spotsylvania Court House, Virginia	Point Lookout, Maryland, transferred to Elmira Prison, NY, July 30, 1864	Oath of Allegiance June 17, 1865
Renfroe, James F. Sergeant	Unk	June 15, 1861, Jones County, Georgia	Co. A, 12th Georgia Infantry	May 10, 1864, Spotsylvania Court House, Virginia	Point Lookout, Maryland, transferred to Elmira Prison, NY, July 30, 1864	Oath of Allegiance June 27, 1865
Renn, Joseph J. Private	22	May 4, 1861, Warrenton, North Carolina	Co. C, 12 North Carolina Infantry	May 12, 1864, Spotsylvania Court House, Virginia	Old Capital Prison, Washington DC. Transferred to Elmira Prison Camp, New York, July 25, 1864.	Oath of Allegiance June 19, 1865
Renneker, F. W. Private	Unk	February 24, 1862, Charleston, South Carolina	Co. B, 25th South Carolina Infantry	January 15, 1865, Fort Fisher, North Carolina	February 1, 1865, Elmira Prison Camp, New York	Exchanged March 14, 1865 at Boulware's Wharf on the James River, Virginia
Renneker, John H. Private	Unk	March 21, 1863, Charleston, South Carolina	Co. B, 25th South Carolina Infantry	January 15, 1865, Fort Fisher, North Carolina	February 1, 1865, Elmira Prison Camp, New York	Oath of Allegiance June 23, 1865
Rentfrow, James Private	Unk	July 11, 1863, Smithville, North Carolina	Co. F, 10th Regiment, 1st North Carolina Artillery	January 15, 1865, Fort Fisher, North Carolina	February 1, 1865, Elmira Prison Camp, New York	Died March 4, 1865 of Pneumonia, Grave No. 1988. Headstone has Rentford.
Rentz, Charles Private	Unk	October 17, 1861, Camp Style, Georgia	Co. H, 26th Georgia Infantry	May 6, 1864, Wilderness, Virginia	Point Lookout, Maryland, transferred to Elmira Prison, NY, August 17, 1864	Exchanged March 2, 1865 at Akins Landing on the James River, Virginia
Rentz, George W. Sergeant	33	December 23, 1861, Colleton, South Carolina	Co. K, 11th South Carolina Infantry	October 21, 1864, Weldon Railroad, Near Petersburg, VA. Gunshot Wound Left Hip.	Old Capital Prison, Washington, DC transferred to Elmira Prison, NY, August 27, 1864	Died December 29, 1864 of Pneumonia, Grave No. 1305

Name & Rank	Age	Enlisted	Regiment and State	Where Captured	Prison	Remarks
Rentz, Samuel R. Private	Unk	June 14, 1861, Valdosta, Georgia	Co. J, 12th Georgia Infantry	May 10, 1864, Spotsylvania Court House, Virginia	Point Lookout, Maryland, transferred to Elmira Prison, NY, July 25, 1864	Oath of Allegiance June 21, 1865
Revel, John W. Private	22	March 15, 1863, Wilmington, North Carolina	Co. F, 56th North Carolina Infantry	June 17, 1864, Petersburg, Virginia	Point Lookout, Maryland, transferred to Elmira Prison, NY, July 23, 1864	Oath of Allegiance May 15, 1865
Revill, Henry Private	21	September 6, 1861, Lumberton, North Carolina	Co. E, 31st North Carolina Infantry	June 3, 1864, Gaines Farm Cold Harbor, Virginia	Transferred From Point Lookout Prison, MD, July 12, 1864. Train Never Arrived at Elmira Prison Camp, NY.	Died July 15, 1864 in Train Wreck at Shohola, Pennsylvania.
Revis, John E. Private	19	June 4, 1861, Mocksville, North Carolina	Co. G, 4th North Carolina Infantry	July 9, 1864, Harpers Ferry, Virginia	Old Capital Prison, Washington DC. Transferred to Elmira Prison Camp, New York, July 25, 1864.	Oath of Allegiance May 29, 1865
Rexroad, Aaron Private	Unk	June 9, 1861, Highland County Courthouse, Virginia	Co. E, 25th Virginia Infantry	May 12, 1864, Spotsylvania Court House, Virginia	Point Lookout, Maryland, transferred to Elmira Prison, NY, August 12, 1864	Exchanged October 29, 1864, at Venus Point, Savannah River, GA.
Rexroad, Addison Private	Unk	May 18, 1861, Franklin, Virginia	Co. G, 25th Virginia Infantry	May 15, 1864, Wilderness, Virginia	Point Lookout, Maryland, transferred to Elmira Prison, NY, August 14, 1864	Oath of Allegiance June 14, 1865
Rexrode, Henry Private	Unk	February 16, 1864, Pendleton County, Virginia	Co. E, 25th Virginia Infantry	May 12, 1864, Spotsylvania Court House, Virginia	Point Lookout, Maryland, transferred to Elmira Prison, NY, August 12, 1864	Exchanged October 29, 1864, at Venus Point, Savannah River, GA.
Reynolds, Benjamin F. Private	Unk	January 24, 1864, Columbia, South Carolina	Co. C, 22nd South Carolina Infantry	July 30, 1864, Petersburg, Virginia	Point Lookout, Maryland, transferred to Elmira Prison, NY, August 12, 1864	Died November 14, 1864 of Scorbutus (Scurvy) Grave No. 797

Name & Rank	Age	Enlisted	Regiment and State	Where Captured	Prison	Remarks
Reynolds, Charles H. Private	Unk	August 17, 1861, Camp Walker, Virginia	Co. H, 12th Alabama Infantry	May 31, 1864 Mechanicsville, Virginia	Point Lookout, Maryland, transferred to Elmira Prison, NY, July 11, 1864	Oath of Allegiance May 29, 1865
Reynolds, David Private	Unk	May 1, 1862, White Sulfur Springs, Virginia	Co. F, 22nd Virginia Infantry	May 31, 1864, Cold Harbor, Virginia	Point Lookout, Maryland, transferred to Elmira Prison, NY, July 12, 1864	Died November 28, 1864 of Chronic Diarrhea, Grave No. 2758
Reynolds, James Private	37	May 4, 1863, Fort Caswell, Brunswick County, North Carolina	Co. F, 36th Regiment 2nd North Carolina Artillery	January 15, 1865, Fort Fisher, North Carolina	February 1, 1865, Elmira Prison Camp, New York	Exchanged February 20, 1865 at Boulware's or Cox Wharf on the James River, Virginia. Woodlawn Cemetery also has J. W. Reynolds Grave No. 2619.
Reynolds, Jasper M. Private	Unk	September 17, 1863, Cable County, Virginia	Co. C, 36th Virginia Cavalry	July 16, 1864, Loudon County, Virginia	Old Capital Prison, Washington DC. Transferred to Elmira Prison Camp, New York, July 25, 1864.	Oath of Allegiance May 29, 1865
Reynolds, John R. Private	26	July 7, 1861, Camp Moore, New Orleans, Louisiana	Co. C, 9th Louisiana Infantry	July 15, 1864, Loudoun County, Virginia	Old Capital Prison, Washington DC. Transferred to Elmira Prison Camp, New York, July 25, 1864.	Exchanged October 29, 1864 at Venus Point, Savannah River, GA.
Reynolds, John R. Private	24	September 1, 1861, Sampson County, North Carolina	Co. A, 30th North Carolina Infantry	May 12, 1864, Near Spotsylvania Court House, Virginia	Point Lookout, Maryland, transferred to Elmira Prison, NY, August 14, 1864	Died March 29, 1865 of Typhoid Fever, Grave No. 2526
Reynolds, Jonathan Private	Unk	March 24, 1862, Lewisburg, Virginia	Co. E, 26th Battalion, Virginia Infantry	June 3, 1864, Gaines Farm Cold Harbor, Virginia	Point Lookout, Maryland, transferred to Elmira Prison, NY, July 17, 1864	Died November 28, 1864 of Chronic Diarrhea, Grave No. 897

Name & Rank	Age	Enlisted	Regiment and State	Where Captured	Prison	Remarks
Reynolds, William Private	37	February 19, 1862, Sampson County, North Carolina	Co. A, 36th Regiment 2nd North Carolina Artillery	January 15, 1865, Fort Fisher, North Carolina	February 1, 1865, Elmira Prison Camp, New York	Died March 5, 1865 of Pneumonia, Grave No. 1971
Reynolds, William H. Private	39	February 19, 1862, Smithville, Brunswick County, North Carolina	Co. K, 36th Regiment 2nd North Carolina Artillery	January 15, 1865, Fort Fisher, North Carolina	February 1, 1865, Elmira Prison Camp, New York	Died April 9, 1865 of Pneumonia, Grave No. 1971. Headstone has J. W. Reynolds
Reynolds, William P. Private	Unk	July 19, 1861, Montgomery, Alabama	Co. D, 13th Alabama Infantry	May 12, 1864, Spotsylvania Court House, Virginia	Point Lookout, Maryland, transferred to Elmira Prison, NY, August 2, 1864	Oath of Allegiance June 21, 1865
Rhames, Nathanial Private	Unk	March 24, 1864, Charleston, South Carolina	Co. A, 21st South Carolina Infantry	January 15, 1865, Fort Fisher, North Carolina	February 1, 1865, Elmira Prison Camp, New York	Died June 10, 1865 of Chronic Diarrhea, Grave No. 2887. Headstone has Reams.
Rhine, William A. Private	18	September 5, 1861, Newton, North Carolina	Co. E, 32nd North Carolina Infantry	May 10, 1864, Wilderness, Virginia	Point Lookout, Maryland, transferred to Elmira Prison, NY, August 6, 1864	Oath of Allegiance June 21, 1865
Rhineheart, Dewitt C. Private	Unk	September 23, 1862, Jefferson, Virginia	Co. H, 7th Virginia Cavalry	September 14, 1863, Near Culpepper Court House, Virginia	Point Lookout, Maryland, transferred to Elmira Prison, NY, August 18, 1864	Exchanged March 10, 1865 at Boulware's Wharf on the James River, Virginia
Rhoden, William W. Private	Unk	September 12, 1862, Calhoun, Georgia	Co. G, 16th Georgia Infantry	May 25, 1864, Spotsylvania Court House, Virginia	Point Lookout, Maryland, transferred to Elmira Prison, NY, July 11, 1864	Died September 10, 1864, Chronic Diarrhea, Grave No. 199
Rhodes, A. J. Private	Unk	October 23, 1863, Darlington, South Carolina	Co. B, 21st South Carolina Infantry	January 15, 1865, Fort Fisher, North Carolina	February 1, 1865, Elmira Prison Camp, New York	Oath of Allegiance July 7, 1865
Rhodes, E. W. Private	Unk	July 15, 1861, Salem, Virginia	Co. D, 5th Virginia Cavalry	May 11, 1864, Yellow Tavern, Hanover County, Virginia	Point Lookout, Maryland, transferred to Elmira Prison, NY, August 17, 1864	Oath of Allegiance June 21, 1865

Name & Rank	Age	Enlisted	Regiment and State	Where Captured	Prison	Remarks
Rhodes, Hiram J. Private	Unk	July 19, 1861, Montgomery, Alabama	Co. D, 13th Alabama Infantry	May 12, 1864, Spotsylvania Court House, Virginia	Point Lookout, Maryland, transferred to Elmira Prison, NY, August 2, 1864	Oath of Allegiance May 17, 1865
Rhodes, Horace L. Private	18	July 7, 1861, Camp Moore, Louisiana	Co. C, 9th Louisiana Infantry	May 12, 1864, Spotsylvania Court House, Virginia	Point Lookout, Maryland, transferred to Elmira Prison, NY, August 17, 1864	Oath of Allegiance June 14, 1865
Rhodes, J. W. Private	Unk	May 26, 1862, Richmond, Virginia	Co. G, 1st Louisiana Cavalry	August 25, 1864, Near Clinton, Louisiana	New Orleans, Louisiana, Transferred to Elmira Prison, New York, November 19, 1864	Exchanged February 25, 1865 at Boulware's or Cox Wharf on the James River, Virginia
Rhodes, John Private	22	November 15. 1861, Portsmouth, Virginia	Co. A, 32nd North Carolina Infantry	May 10, 1864, Near Spotsylvania Court House, Virginia	Point Lookout, Maryland, transferred to Elmira Prison, NY, August 6, 1864	Oath of Allegiance July 3, 1865
Rhodes, John A. Private	Unk	March 31, 1863, Jacksonville, Alabama	Co. G, 10th Alabama Infantry	May 11, 1864, Spotsylvania Court House, Virginia	Point Lookout, Maryland, transferred to Elmira Prison, NY, August 17, 1864	Exchanged March 14, 1865 at Boulware's Wharf on the James River, Virginia
Rhodes, John D. Private	18	March 26, 1862, Fort Caswell, Brunswick County, North Carolina	Co. F, 36th Regiment 2nd North Carolina Artillery	January 15, 1865, Fort Fisher, North Carolina	February 1, 1865, Elmira Prison Camp, New York	Oath of Allegiance July 7, 1865
Rhodes, Lyman P. Private	Unk	June 30, 1863, Pocahontas County, Virginia	Co. C, 19th Virginia Cavalry	July 16, 1864, Loudon County, Virginia	Old Capital Prison, Washington DC. Transferred to Elmira Prison Camp, New York, July 25, 1864.	Oath of Allegiance June 14, 1865
Rhodes, William A. Private	Unk	September 6, 1861, Lumberton, North Carolina	Co. A, 31st North Carolina Infantry	June 1, 1864, Gaines Farm, Cold Harbor, Virginia	Point Lookout, Maryland, transferred to Elmira Prison, NY, July 12, 1864	Died October 29, 1864 of Pneumonia, Grave No. 730

Name & Rank	Age	Enlisted	Regiment and State	Where Captured	Prison	Remarks
Rhodes, William B. Private	29	July 29, 1861, Camden Court House, North Carolina	Co. A, 8th, North Carolina Infantry	May 31, 1864, Cold Harbor, Virginia	Point Lookout, Maryland, transferred to Elmira Prison, NY, July 12, 1864	Died May 24, 1865 of Pneumonia, Grave No. 2922
Rhodes, William W. Private	21	September 21, 1862, Camp Holmes, North Carolina	Co. C, 26th North Carolina Infantry	July 14, 1863, Falling Waters, Maryland	Old Capital Prison, Washington, DC, transferred to Elmira Prison, NY, August 18, 1864	Exchanged March 10, 1865 at Boulware's Wharf on the James River, Virginia
Rhudy, James L. Private	25	April 24, 1861, Elk Creek, Virginia	Co. F, 4th Virginia Infantry	May 12, 1864, Spotsylvania Court House, Virginia	Point Lookout, Maryland, transferred to Elmira Prison, NY, August 2, 1864	Oath of Allegiance June 30, 1865
Rhyne, George C. Private	31	August 6, 1861, Brevard's Station, North Carolina	Co. B, 28th North Carolina Infantry	May 12, 1864, Spotsylvania Court House, VA. Gunshot Right Elbow and Forearm. Arm Amputated.	Old Capital Prison, Washington, DC transferred to Elmira Prison, NY, August 27, 1864	Exchanged February 13, 1865 at Boulware's Wharf on the James River, Virginia
Rice, Charles H. Sergeant	Unk	July 26, 1861, Montgomery, Alabama	Co. D, 13th Alabama Infantry	May 12, 1864, Spotsylvania Court House, Virginia	Point Lookout, Maryland, transferred to Elmira Prison, NY, August 2, 1864	Oath of Allegiance June 30, 1865
Rice, Henry Private	21	May 30, 1861, Webster, North Carolina	Co. B, 25th North Carolina Infantry	June 17, 1864, Petersburg, Virginia	Point Lookout, Maryland, transferred to Elmira Prison, NY, July 30, 1864	Died November 16, 1864 of Pneumonia, Grave No. 951
Rice, John W. Private	26	August 28, 1861, Memphis, Tennessee	Co. B, Woods Regiment, C. S. A.	May 16, 1862, Champion Hill, Mississippi	Point Lookout, Maryland, transferred to Elmira Prison, NY, August 18, 1864	Exchanged October 29, 1864, at Venus Point, Savannah River, GA.
Rice, Thomas C. Private	21	July 27, 1861, Big Island, Virginia	Co. C, 58th Virginia Infantry	May 20, 1864, Spotsylvania Court House, Virginia	Point Lookout, Maryland, transferred to Elmira Prison, NY, July 3, 1864	Transferred for Exchange 10/11/64. Died 11/2/64 of Chronic Diarrhea at US Army Hospital, Baltimore, MD

Name & Rank	Age	Enlisted	Regiment and State	Where Captured	Prison	Remarks
Rice, Thomas N. Private	Unk	February 1, 1864, Big Island, Virginia	Co. C, 58th Virginia Infantry	May 20, 1864, Spotsylvania Court House, Virginia	Point Lookout, Maryland, transferred to Elmira Prison, NY, July 3, 1864	Died August 27, 1864 of Typhoid Fever, Grave No. 99
Rich, Albert Private	20	July 23, 1862, North Carolina	Co. G, 3rd North Carolina Infantry	May 12, 1864, Near Spotsylvania County Court House, Virginia	Point Lookout, Maryland, transferred to Elmira Prison, NY, August 14, 1864	Oath of Allegiance June 23, 1865
Richard, Joseph Private	25	July 22, 1861, Camp Moore, Louisiana	Co. K, 10th Louisiana Infantry	May 12, 1864, Spotsylvania Court House, Virginia	Point Lookout, Maryland, transferred to Elmira Prison, NY, July 25, 1864	Exchanged February 25, 1865 at Boulware's or Cox Wharf on the James River, Virginia
Richard, Myer Sergeant	Unk	April 20, 1862, Marion Court House, South Carolina	Co. D, 25th South Carolina Infantry	January 15, 1865, Fort Fisher, North Carolina	February 1, 1865, Elmira Prison Camp, New York	Oath of Allegiance May 13, 1865
Richardson, Dellett B. Private	22	October 28, 1861, Hempstead, Texas	Co. F, 12th Texas Cavalry	August 25, 1864, Bullitt's Bayou, Concordia Parish, Louisiana	New Orleans, Louisiana, Transferred to Elmira Prison, New York, November 19, 1864	Exchanged March 14, 1865 at Boulware's Wharf on the James River, Virginia
Richardson, George P. Private	Unk	March 29, 1862, Camp Moore, Louisiana	Co. A, 27th Louisiana Infantry	October 6, 1864, Clinton, Louisiana	New Orleans, Louisiana transferred to Elmira November 19, 1864.	Died January 11, 1865 of Typhoid-Pneumonia, Grave No. 1495. Headstone has 2nd Louisiana.
Richardson, Henry D. Private	Unk	June 22, 1861, Wytheville, Virginia	Co. A, 50th Virginia Infantry	May 12, 1864, Spotsylvania Court House, Virginia	Point Lookout, Maryland, transferred to Elmira Prison, NY, August 2, 1864	Died March 3, 1865 of Diarrhea, Grave No. 1983
Richardson, Henry E. Private	Unk	April 24, 1861, Richmond, Virginia	Captain Young's Battery Virginia Artillery	June 15, 1864, Petersburg, Virginia	Point Lookout, Maryland, transferred to Elmira Prison, NY, July 25, 1864	Died October 5, 1864 of Typhoid Fever, Grave No. 602
Richardson, Henry V. Civilian	Unk	Unknown	Citizen Refugee, Virginia	May 12, 1864, Spotsylvania County, Virginia	Point Lookout, Maryland, transferred to Elmira Prison, NY, July 25, 1864	Oath of Allegiance June 30, 1865

Name & Rank	Age	Enlisted	Regiment and State	Where Captured	Prison	Remarks
Richardson, Horatio N. Private	31	May 10, 1861, Washington, North Carolina	Co. J, 3rd North Carolina Infantry	May 12, 1864, Near Spotsylvania County Court House, Virginia	Point Lookout, Maryland, transferred to Elmira Prison, NY, August 14, 1864	Exchanged October 29, 1864, at Venus Point, Savannah River, GA.
Richardson, J. S. Private	Unk	January 27, 1864, Marion, South Carolina	Co. J, 21st South Carolina Infantry	January 15, 1865, Fort Fisher, North Carolina	February 1, 1865, Elmira Prison Camp, New York	Oath of Allegiance August 7, 1865
Richardson, James Private	Unk	March 1, 1864, Decatur, Georgia	Co. C, Cobb's Legion Georgia	August 16, 1864, Front Royal, Virginia	Old Capital Prison, Washington, DC transferred to Elmira Prison, NY, August 29, 1864	Oath of Allegiance June 23, 1865
Richardson, James H. Private	19	June 7, 1861, King and Queen Court House, Virginia	Co. E, 5th Virginia Cavalry	May 11, 1864, Yellow Tavern, Hanover County, Virginia	Point Lookout, Maryland, transferred to Elmira Prison, NY, August 17, 1864	Died November 1, 1864 of Pneumonia, Grave No. 754
Richardson, Joseph Corporal	20	April 2, 1862, Surrey County, North Carolina	Co. E, 53rd North Carolina Infantry	July 12, 1864, Near Washington, DC	Old Capital Prison, Washington DC. Transferred to Elmira Prison Camp, New York, July 25, 1864.	Exchanged October 29, 1864, at Venus Point, Savannah River, GA.
Richardson, L. M. Private	Unk	Unknown	Co. B, 6th North Carolina Infantry	July 14, 1864, Near Washington, DC	Old Capital Prison, Washington DC. Transferred to Elmira Prison Camp, NY, July 25, 1864.	Died January 27, 1865 of Chronic Diarrhea, Grave No. 1646
Richardson, P. G. Private	Unk	January 8, 1862, Camp Harlee, South Carolina	Co. J, 21st South Carolina Infantry	January 15, 1865, Fort Fisher, North Carolina	February 1, 1865, Elmira Prison Camp, New York	Oath of Allegiance July 11, 1865
Richardson, Robert S. Private	Unk	June 8, 1861, Isbell's Store, Virginia	Co. D, 44th Virginia Infantry	May 12, 1864, Spotsylvania Court House, Virginia	Point Lookout, Maryland, transferred to Elmira Prison, NY, August 2, 1864	Oath of Allegiance July 11, 1865
Richardson, Samuel Private	Unk	May 9, 1862, Johnson's Station, Reidsville, Georgia	Co. H, 61st Georgia Infantry	May 12, 1864, Spotsylvania Court House, Virginia	Point Lookout, Maryland, transferred to Elmira Prison, NY, July 30, 1864	Oath of Allegiance June 27, 1865

Name & Rank	Age	Enlisted	Regiment and State	Where Captured	Prison	Remarks
Richardson, Thomas Sergeant	Unk	September 26, 1863, Orange County, Virginia	Co. K, 42nd Virginia Infantry	May 12, 1864, Spotsylvania Court House, Virginia	Point Lookout, Maryland, transferred to Elmira Prison, NY, August 2, 1864	Oath of Allegiance June 16, 1865
Richardson, William M. Private	Unk	August 22, 1862, Camp Randolph, Georgia	Co. A, 44th Georgia Infantry	July 8, 1864, Harpers Ferry, Virginia	Old Capital Prison, Washington DC. Transferred to Elmira Prison Camp, NY July 25, 1864.	Oath of Allegiance May 19, 1865
Richburg, Benjamin D. Private	Unk	February 23, 1863, James Island, South Carolina	Co. J, 25th South Carolina Infantry	January 15, 1865, Fort Fisher, North Carolina	February 1, 1865, Elmira Prison Camp, New York	Died April 24, 1865 of Pneumonia, Grave No. 1409. Headstone has R. D. Richbourg.
Richburgh, J. E. Private	18	January 1, 1862, Camp Harlee, Georgetown, South Carolina	Co. I, 25th South Carolina Infantry	January 15, 1865, Fort Fisher, North Carolina	February 1, 1865, Elmira Prison Camp, New York	Oath of Allegiance June 23, 1865
Richey, J. J. Private	Unk	December 28, 1861, Camp Hampton Legion, South Carolina	Co. F, Holcombe Legion, South Carolina	May 8, 1864, Jarrett's Depot, Virginia	Point Lookout, Maryland, transferred to Elmira Prison, NY, August 17, 1864	Exchanged March 2, 1865 at Akins Landing on the James River, Virginia
Richey, James A. Private	Unk	November 14, 1861, Calhoun, Georgia	Co. E, 18th Georgia Infantry	June 1, 1864, Cold Harbor, Virginia	Point Lookout, Maryland, transferred to Elmira Prison, NY, July 17, 1864	Oath of Allegiance July 7, 1865
Rickets, James Ervin Private	Unk	December 26, 1861, Cheraw, South Carolina	Co. A, 4th South Carolina Cavalry	June 11, 1864, Trevilian Station, Louisa Court House, Virginia	Point Lookout, Maryland, transferred to Elmira Prison, NY, July 25, 1864	Oath of Allegiance July 26, 1865
Ricketts, James W. Sergeant		May 19, 1861, Nashville, Tennessee	Co. F, 7th Tennessee Infantry	May 31, 1864, Cold Harbor, Virginia	Point Lookout, Maryland, transferred to Elmira Prison, NY, July 12, 1864	Transferred for Exchange October 11, 1864
Rickman, John J. Private	25	September 10, 1862, Raleigh, North Carolina	Co. B, 18th North Carolina Infantry	July 29, 1864, Petersburg, Virginia	Point Lookout, Maryland, transferred to Elmira Prison, NY, August 12, 1864	Died September 2, 1864 of Chronic Diarrhea, Grave No. 61

Name & Rank	Age	Enlisted	Regiment and State	Where Captured	Prison	Remarks
Ricks, Robert V. B. Corporal	26	May 10, 1862, Greenville, North Carolina	Co. E, 55th North Carolina Infantry	May 5, 1864, wilderness, Virginia. Gunshot Wound of Neck and Left Lower Jaw.	Old Capital Prison, Washington DC. Transferred to Elmira Prison Camp, New York, July 25, 1864.	Exchanged February 20, 1865 at Boulware's or Cox Wharf on the James River, Virginia
Ricks, Warren W. Private	Unk	June 10, 1862, Savannah, Georgia	Co. B, 7th Georgia Cavalry	June 11, 1864, Trevilian Station, Louisa Court House, Virginia	Point Lookout, Maryland, transferred to Elmira Prison, NY, July 25, 1864	Exchanged February 13, 1865 at Boulware's wharf on the James River, Virginia
Rickson, William Sailor	Unk	Unknown	Confederate States Navy	January 15, 1865, Fort Fisher, North Carolina	February 1, 1865, Elmira Prison Camp, New York	Exchanged March 2, 1865 at Akins Landing on the James River, Virginia
Riddle, Austin Private	30	August 12, 1862, Knoxville, Tennessee	Co. C, 2nd Tennessee Cavalry	May 3, 1863, Mill Springs, Kentucky	Point Lookout, Maryland, transferred to Elmira Prison, NY, July 23, 1864	Died August 27, 1864 Chronic Diarrhea, Grave No. 102
Riddle, David C. Private	Unk	December 16, 1863, Surry County, North Carolina	Co. E, 53rd North Carolina Infantry	May 24, 1864, Hanover Junction, Virginia	Point Lookout, Maryland, transferred to Elmira Prison, NY, July 11, 1864	Died September 19, 1864 of Pneumonia, Grave No. 332
Riddle, George W. Private	Unk	May 8, 1861, Richmond, Virginia	Co. J, 53rd Virginia Infantry	May 10, 1864, Near Petersburg, Virginia	Point Lookout, Maryland, transferred to Elmira Prison, NY, August 17, 1864	Died March 4, 1865 of Chronic Diarrhea, Grave No. 2000. Headstone has G. W. Biddle.
Riddle, James A. Private	17	December 23, 1863, Chatham County, North Carolina	Co. C, 61st North Carolina Infantry	June 16, 1864, Petersburg, Virginia	Point Lookout, Maryland, transferred to Elmira Prison, NY, July 25, 1864	Oath of Allegiance June 21, 1865
Riddle, S. T. Private	Unk	October 1, 1862, Spartanburg, South Carolina	Co. G, 27th South Carolina Infantry	June 24, 1864, Near Petersburg, Virginia	Point Lookout, Maryland, transferred to Elmira Prison, NY, August 18, 1864	Exchanged March 2, 1865 at Akins Landing on the James River, Virginia

Name & Rank	Age	Enlisted	Regiment and State	Where Captured	Prison	Remarks
Riddle, W. S. Private	Unk	March 16, 1864, Fort Morgan, Alabama	Co. B, 1st Jackson's Tennessee Heavy Artillery	August 23, 1864, Fort Morgan, Alabama.	New Orleans, Louisiana transferred to Elmira Prison, NY, December 4, 1864.	Exchanged February 13, 1865 at Boulware's wharf on the James River, Virginia
Riddle, William S. Private	Unk	October 1, 1862, Spartanburg, South Carolina	Co. G, 27th South Carolina Infantry	June 24, 1864, Near Petersburg, Virginia	Point Lookout, Maryland, transferred to Elmira Prison, NY, August 18, 1864	Oath of Allegiance July 3, 1865
Rider, Richard Sergeant	Unk	October 1, 1862, Little Rock, Arkansas	Co. B, Jackson's 1st Regiment, Tennessee Heavy Artillery	August 23, 1864, Fort Morgan, Alabama	New Orleans, Louisiana transferred to Elmira Prison, NY, December 4, 1864.	Exchanged February 25, 1865 at Boulware's or Cox Wharf on the James River, Virginia
Ridgeway, Joseph M. Private	Unk	November 15, 1861, James Island, South Carolina	Co. J, 25th South Carolina Infantry	January 15, 1865, Fort Fisher, North Carolina	February 1, 1865, Elmira Prison Camp, New York	Died April 6, 1865 of Pneumonia, Grave No. 2549
Ridgeway, J. N. Private	33	January 1, 1862, Camp Harlee, Georgetown, South Carolina	Co. J, 25th South Carolina Infantry	January 15, 1865, Fort Fisher, North Carolina	February 1, 1865, Elmira Prison Camp, New York	Exchanged March 14, 1865 at Boulware's Wharf on the James River, Virginia
Ridgeway, Rueben F. Sergeant	30	October 24, 1862, James Island, South Carolina	Co. I, 25th South Carolina Infantry	January 15, 1865, Fort Fisher, North Carolina	February 1, 1865, Elmira Prison Camp, New York	Exchanged February 20, 1865 at Boulware's or Cox Wharf on the James River, Virginia
Ridgeway, William Sergeant	Unk	July 2, 1861, Bethel, Virginia	Co. F, 50th Virginia Infantry	May 12, 1864, Spotsylvania Court House, Virginia	Point Lookout, Maryland, transferred to Elmira Prison, NY, July 30, 1864	Exchanged February 25, 1865 at Boulware's or Cox Wharf on the James River, Virginia
Rieves, Peter Private	Unk	October 13, 1861, Hall's Mill, Alabama	Co. A, 21st Alabama Infantry	August 23, 1864, Fort Morgan, Alabama	Steam Press No. 4 New Orleans, Louisiana transferred to Elmira Prison, NY, October 8, 1864.	Oath of Allegiance May 17, 1865

Name & Rank	Age	Enlisted	Regiment and State	Where Captured	Prison	Remarks
Riffey, George W. Private	20	June 20, 1861, Abingdon, Virginia	Co. B, 48th Virginia Infantry	May 12, 1864, Spotsylvania Court House, Virginia	Point Lookout, Maryland, transferred to Elmira Prison, NY, August 12, 1864	Exchanged October 29, 1864, at Venus Point, Savannah River, GA.
Rigand, L. S. H. Private	25	February 15, 1863, Camp Maynard, Georgia	Co. E, 16th Georgia Infantry	June 1, 1864, Cold Harbor, Virginia	Point Lookout, Maryland, transferred to Elmira Prison, NY, July 12, 1864	Oath of Allegiance July 3, 1865
Rigby, John Private	Unk	September 23, 1861, Atlanta, Georgia	Co. D, 35th Georgia Infantry	May 5, 1864, Wilderness, Virginia	Point Lookout, Maryland, transferred to Elmira Prison, NY, August 17, 1864	Died May 4, 1865 of Acute Bronchitis, Grave No. 2756
Riggan, Isham S. Private	35	July 16, 1863, Raleigh, North Carolina	Co. B, 30th North Carolina Infantry	May 6, 1864, Wilderness, Virginia	Point Lookout, Maryland, transferred to Elmira Prison, NY, August 14, 1864	Died September 27, 1864 of Typhoid-Pneumonia, Grave No. 387. Name J. S. Riggan on Headstone.
Riggan, J. J. Private	19	September 15, 1862, Raleigh, North Carolina	Co. E, 31st North Carolina Infantry	June 1, 1864, Gaines Farm Cold Harbor, Virginia	Point Lookout, Maryland, transferred to Elmira Prison, NY, July 12, 1864	Died November 14, 1864 of Pneumonia, Grave No. 807
Riggin, James J. Private	19	September 15, 1862, Raleigh, North Carolina	Co. E, 31st North Carolina Infantry	June 1, 1864, Gaines Farm, Cold Harbor, Virginia	Point Lookout, Maryland, transferred to Elmira Prison, NY, July 17,1864	Died November 14, 1864 of Pneumonia, Grave No. 387
Riggin, Shugar A. Private	41	April 14, 1862, Camp Saunders, North Carolina	Co. A, 30th North Carolina Infantry	May 12, 1864, Near Spotsylvania Court House, Virginia	Point Lookout, Maryland, transferred to Elmira Prison, NY, August 14, 1864	Died November 29, 1864 of Chronic Diarrhea, Grave No. 1000. Name Sugar A. Regan on Headstone.
Riggins, Robert G. Private	Unk	August 26, 1861, Waresboro, Georgia	Co. F, 26th Georgia Infantry	May 20, 1864, Spotsylvania Court House, Virginia	Point Lookout, Maryland, transferred to Elmira Prison, NY, July 3, 1864	Died May 2, 1865 of Erysipelas, Grave No. 2745

Name & Rank	Age	Enlisted	Regiment and State	Where Captured	Prison	Remarks
Riggleman, Jacob Corporal	Unk	May 24, 1861, Huttonsville, Virginia	Co. F, 31st Virginia Infantry	May 5, 1864, Wilderness, Virginia	Point Lookout, Maryland, transferred to Elmira Prison, NY, August 2, 1864	Oath of Allegiance June 27, 1865
Riggs, Benjamin S. Private	Unk	July 29, 1861, Columbia, South Carolina	Co. C, 1st South Carolina Infantry	July 29, 1864, Petersburg, Virginia	Point Lookout, Maryland, transferred to Elmira Prison, NY, August 12, 1864	Oath of Allegiance May 29, 1865
Riggs, George C. Private	18	July 1, 1861, Jacksonville, Onslow County, North Carolina	Co. G, 3rd North Carolina Infantry	May 30, 1864 Mechanicsville, Virginia	Point Lookout, Maryland, transferred to Elmira Prison, NY, July 11, 1864	Oath of Allegiance June 13, 1865
Riggsbee, John Private	24	February 25, 1862, Riggsbee's Store, North Carolina	Co. D, 15th North Carolina Infantry	May 12, 1864, Spotsylvania Court House, Virginia	Point Lookout, Maryland, transferred to Elmira Prison, NY, August 12, 1864	Died September 16, 1864 of Chronic Diarrhea, Grave No. 297. Jones E. Riggsbee on Headstone.
Rightsel, Samuel Private	18	September 10, 1862, Raleigh, North Carolina	Co. G, 26th North Carolina Infantry	May 12, 1864, Spotsylvania Court House, Virginia	Point Lookout, Maryland, transferred to Elmira Prison, NY, July 30, 1864	Exchanged October 29, 1864, at Venus Point, Savannah River, GA.
Rigney, John Private	46	August 26, 1861, Bethel, Tennessee	Co. A, 1st Tennessee Heavy Artillery	August 23, 1864, Fort Morgan, Alabama	Fort Columbus, New York Harbor. Transferred February 4, 1865 Elmira, Prison Camp, NY	Died March 25, 1865 of Pneumonia, Grave No. 2461
Rikard, James P. Private	22	August 23, 1861, Newberry Court House, Newberry District, South Carolina	Co. D, 13th South Carolina Infantry	July 21, 1864, Deep Bottom, Virginia	Point Lookout, Maryland, transferred to Elmira Prison, NY, August 18, 1864	Oath of Allegiance July 3, 1865
Rike, Benjamin L. Corporal	26	May 3, 1861, Graham, North Carolina	Co. E, 13th North Carolina Infantry	May 6, 1864, Wilderness, Virginia	Point Lookout, Maryland, transferred to Elmira Prison, NY, August 14, 1864	Oath of Allegiance July 11, 1865

Name & Rank	Age	Enlisted	Regiment and State	Where Captured	Prison	Remarks
Rilee, Joshua L. Corporal	Unk	July 22, 1861, Gloucester Point, Virginia	Co. H, 26th North Carolina Infantry	June 17, 1864, Near Petersburg, Virginia	Point Lookout, Maryland, transferred to Elmira Prison, NY, July 30, 1864	Died December 6, 1864 of Pneumonia, Grave No. 1023
Riley, Calvin P. Private	Unk	July 18, 1862, Cumberland County, North Carolina	Co. C, 3rd North Carolina Infantry	May 12, 1864, Near Spotsylvania County Court House, Virginia	Point Lookout, Maryland, transferred to Elmira Prison, NY, August 14, 1864	Died November 26, 1864 of Chronic Diarrhea, Grave No. 899
Riley, Daniel Private	32	March 15, 1863, Fort Fisher, New Hanover County, North Carolina	Co. D, 36th Regiment 2nd North Carolina Artillery	January 15, 1865, Fort Fisher, North Carolina	February 1, 1865, Elmira Prison Camp, New York	Died February 16, 1865 of Pneumonia, Grave No. 2203
Riley, George W. Private	Unk	July 1, 1863, Butler County, Alabama	Co. G, 61st Alabama Infantry	May 12, 1864, Spotsylvania Court House, Virginia	Point Lookout, Maryland, transferred to Elmira Prison, NY, July 30, 1864	Oath of Allegiance June 14, 1865
Riley, Jackson W. Private	Unk	May 11, 1861, New Orleans, Louisiana	Co. K, 2nd Louisiana Infantry	May 12, 1864, Spotsylvania Court House, Virginia	Point Lookout, Maryland, transferred to Elmira Prison, NY, August 17, 1864	Oath of Allegiance May 29, 1865
Riley, James Sergeant	Unk	March 15, 1862, Charleston, South Carolina	Co. C, 27th South Carolina Infantry	June 24, 1864, Near Petersburg, Virginia	Point Lookout, Maryland, transferred to Elmira Prison, NY, July 23, 1864	Oath of Allegiance May 29, 1865
Riley, John W. Private	33	April 25, 1861, Warrenton, Virginia	Co. H, 4th Virginia Cavalry	July 31, 1864, Sharpsburg, Maryland	Old Capital Prison, Washington D. C. Transferred to Elmira Prison, NY, August 12, 1864	Oath of Allegiance May 29, 1865
Riley, Judson Private	18	April 28, 1862, Jonesville, North Carolina	Co. H, 54th North Carolina Infantry	August 22, 1864, Charlestown, Virginia	Old Capital Prison, Washington, DC transferred to Elmira Prison, NY, August 29, 1864	Died May 30, 1865 of Acute Diarrhea, Grave No. 2910

Name & Rank	Age	Enlisted	Regiment and State	Where Captured	Prison	Remarks
Riley, Patrick Sergeant	24	April 25, 1861, Alexandria, Virginia	Co. G, 17th Virginia Infantry	July 21, 1863, Manassas Gap, Virginia	Point Lookout, Maryland, transferred to Elmira Prison, NY, August 18, 1864	Exchanged February 20, 1865 at Boulware's or Cox Wharf on the James River, Virginia
Riley, Phillip G. Private	19	June 23, 1861, Goldsboro, North Carolina	Co. F, 1st North Carolina Cavalry	September 13, 1863, Near Culpepper Court House, Virginia	Point Lookout, Maryland, transferred to Elmira Prison, NY, August 18, 1864	Exchanged March 10, 1865 at Boulware's Wharf on the James River, Virginia
Riley, Timothy Private	Unk	March 27, 1863, Lewisburg, Virginia	Captain Bryan's Co., Virginia Artillery	July 15, 1864, Near Washington, DC	Old Capital Prison, Washington, DC. Transferred to Elmira Prison, New York August 17 1864	Died March 4, 1865 of Diarrhea, Grave No. 2005
Riley, Thomas J. Corporal	24	September 30, 1863, Drury's Bluff, Virginia	Co. C, 45th North Carolina Infantry	July 12, 1864, Near Washington, DC	Old Capital Prison, Washington, DC. Transferred to Elmira Prison Camp, NY, July 25, 1864.	Died March 26, 1865 of Pneumonia, Grave No. 2475
Rills, Edward H. Corporal	Unk	September 1, 1862, Camp Thompson, New Road, Louisiana	Co. J, 2nd Louisiana Cavalry	October 27, 1864, Bayou Grosstete, Point Coupee Parish, Louisiana	New Orleans, Louisiana transferred to Elmira November 19, 1864.	Exchanged March 10, 1865 at Boulware's Wharf on the James River, Virginia
Rimal, George W. Corporal	Unk	April 19, 1861, Harrisonburg, Virginia	Co. B, 10th Virginia Infantry	May 12, 1864, Spotsylvania Court House, Virginia	Point Lookout, Maryland, transferred to Elmira Prison, NY, August 2, 1864	Oath of Allegiance June 27, 1865
Rinaldi, Eugene W. Private	17	August 21, 1864, Fort Holmes, New Hanover County, North Carolina	Co. K, 40th 3rd Regiment North Carolina Artillery	January 15, 1865, Fort Fisher, North Carolina	February 1, 1865, Elmira Prison Camp, New York	Died April 26, 1865 of Chronic Diarrhea, Grave 1426. Headstone has E. W. Renalde.
Rinehardt, Michael C. Private	18	October 21, 1863, Mount Pleasant, North Carolina	Co. H, 8th North Carolina Infantry	June 1, 1864, Gaines Mill, Cold Harbor, Virginia	Point Lookout, Maryland, transferred to Elmira Prison, NY, July 17,1864	Oath of Allegiance June 12, 1865

Name & Rank	Age	Enlisted	Regiment and State	Where Captured	Prison	Remarks
Riner, J. Corporal	Unk	September 4, 1863, Camp Sam Jones, Virginia	Co. H, 26th Battalion, Virginia Infantry	June 3, 1864, Gaines Farm Cold Harbor, Virginia	Point Lookout, Maryland, transferred to Elmira Prison, NY, July 17, 1864	Oath of Allegiance July 16, 1865
Riner, James Private	Unk	July 3, 1861, Peterstown, Virginia	Co. H, 26th Battalion, Virginia Infantry	June 3, 1864, Gaines Mill Cold Harbor, Virginia	Point Lookout, Maryland, transferred to Elmira Prison, NY, July 17, 1864	Oath of Allegiance July 3, 1865
Rinka, Jacob Private	Unk	March 27, 1863, Grace Church, Virginia	Co. D, 5th Alabama Infantry	July 18, 1864, Snickers' Gap, Virginia	Old Capital Prison, Washington D. C. Transferred to Elmira Prison, NY, August 12, 1864	Died December 11, 1864 of Pneumonia, Grave No. 1052
Rinker, James W. Private	Unk	March 20, 1864, Brownsburg, Virginia	Co. E, 11th Virginia Cavalry	May 12, 1864, Spotsylvania Court House, Virginia	Point Lookout, Maryland, transferred to Elmira Prison, NY, August 12, 1864	Exchanged February 20, 1865 at Boulware's or Cox Wharf on the James River, Virginia
Riordan, Daniel Private	Unk	Unknown	Co. F, 6th Louisiana Infantry	May 5, 1864, Wilderness, Virginia	Point Lookout, Maryland, transferred to Elmira Prison, NY, August 17, 1864	Exchanged March 10, 1865 at Boulware's Wharf on the James River, Virginia
Riordan, J. Private	Unk	Unknown	Co. F, 6th Louisiana Infantry	May 5, 1864, Wilderness, Virginia	Point Lookout, Maryland, transferred to Elmira Prison, NY, August 17, 1864	Oath of Allegiance May 15, 1865
Ripley, J. Private	Unk	April 30, 1864, Lewisburg, Virginia	Co. A, 26th Battalion, Virginia Infantry	June 3, 1864, Gaines Mill Cold Harbor, Virginia	Point Lookout, Maryland, transferred to Elmira Prison, NY, July 17, 1864	Oath of Allegiance June 19, 1865
Ripley, James L. Private	Unk	February 9, 1863, Centerville, Virginia	Co. E, 26th Battalion, Virginia Infantry	June 3, 1864, Gaines Mill Cold Harbor, Virginia	Point Lookout, Maryland, transferred to Elmira Prison, NY, July 17, 1864	Oath of Allegiance June 19, 1865

Name & Rank	Age	Enlisted	Regiment and State	Where Captured	Prison	Remarks
Rissler, Samuel J. Private	34	December 4, 1862, Guinea Station, Virginia	Co. G, 2nd Virginia Infantry	July 2, 1864, Near Harpers Ferry, Virginia	Old Capital Prison, Washington DC. Transferred to Elmira Prison Camp, New York, July 25, 1864.	Exchanged March 10, 1865 at Boulware's Wharf on the James River, Virginia
Rist, John Private	Unk	June 7, 1861, Camp Moore, Louisiana	Co. B, 7th Louisiana Infantry	May 11, 1864, Near Spotsylvania Court House, Virginia	Point Lookout, Maryland, transferred to Elmira Prison, NY, August 17, 1864	Exchanged February 25, 1865 at Boulware's or Cox Wharf on the James River, Virginia
Ritter, Joseph Private	20	August 20, 1861 E. City, North Carolina	Co. A, 8th, North Carolina Infantry	May 31, 1864, Cold Harbor, Virginia	Point Lookout, Maryland, transferred to Elmira Prison, NY, July 12, 1864	Oath of Allegiance May 29, 1865
Rivers, James D. Private	Unk	December 26, 1861, Savannah, Georgia	Co. C, 26th Georgia Infantry	July 11, 1864, Frederick, Maryland	Old Capital Prison, Washington, DC. Transferred to Elmira Prison Camp, NY, July 25, 1865	Died March 16, 1865 Diarrhea, Grave No. 1677
Rivers, Jacob J. Private	Unk	June 10, 1861, Morgan, Georgia	Co. D, 12th Georgia Infantry	May 10, 1864, Spotsylvania Court House, Virginia	Point Lookout, Maryland, transferred to Elmira Prison, NY, July 30, 1864	Died March 22, 1865 of Variola (Smallpox). Listed as Grave 1613 But No Grave Found in Woodlawn Cemetery.
Rivers, Jacob M. Private	25	July 15, 1861, Whippy Swamp, South Carolina	Co. G, 11th South Carolina Infantry	January 15, 1865, Fort Fisher, North Carolina	February 1, 1865, Elmira Prison Camp, New York	Exchanged March 2, 1865 at Akins Landing on the James River, Virginia
Rivers, L. J. Corporal	Unk	July 2, 1863, Mississippi	Co. B, 26th South Carolina Infantry	July 30, 1864, Petersburg, Virginia	Point Lookout, Maryland, transferred to Elmira Prison, NY, August 12, 1864	Exchanged October 29, 1864, at Venus Point, Savannah River, GA.
Rivers, M. J. Corporal	Unk	May 4, 1862, Chesterfield, South Carolina	Co. B, 26th South Carolina Infantry	July 30, 1864, Petersburg, Virginia	Point Lookout, Maryland, transferred to Elmira Prison, NY, August 12, 1864	Exchanged March 14, 1865 at Boulware's Wharf on the James River, Virginia

Name & Rank	Age	Enlisted	Regiment and State	Where Captured	Prison	Remarks
Rives, Robert L. Corporal	Unk	July 8, 1861, Griffin, Georgia	Co. I, 13th Georgia Infantry	July 8, 1864, Harpers Ferry, Virginia	Old Capital Prison, Washington, DC. Transferred to Elmira July 25, 1864	Died September 20, 1864 of Chronic Diarrhea, Grave No. 505
Rives, William C. Private	20	May 11, 1862, Secessionville, James Island, South Carolina	Co. G, 25th South Carolina Infantry	January 15, 1865, Fort Fisher, North Carolina	February 1, 1865, Elmira Prison Camp, New York	Oath of Allegiance June 16, 1865
Roach, Charles B. Private	Unk	August 22, 1862, Muddy Creek, Virginia	Co. E, 26th Battalion, Virginia Infantry	June 3, 1864, Gaines Farm Cold Harbor, Virginia	Point Lookout, Maryland, transferred to Elmira Prison, NY, July 17, 1864	Died September 28, 1864 of Typhoid Fever, Grave 440
Roach, John A. Sergeant	23	February 27, 1862, Reidsville, North Carolina	Co. E, 45th North Carolina Infantry	May 10, 1864, Spotsylvania Court House, Virginia	Point Lookout, Maryland, transferred to Elmira Prison, NY, August 6, 1864	Exchanged March 10, 1865 at Boulware's Wharf on the James River, Virginia
Roach, John H. Private	23	March 11, 1862, Spring Garden, North Carolina	Co. A, 45th North Carolina Infantry	May 10, 1864, Spotsylvania Court House, Virginia	Point Lookout, Maryland, transferred to Elmira Prison, NY, August 6, 1864	Oath of Allegiance June 12, 1865
Roach, William Sergeant	Unk	May 5, 1862, Sumpter, Texas	Co. F, 1st Texas Infantry	May 12, 1864, Spotsylvania Court House, Virginia	Point Lookout, Maryland, transferred to Elmira Prison, NY, August 12, 1864	Oath of Allegiance June 19, 1865
Roane, William L. Private	Unk	March 28, 1862, Gloucester Point, Virginia	Co. E, 5th Virginia Cavalry	May 11, 1864, Yellow Tavern, Hanover County, Virginia	Point Lookout, Maryland, transferred to Elmira Prison, NY, August 17, 1864	Died April 8, 1865 of Variola (Smallpox), Grave No. 2617
Robb, Benjamin F. Private	22	April 13, 1862, Centerville, Alabama	Co. C, 1st Battalion Alabama Artillery	August 23, 1864, Fort Morgan, Alabama	New Orleans, Louisiana transferred to Elmira Prison, NY, December 4, 1864.	Died January 13, 1865 of Chronic Diarrhea, Grave No. 1474
Roberson, Edwin B. Private	26	July 1, 1861, Jacksonville, Onslow County, North Carolina	Co. G, 3rd North Carolina Infantry	May 10, 1864, Near Spotsylvania County Court House, Virginia	Point Lookout, Maryland, transferred to Elmira Prison, NY, August 14, 1864	Oath of Allegiance June 23, 1865

Name & Rank	Age	Enlisted	Regiment and State	Where Captured	Prison	Remarks
Roberson, Gideon S. Private	46	March 4, 1863, Roxboro, North Carolina	Co. E, 35th North Carolina Infantry	June 17, 1864, Petersburg, Virginia	Point Lookout, Maryland, transferred to Elmira Prison, NY, July 30, 1864	Died September 25, 1864 of Typhoid-Pneumonia, Grave No. 363
Roberson, Green M. Private	Unk	July 3, 1863, Camp of Instruction, Virginia	Co. I, 26th Battalion, Virginia Infantry	June 2, 1864, Gaines Farm Cold Harbor, Virginia	Point Lookout, Maryland, transferred to Elmira Prison, NY, July 17, 1864	Oath of Allegiance July 3, 1865
Roberson, J. William Private	26	July 14, 1862, Oxford, North Carolina	Co. D, 8th North Carolina Infantry	June 1, 1864, Gaines Farm Cold Harbor, Virginia	Point Lookout, Maryland, transferred to Elmira Prison, NY, July 12, 1864	Oath of Allegiance July 3, 1865
Roberson, John W. Private	Unk	March 29, 1861, Montgomery, Alabama	Co. E, 1st Battalion Alabama Artillery	August 23, 1864, Fort Morgan, Alabama	Steam Press No. 4, New Orleans, Louisiana transferred to Elmira October 8, 1864.	Exchanged March 2, 1865 at Akins Landing on the James River, Virginia
Roberson, Noah Perry Private	34	June 24, 1861, Williamston, North Carolina	Co. H, 1st North Carolina Infantry	May 12, 1864, Spotsylvania Court House, Virginia	Point Lookout, Maryland, transferred to Elmira Prison, NY, August 6, 1864	Oath of Allegiance June 27, 1865
Roberson, Samuel Private	Unk	February 12, 1864, Quitman County, Georgia	Co. F, 61st Georgia Infantry	May 12, 1864, Spotsylvania Court House, Virginia	Point Lookout, Maryland, transferred to Elmira Prison, NY, July 30, 1864	Died April 7, 1865 of Chronic Diarrhea, Grave No. 2656
Roberson, Samuel H. Private	Unk	December 29, 1863, Montgomery, Alabama	Co. E, 1st Battalion Alabama Artillery	August 23, 1864, Fort Morgan, Alabama	Steam Press No. 4, New Orleans, Louisiana transferred to Elmira October 8, 1864.	Oath of Allegiance to June 21, 1865
Roberts, E. A. Private	Unk	July 15, 1862, Camp Butler, Natchez Parish, Louisiana	Co. K, 2nd Louisiana Cavalry	October 19, 1864, Lavinia, Pointe Coupee, Louisiana	New Orleans, Louisiana transferred to Elmira November 19, 1864.	Exchanged February 25, 1865 at Boulware's or Cox Wharf on the James River, Virginia

Name & Rank	Age	Enlisted	Regiment and State	Where Captured	Prison	Remarks
Roberts, E. J. Private	Unk	April 7, 1864, Cropwell, Alabama	Co. F, 10th Alabama Infantry	May 13, 1864, Spotsylvania Court House, Virginia	Point Lookout, Maryland, transferred to Elmira Prison, NY, August 17, 1864	Exchanged March 14, 1865 at Boulware's Wharf on the James River, Virginia
Roberts, Frank B. Private	Unk	July 1, 1863, G. Court House, Virginia	Co. F, 4th Virginia Infantry	May 12, 1864, Spotsylvania Court House, Virginia	Point Lookout, Maryland, transferred to Elmira Prison, NY, August 2, 1864	Oath of Allegiance June 19, 1865
Roberts, George M. Private	27	May 13, 1862, Loachapoka, Tallapoosa County, Alabama	Co. F, 47th Alabama Infantry	May 6, 1864, Wilderness, Virginia	Point Lookout, Maryland, transferred to Elmira Prison, NY, August 17, 1864	Oath of Allegiance June 14, 1865
Roberts, Isaac Private	Unk	March 1, 1862, Luray, Virginia	Co. K, 10th Virginia Infantry	May 12, 1864, Spotsylvania Court House, Virginia	Point Lookout, Maryland, transferred to Elmira Prison, NY, August 2, 1864	Oath of Allegiance May 29, 1865
Roberts, James C. Private	24	July 15, 1862, Raleigh, North Carolina	Co. E, 1st North Carolina Infantry	May 12, 1864, Near Spotsylvania Court House, Virginia	Point Lookout Prison, Maryland. Transferred to Elmira Prison Camp New York August 6, 1864.	Oath of Allegiance May 19, 1865
Roberts, James M. Private	19	September 1, 1861, Camp Beauregard, Marshall, Texas	Co. J, 7th Texas Infantry	February 12, 1863, Raymond, Mississippi	Point Lookout, Maryland, transferred to Elmira Prison, NY, August 18, 1864	Oath of Allegiance June 16, 1865
Roberts, John Private	Unk	Unknown	Co. C, 3rd Alabama Infantry	June 6,1864, Gave Himself Up	Point Lookout, Maryland, transferred to Elmira Prison, NY, July 11, 1864	Oath of Allegiance May 17, 1865
Roberts, John S. Private	Unk	June 15, 1861, Jones County, Georgia	Co. A, 12th Georgia Infantry	May 10, 1864, Spotsylvania Court House, Virginia	Point Lookout, Maryland, transferred to Elmira Prison, NY, July 30, 1864	Oath of Allegiance July 11, 1865

Name & Rank	Age	Enlisted	Regiment and State	Where Captured	Prison	Remarks
Roberts, John T. Private	Unk	October 15, 1861, Haley's Store, Georgia	Co. F, 38th Georgia Infantry	August 10, 1864, Berryville, Virginia	Old Capital Prison, Washington, DC transferred to Elmira Prison, NY, August 29, 1864	Died April 23, 1865 of Variola (Smallpox), Grave No. 1399
Roberts, John Troy Private	17	June 21, 1864, Fort Fisher, New Hanover County, North Carolina	Co. G, 36th Regiment 2nd North Carolina Artillery	January 15, 1865, Fort Fisher, North Carolina	February 1, 1865, Elmira Prison Camp, New York	Oath of Allegiance July 11, 1865
Roberts, M. V. B Private	Unk	September 24, 1861, Hall & Gwinnett Counties, Georgia	Co. H, 35th Georgia Infantry	May 24, 1864, Hanover Junction, Virginia	Point Lookout, Maryland, transferred to Elmira Prison, NY, July 11, 1864	Oath of Allegiance June 14, 1865
Roberts, Richard Private	Unk	February 20, 1864, Dublin, Virginia	Co. F, 4th Virginia Infantry	May 12, 1864, Spotsylvania Court House, Virginia	Point Lookout, Maryland, transferred to Elmira Prison, NY, August 2, 1864	Oath of Allegiance June 27, 1865
Roberts, Rufus F. Private	26	September 24, 1861, Wilkesboro, North Carolina	Co. F, 37th North Carolina Infantry	May 12, 1864, Near Spotsylvania Court House, Virginia	Point Lookout, Maryland, transferred to Elmira Prison, NY, August 14, 1864	Oath of Allegiance June 12, 1865
Roberts, Samuel L. Private	21	September 3, 1861, Mecklenburg County, North Carolina	Co. H, 35th North Carolina Infantry	June 17, 1864, Petersburg, Virginia	Point Lookout, Maryland, transferred to Elmira Prison, NY, July 30, 1864	Oath of Allegiance June 12, 1865
Roberts, Stephen Private	Unk	May 19, 1862, Fredrickburg, Virginia	Co. E, 16th Georgia Infantry	June 1, 1864, Cold Harbor, Virginia	Point Lookout, Maryland, transferred to Elmira Prison, NY, July 12, 1864	Transferred for Exchange 10/11/64. Died 10/22/64, of Unknown Disease Point Lookout, MD.
Roberts, Thomas H. Private	21	June 8, 1861, Lexington, Virginia	Co. J, 4th Virginia Infantry	May 12, 1864, Near Spotsylvania Court House, Virginia	Point Lookout, Maryland, transferred to Elmira Prison, NY, August 6, 1864	Exchanged October 29, 1864, at Venus Point, Savannah River, GA.

Name & Rank	Age	Enlisted	Regiment and State	Where Captured	Prison	Remarks
Roberts, Wade G. Private	25	May 9, 1861, Chadbourne, Texas	Co. K, Yager's 1st Texas Cavalry	August 8, 1864, Williamsport, Louisiana	New Orleans, Louisiana, Transferred to Elmira Prison, New York, November 19, 1864	Oath of Allegiance June 19, 1865
Roberts, William C. Private	Unk	July 14, 1862, Richland, South Carolina	Co. H, 7th Battalion South Carolina Infantry	May 16, 1864, Near Drury's Bluff, Virginia	Point Lookout, Maryland, transferred to Elmira Prison, NY, August 17, 1864	Exchanged October 29, 1864, at Venus Point, Savannah River, GA.
Roberts, William C. Corporal	23	August 26, 1861, Lancaster Court House, South Carolina	Co. E, 12th South Carolina Infantry	May 12, 1864, Spotsylvania Court House, VA. Gunshot Wound Ear, Left Side of Face and Left Arm.	Old Capital Prison, Washington D. C. Transferred to Elmira Prison, NY, August 12, 1864	Exchanged October 29, 1864, at Venus Point, Savannah River, GA.
Roberts, William H. Private	Unk	February 7, 1863, Selma, Alabama	Co. A, 1st Battalion Alabama Artillery	August 23, 1864, Fort Morgan, Alabama	New Orleans, Louisiana transferred to Elmira Prison, NY, December 4, 1864.	Died July 25, 1865 of Unknown Causes, Grave No. 2864
Roberts, Willis W. Private	Unk	September 10, 1861, Covington, Georgia	Co. A, Cobb's Legion, Georgia Infantry	May 6, 1864, Wilderness, Virginia	Point Lookout, Maryland, transferred to Elmira Prison, NY, August 17, 1864	Exchanged March 2, 1865 at Akins Landing on the James River, Virginia
Robertson, C. P. Private	Unk	November 13, 1861, White County, Georgia	Co. E, 24th Georgia Infantry	August 16, 1864, Front Royal, Virginia	Old Capital Prison, Washington, DC transferred to Elmira Prison, NY, August 29, 1864	Exchanged February 20, 1865 at Boulware's or Cox Wharf on the James River, Virginia
Robertson, Green M. Private	Unk	July 3, 1863, Camp of Instruction, Virginia	Co. I, 26th Battalion Infantry	June 3, 1864, Gaines Farm, Cold Harbor, Virginia	Point Lookout, Maryland, transferred to Elmira Prison, NY, July 17,1864	Oath of Allegiance July 3, 1865
Robertson, Harrison Private	Unk	April 1, 1862, Williamston, North Carolina	Co. K, 10th Regiment, 1st North Carolina Artillery	January 15, 1865, Fort Fisher, North Carolina	February 1, 1865, Elmira Prison Camp, New York	Died March 7, 1865 of Pneumonia, Grave No. 2405.

Name & Rank	Age	Enlisted	Regiment and State	Where Captured	Prison	Remarks
Robertson, J. E. Private	Unk	February 10, 1864, Columbia, South Carolina	Co. C, 22nd South Carolina Infantry	July 30, 1864, Petersburg, Virginia	Point Lookout, Maryland, transferred to Elmira Prison, NY, August 12, 1864	Died October 1, 1864 of Chronic Diarrhea, Grave No. 412. Name Robinson on Headstone.
Robertson, John Private	45	March 10, 1864, Green County, Tennessee	Co. D, 7th Tennessee Infantry	May 6, 1864, Wilderness, Virginia	Point Lookout, Maryland, transferred to Elmira Prison, NY, July 23, 1864	Oath of Allegiance May 12, 1865
Robertson, Joseph C. G. Private	20	March 11, 1862, Spring Garden, North Carolina	Co. I, 45th North Carolina Infantry	May 10, 1864, Spotsylvania Court House, Virginia	Point Lookout, Maryland, transferred to Elmira Prison, NY, August 6, 1864	Oath of Allegiance June 12, 1865
Robertson, Robert Private	20	June 22, 1863, Raleigh, North Carolina	Co. K, 14th, North Carolina Infantry	May 30, 1864, Old Church, Cold Harbor, Virginia	Point Lookout, Maryland, transferred to Elmira Prison, NY, July 12, 1864	Exchanged February 13, 1865 at Boulware's wharf on the James River, Virginia
Robertson, Thomas Private	23	April 26, 1861, Townsville, North Carolina	Co. D, 12th North Carolina Infantry	July 4, 1864, Harper's Ferry, Virginia	Old Capital Prison, Washington D. C. Transferred to Elmira Prison, NY, August 12, 1864	Oath of Allegiance May 19, 1865
Robertson, William Private	Unk	January 29, 1864, Bristol, Tennessee	Co. J, 14th Tennessee Infantry	May 26, 1864, Hanover Junction, Virginia	Point Lookout, Maryland, transferred to Elmira Prison, NY, July 23, 1864	Oath of Allegiance May 29, 1865
Robertson, William Private	Unk	June 11, 1861, Hevener's Store, Virginia	Co. E, 31st Virginia Infantry	May 30, 1864, Old Church, Cold Harbor, Virginia	Point Lookout, Maryland, transferred to Elmira Prison, NY, July 12, 1864	Oath of Allegiance May 29, 1865
Robertson, William Private	Unk	June 15, 1861, Lynchburg, Virginia	Co. H, 42nd Virginia Infantry	May 12, 1864, Near Spotsylvania Court House, Virginia	Point Lookout, Maryland, transferred to Elmira Prison, NY, August 6, 1864	Died March 10, 1865 of Chronic Diarrhea, Grave No. 1870

Name & Rank	Age	Enlisted	Regiment and State	Where Captured	Prison	Remarks
Robeson, Albert, Private	18	December 2, 1863, Fort Pender, North Carolina	Co. H, 36th Regiment 2nd North Carolina Artillery	January 15, 1865, Fort Fisher, North Carolina	February 1, 1865, Elmira Prison Camp, New York	Exchanged March 14, 1865 at Boulware's Wharf on the James River, Virginia
Robeson, Matthew P., Private	42	March 15, 1862, Elizabethtown, Bladen County, North Carolina	Co. H, 36th Regiment 2nd North Carolina Artillery	January 15, 1865, Fort Fisher, North Carolina	February 1, 1865, Elmira Prison Camp, New York	Died February 22, 1865 of Variola (Smallpox), Grave No. 2247. Headstone has M. P. Robinson.
Robins, Elias, Private	30	November 7, 1862, Randolph County, North Carolina	Co. B, 52nd North Carolina Infantry	June 13, 1864, Gaines Mill, Virginia	Point Lookout, Maryland, transferred to Elmira Prison, NY, July 23, 1864	Died December 24, 1864 of Chronic Diarrhea, Grave No. 1105
Robins, John W., Private	37	April 20, 1861, Belle Roi., Virginia	Co. A, 26th Virginia Infantry	June 15, 1864, Near Petersburg, Virginia	Point Lookout, Maryland, transferred to Elmira Prison, NY, July 12, 1864	Died March 7, 1865 of Chronic Diarrhea, Grave No. 2393
Robins, William W., Private	36	August 29, 1863, Fort Caswell, Brunswick County, North Carolina	Co. G, 36th Regiment 2nd North Carolina Artillery	January 15, 1865, Fort Fisher, North Carolina. Wounded	February 1, 1865, Elmira Prison Camp, New York	Died March 22, 1865 of Variola (Smallpox), Grave No. 1538
Robinson, Alexander, Private	Unk	October 20, 1863, Camp Holmes, Wilkesboro, North Carolina	Co. F, 37th North Carolina Infantry	July 29, 1864, Near Darby Town, Petersburg Virginia	Point Lookout, Maryland, transferred to Elmira Prison, NY, August 12, 1864	Died 9/15/64 of Chronic Diarrhea, Grave No. 281. Robertson on Headstone.
Robinson, Allen J., Private	Unk	March 15, 1864, Burnett's Farm, Green Pond, South Carolina	Co. J, 17th South Carolina Infantry	July 30, 1864, Petersburg, Virginia	Point Lookout, Maryland, transferred to Elmira Prison, NY, August 12, 1864	Died November 8, 1864 of Chronic Diarrhea, Grave No. 781
Robinson, Augustus, Private	18	March 10, 1864, Camp Holmes, North Carolina	Co. B, 32nd North Carolina Infantry	May 10, 1864, Spotsylvania Court House, Virginia	Old Capital Prison, Washington D. C. Transferred to Elmira Prison, NY, August 12, 1864	Exchanged March 14, 1865 at Boulware's Wharf on the James River, Virginia

Name & Rank	Age	Enlisted	Regiment and State	Where Captured	Prison	Remarks
Robinson, Benjamin F. Corporal	36	March 14, 1862, Camp Leon, Florida	Co. J, 5th Florida Infantry	May 5, 1864, Wilderness, Virginia	Point Lookout, Maryland, transferred to Elmira Prison, NY, August 12, 1864	Exchanged March 2, 1865 at Akins Landing on the James River, Virginia
Robinson, Benjamin F. Private	35	September 5, 1861, Luka, Mississippi	Co. A, 26th Mississippi Infantry	May 16, 1863, Champion Hill, Mississippi	Point Lookout, Maryland, transferred to Elmira Prison, NY, July 25, 1864	Oath of Allegiance May 19, 1865
Robinson, Clark H. Private	Unk	May 13, 1861, Camp Peery, Tazewell County, Virginia	Co. C, 29th Virginia Infantry	June 3, 1864, Gaines Mill Cold Harbor, Virginia	Point Lookout, Maryland, transferred to Elmira Prison, NY, July 12, 1864	Oath of Allegiance July 3, 1865
Robinson, Columbus H. Private	Unk	May 16, 1861, Montgomery, Alabama	Co. J, 6th Alabama Infantry	May 20, 1864, Spotsylvania Court House, Virginia	Point Lookout, Maryland, transferred to Elmira Prison, NY, July 3, 1864	Exchanged March 14, 1865 at Boulware's Wharf on the James River, Virginia
Robinson, Daniel Private	26	July 9, 1861, Fayetteville, North Carolina	Co. C, 3rd North Carolina Infantry	May 10, 1864, Near Spotsylvania County Court House, Virginia	Point Lookout, Maryland, transferred to Elmira Prison, NY, August 14, 1864	Oath of Allegiance June 27, 1865
Robinson, Franklin Private	18	Unknown	Co. C, 18th South Carolina Infantry	July 30, 1864, Petersburg, Virginia	Point Lookout, Maryland, transferred to Elmira Prison, NY, August 12, 1864	Oath of Allegiance July 3, 1865
Robinson, George Drummer, Private	Unk	September 6, 1862, Fort Morgan, Alabama	Co. C, 1st Battalion Alabama Artillery	August 23, 1864, Fort Morgan, Alabama	New Orleans, Louisiana transferred to Elmira Prison, NY, December 4, 1864.	Oath of Allegiance May 13, 1865
Robinson, H. M. Private	Unk	April 26, 1864, Fort Morgan, Alabama	Co. A, Jackson's 1st Regiment, Tennessee Heavy Artillery	August 23, 1864, Fort Morgan, Alabama	New Orleans, Louisiana transferred to Elmira Prison, NY, December 4, 1864.	Exchanged February 25, 1865 at Boulware's or Cox Wharf on the James River, Virginia

Name & Rank	Age	Enlisted	Regiment and State	Where Captured	Prison	Remarks
Robinson, J. A. Private	Unk	Unknown	Co. B, 36th Georgia Infantry	May 20, 1864, Spotsylvania Court House, Virginia	Point Lookout Prison Camp, Maryland. Transferred to Elmira Prison Camp, NY, July 6, 1864	Died May 4, 1865 of Pneumonia, Grave No. 2761
Robinson, J. H. Private	24	July 8, 1862, Camp Drury, North Carolina	Co. F, 26th North Carolina Infantry	May 12, 1864, Spotsylvania Court House, Virginia	Point Lookout, Maryland, transferred to Elmira Prison, NY, August 6, 1864	Oath of Allegiance May 29, 1865
Robinson, J. R. Private	Unk	May 16, 1863, Augusta, Georgia	Co. I, 16th Georgia Infantry	June 1, 1864, Gaines Farm Cold Harbor, Virginia	Point Lookout, Maryland, transferred to Elmira Prison, NY, July 12, 1864	Oath of Allegiance July 7, 1865
Robinson, Jesse Private	36	July 3, 1861, Goldsboro, North Carolina	Co. F, 10th Regiment, 1st North Carolina Artillery	January 15, 1865, Fort Fisher, North Carolina	February 1, 1865, Elmira Prison Camp, New York	Died February 19, 1865 of Rubeola (Measles), Grave No. 2337. Headstone has Robertson.
Robinson, John S. Private	19	May 27, 1861, Troy, North Carolina	Co. C, 23rd North Carolina Infantry	May 20, 1864, Spotsylvania Court House, Virginia	Point Lookout, Maryland, transferred to Elmira Prison, NY, July 3, 1864	Died January 29, 1865 of Typhoid-Pneumonia, Grave No. 1656
Robinson, Joseph J. Private	Unk	September 20, 1862, Shepherds-town, Virginia	Co. G, 3rd Virginia Cavalry	May 9, 1864, Spotsylvania Court House, Virginia	Point Lookout, Maryland, transferred to Elmira Prison, NY, August 17, 1864	Exchanged March 14, 1865 at Boulware's Wharf on the James River, Virginia
Robinson, Julius C. Private	18	March 1, 1864, Fort Fisher, New Hanover County, North Carolina	Co. G, 36th Regiment 2nd North Carolina Artillery	January 15, 1865, Fort Fisher, North Carolina	February 1, 1865, Elmira Prison Camp, New York	Died February 15, 1865 of Chronic Diarrhea, Grave No. 2170
Robinson, Napoleon A. Private	17	July 9, 1863, Fort Branch, Martin County, North Carolina	Co. G, 40th Regiment, 3rd North Carolina Artillery	January 15, 1865, Fort Fisher, North Carolina	February 1, 1865, Elmira Prison Camp, New York	Oath of Allegiance June 12, 1865
Robinson, Newton L. Private	18	February 23, 1862, Catawba Station, North Carolina	Co. F, 32nd North Carolina Infantry	May 10, 1864, Wilderness, Virginia	Point Lookout, Maryland, transferred to Elmira Prison, NY, August 6, 1864	Exchanged October 29, 1864, at Venus Point, Savannah River, GA.

Name & Rank	Age	Enlisted	Regiment and State	Where Captured	Prison	Remarks
Robinson, Simeon C. Private	Unk	July 10, 1862, Covington, Louisiana	Co. B, Wingfield's 3rd Louisiana Cavalry	October 6, 1864, Clinton, Louisiana	New Orleans, Louisiana transferred to Elmira November 19, 1864.	Oath of Allegiance May 29, 1865
Robinson, Stephert G. Private	Unk	September 22, 1862, Waynesville, Georgia	Co. G, 7th Georgia Cavalry	June 11, 1864, Trevilian Station, Louisa Court House, Virginia	Point Lookout, Maryland, transferred to Elmira Prison, NY, July 25, 1864	Died September 24, 1864 of Typhoid-Pneumonia, Grave No. 460
Robinson, W. E. Private	Unk	Unknown	Co. J, 12th Alabama Infantry	May 12, 1864, Spotsylvania Court House, Virginia	Point Lookout, Maryland, transferred to Elmira Prison, NY, August 6, 1864	Exchanged October 29, 1864, at Venus Point, Savannah River, GA.
Robinson, Wesley Civilian	Unk	Unknown	Citizen of Calhoun County, Virginia	June 10, 1864, Newton, Virginia	Point Lookout, Maryland, transferred to Elmira Prison, NY, July 25, 1864	Oath of Allegiance June 30, 1865
Robinson, William Private	Unk	August 23, 1863, Goldsboro, North Carolina	Co. F, 10th Regiment, 1st North Carolina Artillery	January 15, 1865, Fort Fisher, North Carolina	February 1, 1865, Elmira Prison Camp, New York	Died March 7, 1865 of Pneumonia, Grave No. 2407. Headstone has Robertson.
Robinson, William H. Private	35	September 13, 1861, Mecklenburg County, North Carolina	Co. K, 30th North Carolina Infantry	July 12, 1864, Near Washington, DC	Old Capital Prison, Washington, DC. Transferred to Elmira Prison Camp, NY, July 25, 1865	Died January 30, 1865 of Acute Bronchitis, Grave No. 1792
Robinson, William L. Private	Unk	August 16, 1863, Fredericks-burg, Virginia	Co. G, 3rd Virginia Cavalry	May 9, 1864, Spotsylvania Court House, Virginia	Point Lookout, Maryland, transferred to Elmira Prison, NY, August 17, 1864	Exchanged February 25, 1865 at Boulware's or Cox Wharf on the James River, Virginia
Robinson, William S. B. Private	Unk	November 18, 1861, Columbia, South Carolina	Co. A, 18th South Carolina Infantry	July 30, 1864, Battle of the Crater, Petersburg, Virginia	Point Lookout, Maryland, transferred to Elmira Prison, NY, August 12, 1864	Transferred for Exchange 10/11/64. Died 10/28/64 of Chronic Diarrhea at Point Lookout, MD.

Name & Rank	Age	Enlisted	Regiment and State	Where Captured	Prison	Remarks
Robison, Joseph A. Private	Unk	April 1, 1864, Orange County Court House, North Carolina	Co. H, 1st North Carolina Infantry	May 12, 1864, Spotsylvania Court House, Virginia	Point Lookout, Maryland, transferred to Elmira Prison, NY, August 6, 1864	Exchanged March 14, 1864 at Boulware's Wharf on the James River, Virginia
Robison, Samuel L. Private	Unk	September 27, 1861, Augusta, Georgia	Co. B, 7th Georgia Cavalry	June 11, 1864, Trevilian Station, Louisa Court House, Virginia	Point Lookout, Maryland, transferred to Elmira Prison, NY, July 25, 1864	Oath of Allegiance June 27, 1865
Robison, Thomas G. Private	Unk	June 17, 1861, Camp Bradford, Coosa County, Alabama	Co. B, 12th Alabama Infantry	July 8, 1864, Harpers Ferry, Virginia	Old Capital Prison, Washington DC. Transferred to Elmira Prison Camp, New York, July 25, 1864.	Oath of Allegiance June 16, 1865
Rocket, Richard B. Private	Unk	May 4, 1862, Sandersville, Georgia	Co. H, 49th Georgia Infantry	May 6, 1864, Wilderness, Virginia	Point Lookout, Maryland, transferred to Elmira Prison, NY, August 14, 1864	Oath of Allegiance June 14, 1865
Rodgers, Elbert S. Private	18	August 1, 1861, Asheville, North Carolina	Co. G, 25th North Carolina Infantry	June 17, 1864, Petersburg, Virginia	Point Lookout, Maryland, transferred to Elmira Prison, NY, July 30, 1864	Oath of Allegiance July 3, 1865
Rodgers, John C. Private	Unk	May 20, 1864, Randolph, North Carolina	Co. L, 22nd North Carolina Infantry	May 24, 1864, Hanover Junction, Virginia	Point Lookout, Maryland, transferred to Elmira Prison, NY, July 11, 1864	Oath of Allegiance May 13, 1865
Rodgers, L. P. Private	Unk	January 2, 1864, Laurens, South Carolina	Co. G, 27th South Carolina Infantry	June 24, 1864, Near Petersburg, Virginia	Point Lookout, Maryland, transferred to Elmira Prison, NY, August 18, 1864	Exchanged March 2, 1865 at Akins Landing on the James River, Virginia
Rodgers, Thomas Private	22	Unknown	Co. H, 1st North Carolina Infantry	May 12, 1864, Spotsylvania Court House, Virginia	Point Lookout, Maryland, transferred to Elmira Prison, NY, August 6, 1864	Oath of Allegiance June 12, 1865

Name & Rank	Age	Enlisted	Regiment and State	Where Captured	Prison	Remarks
Rodgers, Thomas J. Private	Unk	Unknown	Co. A, 1st Battalion Alabama Artillery	August 23, 1864, Fort Morgan, Alabama	Steam Press No. 4 New Orleans, Louisiana transferred to Elmira Prison, NY, October 8, 1864.	Oath of Allegiance June 16, 1865
Rodgers, William H. Private	Unk	December 17, 1862, Richmond, Virginia	Co. G, 24th Virginia Cavalry	July 8, 1864, Deserted to Enemy at Mayanock, Virginia	Point Lookout, Maryland, transferred to Elmira Prison, NY, July 25, 1864	Oath of Allegiance May 17, 1865
Rodgers, William J. J. Private	Unk	October 9, 1861, Enfield, Halifax County, North Carolina	Co. F, 36th Regiment 2nd North Carolina Artillery	January 15, 1865, Fort Fisher, North Carolina	February 1, 1865, Elmira Prison Camp, New York	Died February 27, 1865 of Typhoid Fever, Grave No. 2120. Headstone has W. J. Rogers.
Rodman, John F. Sergeant	17	June 10, 1861, Salisbury, North Carolina	Co. K, 5th North Carolina Infantry	July 11, 1864, Leasburg, Virginia. Deserted to Union Lines.	Old Capital Prison, Washington D. C. Transferred to Elmira Prison, NY, August 12, 1864	Oath of Allegiance September 16, 1864. Early Release per Lincoln's Proclamation, 12/8/1863.
Rodriguez, Raymond Private	Unk	June 23, 1861, Camp Moore, Louisiana	Co. G, 8th Louisiana Infantry	May 12, 1864, Spotsylvania Court House, Virginia	Point Lookout, Maryland, transferred to Elmira Prison, NY, August 17, 1864	Exchanged February 25, 1865 at Boulware's or Cox Wharf on the James River, Virginia
Roemer, Adolph Private	Unk	February 17, 1864, Montgomery, Alabama	Co. F, 1st Battalion Alabama Artillery	August 23, 1864, Fort Morgan, Alabama	Steam Press No. 4 New Orleans, Louisiana transferred to Elmira Prison, NY, October 8, 1864.	Oath of Allegiance December 15, 1864. Early Release per Lincoln's Proclamation, 12/8/1863.
Rogan, Owen Private	Unk	March 10, 1862, Cohaba, Alabama	Co. F, 5th Alabama Infantry	May 20, 1864, Spotsylvania Court House, Virginia	Point Lookout, Maryland, transferred to Elmira Prison, NY, July 3, 1864	Oath of Allegiance June 19, 1865
Rogers, Arthur M. Private	Unk	February 11, 1863, Charleston, South Carolina	Co. G, 27th South Carolina Infantry	June 24, 1864, Near Petersburg, Virginia	Point Lookout, Maryland, transferred to Elmira Prison, NY, August 18, 1864	Transferred for Exchange February 20, 1865. Died Unknown Date and Cause on Exchange Boat.

Name & Rank	Age	Enlisted	Regiment and State	Where Captured	Prison	Remarks
Rogers, B. F. Private	Unk	Unknown	Co. B, 1st Jackson's Tennessee Heavy Artillery	August 23, 1864, Fort Morgan, Alabama.	New Orleans, Louisiana transferred to Elmira Prison, NY, December 4, 1864.	Exchanged February 25, 1865 at Boulware's or Cox Wharf on the James River, Virginia
Rogers, Charles A. Private	Unk	July 2, 1861, Bethel, Virginia	Co. F, 50th Virginia Infantry	May 12, 1864, Spotsylvania Court House, Virginia	Point Lookout, Maryland, transferred to Elmira Prison, NY, July 25, 1864	Died January 30, 1865 of Variola (Smallpox), Grave No. 1801. Has 4th Virginia on Headstone.
Rogers, David Private	27	May 20, 1861, Carroll, Louisiana	Co. C, 14th Louisiana Infantry	May 20, 1864, Spotsylvania Court House, Virginia	Point Lookout, Maryland, transferred to Elmira Prison, NY, July 3, 1864	Died October 11, 1864 of Chronic Diarrhea, Grave No. 692
Rogers, Enoch Private	Unk	January 13, 1863, Georgetown, South Carolina	Co. J, 4th South Carolina Cavalry	June 11, 1864, Trevilian Station, Louisa Court House, Virginia	Point Lookout, Maryland, transferred to Elmira Prison, NY, July 25, 1864	Oath of Allegiance June 14, 1865
Rogers, George Private	Unk	March 15, 1861, Pineville, Alabama	Co. C, 5th Alabama Infantry	July 16, 1864, Loudoun County, Virginia	Old Capital Prison, Washington, DC. Transferred to Elmira Prison Camp, NY, July 25, 1864.	Died February 13, 1865 of Variola (Smallpox), Grave No. 2040
Rogers, J. C. Private	Unk	Unknown	Co. H, 16th Georgia Infantry	May 6, 1864, Wilderness, Virginia	Point Lookout, Maryland, transferred to Elmira Prison, NY, August 14, 1864	Oath of Allegiance June 19, 1865
Rogers, James C. Private	Unk	February 28, 1861, Selma, Alabama	Co. C, 1st Battalion Alabama Artillery	August 23, 1864, Fort Morgan, Alabama	New Orleans, Louisiana transferred to Elmira Prison, NY, December 4, 1864.	Died March 17, 1865 of Diarrhea, Grave No. 1715
Rogers, Jared Private	33	April 14, 1863, Pocahontas County, Virginia	Co. A, 20th Virginia Cavalry	July 16, 1864, Loudon County, Virginia	Old Capital Prison, Washington DC. Transferred to Elmira Prison Camp, New York, July 25, 1864.	Oath of Allegiance May 29, 1865

Name & Rank	Age	Enlisted	Regiment and State	Where Captured	Prison	Remarks
Rogers, Jobe Private	45	September 16, 1863, Union County, North Carolina	Co. E, 30th North Carolina Infantry	May 31, 1864, Old Church, Cold Harbor, Virginia	Point Lookout, Maryland, transferred to Elmira Prison, NY, July 11, 1864	Died January 28, 1865 of Chronic Diarrhea, Grave No. 1659
Rogers, John Private	22	June 7, 1861, Camp Moore, New Orleans, Louisiana	Co. D, 7th Louisiana Infantry	November 7, 1863, Rappahannock Station, Virginia	Point Lookout, Maryland, transferred to Elmira Prison, NY, July 25, 1864	Oath of Allegiance May 15, 1865
Rogers, John A. Private	Unk	January 10, 1862, Columbia, South Carolina	Co. C, 22nd South Carolina Infantry	July 30, 1864, Petersburg, Virginia	Point Lookout, Maryland, transferred to Elmira Prison, NY, August 12, 1864	Oath of Allegiance June 14, 1865
Rogers, John Dew Private	Unk	August 26, 1861, Marion District, South Carolina	Co. E, 1st South Carolina Infantry	July 29, 1864, Petersburg, Virginia	Point Lookout, Maryland, transferred to Elmira Prison, NY, August 12, 1864	Oath of Allegiance July 3, 1865
Rogers, John H. Private	22	April 19, 1862, Wake County, North Carolina	Co. D, 30th North Carolina Infantry	May 6, 1864, Wilderness, Virginia	Point Lookout, Maryland, transferred to Elmira Prison, NY, August 14, 1864	Died January 22, 1865 of Variola (Smallpox), Grave No. 1595. Headstone has Rodgers.
Rogers, Joseph Private	Unk	April 7, 1862, Petersburg, Virginia	Co. K, 5th Virginia Cavalry	May 11, 1864, Yellow Tavern, Hanover County, Virginia	Point Lookout, Maryland, transferred to Elmira Prison, NY, August 17, 1864	Died September 22, 1864 of Pneumonia, Grave No. 492. Headstone has Rodgers, 1st Cav.
Rogers, Lewis L. Private	25	July 15, 1862, Raleigh, North Carolina	Co. G, 1st North Carolina Infantry	May 12, 1864, Spotsylvania Court House, Virginia	Point Lookout, Maryland, transferred to Elmira Prison, NY, August 6, 1864	Died May 17, 1865 of Chronic Diarrhea, Grave No. 2955
Rogers, Robert C. Seaman	Unk	Unknown	Confederate States Navy	May 5, 1864, Albemarle Sound on Steamer CSS Bombshell	Point Lookout, Maryland, transferred to Elmira Prison, NY, August 17, 1864	Transferred For Exchange October 11, 1864 to Point Lookout Prison Camp, MD. Nothing Further.

Name & Rank	Age	Enlisted	Regiment and State	Where Captured	Prison	Remarks
Rogers, Robert H. Private	Unk	July 2, 1861, Bethel Am., Virginia	Co. F, 50th Virginia Infantry	May 12, 1864, Spotsylvania Court House, Virginia	Point Lookout, Maryland, transferred to Elmira Prison, NY, August 12, 1864	Oath of Allegiance June 23, 1865
Rogers, Rueben Private	22	October 24, 1861, Camp Burnett, Kentucky	Co. G, 7th Kentucky Mounted Infantry	May 16, 1863, Champion Hill, Mississippi	Point Lookout, Maryland, transferred to Elmira Prison, NY, July 23, 1864	Oath of Allegiance May 15, 1865
Rogers, Samuel Private	Unk	Unknown	Co. K, Mosby's Regiment Virginia Cavalry	April 10, 1865, Fairfax Station, Virginia	Old Capital Prison, Washington D. C. Transferred to Elmira Prison, NY, May 2, 1865.	Oath of Allegiance July 7, 1865
Rogers, Samuel B. Private	Unk	May 9, 1861, Reidsville, Georgia	Co. H, 61st Georgia Infantry	May 12, 1864, Spotsylvania Court House, Virginia	Point Lookout, Maryland, transferred to Elmira Prison, NY, July 25, 1864	Oath of Allegiance July 11, 1865
Rogers, Samuel S. Private	Unk	July 11, 1861, Athens, Texas	Co. K, 4th Texas Infantry	May 12, 1864, Spotsylvania Court House, Virginia	Point Lookout, Maryland, transferred to Elmira Prison, NY, July 30, 1864	Oath of Allegiance June 19, 1865
Rogers, Sanford V. Private	Unk	January 10, 1862, Columbia, South Carolina	Co. C, 22nd South Carolina Infantry	July 30, 1864, Petersburg, Virginia	Point Lookout, Maryland, transferred to Elmira Prison, NY, August 12, 1864	Died October 31, 1864 of Chronic Diarrhea, Grave No. 749
Rogers, Stephen Private	22	April 29, 1862, Wilson, North Carolina	Co. F, 61st North Carolina Infantry	June 16, 1864, Petersburg, Virginia	Point Lookout, Maryland, transferred to Elmira Prison, NY, July 25, 1864	Died October 17, 1864 of Chronic Diarrhea, Grave No. 544
Rogers, Thomas E. Private	30	June 13, 1862, Savannah, Georgia	Co. B, 7th Georgia Cavalry	June 11, 1864, Trevilian Station, Louisa Court House, Virginia	Point Lookout, Maryland, transferred to Elmira Prison, NY, July 25, 1864	Transferred for Exchange 10/11/64. Died 10/13/64 at US Army Hospital, Baltimore, MD.

Name & Rank	Age	Enlisted	Regiment and State	Where Captured	Prison	Remarks
Rogers, Thomas G. Private	27	December 20, 1861, Brittons Neck, South Carolina	Co. J, 21st South Carolina Infantry	January 15, 1865, Fort Fisher, North Carolina	February 1, 1865, Elmira Prison Camp, New York	Died February 16, 1865 of Chronic Diarrhea, Grave No. 2188. Headstone has T. C. Rodgers.
Rogers, William D. Private	Unk	June 15, 1861, Macon, Georgia	Co. C, 12th Georgia Infantry	May 10, 1864, Spotsylvania Court House, Virginia	Point Lookout, Maryland, transferred to Elmira Prison, NY, July 30, 1864	Oath of Allegiance June 27, 1865
Rogers, William W. Private	26	July 29, 1861, Forestville, Wake County, North Carolina	Co J, 1st North Carolina Infantry	May 12, 1864, Spotsylvania Court House, Virginia	Point Lookout, Maryland, transferred to Elmira Prison, NY, August 6,1864	Oath of Allegiance June 27, 1865
Rogers, Wood M. Private	22	March 21, 1862, Charlotte, North Carolina	Co. F, 1st North Carolina Cavalry	September 22, 1863, Jack's Shop, Near Madison County House, Virginia	Point Lookout, Maryland, transferred to Elmira Prison, NY, August 18, 1864	Exchanged March 10, 1865 at Boulware's Wharf on the James River, Virginia
Rolack, J. B. Private	Unk	Unknown	Captain Norwood's Home Guard, Florida	September 27, 1864, Marianna, Florida	New Orleans, Louisiana transferred to Elmira November 19, 1864.	Oath of Allegiance December 12, 1864. Early Release per Commissary General of Prisoners.
Rolan, Robert J. Private	Unk	September 10, 1861, Griffin, Georgia	Co. K, 27th Georgia Infantry	June 1, 1864, Gaines Mill Cold Harbor, Virginia	Point Lookout, Maryland, transferred to Elmira Prison, NY, July 12, 1864	Transferred for Exchange February 9, 1865, at James River, Virginia
Roland, Chesley H. Private	23	July 30, 1862, Franklin, North Carolina	Co. C, 8th, North Carolina Infantry	May 31, 1864, Cold Harbor, Virginia	Point Lookout, Maryland, transferred to Elmira Prison, NY, July 12, 1864	Died October 2, 1864 of Chronic Diarrhea, Grave No. 627. Last Name Rowland on Headstone.
Roland, J. Private	Unk	May 7, 1861, New Prospect, Virginia	Co. D, 26th Virginia Infantry	June 15, 1864, Near Petersburg, Virginia	Point Lookout, Maryland, transferred to Elmira Prison, NY, July 12, 1864	Transferred for Exchange October 11, 1864. Nothing Further

Name & Rank	Age	Enlisted	Regiment and State	Where Captured	Prison	Remarks
Roland, Richard N. Sergeant	25	April 17, 1861, Alexandria, Virginia	Co. F, 14th Virginia Infantry	July 21, 1863, Manassas Gap, Virginia	Point Lookout, Maryland, transferred to Elmira Prison, NY, August 18, 1864	Exchanged February 20, 1865 at Boulware's or Cox Wharf on the James River, Virginia
Rollins, Offie Private	Unk	December 19, 1863, Charleston, South Carolina	Co. J, 18th South Carolina Infantry	July 30, 1864, Petersburg, Virginia	Point Lookout, Maryland, transferred to Elmira Prison, NY, August 12, 1864	Died September 1, 1864 of Chronic Diarrhea, Grave No. 75
Rollins, William A. Corporal	Unk	September 9, 1861, Middleton, North Carolina	Co. F, 33rd North Carolina Infantry	July 29, 1864, Petersburg, Virginia	Point Lookout, Maryland, transferred to Elmira Prison, NY, August 12, 1864	Oath of Allegiance July 3, 1865
Rollo, Thomas H. Private	Unk	May 21, 1863, Pike County, Alabama	Co. A, 61st Alabama Infantry	May 12, 1864, Spotsylvania Court House, Virginia	Point Lookout, Maryland, transferred to Elmira Prison, NY, July 30, 1864	Oath of Allegiance June 30, 1865
Rome, S. R. Private	Unk	Unknown	Co. B, 1st Jackson's Tennessee Heavy Artillery	August 23, 1864, Fort Morgan, Alabama.	New Orleans, Louisiana transferred to Elmira Prison, NY, December 4, 1864.	Exchanged February 25, 1865 at Boulware's or Cox Wharf on the James River, Virginia
Romines, James Private	Unk	August 28, 1861, Summerville, Georgia	Co. K, 21st Georgia Infantry	June 4, 1864, Gaines Mill Cold Harbor, Virginia	Point Lookout, Maryland, transferred to Elmira Prison, NY, July 12, 1864. Ward No. 17	Died July 18, 1864 of Heart Disease, Grave No. 2851
Rominger, Leander M. Private	28	March 24, 1862, Forsyth County, North Carolina	Co. E, 53rd North Carolina Infantry	May 20, 1864, Spotsylvania Court House, Virginia	Point Lookout, Maryland, transferred to Elmira Prison, NY, July 3, 1864	Oath of Allegiance May 17, 1865
Rook, E. C. Private	Unk	April 11, 1862, Coles Island, South Carolina	Co. F, 25th South Carolina Infantry	January 15, 1865, Fort Fisher, North Carolina	February 1, 1865, Elmira Prison Camp, New York	Exchanged March 2, 1865 at Akins Landing on the James River, Virginia

Name & Rank	Age	Enlisted	Regiment and State	Where Captured	Prison	Remarks
Rook, Samuel L. Private	42	February 29, 1864, James Island, South Carolina	Co. A, 27th South Carolina Infantry	August 19, 1864, Weldon Railroad, Near Petersburg, VA. Gunshot Wound Right Leg.	DeCamp General Hospital, David's Island New York Harbor.	Died January 16, 1865, of Acute Bronchitis, Grave No. 1446
Rooke, Artemis V. Private	27	July 1, 1862, Orangeburg, South Carolina	Co. G, 27th South Carolina Infantry	June 24, 1864, Near Petersburg, Virginia	Point Lookout, Maryland, transferred to Elmira Prison, NY, August 18, 1864	Exchanged February 20, 1865 at Boulware's or Cox Wharf on the James River, Virginia
Rooks, Archibald B. Private	21	May 17, 1861, Lower Black River District, North Carolina	Co. B, 18th North Carolina Infantry	May 12, 1864, Spotsylvania Court House, Virginia	Point Lookout, Maryland, transferred to Elmira Prison, NY, August 6, 1864	Oath of Allegiance June 12, 1865
Roper, John E. Private	Unk	January 25, 1864, Montgomery, Alabama	Co. F, 1st Battalion Alabama Artillery	August 23, 1864, Fort Morgan, Alabama	Steam Press No. 4 New Orleans, Louisiana transferred to Elmira Prison, NY, October 8, 1864.	Oath of Allegiance July 11, 1865
Roper, M. P. Private	Unk	January 25, 1864, Montgomery, Alabama	Co. F, 1st Battalion Alabama Artillery	August 23, 1864, Fort Morgan, Alabama	Steam Press No. 4 New Orleans, Louisiana transferred to Elmira Prison, NY, October 8, 1864.	Exchanged March 2, 1865 at Akins Landing on the James River, Virginia
Rose, H. B. Sergeant	Unk	Unknown	Co. H, 30th North Carolina Infantry	May 12, 1864, Spotsylvania Court House, Virginia	Point Lookout, Maryland, transferred to Elmira Prison, NY, July 11, 1864	Oath of Allegiance May 29, 1865
Rose, James Private	Unk	Unknown	Co. E, 37th Virginia Infantry	May 6, 1864, Wilderness, Virginia	Point Lookout, Maryland, transferred to Elmira Prison, NY, July 23, 1864	Died October 16, 1864 of Chronic Diarrhea, Grave No. 562
Rose, Washington Private	Unk	June 4, 1861, Camp Moore, Louisiana	Co. C, 6th Louisiana Infantry	May 5, 1864, Wilderness, Virginia	Point Lookout, Maryland, transferred to Elmira Prison, NY, August 17, 1864	Exchanged February 25, 1865 at Boulware's or Cox Wharf on the James River, Virginia

Name & Rank	Age	Enlisted	Regiment and State	Where Captured	Prison	Remarks
Rose, William H. Corporal	Unk	May 18, 1861, Lisbon, Virginia	Co. C, 42nd Virginia Infantry	May 12, 1864, Spotsylvania Court House, Virginia	Point Lookout, Maryland, transferred to Elmira Prison, NY, August 2,1864	Died October 30, 1864 of Chronic Diarrhea, Grave No. 737
Rosenberger, John A. Private	Unk	April 18, 1861, Harrisonburg, Virginia	Co. D, 10th Virginia Infantry	May 12, 1864, Spotsylvania Court House, Virginia	Point Lookout, Maryland, transferred to Elmira Prison, NY, August 2, 1864	Exchanged March 2, 1865 at Akins Landing on the James River, Virginia
Rosette, John Sergeant	Unk	October 13, 1861, Mobile, Alabama	Co. A, 21st Alabama Infantry	August 23, 1864, Fort Morgan, Alabama	Steam Press No. 4 New Orleans, Louisiana transferred to Elmira Prison, NY, October 8, 1864.	Exchanged March 14, 1865 at Boulware's Wharf on the James River, Virginia
Ross, James P. Corporal	Unk	June 9, 1861, Bibb County, Georgia	Co. H, 12th Georgia Infantry	July 12, 1864, Near Washington, DC	Old Capital Prison, Washington DC. Transferred to Elmira Prison Camp, New York, July 25, 1864.	Oath of Allegiance June 19, 1865
Ross, R. B. Private	Unk	Unknown	Co. D, 50th Virginia Infantry	May 12, 1864, Spotsylvania Court House, Virginia	Point Lookout, Maryland, transferred to Elmira Prison, NY, August 2, 1864	Oath of Allegiance June 27, 1865
Ross, William M. Private	Unk	March 4, 1862, Forsyth, Georgia	Co. D, 45th Georgia Infantry	May 6, 1864, Wilderness, Virginia	Point Lookout, Maryland, transferred to Elmira Prison, NY, August 17, 1864	Oath of Allegiance June 19, 1865
Rosseaux, William N. Private	Unk	August 20, 1862, Camp Moore, Louisiana	Co. B, 3rd Battalion Louisiana Cavalry	July 5, 1863, Pearl River, Louisiana	New Orleans, Louisiana, Transferred to Elmira Prison, New York, November 19, 1864	Died December 5, 1864 of Chronic Diarrhea, Grave No. 1021
Rosser, James W. Sergeant	Unk	June 15, 1861, Buena Vista, Georgia	Co. K, 12th Georgia Infantry	May 10, 1864, Spotsylvania, Virginia	Point Lookout, Maryland, transferred to Elmira Prison, NY, July 28,1864	Oath of Allegiance June 21, 1865

Name & Rank	Age	Enlisted	Regiment and State	Where Captured	Prison	Remarks
Roszell, Dulany DeButts Private	19	September 4, 1862, Leesburg, Virginia	Co. A, 6th Virginia Cavalry	May 31, 1864, Cold Harbor, Virginia	Point Lookout, Maryland, transferred to Elmira Prison, NY, July 11, 1864	Oath of Allegiance May 29, 1965
Roten, Josiah G. Private	19	August 15, 1862, Statesville, North Carolina	Co. A, 37th North Carolina Infantry	May 12, 1864, Spotsylvania Court House, Virginia	Point Lookout, Maryland, transferred to Elmira Prison, NY, August 12, 1864	Exchanged October 29, 1864, at Venus Point, Savannah River, GA.
Roth, Gustavus A. Private	23	June 25, 1862, Charleston, Mississippi	Co. F, 21st Mississippi Infantry	May 6, 1864, Wilderness, Virginia	Point Lookout, Maryland, transferred to Elmira Prison, NY, August 18, 1864	Oath of Allegiance June 19, 1865
Roubleau, Emile Sergeant	Unk	July 22, 1861, Camp Moore, Louisiana	Co. H, 10th Louisiana Infantry	May 12, 1864, Spotsylvania Court House, Virginia	Point Lookout, Maryland, transferred to Elmira Prison, NY, July 25, 1864	Died December 6, 1864 of Chronic Diarrhea, Grave No. 1018
Roundtree, John M. Private	Unk	June 5, 1863, Henry County, Alabama	Co. A, 61st Alabama Infantry	May 8, 1864, Wilderness, Virginia	Point Lookout, Maryland, transferred to Elmira Prison, NY, July 30, 1864	Oath of Allegiance July 7, 1865
Rourke, James Private	25	March 5, 1862, New Orleans, Louisiana	Co. J, 7th Louisiana Infantry	May 11, 1864, Spotsylvania Court House, Virginia	Point Lookout, Maryland, transferred to Elmira Prison, NY, August 17, 1864	Exchanged February 20, 1865 at Boulware's or Cox Wharf on the James River, Virginia
Rouse, Noah Private	21	February 9, 1863, Fort Fisher, New Hanover County, North Carolina	Co. K, 40th 3rd Regiment North Carolina Artillery	January 15, 1865, Fort Fisher, North Carolina	February 1, 1865, Elmira Prison Camp, New York	Oath of Allegiance June 12, 1865
Rouseau, A. Private	Unk	Unknown	Co. D, Gober's Battalion Cavalry	September 20, 1864, Amite River, Louisiana	New Orleans, Louisiana transferred to Elmira November 19, 1864.	Oath of Allegiance May 19, 1865

Name & Rank	Age	Enlisted	Regiment and State	Where Captured	Prison	Remarks
Rousey, A. Private	Unk	October 15, 1861, Elbert County, Georgia	Co. H, 38th Georgia Infantry	August 10, 1864, Berryville, Virginia	Old Capital Prison, Washington, DC transferred to Elmira Prison, NY, August 29, 1864	Oath of Allegiance June 23, 1865
Row, E. L. Private	Unk	Unknown	Co. J, 3rd Louisiana Cavalry	August 25, 1864, Near Clinton, Louisiana	New Orleans, Louisiana, Transferred to Elmira Prison, New York, November 19, 1864	Exchanged February 25, 1865 at Boulware's or Cox Wharf on the James River, Virginia
Row, Jacob A. Private	Unk	Unknown	Co. J, 3rd Louisiana Cavalry	August 25, 1864, Near Clinton, Louisiana	New Orleans, Louisiana, Transferred to Elmira Prison, New York, November 19, 1864	Exchanged February 25, 1865 at Boulware's or Cox Wharf on the James River, Virginia
Rowe, John W. Sergeant	20	June 10, 1861, Burgaw, North Carolina	Co. K, 3rd North Carolina Infantry	May 12, 1864, Near Spotsylvania County Court House, Virginia	Point Lookout, Maryland, transferred to Elmira Prison, NY, August 14, 1864	Exchanged February 13, 1865 at Boulware's wharf on the James River, Virginia
Rowe, Noah J. Private	35	October 16, 1861, Newton, North Carolina	Co. A, 12th North Carolina Infantry	May 12, 1864, Spotsylvania Court House, Virginia	Point Lookout, Maryland, transferred to Elmira Prison, NY, August 14, 1864	Oath of Allegiance June 27, 1865
Rowe, Samuel M. Corporal	28	March 20, 1861, E. H. Rowe's Store, Virginia	Co. F, 26th North Carolina Infantry	June 17, 1864, Near Petersburg, Virginia	Point Lookout, Maryland, transferred to Elmira Prison, NY, July 30, 1864	Oath of Allegiance June 16, 1865
Rowe, Sidney H. Corporal	26	June 6, 1861, Newton, North Carolina	Co. A, 12th North Carolina Infantry	May 12, 1864, Spotsylvania Court House, Virginia	Point Lookout, Maryland, transferred to Elmira Prison, NY, August 14, 1864	Died December 20, 1864 of Pneumonia, Grave No. 1077
Rowe, Wiley Sergeant	Unk	Unknown	Co. B, 11th North Carolina Infantry	August 8, 1863, Big Black, Mississippi	Point Lookout, Maryland, transferred to Elmira Prison, NY, August 18, 1864	Exchanged October 29, 1864, at Venus Point, Savannah River, GA.

Name & Rank	Age	Enlisted	Regiment and State	Where Captured	Prison	Remarks
Rowell, Henry A. Private	Unk	April 31, 1862, Camp Leon, Madison, Florida	Co. D, 5th Florida Infantry	May 12, 1864, Spotsylvania Court House, Virginia	Point Lookout, Maryland, transferred to Elmira Prison, NY, July 30, 1864	Exchanged February 20, 1865 at Boulware's or Cox Wharf on the James River, Virginia
Rowell, J. Private	Unk	Unknown	Co. H, 16th Georgia Infantry	May 6, 1864, Wilderness, Virginia	Point Lookout, Maryland, transferred to Elmira Prison, NY, August 14, 1864	Oath of Allegiance June 14, 1865
Rowell, James V. Private	Unk	November 10, 1861, Camp Green, James Island, South Carolina	Co. H, 23rd South Carolina Infantry	June 17, 1864, Near Petersburg, Virginia	Point Lookout, Maryland, transferred to Elmira Prison, NY, July 30, 1864	Died December 20, 1864 of Pleuro Pneumonia, Grave No. 1073
Rowland, Benjamin W. Private	18	August 2, 1863, Fort Caswell, Brunswick County, North Carolina	Co. F, 36th Regiment 2nd North Carolina Artillery	January 15, 1865, Fort Fisher, North Carolina	February 1, 1865, Elmira Prison Camp, New York	Oath of Allegiance June 12, 1865
Rowland, Hinton A. Private	18	July 1, 1863, Raleigh, North Carolina	Co. J, 1st North Carolina Infantry	May 12, 1864, Spotsylvania Court House, Virginia	Point Lookout, Maryland, transferred to Elmira Prison, NY, August 6, 1864	Died March 19, 1865 of Pneumonia, Grave No. 1576. Name Rollan on Headstone.
Rowland, W. R. Private	Unk	March 18, 1862, Charleston, South Carolina	Co. G, 22nd South Carolina Infantry	July 30, 1864, Petersburg, Virginia	Point Lookout, Maryland, transferred to Elmira Prison, NY, August 12, 1864	Oath of Allegiance May 19, 1865
Rowland, William E. Private	24	March 20, 1862, union County, North Carolina	Co. J, 53rd North Carolina Infantry	July 12, 1864, Near Washington, DC	Old Capital Prison, Washington DC. Transferred to Elmira Prison Camp, New York, July 25, 1864.	Oath of Allegiance June 19, 1865
Rowling, John Private	25	March 8, 1862, Lake City, Florida	Co. B, 5th Florida Infantry	May 12, 1864, Spotsylvania Court House, Virginia	Point Lookout, Maryland, transferred to Elmira Prison, NY, August 12, 1864	Oath of Allegiance June 23, 1865

Name & Rank	Age	Enlisted	Regiment and State	Where Captured	Prison	Remarks
Rowsey, Henry A. Private	24	July 27, 1861, Big Island, Virginia	Co. C, 58th Virginia Infantry	May 20, 1864, Spotsylvania Court House, Virginia	Point Lookout, Maryland, transferred to Elmira Prison, NY, July 3, 1864	Died October 22, 1864 of Pneumonia, Grave No. 863
Royal, Archibald Private	26	April 24, 1862, Clinton, North Carolina	Co. D, 46th North Carolina Infantry	May 12, 1864, Spotsylvania Court House, Virginia	Point Lookout, Maryland, transferred to Elmira Prison, NY, July 30, 1864	Exchanged September 18, 1864 at Akins Landing on the James River, Virginia
Royal, Molton Private	22	October 31, 1862, Fort Fisher, New Hanover County, North Carolina	Co. C, 36th Regiment 2nd North Carolina Artillery	January 15, 1865, Fort Fisher, North Carolina	February 1, 1865, Elmira Prison Camp, New York	Exchanged March 2, 1865 at Akins Landing on the James River, Virginia
Royal, Noah Private	Unk	July 1, 1861, Portsmouth, Virginia	Co. E, Cobb's Legion Georgia	August 16, 1864, Front Royal, Virginia	Old Capital Prison, Washington, DC transferred to Elmira Prison, NY, August 29, 1864	Died February 2, 1865 of Pneumonia, Grave No. 1767
Royal, Ollin Private	35	February 18, 1863, Sampson County, North Carolina	Co. A, 36th Regiment 2nd North Carolina Artillery	January 15, 1865, Fort Fisher, North Carolina	February 1, 1865, Elmira Prison Camp, New York	Oath of Allegiance June 12, 1865
Royal, Peter J. Sergeant	Unk	April 20, 1861, Petersburg, Virginia	Capt. Pegram's Battery Virginia Light Artillery	July 30, 1864, Petersburg, Virginia	Point Lookout, Maryland, transferred to Elmira Prison, NY, August 12, 1864	Exchanged March 14, 1865 at Boulware's Wharf on the James River, Virginia
Royal, William M. Private	28	May 1, 1862, Jefferson, North Carolina	Co. A, 37th North Carolina Infantry	May 12, 1864, Spotsylvania Court House, Virginia	Point Lookout, Maryland, transferred to Elmira Prison, NY, August 12, 1864	Died March 19, 1865 of Diarrhea, Grave No. 1569
Royal, Wilson Private	Unk	January 14, 1864, Black Water, North Carolina	Co. J, 61st North Carolina Infantry	June 16, 1864, Petersburg, Virginia	Point Lookout, Maryland, transferred to Elmira Prison, NY, July 23, 1864	Died September 18, 1864 of Chronic Diarrhea, Grave No. 315. Name Joseph Ryals on Headstone.

Name & Rank	Age	Enlisted	Regiment and State	Where Captured	Prison	Remarks
Royals, William B. Private	Unk	August 1, 1863, Dawson, Georgia	Co. H, 64th Georgia Infantry	June 17, 1864, Petersburg, Virginia	Point Lookout, Maryland, transferred to Elmira Prison, NY, July 30, 1864	Died November 28, 1864 of Pleuro Pneumonia, Grave No. 988
Royster, Charles E. Sergeant	Unk	June 7, 1862, Nashville, Tennessee	Co. A, 23rd Tennessee Infantry	June 17, 1864, Petersburg, Virginia	Point Lookout, Maryland, transferred to Elmira Prison, NY, July 30, 1864	Exchanged February 25, 1865 at Boulware's or Cox Wharf on the James River, Virginia
Rozier, Amos L. Private	28	April 7, 1862, Fayetteville, North Carolina	Co. D, 51st North Carolina Infantry	May 16, 1864, Near Drury's Bluff, Virginia	Point Lookout, Maryland, transferred to Elmira Prison, NY, August 18, 1864	Exchanged March 2, 1865. Died March 26, 1865 of Chronic Diarrhea, Place Unknown.
Rozier, Evander C. Private	Unk	December 1, 1862, Howellsville, North Carolina	Co. D, 51st North Carolina Infantry	June 1, 1864, Cold Harbor, Virginia	Point Lookout, Maryland, transferred to Elmira Prison, NY, July 17, 1864	Died November 23, 1864 of Pneumonia, Grave No. 922
Rozier, Robert A. Private	Unk	April 26, 1862, Camp Holmes, Crossroads, North Carolina	Co. E, 51st North Carolina Infantry	June 16, 1864, Near Petersburg, Virginia	Point Lookout, Maryland, transferred to Elmira Prison, NY, July 12, 1864	Exchanged March 2, 1865 at Akins Landing on the James River, Virginia
Rozier, Rueben Private	43	August 1, 1863, Fort Fisher, New Hanover County, North Carolina	Co. K, 40th 3rd Regiment North Carolina Artillery	January 15, 1865, Fort Fisher, North Carolina	February 1, 1865, Elmira Prison Camp, New York	Oath of Allegiance June 12, 1865
Rucker, S. B. Private	Unk	March 12, 1864, Amherst, Virginia	Co. F, 6th Virginia Cavalry	June 11, 1864, Louisa Court House, Trevilian Station, Virginia	Point Lookout, Maryland, transferred to Elmira Prison, NY, August 12, 1864	Oath of Allegiance June 14, 1865
Rudaciller, Isaac Private	Unk	June 17, 1861, Front Royal, Virginia	Co. D, 49th Virginia Cavalry	May 31, 1864, Cold Harbor, Virginia	Point Lookout, Maryland, transferred to Elmira Prison, NY, July 12, 1864	Oath of Allegiance June 16, 1965

Name & Rank	Age	Enlisted	Regiment and State	Where Captured	Prison	Remarks
Rudd, Ruben A. Private	42	September 1, 1863, Mecklenburg, Virginia	Co. B, 34th Virginia Infantry	June 18, 1864, Petersburg, Virginia	Point Lookout, Maryland, transferred to Elmira Prison, NY, July 30, 1864	Oath of Allegiance June 21, 1865
Rudder, William H. Private	17	March 5, 1862, Milton, North Carolina	Co. J, 45th North Carolina Infantry	May 10, 1864, Spotsylvania Court House, Virginia	Point Lookout, Maryland, transferred to Elmira Prison, NY, August 6, 1864	Exchanged March 14, 1865 at Boulware's Wharf on the James River, Virginia
Ruddle, James H. Private	Unk	Unknown	Co. F, 62nd Georgia Infantry	July 16, 1864, Near Harpers Ferry, Loudoun County, Virginia	Old Capital Prison, Washington DC. Transferred to Elmira Prison Camp, New York, July 25, 1864.	Oath of Allegiance June 27, 1865
Rudisail, G. A. Corporal	Unk	June 27, 1863, Spartanburg, South Carolina	Co. H, 6th South Carolina Cavalry	June 11, 1864, Trevilian Station, Louisa Court House, Virginia	Point Lookout, Maryland, transferred to Elmira Prison, NY, July 25, 1864	Died August 19, 1864 of Chronic Diarrhea, Grave No. 119
Rudisell, Eli Private	Unk	August 12, 1862, Statesville, North Carolina	Co. H, 37th North Carolina Infantry	July 29, 1864, Petersburg, Virginia	Point Lookout, Maryland, transferred to Elmira Prison, NY, August 12, 1864	Oath of Allegiance May 29, 1865
Rudisil, Wiley V. Corporal	Unk	January 14, 1862, Camp Hampton, South Carolina	Co. D, 17th South Carolina Infantry	July 30, 1864, Petersburg, Virginia	Point Lookout, Maryland, transferred to Elmira Prison, NY, August 12, 1864	Died May 28, 1865 of Chronic Diarrhea, Grave No. 2911
Ruels, J. W. Private	Unk	Unable to Find Soldier's Record	Co. E, 31st North Carolina Infantry	June 1, 1864, Gaines Mill, Cold Harbor, Virginia	Transferred from Point Lookout Prison, Maryland, July 12, 1864. Train Never Arrived at Elmira Prison, New York.	Died July 15, 1864 in Train Wreck at Shohola, Pennsylvania.
Ruff, Benjamin A. Private	25	May 13, 1862, Goldsboro, North Carolina	Co. A, 3rd North Carolina Infantry	May 12, 1864, Near Spotsylvania County Court House, Virginia	Point Lookout, Maryland, transferred to Elmira Prison, NY, August 14, 1864	Oath of Allegiance June 17, 1865

Name & Rank	Age	Enlisted	Regiment and State	Where Captured	Prison	Remarks
Ruff, James R. Private	31	May 2, 1862, Maysville, North Carolina	Co. F, 61st North Carolina Infantry	June 16, 1864, Petersburg, Virginia	Point Lookout, Maryland, transferred to Elmira Prison, NY, July 25, 1864	Oath of Allegiance June 30, 1865
Ruff, John Private	26	April 23, 1861, Snow Hill, North Carolina	Co. A, 3rd North Carolina Infantry	May 12, 1864, Near Spotsylvania County Court House, Virginia	Point Lookout, Maryland, transferred to Elmira Prison, NY, August 14, 1864	Oath of Allegiance June 23, 1865
Ruff, Thomas Private	17	July 7, 1861, Camp Moore, New Orleans, Louisiana	Co. C, 9th Louisiana Infantry	July 16, 1864, Loudon County, Virginia	Old Capital Prison, Washington DC. Transferred to Elmira Prison Camp, New York, July 25, 1864.	Exchanged February 25, 1865 at Boulware's or Cox Wharf on the James River, Virginia
Rumage, Nathaniel Private	33	August 8, 1862, Stanley County, North Carolina	Co. F, 5th North Carolina Infantry	May 20, 1864, Spotsylvania Court House, Virginia	Point Lookout, Maryland, transferred to Elmira Prison, NY, July 3, 1864	Died October 3, 1864 of Chronic Diarrhea, Grave No. 617
Rumsey, Harris M. Private	Unk	July 13, 1861, Hartwell, Georgia	Co. C, 16th Georgia Infantry	August 16, 1864, Front Royal, Virginia	Old Capital Prison, Washington, DC transferred to Elmira Prison, NY, August 29, 1864	Exchanged February 13, 1865. Died February 25, 1865 of Chronic Diarrhea at Jackson Hospital, Richmond, VA.
Runkle, Charles E. Corporal	Unk	April 16, 1862, Rudes Hill, Virginia	Co. F, 2nd Virginia Infantry	May 12, 1864, Near Spotsylvania Court House, Virginia	Point Lookout, Maryland, transferred to Elmira Prison, NY, August 6, 1864	Died September 16, 1864 of Continued Fever, Grave No. 307
Ruppe, James D. Corporal	Unk	May 1, 1862, Adams Run, South Carolina	Co. K, Holcombe Legion, South Carolina Infantry	May 7, 1864, Stony Creek, Virginia	Point Lookout, Maryland, transferred to Elmira Prison, NY, August 17, 1864	Exchanged February 20, 1865 at Boulware's or Cox Wharf on the James River, Virginia
Ruppe, William W. Corporal	Unk	May 1, 1862, Adams Run, South Carolina	Co. K, Holcombe Legion, South Carolina Infantry	May 7, 1864, Stony Creek, Virginia	Point Lookout, Maryland, transferred to Elmira Prison, NY, August 17, 1864	Died September 9, 1864 of Chronic Diarrhea, Grave No. 204

Name & Rank	Age	Enlisted	Regiment and State	Where Captured	Prison	Remarks
Rush, Alfred C. Private	18	May 9, 1862, Asheboro, North Carolina	Co. K, 54th North Carolina Infantry	November 7, 1863, Rappahannock Station, Virginia	Point Lookout, Maryland, transferred to Elmira Prison, NY, July 12, 1864	Oath of Allegiance June 19, 1965
Rush, Henry, B. Sergeant	20	June 5, 1861, Asheboro, North Carolina	Co. I, 22nd North Carolina Infantry	May 24, 1864, Hanover Junction, Virginia	Point Lookout, Maryland, transferred to Elmira Prison, NY, July 11, 1864	Oath of Allegiance May 17, 1865
Rush, J. Private	Unk	Unknown	Co. H, 16th Georgia Infantry	May 6, 1864, Wilderness, Virginia	Point Lookout, Maryland, transferred to Elmira Prison, NY, August 14, 1864	Died March 25, 1865 of Diarrhea, Grave No. 2459. Name Rutherford on Headstone.
Rush, Robert T. Private	18	July 20, 1863, Fort Branch, Near Hamilton, Martin County, North Carolina	Co. G, 40th 3rd Regiment North Carolina Artillery	January 15, 1865, Fort Fisher, North Carolina	February 1, 1865, Elmira Prison Camp, New York	Exchanged March 2, 1865 at Akins Landing on the James River, Virginia
Rushing, James B. Private	Unk	April 20, 1862, Marion Court House, South Carolina	Co. D, 25th South Carolina Infantry	January 15, 1865, Fort Fisher, North Carolina	February 1, 1865, Elmira Prison Camp, New York	Exchanged February 20, 1865 at Boulware's or Cox Wharf on the James River, Virginia
Rusmisle, John J. Sergeant	Unk	June 11, 1861, Hevener's Store, Virginia	Co. F, 25th Virginia Infantry	May 5, 1864, Wilderness, Virginia	Point Lookout, Maryland, transferred to Elmira Prison, NY, August 14, 1864	Oath of Allegiance June 27, 1865
Russ, Isham Private	Unk	December 20, 1863, Camp Harleston, Ashford, South Carolina	Co. D, 6th South Carolina Cavalry	June 11, 1864, Trevilian Station, Louisa Court House, Virginia	Point Lookout, Maryland, transferred to Elmira Prison, NY, July 25, 1864	Exchanged March 14, 1865 at Boulware's Wharf on the James River, Virginia
Russ, William Corporal	18	June 22, 1861, Wilmington, North Carolina	Co. C, 8th, North Carolina Infantry	May 31, 1864, Cold Harbor, Virginia	Point Lookout, Maryland, transferred to Elmira Prison, NY, July 12, 1864	Died April 8, 1865 of Variola (Smallpox), Grave No. 2622
Russ, William Charles Private	18	June 24, 1861, Williamston, North Carolina	Co. H, 1st North Carolina Infantry	May 12, 1864, Wilderness, Spotsylvania Court House, Virginia	Point Lookout, Maryland, transferred to Elmira Prison, NY, August 6, 1864	Oath of Allegiance June 14, 1865

Name & Rank	Age	Enlisted	Regiment and State	Where Captured	Prison	Remarks
Russ, William H. Private	17	January 16, 1864, Fort Campbell, Brunswick County, North Carolina	Co. G, 36th Regiment 2nd North Carolina Artillery	January 15, 1865, Fort Fisher, North Carolina	February 1, 1865, Elmira Prison Camp, New York	Oath of Allegiance July 7, 1865
Russau, Ezekiel Private	Unk	June 15, 1861, Jones County, Georgia	Co. A, 12th Georgia Infantry	May 10, 1864, Spotsylvania Court House, Virginia	Point Lookout, Maryland, transferred to Elmira Prison, NY, July 30, 1864	Exchanged October 29, 1864, at Venus Point, Savannah River, GA.
Russell, Arnold J. Private	Unk	May 16, 1861, Montgomery, Alabama	Co. K, 5th Alabama Infantry	May 5, 1864, Wilderness, Virginia	Point Lookout, Maryland, transferred to Elmira Prison, NY, August 17, 1864	Exchanged February 13, 1865 at Boulware's wharf on the James River, Virginia
Russell, Benjamin F. Corporal	30	February 20, 1862, Washington, North Carolina	Co. F, 3rd North Carolina Infantry	May 12, 1864, Near Spotsylvania County Court House, Virginia	Point Lookout, Maryland, transferred to Elmira Prison, NY, August 14, 1864	Oath of Allegiance July 11, 1865
Russell, Charles Private	30	March 27, 1862, Salisbury, North Carolina	Co. D, 42nd North Carolina Infantry	June 3, 1864, Gaines Mill Cold Harbor, Virginia	Point Lookout, Maryland, transferred to Elmira Prison, NY, August 12, 1864	Oath of Allegiance June 21, 1865
Russell, David D. Private	Unk	November 1, 1863, Raleigh, North Carolina	Co. H, 21st North Carolina Infantry	August 22, 1864, Charlestown, Virginia	Old Capital Prison, Washington, DC transferred to Elmira Prison, NY, August 29, 1864	Died December 25, 1864 of Pneumonia, Grave No. 1108
Russell, E. F. Corporal	Unk	May 16, 1861, Alisona, Tennessee	Co. A, 17th Tennessee Infantry	June 17, 1864, Petersburg, Virginia	Point Lookout, Maryland, transferred to Elmira Prison, NY, July 30, 1864	Exchanged March 2, 1865 at Akins Landing on the James River, Virginia
Russell, James B. Private	Unk	June 22, 1862, Camp Norton, South Carolina	Co. A, 1st South Carolina Infantry	July 14, 1863, Falling Waters, Maryland	Point Lookout, Maryland, transferred to Elmira Prison, NY, August 18, 1864	Died September 13, 1864 of Chronic Diarrhea, Grave No. 267

Name & Rank	Age	Enlisted	Regiment and State	Where Captured	Prison	Remarks
Russell, James Hannibal Private	23	May 4, 1861, Warrenton, North Carolina	Co. C, 12th North Carolina Infantry	October 3, 1864, Brandy Station, Virginia	Old Capital Prison, Washington, DC transferred to Elmira Prison, NY, August 27, 1864	Oath of Allegiance June 19, 1865
Russell, Joel Private	32	August 8, 1862, Raleigh, North Carolina	Co. B, 5th North Carolina Infantry	May 12, 1864, Spotsylvania Court House, Virginia	Point Lookout, Maryland, transferred to Elmira Prison, NY, August 6, 1864	Died February 4, 1865 of Chronic Diarrhea, Grave No. 1744
Russell, John Private	42	July 28, 1863, Fort Branch, Martin County, North Carolina	Co. G, 40th Regiment, 3rd North Carolina Artillery	January 15, 1865, Fort Fisher, North Carolina	January 30, 1865, Elmira Prison Camp, New York.	Died March 4, 1865 of Pneumonia, Grave No. 1975
Russell, L. W. Private	Unk	August 14, 1862, Statesville, North Carolina	Co. G, 18th North Carolina Infantry	May 12, 1864, Spotsylvania Court House, Virginia	Point Lookout, Maryland, transferred to Elmira Prison, NY, July 17, 1864	Exchanged March 14, 1865 at Boulware's Wharf on the James River, Virginia
Russell, Patrick F. Private	Unk	May 15, 1861, Thompson's Crossroads, Virginia	Co. A, 23rd Virginia Infantry	May 17, 1864, Spotsylvania Court House, Virginia	Point Lookout, Maryland, transferred to Elmira Prison, NY, July 3, 1864	Oath of Allegiance June 16, 1865
Russell, Warren Private	Unk	May 5, 1864, Petersburg, Virginia	Co. D, 3rd Battalion Virginia Reserves	June 9, 1864, Near Petersburg, Virginia	Point Lookout, Maryland, transferred to Elmira Prison, NY, July 23, 1864	Oath of Allegiance August 25, 1864. Early Release per Lincoln's Proclamation, 12/8/1863.
Russell, William Private	Unk	February 15, 1861, Gloucester Point, Virginia	Co. A, 26th Virginia Infantry	June 15, 1864, Near Petersburg, Virginia	Point Lookout, Maryland, transferred to Elmira Prison, NY, July 12, 1864	Exchanged March 14, 1865 at Boulware's Wharf on the James River, Virginia
Rust, Thomas G. Private	23	April 18, 1861, Jefferson Court House, Virginia	Co. A, 2nd Virginia Infantry	May 12, 1864, Near Spotsylvania Court House, Virginia	Point Lookout, Maryland, transferred to Elmira Prison, NY, August 6, 1864	Oath of Allegiance May 29, 1865

Name & Rank	Age	Enlisted	Regiment and State	Where Captured	Prison	Remarks
Rustin, Benjamin W. Private	Unk	August 29, 1863, Bryan County, Georgia	Co. H, 7th Georgia Cavalry	June 11, 1864, Trevilian Station, Louisa Court House, Virginia	Point Lookout, Maryland, transferred to Elmira Prison, NY, July 25, 1864	Died August 19, 1864 of Remittent Fever, Grave No. 120
Ruth, A. J. Private	Unk	Unknown	Co. E, 11th South Carolina Infantry	June 24, 1864, Near Petersburg, Virginia	Point Lookout, Maryland, transferred to Elmira Prison, NY, August 18, 1864	Exchanged March 2, 1865 at Akins Landing on the James River, Virginia
Rutherford, J. Private	Unk	Unknown	Co. H, 16th Georgia Infantry	May 6, 1864, wilderness, Virginia	Point Lookout, Maryland, transferred to Elmira Prison, New York, August 14, 1864	Oath of Allegiance June 14, 1865
Rutherford, John A. Private	22	April 20, 1862, Swift River Gap, Virginia	Co. E, 11th Virginia Cavalry	September 14, 1863, Near Culpepper Court House, Virginia	Point Lookout, Maryland, transferred to Elmira Prison, NY, August 18, 1864	Exchanged March 10, 1865 at Boulware's Wharf on the James River, Virginia
Rutherford, John C. Corporal	Unk	July 31, 1861, Staunton, Virginia	Co. F, 52nd Virginia Infantry	May 31, 1864 Mechanicsville, Virginia	Point Lookout, Maryland, transferred to Elmira Prison, NY, July 9, 1864	Oath of Allegiance June 30, 1865
Rutherford, John James Sergeant	Unk	July 17, 1861, Wyhteville, Virginia	Co. B, 50th Virginia Infantry	May 12, 1864, Spotsylvania Court House, Virginia	Point Lookout, Maryland, transferred to Elmira Prison, NY, August 2, 1864	Transferred For Exchange October 11, 1864 to Point Lookout Prison Camp, MD. Nothing Further.
Rutland, John D. Private	Unk	July 29, 1863, Quincy, Florida	Co. D, 64th Georgia Infantry	August 16, 1864, New Market, Virginia	Old Capital Prison, Washington, DC transferred to Elmira Prison, NY, August 27, 1864	Exchanged March 2, 1865 at Akins Landing on the James River, Virginia
Rutland, William T. Private	Unk	June 11, 1861, Drayton, Georgia	Co. F, 12th Georgia Infantry	May 10, 1864, Spotsylvania Court House, Virginia	Point Lookout, Maryland, transferred to Elmira Prison, NY, July 25, 1864	Exchanged February 20, 1865 at Boulware's or Cox Wharf on the James River, Virginia

Name & Rank	Age	Enlisted	Regiment and State	Where Captured	Prison	Remarks
Rutledge, George Private	Unk	July 7, 1861, Camp Moore, Louisiana	Co. E, 9th Louisiana Infantry	May 12, 1864, Spotsylvania Court House, Virginia	Point Lookout, Maryland, transferred to Elmira Prison, NY, August 17, 1864	Exchanged October 29, 1864, at Venus Point, Savannah River, GA.
Rutledge, James Private	Unk	July 3, 1861, Eufaula, Alabama	Co. K, 15th Alabama Infantry	May 12, 1864, Spotsylvania Court House, Virginia	Point Lookout, Maryland, transferred to Elmira Prison, NY, July 23, 1864	Oath of Allegiance March 24, 1865
Rutledge, Joseph M. Private	Unk	August 11, 1861, Gwinnett, Georgia	Co. H, 16th Georgia Infantry	August 16, 1864, Front Royal, Virginia	Old Capital Prison, Washington, DC transferred to Elmira Prison, NY, August 29, 1864	Oath of Allegiance June 23, 1865
Ryan, Isaac Corporal	Unk	April 16, 1862, Rudes Hill, Virginia	Co. F, 2nd Virginia Infantry	May 12, 1864, Near Spotsylvania Court House, Virginia	Point Lookout, Maryland, transferred to Elmira Prison, NY, August 6, 1864	Oath of Allegiance June 19, 1865
Ryan, J. C. Private	Unk	Unknown	Co. L, 16th North Carolina Infantry	July 14, 1863, Falling Waters, Maryland	Point Lookout, Maryland, transferred to Elmira Prison, NY, August 18, 1864	Died September 17, 1864 of Chronic Diarrhea, Grave No. 317
Ryan, James T. Private	18	July 1, 1863, Fort Caswell, North Carolina	Co. F, 36th Regiment, 2nd North Carolina Artillery	January 15, 1865, Fort Fisher, North Carolina	Elmira Prison Camp New York February 1, 1865	Oath of Allegiance July 7, 1865
Ryan, John Sergeant	Unk	June 19, 1861, Camp Moore, Louisiana	Co. J, 8th Louisiana Infantry	May 12, 1864, Spotsylvania Court House, Virginia	Point Lookout, Maryland, transferred to Elmira Prison, NY, August 17, 1864	Exchanged February 25, 1865 at Boulware's or Cox Wharf on the James River, Virginia
Ryan, John Private	Unk	August 1, 1863, Charleston, South Carolina	Co. G, 27th South Carolina Infantry	June 24, 1864, Near Petersburg, Virginia	Point Lookout, Maryland, transferred to Elmira Prison, NY, August 18, 1864	Exchanged March 2, 1865 at Akins Landing on the James River, Virginia

Name & Rank	Age	Enlisted	Regiment and State	Where Captured	Prison	Remarks
Ryan, P. H. Corporal	Unk	April 8, 1861, Camden, South Carolina	Co. E, 2nd South Carolina Infantry	July 29, 1864, Petersburg, Virginia	Point Lookout, Maryland, transferred to Elmira Prison, NY, August 12, 1864	Exchanged March 14, 1865 at Boulware's Wharf on the James River, Virginia
Ryan, Philip Private	Unk	July 22, 1861, Camp Moore, Louisiana	Co. B, 10th Louisiana Infantry	May 12, 1864, Spotsylvania Court House, Virginia	Point Lookout, Maryland, transferred to Elmira Prison, NY, July 25, 1864	Oath of Allegiance May 17, 1865
Ryan, Samuel E. Private	20	July 13, 1862, Leesburg, Virginia	Co. H, 8th Virginia Infantry	June 14, 1864, Leesburg, Virginia	Point Lookout, Maryland, transferred to Elmira Prison, NY, July 25, 1864	Oath of Allegiance May 19, 1865
Rykard, John H. Private	Unk	August 15, 1863, Abbeville, South Carolina	Co. C, 6th South Carolina Cavalry	June 11, 1864, Trevilian Station, Louisa Court House, Virginia	Point Lookout, Maryland, transferred to Elmira Prison, NY, July 25, 1864	Died September 6, 1864 of Typhoid Fever, Grave No. 243
Ryland, Talbot Sergeant	24	April 21, 1862, Jonesboro, Tennessee	Co. D, 63rd Tennessee Infantry	June 17, 1864, Petersburg, Virginia	Point Lookout, Maryland, transferred to Elmira Prison, NY, July 30, 1864	Exchanged February 25, 1865 at Boulware's or Cox Wharf on the James River, Virginia
Rylander, Joel F. Private	Unk	September 11, 1863, Fort Morgan, Alabama	Co. A, 1st Battalion Alabama Artillery	August 23, 1864, Fort Morgan, Alabama	New Orleans, Louisiana transferred to Elmira Prison, NY, December 4, 1864.	Died April 9, 1865 of Chronic Diarrhea, Grave No. 2604
Rylander, John D. P. Sergeant	Unk	September 15, 1862, Loundes, Alabama	Co. A, 1st Alabama Artillery	August 23, 1864, Fort Morgan, Alabama.	New Orleans, Louisiana transferred to Elmira Prison, NY, December 4, 1864.	Oath of Allegiance May 17, 1865

Name & Rank	Age	Enlisted	Regiment and State	Where Captured	Prison	Remarks
Saddler, Green B. Private	Unk	July 1, 1861, Lafayette, Alabama	Co. E, 14th Alabama Infantry	May 31, 1864, Mechanicsville, Virginia	Point Lookout, Maryland, transferred to Elmira Prison, NY, July 12, 1864	Died December 28, 1864 of Pneumonia, Grave No. 1303

Name & Rank	Age	Enlisted	Regiment and State	Where Captured	Prison	Remarks
Sadler, Absalom M. Private	Unk	May 28, 1861, Matthews Court House, Virginia	Co. D, 26th Virginia Infantry	May 8, 1864, Nottoway, Virginia	Point Lookout, Maryland, transferred to Elmira Prison, NY, August 17, 1864	Exchanged March 2, 1865 at Akins Landing on the James River, Virginia
Sadler, B. F. Private	30	August 20, 1862, Camp Moore, Louisiana	Co. B, 3rd Battalion Louisiana Cavalry	August 25, 1864, Near Clinton, Louisiana	New Orleans, Louisiana, Transferred to Elmira Prison, New York, November 19, 1864	Exchanged February 25, 1865 at Boulware's or Cox Wharf on the James River, Virginia
Sadler, Isaac Private	Unk	December 28, 1861, Anderson District, South Carolina	Co. E, 20th South Carolina Infantry	July 29, 1864, Petersburg, Virginia	Point Lookout, Maryland, transferred to Elmira Prison, NY, August 12, 1864	Transferred for Exchange 2/20/65. Died 2/20/65. Record has "Dead on Boat".
Sadler, John Private	Unk	August 20, 1862, Camp Moore, Louisiana	Co. B, Ogden's Louisiana Cavalry	July 5, 1863, Pearl River, Louisiana	New Orleans, Louisiana, Transferred to Elmira Prison, New York, November 19, 1864	Exchanged February 25, 1865 at Boulware's or Cox Wharf on the James River, Virginia
Sadler, Robert Private	37	February 28, 1862, Young's Crossroads, North Carolina	Co. J, 23rd North Carolina Infantry	May 12, 1864, Near Spotsylvania Court House, Virginia	Point Lookout, Maryland, transferred to Elmira Prison, NY, August 14, 1864	Exchanged October 29, 1864, at Venus Point, Savannah River, GA.
Sadler, William Private	Unk	June 30, 1862, Anderson District, South Carolina	Co. E, 20th South Carolina Infantry	July 29, 1864, Petersburg, Virginia	Point Lookout, Maryland, transferred to Elmira Prison, NY, August 12, 1864	Died January 19, 1865 of Chronic Diarrhea, Grave No. 1205
Safiet, Alexander C. Private	21	August 6, 1861, Mount Pleasant North Carolina	Co. H, 8th North Carolina Infantry	May 31, 1864, Cold Harbor, Virginia	Point Lookout, Maryland, transferred to Elmira Prison, NY, July 12, 1864	Oath of Allegiance July 7, 1865
Sahr, Simon M. Private	Unk	July 22, 1861, Camp Moore, Louisiana	Co. A, 10th Louisiana Infantry	May 12, 1864, Spotsylvania Court House, Virginia	Point Lookout, Maryland, transferred to Elmira Prison, NY, July 25, 1864	Oath of Allegiance May 29, 1865

Name & Rank	Age	Enlisted	Regiment and State	Where Captured	Prison	Remarks
Sale, William J. Sergeant	18	April 20, 1861, Belle Roi, Virginia	Co. A, 26th Virginia Infantry	June 15, 1864, Petersburg, Virginia	Point Lookout, Maryland, transferred to Elmira Prison, NY, July 30, 1864	Oath of Allegiance June 16, 1865
Salley, Nathan A. Private	Unk	Unknown	Co. A, 50th Virginia Infantry	May 12, 1864, Spotsylvania Court House, Virginia	Point Lookout, Maryland, transferred to Elmira Prison, NY, August 2, 1864	Oath of Allegiance June 16, 1865
Salmon, Rueben Private	21	March 1, 1862, Bane Creek, North Carolina	Co. E, 44th North Carolina Infantry	June 2, 1864, Gaines Farm Cold Harbor, Virginia	Point Lookout, Maryland, transferred to Elmira Prison, NY, July 12, 1864	Exchanged March 2, 1865 at Akins Landing on the James River, Virginia
Salmon, Sidney Private	18	March 26, 1863, Chatham County, North Carolina	Co. G, 40th Regiment, 3rd North Carolina Artillery	January 15, 1865, Fort Fisher, North Carolina	February 1, 1865, Elmira Prison Camp, New York	Died of unknown Disease March 2, 1865. Could find no grave In Woodlawn Cemetery, Elmira, NY
Salmons, Nelson Private	Unk	August 18, 1861, Camp Moore, Louisiana	Co. C, 12th Louisiana Infantry	May 16, 1863, Baker's Creek, Champion Hill, Mississippi	Point Lookout, Maryland, transferred to Elmira Prison, NY, August 18, 1864	Exchanged March 10, 1865 at Boulware's wharf on the James River, Virginia
Salter, A. L. Private	Unk	Unknown	Co. H, 6th Alabama Infantry	May 20, 1864, Spotsylvania Court House, Virginia	Point Lookout Prison. Transferred to Elmira Prison, New York, July 6, 1864.	Exchanged March 2, 1865 at Akins Landing on the James River, Virginia
Salyer, Jesse Private	Unk	August 15, 1862, Bristol, Tennessee	Co. F, 37th North Carolina Infantry	May 24, 1864, Hanover Junction, Virginia	Point Lookout, Maryland, transferred to Elmira Prison, NY, July 25, 1864	Oath of Allegiance June 30, 1865
Sammons, Charles B. Private	Unk	May 1, 1862 White Sulfur Springs, Virginia	Co. C, 22nd Virginia Infantry	July 14, 1864, Near Washington, DC	Old Capital Prison, Washington, DC, transferred to Elmira Prison, NY, July 23, 1864	Oath of Allegiance June 21, 1865

Name & Rank	Age	Enlisted	Regiment and State	Where Captured	Prison	Remarks
Sampkin, J. C. Private	Unk	Unknown	Co. E, 40th Virginia Infantry	June 2, 1864, Near Old Church, Cold Harbor, Virginia	Point Lookout, Maryland, transferred to Elmira Prison, NY, July 12, 1864	Exchanged March 14, 1865 at Boulware's Wharf on the James River, Virginia
Sampson, John W. Private	28	June 4, 1861, Wilmington, North Carolina	Co. F, 3rd North Carolina Infantry	May 12, 1864, Near Spotsylvania County Court House, Virginia	Point Lookout, Maryland, transferred to Elmira Prison, NY, August 14, 1864	Oath of Allegiance May 19, 1865
Sampson, William J. Private	Unk	April 15, 1864, Rudes Hill, Virginia	Co. A, 2nd Virginia Infantry	May 12, 1864, Near Spotsylvania Court House, Virginia	Point Lookout, Maryland, transferred to Elmira Prison, NY, August 6, 1864	Oath of Allegiance June 27, 1865
Sams, William A. Private	17	September 1, 1862, Francisco, Stokes County, North Carolina	Co. A, 2nd Battalion North Carolina Infantry	May 20, 1864, Spotsylvania Court House, Virginia	Point Lookout, Maryland, transferred to Elmira Prison, NY, July 3, 1864	Oath of Allegiance May 21, 1865
Samuel, Albert H. Private	20	July 25, 1863, Danbury, North Carolina	Co. G, 21st North Carolina Infantry	July 10, 1864, Harper's Ferry, Virginia	Old Capital Prison, Washington, DC, transferred to Elmira Prison, NY, July 23, 1864	Oath of Allegiance June 16, 1865
Samuel, Richard H. Private	Unk	March 10, 1862, Fort Lowry, Virginia	Co. E, 55th Virginia Infantry	May 6, 1864, Wilderness, Virginia	Point Lookout, Maryland, transferred to Elmira Prison, NY, August 14, 1864	Exchanged March 2, 1865 at Akins Landing on the James River, Virginia
Sanchez, Joseph E. Private	Unk	May 25, 1861, Camp Moore, Tangipahoe, Louisiana	Co. F, 4th Louisiana Infantry	September 5, 1864, St. Francisville, Louisiana	New Orleans, Louisiana transferred to Elmira Prison November 19, 1864	Exchanged February 13, 1865 at Boulware's Wharf on the James River, Virginia
Sanderford, N. Green Private	26	July 26, 1861, Forestville, North Carolina	Co. I, 1st North Carolina Infantry	May 12, 1864, Spotsylvania Court House, Virginia	Point Lookout, Maryland, transferred to Elmira Prison, NY, August 6, 1864	Exchanged February 20, 1865 at Boulware's or Cox Wharf on the James River, Virginia

Name & Rank	Age	Enlisted	Regiment and State	Where Captured	Prison	Remarks
Sanders, Alfred Private	Unk	March 10, 1864, Danville, Virginia	Co. G, 45th North Carolina Infantry	May 10, 1864, Spotsylvania Court House, Virginia	Point Lookout, Maryland, transferred to Elmira Prison, NY, August 6, 1864	Died February 3, 1865 of Variola (Smallpox), Grave No. 1755. Name Aaron Saunders on Headstone.
Sanders, B. T. Private	Unk	September 5, 1861, Hartwell, Georgia	Co. C, 16th Georgia Infantry	August 16, 1864, Front Royal, Virginia	Old Capital Prison, Washington, DC transferred to Elmira Prison, NY, August 29, 1864	Died March 1, 1865 of Continued Fever, Grave No. 2108
Sanders, Benjamin H. Private	Unk	April 11, 1862, Coles Island, South Carolina	Co. G, 25th South Carolina Infantry	January 15, 1865, Fort Fisher, North Carolina	January 30, 1865, Elmira Prison Camp, New York	Oath of Allegiance June 7, 1865
Sanders, G. W. Civilian	Unk	Unknown	Citizen of Louisiana	September 19, 1864, Tensan Parish, Louisiana	New Orleans, Louisiana, Transferred to Elmira Prison, New York, November 19, 1864	Oath of Allegiance February 2, 1865. Early Release per Lincoln's Proclamation, 12/8/1863.
Sanders, James A. Corporal	30	January 14, 1862, Columbia, South Carolina	Co. E, 7th Battalion, South Carolina	August 21, 1864, Weldon Railroad, Virginia. Gunshot wound Left Thigh. Leg Amputated.	Old Capital Prison, Washington D. C. Transferred to Elmira Prison, NY, March 3, 1865.	Exchanged March 14, 1865 at Boulware's Wharf on the James River, Virginia
Sanders, John A. Private	Unk	March 10, 1864, Danville, Virginia	Co. G, 45th North Carolina Infantry	May 20, 1864, Spotsylvania Court House, Virginia	Point Lookout, Maryland, transferred to Elmira Prison, NY, July 3, 1864	Oath of Allegiance July 11, 1865
Sanders, Joseph T. Sergeant	19	April 1, 1862, Charleston, South Carolina	Co. E, 25th South Carolina Infantry	January 15, 1865, Fort Fisher, North Carolina	February 1, 1865, Elmira Prison Camp, New York	Exchanged February 20, 1865 at Boulware's or Cox Wharf on the James River, Virginia

Name & Rank	Age	Enlisted	Regiment and State	Where Captured	Prison	Remarks
Sanders, Malachi M. Private	Unk	May 9, 1862, Gordon, Georgia	Co. B, 14th Georgia Infantry	May 12, 1864, Spotsylvania Court House, Virginia	Point Lookout, Maryland, transferred to Elmira Prison, NY, July 30, 1864	Oath of Allegiance June 19, 1865
Sanders, S. H. Corporal	Unk	July 13, 1861, Hartwell, Georgia	Co. C, 16th Georgia Infantry	August 16, 1864, Front Royal, Virginia	Old Capital Prison, Washington, DC transferred to Elmira Prison, NY, August 29, 1864	Oath of Allegiance June 19, 1865
Sanders, Samuel M. Sergeant	Unk	June 4, 1861, Warsaw, Virginia	Co. D, 40th Virginia Infantry	July 14, 1863, Falling Waters, Maryland	Point Lookout, Maryland, transferred to Elmira Prison, NY, August 18, 1864	Exchanged March 10, 1865 at Boulware's Wharf on the James River, Virginia
Sanderson, Isaac Private	Unk	April 24, 1862, Kenansville, North Carolina	Co. B, 51st North Carolina Infantry	June 16, 1864, Near Petersburg, Virginia	Point Lookout, Maryland, transferred to Elmira Prison, NY, July 12, 1864	Oath of Allegiance June 14, 1865
Sanderson, Samuel Private	Unk	August 23, 1862, Washington County, Alabama	Co. E, 1st Battalion Alabama Artillery	August 23, 1864, Fort Morgan, Alabama	Steam Press No. 4 New Orleans, Louisiana transferred to Elmira Prison, NY, October 8, 1864.	Died January 19, 1865, Chronic Diarrhea, Grave No. 1196
Sandford, James F. Private	20	February 22, 1862, Granville County, North Carolina	Co. A, 44th North Carolina Infantry	June 1, 1864, Shady Grove Church, Cold Harbor, Virginia	Transferred From Point Lookout Prison, MD, July 12, 1864. Train Never Arrived at Elmira Prison Camp, NY.	Died July 15, 1864 in Train Wreck at Shohola, Pennsylvania.
Sandlin, Daniel S. Private	25	May 16, 1861, Columbia, North Carolina	Co. A, 32nd North Carolina Infantry	May 10, 1864, Near Mine Run Spotsylvania, Virginia	Point Lookout, Maryland, transferred to Elmira Prison, NY, August 6, 1864	Oath of Allegiance June 27, 1865
Sandlin, Robert Private	18	July 1, 1861, Jacksonville, Onslow County, North Carolina	Co. G, 3rd North Carolina Infantry	May 12, 1864, Near Spotsylvania County Court House, Virginia	Point Lookout, Maryland, transferred to Elmira Prison, NY, August 14, 1864	Oath of Allegiance June 21, 1865

Name & Rank	Age	Enlisted	Regiment and State	Where Captured	Prison	Remarks
Sanfley, James M. Private	Unk	August 20, 1863, Harrisonburg, Virginia	Co. C, 6th Virginia Cavalry	May 31, 1864, Cold Harbor, Virginia	Point Lookout, Maryland, transferred to Elmira Prison, NY, July 12, 1864	Oath of Allegiance May 29, 1865
Sanford, Jesse Private	Unk	August 13, 1864, Columbia, Richland County, South Carolina	Co. G, 25th South Carolina Infantry	January 15, 1865, Fort Fisher, North Carolina	February 1, 1865, Elmira Prison Camp, New York	Died March 20, 1865 of Chronic Diarrhea, Grave No. 1549
Sanford, William P. Private	Unk	May 29, 1863, Tallapoosa County, Alabama	Co. E, 61st Alabama Infantry	May 12, 1864, Spotsylvania Court House, Virginia	Point Lookout, Maryland, transferred to Elmira Prison, NY, July 30, 1864	Died February 14, 1864 of Pneumonia, Grave No. 2035
Sanner, Joseph H. Private	24	May 14, 1861, Louis County, Virginia	Co. B, 13th Virginia Infantry	May 30, 1864, Gaines Mill Cold Harbor, Virginia	Point Lookout, Maryland, transferred to Elmira Prison, NY, July 11, 1864	Oath of Allegiance June 19, 1865
Sapp, F. W. Private	Unk	March 14, 1864, Raleigh, North Carolina	Co. A, 2nd North Carolina Cavalry	June 1, 1864, Hanover Court House, Cold Harbor, Virginia	Transferred From Point Lookout Prison, MD, July 12, 1864. Train Never Arrived at Elmira Prison Camp, NY.	Died July 15, 1864 in Train Wreck at Shohola, Pennsylvania.
Sapp, Lemuel Private	Unk	September 24, 1863, Macon, Georgia	Co. J, 21st Georgia Infantry	July 12, 1864, Near Washington, DC	Old Capital Prison, Washington, DC, transferred to Elmira Prison, NY, July 23, 1864	Died December 22, 1864 of Pneumonia, Grave No. 1088
Sarratt, J. G. Private	20	June 18, 1862, Columbia, South Carolina	Co. G, 6th South Carolina Cavalry	June 11, 1864, Trevilian Station, Louisa Court House, Virginia	Point Lookout, Maryland, transferred to Elmira Prison, NY, July 25, 1864	Exchanged March 2, 1865 at Akins Landing on the James River, Virginia
Sartin, Aaron H. Sergeant	Unk	December 9, 1861, Camp Trousdale, Tennessee	Co. K, 44th Tennessee Infantry	June 17, 1864, Petersburg, Virginia	Point Lookout, Maryland, transferred to Elmira Prison, NY, July 30, 1864	Died July 18, 1865 at US Army Hospital, Elmira, NY. No Grave in Woodlawn Cemetery.

Name & Rank	Age	Enlisted	Regiment and State	Where Captured	Prison	Remarks
Satterfield, Jacob Private	28	March 9, 1862, Salem, North Carolina	Co. G, 7th North Carolina Infantry	May 6, 1864, Wilderness, Virginia	Point Lookout, Maryland, transferred to Elmira Prison, NY, August 14, 1864	Died January 5, 1865 of Pneumonia, Grave No. 1244. Headstone has 37th NC.
Satterwhite, John Private	Unk	September 3, 1862, Jefferson County, Alabama	Co. A, 1st Battalion Alabama Artillery	August 23, 1864, Fort Morgan, Alabama	Steam Press No. 4 New Orleans, Louisiana transferred to Elmira Prison, NY, October 8, 1864.	Died March 19, 1865 of Pneumonia, Grave No. 1582
Satterwhite, John Private	Unk	August 3, 1862 Jefferson County, Alabama	Co. A, 21st Alabama Infantry	August 23, 1864 Fort Morgan, Alabama	New Orleans, Louisiana. Transferred to Elmira Prison Camp October 8, 1864	Died March 19, 1865 of Pneumonia, Grave No. 1582
Satterwhite, Lenn H. Sergeant	17	July 15, 1861, Henderson, North Carolina	Co. D, 8th North Carolina Infantry	June 1, 1864, Gaines Farm, Cold Harbor, Virginia	Point Lookout Prison Camp, Maryland. Transferred to Elmira Prison Camp, NY, July 7, 1864	Died June 24, 1865 of Chronic Diarrhea, Grave No. 2821. Headstone has Satterfield.
Satterwhite, Philip Private	Unk	August 28, 1862, Jefferson County, Alabama	Co. A, 1st Battalion Alabama Artillery	August 23, 1864, Fort Morgan, Alabama	Steam Press No. 4 New Orleans, Louisiana transferred to Elmira Prison, NY, October 8, 1864.	Died April 5, 1865 of Chronic Diarrhea, Grave No. 2546
Saturday, George W. Private	25	September 1, 1861, Reidsville, Tattnall County, Georgia	Co. B, 61st Georgia Infantry	May 12, 1864, Spotsylvania Court House, Virginia	Point Lookout, Maryland, transferred to Elmira Prison, NY, July 30, 1864	Exchanged March 2, 1865 at Akins Landing on the James River, Virginia
Saul, A. F. Corporal	Unk	June 17, 1861, Rocky Mount, Virginia	Co. K, 4th Virginia Infantry	May 12, 1864, Spotsylvania Court House, Virginia	Point Lookout, Maryland, transferred to Elmira Prison, NY, August 2, 1864	Oath of Allegiance April 26, 1865
Saunders, Adison Private	Unk	May 1, 1864, Pisgah Church, Virginia	Co. H, 42nd Virginia Infantry	May 12, 1864, Near Spotsylvania Court House, Virginia	Point Lookout, Maryland, transferred to Elmira Prison, NY, August 6, 1864	Exchanged October 29, 1864, at Venus Point, Savannah River, GA.

Name & Rank	Age	Enlisted	Regiment and State	Where Captured	Prison	Remarks
Saunders, Britton Private	30	July 15, 1862, Moore County, North Carolina	Co. F, 3rd North Carolina Infantry	May 12, 1864, Near Spotsylvania Court House, Virginia	Point Lookout, Maryland, transferred to Elmira Prison, NY, August 14, 1864	Oath of Allegiance July 7, 1865
Saunders, E. M. Private	27	August 1, 1862, Statesville, North Carolina	Co. I, 5th North Carolina Infantry	May 12, 1864, Near Spotsylvania County Court House, Virginia	Point Lookout, Maryland, transferred to Elmira Prison, NY, August 14, 1864	Died May 5, 1865 of Pneumonia, Grave No. 2763
Saunders, Jackson P. Private	28	March 17, 1862, Tatum's Store, Patrick County, Virginia	Co. H, 42nd Virginia Infantry	May 12, 1864, Near Spotsylvania Court House, Virginia	Point Lookout, Maryland, transferred to Elmira Prison, NY, August 2, 1864	Exchanged March 2, 1865 at Akins Landing on the James River, Virginia
Saunders, James R. Private	18	July 15, 1863, Fort Caswell, Brunswick County, North Carolina	Co. F, 36th Regiment, 2nd North Carolina Artillery	January 15, 1865, Fort Fisher, North Carolina	February 1, 1865, Elmira Prison Camp, New York	Exchanged March 14, 1865 at Boulware's Wharf on the James River, Virginia
Saunders, P. A. Private	Unk	May 11, 1861, New Orleans, Louisiana	Co. D, 2nd Louisiana Infantry	May 12, 1864, Spotsylvania Court House, Virginia	Point Lookout, Maryland, transferred to Elmira Prison, NY, July 6, 1864	Exchanged October 29, 1864, at Venus Point, Savannah River, GA.
Saunders, Robert J. Private	18	May 30, 1861, Weldon, North Carolina	Co. H, 5th North Carolina Infantry	May 12, 1864, Near Spotsylvania County Court House, Virginia	Point Lookout, Maryland, transferred to Elmira Prison, NY, August 14, 1864	Oath of Allegiance June 27, 1865
Saunders, Silas G. Private	Unk	May 22, 1861, Spoon Creek, Virginia	Co. H, 42nd Virginia Infantry	May 12, 1864, Near Spotsylvania Court House, Virginia	Point Lookout, Maryland, transferred to Elmira Prison, NY, August 6, 1864	Oath of Allegiance June 21, 1865
Saunders, Stephen Private	28	February 2, 1862, Salisbury, North Carolina	Co. C, 42nd North Carolina Infantry	June 1, 1864, Gaines Farm Cold Harbor, Virginia	Point Lookout, Maryland, transferred to Elmira Prison, NY, July 12, 1864	Died September 14, 1864 of Chronic Diarrhea, Grave No. 294
Saunders, Vincent W. Private	Unk	Unknown	Co. K, 50th Virginia Infantry	May 6, 1864, Wilderness, Virginia	Point Lookout, Maryland, transferred to Elmira Prison, NY, August 14, 1864	Died October 8, 1864 of Chronic Diarrhea, Grave No. 654

Name & Rank	Age	Enlisted	Regiment and State	Where Captured	Prison	Remarks
Saunders, William K. Private	Unk	June 8, 1861, Isbell's Store, Virginia	Co. D, 44th Virginia Infantry	May 12, 1864, Spotsylvania Court House, Virginia	Point Lookout, Maryland, transferred to Elmira Prison, NY, August 12, 1864	Died June 29, 1865 of Chronic Diarrhea, Grave No. 2828.
Saurin, Frank E. Private	Unk	April 26, 1861, Montgomery, Alabama	Co. F, 3rd Alabama Infantry	May 12, 1864, Spotsylvania Court House, Virginia	Point Lookout, Maryland, transferred to Elmira Prison, NY, August 12, 1864	Oath of Allegiance June 19, 1865
Saussy, G. Nowlan Private	23	September 17, 1861, Savannah, Georgia	Co. F, Jeff Davis Legion Mississippi Cavalry	September 22, 1863, Near Madison Court House, Virginia	Point Lookout, Maryland, transferred to Elmira Prison, NY, August 18, 1864	Died February 25, 1865 of Variola (Smallpox). No Grave at Woodlawn Cemetery, NY
Savage, Richard S. Private	Unk	May 16, 1861, Montgomery, Alabama	Co. K, 5th Alabama Infantry	August 12, 1864, Winchester, Virginia	Old Capital Prison, Washington, DC transferred to Elmira Prison, NY, August 29, 1864	Exchanged February 20, 1865 at Boulware's or Cox Wharf on the James River, Virginia
Savage, Southey L. Private	29	June 28, 1861, New Kent Court House, Virginia	Co. H, 3rd Virginia Cavalry	May 15, 1864, Between King George Court House, Potomac Creek, Virginia	Point Lookout, Maryland, transferred to Elmira Prison, NY, July 3, 1864	Exchanged March 10, 1865 at Boulware's Wharf on the James River, Virginia
Savage, Wesley Private	41	September 7, 1863, Garysburg, North Carolina	Co. D, 24th North Carolina Infantry	June 17, 1864, Petersburg, Virginia	Point Lookout, Maryland, transferred to Elmira Prison, NY, July 30, 1864	Died September 14, 1864 of Typhoid Fever, Grave No. 280
Savage, Willoughbey Private	Unk	August 30, 1862, Manassas, Virginia	Co. D, 4th Virginia Infantry	May 12, 1864 Spotsylvania Court House, Virginia	Point Lookout, Maryland, transferred to Elmira Prison, NY, August 2, 1864	Exchanged 2/20/65. Died 3/11/65 of Chronic Diarrhea at Hospital No. 9, Richmond, VA
Saville, John F. Private	22	May 6, 1862, Knoxville, Tennessee	Co. G, 63rd Tennessee Infantry	June 17, 1864, Near Petersburg, Virginia	Point Lookout, Maryland, transferred to Elmira Prison, NY, July 30, 1864	Oath of Allegiance May 29, 1865

Name & Rank	Age	Enlisted	Regiment and State	Where Captured	Prison	Remarks
Saville, Peter A. Private	30	December 1, 1863, Hampshire, Virginia	Co. K, 18th Virginia Cavalry	July 16, 1864, Loudoun County, Virginia	Old Capital Prison, Washington, DC, transferred to Elmira Prison, NY, July 23, 1864	Exchanged March 2, 1865 at Akins Landing on the James River, Virginia
Sawyer, Charles H. H. Corporal	24	May 16, 1861, Columbia, North Carolina	Co. A, 32nd North Carolina Infantry	May 10, 1864, Near Mine Run Spotsylvania, Virginia	Point Lookout, Maryland, transferred to Elmira Prison, NY, August 6, 1864	Died March 15, 1865 of Chronic Diarrhea, Grave No. 1667
Sawyer, Edwin Private	Unk	February 10, 1862, Intrenchment Line, Norfolk, Virginia	Co. B, 6th Virginia Infantry	May 12, 1864, Near Spotsylvania Court House, Virginia	Point Lookout, Maryland, transferred to Elmira Prison, NY, August 6, 1864	Died December 16, 1864 of Typhoid Pneumonia, Grave No. 1272
Sawyer, George W. Private	Unk	October 1, 1861, Lynn Beach, Virginia	Co. J, 15th Virginia Cavalry	May 9, 1864, Spotsylvania Court House, Virginia	Point Lookout, Maryland, transferred to Elmira Prison, NY, August 17, 1864	Oath of Allegiance June 16, 1865
Sawyer, John F. Private	20	May 30, 1861, Camden County, North Carolina	Co. B, 32nd North Carolina Infantry	May 10, 1864, Near Mine Run Spotsylvania, Virginia	Point Lookout, Maryland, transferred to Elmira Prison, NY, August 6, 1864	Died March 26, 1865 of Diarrhea, Grave No. 2469
Sawyer, Simeon T. Sergeant	26	May 16, 1861, Columbia, North Carolina	Co. A, 32nd North Carolina Infantry	May 10, 1864, Near Mine Run Spotsylvania, Virginia	Point Lookout, Maryland, transferred to Elmira Prison, NY, August 6, 1864	Died January 5, 1865 of Typhoid Fever, Grave No. 1255
Sawyer, William A. Private	18	August 1, 1861, Salisbury, North Carolina	Co. K, 8th North Carolina Infantry	May 31, 1864, Cold Harbor, Virginia	Point Lookout, Maryland, transferred to Elmira Prison, NY, July 12, 1864	Exchanged October 29, 1864, at Venus Point, Savannah River, GA.
Sawyers, H. P. Private	Unk	Unknown	Co. H, 50th Virginia Infantry	May 12, 1864, Spotsylvania Court House, Virginia	Point Lookout, Maryland, transferred to Elmira Prison, NY, August 2, 1864	Oath of Allegiance June 14, 1865

Name & Rank	Age	Enlisted	Regiment and State	Where Captured	Prison	Remarks
Sawyers, Lewis Private	31	September 5, 1862, Butler County, Alabama	Co. C, 1st Battalion Alabama Artillery	August 23, 1864, Fort Morgan, Alabama	New Orleans, Louisiana transferred to Elmira Prison, NY, December 4, 1864.	Oath of Allegiance June 21, 1865
Sawyers, William Private	Unk	Unknown	Co. K, 50th Virginia Infantry	May 12, 1864, Spotsylvania Court House, Virginia	Point Lookout, Maryland, transferred to Elmira Prison, NY, August 2, 1864	Exchanged October 29, 1864, at Venus Point, Savannah River, GA.
Saxon, James W. Private	Unk	April 24, 1862, Arbacoocha, Alabama	Co. E, 13th Alabama Infantry	May 12, 1864, Spotsylvania Court House, Virginia	Point Lookout, Maryland, transferred to Elmira Prison, NY, August 2, 1864	Exchanged March 2, 1865 at Akins Landing on the James River, Virginia
Sayer, William T. Private	Unk	October 15, 1861, Haley's Store, Georgia	Co. F, 38th Georgia Infantry	May 20, 1864, Spotsylvania Court House, Virginia	Point Lookout, Maryland, transferred to Elmira Prison, NY, July 3, 1864	Exchanged March 2, 1865 at Akins Landing on the James River, Virginia
Scaff, Charles S. Private	Unk	February 12, 1862, Blinkhorn Point, Virginia	Co. B, 61st Virginia Infantry	June 6, 1864, Cold Harbor, Virginia	Point Lookout, Maryland, transferred to Elmira Prison, NY, July 25, 1864	Oath of Allegiance May 29, 1865
Scarborough, A. Private	Unk	Unknown	6th Field Battery Louisiana Light Artillery	October 22, 1864, Grosstete, Louisiana	New Orleans, Louisiana transferred to Elmira November 19, 1864.	Exchanged February 25, 1865 at Boulware's or Cox Wharf on the James River, Virginia
Scarborough, Joseph L. Private	25	April 28, 1861, New Orleans, Louisiana	Nelligan's Co. A, 1st Louisiana Infantry	May 12, 1864, Spotsylvania Court House, Virginia	Point Lookout, Maryland, transferred to Elmira Prison, NY, July 12, 1864	Exchanged February 25, 1865 at Boulware's or Cox Wharf on the James River, Virginia
Scates, Zebulan B. Private	24	May 18, 1861, Seven Mile Ford, Virginia	Co. D, 48th Virginia Infantry	May 12, 1864, Near Spotsylvania Court House, Virginia	Point Lookout, Maryland, transferred to Elmira Prison, NY, August 2, 1864	Oath of Allegiance, June 19, 1865

Name & Rank	Age	Enlisted	Regiment and State	Where Captured	Prison	Remarks
Schaff, Nicholas Private	20	June 22, 1861, New Orleans, Louisiana	Co. D, 14th Louisiana Infantry	May 12, 1864, Spotsylvania Court House, Virginia	Point Lookout, Maryland, transferred to Elmira Prison, NY, July 25, 1864	Exchanged February 25, 1865 at Boulware's or Cox Wharf on the James River, Virginia
Scheel, William Private	19	October 8, 1864, the Camp of 4th Regiment, Texas	Co. B, 7th Texas Cavalry	July 22, 1864, Concordia Parish, Louisiana	New Orleans, Louisiana, Transferred to Elmira Prison, New York, November 19, 1864	Oath of Allegiance May 19, 1865
Schirer, John Private	Unk	July 20, 1862, James Island, South Carolina	Co. B, 25th South Carolina Infantry	January 15, 1865, Fort Fisher, North Carolina	February 1, 1865, Elmira Prison Camp, New York	Oath of Allegiance May 29, 1865
Schmotzard, Joseph Private	34	May 22, 1861, New Orleans, Louisiana	Co. E, 7th Louisiana Infantry	May 5, 1864, Wilderness, Virginia	Point Lookout, Maryland, transferred to Elmira Prison, NY, August 17, 1864	Exchanged February 25, 1865 at Boulware's or Cox Wharf on the James River, Virginia
Schneider, Martin Private	Unk	Unknown	Co. A, 13th North Carolina Infantry	October 25, 1864, Weldon Railroad, Near Petersburg, Virginia	Old Capital Prison, Washington, DC transferred to Elmira Prison, NY, August 27, 1864	Oath of Allegiance November 29, 1864. Early Release per Lincoln's Proclamation, 12/8/1863.
Schonigal, Gustave Sergeant	26	April 24, 1861, New Orleans, Louisiana	Co. F, 1st Louisiana Infantry	May 20, 1864, Spotsylvania Court House, Virginia	Point Lookout, Maryland, transferred to Elmira Prison, NY, August 17, 1864	Oath of Allegiance May 19, 1865
Schooler, Rice L. Private	23	May 12, 1862, Knoxville, Tennessee	Co. G, 63rd Tennessee Infantry	June 17, 1864, Petersburg, Virginia	Point Lookout, Maryland, transferred to Elmira Prison, NY, July 30, 1864	Oath of Allegiance May 29, 1865
Schools, Thomas Private	35	June 13, 1861, Clarkson, Virginia	Co. J, 26th North Carolina Infantry	June 17, 1864, Near Petersburg, Virginia	Point Lookout, Maryland, transferred to Elmira Prison, NY, July 30, 1864	Died March 7, 1865 of Variola (smallpox), Grave No. 2389

Name & Rank	Age	Enlisted	Regiment and State	Where Captured	Prison	Remarks
Schrader, Ammi Private	Unk	May 18, 1861, Franklin, Virginia	Co. K, 25th Virginia Infantry	May 12, 1864, Spotsylvania Court House, Virginia	Point Lookout, Maryland, transferred to Elmira Prison, NY, August 12, 1864	Exchanged March 2, 1865 at Akins Landing on the James River, Virginia
Schroder, Henry Private	Unk	May 15, 1863, Charleston, South Carolina	Co. C, 27th South Carolina Infantry	June 24, 1864, Near Petersburg, Virginia	Point Lookout, Maryland, transferred to Elmira Prison, NY, August 18, 1864	Died March 4, 1865 of Pneumonia, Grave No. 1978. Headstone has Selroder.
Schulte, J. H. Private	Unk	April 4, 1862, Charleston, South Carolina	Co. B, 25th South Carolina Infantry	January 15, 1865, Fort Fisher, North Carolina	February 1, 1865, Elmira Prison Camp, New York	Oath of Allegiance June 16, 1865
Schultz, George E. Sergeant	24	December 31, 1861, Springfield, Missouri	Co. G, 1st Missouri Cavalry	May 17, 1863, Big Black Bridge, Champion Hill, Mississippi	Point Lookout, Maryland, transferred to Elmira Prison, NY, August 18, 1864	Exchanged February 13, 1865 at Boulware's wharf on the James River, Virginia
Schwing, George B. Private	30	September 1, 1862, New Road, Louisiana	Co. J, 2nd Louisiana Cavalry	September 16, 1864, Stone's Plantation, Louisiana	Fort Columbus, N Y Harbor, transferred to Elmira December 4, 1864.	Exchanged March 2, 1865 at Boulware's Wharf on the James River, Virginia
Schwing, J. T. Private	Unk	September 8, 1862, Camp Thompson, False River, Louisiana	Co. J, 2nd Louisiana Cavalry	October 10, 1864, Atchafalia, Louisiana	New Orleans, Louisiana transferred to Elmira November 19, 1864.	Exchanged February 25, 1865 at Boulware's or Cox Wharf on the James River, Virginia
Scoggin, Aaron J. Corporal	22	March 5, 1862, Yanceyville, North Carolina	Co. I, 45th North Carolina Infantry	May 10, 1864, Spotsylvania Court House, Virginia	Point Lookout, Maryland, transferred to Elmira Prison, NY, August 6, 1864	Died June 22, 1865 of Chronic Diarrhea, Grave No. 2814
Scoggins, J. Private	Unk	May 10, 1862, Farrant, Texas	Co. J, 23rd Texas Cavalry	August 8, 1864, Near Simsport, Louisiana	New Orleans, Louisiana, Transferred to Elmira Prison, New York, November 19, 1864	Died March 9, 1865 of Pneumonia, Grave No. 2360

Name & Rank	Age	Enlisted	Regiment and State	Where Captured	Prison	Remarks
Scoggins, John M. Private	Unk	March 15, 1863, Atlanta, Georgia	Co. C, 64th Georgia Infantry	August 16, 1864, New Market, Virginia	Old Capital Prison, Washington, DC transferred to Elmira Prison, NY, August 27, 1864	Died December 26, 1864 of Chronic Diarrhea, Grave No. 1285
Scott, Andrew D. Private	Unk	August 1, 1861, Marion District, South Carolina	Co. E, 1st South Carolina Infantry	July 29, 1864, Petersburg, Virginia	Point Lookout, Maryland, transferred to Elmira Prison, NY, August 12, 1864	Oath of Allegiance July 3, 1865
Scott, Benjamin S. Sergeant	32	March 22, 1862, Forsyth, Georgia	Co. B, 45th Georgia Infantry	March 25, 1865, Fort Fisher, Virginia. Gunshot Wound Right Side.	Old Capital Prison, Washington D. C. Transferred to Elmira Prison, NY, May 2, 1865.	Oath of Allegiance July 7, 1865
Scott, Charles H. Private	Unk	December 22, 1863, Fort Morgan, Alabama	Co. F, 1st Battalion Alabama Artillery	August 23, 1864, Fort Morgan, Alabama	Steam Press No. 4 New Orleans, Louisiana transferred to Elmira Prison, NY, October 8, 1864.	Oath of Allegiance December 17, 1864. Early Release per Lincoln's Proclamation, 12/8/1863.
Scott, Henry M. Private	Unk	December 1, 1863, Yadkinville, North Carolina	Co. J, 21st North Carolina Infantry	July 10, 1864, Harper's Ferry, Virginia	Old Capital Prison, Washington, DC, transferred to Elmira Prison, NY, July 23, 1864	Died February 13, 1865 of Chronic Diarrhea, Grave No. 2070
Scott, J. Private	Unk	Unknown	Co. C, 16th Georgia Infantry	August 16, 1864, Front Royal, Virginia	Old Capital Prison, Washington, DC transferred to Elmira Prison, NY, August 29, 1864	Oath of Allegiance June 21, 1865
Scott, J. E. Private	Unk	May 16, 1863, James Island, South Carolina	Co. C, 25th South Carolina Infantry	January 15, 1865, Fort Fisher, North Carolina	February 1, 1865, Elmira Prison Camp, New York	Oath of Allegiance June 30, 1865
Scott, John D. Private	Unk	February 24, 1862, Conyers, Georgia	Co. K, 35th Georgia Infantry	May 31, 1864, Hanover Junction, Virginia	Point Lookout, Maryland, transferred to Elmira Prison, NY, July 12, 1864	Died September 12, 1864 of Chronic Diarrhea, Grave No. 175

Name & Rank	Age	Enlisted	Regiment and State	Where Captured	Prison	Remarks
Scott, John L. Private	Unk	August 29, 1863 James Island, South Carolina	Co. G, 25th South Carolina Infantry	January 15, 1865, Fort Fisher, North Carolina	February 1, 1865, Elmira Prison Camp, New York	Oath of Allegiance July 11, 1865
Scott, John L. Private	22	July 22, 1862, Camp Turner, Louisiana	Co. G, 3rd Louisiana Cavalry	October 1, 1864, East Baton Rouge, Louisiana	New Orleans, Louisiana transferred to Elmira November 19, 1864.	Oath of Allegiance May 15, 1865
Scott, Thomas B. Private	Unk	March 1, 1864, Greensboro, North Carolina	Co. B, 45th North Carolina Infantry	May 10, 1864, Spotsylvania Court House, Virginia	Point Lookout, Maryland, transferred to Elmira Prison, NY, August 6, 1864	Exchanged October 29, 1864, at Venus Point, Savannah River, GA.
Scott, Thomas M. Private	32	July 25, 1862, Danbury, North Carolina	Co. J, 21st South Carolina Infantry	May 16, 1864, Near Drury's Bluff, Virginia	Point Lookout, Maryland, transferred to Elmira Prison, NY, August 17, 1864	Died December 21, 1865 of Pneumonia, Grave No. 1082
Scott, William H. Private	22	March 7, 1862, Fayetteville, North Carolina	Co. E, 51st North Carolina Infantry	June 16, 1864, Near Petersburg, Virginia	Point Lookout, Maryland, transferred to Elmira Prison, NY, July 12, 1864	Died January 23, 1865 of Pneumonia, Grave No. 1600
Scott, William T. Private	21	April 1, 1861, Norfolk, Virginia	CO. H, 1ST Virginia Infantry	July 30, 1864, Petersburg, Virginia	Point Lookout, Maryland, transferred to Elmira Prison, NY, August 12, 1864	Oath of Allegiance May 14, 1865
Scroggins, William C. Private	Unk	March 19, 1861, Union Springs, Alabama	Co. A, 1st Battalion Alabama Artillery	August 23, 1864, Fort Morgan, Alabama	New Orleans, Louisiana transferred to Elmira Prison, NY, December 4, 1864.	Oath of Allegiance May 29, 1865
Scruggs, B. O. Private	17	November 21, 1861, Spartanburg, South Carolina	Co. A, Holcombe Legion, South Carolina Infantry	May 7, 1864, Stony Creek, Virginia	Point Lookout, Maryland, transferred to Elmira Prison, NY, August 17, 1864	Exchanged February 20, 1865 at Boulware's or Cox Wharf on the James River, Virginia
Scruggs, J. P. Sergeant	Unk	March 19, 1862, Orange, Virginia	Co. K, Holcombe Legion, South Carolina Infantry	May 7, 1864, Stony Creek, Virginia	Point Lookout, Maryland, transferred to Elmira Prison, NY, August 17, 1864	Escaped October 27, 1864 by Tunneling Under Fence.

Name & Rank	Age	Enlisted	Regiment and State	Where Captured	Prison	Remarks
Scruggs, J. W. Sergeant	Unk	March 19, 1862, Orange, Virginia	Co. K, Holcombe Legion, South Carolina Infantry	May 7, 1864, Stony Creek, Virginia	Point Lookout, Maryland, transferred to Elmira Prison, NY, August 17, 1864	Exchanged February 20, 1865 at Boulware's or Cox Wharf on the James River, Virginia
Scruggs, Joseph A. Private	32	May 9, 1861, Amelia Court House, Virginia	Co. G, 1st Virginia Cavalry	May 9, 1864, Spotsylvania Court House, Virginia. Gunshot Wound Left Thigh. Left Leg Amputated.	Old Capital Prison, Washington D. C. Transferred to Elmira Prison, NY, March 27, 1865.	Oath of Allegiance June 19, 1865
Scruggs, Lovenzo B. Private	28	August 22, 1861, Cleveland County, North Carolina	Co. H, 33rd North Carolina Infantry	May 12, 1864, Spotsylvania County Court House, Virginia	Point Lookout, Maryland, transferred to Elmira Prison, NY, August 14, 1864	Exchanged October 29, 1864, at Venus Point, Savannah River, GA.
Scruggs, W. H. Private	Unk	November 28, 1861, Troy, Tennessee	Co. B, 1st Jackson's Tennessee Heavy Artillery	August 23, 1864, Fort Morgan, Alabama.	New Orleans, Louisiana transferred to Elmira Prison, NY, December 4, 1864.	Exchanged 2/13/65. Died of Chronic Diarrhea and Debility at Chimborazo, Hospital No. 4, Richmond, VA
Scruggs, W. W. Private	19	November 21, 1861, Spartanburg, South Carolina	Co. A, Holcombe Legion, South Carolina Infantry	May 7, 1864, Stony Creek, Virginia	Point Lookout, Maryland, transferred to Elmira Prison, NY, August 17, 1864	Transferred for Exchange February 20, 1865. Died on boat February 28, 1865 US Army Hospital, Baltimore, MD.
Sculthorp, John L. Private	23	June 20, 1861, Christianville, Virginia	Co. C, 21st Virginia Infantry	May 12, 1864, Spotsylvania Court House, Virginia	Point Lookout, Maryland, transferred to Elmira Prison, NY, August 2, 1864	Oath of Allegiance June 19, 1865
Seaborn, David Private	Unk	May 5, 1862, Macon, Georgia	Co. I, 61st Georgia Infantry	May 12, 1864, Spotsylvania Court House, Virginia	Point Lookout, Maryland, transferred to Elmira Prison, NY, July 30, 1864	Oath of Allegiance June 30, 1865

Name & Rank	Age	Enlisted	Regiment and State	Where Captured	Prison	Remarks
Seachrist, Amos L. Private	24	May 14, 1861, Lexington, North Carolina	Co. J, 14th North Carolina Infantry	July 12, 1864, Near Washington, DC	Old Capital Prison, Washington, DC, transferred to Elmira Prison, NY, July 23, 1864	Oath of Allegiance May 29, 1865
Seachrist, James M. Private	19	May 14, 1861, Lexington, North Carolina	Co. J, 14th North Carolina Infantry	July 12, 1864, Near Washington, DC	Old Capital Prison, Washington, DC, transferred to Elmira Prison, NY, July 23, 1864	Died May 10, 1865 of Chronic Diarrhea, Grave No. 2790
Seago, Patrick H. Private	21	September 15, 1862, Camp Mangum, Raleigh, North Carolina	Co. B, 31st North Carolina Infantry	June 1, 1864, Cold Harbor, Virginia	Transferred From Point Lookout Prison, MD, July 12, 1864. Train Never Arrived at Elmira Prison Camp, NY.	Died July 15, 1864 in Train Wreck at Shohola, Pennsylvania.
Seagraves, James M. Private	Unk	August 8, 1862, Camp Hill, North Carolina	Co. C, 3rd Battalion North Carolina Light Artillery	January 15, 1865, Fort Fisher, North Carolina	February 1, 1865, Elmira Prison Camp, New York	Exchanged March 14, 1865 at Boulware's Wharf on the James River, Virginia
Seahorn, William A. Private	20	May 6, 1862, Jonesboro, Tennessee	Co. D, 63rd Tennessee Infantry	June 17, 1864, Near Petersburg, Virginia	Point Lookout, Maryland, transferred to Elmira Prison, NY, July 30, 1864	Exchanged February 25, 1865 at Boulware's or Cox Wharf on the James River, Virginia
Sealy, Allen H. Private	17	September 6, 1861, Lumberton, North Carolina	Co. A, 31st North Carolina Infantry	June 1, 1864, Gaines Farm Cold Harbor, Virginia	Point Lookout, Maryland, transferred to Elmira Prison, NY, July 12, 1864	Exchanged October 29, 1864, at Venus Point, Savannah River, GA.
Searbery, William H. Private	Unk	June 22, 1861, Henry County, Virginia	Co. F, 42nd Virginia Infantry	May 12, 1864, Near Spotsylvania Court House, Virginia	Point Lookout, Maryland, transferred to Elmira Prison, NY, August 6, 1864	Transferred for Exchange 10/11/64. Died 10/24/64 of Inflammation of Lungs at Point Lookout, MD.

Name & Rank	Age	Enlisted	Regiment and State	Where Captured	Prison	Remarks
Searcy, Bennett Sergeant	Unk	Unknown	Co. J, 3rd Louisiana Cavalry	September 14, 1864, Tunica, Louisiana	New Orleans, Louisiana transferred to Elmira November 19, 1864.	Exchanged February 25, 1865 at Boulware's or Cox Wharf on the James River, Virginia
Searcy, William G. Private	Unk	July 15, 1862, Macon, Georgia	Captain Slaten's Battery, Georgia Artillery	June 17, 1864, Petersburg, Virginia	Point Lookout, Maryland, transferred to Elmira Prison, NY, July 30, 1864	Transferred For Exchange October 11, 1864 to Point Lookout Prison Camp, MD. Nothing Further.
Searle, Ed B. Sergeant	Unk	May 19, 1861, New Orleans, Louisiana	Co. C, 1st Texas Infantry	July 29, 1864, Petersburg, Virginia. Deserted 3rd Delaware	Point Lookout, Maryland, transferred to Elmira Prison, NY, August 12, 1864	Oath of Allegiance September 30, 1864. Early Release per Lincoln's Proclamation, 12/8/1863.
Sears, Henry T. Private	Unk	February 15, 1862, Gloucester Point, Virginia	Co. B, 26th Virginia Infantry	June 15, 1864, Near Petersburg, Virginia	Point Lookout, Maryland, transferred to Elmira Prison, NY, July 12, 1864	Oath of Allegiance June 19, 1865
Sears, William A. Private	Unk	February 7, 1862, Gloucester Point, Virginia	Co. B, 26th Virginia Infantry	June 15, 1864, Near Petersburg, Virginia	Point Lookout, Maryland, transferred to Elmira Prison, NY, July 12, 1864	Oath of Allegiance June 19, 1865
Seay, Daniel E. Private	Unk	January 1, 1862, Lexington, South Carolina	Co. F, 5th South Carolina Cavalry	May 28, 1864, Hall's Shop, Virginia	Point Lookout, Maryland, transferred to Elmira Prison, NY, July 12, 1864	Died January 30, 1865 of Variola (Smallpox), Grave No. 1786
Seay, W. F. Private	Unk	January 1, 1862, Lexington, South Carolina	Co. H, Nelson's Battalion, 7th South Carolina Infantry	June 1, 1864, Gaines Mill Cold Harbor, Virginia	Point Lookout, Maryland, transferred to Elmira Prison, NY, July 11,1864	Exchanged October 29, 1864, at Venus Point, Savannah River, GA.
Sebert, Lanty L. Corporal	Unk	May 18, 1861, Huntersville, Virginia	Co. I, 25th Virginia Infantry	May 12, 1864, Spotsylvania Court House, Virginia	Point Lookout, Maryland, transferred to Elmira Prison, NY, August 12, 1864	Died November 11, 1864 of Pneumonia, Grave No. 825. Name Seebert on Headstone.

Name & Rank	Age	Enlisted	Regiment and State	Where Captured	Prison	Remarks
Secrest, Adam J. Private	Unk	April 20, 1863, Camp Lay, South Carolina	Co. B, 4th South Carolina Cavalry	June 11, 1864, Trevilian Station, Louisa Court House, Virginia	Point Lookout, Maryland, transferred to Elmira Prison, NY, July 25, 1864	Oath of Allegiance May 29, 1865
Secrest, Lafayette A. Private	Unk	May 11, 1864, Wilmington, North Carolina	Co. K, 10th Regiment, 1st North Carolina Artillery	January 15, 1865, Fort Fisher, North Carolina	February 1, 1865, Elmira Prison Camp, New York	Died April 13, 1865 of Spasm of Glottis (Larynx), Grave No. 2717
Secrist, Charles N. Private	Unk	April 18, 1862, Rudes Hill, Virginia	Co. B, 2nd Virginia Infantry	May 12, 1864, Near Spotsylvania Court House, Virginia	Point Lookout, Maryland, transferred to Elmira Prison, NY, August 6, 1864	Died October 6, 1864 of Chronic Diarrhea, Grave No. 595. Name Sichrist on Headstone.
Secrist, Daniel W. Corporal	Unk	June 17, 1861, Conrad's Store, Virginia	Co. I, 10th Virginia Infantry	May 12, 1864, Spotsylvania, Virginia	Point Lookout Prison Camp, Maryland. Transferred to Elmira Prison, August 2, 1864	Died March 17, 1865 of Chronic Diarrhea, Grave No. 1714
Secrist, Philip M. Sergeant	Unk	May 25, 1861, Harpers Ferry, Virginia	Co. I, 10th Virginia Infantry	May 12, 1864, Spotsylvania Court House, Virginia	Point Lookout, Maryland, transferred to Elmira Prison, NY, August 2, 1864	Oath of Allegiance June 27, 1865
See, Cyrus Private	Unk	November 4, 1863, Hardy, Virginia	Co. B, 18th Virginia Cavalry	July 16, 1864, Loudoun County, Virginia	Old Capital Prison, Washington, DC, transferred to Elmira Prison, NY, July 23, 1864	Died April 23, 1865 of Chronic Diarrhea, Grave No. 1398. Name on Headstone Cyrus Lee.
Segars, Wiley Private	Unk	October 8, 1862, Macon, Georgia	Co. D, 12th Georgia Infantry	July 16, 1864, Loudoun County, Virginia	Old Capital Prison, Washington, DC, transferred to Elmira Prison, NY, July 23, 1864	Died February 5, 1865 of Variola (Smallpox), Grave No. 1907
Sego, John T. Private	Unk	March 4, 1862, Valdosta, Georgia	Co. D, 50th Georgia Infantry	May 6, 1864, Wilderness, Virginia	Point Lookout, Maryland, transferred to Elmira Prison, NY, August 14, 1864	Oath of Allegiance June 19, 1865

Name & Rank	Age	Enlisted	Regiment and State	Where Captured	Prison	Remarks
Segraves, C. N. Private	Unk	August 24, 1861, Lawrenceville, Georgia	Co. F, 24th Georgia Infantry	August 16, 1864, Front Royal, Virginia	Old Capital Prison, Washington, DC transferred to Elmira Prison, NY, August 29, 1864	Oath of Allegiance July 7, 1865
Seitz, Julius Private	18	June 6, 1861, Newton, North Carolina	Co. F, 23rd North Carolina Infantry	May 12, 1864, Near Spotsylvania Court House, Virginia	Point Lookout, Maryland, transferred to Elmira Prison, NY, August 14, 1864	Oath of Allegiance June 27, 1865
Self, William J. Private	Unk	March 8, 1862, Henry County, Virginia	Co. H, 24th Virginia Cavalry	May 16, 1864, Near Drury's Bluff, Virginia	Point Lookout, Maryland, transferred to Elmira Prison, NY, August 18, 1864	Oath of Allegiance June 27, 1865
Sell, Andrew Private	Unk	November 13, 1863, Raleigh, North Carolina	Co. G, 21st North Carolina Infantry	July 8, 1864, Harper's Ferry, Virginia	Old Capital Prison, Washington, DC, transferred to Elmira Prison, NY, July 23, 1864	Died February 16, 1865 of Pneumonia, Grave No. 2187
Sellers, David Private	35	October 20, 1863, Fort Caswell, Brunswick County, North Carolina	Co. D, 36th Regiment, 2nd North Carolina Artillery	January 15, 1865, Fort Fisher, North Carolina	February 1, 1865, Elmira Prison Camp, New York	Died March 20, 1865 of Variola (Smallpox), Grave No. 1544
Sellers, Duncan C. Private	26	January 28, 1862, Bladen County, North Carolina	Co. B, 36th Regiment 2nd North Carolina Artillery	January 15, 1865, Fort Fisher, North Carolina	February 1, 1865, Elmira Prison Camp, New York	Oath of Allegiance July 3, 1865
Sellers, George Private	19	October 28, 1861, Wilmington, New Hanover County, North Carolina	Co. D, 36th Regiment, 2nd North Carolina Artillery	January 15, 1865, Fort Fisher, North Carolina	February 1, 1865, Elmira Prison Camp, New York	Died May 27, 1865 of Chronic Diarrhea, Grave No. 2916
Sellers, James B. Private	17	May 23, 1864, Fort Fisher, New Hanover County, North Carolina	Co. G, 36th Regiment 2nd North Carolina Artillery	January 15, 1865, Fort Fisher, North Carolina	February 1, 1865, Elmira Prison Camp, New York	Oath of Allegiance July 7, 1865

Name & Rank	Age	Enlisted	Regiment and State	Where Captured	Prison	Remarks
Sellers, Joel S. Private	Unk	September 1, 1863, Troy, Alabama	Co. G, 59th Alabama Infantry	June 17, 1864, Near Petersburg, Virginia	Point Lookout, Maryland, transferred to Elmira Prison, NY, July 30, 1864	Oath of Allegiance July 26, 1865
Sellers, John Sergeant	34	March 14, 1862, Fort St. Philip, Brunswick County, North Carolina	Co. G, 36th Regiment 2nd North Carolina Artillery	January 15, 1865, Fort Fisher, North Carolina	February 1, 1865, Elmira Prison Camp, New York	Died March 29, 1865 of Diarrhea, Grave No. 2023
Sellers, John Private	38	March 3, 1862, Wilmington, New Hanover County, North Carolina	Co. D, 36th Regiment 2nd North Carolina Artillery	January 15, 1865, Fort Fisher, North Carolina	February 1, 1865, Elmira Prison Camp, New York	Died March 1, 1865 of Variola (Smallpox), Grave No. 2023
Sellers, John M. Private	41	April 16, 1862, Old Brunswick Town, North Carolina	Co. G, 36th Regiment 2nd North Carolina Artillery	January 15, 1865, Fort Fisher, North Carolina	February 1, 1865, Elmira Prison Camp, New York	Died March 20, 1865 of Variola (Smallpox), Grave No. 1560
Sellers, John W. Private	37	February 24, 1863, Fort Caswell, Brunswick County, North Carolina	Co. G, 36th Regiment, 2nd North Carolina Artillery	January 15, 1865, Fort Fisher, North Carolina	February 1, 1865, Elmira Prison Camp, New York	Died May 14, 1865 of Variola (Smallpox), Grave No. 2804
Sellers, Joseph D. Private	26	June 6, 1861, Wilmington, North Carolina	Co. F, 3rd North Carolina Infantry	May 12, 1864, Near Spotsylvania Court House, Virginia	Point Lookout, Maryland, transferred to Elmira Prison, NY, August 14, 1864	Oath of Allegiance May 15, 1865
Sellers, Lorenzo Private	21	September 25, 1862, Fort Caswell, Brunswick County, North Carolina	Co. G, 36th Regiment 2nd North Carolina Artillery	January 15, 1865, Fort Fisher, North Carolina	February 1, 1865, Elmira Prison Camp, New York	Exchanged March 14, 1865 at Boulware's Wharf on the James River, Virginia
Sellers, Rilah Private	Unk	September 19, 1862, Henry, Alabama	Co. F, 1st Battalion Alabama Artillery	August 23, 1864, Fort Morgan, Alabama	Steam Press No. 4 New Orleans, Louisiana transferred to Elmira Prison, NY, October 8, 1864.	Oath of Allegiance June 21, 1865
Sellers, Robert A. Private	17	May 16, 1863, Fort Johnson, North Carolina	Co. G, 40th Regiment, 3rd North Carolina Artillery	January 15, 1865, Fort Fisher, North Carolina	February 1, 1865, Elmira Prison Camp, New York	Oath of Allegiance June 12, 1865

Name & Rank	Age	Enlisted	Regiment and State	Where Captured	Prison	Remarks
Sellers, Thomas A. Private	38	February 8, 1863, Fort Caswell, Brunswick County, North Carolina	Co. G, 36th Regiment, 2nd North Carolina Artillery	January 15, 1865, Fort Fisher, North Carolina	February 1, 1865, Elmira Prison Camp, New York	Exchanged February 20, 1865 at Boulware's or Cox Wharf on the James River, Virginia
Sellers, W. P. Private	Unk	June 2, 1862, Chesterfield, South Carolina	Co. D, 6th South Carolina Cavalry	July 30, 1864, Lee's Mill, Petersburg, Virginia	Point Lookout, Maryland, transferred to Elmira Prison, NY, August 12, 1864	Oath of Allegiance June 19, 1865
Sellers, Wiley Private	Unk	January 24, 1864, Macon, Georgia	Co. C, 51st Georgia Infantry	June 3, 1864, Gaines Farm Cold Harbor, Virginia	Point Lookout Prison, Maryland Transferred July 12, 1864 to Elmira, New York	Exchanged February 20, 1865 at Boulware's or Cox Wharf on the James River, Virginia
Sellers, William H. Private	25	March 5, 1862, Cerro Gordo, North Carolina	Co. E, 36th Regiment 2nd North Carolina Artillery	January 15, 1865, Fort Fisher, North Carolina	February 1, 1865, Elmira Prison Camp, New York	Oath of Allegiance July 3, 1865
Sellers, William R. Private	30	August 24, 1863, Brunswick County, North Carolina	Co. D, 36th Regiment, 2nd North Carolina Artillery	January 15, 1865, Fort Fisher, North Carolina	February 1, 1865, Elmira Prison Camp, New York	Died February 10, 1865 of Congestion of Lungs, Grave No. 1944
Sellers, William R. Private	Unk	December 26, 1861, Cheraw, South Carolina	Co. A, 4th South Carolina Cavalry	May 30, 1864, Chickahominy, Cold Harbor, Virginia	Point Lookout, Maryland, transferred to Elmira Prison, NY, July 12, 1864	Died March 23, 1865 of Pneumonia, Grave No. 2438
Sensibaugh, John Private	Unk	May 21, 1861, Brownsburg, Virginia	Co. H, 25th Virginia Infantry	May 12, 1864, Spotsylvania Court House, Virginia	Point Lookout, Maryland, transferred to Elmira Prison, NY, August 12, 1864	Oath of Allegiance June 27, 1865
Sensibaugh, Samuel Private	25	April 23, 1861, Brownsburg, Virginia	Co. H, 25th Virginia Infantry	May 5, 1864, Mine Run Wilderness, Virginia	Point Lookout, Maryland, transferred to Elmira Prison, NY, August 2, 1864	Oath of Allegiance June 14, 1865
Senner, J. M. Private	Unk	Unknown	Co. A, 10th Virginia Infantry	May 12, 1864, Spotsylvania Court House, Virginia	Point Lookout, Maryland, transferred to Elmira Prison, NY, August 2, 1864	Oath of Allegiance June 19, 1865

Name & Rank	Age	Enlisted	Regiment and State	Where Captured	Prison	Remarks
Sennett, Henry Corporal	Unk	May 14, 1861, Franklin, Virginia	Co. E, 25th Virginia Infantry	May 12, 1864, Spotsylvania Court House, Virginia	Point Lookout, Maryland, transferred to Elmira Prison, NY, August 12, 1864	Oath of Allegiance June 27, 1865
Sentell, R. A. Private	Unk	May 1, 1864, Fort Morgan, Alabama	Co. A, 1st Battalion Alabama Artillery	August 23, 1864, Fort Morgan, Alabama	New Orleans, Louisiana transferred to Elmira Prison, NY, December 4, 1864.	Oath of Allegiance July 7, 1865
Senter, Caleb O. Private	32	March 25, 1862, Sharon Station, Lincoln County, North Carolina	Co. H, 52nd North Carolina Infantry	June 2, 1864, Near Talapatomoy Creek, Cold Harbor, Virginia	Transferred From Point Lookout Prison, MD, July 12, 1864. Train Never Arrived at Elmira Prison Camp, NY.	Died July 15, 1864 in Train Wreck at Shohola, Pennsylvania.
Senter, John A. Private	Unk	October 13, 1863, Camp Holmes, Near Raleigh, North Carolina	Co. D, 36th Regiment, 2nd North Carolina Artillery	January 15, 1865, Fort Fisher, North Carolina	February 1, 1865, Elmira Prison Camp, New York	Oath of Allegiance July 3, 1865
Sercey, George Private	Unk	Unknown	Co. D, 12th Alabama Infantry	July 16, 1864, Loudoun County, Virginia	Old Capital Prison, Washington, DC, transferred to Elmira, NY July 23, 1864	Oath of Allegiance June 19, 1865
Sessoms, Neill Private	26	February 26, 1862, Blockersville, Cumberland County, North Carolina	Co. C, 36th Regiment, 2nd North Carolina Artillery	January 15, 1865, Fort Fisher, North Carolina	February 1, 1865, Elmira Prison Camp, New York	Oath of Allegiance June 12, 1865
Sessoms, Thomas S. Private	21	November 4, 1861, Wilmington, New Hanover County, North Carolina	Co. J, 36th Regiment, 2nd North Carolina Artillery	January 15, 1865, Fort Fisher, North Carolina	February 1, 1865, Elmira Prison Camp, New York	Oath of Allegiance June 12, 1865
Settlemyer, Daniel S. Private	23	April 27, 1861, Newton, North Carolina	Co. A, 12th North Carolina Infantry	May 12, 1864, Spotsylvania Court House, Virginia	Point Lookout, Maryland, transferred to Elmira Prison, NY, August 14, 1864	Oath of Allegiance May 13, 1865

Name & Rank	Age	Enlisted	Regiment and State	Where Captured	Prison	Remarks
Setzer, John S. Private	20	August 14, 1861, Newton, North Carolina	Co. E, 32nd North Carolina Infantry	May 10, 1864, Wilderness, Virginia	Point Lookout, Maryland, transferred to Elmira Prison, NY, August 6, 1864	Exchanged February 20, 1865 at Boulware's or Cox Wharf on the James River, Virginia
Seward, Robert B. Private	22	June 2, 1861, Little Plymouth, Virginia	Co. G, 26th Virginia Infantry	June 15, 1864, Near Petersburg, Virginia	Point Lookout, Maryland, transferred to Elmira Prison, NY, July 12, 1864. Ward No. 19	Died August 11, 1864 of Chronic Diarrhea, Grave No. 131
Sexton, Alsey Private	33	September 27, 1862, Wake County, North Carolina	Co. C, 31st North Carolina Infantry	May 31, 1864, Gaines Farm, Cold Harbor, Virginia	Point Lookout, Maryland, transferred to Elmira Prison, NY, July 17, 1864	Died February 19, 1865 of Variola (Smallpox), Grave No. 2330
Sexton, Archibald S. Private	Unk	Unknown	Co. D, 50th Virginia Infantry	May 12, 1864, Spotsylvania Court House, Virginia	Point Lookout, Maryland, transferred to Elmira Prison, NY, August 2, 1864	Exchanged October 29, 1864, at Venus Point, Savannah River, GA.
Sexton, Augustine Private	Unk	April 15, 1864, Wake County, North Carolina	Co. C, 31st North Carolina Infantry	May 31, 1864, Gaines Farm, Cold Harbor, Virginia	Point Lookout, Maryland, transferred to Elmira Prison, NY, July 17, 1864	Died July 13, 1864 of Unknown Causes While in Transit.
Sexton, John H. Private	Unk	March 12, 1861, Prattville, Alabama	Co. E, 1st Battalion Alabama Artillery	August 23, 1864, Fort Morgan, Alabama	Steam Press No. 4 New Orleans, Louisiana transferred to Elmira Prison, NY, October 8, 1864.	Oath of Allegiance July 7, 1865
Sexton, John T. Private	38	March 1, 1861, Nashville, North Carolina	Co. H, 32nd North Carolina Infantry	May 10, 1864, Near Mine Run Spotsylvania, Virginia	Point Lookout, Maryland, transferred to Elmira Prison, NY, August 6, 1864	Exchanged March 10, 1865 at Boulware's Wharf on the James River, Virginia
Sexton, John W. Sergeant	Unk	October 1, 1862, Snickersville, Virginia	Co. C, 35th Battalion Virginia Cavalry	July 17, 1863, Snickers Gap, Virginia	Point Lookout, Maryland, transferred to Elmira Prison, NY, August 18, 1864	Exchanged February 25, 1865 at Boulware's or Cox Wharf on the James River, Virginia

Name & Rank	Age	Enlisted	Regiment and State	Where Captured	Prison	Remarks
Sexton, Joseph Private	28	August 15, 1862, Statesville, North Carolina	Co. H, 37th North Carolina Infantry	July 29, 1864, Petersburg, Virginia	Point Lookout, Maryland, transferred to Elmira Prison, NY, August 12, 1864	Died January 15, 1865 of Variola (Smallpox) Grave No. 1444
Shackleford, Jonathan C. Private	18	December 25, 1861, Spartanburg, South Carolina	Co. E, 18th South Carolina Infantry	July 30, 1864, Petersburg, Virginia	Point Lookout, Maryland, transferred to Elmira Prison, NY, August 12, 1864	Exchanged October 29, 1864, at Venus Point, Savannah River, GA.
Shackleford, William C. Private	Unk	October 19, 1861, Gloucester Point, Virginia	Co. B, 26th Virginia Infantry	June 15, 1864, Near Petersburg, Virginia	Point Lookout, Maryland, transferred to Elmira Prison, NY, July 12, 1864	Oath of Allegiance July 11, 1865
Shadding, Henry J. Private	18	December 7, 1863, Fort Pender, Brunswick County, North Carolina	Co. H, 36th Regiment, 2nd North Carolina Artillery	January 15, 1865, Fort Fisher, North Carolina	February 1, 1865, Elmira Prison Camp, New York	Died March 31, 1865 of Chronic Diarrhea, Grave No. 2598
Shaffer, R. R. Private	33	February 24, 1862, Charleston, South Carolina	Co. B, 25th South Carolina Infantry	January 15, 1865, Fort Fisher, North Carolina	February 1, 1865, Elmira Prison Camp, New York	Oath of Allegiance July 11, 1865
Shamel, Junius T. Private	22	July 8, 1862, Winston, Forsyth County, North Carolina	Co. K, 21st North Carolina Infantry	May 22, 1864, Milford Station, North Anna, Virginia	Point Lookout, Maryland, transferred to Elmira Prison, NY, July 23, 1864	Oath of Allegiance May 17, 1865
Shankle, Eli Private	32	August 8, 1862, Camp Hill, Stanley County, North Carolina	Co. F, 5th North Carolina Infantry	May 12, 1864, Spotsylvania Court House, Virginia	Point Lookout, Maryland, transferred to Elmira Prison, NY, August 6, 1864	Exchanged October 29, 1864, at Venus Point, Savannah River, GA.
Shannon, John A. Private	Unk	June 11, 1863, Tallapoosa County, Alabama	Co. L, 61st Alabama Infantry	May 20, 1864, Spotsylvania Court House, Virginia	Point Lookout, Maryland, transferred to Elmira Prison, NY, July 3, 1864	Died April 6, 1865 of Pneumonia, Grave No. 2630
Sharbutt, Warner B. Private	Unk	January 14, 1862, Camp Walsh, South Carolina	Co. J, Holcombe Legion, South Carolina Infantry	May 7, 1864, Stony Creek, Virginia	Point Lookout, Maryland, transferred to Elmira Prison, NY, August 17, 1864	Oath of Allegiance July 19, 1865

Name & Rank	Age	Enlisted	Regiment and State	Where Captured	Prison	Remarks
Sharp, John Private	38	October 17, 1864, Rockingham, North Carolina	Co. F, 45th North Carolina Infantry	April 2, 1865, Petersburg, Virginia. Gunshot Wound of Nose.	Old Capital Prison, Washington D. C. Transferred to Elmira Prison, NY, May 2, 1865.	Oath of Allegiance July 7, 1865
Sharp, Miner Private	18	April 1, 1864, Oakland Depot, Virginia	Co. D, 20th Virginia Cavalry	July 10, 1864, Frederick, Maryland	Old Capital Prison, Washington, DC, transferred to Elmira Prison, NY, July 23, 1864	Oath of Allegiance May 29, 1865
Sharp, Peter B. Private	37	February 12, 1863, Hillsboro, North Carolina	Co. E, 31st North Carolina Infantry	June 1, 1864, Gaines Farm Cold Harbor, Virginia	Point Lookout, Maryland, transferred to Elmira Prison, NY, July 12, 1864	Died October 10, 1864 of Chronic Diarrhea, Grave No. 676
Sharp, S. M. Private	Unk	Unknown	Co. F, 10th Georgia Infantry	May 6, 1864, Mine Run Wilderness, Virginia	Point Lookout, Maryland, transferred to Elmira Prison, NY, August 14, 1864	Oath of Allegiance June 30, 1865
Sharp, Sherad L. Private	23	March 4, 1862, Georgetown, Georgia	Co. G, 51st Georgia Infantry	June 3, 1864, Gaines Farm Cold Harbor, Virginia	Point Lookout, Maryland, transferred to Elmira Prison, NY, July 12, 1864	Exchanged October 29, 1864, at Venus Point, Savannah River, GA.
Sharpe, Wiley Corporal	Unk	May 9, 1862, Johnson's Station, Reidsville, Georgia	Co. H, 61st Georgia Infantry	May 12, 1864, Spotsylvania Court House, Virginia	Point Lookout, Maryland, transferred to Elmira Prison, NY, July 25, 1864	Exchanged March 10, 1865 at Boulware's Wharf on the James River, Virginia
Shaver, John J. Private	19	August 8, 1862, Statesville, North Carolina	Co. H, 5th North Carolina Infantry	May 12, 1864, Near Spotsylvania County Court House, Virginia	Point Lookout, Maryland, transferred to Elmira Prison, NY, August 14, 1864	Oath of Allegiance June 27, 1865
Shaver, S. C. Private	Unk	Unknown	Co. B, 5th North Carolina Infantry	May 12, 1864, Spotsylvania Court House, Virginia	Old Capital Prison, Washington, DC transferred to Elmira Prison, NY, August 29, 1864	Exchanged March 2, 1865 at Akins Landing on the James River, Virginia

Name & Rank	Age	Enlisted	Regiment and State	Where Captured	Prison	Remarks
Shaw, Alexander E. Private	Unk	April 22, 1864, Greensboro, Georgia	Co. E, 3rd Georgia Sharp Shooters	August 16, 1864, Front Royal, Virginia	Old Capital Prison, Washington, DC transferred to Elmira Prison, NY, August 29, 1864	Died May 8, 1865 of Diarrhea, Grave No. 2777
Shaw, Archibald J. Private	23	March 7, 1862, Lumber Bridge, North Carolina	Co. D, 51st North Carolina Infantry	June 16, 1864, Near Petersburg, Near Bermuda Hundred, Virginia	Point Lookout, Maryland, transferred to Elmira Prison, NY, July 12, 1864	Died March 24, 1865 of Pneumonia, Grave No. 2449
Shaw, Bennett Private	22	May 6, 1862, Elizabethtown, Bladen County, North Carolina	Co. K, 40th Regiment, 3rd North Carolina Artillery	January 15, 1865, Fort Fisher, North Carolina	February 1, 1865, Elmira Prison Camp, New York	Oath of Allegiance June 12, 1865
Shaw, Daniel M. Private	41	September 19, 1863, Fort Caswell, Brunswick County, North Carolina	Co. E, 40th Regiment, 3rd North Carolina Artillery	January 15, 1865, Fort Fisher, North Carolina	February 1, 1865, Elmira Prison Camp, New York	Exchanged March 2, 1865 at Akins Landing on the James River, Virginia
Shaw, David F. Private	33	May 6, 1862, Elizabethtown, Bladen County, North Carolina	Co. K, 40th Regiment, 3rd North Carolina Artillery	January 15, 1865, Fort Fisher, North Carolina	February 1, 1865, Elmira Prison Camp, New York	Oath of Allegiance June 12, 1865
Shaw, Duncan Private	Unk	May 6, 1862, Elizabethtown, Bladen County, North Carolina	Co. K, 40th Regiment, 3rd North Carolina Artillery	January 15, 1865, Fort Fisher, North Carolina	February 1, 1865, Elmira Prison Camp, New York	Oath of Allegiance June 12, 1865
Shaw, Frederick E. Private	22	February 22, 1862, Greensboro, North Carolina	Co. E, 22nd North Carolina Infantry	May 6, 1864, Wilderness, Virginia	Point Lookout, Maryland, transferred to Elmira Prison, NY, August 14, 1864	Died March 6, 1865 of Variola (Smallpox), Grave No. 2415. Headstone has 32nd NC.
Shaw, H. D. Private	17	April 12, 1862, Battery Island, South Carolina	Co. C, 25th South Carolina Infantry	January 15, 1865, Fort Fisher, North Carolina	February 1, 1865, Elmira Prison Camp, New York	Oath of Allegiance July 11, 1865
Shaw, James P. Private	23	July 15, 1862, Alamance County, North Carolina	Co. B, 1st North Carolina Infantry	May 12, 1864, Spotsylvania Court House, Virginia	Point Lookout, Maryland, transferred to Elmira Prison, NY, August 6, 1864	Exchanged October 29, 1864, at Venus Point, Savannah River, GA.

Name & Rank	Age	Enlisted	Regiment and State	Where Captured	Prison	Remarks
Shaw, Jesse T. Private	20	November 4, 1861, Randolph County, North Carolina	Co. H, 38th North Carolina Infantry	July 14, 1863, Falling Waters, Maryland	Point Lookout, Maryland, transferred to Elmira Prison, NY, August 18, 1864	Exchanged March 10, 1865 at Boulware's Wharf on the James River, Virginia
Shaw, John Private	40	December 28, 1861, Wilmington, North Carolina	Co. D, 36th Regiment 2nd North Carolina Artillery	January 15, 1865, Fort Fisher, North Carolina	February 1, 1865, Elmira Prison Camp, New York	Oath of Allegiance July 3, 1865
Shaw, John A. Private	33	March 5, 1862, Lumber Bridge, North Carolina	Co. D, 51st North Carolina Infantry	June 16, 1864, Near Petersburg, Near Bermuda Hundred, Virginia	Point Lookout, Maryland, transferred to Elmira Prison, NY, July 12, 1864	Transferred for Exchange 10/11/64, Died 10/14/64 at U. S. Army Hospital, Baltimore, MD.
Shaw, John W. Private	18	May 6, 1862, Elizabethtown, Bladen County, North Carolina	Co. K, 40th Regiment, 3rd North Carolina Artillery	January 15, 1865, Fort Fisher, North Carolina	February 1, 1865, Elmira Prison Camp, New York	Oath of Allegiance June 12, 1865
Shaw, Malcom Private	16	February 7, 1863, Fort St. Philip, Brunswick County, North Carolina	Co. K, 36th Regiment, 2nd North Carolina Artillery	January 15, 1865, Fort Fisher, North Carolina	February 1, 1865, Elmira Prison Camp, New York	Oath of Allegiance July 7, 1865
Shaw, Martin Private	33	May 27, 1861, Troy, North Carolina	Co. J, 32nd North Carolina Infantry	June 10, 1864, Spotsylvania, Virginia	Point Lookout, Maryland, transferred to Elmira Prison, NY, July 25, 1864	Exchanged March 14, 1865 at Boulware's Wharf on the James River, Virginia
Shaw, Mitchell Private	41	October 26, 1864, Fort Holmes, New Hanover County, North Carolina	Co. K, 40th Regiment, 3rd North Carolina Artillery	January 15, 1865, Fort Fisher, North Carolina	February 1, 1865, Elmira Prison Camp, New York	Exchanged March 2, 1865 at Akins Landing on the James River, Virginia
Shaw, Percival N. Private	22	February 12, 1862, Waterproof, Louisiana	Co. A, 14th Louisiana Infantry	May 12, 1864, Spotsylvania, Virginia. Gunshot Wound Right Thigh.	Old Capital Prison, Washington, DC, transferred to Elmira Prison, NY, December 17, 1864	Exchanged February 25, 1865 at Boulware's or Cox Wharf on the James River, Virginia

Name & Rank	Age	Enlisted	Regiment and State	Where Captured	Prison	Remarks
Shaw, Robert Private	34	July 15, 1862, Alamance County, North Carolina	Co. B, 1st North Carolina Infantry	May 12, 1864, Spotsylvania Court House, Virginia	Point Lookout, Maryland, transferred to Elmira Prison, NY, August 6, 1864	Exchanged February 20, 1865 at Boulware's or Cox Wharf on the James River, Virginia
Shaw, Robert Private	18	June 10, 1861, Halifax County, North Carolina	Co. K, 1st North Carolina Infantry	May 12, 1864, Spotsylvania Court House, Virginia	Point Lookout, Maryland, transferred to Elmira Prison, NY, August 6, 1864	Exchanged February 20, 1865 at Boulware's or Cox Wharf on the James River, Virginia
Shaw, Solomon Private	36	February 7, 1863, Fort Philip, Brunswick County, North Carolina	Co. E, 36th Regiment, 2nd North Carolina Artillery	January 15, 1865, Fort Fisher, North Carolina	February 1, 1865, Elmira Prison Camp, New York	Exchanged March 14, 1865 at Boulware's Wharf on the James River, Virginia
Shaw, Thomas Private	45	February 15, 1862, Camp Bee, North Carolina	Co. K, 1st North Carolina Infantry	May 12, 1864, Spotsylvania Court House, Virginia	Point Lookout, Maryland, transferred to Elmira Prison, NY, August 6, 1864	Oath of Allegiance June 12, 1865
Shawkey, Andrew Private	Unk	April 23, 1861, Memphis, Tennessee	Co. A, Jackson's 1st Regiment, Tennessee Heavy Artillery	August 23, 1864, Fort Morgan, Alabama	New Orleans, Louisiana transferred to Elmira Prison, NY, December 4, 1864.	Oath of Allegiance May 17, 1865
Shay, Martin Private	Unk	October 13, 1861, Mobile, Alabama	Co. A, 21st Alabama Infantry	August 23, 1864, Fort Morgan, Alabama	Steam Press No. 4 New Orleans, Louisiana transferred to Elmira Prison, NY, October 8, 1864.	Oath of Allegiance July 7, 1865
Shea, John Private	Unk	May 27, 1861, New Orleans, Louisiana	Co. B, 15th Louisiana Infantry	May 12, 1864, Spotsylvania Court House, Virginia	Point Lookout, Maryland, transferred to Elmira Prison, NY, July 25, 1864	Died December 1, 1864 of Pneumonia, Grave No. 1014
Sheahan, William S. Private	Unk	May 2, 1862, St. John, Hertford County, North Carolina	Co. C, 3rd Battalion North Carolina Light Artillery	January 15, 1865, Fort Fisher, North Carolina	February 1, 1865, Elmira Prison Camp, New York	Oath of Allegiance August 7, 1865

Name & Rank	Age	Enlisted	Regiment and State	Where Captured	Prison	Remarks
Shearer, B. H. Private	Unk	February 11, 1863, Pendleton, South Carolina	Co. A, 7th South Carolina Cavalry	May 30, 1864, Old Church, Cold Harbor, Virginia	Point Lookout, Maryland, transferred to Elmira Prison, NY, July 12, 1864	Died August 10, 1864 of Chronic Diarrhea, Grave No. 14
Shearin, Edward A. Private	38	February 25, 1862, Halifax County, North Carolina	Co. I, 12th North Carolina Infantry	May 20, 1864, Spotsylvania Court House, Virginia	Point Lookout, Maryland, transferred to Elmira Prison, NY, July 3, 1864	Exchanged October 29, 1864, at Venus Point, Savannah River, GA.
Shearin, H. L. W. Private	Unk	December 9, 1861, Camp Trousdale, Tennessee	Co. B, 44th Tennessee Infantry	June 17, 1864, Petersburg, Virginia	Point Lookout, Maryland, transferred to Elmira Prison, NY, July 30, 1864	Died October 21, 1864 of Chronic Diarrhea, Grave No. 873
Shearin, John D. Private	25	August 16, 1861, Warren County, North Carolina	Co. B, 30th North Carolina Infantry	May 8, 1864, Wilderness, Virginia	Point Lookout, Maryland, transferred to Elmira Prison, NY, August 14, 1864	Died October 4, 1864 of Chronic Diarrhea, Grave No. 639. Name Sharing on Headstone.
Shearin, Thomas W. Private	30	July 22, 1861, Warrenton, North Carolina	Co. K, 5th North Carolina Infantry	May 12, 1864, Spotsylvania Court House, Virginia	Point Lookout, Maryland, transferred to Elmira Prison, NY, August 6, 1864	Died December 30, 1864 of Pneumonia, Grave No. 1320. Wrong Name on Headstone Abner Harrell.
Shearin, Zachariah T. Private	19	March 30, 1861, Littleton, North Carolina	Co. A, 14th North Carolina Infantry	May 8, 1864, Wilderness, Virginia	Point Lookout, Maryland, transferred to Elmira Prison, NY, August 14, 1864	Exchanged March 10, 1865 on the James River, Virginia
Sheaves, Joseph A. Private	17	December 31, 1861, Richmond, Virginia	Co. A, 26th Battalion, Virginia Infantry	June 3, 1864, Gaines Mill Cold Harbor, Virginia	Point Lookout, Maryland, transferred to Elmira Prison, NY, July 17, 1864	Oath of Allegiance June 23, 1865
Sheets, David H. L. Sergeant	27	May 18, 1861, Seven Mile Ford, Virginia	Co. D, 48th Virginia Infantry	May 12, 1864, Spotsylvania Court House, Virginia	Point Lookout, Maryland, transferred to Elmira Prison, NY, August 2, 1864	Oath of Allegiance, May 29, 1865

Name & Rank	Age	Enlisted	Regiment and State	Where Captured	Prison	Remarks
Sheets, John II. Private	Unk	May 22, 1861, Harrisonburg, Virginia	Co. C, 1st Virginia Cavalry	September 14, 1863, Near Culpepper, Virginia	Point Lookout, Maryland, transferred to Elmira Prison, NY, August 12, 1864	Exchanged March 14, 1865 at Boulware's Wharf on the James River, Virginia
Sheetz, Daniel H. Sergeant	Unk	April 16, 1862, Rudes Hill, Virginia	Co. K, 2nd Virginia Infantry	May 12, 1864, Near Spotsylvania Court House, Virginia	Point Lookout, Maryland, transferred to Elmira Prison, NY, August 2, 1864	Exchanged October 29, 1864, at Venus Point, Savannah River, GA.
Sheetz, George W. Private	Unk	April 14, 1862, Rudes Hill, Virginia	Co. K, 2nd Virginia Infantry	May 12, 1864, Spotsylvania Court House, Virginia	Point Lookout, Maryland, transferred to Elmira Prison, NY, August 2, 1864	Oath of Allegiance June 27, 1865
Sheetz, Samuel W. Private	Unk	April 16, 1862, Rudes Hill, Virginia	Co. G, 2nd Virginia Infantry	May 12, 1864, Near Spotsylvania Court House, Virginia	Point Lookout, Maryland, transferred to Elmira Prison, NY, August 2, 1864	Died March 1, 1865 of Congestion of Lungs, Grave No. 2101
Sheetz, William L. Private	Unk	April 14, 1862, Rudes Hill, Virginia	Co. K, 2nd Virginia Infantry	May 12, 1864, Spotsylvania Court House, Virginia	Point Lookout, Maryland, transferred to Elmira Prison, NY, August 2, 1864	Died February 12, 1865 of Chronic Diarrhea, Grave No. 2076
Sheffey, William B. Private	Unk	July 30, 1861, Marion, Virginia	Co. D, 4th Virginia Infantry	May 12, 1864 Spotsylvania Court House, Virginia	Point Lookout, Maryland, transferred to Elmira Prison, NY, August 2, 1864	Died September 2, 1864 of Chronic Diarrhea, Grave No. 64
Sheffield, James Private	Unk	Unknown	Co. B, Hood's Battalion, Virginia Reserves	June 15, 1864, Petersburg, Virginia	Point Lookout, Maryland, transferred to Elmira Prison, NY, July 30, 1864	Exchanged March 14, 1865 at Boulware's Wharf on the James River, Virginia
Sheffield, Newton Private	Unk	November 9, 1863, Talladega, Alabama	Jeff Davis Alabama Artillery	May 5, 1864, Wilderness, Virginia	Point Lookout, Maryland, transferred to Elmira Prison, NY, August 17, 1864	Exchanged February 20, 1865 at Boulware's or Cox Wharf on the James River, Virginia

Name & Rank	Age	Enlisted	Regiment and State	Where Captured	Prison	Remarks
Shelby, William J. Private	Unk	January 13, 1864, Montgomery, Alabama	Co. F, 1st Battalion Alabama Artillery	August 23, 1864, Fort Morgan, Alabama	Steam Press No. 4 New Orleans, Louisiana transferred to Elmira Prison, NY, October 8, 1864.	Died October 31, 1864, Chronic Diarrhea, Grave No 741.
Shelfer, Elijah K. Private	Unk	November 5, 1861, Camp Gaston, North Carolina	Co. E, 3rd North Carolina Cavalry	May 27, 1864, Nelson Ford, Virginia	Point Lookout, Maryland, transferred to Elmira Prison, NY, July 12, 1864	Died of October 1, 1864 Chronic Diarrhea, Grave No. 402
Shelfer, Jesse Private	Unk	May 15, 1862, Lenoir County, North Carolina	Co. E, 3rd North Carolina Cavalry	May 24, 1864, Hanover Junction, Virginia	Point Lookout, Maryland, transferred to Elmira Prison, NY, July 12, 1864	Exchanged February 20, 1865 at Boulware's or Cox Wharf on the James River, Virginia
Shell, George W. Private	Unk	Unknown	Co. C, 37th Virginia Infantry	May 12, 1864, Spotsylvania Court House, Virginia	Point Lookout, Maryland, transferred to Elmira Prison, NY, August 2, 1864	Exchanged March 2, 1865 at Akins Landing on the James River, Virginia
Shell, William D. Private	20	June 6, 1861, Newton, North Carolina	Co. F, 23rd North Carolina Infantry	May 12, 1864, Near Spotsylvania Court House, Virginia	Point Lookout, Maryland, transferred to Elmira Prison, NY, August 14, 1864	Oath of Allegiance June 27, 1865
Shelor, John B. Private	Unk	June 22, 1861, Wytheville, Virginia	Co. K, 50th Virginia Infantry	May 12, 1864, Spotsylvania Court House, Virginia	Point Lookout Prison Camp, Maryland. Transferred to Elmira Prison, NY, August 2, 1864	Died February 16, 1865 of Anasarca (Edema or Dropsy), Grave No. 2181
Shelton, Alfred Private	Unk	April 29, 1861, Marshall, North Carolina	Co. H, 6th North Carolina Infantry	July 10, 1864, Frederick, Maryland	Old Capital Prison, Washington, DC, transferred to Elmira Prison, NY, July 23, 1864	Died September 25, 1864 of Chronic Diarrhea. Grave No. 372
Shelton, Edward B. Sergeant	Unk	March 19, 1862, Richmond, Virginia	Co. A, 24th Virginia Cavalry	May 16, 1864, Near Drury's Bluff, Virginia	Point Lookout, Maryland, transferred to Elmira Prison, NY, August 17, 1864	Died September 21, 1864 of Chronic Diarrhea, Grave No. 347. Headstone has 40th Virginia.

Name & Rank	Age	Enlisted	Regiment and State	Where Captured	Prison	Remarks
Shelton, George A. Private	Unk	February 18, 1864, Henry County, Virginia	Co. H, 42nd Virginia Infantry	May 12, 1864, Near Spotsylvania Court House, Virginia	Point Lookout, Maryland, transferred to Elmira Prison, NY, August 6, 1864	Exchanged October 29, 1864, at Venus Point, Savannah River, GA.
Shelton, J. Private	Unk	Unknown	Co. A, Jackson's 1st Regiment, Tennessee Heavy Artillery	August 23, 1864, Fort Morgan, Alabama	New Orleans, Louisiana transferred to Elmira Prison, NY, December 4, 1864.	Exchanged February 25, 1865 at Boulware's or Cox Wharf on the James River, Virginia
Shelton, Joshua John Private	18	May 22, 1861, Spoon Creek, Virginia	Co. H, 42nd Virginia Infantry	May 12, 1864, Spotsylvania Court House, Virginia. Gunshot Wound Left Shoulder.	Old Capital Prison, Washington, DC transferred to Elmira Prison, NY, August 27, 1864	Oath of Allegiance June 19, 1865
Shelton, S. M. Sergeant	Unk	Unknown	Co. E, 44th Virginia Infantry	May 12, 1864, Spotsylvania Court House, Virginia	Point Lookout, Maryland, transferred to Elmira Prison, NY, August 12, 1864	Exchanged February 25, 1865 at Boulware's or Cox Wharf on the James River, Virginia
Shelton, William H. Private	Unk	May 22, 1861, Spoon Creek, Virginia	Co. H, 42nd Virginia Infantry	May 12, 1864, Near Spotsylvania Court House, Virginia	Point Lookout, Maryland, transferred to Elmira Prison, NY, August 6, 1864	Died January 27, 1865 of Pneumonia, Grave No. 1645
Shepard, Daniel Private	23	July 8, 1861, Salisbury, North Carolina	Co. K, 8th North Carolina Infantry	May 31, 1864, Cold Harbor, Virginia	Point Lookout, Maryland, transferred to Elmira Prison, NY, July 12, 1864	Died September 18, 1864 of Chronic Diarrhea, Grave No. 151. Headstone has 1st Regiment.
Shepard, John J. Private	17	February 13, 1862, Wilmington, New Hanover County, North Carolina	Co. J, 36th Regiment, 2nd North Carolina Artillery	January 15, 1865, Fort Fisher, North Carolina	February 1, 1865, Elmira Prison Camp, New York	Exchanged March 14, 1865 at Boulware's Wharf on the James River, Virginia
Shepard, W. J. Private	Unk	May 24, 1862, Macon, Georgia	Captain Slaten's Battery, Georgia Artillery	June 17, 1864, Petersburg, Virginia	Point Lookout, Maryland, transferred to Elmira Prison, NY, July 30, 1864	Oath of Allegiance May 29, 1865

Name & Rank	Age	Enlisted	Regiment and State	Where Captured	Prison	Remarks
Sheperd, Daniel Private	30	July 15, 1862, Alamance County, North Carolina	Co. B, 1st North Carolina Infantry	May 12, 1864, Near Spotsylvania Court House, Virginia	Point Lookout Prison, Maryland. Transferred to Elmira Prison Camp New York August 6, 1864.	Oath of Allegiance June 27, 1865
Sheperd, Elijah Private	21	March 4, 1862, Dublin, Georgia	Co. H, 14th Georgia Infantry	May 6, 1864, Mine Run Wilderness, Virginia	Point Lookout, Maryland, transferred to Elmira Prison, NY, August 6, 1864	Oath of Allegiance June 19, 1865
Shephard, John J. Private	17	February 13, 1862, Wilmington, New Hanover County, North Carolina	2nd Co. D, 36th Regiment North Carolina, 2nd Artillery	January 15, 1865, Fort Fisher, North Carolina	February 1, 1865, Elmira Prison Camp, New York	Exchanged March 14, 1865 at Boulware's Wharf on the James River, Virginia
Shepherd, Ethemore Private	18	March 1, 1862, Cerro Gordo, North Carolina	Co. E, 36th Regiment, 2nd North Carolina Artillery	January 15, 1865, Fort Fisher, North Carolina	February 1, 1865, Elmira Prison Camp, New York	Oath of Allegiance July 26, 1865
Shepherd, Henry Private	Unk	May 1, 1862, Richmond, Virginia	Sturdivant's Co. A, Virginia Light Artillery	June 15, 1864, Petersburg, Virginia	Point Lookout, Maryland, transferred to Elmira Prison, NY, July 12, 1864	Exchanged March 10, 1865 at Boulware's Wharf on the James River, Virginia
Shepherd, James K. Private	18	March 14, 1862, Whiteville, North Carolina	Co. H, 51st North Carolina Infantry	June 1, 1864, Cold Harbor, Virginia	Point Lookout, Maryland, transferred to Elmira Prison, NY, July 12, 1864	Oath of Allegiance July 3, 1865
Shepherd, Joseph H. Private	20	May 11, 1861, Sangerville, Virginia	Co. I, 5th Virginia Infantry	May 20, 1864, Spotsylvania Court House, Virginia	Point Lookout, Maryland, transferred to Elmira Prison, NY, July 3, 1864	Exchanged March 14, 1865 at Boulware's Wharf on the James River, Virginia
Shepherd, Robert S. Private	Unk	April 26, 1861, Lagrange, Georgia	Co. B, 4th Georgia Infantry	May 20, 1864, Spotsylvania Court House, Virginia	Point Lookout, Maryland, transferred to Elmira Prison, NY, July 3, 1864	Exchanged March 10, 1865 at Boulware's Wharf on the James River, Virginia

Name & Rank	Age	Enlisted	Regiment and State	Where Captured	Prison	Remarks
Shepherd, William M. B. Sergeant	Unk	May 20, 1861, Palmyra, Virginia	Co. F, 44th Virginia Infantry	May 12, 1864, Spotsylvania Court House, Virginia	Point Lookout, Maryland, transferred to Elmira Prison, NY, August 2, 1864	Oath of Allegiance June 14, 1865
Sheppard, George W. Private	Unk	May 6, 1861, Grove Hill, Alabama	Co. J, 5th Alabama Infantry	July 15, 1864, Leasburg, Virginia	Old Capital Prison, Washington D. C. Transferred to Elmira Prison, NY, August 12, 1864	Died November 19, 1864 of Chronic Diarrhea, Grave No. 946
Sheppard, Richard T. Private	21	April 23, 1861, Gloucester Court House, Virginia	Co. B, 26th Virginia Infantry	June 3, 1864, Gaines Farm Cold Harbor, Virginia	Point Lookout, Maryland, transferred to Elmira Prison, NY, July 12, 1864	Oath of Allegiance July 3, 1865
Sheriff, Thomas M. Private	21	August 24, 1861, Habersham County, Georgia	Co. H, 24th Georgia Infantry	June 3, 1864, Gaines Mill Cold Harbor, Virginia	Point Lookout, Maryland, transferred to Elmira Prison, NY, July 12, 1864	Died February 25, 1865 of Chronic Diarrhea, Grave No. 2291
Sherman, Daniel W. Private	Unk	August 27, 1863, Harrisonburg, Virginia	Co. H, 12th Virginia Cavalry	July 24, 1864, Lewisville, Virginia	Old Capital Prison, Washington D. C. Transferred to Elmira Prison, NY, August 12, 1864	Oath of Allegiance May 17, 1865
Sherman, John Private	Unk	November 4, 1863, Hardy, Virginia	Co. B, 18th Virginia Cavalry	July 16, 1864, Loudoun County, Virginia	Old Capital Prison, Washington, DC, transferred to Elmira Prison, NY, July 23, 1864	Died October 3, 1864 of Chronic Diarrhea, Grave No. 637
Sherriff, W. W. Private	Unk	November 1, 1863, Pocotaligo, South Carolina	Co. C, 4th South Carolina Cavalry	June 11, 1864, Trevilian Station, Louisa Court House, Virginia	Point Lookout, Maryland, transferred to Elmira Prison, NY, July 25, 1864	Died February 16, 1865 of Variola (Smallpox), Grave No. 2198
Sherril, Miles Sergeant	19	April 27, 1861, Newton, North Carolina	Co. A, 12th North Carolina Infantry	May 9, 1864, Spotsylvania, Virginia. Gunshot Wound Fracture of Right Knee, Amputated	Old Capital Prison, Washington, DC, transferred to Elmira Prison, NY, December 17, 1864	Exchanged February 13, 1865 at Boulware's Wharf on the James River, Virginia

Name & Rank	Age	Enlisted	Regiment and State	Where Captured	Prison	Remarks
Sherrill, James M. Private	Unk	February 22, 1864, Newton, North Carolina	Co. E, 32nd North Carolina Infantry	May 10, 1864, Wilderness, Virginia	Point Lookout, Maryland, transferred to Elmira Prison, NY, August 6, 1864	Exchanged October 29, 1864, at Venus Point, Savannah River, GA.
Sherrill, Nicholas Private	20	August 14, 1861, Newton, North Carolina	Co. F, 32nd North Carolina Infantry	May 10, 1864, Wilderness, Virginia	Point Lookout, Maryland, transferred to Elmira Prison, NY, August 6, 1864	Died March 29, 1865 of Chronic Diarrhea, Grave No. 2538
Sherrill, William P. Private	25	April 27, 1861, Newton, North Carolina	Co. E, 32nd North Carolina Infantry	May 10, 1864, Wilderness, Virginia	Point Lookout, Maryland, transferred to Elmira Prison, NY, August 6, 1864	Died January 27, 1865 of Chronic Diarrhea, Grave No. 1644
Sherry, Charles Private	Unk	July 13, 1863, Richmond, Virginia	Co. F, 1st Maryland Cavalry	July 12, 1864, Near Washington, DC	Old Capital Prison, Washington, DC, transferred to Elmira Prison, NY, July 23, 1864	Oath of Allegiance May 29, 1865
Shew, Constance Private	Unk	March 1, 1864, Camp Vance, North Carolina	Co. F, 37th North Carolina Infantry	May 12, 1864, Near Spotsylvania Court House, Virginia	Point Lookout, Maryland, transferred to Elmira Prison, NY, August 14, 1864	Died September 18, 1864 of Chronic Diarrhea, Grave No. 513. Name Constin Shoe on Headstone.
Shield, Michael Private	Unk	October 25, 1861, Richmond, Virginia	Captain Brocken-brough's 2nd battery Maryland Artillery	July 16, 1864, Loudoun County, Virginia	Old Capital Prison, Washington, DC, transferred to Elmira Prison, NY, July 23, 1864	Oath of Allegiance July 11, 1865
Shields, Jesse W. Private	Unk	March 8, 1862, Norfolk, Virginia	Co. B, 6th Virginia Infantry	July 30, 1864, Petersburg, Virginia	Point Lookout, Maryland, transferred to Elmira Prison, NY, August 12, 1864	Oath of Allegiance May 29, 1865
Shifflett, Benjamin F. Private	Unk	June 15, 1861, Ch'Ville, Virginia	Co. D, 46th Virginia Infantry	June 17, 1864, Near Petersburg, Virginia	Point Lookout Prison Camp, Maryland. Transferred to Elmira Prison Camp, NY, July 28, 1864	Died June 26, 1865 of Variola (Smallpox), Grave No. 2824. Name B. F. Sheflet on Headstone.

Name & Rank	Age	Enlisted	Regiment and State	Where Captured	Prison	Remarks
Shifflett, Eli Private	Unk	April 6, 1864, Wilkes, Virginia	Co. D, 46th Virginia Infantry	June 17, 1864, Near Petersburg, Virginia	Point Lookout, Maryland, transferred to Elmira Prison, NY, July 25, 1864	Oath of Allegiance July 3, 1865
Shifflett, William L Private	Unk	February 18, 1864, Harrisonburg, Virginia	Co. C, 10th Virginia Infantry	May 12, 1864, Spotsylvania Court House, Virginia	Point Lookout, Maryland, transferred to Elmira Prison, NY, August 2, 1864	Exchanged March 2, 1865 at Akins Landing on the James River, Virginia
Shiflett, Montgomery Private	Unk	February 26, 1864, John's Island, South Carolina	Co. D, 46th Virginia Infantry	June 17, 1864, Petersburg, Virginia	Point Lookout, Maryland, transferred to Elmira Prison, NY, July 23, 1864	Died February 27, 1865 of Diarrhea, Grave No. 2156
Shilling, William R. Private	19	March 8, 1862, Floyd Court House, Virginia	Co. B, 42nd Virginia Infantry	May 12, 1864, Spotsylvania Court House, Virginia	Point Lookout, Maryland, transferred to Elmira Prison, NY, July 30, 1864	Oath of Allegiance May 29, 1865
Shinard, John Jr. Private	Unk	Unknown	Co. J, 14th Virginia Infantry	May 27, 1864, Caroline County, Virginia	Point Lookout, Maryland, transferred to Elmira Prison, NY, July 23, 1864	Died April 6, 1865 of Pneumonia, Grave No. 2628
Shinault, Hiter Private	17	Unknown	Co. I, 2nd Virginia Infantry, Local Defense	May 28, 1864, Reader Mills, Virginia	Point Lookout, Maryland, transferred to Elmira Prison, NY, July 11, 1864	Exchanged October 29, 1864, at Venus Point, Savannah River, GA.
Shinault, V. Private	Unk	Unknown	Co. I, 2nd Virginia Infantry, Local Defense	May 28, 1864, Reader Mills, Virginia	Point Lookout, Maryland, transferred to Elmira Prison, NY, July 11, 1864	Oath of Allegiance May 29, 1865
Shingleton, Elisha Private	Unk	February 7, 1863, New Market, Virginia	Co. D, 11th Virginia Cavalry	September 22, 1863, Rexeyville, Near Madison Court House, Virginia	Point Lookout, Maryland, transferred to Elmira Prison, NY, August 18, 1864	Exchanged March 10, 1865 at Boulware's Wharf on the James River, Virginia

Name & Rank	Age	Enlisted	Regiment and State	Where Captured	Prison	Remarks
Shinn, Samuel J. Private	Unk	Unknown	Co. G, 6th North Carolina Infantry	July 8, 1864, Harper's Ferry, Virginia	Old Capital Prison, Washington, DC, transferred to Elmira Prison, NY, July 23, 1864	Oath of Allegiance May 29, 1865
Shipes, Jacob Private	16	July 15, 1861, Whippy Swamp, South Carolina	Co. D, 11th South Carolina Infantry	June 16, 1864, Petersburg, Virginia	Point Lookout Prison Camp, Maryland. Transferred to Elmira Prison, July 28, 1864	Died December 8, 1864 of Chronic Diarrhea, Grave No. 1174
Shipman, J. K. P. Sergeant	16	May 20, 1861, Nashville, North Carolina	Co. G, 1st North Carolina Cavalry	September 22, 1863, Jack's Shop, Near Madison County House, Virginia	Point Lookout, Maryland, transferred to Elmira Prison, NY, August 18, 1864	Transferred For Exchange 10/11/64 to Point Lookout Prison Camp, MD. Died 10/22/64 of Chronic Diarrhea.
Shipman, William Private	24	July 8, 1862, Bladen County, North Carolina	Co. B, 36th Regiment, 2nd North Carolina Artillery	January 15, 1865, Fort Fisher, North Carolina	February 1, 1865, Elmira Prison Camp, New York	Oath of Allegiance July 7, 1865
Shipp, William L. Private	Unk	May 18, 1861, Cusseta, Georgia	Co. C, 31st Georgia Infantry	May 20, 1864, Spotsylvania Court House, Virginia	Point Lookout, Maryland, transferred to Elmira Prison, NY, July 3, 1864	Died September 26, 1864 of Acute Diarrhea, Grave No. 370
Shireman, Eli Private	Unk	Unknown	Co. A, 23rd Virginia Cavalry	July 16, 1864, Loudoun County, Virginia	Old Capital Prison, Washington, DC, transferred to Elmira Prison, NY, July 23, 1864	Oath of Allegiance July 11, 1865
Shirier, Henry W. Private	Unk	April 11, 1862, Coles Island, South Carolina	Co. F, 25th South Carolina Infantry	January 15, 1865, Fort Fisher, North Carolina	February 1, 1865, Elmira Prison Camp, New York	Died June 30, 1865 of Variola (Smallpox), Grave No. 2830
Shirley, Bird Private	Unk	October 3, 1861, Clarksville, Georgia	Co. K, 24th Georgia infantry	August 16, 1864, Front Royal, Virginia	Old Capital Prison, Washington, DC transferred to Elmira Prison, NY, August 29, 1864	Oath of Allegiance July 7, 1865

Name & Rank	Age	Enlisted	Regiment and State	Where Captured	Prison	Remarks
Shirley, Hambleton Private	Unk	August 13, 1861, Camp Moore, Louisiana	Co. K, 12th Louisiana Infantry	May 16, 1863, Baker's Creek, Champion Hill, Mississippi	Point Lookout, Maryland, transferred to Elmira Prison, NY, August 18, 1864	Exchanged February 25, 1865 at Boulware's wharf on the James River, Virginia
Shirley, James M. Civilian	Unk	Unknown	Citizen of Prince William County, Virginia	December 29, 1863, Prince William County, Virginia	Point Lookout, Maryland, transferred to Elmira Prison, NY, July 25, 1864	Exchanged March 10, 1865 at Boulware's Wharf on the James River, Virginia
Shirley, John Private	25	December 25, 1861, Fort Ellis, Craven County, North Carolina	Co. F, 36th Regiment, 2nd North Carolina Artillery	January 15, 1865, Fort Fisher, North Carolina	February 1, 1865, Elmira Prison Camp, New York	Exchanged February 20, 1865 at Boulware's or Cox Wharf on the James River, Virginia
Shirley, John A. Private	Unk	September 1, 1862, Macon, Georgia	Co. B, 2nd Battalion Georgia Infantry	May 24, 1864, North Anna, Virginia	Point Lookout, Maryland, transferred to Elmira Prison, NY, July 11, 1864	Oath of Allegiance June 14, 1865
Shirley, Robert Private	20	April 23, 1861, Snow Hill, North Carolina	Co. A, 3rd North Carolina Infantry	June 10, 1864, Spotsylvania, Virginia	Point Lookout, Maryland, transferred to Elmira Prison, NY, July 25, 1864	Oath of Allegiance June 23, 1865
Shirley, Thomas S. Sergeant	36	April 23, 1861, Brentsville, Virginia	Co. A, 4th Virginia Cavalry	August 7, 1863, Kelly's Ford, Maryland	Point Lookout, Maryland, transferred to Elmira Prison, NY, August 18, 1864	Transferred For Exchange 10/11/64 to Point Lookout Prison Camp, MD. Died 11/11/64 of Unknown Causes at Port Royal, SC.
Shirley, William Private	23	April 26, 1861, Snow Hill, North Carolina	Co. A, 3rd North Carolina Infantry	May 12, 1864, Near Spotsylvania Court House, Virginia	Point Lookout, Maryland, transferred to Elmira Prison, NY, August 14, 1864	Oath of Allegiance June 23, 1865
Shiver, William N. W. Private	Unk	May 2, 1864, Marianna, Florida	Co. C, 1st Reserves Florida Infantry	September 27, 1864, Marianna, Florida	New Orleans, Louisiana transferred to Elmira November 19, 1864.	Died December 1, 1864 of Pleuro-Pneumonia, Grave No. 1004

Name & Rank	Age	Enlisted	Regiment and State	Where Captured	Prison	Remarks
Shober, Charles B. Private	Unk	March 4, 1862, Winchester, Virginia	Co. D, 2nd Virginia Infantry	July 14, 1864, Rockville, Virginia	Old Capital Prison, Washington D. C. Transferred to Elmira Prison, NY, August 12, 1864	Oath of Allegiance June 19, 1865
Shockley, W. S. Private	Unk	June 14, 1861, Camp McDonald, Georgia	Co. C, 18th Georgia Infantry	June 1, 1864, Cold Harbor, Virginia	Point Lookout, Maryland, transferred to Elmira Prison, NY, July 17, 1864	Died February 5, 1865 of Pneumonia, Grave No. 1902
Shockley, William D. Private	Unk	April 29, 1862, Auburn, Alabama	Co. D, 37th Alabama Infantry	June 11, 1864, Trevilian Station, Louisa Court House, Virginia	Point Lookout, Maryland, transferred to Elmira Prison, NY, July 23, 1864	Died September 14, 1864 of Pneumonia, Grave No. 291
Shoemaker, Charles S. Private	32	December 5, 1861, Sac River, St. Clair County, Missouri	Co. G, 1st Missouri Cavalry	May 17, 1863, Big Black Bridge, Champion Hill, Mississippi	Point Lookout, Maryland, transferred to Elmira Prison, NY, August 18, 1864	Exchanged February 13, 1865 at Boulware's wharf on the James River, Virginia
Shoemaker, Ira Thomas Sergeant	Unk	April 11, 1862, Coles Island, South Carolina	Co. F, 25th South Carolina Infantry	January 15, 1865, Fort Fisher, North Carolina	February 1, 1865, Elmira Prison Camp, New York	Oath of Allegiance June 14, 1865
Shoffner, George W. Private	19	March 5, 1862, Alamance County, North Carolina	Co. F, 53rd North Carolina Infantry	May 11, 1864, Spotsylvania Court House, VA. Gunshot Laceration of Face, Injury to Eye.	Old Capital Prison, Washington D. C. Transferred to Elmira Prison, NY, August 12, 1864	Died March 15, 1865 of Variola (Smallpox), Grave No. 1683. Shaffner on Headstone.
Shokey, Alexander H. Sergeant	24	May 16, 1861, Camp Moore, New Orleans, Louisiana	Co. G, 5th Louisiana Infantry	May 4, 1864, Wilderness, Virginia	Point Lookout, Maryland, transferred to Elmira Prison, NY, July 25, 1864	Oath of Allegiance May 17, 1865
Shook, Henry Private	28	August 14, 1862, Statesville, North Carolina	Co. A, 18th North Carolina Infantry	May 12, 1864, Spotsylvania Court House, Virginia	Point Lookout, Maryland, transferred to Elmira Prison, NY, August 6, 1864	Died August 16, 1864 of Pneumonia, Grave No. 24

Name & Rank	Age	Enlisted	Regiment and State	Where Captured	Prison	Remarks
Shoop, John A. Private	Unk	June 29, 1861, Wytheville, Virginia	Co. B, 50th Virginia Infantry	May 12, 1864, Spotsylvania Court House, Virginia	Point Lookout, Maryland, transferred to Elmira Prison, NY, August 2, 1864	Oath of Allegiance June 27, 1865
Shores, Sanford Private	24	October 18, 1863, Camp Holmes, North Carolina	Co. F, 32nd North Carolina Infantry	May 10, 1864, Wilderness, Virginia	Point Lookout, Maryland, transferred to Elmira Prison, NY, August 6, 1864	Died April 18, 1865 of Chronic Diarrhea, Grave No. 1359
Shores, Walter L. Private	Unk	June 11, 1861, Bledsoe's Store, Virginia	Co. K, 44th Virginia Infantry	May 12, 1864, Spotsylvania Court House, Virginia	Point Lookout, Maryland, transferred to Elmira Prison, NY, August 2, 1864	Oath of Allegiance June 27, 1865
Short, Benjamin Private	25	July 15, 1862, Raleigh, North Carolina	Co. K, 5th North Carolina Infantry	May 12, 1864, Spotsylvania Court House, Virginia	Point Lookout, Maryland, transferred to Elmira Prison, NY, August 6, 1864	Exchanged October 29, 1864, at Venus Point, Savannah River, GA.
Short, Daniel Private	38	April 1, 1864, Pittsboro, North Carolina	Co. G, 5th North Carolina Infantry	May 31, 1864, Hanover Court House, Virginia	Point Lookout, Maryland, transferred to Elmira Prison, NY, July 12, 1864	Oath of Allegiance March 22, 1865
Shotwell, John L. Sergeant	Unk	July 29, 1861, Columbia, South Carolina	Co. C, 1st South Carolina Infantry	July 28, 1864, Petersburg, Virginia	Point Lookout, Maryland, transferred to Elmira Prison, NY, August 12, 1864	Oath of Allegiance December 20, 1864. Early Release per Lincoln's Proclamation, 12/8/1863.
Shrewsberry, John Gabriel Private	Unk	June 4, 1861, Salem, Virginia	Co. E, 42nd Virginia Infantry	May 12, 1864, Near Spotsylvania Court House, Virginia	Point Lookout, Maryland, transferred to Elmira Prison, NY, August 6, 1864	Oath of Allegiance June 19, 1865
Shriver, John A. Sergeant	Unk	June 11, 1861, Tangipaho, Louisiana	Co. G, 6th Louisiana Infantry	May 5, 1864, Near Mine Run Wilderness, Virginia	Point Lookout, Maryland, transferred to Elmira Prison, NY, August 17, 1864	Exchanged February 25, 1865 at Boulware's or Cox Wharf on the James River, Virginia

Name & Rank	Age	Enlisted	Regiment and State	Where Captured	Prison	Remarks
Shriver, John J. Private	36	October 3, 1861, Vidalia, Louisiana	Co. A, 1st Louisiana Cavalry	October 6, 1864, Near Hampton's Ferry, Louisiana	New Orleans, Louisiana transferred to Elmira November 19, 1864.	Oath of Allegiance May 19, 1865
Shuchard, Lewis Private	Unk	Unknown	Co. B, 6th Texas Cavalry	September 19, 1864, Tensan Parish, Louisiana	New Orleans, Louisiana, Transferred to Elmira Prison, New York, November 19, 1864	Oath of Allegiance May 19, 1865
Shufflebarger, Mazarine Private	20	April 17, 1861, Christiansburg, Virginia	Co. G, 4th Virginia Infantry	May 12, 1864, Spotsylvania Court House, Virginia	Point Lookout, Maryland, transferred to Elmira Prison, NY, August 2, 1864	Oath of Allegiance July 11, 1865
Shuffler, Noah Private	25	April 15, 1862, Morganton, North Carolina	Co. B, 54th North Carolina Infantry	May 16, 1864, Near Drury's Bluff, Virginia	Point Lookout, Maryland, transferred to Elmira Prison, NY, August 17, 1864	Exchanged February 25, 1865 at Boulware's or Cox Wharf on the James River, Virginia
Shuford, Jacob M. Private	17	March 15, 1862, Lincolnton, North Carolina	Co. B, 23rd North Carolina Infantry	August 3, 1863, Gaines Crossroad, Chester Gap, Virginia	Point Lookout, Maryland, transferred to Elmira Prison, NY, August 18, 1864	Exchanged March 10, 1865 at Boulware's Wharf on the James River, Virginia
Shugart, T. C. Private	Unk	November 9, 1864, Camp McGinnis, Tullahoma, Tennessee	Co. E, 25th Tennessee Infantry	June 17, 1864, Near Petersburg, Virginia	Point Lookout, Maryland, transferred to Elmira Prison, NY, August 17, 1864	Exchanged February 25, 1865 at Boulware's or Cox Wharf on the James River, Virginia
Shuler, F. P. H. Private	Unk	April 11, 1862, Coles Island, South Carolina	Co. F, 25th South Carolina Infantry	January 15, 1865, Fort Fisher, North Carolina	February 1, 1865, Elmira Prison Camp, New York	Exchanged March 2, 1865. Died April 7, 1865 at Jackson Hospital, Richmond, Virginia.
Shuler, G. L. V. S. Private	Unk	April 11, 1862, Coles Island, South Carolina	Co. F, 25th South Carolina Infantry	January 15, 1865, Fort Fisher, North Carolina	February 1, 1865, Elmira Prison Camp, New York	Exchanged March 2, 1865 at Akins Landing on the James River, Virginia

Name & Rank	Age	Enlisted	Regiment and State	Where Captured	Prison	Remarks
Shull, Anthony Private	28	March 15, 1862, Lincolnton, North Carolina	Co. J, 11th North Carolina Infantry	July 14, 1863, Falling Waters, Maryland	Point Lookout, Maryland, transferred to Elmira Prison, NY, August 18, 1864	Died October 7, 1864 of Chronic Diarrhea, Grave No. 651. Headstone has Schull.
Shull, Charles D. Private	18	August 31, 1861, Lincolnton, North Carolina	Co. E, 34th North Carolina Infantry	May 6, 1864, Wilderness, Virginia	Point Lookout, Maryland, transferred to Elmira Prison, NY, August 14, 1864	Exchanged 10/11/64. Exchanged 10/29/64. Died 2/6/65 at General Hospital Lynchburg, VA.
Shull, Moses Private	Unk	Unknown	Co. K, 49th North Carolina Infantry	March 25, 1865, Petersburg, VA. Gunshot Wound of Neck.	Old Capital Prison, Washington D. C. Transferred to Elmira Prison, NY, May 2, 1865.	Oath of Allegiance July 7, 1865
Shull, Simon P. Sergeant	21	September 18, 1861, Boone, North Carolina	Co. E, 37th North Carolina Infantry	May 12, 1864, Near Spotsylvania Court House, Virginia	Point Lookout, Maryland, transferred to Elmira Prison, NY, August 14, 1864	Oath of Allegiance June 23, 1865
Shults, G. E. Private	Unk	March 15, 1864, Raleigh, North Carolina	Co. H, 57th North Carolina Infantry	July 8, 1864, Harper's Ferry, Virginia	Old Capital Prison, Washington, DC, transferred to Elmira Prison, NY, July 23, 1864	Oath of Allegiance March 9, 1865
Shultz, John H. Private	28	March 20, 1862, Vienna, North Carolina	Co. I, 33rd North Carolina Infantry	May 24, 1864, North Anna, Virginia	Point Lookout, Maryland, transferred to Elmira Prison, NY, July 11, 1864	Oath of Allegiance June 30, 1865
Shultz, Samuel T. Corporal	25	June 20, 1861, Abingdon, Virginia	Co. B, 48th Virginia Infantry	May 12, 1864, Spotsylvania Court House, Virginia	Point Lookout, Maryland, transferred to Elmira Prison, NY, August 12, 1864	Exchanged October 29, 1864, at Venus Point, Savannah River, GA.
Shuman, Stephen A. Sergeant	16	July 6, 1861, Salisbury, North Carolina	Co. K, 8th North Carolina Infantry	June 1, 1864, Gaines Farm Cold Harbor, Virginia	Point Lookout, Maryland, transferred to Elmira Prison, NY, July 12, 1864	Oath of Allegiance June 21, 1865

Name & Rank	Age	Enlisted	Regiment and State	Where Captured	Prison	Remarks
Shuman, W. S. Private	Unk	October 17, 1862, Braddock's Point, South Carolina	Co. E, 11th South Carolina Infantry	June 16, 1864, Petersburg, Virginia	Point Lookout, Maryland, transferred to Elmira Prison, NY, July 25, 1864	Exchanged March 14, 1865 at Boulware's Wharf on the James River, Virginia
Shumate, Daniel Private	24	September 22, 1863, Camp French, Virginia	Co. F, 52nd North Carolina Infantry	May 12, 1864, Spotsylvania Court House, Virginia	Point Lookout, Maryland, transferred to Elmira Prison, NY, August 12, 1864	Died January 6, 1865 of Pneumonia, Grave No. 1235
Shumate, L. J. Private	Unk	February 18, 1864, Henry County, Virginia	Co. F, 42nd Virginia Infantry	May 12, 1864, Near Spotsylvania Court House, Virginia	Point Lookout, Maryland, transferred to Elmira Prison, NY, August 6, 1864	Transferred for Exchange 10/11/64. Died 10/28/64 of Typhoid Fever at Point Lookout, MD
Shumate, Samuel P. Corporal	Unk	June 22, 1861, Henry County, Virginia	Co. F, 42nd Virginia Infantry	May 12, 1864, Near Spotsylvania Court House, Virginia	Point Lookout, Maryland, transferred to Elmira Prison, NY, August 6, 1864	Oath of Allegiance July 11, 1865
Shuping, Noah R. Private	21	May 29, 1861, Charlotte, North Carolina	Co. G, 6th North Carolina Infantry	July 16, 1864, Frederick, Maryland	Old Capital Prison, Washington D. C. Transferred to Elmira Prison, NY, August 12, 1864	Oath of Allegiance July 11, 1865
Shurbutt, Aaron M. Private	19	December 28, 1861, Columbia, South Carolina	Co. E, 18th South Carolina Infantry	July 30, 1864, Petersburg, Virginia	Point Lookout, Maryland, transferred to Elmira Prison, NY, August 12, 1864	Oath of Allegiance May 29, 1865
Shurley, James M. Private	21	May 31, 1861, Smithfield, North Carolina	Co. E, 24th North Carolina Infantry	June 17, 1864, Petersburg, Virginia	Point Lookout, Maryland, transferred to Elmira Prison, NY, July 30, 1864	Oath of Allegiance July 3, 1865
Shuttlesworth, H. Private	Unk	January 10, 1864, Centerville, Alabama	Co. C, 1st Battalion Alabama Artillery	August 23, 1864, Fort Morgan, Alabama	New Orleans, Louisiana transferred to Elmira Prison, NY, December 4, 1864.	Died April 9, 1865 of Chronic Diarrhea, Grave No. 2623

Name & Rank	Age	Enlisted	Regiment and State	Where Captured	Prison	Remarks
Shuttlesworth, Q. Private	Unk	January 10, 1864, Centerville, Alabama	Co. C, 1st Battalion Alabama Artillery	August 23, 1864, Fort Morgan, Alabama	New Orleans, Louisiana transferred to Elmira Prison, NY, December 4, 1864.	Oath of Allegiance June 21, 1865
Shwabackner, Henry Private	Unk	August 23, 1864, Fort Morgan, Alabama	Co. F, 1st Battalion Alabama Artillery	August 23, 1864, Fort Morgan, Alabama	Steam Press No. 4 New Orleans, Louisiana transferred to Elmira Prison, NY, October 8, 1864.	Oath of Allegiance February 13, 1865. Early Release per Lincoln's Proclamation, 12/8/1863.
Shytle, Andrew Private	28	March 14, 1862, Lincoln County, North Carolina	Co. D, 1st North Carolina Infantry	May 12, 1864, Near Spotsylvania Court House, Virginia	Point Lookout Prison, Maryland. Transferred to Elmira Prison Camp New York August 6, 1864.	Died June 19, 1865 of Chronic Diarrhea, Grave No. 2809
Sibbett, John William Private	39	March 7, 1862, Wilmington, North Carolina	Co. H, 51st North Carolina Infantry	June 1, 1864, Cold Harbor, Virginia	Old Capital Prison, Washington, DC, transferred to Elmira Prison, NY, July 23, 1864	Exchanged February 13, 1865 at Boulware's wharf on the James River, Virginia
Sicard, F. C. Private	Unk	Unknown	6th Field Battery Louisiana Light Artillery	October 22, 1864, Grosstete, Louisiana	New Orleans, Louisiana transferred to Elmira November 19, 1864.	Exchanged February 13, 1865 at Boulware's wharf on the James River, Virginia
Sichler, Enos Private	27	August 8, 1862, Statesville, North Carolina	Co. I, 5th North Carolina Infantry	May 12, 1864, Spotsylvania Court House, Virginia	Point Lookout, Maryland, transferred to Elmira Prison, NY, August 6, 1864	Oath of Allegiance June 30, 1865
Siddons, Benjamin F. Private	35	April 1, 1861, Lacy's Store, Virginia	Co. B, 44th Virginia Infantry	May 12, 1864, Spotsylvania Court House, Virginia	Point Lookout, Maryland, transferred to Elmira Prison, NY, August 2, 1864	Exchanged October 29, 1864, at Venus Point, Savannah River, GA.
Sides, Charles D. Private	33	August 8, 1862, Statesville, North Carolina	Co. I, 5th North Carolina Infantry	May 12, 1864, Spotsylvania Court House, Virginia	Point Lookout, Maryland, transferred to Elmira Prison, NY, August 6, 1864	Died February 8, 1865 of Variola (Smallpox), Grave No. 1956

Name & Rank	Age	Enlisted	Regiment and State	Where Captured	Prison	Remarks
Siebert, Charles J. Private	Unk	Unknown	Co. D, 11th Virginia Cavalry	October 30, 1864, Hampshire County, Virginia	Old Capital Prison, Washington, DC, transferred to Elmira Prison, NY, December 17, 1864	Exchanged March 10, 1865 at Boulware's Wharf on the James River, Virginia
Siebert, Joseph M. Private	Unk	April 14, 1862, Rudes Hill, Virginia	Co. B, 2nd Virginia Infantry	May 12, 1864, Spotsylvania Court House, Virginia	Point Lookout, Maryland, transferred to Elmira Prison, NY, August 2, 1864	Oath of Allegiance June 27, 1865
Sievers, William Fredrick Private	Unk	June 21, 1861, New Orleans, Louisiana	Co. F, 15th Louisiana Infantry	August 12, 1864, Winchester, Virginia	Old Capital Prison, Washington, DC transferred to Elmira Prison, NY, August 29, 1864	Died November 24, 1864 of Pneumonia, Grave No. 915
Sigman, Alfred P. Private	Unk	April 14, 1863, Newton, North Carolina	Co. C, 28th North Carolina Infantry	May 12, 1864, Spotsylvania County Court House, Virginia	Point Lookout, Maryland, transferred to Elmira Prison, NY, August 14, 1864	Oath of Allegiance June 27, 1865
Sigman, Martin M. Private	35	March 15, 1862, Newton, North Carolina	Co. C, 28th North Carolina Infantry	May 12, 1864, Spotsylvania County Court House, Virginia	Point Lookout, Maryland, transferred to Elmira Prison, NY, August 14, 1864	Died November 14, 1864 of Chronic Diarrhea, Grave No. 809
Sigman, Miles S. Private	Unk	March 1, 1864, Newton, North Carolina	Co. F, 23rd North Carolina Infantry	May 20, 1864, Spotsylvania Court House, Virginia	Point Lookout, Maryland, transferred to Elmira Prison, NY, July 3, 1864	Oath of Allegiance June 12, 1865
Sikes, Amos Private	42	September 28, 1863, Fort Fisher, New Hanover County, North Carolina	Co. J, 36th Regiment, 2nd North Carolina Artillery	January 15, 1865, Fort Fisher, North Carolina	February 1, 1865, Elmira Prison Camp, New York	Died May 6, 1865 of Typhoid Fever, Grave No. 2766
Sikes, David A. Sergeant	22	June 29, 1861, Randolph County, North Carolina	Co. H, 3rd North Carolina Infantry	May 12, 1864, Near Spotsylvania Court House, Virginia	Point Lookout, Maryland, transferred to Elmira Prison, NY, August 14, 1864	Oath of Allegiance May 19, 1865

Name & Rank	Age	Enlisted	Regiment and State	Where Captured	Prison	Remarks
Sikes, Lucian Private	28	May 12, 1862, Fort Fisher, New Hanover County, North Carolina	Co. J, 36th Regiment, 2nd North Carolina Artillery	January 15, 1865, Fort Fisher, North Carolina	February 1, 1865, Elmira Prison Camp, New York	Exchange March 14, 1865. Died April 7, 1865 of Debility at Jackson Hospital, Richmond, VA.
Sillivent, Hardy Private	Unk	August 27, 1863, Goldsboro, North Carolina	Co. F, 10th Regiment, 1st North Carolina Artillery	January 15, 1865, Fort Fisher, North Carolina	February 1, 1865, Elmira Prison Camp, New York	Died April 20, 1865 of Typhoid Fever, Grave No. 1383. Headstone has Sullivan.
Sills, Levi Private	18	August 15, 1863, Raleigh, North Carolina	Co. F, 2nd North Carolina Infantry	May 31, 1864 Mechanicsville, Virginia	Point Lookout, Maryland, transferred to Elmira Prison, NY, July 11, 1864	Died December 10, 1864 of Congestion of Lungs (Pneumonia), Grave No. 1035
Silvers, Jackson A. Private	Unk	March 11, 1862, Newbern, Virginia	Co. C, 4th Virginia Infantry	May 12, 1864 Spotsylvania Court House, Virginia	Point Lookout, Maryland, transferred to Elmira Prison, NY, August 2, 1864	Exchanged March 14, 1865 at Boulware's Wharf on the James River, Virginia
Simmerman, John Henry Private	Unk	February 1, 1863, Wytheville, Virginia	Co. C, 51st Virginia Infantry	July 10, 1864, Frederick, Maryland	Old Capital Prison, Washington, DC, transferred to Elmira Prison, NY, July 23, 1864	Oath of Allegiance May 29, 1865
Simmerman, Robert Private	Unk	May 1, 1862, Wytheville, Virginia	Co. C, 51st Virginia Infantry	July 10, 1864, Frederick, Maryland	Old Capital Prison, Washington, DC, transferred to Elmira Prison, NY, July 23, 1864	Oath of Allegiance May 29, 1865
Simmons, Alfred N. Private	Unk	May 15, 1862, Trenton, North Carolina	Co. F, 66th North Carolina Infantry	June 16, 1864, Petersburg, Virginia	Point Lookout, Maryland, transferred to Elmira Prison, NY, July 30, 1864	Exchanged October 29, 1864, at Venus Point, Savannah River, GA.
Simmons, Ammi Private	Unk	June 9, 1861, Hevener's Store, Highland County, Virginia	Co. E, 25th Virginia Infantry	May 12, 1864, Spotsylvania Court House, Virginia	Point Lookout, Maryland, transferred to Elmira Prison, NY, August 12, 1864	Oath of Allegiance June 27, 1865

Name & Rank	Age	Enlisted	Regiment and State	Where Captured	Prison	Remarks
Simmons, Asberry Private	33	May 13, 1863, Fort St. Philip, Brunswick County, North Carolina	Co. G, 36th Regiment 2nd North Carolina Artillery	January 15, 1865, Fort Fisher, North Carolina	February 1, 1865, Elmira Prison Camp, New York	Oath of Allegiance June 23, 1865
Simmons, Calvin Private	20	June 21, 1861, Wilkesboro, North Carolina	Co. C, 26th North Carolina Infantry	May 12, 1864, Spotsylvania Court House, Virginia	Point Lookout, Maryland, transferred to Elmira Prison, NY, July 30, 1864	Died March 25, 1865 of Diarrhea, Grave No. 2452
Simmons, Christian Private	Unk	October 13, 1862, Camp near Bunker Hill, Virginia	Co. F, 25th Virginia Infantry	May 5, 1864, Wilderness, Virginia	Point Lookout, Maryland, transferred to Elmira Prison, NY, August 17, 1864	Oath of Allegiance June 30, 1865
Simmons, Edward J. Private	27	February 24, 1863, Stokes County, North Carolina	Co. C, 2nd Battalion North Carolina Infantry	May 10, 1864, Near Spotsylvania County Court House, Virginia	Point Lookout, Maryland, transferred to Elmira Prison, NY, August 14, 1864	Died September 29, 1864 of Chronic Diarrhea, Grave No. 634
Simmons, Elvin Isaac Private	Unk	March 1, 1863, Troy, Alabama	Co. F, 1st Battalion Alabama Artillery	August 23, 1864, Fort Morgan, Alabama	Steam Press No. 4 New Orleans, Louisiana transferred to Elmira Prison, NY, October 8, 1864.	Died February 17, 1865 of Chronic Diarrhea, Grave No. 2207
Simmons, James Private	28	March 27, 1862, Clinton, North Carolina	Co. I, 51st North Carolina Infantry	June 1, 1864, Cold Harbor, Virginia	Point Lookout, Maryland, transferred to Elmira Prison, NY, July 12, 1864	Exchanged October 29, 1864, at Venus Point, Savannah River, GA.
Simmons, Jesse Private	45	July 4, 1861, Columbus, North Carolina	Co. D, 20th North Carolina Infantry	July 10, 1864, Frederick, Maryland	Old Capital Prison, Washington, DC, transferred to Elmira Prison, NY, July 23, 1864	Died March 22, 1865 of Typhoid Fever, Grave No. 1540
Simmons, Jesse Private	Unk	July 15, 1861, Salem, Virginia	Co. D, 5th Virginia Cavalry	May 11, 1864, Yellow Tavern, Hanover County, Virginia	Point Lookout, Maryland, transferred to Elmira Prison, NY, August 17, 1864	Transferred For Exchange 10/11/64 to Point Lookout Prison Camp, MD. Died 10/18/64 of Intermittent Fever.

Name & Rank	Age	Enlisted	Regiment and State	Where Captured	Prison	Remarks
Simmons, Jesse W. Private	Unk	February 15, 1862, New Orleans, Louisiana	Co. D, 5th Louisiana Infantry	May 12, 1864, Spotsylvania Court House, Virginia	Point Lookout, Maryland, transferred to Elmira Prison, NY, August 17, 1864	Exchanged March 14, 1865 at Boulware's Wharf on the James River, Virginia
Simmons, John F. Private	28	February 24, 1863, Stokes County, North Carolina	Co. A, 2nd Battalion North Carolina Infantry	May 10, 1864, Near Spotsylvania County Court House, Virginia	Point Lookout, Maryland, transferred to Elmira Prison, NY, August 14, 1864	Died March 13, 1865 of Chronic Diarrhea, Grave No. 1834
Simmons, John H. Private	18	March 15, 1863, Fort Fisher, New Hanover County, North Carolina	Co. C, 36th Regiment, 2nd North Carolina Artillery	January 15, 1865, Fort Fisher, North Carolina	February 1, 1865, Elmira Prison Camp, New York	Died February 24, 1865 of Chronic Diarrhea-Pneumonia, Grave No. 2269
Simmons, John W. Private	36	June 11, 1864, Fort Fisher, New Hanover County, North Carolina	Co. J, 36th Regiment, 2nd North Carolina Artillery	January 15, 1865, Fort Fisher, North Carolina	February 1, 1865, Elmira Prison Camp, New York	Exchanged March 14, 1865 at Boulware's Wharf on the James River, Virginia
Simmons, Joseph W. Private	Unk	Unknown	Co. B, Hood's Battalion, Virginia Reserves	June 15, 1864, Petersburg, Virginia	Point Lookout, Maryland, transferred to Elmira Prison, NY, July 30, 1864	Died February 18, 1865 of Chronic Diarrhea, Grave No. 2222
Simmons, Joshua M. Private	25	June 15, 1861, Wilmington, North Carolina	Co. A, 18th North Carolina Infantry	May 12, 1864, Spotsylvania Court House, Virginia	Point Lookout, Maryland, transferred to Elmira Prison, NY, August 6, 1864	Died March 3, 1865 of Variola (Smallpox), Grave No. 1989
Simmons, Love Private	28	August 20, 1862, Statesville, North Carolina	Co. B, 18th North Carolina Infantry	July 30, 1864, Petersburg, Virginia	Point Lookout, Maryland, transferred to Elmira Prison, NY, August 12, 1864	Exchanged October 29, 1864, at Venus Point, Savannah River, GA.
Simmons, Malcom L. Private	Unk	May 23. 1863, Cumberland County, North Carolina	Co. I, 51st North Carolina Infantry	June 1, 1864, Cold Harbor, Virginia	Point Lookout, Maryland, transferred to Elmira Prison, NY, July 12, 1864	Died November 28, 1864 of Hospital Gangrene, Grave No. 990
Simmons, Moses Private	21	May 25, 1861, Camp Howard, Brunswick County, North Carolina	Co. G, 3rd North Carolina Infantry	May 12, 1864, Near Spotsylvania Court House, Virginia	Point Lookout, Maryland, transferred to Elmira Prison, NY, August 14, 1864	Died September 14, 1864 of Pneumonia, Grave No. 275

Name & Rank	Age	Enlisted	Regiment and State	Where Captured	Prison	Remarks
Simmons, Noah Private	Unk	February 24, 1863, Stokes County, North Carolina	Co. C, 28th North Carolina Infantry	May 12, 1864, Near Spotsylvania County Court House, Virginia	Point Lookout, Maryland, transferred to Elmira Prison, NY, August 14, 1864	Died April 10, 1865 of Chronic Diarrhea, Grave No. 2672. Name H. Simmons on Headstone.
Simmons, Peter M. Private	24	May 4, 1861, Stokes County, North Carolina	Co. A, 2nd Battalion North Carolina Infantry	May 12, 1864, Near Spotsylvania County Court House, Virginia	Point Lookout, Maryland, transferred to Elmira Prison, NY, August 14, 1864	Died September 29, 1864 of Chronic Diarrhea, Grave No. 426
Simmons, Samuel Private	Unk	July 13, 1864, Fort Fisher, New Hanover County, North Carolina	Co. G, 36th Regiment, 2nd North Carolina Artillery	January 15, 1865, Fort Fisher, North Carolina	February 1, 1865, Elmira Prison Camp, New York	Exchanged March 2, 1865 at Akins Landing on the James River, Virginia
Simmons, William Private	Unk	Unknown	Co. A, 12th Battalion North Carolina Cavalry	July 31, 1864, Sharpsburg, Maryland	Old Capital Prison, Washington D. C. Transferred to Elmira Prison, NY, August 12, 1864	Oath of Allegiance May 19, 1865
Simms, John Corporal	22	May 9, 1861, Jacksonville, Florida	Co. M, 2nd Florida Infantry	July 29, 1864, Deserted to Union Lines, Petersburg, Virginia	Point Lookout, Maryland, transferred to Elmira Prison, NY, August 12, 1864	Oath of Allegiance January 30, 1865. Early Release per Lincoln's Proclamation, 12/8/1863.
Simms, John H. Private	18	March 15, 1863, Fort Fisher, New Hanover County, North Carolina	2nd Co. C, 36th Regiment North Carolina, 2nd Artillery	January 15, 1865, Fort Fisher, North Carolina	February 1, 1865, Elmira Prison Camp, New York	Died of Chronic Diarrhea/Pneumonia 2/24/1865, Grave No. 2269. Headstone has Simmons.
Simms, Julius C. Private	Unk	April 28, 1862, Aberdeen, Mississippi	Co. C, 43rd Mississippi Infantry	May 18, 1863, Chickasaw Bayou, Mississippi	Point Lookout, Maryland, transferred to Elmira Prison, NY, August 18, 1864	Exchanged October 29, 1864, at Venus Point, Savannah River, GA.

Name & Rank	Age	Enlisted	Regiment and State	Where Captured	Prison	Remarks
Simms, Miles Private	Unk	May 2, 1864, Marianna, Florida	Co. C, 1st Reserves Florida Infantry	September 27, 1864, Marianna, Florida	New Orleans, Louisiana transferred to Elmira November 19, 1864.	Died March 19, 1865 of Chronic Diarrhea, Grave No. 1571
Simms, Simon Private	Unk	August 18, 1862, Exact Location Unknown. Kentucky	Co E, 6th Kentucky Mounted Infantry	Deserted to Union Lines May 1, 1863 in Lawrence County, Kentucky	Point Lookout, Maryland, transferred to Elmira Prison, NY, August 14, 1864	Oath of Allegiance February 17, 1865 Early Release per Lincoln's Proclamation, 12/8/1863.
Simons, W. Lucas Private	19	May 1, 1862, James Island, South Carolina	Co. B, 25th South Carolina Infantry	January 15, 1865, Fort Fisher, North Carolina	February 1, 1865, Elmira Prison Camp, New York	Exchanged March 10, 1865 at Boulware's Wharf on the James River, Virginia
Simonton, Joseph V. Private	Unk	May 21, 1862, Richmond, Virginia	Co. J, 16th Georgia Infantry	August 16, 1864, Front Royal, Virginia	Old Capital Prison, Washington, DC transferred to Elmira Prison, NY, August 29, 1864	Oath of Allegiance July 7, 1865
Simpkins, James G. Private	20	August 2, 1861, New Orleans, Louisiana	Co. B, 1st Louisiana Infantry	May 20, 1864, Spotsylvania Court House, Virginia	Point Lookout, Maryland, transferred to Elmira Prison, NY, July 3, 1864	Exchanged February 25, 1865 at Boulware's or Cox Wharf on the James River, Virginia
Simpkins, Lawrence W. Private	Unk	August 14, 1862, King and Queen County, Virginia	Co. H, 26th North Carolina Infantry	June 17, 1864, Near Petersburg, Virginia	Point Lookout, Maryland, transferred to Elmira Prison, NY, July 30, 1864	Oath of Allegiance June 21, 1865
Simpson, Albert J. Private	Unk	March 8, 1862, Lynnhaven Beach, Virginia	Co. K, 15th Virginia Cavalry	November 14, 1863, Near Culpepper Court House, Virginia	Point Lookout, Maryland, transferred to Elmira Prison, NY, August 18, 1864	Exchanged March 10, 1865 at Boulware's Wharf on the James River, Virginia
Simpson, E. F. Civilian	Unk	Unknown	Citizen of Fairfax County, Virginia	November 26, 1863, Fairfax County, Virginia	Point Lookout, Maryland, transferred to Elmira Prison, NY, July 25, 1864	Exchanged March 10, 1865 at Boulware's Wharf on the James River, Virginia

Name & Rank	Age	Enlisted	Regiment and State	Where Captured	Prison	Remarks
Simpson, George B. Private	Unk	Unknown	Co. A, Bryant's Louisiana Cavalry	August 25, 1864, Near Clinton, Louisiana	New Orleans, Louisiana, Transferred to Elmira Prison, New York, November 19, 1864	Exchanged February 25, 1865 at Boulware's or Cox Wharf on the James River, Virginia
Simpson, George R. Corporal		September 20, 1863, Winchester, Virginia	Co. D, 1st Maryland Cavalry	May 24, 1864, Hanover Junction, Virginia	Point Lookout, Maryland, transferred to Elmira Prison, NY, July 11, 1864	Exchanged February 20, 1865 at Boulware's or Cox Wharf on the James River, Virginia
Simpson, Green M. Private	Unk	May 3, 1864, Taylorsville, North Carolina	Co. G, 5th North Carolina Infantry	May 12, 1864, Spotsylvania Court House, Virginia	Point Lookout, Maryland, transferred to Elmira Prison, NY, August 6, 1864	Oath of Allegiance June 30, 1865
Simpson, First Name Unknown Private	Unk	Unknown	Co. E, 38th North Carolina Infantry	May 20, 1864, Spotsylvania Court House, Virginia	Point Lookout, Maryland, transferred to Elmira Prison, NY, July 12, 1864	Oath of Allegiance June 12, 1865
Simpson, John F. Civilian	Unk	Unknown	Citizen of Prince William County, Virginia	November 26, 1863, Prince William County, Virginia	Point Lookout, Maryland, transferred to Elmira Prison, NY, July 25, 1864	Transferred For Exchange October 11, 1864 to Point Lookout Prison Camp, MD. Nothing Further.
Simpson, John F. Private	Unk	March 3, 1863, Columbia, South Carolina	Co. F, Holcombe Legion, South Carolina	May 8, 1864, Jarrett's Depot, Virginia	Point Lookout, Maryland, transferred to Elmira Prison, NY, August 17, 1864	Died January 19, 1865 of Variola (Smallpox), Grave No. 1429
Simpson, Peter Private	23	October 22, 1863, Richmond, North Carolina	Co. D, 45th North Carolina Infantry	May 20, 1864, Spotsylvania Court House, Virginia	Point Lookout, Maryland, transferred to Elmira Prison, NY, July 3, 1864	Exchanged October 29, 1864, at Venus Point, Savannah River, GA.
Simpson, Robert C. Private	24	March 2, 1862, McCollum's Schoolhouse, Reidsville, North Carolina	Co. G, 45th North Carolina Infantry	May 10, 1864, Spotsylvania Court House, Virginia	Point Lookout, Maryland, transferred to Elmira Prison, NY, August 6, 1864	Exchanged March 10, 1865 at Boulware's Wharf on the James River, Virginia

Name & Rank	Age	Enlisted	Regiment and State	Where Captured	Prison	Remarks
Simpson, William A. Private	19	July 1, 1861, Jacksonville, Onslow County, North Carolina	Co. C, 3rd North Carolina Infantry	May 12, 1864, Near Spotsylvania County Court House, Virginia	Point Lookout, Maryland, transferred to Elmira Prison, NY, August 14, 1864	Died December 5, 1864 of Chronic Diarrhea, Grave No. 1029. Headstone has 3rd SC.
Sims, George Private	19	November 5, 1864, Butler County, Alabama	Co. D, 61st Alabama Infantry	July 12, 1864, Silver Springs, Virginia. Gunshot Wound Fracture of Elbow. Amputated Arm.	Old Capital Prison, Washington, DC transferred to Elmira Prison, NY, August 27, 1864	Exchanged 2/20/65. Died 3/9/65 of Pleuro--Pneumonia at Howard's Grove General Hospital, Richmond, VA.
Sims, John T. Sergeant	Unk	March 27, 1862, Lewisburg, Virginia	Captain Bryan's Battery, Virginia Artillery	July 10, 1864, German Town, Maryland	Old Capital Prison, Washington, DC, transferred to Elmira Prison, NY, July 23, 1864	Oath of Allegiance June 21, 1865
Sinclair, James J. Private	18	Fort Holmes, New Hanover County, North Carolina	Co. G, 36th Regiment, 2nd North Carolina Artillery	January 15, 1865, Fort Fisher, North Carolina	February 1, 1865, Elmira Prison Camp, New York	Exchanged March 2, 1865 at Akins Landing on the James River, Virginia
Singer, Edward A. Private	Unk	June 2, 1862, Luray, Virginia	Co. K, 10th Virginia Infantry	May 12, 1864, Spotsylvania Court House, Virginia	Point Lookout, Maryland, transferred to Elmira Prison, NY, August 2, 1864	Oath of Allegiance June 19, 1865
Singletary, Amos D. Private	21	October 28, 1861, Fayetteville, North Carolina	Co. G, 33rd North Carolina Infantry	May 13, 1864, Wilderness Spotsylvania, Virginia	Point Lookout, Maryland, transferred to Elmira Prison, NY, August 14, 1864	Oath of Allegiance May 29, 1865
Singletary, Calvin Private	33	May 6, 1862, Elizabethtown, Bladen County, North Carolina	Co. G, 36th Regiment, 2nd North Carolina Artillery	January 15, 1865, Fort Fisher, North Carolina	February 1, 1865, Elmira Prison Camp, New York	Died February 24, 1865 of Pneumonia, Grave No. 2287
Singletary, Dennis Lennon Private	Unk	May 6, 1862, Elizabethtown, Bladen County, North Carolina	Co. K, 40th Regiment, 3rd North Carolina Artillery	January 15, 1865, Fort Fisher, North Carolina	February 1, 1865, Elmira Prison Camp, New York	Exchanged March 2, 1865 at Akins Landing on the James River, Virginia

Name & Rank	Age	Enlisted	Regiment and State	Where Captured	Prison	Remarks
Singletary, George S. Private	23	May 6, 1862, Elizabethtown, Bladen County, North Carolina	Co. K, 40th Regiment, 3rd North Carolina Artillery	January 15, 1865, Fort Fisher, North Carolina	February 1, 1865, Elmira Prison Camp, New York	Oath of Allegiance June 12, 1865
Singletary, John Y. Private	18	May 3, 1861, Elizabethtown, North Carolina	Co. K, 18th North Carolina Infantry	May 12, 1864, Spotsylvania Court House, Virginia	Point Lookout, Maryland, transferred to Elmira Prison, NY, August 6, 1864	Died March 6, 1865 of Variola (smallpox), Grave No. 2390. Name J. T. Singleterry on Headstone.
Singletary, Jonathan L. Private	20	May 6, 1862, Elizabethtown, Bladen County, North Carolina	Co. K, 40th Regiment, 3rd North Carolina Artillery	January 15, 1865, Fort Fisher, North Carolina	February 1, 1865, Elmira Prison Camp, New York	Oath of Allegiance June 12, 1865
Singletary, Joshua K. Private	20	August 28, 1862, Bladen County, North Carolina	Co. B, 36th Regiment, 2nd North Carolina Artillery	January 15, 1865, Fort Fisher, North Carolina	February 1, 1865, Elmira Prison Camp, New York	Exchanged March 2, 1865 at Akins Landing on the James River, Virginia
Singletary, Matthew Young Private	25	December 20, 1861, Bladen County, North Carolina	Co. B, 36th Regiment, 2nd North Carolina Artillery	January 15, 1865, Fort Fisher, North Carolina	February 1, 1865, Elmira Prison Camp, New York	Exchanged February 20, 1865 at Boulware's or Cox Wharf on the James River, Virginia
Singletary, Wright Private	30	January 1, 1862, Wilmington, New Hanover County, North Carolina	Co. B, 36th 2nd Regiment North Carolina Artillery	January 15, 1865, Fort Fisher, North Carolina	February 1, 1865, Elmira Prison Camp, New York	Oath of Allegiance July 7, 1865
Singleton, A. R. Private	Unk	June 26, 1861, Coalsmouth, Virginia	Co. H, 22nd Virginia Infantry	June 3, 1864, Gaines Farm Cold Harbor, Virginia	Point Lookout, Maryland, transferred to Elmira Prison, NY, July 12, 1864	Oath of Allegiance May 13, 1865
Singleton, Champion Private	Unk	February 15, 1862, Pike County, Mississippi	Co. K, 33rd Mississippi Infantry	May 16, 1863, Champion Hill, Mississippi	Point Lookout, Maryland, transferred to Elmira Prison, NY, August 18, 1864	Exchanged October 29, 1864, at Venus Point, Savannah River, GA.

Name & Rank	Age	Enlisted	Regiment and State	Where Captured	Prison	Remarks
Singleton, David D. Private	Unk	June 15, 1861, Columbus, Georgia	Co. E, 12th Georgia Infantry	May 10, 1864, Spotsylvania Court House, Virginia	Point Lookout, Maryland, transferred to Elmira Prison, NY, July 30, 1864	Exchanged February 20, 1865 at Boulware's or Cox Wharf on the James River, Virginia
Singleton, Francis M. Private	Unk	October 29, 1862, Clayton, Georgia	Co. E, 24th Georgia Infantry	August 16, 1864, Front Royal, Virginia	Old Capital Prison, Washington, DC transferred to Elmira Prison, NY, August 29, 1864	Died January 29, 1865 of Pneumonia, Grave No. 1806
Singleton, George Hospital Steward	Unk	June 4, 1861, Camp Moore, Louisiana	Co. H, 6th Louisiana Infantry	September 19, 1864, Winchester, Virginia	Old Capital Prison, Washington, DC, transferred to Elmira Prison, NY, December 17, 1864	Died March 30, 1865 of Pneumonia, Grave. 2533
Singleton, Obadiah W. Corporal	Unk	March 6, 1861, Winchester, Virginia	Co. F, 2nd Virginia Infantry	May 12, 1864, Near Spotsylvania Court House, Virginia	Point Lookout, Maryland, transferred to Elmira Prison, NY, August 6, 1864	Died December 26, 1864 of gangrene of the Lungs, Grave No. 1107
Singleton, P. V. Private	Unk	July 16, 1861, Lawrenceville, Georgia	Co. J, 16th Georgia Infantry	August 16, 1864, Front Royal, Virginia	Old Capital Prison, Washington, DC transferred to Elmira Prison, NY, August 29, 1864	Exchanged March 14, 1865 at Boulware's Wharf on the James River, Virginia
Singleton, Patrick H. Private	Unk	June 10, 1861, Morgan, Georgia	Co. D, 12th Georgia Infantry	May 10, 1864, Spotsylvania Court House, Virginia	Point Lookout, Maryland, transferred to Elmira Prison, NY, July 30, 1864	Oath of Allegiance June 30, 1865
Singleton, Samuel Private	Unk	May 14, 1862, Milledgeville, Georgia	Co. H, 4th Georgia Infantry	May 20, 1864, Spotsylvania Court House, Virginia	Point Lookout, Maryland, transferred to Elmira Prison, NY, July 3, 1864	Died February 28, 1865 of Variola (Smallpox), Grave No. 2114

Name & Rank	Age	Enlisted	Regiment and State	Where Captured	Prison	Remarks
Sipe, Jacob F. Corporal	Unk	April 18, 1861, McGaheysville, Virginia	Co. E, 10th Virginia Infantry	May 12, 1864, Spotsylvania Court House, Virginia	Point Lookout, Maryland, transferred to Elmira Prison, NY, August 2, 1864	Died January 5, 1865 of Variola (Smallpox), Grave No. 1249
Siple, Josiah Private	Unk	May 14, 1861, Franklin, Virginia	Co. E, 25th Virginia Infantry	May 12, 1864, Spotsylvania Court House, Virginia	Point Lookout, Maryland, transferred to Elmira Prison, NY, August 12, 1864	Exchanged October 29, 1864, at Venus Point, Savannah River, GA.
Sisk, Charles H. Private	21	June 1, 1861, Romney, Virginia	Co. C, 7th Virginia Cavalry	September 14, 1863, Near Culpepper, Virginia	Point Lookout, Maryland, transferred to Elmira Prison, NY, August 18, 1864	Exchanged March 10, 1865 at Boulware's Wharf on the James River, Virginia
Sisson, James C. Private	Unk	March 12, 1862, Beaulien, Georgia	Co. G, 61st Georgia Infantry	July 6, 1864, Harper's Ferry, Virginia	Old Capital Prison, Washington, DC, transferred to Elmira Prison, NY, July 23, 1864	Oath of Allegiance May 19, 1865
Sisson, M. Henry Private		April 20, 1861, Macon, Georgia	Co. L, 2nd Battalion Georgia Infantry	May 24, 1864, North Anna, Virginia	Point Lookout, Maryland, transferred to Elmira Prison, NY, July 11,1864	Exchanged October 29, 1864, at Venus Point, Savannah River, GA.
Sisson, Nathan H. Sergeant	Unk	September 23, 1861, Tappahannock, Virginia	Co. E, 55th Virginia Infantry	July 14, 1863, Falling Waters, Maryland	Point Lookout, Maryland, transferred to Elmira Prison, NY, August 18, 1864	Exchanged March 10, 1865 at Boulware's Wharf on the James River, Virginia
Sites, John A. Private	Unk	June 12, 1861, Harrisonburg, Virginia	Co. G, 10th Virginia Infantry	May 12, 1864, Spotsylvania Court House, Virginia	Point Lookout, Maryland, transferred to Elmira Prison, NY, August 2, 1864	Exchanged October 29, 1864 at Venus Point, Savannah River, GA.
Sitton, John R. Private	Unk	Unknown	Co. A, 50th Virginia Infantry	May 12, 1864, Spotsylvania Court House, Virginia	Point Lookout, Maryland, transferred to Elmira Prison, NY, August 2, 1864	Oath of Allegiance June 16, 1865

Name & Rank	Age	Enlisted	Regiment and State	Where Captured	Prison	Remarks
Sizemore, Aaron Private	Unk	March 4, 1861, Selma, Alabama	Co. C, 1st Battalion Alabama Artillery	August 23, 1864, Fort Morgan, Alabama	New Orleans, Louisiana transferred to Elmira Prison, NY, December 4, 1864.	Died March 1, 1865 of Pneumonia, Grave No. 2104
Sizemore, Edward Private	Unk	April 27, 1862, Charleston, South Carolina	Co. C, 22nd South Carolina Infantry	July 30, 1864, Petersburg, Virginia	Point Lookout, Maryland, transferred to Elmira Prison, NY, August 12, 1864	Died November 19, 1864 of Chronic Diarrhea, Grave No. 948
Sizemore, J. Thomas Sergeant	Unk	January 10, 1862, Columbia, South Carolina	Co. C, 22nd South Carolina Infantry	July 30, 1864, Petersburg, Virginia	Point Lookout, Maryland, transferred to Elmira Prison, NY, August 12, 1864	Exchanged 2/20/65. Died 3/22/65 of Chronic Diarrhea at CSA Hospital, No. 11, Charlotte, NC.
Sizemore, R. P. Private	Unk	August 31, 1861, Spartanburg, South Carolina	Co. C, 22nd South Carolina Infantry	July 30, 1864, Petersburg, Virginia	Point Lookout, Maryland, transferred to Elmira Prison, NY, August 12, 1864	Oath of Allegiance July 3, 1865
Sizemore, William J. Private	37	March 26, 1863, Chatham County, North Carolina	Co. B, 40th Regiment, 3rd North Carolina Artillery	January 15, 1865, Fort Fisher, North Carolina	February 1, 1865, Elmira Prison Camp, New York	Died March 21, 1865 of Pneumonia, Grave No. 1528
Skates, James W. Private	Unk	Unknown	Co. D, 7th Georgia Cavalry	June 21, 1864, Near Wilmington, North Carolina	Point Lookout, Maryland, transferred to Elmira Prison, NY, July 23, 1864	Exchanged October 29, 1864, at Venus Point, Savannah River, GA.
Skeen, Pernal A. Private	Unk	Unknown	Co. A, Jackson's 1st Regiment, Tennessee Heavy Artillery	August 23, 1864, Fort Morgan, Alabama	New Orleans, Louisiana transferred to Elmira Prison, NY, December 4, 1864.	Exchanged March 10, 1865 at Boulware's Wharf on the James River, Virginia
Skeen, William Park Private	19	November 1, 1861, Lebanon, Tennessee	Co. A, Jackson's 1st Regiment, Tennessee Heavy Artillery	August 23, 1864, Fort Morgan, Alabama	New Orleans, Louisiana transferred to Elmira Prison, NY, December 4, 1864.	Exchanged March 10, 1865 at Boulware's Wharf on the James River, Virginia

Name & Rank	Age	Enlisted	Regiment and State	Where Captured	Prison	Remarks
Skeheil, John Private	24	July 22, 1861, Camp Moore, Louisiana	Co. A, 10th Louisiana Infantry	May 12, 1864, Spotsylvania Court House, Virginia	Point Lookout, Maryland, transferred to Elmira Prison, NY, July 25, 1864	Oath of Allegiance May 15, 1865
Skelton, William M. Private	Unk	March 10, 1862, Luray, Virginia	Co. K, 10th Virginia Infantry	May 12, 1864, Spotsylvania Court House, Virginia	Point Lookout, Maryland, transferred to Elmira Prison, NY, August 2, 1864	Oath of Allegiance May 29, 1865
Skidmore, John S. Private	Unk	July 21, 1863, Orange County Court House, Virginia	Co. 39th Battalion Virginia Infantry	August 6, 1864, Falls Church, Virginia	Old Capital Prison, Washington D. C. Transferred to Elmira Prison, NY, August 12, 1864	Exchanged March 14, 1865 at Boulware's Wharf on the James River, Virginia
Skinner, Benjamin S. Private	18	May 18, 1861, Edenton, North Carolina	Co. A, 1st North Carolina Infantry	May 12, 1864, Spotsylvania, Virginia	Point Lookout Prison Camp, Maryland. Transferred to Elmira Prison Camp, New York August 6, 1864	Died September 23, 1864 of Chronic Diarrhea, Grave No. 470
Skinner, C. A. Private	Unk	Unknown	Co. J, 2nd Louisiana Cavalry	October 20, 1864, Bayou Fordorche, Louisiana	New Orleans, Louisiana transferred to Elmira November 19, 1864.	Exchanged February 13, 1865 at Boulware's wharf on the James River, Virginia
Skinner, Franklin Private	Unk	September 1, 1863, James Island, South Carolina	Co. H, 21st South Carolina Infantry	January 15, 1865, Fort Fisher, North Carolina	February 1, 1865, Elmira Prison Camp, New York	Died April 9, 1865 of Chronic Diarrhea, Grave No. 2612
Skinner, Jesse J. Private	Unk	March 1, 1863, Atlanta, Georgia	Co. E, 64th Georgia Infantry	August 16, 1864, New Market, Virginia	Old Capital Prison, Washington, DC transferred to Elmira Prison, NY, August 27, 1864	Oath of Allegiance July 11, 1865
Skinner, Joel J. Sergeant	Unk	July 16, 1861, Lawrenceville, Georgia	Co. I, 16th Georgia Infantry	June 1, 1864, Gaines Farm Cold Harbor, Virginia	Point Lookout, Maryland, transferred to Elmira Prison, NY, July 12, 1864	Died January 1, 1865 of Pneumonia, Grave No. 1342

Name & Rank	Age	Enlisted	Regiment and State	Where Captured	Prison	Remarks
Skinner, M. P. Private	Unk	Unknown	Co. H, 14th Louisiana Infantry	May 12, 1864, Spotsylvania Court House, Virginia	Point Lookout, Maryland, transferred to Elmira Prison, NY, July 25, 1864	Exchanged February 25, 1865 at Boulware's or Cox Wharf on the James River, Virginia
Skinner, William Private	21	April 27, 1861, Snow Hill, North Carolina	Co. A, 3rd North Carolina Infantry	May 12, 1864, Near Spotsylvania County Court House, Virginia	Point Lookout, Maryland, transferred to Elmira Prison, NY, August 14, 1864	Oath of Allegiance June 27, 1865
Skipper, Daniel Private	Unk	May 21, 1863, Henry County, Alabama	Co. A, 61st Alabama Infantry	May 12, 1864, Spotsylvania Court House, Virginia	Point Lookout, Maryland, transferred to Elmira Prison, NY, July 30, 1864	Transferred for Exchange February 20, 1865. Died on the Route to be Exchanged.
Skipper, Henry J. Private	Unk	January 22, 1864, Montgomery, Alabama	Co. E, 1st Battalion Alabama Artillery	August 23, 1864, Fort Morgan, Alabama	Steam Press No. 4 New Orleans, Louisiana transferred to Elmira Prison, NY, October 8, 1864.	Oath of Allegiance July 7, 1865
Skipper, James H. Private	Unk	September 17, 1862, Mobile, Alabama	Co. E, 1st Battalion Alabama Artillery	August 23, 1864, Fort Morgan, Alabama	Steam Press No. 4 New Orleans, Louisiana transferred to Elmira Prison, NY, October 8, 1864.	Exchanged February 20, 1865 at Boulware's or Cox Wharf on the James River, Virginia
Skipper, Murdock Private	26	May 8, 1862, Old Hundred, North Carolina	Co. D, 46th North Carolina Infantry	May 5, 1864, Wilderness, Virginia	Point Lookout, Maryland, transferred to Elmira Prison, NY, July 30, 1864	Transferred for Exchange 10/11/64. Died 10/14/64 at US Army Hospital, Baltimore, MD. Brought to the Hospital Dead.
Skipper, William M. Corporal	Unk	March 8, 1861, Davidson, Alabama	Co. E, 1st Battalion Alabama Artillery	August 23, 1864, Fort Morgan, Alabama	New Orleans, Louisiana transferred to Elmira Prison, NY, December 4, 1864.	Oath of Allegiance June 21, 1865

Name & Rank	Age	Enlisted	Regiment and State	Where Captured	Prison	Remarks
Skipper, William M. Private	15	April 23, 1862, Old Brunswick Town, North Carolina	Co. G, 36th Regiment 2nd North Carolina Artillery	January 15, 1865, Fort Fisher, North Carolina	February 1, 1865, Elmira Prison Camp, New York	Exchanged March 2, 1865 at Akins Landing on the James River, Virginia
Slack, Charles D. Private	Unk	June 7, 1861, Camp Moore, Louisiana	Co. G, 7th Louisiana Infantry	May 5, 1864, Wilderness, Virginia	Point Lookout, Maryland, transferred to Elmira Prison, NY, July 3, 1864	Escaped the Night of July 8, 1864. Was Arrested at Newport, PA. Oath of Allegiance June 29, 1865
Slade, Benjamin S. Private	Unk	April 11, 1862, H. Barracks, Petersburg, Virginia	Co. F, 16th Virginia Infantry	May 6, 1864, Wilderness, Virginia	Point Lookout, Maryland, transferred to Elmira Prison, NY, July 30, 1864	Oath of Allegiance June 14, 1865
Slade, Henry Clay Private	26	June 15, 1861, Harrison's Church, North Carolina	Co. I, 5th North Carolina Infantry	May 12, 1864, Spotsylvania Court House, Virginia	Point Lookout, Maryland, transferred to Elmira Prison, NY, August 6, 1864	Died February 1, 1865 of Variola (Smallpox), Grave No. 1764
Slade, Jerry Z. Private	Unk	June 11, 1861, Drayton, Georgia	Co. F, 12th Georgia Infantry	May 10, 1864, Spotsylvania Court House, Virginia	Point Lookout, Maryland, transferred to Elmira Prison, NY, July 25, 1864	Oath of Allegiance June 27, 1865
Slade, William Private	Unk	June 13, 1864, Jacksonville, Georgia	Co. F, 12th Georgia Infantry	May 10, 1864, Spotsylvania Court House, Virginia	Point Lookout, Maryland, transferred to Elmira Prison, NY, July 25, 1864	Oath of Allegiance June 27, 1865
Slade, William F. Private	Unk	February 1, 1863, Choctaw Bluff, Alabama	Co. A, 21st Alabama Infantry	August 23, 1864, Fort Morgan, Alabama	Steam Press no. 4, New Orleans, Louisiana. Transferred to Elmira Prison October 8, 1864.	Died January 1, 1865 of Chronic Diarrhea, Grave No. 1332
Slagle, John H. Private	Unk	July 2, 1861, Bethel Am., Virginia	Co. F, 50th Virginia Infantry	May 12, 1864, Spotsylvania Court House, Virginia	Point Lookout, Maryland, transferred to Elmira Prison, NY, August 2, 1864	Oath of Allegiance May 19, 1865

Name & Rank	Age	Enlisted	Regiment and State	Where Captured	Prison	Remarks
Slater, Charles Private	Unk	July 15, 1862, Forsyth County, North Carolina	Co. G, 33rd North Carolina Infantry	May 6, 1864, Mine Run Wilderness, Virginia	Point Lookout, Maryland, transferred to Elmira Prison, NY, August 17, 1864	Oath of Allegiance June 30, 1865
Slatern, George W. Private	Unk	August 14, 1861, Atlanta, Georgia	Co. B, Cobb's Legion Georgia	September 22, 1863, Jack's Shop, Near Madison County House, Virginia	Point Lookout, Maryland, transferred to Elmira Prison, NY, August 18, 1864	Exchanged October 29, 1864, at Venus Point, Savannah River, GA.
Slaughter, James Private	Unk	January 5, 1862, Monticello, Florida	Co. A, 5th Florida Infantry	May 6, 1864, Wilderness, Virginia. Gunshot Wound Lower Forearm.	Old Capital Prison, Washington, DC, transferred to Elmira Prison, NY, July 23, 1864	Exchanged February 20, 1865 at Boulware's or Cox Wharf on the James River, Virginia
Slaughter, James N. Private	27	May 4, 1861, Stokes County, North Carolina	Co. A, 2nd Battalion North Carolina Infantry	June 10, 1864, Spotsylvania, Virginia	Point Lookout, Maryland, transferred to Elmira Prison, NY, July 25, 1864	Exchanged March 2, 1865 at Akins Landing on the James River, Virginia
Slaughter, W. B. Private	Unk	Unknown	Co. H, 16th Georgia Infantry	May 6, 1864, Wilderness, Virginia	Point Lookout, Maryland, transferred to Elmira Prison, NY, August 14, 1864	Oath of Allegiance July 27, 1865
Slavin, Newton C. Sergeant	24	October 1, 1861, Marshall, Texas	Co. A, 7th Texas Infantry	February 12, 1863, Raymond, Mississippi	Point Lookout, Maryland, transferred to Elmira Prison, NY, August 18, 1864	Exchanged February 25, 1865 at Boulware's wharf on the James River, Virginia
Slayden, James B. Private	Unk	April 1, 1861, Lacy's Store, Virginia	Co. B, 44th Virginia Infantry	May 5, 1864, Orange County Court House, Virginia	Point Lookout, Maryland, transferred to Elmira Prison, NY, August 2, 1864	Oath of Allegiance June 27, 1865
Slayden, Joseph T. Private	Unk	April 1, 1861, Lacy's Store, Virginia	Co. B, 44th Virginia Infantry	May 5, 1864, Orange County Court House, Virginia	Point Lookout, Maryland, transferred to Elmira Prison, NY, August 2, 1864	Oath of Allegiance June 27, 1865

Name & Rank	Age	Enlisted	Regiment and State	Where Captured	Prison	Remarks
Slayden, William J. Private	Unk	April 1, 1861, Lacy's Store, Virginia	Co. B, 44th Virginia Infantry	May 12, 1864, Spotsylvania Court House, Virginia	Point Lookout, Maryland, transferred to Elmira Prison, NY, August 2, 1864	Oath of Allegiance June 27, 1865.
Slessinger, Philip Corporal	21	June 12, 1861, New Orleans, Louisiana	Co. K, 14th Louisiana Infantry	May 12, 1864, Spotsylvania Court House, Virginia	Point Lookout, Maryland, transferred to Elmira Prison, NY, July 25, 1864	Exchanged February 25, 1865 at Boulware's or Cox Wharf on the James River, Virginia
Slingluff, Truman Private	Unk	Unknown	Co. F, 1st Maryland Cavalry	July 8, 1864, Boonesboro, Maryland	Old Capital Prison, Washington, DC, transferred to Elmira Prison, NY, July 23, 1864	Exchanged March 10, 1865 at Boulware's Wharf on the James River, Virginia
Slipp, J. M. Private	Unk	Unknown	Co. K, 26th Virginia Infantry	June 15, 1864, Near Petersburg, Virginia	Point Lookout, Maryland, transferred to Elmira Prison, NY, July 12, 1864	Transferred for Exchange October 11, 1864. Nothing Further.
Sloan, Dudley Private	Unk	Unknown	Co. A, Ogden's Louisiana Cavalry	November 5, 1864, Near Baton Rouge, Louisiana	New Orleans, Louisiana transferred to Elmira November 19, 1864.	Exchanged February 25, 1865 at Boulware's or Cox Wharf on the James River, Virginia
Sluppey, William Augustus Private	Unk	April 1, 1864, Augusta County, Georgia	Co. C, 12th Georgia Infantry	May 10, 1864, Spotsylvania Court House, Virginia	Point Lookout, Maryland, transferred to Elmira Prison, NY, July 30, 1864	Oath of Allegiance June 30, 1865
Slusser, John H. Sergeant	Unk	October 22, 1861, Centreville, Virginia	Co. E, 4th Virginia Infantry	May 12, 1864, Near Spotsylvania Court House, Virginia	Point Lookout, Maryland, transferred to Elmira Prison, NY, August 2, 1864	Exchanged February 13, 1865 at Boulware's wharf on the James River, Virginia
Small, Amos C. Private	Unk	January 1, 1862, Blanton's Crossroads, South Carolina	Co. K, 26th South Carolina Infantry	July 30, 1864, Petersburg, Virginia	Point Lookout, Maryland, transferred to Elmira Prison, NY, August 12, 1864	Died December 7, 1864 of Chronic Diarrhea, Grave No. 1185

Name & Rank	Age	Enlisted	Regiment and State	Where Captured	Prison	Remarks
Small, James N. Private	21	September 16, 1861, Jefferson County Courthouse, Virginia	Co. A, 2nd Virginia Infantry	July 28, 1863, Newtown, Virginia	Point Lookout, Maryland, transferred to Elmira Prison, NY, August 18, 1864	Exchanged March 10, 1865 at Boulware's Wharf on the James River, Virginia
Small, James P. Private	Unk	May 12, 1862, Troy, Alabama	Co. G, 59th Alabama Infantry	June 17, 1864, Near Petersburg, Virginia	Point Lookout, Maryland, transferred to Elmira Prison, NY, July 30, 1864	Oath of Allegiance July 7, 1865
Small, Thomas J. Sergeant	Unk	May 9, 1861, New Orleans, Louisiana	Co. H, 2nd Louisiana Infantry	May 12, 1864, Wilderness Spotsylvania, Virginia	Point Lookout, Maryland, transferred to Elmira Prison, NY, August 17, 1864	Exchanged February 25, 1865 at Boulware's or Cox Wharf on the James River, Virginia
Smalley, G. T. Private	Unk	March 16, 1863, Virginia	Co. C, Phillips Legion Georgia Infantry	June 1, 1864, Gaines Farm, Cold Harbor, Virginia	Transferred From Point Lookout Prison, MD, July 12, 1864. Train Never Arrived at Elmira Prison Camp, NY.	Died July 15, 1864 in Train Wreck at Shohola, Pennsylvania.
Smallwood, Charles F. Private	Unk	March 1, 1862, Union, Virginia	Co. H, 1st Virginia Cavalry	August 16, 1864, Front Royal, Virginia	Old Capital Prison, Washington, DC transferred to Elmira Prison, NY, August 29, 1864	Oath of Allegiance June 21, 1865
Smals, Newton M. Corporal	Unk	April 18, 1861, Harrisonburg, Virginia	Co. D, 10th Virginia Infantry	May 12, 1864, Spotsylvania Court House, Virginia	Point Lookout, Maryland, transferred to Elmira Prison, NY, August 2, 1864	Oath of Allegiance June 14, 1865
Smart, James P. Private	Unk	May 20, 1861, Nashville, Tennessee	Co. K, 7th Tennessee Infantry	June 2, 1864, Gaines Mill Cold Harbor, Virginia	Point Lookout, Maryland, transferred to Elmira Prison, NY, July 12, 1864	Oath of Allegiance March 31, 1865
Smith, A. J. Private	Unk	December 28, 1861, Camp Hampton, South Carolina	Co. F, Holcombe Legion, South Carolina	May 8, 1864, Jarrett's Depot, Virginia	Point Lookout, Maryland, transferred to Elmira Prison, NY, August 17, 1864	Died September 5, 1864 of Scorbutus (Scurvy), Grave No. 239

Name & Rank	Age	Enlisted	Regiment and State	Where Captured	Prison	Remarks
Smith, Albert Private	Unk	January 22, 1864, Camp Watts, Alabama	Co. A, Jackson's 1st Regiment, Tennessee Heavy Artillery	August 23, 1864, Fort Morgan, Alabama	New Orleans, Louisiana transferred to Elmira Prison, NY, December 4, 1864.	Exchanged February 13, 1865 at Boulware's wharf on the James River, Virginia
Smith, Albert G. Private	Unk	Unknown	Co. F, 45th North Carolina Infantry	June 3, 1864, Gaines Mill Cold Harbor, Virginia	Point Lookout, Maryland, transferred to Elmira Prison, NY, July 12, 1864	Died August 31, 1864 of Chronic Diarrhea, Grave No. 91
Smith, Alfred H. Private	18	April 23, 1861, Lexington, North Carolina	Co. B, 14th North Carolina Infantry	May 30, 1864 Mechanicsville, Virginia	Point Lookout, Maryland, transferred to Elmira Prison, NY, July 11, 1864	Oath of Allegiance June 19, 1865
Smith, Alfred H. Sergeant	32	March 8, 1862, Concorde, North Carolina	Co. A, 52nd North Carolina Infantry	May 12, 1864, Spotsylvania Court House, Virginia	Point Lookout, Maryland, transferred to Elmira Prison, NY, July 30, 1864	Oath of Allegiance June 12, 1865
Smith, Alonzo M. Private	19	March 6, 1862, Fort Pillow, Tennessee	Co. B, 1st Jackson's Tennessee Heavy Artillery	August 23, 1864, Fort Morgan, Alabama.	New Orleans, Louisiana transferred to Elmira Prison, NY, December 4, 1864.	Orders for Elmira, New York. Died December 20, 1864 of Chronic Diarrhea at US Army Hospital Fort Columbus, NY Harbor.
Smith, Amos J. Private	Unk	March 1, 1863, Saint Andrews, South Carolina	Co. B, 51st North Carolina Infantry	June 16, 1864, Petersburg, Virginia	Point Lookout, Maryland, transferred to Elmira Prison, NY, July 9, 1864	Oath of Allegiance July 3, 1865
Smith, Andrew Private	Unk	Unkown	Co. B, 8th Texas Infantry	September 2, 1863, Aranzas's Pass, Texas	New Orleans, Louisiana, Transferred to Elmira Prison, New York, November 19, 1864	Oath of Allegiance May 19, 1865
Smith, Appleton Corporal	Unk	March 4, 1862, Albany, Georgia	Co. K, 51st Georgia Infantry	June 3, 1864, Gaines Farm Cold Harbor, Virginia	Point Lookout, Maryland, transferred to Elmira Prison, NY, July 12, 1864	Oath of Allegiance June 30, 1865

Name & Rank	Age	Enlisted	Regiment and State	Where Captured	Prison	Remarks
Smith, Archibald Private	45	October 16, 1863, Fort Fisher, New Hanover County, North Carolina	Co. I, 36th Regiment 2nd North Carolina Artillery	January 15, 1865, Fort Fisher, North Carolina	February 1, 1865, Elmira Prison Camp, New York	Oath of Allegiance June 12, 1865
Smith, B. T. Corporal	Unk	October 3, 1862, Homer, Georgia	Co. A, 24th Georgia Infantry	August 16, 1864, Front Royal, Virginia	Old Capital Prison, Washington, DC transferred to Elmira Prison, NY, August 29, 1864	Exchanged March 14, 1865 at Boulware's Wharf on the James River, Virginia
Smith, Benjamin Private	21	June 12, 1861, Weldon, North Carolina	Co. B, 5th North Carolina Infantry	May 20, 1864, Spotsylvania Court House, Virginia	Point Lookout, Maryland, transferred to Elmira Prison, NY, July 3, 1864	Oath of Allegiance June 20, 1865
Smith, Bracy Private	Unk	May 2, 1862, Wilmington, North Carolina	Co. G, 51st North Carolina Infantry	June 3, 1864, Gaines Mill Cold Harbor, Virginia	Point Lookout, Maryland, transferred to Elmira Prison, NY, July 9, 1864	Died September 20, 1864 of Remittent Fever Grave No. 194
Smith, Bunyon M. Private	18	October 19, 1861, Elizabethtown, Bladen County, North Carolina	Co. J, 36th Regiment, 2nd North Carolina Artillery	January 15, 1865, Fort Fisher, North Carolina	February 1, 1865, Elmira Prison Camp, New York	Oath of Allegiance June 12, 1865
Smith, Calvin M. Private	Unk	May 12, 1862, Tuscaloosa, Alabama	Co. A, 41st Alabama Infantry	May 16, 1864, Near Drury's Bluff, Virginia	Point Lookout, Maryland, transferred to Elmira Prison, NY, August 17, 1864	Oath of Allegiance June 19, 1865
Smith, Charles Private	21	May 16, 1861, Columbia, North Carolina	Co. A, 32nd North Carolina Infantry	May 10, 1864, Near Mine Run Spotsylvania, Virginia	Point Lookout, Maryland, transferred to Elmira Prison, NY, August 6, 1864	Oath of Allegiance August 7, 1865
Smith, Charles Private	40	Unknown	Co. L, 1st Jackson's Tennessee Heavy Artillery	August 23, 1864, Fort Morgan, Alabama.	New Orleans, Louisiana transferred to Elmira Prison, NY, December 4, 1864.	Oath of Allegiance May 19, 1865

Name & Rank	Age	Enlisted	Regiment and State	Where Captured	Prison	Remarks
Smith, Charles W. Private	Unk	April 17, 1861, Wytheville, Virginia	Co. A, 4th Virginia Infantry	May 12, 1864, Spotsylvania Court House, Virginia	Point Lookout, Maryland, transferred to Elmira Prison, NY, August 2, 1864	Oath of Allegiance June 21, 1865
Smith, Chesley Private	38	October 18, 1861, Sampson County, North Carolina	Co. A, 36th Regiment, 2nd North Carolina Artillery	January 15, 1865, Fort Fisher, North Carolina	February 1, 1865, Elmira Prison Camp, New York	Died June 23, 1865 of Chronic Diarrhea, Grave No. 2817
Smith, Cholson Private	30	April 4, 1862, Bennettsville, South Carolina	Co. F, 21st South Carolina Infantry	June 17, 1864, Petersburg, Virginia	Point Lookout, Maryland, transferred to Elmira Prison, NY, July 30, 1864	Exchanged March 2, 1865 at Akins Landing on the James River, Virginia
Smith, Coleman Private	Unk	February 18, 1864, Greenville, Tennessee	Co. B, 1st Tennessee Infantry	May 6, 1864, Wilderness, Virginia	Point Lookout, Maryland, transferred to Elmira Prison, NY, July 25, 1864	Died September 4, 1864 of Chronic Diarrhea, Grave No. 227
Smith, D. Private	18	July 29, 1861, Albmarle, North Carolina	Co. B, 28th North Carolina Infantry	May 12, 1864, Spotsylvania County Court House, Virginia	Point Lookout, Maryland, transferred to Elmira Prison, NY, August 14, 1864	Oath of Allegiance May 29, 1865
Smith, D. L. Private	Unk	February 18, 1863, Marion, Alabama	Co. E, 41st Alabama Infantry	June 15, 1864, Petersburg, Virginia	Point Lookout, Maryland, transferred to Elmira Prison, NY, July 12, 1864	Exchanged March 14, 1865 at Boulware's Wharf on the James River, Virginia
Smith, D. S. Sergeant	Unk	May 8, 1862, Tennille, Georgia	Co. D, 59th Georgia Infantry	May 24, 1864, Hanover Junction, Virginia	Point Lookout, Maryland, transferred to Elmira Prison, NY, July 11,1864	Exchanged October 29, 1864, at Venus Point, Savannah River, GA.
Smith, Daniel Private	27	July 8, 1862, Elizabeth, North Carolina	Co. J, 36th Regiment, 2nd North Carolina Artillery	January 15, 1865, Fort Fisher, North Carolina	Elmira Prison Camp, New York, February 1, 1865	Died March 29, 1865 of Variola (Smallpox), Grave No. 2517
Smith, Daniel Private	Unk	June 22, 1861, Wytheville, Virginia	Co. K, 50th Virginia Infantry	May 12, 1864, Spotsylvania Court House, Virginia	Point Lookout, Maryland, transferred to Elmira Prison, NY, August 2, 1864	Exchanged October 29, 1864, at Venus Point, Savannah River, GA.

Name & Rank	Age	Enlisted	Regiment and State	Where Captured	Prison	Remarks
Smith, David H. Private	Unk	Unknown	Co. C, 11th North Carolina Infantry	April 2, 1865, Hatchers Run, Virginia	Old Capital Prison, Washington D. C. Transferred to Elmira Prison, NY, May 2, 1865.	Oath of Allegiance June 23, 1865
Smith, David H. Private	37	December 28, 1861, Columbia, South Carolina	Co. F, 18th South Carolina Infantry	July 30, 1864, Petersburg, Virginia. Contusion from Explosion.	Old Capital Prison, Washington, DC transferred to Elmira Prison, NY, August 27, 1864	Oath of Allegiance June 21, 1865
Smith, E. B. Private	Unk	April 26, 1864, Marion, South Carolina	Co. D, 21st South Carolina Infantry	January 15, 1865, Fort Fisher, North Carolina	February 1, 1865, Elmira Prison Camp, New York	Died on Route to be Exchanged March 2, 1865.
Smith, E. F. Private	37	July 6, 1861, Hilton Head, South Carolina	Co. C, 11th South Carolina Infantry	June 24, 1864, Near Petersburg, Virginia	Point Lookout, Maryland, transferred to Elmira Prison, NY, August 18, 1864	Died May 31, 1865 of Chronic Diarrhea, Grave No. 2753. Headstone has B. F. Smith.
Smith, E. P. Private	Unk	August 18, 1863, Spartanburg, South Carolina	Co. E, 6th South Carolina Cavalry	July 30, 1864, Lee's Mill, Petersburg, Virginia	Point Lookout, Maryland, transferred to Elmira Prison, NY, August 12, 1864	Died February 20, 1865 of Diarrhea, Grave No. 2322
Smith, E. S. Private	Unk	May 12, 1863, Raleigh, North Carolina	Co. D, 5th North Carolina Infantry	July 4, 1864, Harper's Ferry, Virginia	Old Capital Prison, Washington, DC, transferred to Elmira Prison, NY, July 23, 1864	Exchanged October 29, 1864, at Venus Point, Savannah River, GA.
Smith, Edmund Private	27	February 28, 1863, Weldon, North Carolina	Co. D, 42nd North Carolina Infantry	June 3, 1864, Cold Harbor, Virginia	Point Lookout, Maryland, transferred to Elmira Prison, NY, July 12, 1864	Oath of Allegiance July 3, 1865
Smith, Edmund D. Private	27	February 28, 1863, Weldon, North Carolina	Co. C, 42nd North Carolina Infantry	June 3, 1864, Cold Harbor, Virginia	Point Lookout, Maryland, transferred to Elmira Prison, NY, July 12, 1864	Oath of Allegiance July 3, 1865

Name & Rank	Age	Enlisted	Regiment and State	Where Captured	Prison	Remarks
Smith, Edmund R. Private	19	September 7, 1861, Albemarle, North Carolina	Co. B, 28th North Carolina Infantry	May 12, 1864, Spotsylvania County Court House, Virginia	Point Lookout, Maryland, transferred to Elmira Prison, NY, August 14, 1864	Oath of Allegiance May 29, 1865
Smith, Edom Private	20	June 11, 1863, Fort Fisher, New Hanover County, North Carolina	Co. I, 36th Regiment 2nd North Carolina Artillery	January 15, 1865, Fort Fisher, North Carolina	February 1, 1865, Elmira Prison Camp, New York	Died February 18, 1865 of Pneumonia, Grave No. 2352
Smith, Elias Private	51	August 1, 1862, Drury's Bluff, Virginia	Co. H, 32nd Virginia Infantry	May 10, 1864, Spotsylvania, Virginia	Old Capital Prison, Washington, DC, transferred to Elmira Prison, NY, December 17, 1864	Died February 8, 1865 of Chronic Diarrhea, Grave No. 1931. Headstone has 36th NC.
Smith, Elnathan N. Private	Unk	July 13, 1862, White County, Georgia	Co. C, 24th Georgia Infantry	August 16, 1864, Front Royal, Virginia	Old Capital Prison, Washington, D. C., transferred to Elmira Prison, NY, August 29, 1864	Died February 8, 1865 of Chronic Diarrhea Grave No. 1924
Smith, Emerson Private	39	March 2, 1863, Rogersville, Tennessee	Co. C, 63rd Tennessee Infantry	June 17, 1864, Petersburg, Virginia	Point Lookout, Maryland, transferred to Elmira Prison, NY, July 30, 1864	Exchanged February 25, 1865 at Boulware's or Cox Wharf on the James River, Virginia
Smith, Emmett P. Corporal	Unk	May 11, 1861, Richmond, Virginia	Co. C, 38th Read's Battalion, Virginia Light Artillery	June 3, 1864, Gaines Farm Cold Harbor, Virginia	Point Lookout, Maryland, transferred to Elmira Prison, NY, July 17, 1864	Oath of Allegiance July 3, 1865
Smith, Evan Private	30	September 7, 1861, Albemarle, North Carolina	Co. K, 28th North Carolina Infantry	May 12, 1864, Spotsylvania County Court House, Virginia	Point Lookout, Maryland, transferred to Elmira Prison, NY, August 14, 1864	Died April 2, 1865 of Chronic Diarrhea, Grave No. 2579
Smith, F. C. Private	Unk	Unknown	Co. A, 36th Regiment 2nd North Carolina Artillery	January 15, 1865, Fort Fisher, North Carolina	February 1, 1865, Elmira Prison Camp, New York	Oath of Allegiance July 11, 1865

Name & Rank	Age	Enlisted	Regiment and State	Where Captured	Prison	Remarks
Smith, F. M. Corporal	Unk	Unknown	Co. B, 52nd North Carolina Infantry	May 12, 1864, Spotsylvania Court House, Virginia	Point Lookout, Maryland, transferred to Elmira Prison, NY, August 12, 1864	Oath of Allegiance June 12, 1865
Smith, Frank Private	Unk	August 6, 1863, Camp Laurel, Virginia	Co. A, 21st Virginia Cavalry	July 12, 1864, Beltsville, Maryland	Old Capital Prison, Washington, DC, transferred to Elmira Prison, NY, July 23, 1864	Oath of Allegiance May 29, 1865
Smith, Franklin Corporal	28	March 20, 1862, Danburg, North Carolina	Co. H, 53rd North Carolina Infantry	July 12, 1864, Near Washington, D. C. Gunshot Wound Left Thigh.	Old Capital Prison, Washington, DC, transferred to Elmira Prison, NY, December 17, 1864	Oath of Allegiance July 11, 1865
Smith, Franklin A. Private	20	June 4, 1861, Mocksville, North Carolina	Co. G, 4th North Carolina Infantry	July 12, 1864, Near Washington, DC	Old Capital Prison, Washington, DC, transferred to Elmira Prison, NY, July 23, 1864	Exchanged February 20, 1865 at Boulware's or Cox Wharf on the James River, Virginia
Smith, Frederick Private	22	July 16, 1862, Raleigh, North Carolina	Co. D, 14th North Carolina Infantry	May 20, 1864, Spotsylvania Court House, Virginia	Point Lookout Prison Camp, Maryland. Transferred to Elmira Prison, July 6, 1864	Died March 1, 1865 of Chronic Diarrhea, Grave No. 2105
Smith, Freeman Private	47	March 18, 1862, Dobson, North Carolina	Co. A, 28th North Carolina Infantry	May 12, 1864, Spotsylvania County Court House, Virginia	Point Lookout, Maryland, transferred to Elmira Prison, NY, August 14, 1864	Died February 22, 1865 of Chronic Diarrhea, Grave No. 2303
Smith, General M. Private	Unk	July 29, 1861, Satilla, Georgia	Co. D, 26th Georgia Infantry	May 20, 1864, Spotsylvania Court House, Virginia	Point Lookout, Maryland, transferred to Elmira Prison, NY, July 3, 1864	Died January 31, 1865 of Pneumonia, Grave No. 1782
Smith, George Private	21	September 2, 1861, Orange County, North Carolina	Co. G, 28th North Carolina Infantry	May 12, 1864, Near Spotsylvania Court House, Virginia	Point Lookout, Maryland, transferred to Elmira Prison, NY, August 14, 1864	Died October 25, 1864 of Chronic Diarrhea, Grave No. 855

Name & Rank	Age	Enlisted	Regiment and State	Where Captured	Prison	Remarks
Smith, George Private	37	March 7, 1863, Zollicoffer, Cumberland Gap, Tennessee	Co. F, 63rd Tennessee Infantry	May 16, 1864, Near Drury's Bluff, Virginia	Point Lookout, Maryland, transferred to Elmira Prison, NY, August 17, 1864	Died February 4, 1865 of Variola (Smallpox), Grave No. 1897
Smith, George A. Sergeant	19	February 28, 1862, Lumberton, North Carolina	Co. E, 51st North Carolina Infantry	June 1, 1864, Gaines Mill Cold Harbor, Virginia	Point Lookout, Maryland, transferred to Elmira Prison, NY, July 9, 1864	Exchanged March 2, 1865 at Akins Landing on the James River, Virginia
Smith, George A. Private	Unk	March 1, 1862, Acworth, Georgia	Co. E, 3rd Georgia Sharp Shooters	August 16, 1864, Front Royal, Virginia	Old Capital Prison, Washington, DC transferred to Elmira Prison, NY, August 29, 1864	Exchanged February 13, 1865 at Boulware's wharf on the James River, Virginia
Smith, George F. Private	42	August 10, 1863, Chaffins, Virginia	Co. F, 46th Virginia Infantry	June 17, 1864, Petersburg, Virginia	Point Lookout, Maryland, transferred to Elmira Prison, NY, July 23, 1864	Oath of Allegiance April 1, 1865
Smith, George H. Private	Unk	February 27, 1862, Norfolk, Virginia	Capt. Kevill's Battery, Richmond Howitzers, Virginia Artillery	July 7, 1864, Howlett's Farm, Virginia	Point Lookout, Maryland, transferred to Elmira Prison, NY, August 6, 1864	Exchanged March 14, 1865 at Boulware's Wharf on the James River, Virginia
Smith, Harris G. Corporal	Unk	October 13, 1861, Camp Kirkpatrick, Dawson or Forsyth County, Georgia	Co. K, 38th Georgia Infantry	August 12, 1864, Middletown, Virginia	Old Capital Prison, Washington, DC transferred to Elmira Prison, NY, August 29, 1864	Exchanged March 14, 1865 at Boulware's Wharf on the James River, Virginia
Smith, Henry Private	40	June 12, 1861, New Orleans, Louisiana	Co. K, 14th Louisiana Infantry	May 12, 1864, Spotsylvania Court House, Virginia	Point Lookout, Maryland, transferred to Elmira Prison, NY, July 25, 1864	Exchanged February 13, 1865 at Boulware's wharf on the James River, Virginia
Smith, Henry Private	32	October 20, 1863, Camp Vance, North Carolina	Co. G, 37th North Carolina Infantry	May 6, 1864, Wilderness, Virginia	Point Lookout, Maryland, transferred to Elmira Prison, NY, July 23, 1864	Oath of Allegiance May 29, 1865

Name & Rank	Age	Enlisted	Regiment and State	Where Captured	Prison	Remarks
Smith, Henry Private	21	August 17, 1864, Pitt County, North Carolina	Co. K, 40th Regiment, 3rd North Carolina Artillery	January 15, 1865, Fort Fisher, North Carolina	February 1, 1865, Elmira Prison Camp, New York	Exchanged March 14, 1865 at Boulware's Wharf on the James River, Virginia
Smith, Henry H. Private	Unk	June 26, 1861, Scott County, Virginia	Co. H, 48th Virginia Infantry	May 12, 1864, Near Spotsylvania Court House, Virginia	Point Lookout, Maryland, transferred to Elmira Prison, NY, August 6, 1864	Transferred For Exchange October 11, 1864 to Point Lookout Prison Camp, MD. Nothing Further.
Smith, Henry Paris Corporal	Unk	July 16, 1861, Blacksburg, Virginia	Co. L, 4th Virginia Infantry	May 12, 1864, Near Spotsylvania Court House, Virginia	Point Lookout, Maryland, transferred to Elmira Prison, NY, August 6, 1864	Exchanged February 13, 1865 at Boulware's wharf on the James River, Virginia
Smith, Herbert M. Private	Unk	November 27, 1863, Pocotaligo, South Carolina	Co. E, 4th South Carolina Cavalry	June 11, 1864, Trevilian Station, Louisa Court House, Virginia	Point Lookout, Maryland, transferred to Elmira Prison, NY, July 25, 1864	Died September 16, 1864 of Chronic Diarrhea, Grave No. 304
Smith, Hezekiah Private	Unk	July 11, 1861, Johnson County, Georgia	Co. B, 14th Georgia Infantry	May 12, 1864, Spotsylvania Court House, Virginia	Point Lookout, Maryland, transferred to Elmira Prison, NY, July 30, 1864	Oath of Allegiance July 11, 1865
Smith, Isaac Private	Unk	September 8, 1863, Coffee County, Alabama	Co. H, 6th Alabama Infantry	May 20, 1864, Spotsylvania Court House, Virginia	Point Lookout, Maryland, transferred to Elmira Prison, NY, July 3, 1864	Died September 17, 1864 of Chronic Diarrhea, Grave No. 160
Smith, Isaac Private	Unk	May 7, 1862, Bibb County, Alabama	Co. J, 44th Alabama Infantry	May 6, 1864, Wilderness, Virginia	Point Lookout, Maryland, transferred to Elmira Prison, NY, August 17, 1864	Died November 2, 1864 of Chronic Diarrhea, Grave No. 843
Smith, J. Private	Unk	Unknown	Co. G, 8th Louisiana Infantry	May 12, 1864, Spotsylvania Court House, Virginia	Point Lookout, Maryland, transferred to Elmira Prison, NY, August 17, 1864	Exchanged March 14, 1865 at Boulware's Wharf on the James River, Virginia

Name & Rank	Age	Enlisted	Regiment and State	Where Captured	Prison	Remarks
Smith, J. A. Private	Unk	December 28, 1861, Camp Hampton, South Carolina	Co. F, Holcombe Legion, South Carolina	May 8, 1864, Jarrett's Depot, Virginia	Point Lookout, Maryland, transferred to Elmira Prison, NY, August 17, 1864	Oath of Allegiance June 14, 1865
Smith, J. D. Private	Unk	June 1, 1861, Richmond, Virginia	Co. K, 10th Virginia Cavalry	June 1, 1864, Hanover Court House, Cold Harbor, Virginia	Point Lookout, Maryland, transferred to Elmira Prison, NY, July 17,1864	Exchanged March 10, 1865 at Boulware's wharf on the James River, Virginia
Smith, J. F. Private	Unk	May 15, 1861, Raleigh, North Carolina	Signal Corps Confederate States Army	June 2, 1864, Gaines Mill Cold Harbor, Virginia	Point Lookout, Maryland, transferred to Elmira Prison, NY, July 12, 1864	Exchanged February 25, 1865 at Boulware's or Cox Wharf on the James River, Virginia
Smith, J. H. Private	Unk	May 7, 1862, Thunderbolt, Georgia	Co. B, 7th Georgia Cavalry	June 11, 1864, Trevilian Station, Louisa Court House, Virginia	Point Lookout, Maryland, transferred to Elmira Prison, NY, July 25, 1864	Died October 27, 1864 of Chronic Diarrhea, Grave No. 721
Smith, J. H. Private	Unk	Unknown	Co. E, 11th South Carolina Infantry	June 16, 1864, Petersburg, Virginia	Point Lookout, Maryland, transferred to Elmira Prison, NY, July 25, 1864	Oath of Allegiance July 11, 1865
Smith, J. H. C. Private	Unk	Unknown	Co. I, 50th Virginia Infantry	May 12, 1864, Spotsylvania Court House, Virginia	Point Lookout, Maryland, transferred to Elmira Prison, NY, August 2, 1864	Exchanged October 29, 1864, at Venus Point, Savannah River, GA.
Smith, J. L. Private	Unk	Unknown	Co. G, 7th Kentucky Mounted Infantry	June 30, 1864, Came into Lines at Mecklenberry County, Virginia	Point Lookout, Maryland, transferred to Elmira Prison, NY, July 23, 1864	Oath of Allegiance June 20, 1865
Smith, J. N. Private	Unk	August 15, 1862, Bartow County, Georgia	Co. A, 3rd Georgia Sharp Shooters	August 16, 1864, Front Royal, Virginia	Old Capital Prison, Washington, DC transferred to Elmira Prison, NY, August 29, 1864	Oath of Allegiance June 30, 1865

Name & Rank	Age	Enlisted	Regiment and State	Where Captured	Prison	Remarks
Smith, J. P. Private	Unk	September 1, 1863, Spartanburg, South Carolina	Co. K, 27th South Carolina Infantry	June 24, 1864, Near Petersburg, Virginia	Point Lookout, Maryland, transferred to Elmira Prison, NY, August 18, 1864	Oath of Allegiance June 16, 1865
Smith, J. W. Private	Unk	September 6, 1862, Choctaw County, Alabama	Co. A, 1st Battalion Alabama Artillery	August 23, 1864, Fort Morgan, Alabama	New Orleans, Louisiana transferred to Elmira Prison, NY, December 4, 1864.	Died March 7, 1865 of Diarrhea, Grave No. 2403
Smith, James Private	Unk	Unknown	Co. A, Ogden's Battalion Louisiana Cavalry	September 17, 1864, Greenville Springs, Near East Baton Rouge, Louisiana	New Orleans, Louisiana transferred to Elmira November 19, 1864.	Died December 27, 1864 of Typhoid-pneumonia, Grave No. 1298
Smith, James Private	Unk	February 28, 1862, Columbus, Kentucky	Co. B, 1st Jackson's Tennessee Heavy Artillery	August 23, 1864, Fort Morgan, Alabama.	New Orleans, Louisiana transferred to Elmira Prison, NY, December 4, 1864.	Exchanged March 10, 1865 at Boulware's Wharf on the James River, Virginia
Smith, James C. Private	Unk	July 17, 1861, Yorktown, Virginia	Co. B, 6th Georgia Infantry	June 17, 1864, Near Petersburg, Virginia	Point Lookout, Maryland, transferred to Elmira Prison, NY, July 30, 1864	Oath of Allegiance July 7, 1865
Smith, James C. Corporal	Unk	March 4, 1862, Millen County, Georgia	Co. D, 51st Georgia Infantry	June 3, 1864, Gaines Farm Cold Harbor, Virginia	Point Lookout, Maryland, transferred to Elmira Prison, NY, July 12, 1864	Died May 11, 1865 of Chronic Diarrhea, Grave No. 2796
Smith, James C. Private	Unk	June 25, 1861, Wytheville, Virginia	Co. J, 50th Virginia Infantry	May 6, 1864, Wilderness, Virginia	Point Lookout, Maryland, transferred to Elmira Prison, NY, August 14, 1864	Exchanged February 20, 1865 at Boulware's or Cox Wharf on the James River, Virginia
Smith, James E. Private	Unk	May 5, 1864, Prince George County, Virginia	Co. C, Archer's 3rd Battalion Virginia Reserves	June 15, 1864, Petersburg, Virginia	Point Lookout, Maryland, transferred to Elmira Prison, NY, July 30, 1864	Exchanged October 29, 1864, at Venus Point, Savannah River, GA.

Name & Rank	Age	Enlisted	Regiment and State	Where Captured	Prison	Remarks
Smith, James F. Private	Unk	October 24, 1861, Camp Wayne, Georgia	Co. G, 61st Georgia Infantry	May 12, 1864, Spotsylvania Court House, Virginia	Point Lookout, Maryland, transferred to Elmira Prison, NY, July 30, 1864	Oath of Allegiance June 27, 1865
Smith, James F. Private	Unk	Unknown	Co. J, 25th South Carolina Infantry	Unknown	Point Lookout Prison Camp, Maryland. Transferred to Elmira Prison, Unknown Date	Died March 16, 1865 of Unknown Disease, Grave No. 1554
Smith, James J. Private	24	May 14, 1861, Vicksburg, Mississippi	Co. C, 19th Mississippi Infantry	May 23, 1864, Beaver Dam, Virginia	Point Lookout, Maryland, transferred to Elmira Prison, NY, July 11, 1864	Oath of Allegiance May 17, 1865
Smith, James K. Private	Unk	December 7, 1863, Tullahoma, Tennessee	Co. B, 44th Tennessee Infantry	June 17, 1864, Petersburg, Virginia	Point Lookout, Maryland, transferred to Elmira Prison, NY, July 30, 1864	Oath of Allegiance July 3, 1865
Smith, James P. Private	21	February 28, 1862, Lumberton, North Carolina	Co. E, 51st North Carolina Infantry	June 1, 1864, Gaines Mill Cold Harbor, Virginia	Point Lookout, Maryland, transferred to Elmira Prison, NY, July 9, 1864	Exchanged March 14, 1865 at Boulware's Wharf on the James River, Virginia
Smith, James W. Private	29	November 17, 1861, Camp Stevens, North Carolina	Co. F, 18th North Carolina Infantry	May 12, 1864, Spotsylvania Court House, Virginia	Point Lookout, Maryland, transferred to Elmira Prison, NY, August 6, 1864	Oath of Allegiance June 14, 1865
Smith, Jasper N. Corporal	Unk	July 1, 1863, Butler County, Alabama	Co. G, 61st Alabama Infantry	May 12, 1864, Spotsylvania Court House, Virginia	Point Lookout, Maryland, transferred to Elmira Prison, NY, July 30, 1864	Exchanged October 29, 1864, at Venus Point, Savannah River, GA.
Smith, Jesse L. Sergeant	25	June 10, 1861, Matthews, North Carolina	Co. G, 26th North Carolina Infantry	May 12, 1864, Spotsylvania Court House, Virginia	Point Lookout, Maryland, transferred to Elmira Prison, NY, July 30, 1864	Oath of Allegiance June 23, 1865
Smith, Jesse S. Private	Unk	June 15, 1862, Americus, Georgia	Co. K, 9th Georgia Infantry	May 6, 1864, Mine Run Wilderness, Virginia	Point Lookout, Maryland, transferred to Elmira Prison, NY, August 14, 1864	Died February 1, 1865 of Variola (Smallpox), Grave No. 1763

Name & Rank	Age	Enlisted	Regiment and State	Where Captured	Prison	Remarks
Smith, Job Private	Unk	August 21, 1863, Waller's Tavern, Georgia	Co. I, 16th Georgia Infantry	June 1, 1864, Gaines Farm Cold Harbor, Virginia	Point Lookout, Maryland, transferred to Elmira Prison, NY, July 12, 1864	Exchanged October 29, 1864, at Venus Point, Savannah River, GA.
Smith, John Private	23	July 7, 1861, Camp Moore, Louisiana	Co. B, 9th Louisiana Infantry	May 12, 1864, Spotsylvania Court House, Virginia	Point Lookout, Maryland, transferred to Elmira Prison, NY, August 17, 1864	Exchanged March 10, 1865 at Boulware's Wharf on the James River, Virginia
Smith, John A. Private	31	July 5, 1861, Bladen County, North Carolina	Co. H, 3rd North Carolina Infantry	May 12, 1864, Near Spotsylvania Court House, Virginia	Point Lookout, Maryland, transferred to Elmira Prison, NY, August 14, 1864	Oath of Allegiance June 12, 1865
Smith, John B. Private	24	March 8, 1862, Kinston, North Carolina	Co. C, 35th North Carolina Infantry	June 17, 1864, Petersburg, Virginia	Point Lookout, Maryland, transferred to Elmira Prison, NY, July 30, 1864	Transferred for Exchange 10/11/64. Died 10/24/64 at US Army Hospital, Baltimore, MD.
Smith, John B. Private	45	October 26, 1863, Fort Fisher, New Hanover County, North Carolina	Co. J, 36th Regiment, 2nd North Carolina Artillery	January 15, 1865, Fort Fisher, North Carolina	February 1, 1865, Elmira Prison Camp, New York	Died April 10, 1865 of Pneumonia, Grave No. 2609
Smith, John B. Private	37	March 26, 1863, Chatham County, North Carolina	Co. G, 40th Regiment, 3rd North Carolina Artillery	January 15, 1865, Fort Fisher, North Carolina	February 1, 1865, Elmira Prison Camp, New York	Died February 8, 1865 of Pneumonia, Grave No. 1936
Smith, John D. Private	19	October 19, 1861, Wilmington, New Hanover County, North Carolina	Co. I, 36th Regiment, 2nd North Carolina Artillery	January 15, 1865, Fort Fisher, North Carolina	February 1, 1865, Elmira Prison Camp, New York	Died March 22, 1865 of Chronic Diarrhea, Grave No. 1523
Smith, John E. Private	Unk	May 29, 1864, Petersburg, Virginia	Co. D, 3rd Archer's Battalion, Virginia Reserves Infantry	June 9, 1864, Petersburg, Virginia	Point Lookout, Maryland, transferred to Elmira Prison, NY, July 12,1864	Exchanged October 29, 1864, at Venus Point, Savannah River, GA.
Smith, John F. Private	35	March 1, 1864, Opilika, Alabama	Co. A, 1st Battalion Alabama Artillery	August 23, 1864, Fort Morgan, Alabama	New Orleans, Louisiana transferred to Elmira Prison, NY, December 4, 1864.	Died February 17, 1865 of Chronic Diarrhea, Grave No. 2226

Name & Rank	Age	Enlisted	Regiment and State	Where Captured	Prison	Remarks
Smith, John H. Private	Unk	March 7, 1864, Camp Terrel, Greensboro, North Carolina	Co. B, 45th North Carolina Infantry	May 10, 1864, Spotsylvania Court House, Virginia	Point Lookout, Maryland, transferred to Elmira Prison, NY, August 6, 1864	Died September 27, 1864 of Typhoid-Pneumonia, Grave No. 389
Smith, John H. Private	Unk	July 20, 1861, Wytheville, Virginia	Co. C, 51st Virginia Infantry	July 10, 1864, Frederick, Maryland	Old Capital Prison, Washington, DC, transferred to Elmira Prison, NY, July 23, 1864	Died February 14, 1865 of Variola (Smallpox), Grave No. 2027
Smith, John M. Private	30	September 15, 1863, Albmarle, North Carolina	Co. K, 28th North Carolina Infantry	May 12, 1864, Spotsylvania County Court House, Virginia	Point Lookout, Maryland, transferred to Elmira Prison, NY, August 14, 1864	Died April 9, 1865 of Hospital Gangrene, Grave No. 2627
Smith, John O. Private	Unk	June 25, 1861, Wytheville, Virginia	Co. J, 50th Virginia Infantry	May 6, 1864, Wilderness, Virginia	Point Lookout, Maryland, transferred to Elmira Prison, NY, August 14, 1864	Died December 19, 1864 of Pneumonia, Grave No. 1072
Smith, John W. Private	Unk	April 1, 1862, Montgomery, Alabama	Co. B, 59th Alabama Infantry	June 16, 1864, Petersburg, Virginia	Point Lookout, Maryland, transferred to Elmira Prison, NY, July 12, 1864	Oath of Allegiance June 19, 1865
Smith, John W. Private	Unk	March 30, 1862, Orangeburg, South Carolina	Co. F, 25th South Carolina Infantry	January 15, 1865, Fort Fisher, North Carolina	February 1, 1865, Elmira Prison Camp, New York	Oath of Allegiance July 11, 1865
Smith, John W. Private	Unk	March 10, 1862, Henry County, Virginia	Co. G, 42nd Virginia Infantry	May 12, 1864, Near Spotsylvania Court House, Virginia	Point Lookout, Maryland, transferred to Elmira Prison, NY, August 6, 1864	Died November 20, 1864 of Pneumonia, Grave No. 939
Smith, Jordan Private	18	January 1, 1862, Georgetown, South Carolina	Co. A, 21st South Carolina Infantry	June 24, 1864, Near Petersburg, Virginia	Point Lookout, Maryland, transferred to Elmira Prison, NY, August 18, 1864	Exchanged March 14, 1865 at Boulware's Wharf on the James River, Virginia
Smith, Joseph B. Private	32	April 23, 1861, Madison Court House, Virginia	Co. K, 7th Virginia Infantry	May 16, 1864, Near Drury's Bluff, Virginia	Point Lookout, Maryland, transferred to Elmira Prison, NY, August 17, 1864	Oath of Allegiance June 21, 1865

Name & Rank	Age	Enlisted	Regiment and State	Where Captured	Prison	Remarks
Smith, Joseph E. Private	Unk	July 10, 1861, Auburn, Alabama	Co. K, 12th Alabama Infantry	May 12, 1864, Spotsylvania Court House, Virginia	Point Lookout, Maryland, transferred to Elmira Prison, NY, August 17, 1864	Oath of Allegiance June 21, 1865
Smith, Joseph J. Private	Unk	July 24, 1862, Calhoun, Georgia	Co. B, 16th Georgia Infantry	August 16, 1864, Front Royal, Virginia	Old Capital Prison, Washington, DC transferred to Elmira Prison, NY, August 29, 1864	Died March 2, 1865, Diarrhea, Grave No. 2103
Smith, Joseph W. Private	Unk	December 28, 1861, Camp Hampton, South Carolina	Co. F, Holcombe Legion, South Carolina	May 8, 1864, Jarrett's Depot, Virginia	Point Lookout, Maryland, transferred to Elmira Prison, NY, August 17, 1864	Died February 9, 1865 of Chronic Diarrhea, Grave No. 1932
Smith, Joseph W. Private	Unk	December 27, 1861, York County Court House, South Carolina	Co. C, 17th South Carolina Infantry	July 30, 1864, Petersburg, Virginia	Point Lookout, Maryland, transferred to Elmira Prison, NY, August 12, 1864	Died January 9, 1865 of Pneumonia, Grave No. 1216
Smith, Josephus C. Private	18	June 11, 1863, Fort Fisher, New Hanover County, North Carolina	Co. I, 36th Regiment 2nd North Carolina Artillery	January 15, 1865, Fort Fisher, North Carolina	February 1, 1865, Elmira Prison Camp, New York	Died March 22, 1865 of Diarrhea, Grave No. 1523
Smith, Junius H. Private	45	August 11, 1863, Rogersville, Tennessee	Co. C, 63rd Tennessee Infantry	June 17, 1864, Petersburg, Virginia	Point Lookout, Maryland, transferred to Elmira Prison, NY, July 23, 1864	Died January 9, 1865 of Chronic Diarrhea, Grave No. 1217
Smith, Lauson M. Private	21	July 30, 1861, Dallas, North Carolina	Co. B, 28th North Carolina Infantry	May 12, 1864, Spotsylvania County Court House, Virginia	Point Lookout, Maryland, transferred to Elmira Prison, NY, August 14, 1864	Oath of Allegiance June 19, 1865
Smith, Lewis Private	Unk	May 27, 1861, Staunton, Virginia	Co. D, 25th Virginia Infantry	May 12, 1864, Spotsylvania Court House, Virginia	Point Lookout, Maryland, transferred to Elmira Prison, NY, August 12, 1864	Oath of Allegiance June 19, 1865

Name & Rank	Age	Enlisted	Regiment and State	Where Captured	Prison	Remarks
Smith, Lewis P. Private	44	August 12, 1863, Knoxville, Tennessee	Co. L, 14th Tennessee Infantry	May 6, 1864, Wilderness, Virginia	Point Lookout, Maryland, transferred to Elmira Prison, NY, July 25, 1864	Oath of Allegiance November 16, 1864. Early Release per Lincoln's Proclamation, 12/8/1863.
Smith, Lindsay Private	Unk	August 11, 1861, Gwinnett, Georgia	Co. H, 16th Georgia Infantry	August 16, 1864, Front Royal, Virginia	Old Capital Prison, Washington, DC transferred to Elmira Prison, NY, August 29, 1864	Oath of Allegiance June 14, 1865
Smith, Lorenzo P. Private	23	April 25, 1862, Lewisburg, Virginia	Captain G. B. Chapman's Battery Virginia Light Artillery	July 10, 1864, Frederick, Maryland	Old Capital Prison, Washington, DC, transferred to Elmira Prison, NY, July 23, 1864	Exchanged October 29, 1864, at Venus Point, Savannah River, GA.
Smith, Malery G. Private	22	July 18, 1862, Camp Hill, North Carolina	Co. E, 18th North Carolina Infantry	May 12, 1864, Spotsylvania Court House, Virginia	Point Lookout, Maryland, transferred to Elmira Prison, NY, August 6, 1864	Oath of Allegiance June 12, 1865
Smith, Minett Martin Private	19	April 29, 1861, Cherry Creek, Mississippi	Co. J, 2nd Mississippi Infantry	October 1, 1864, Weldon Railroad, Virginia. Gunshot Wound Abdomen.	Old Capital Prison, Washington, DC, transferred to Elmira Prison, NY, December 17, 1864	Oath of Allegiance June 14, 1865
Smith, Nathan Private	26	May 5, 1864, Fort Fisher, New Hanover County, North Carolina	Co. C, 36th Regiment, 2nd North Carolina Artillery	January 15, 1865, Fort Fisher, North Carolina	February 1, 1865, Elmira Prison Camp, New York	Died February 24, 1865 of Pneumonia, Grave No. 2267
Smith, Neill McN Sergeant	23	June 1, 1861, Richmond County, North Carolina	Co. F, 18th North Carolina Infantry	May 12, 1864, Spotsylvania Court House, Virginia	Point Lookout, Maryland, transferred to Elmira Prison, NY, August 6, 1864	Oath of Allegiance June 12, 1865
Smith, Noah Private	Unk	June 4, 1861, Salem, Virginia	Co. E, 42nd Virginia Infantry	May 12, 1864, Spotsylvania Court House, Virginia	Point Lookout Prison Camp, Maryland. Transferred to Elmira Prison, August 6, 1864	Died February 25, 1865 Chronic Diarrhea, Grave No. 2280

Name & Rank	Age	Enlisted	Regiment and State	Where Captured	Prison	Remarks
Smith, Norman Private	20	May 18, 1861, Edenton, North Carolina	Co. A, 1st North Carolina Infantry	May 12, 1864, Spotsylvania Court House, Virginia	Point Lookout Prison Camp, Maryland. Transferred to Elmira Prison, NY, August 6, 1864	Died March 2, 1865 of Chronic Diarrhea, Grave No. 2006
Smith, Obadiah Private	Unk	July 29, 1861, Wytheville, Virginia	Co. C, 51st Virginia Infantry	July 10, 1864, Frederick, Maryland	Old Capital Prison, Washington, DC, transferred to Elmira Prison, NY, July 23, 1864	Oath of Allegiance June 16, 1865
Smith, Osceola A. Private	18	May 22, 1861, Kilmarnock, Virginia	Co. H, 40th Virginia Infantry	May 6, 1864, Wilderness, Virginia	Point Lookout, Maryland, transferred to Elmira Prison, NY, August 14, 1864	Died December 12, 1864 of Chronic Diarrhea, Grave No. 1147
Smith, P. D. Private	23	January 20, 1862, Darlington, South Carolina	Co. H, 21st South Carolina Infantry	January 15, 1865, Fort Fisher, North Carolina	February 1, 1865, Elmira Prison Camp, New York	Oath of Allegiance July 11, 1865
Smith, Peter Private	Unk	May 27, 1861, New Orleans, Louisiana	Co. F, 15th Louisiana Infantry	May 12, 1864, Spotsylvania Court House, Virginia	Point Lookout, Maryland, transferred to Elmira Prison, NY, July 25, 1864	Exchanged February 25, 1865 at Boulware's or Cox Wharf on the James River, Virginia
Smith, Peter M. Private	Unk	October 3, 1862, Cumberland County, North Carolina	Co. I, 51st North Carolina Infantry	June 1, 1864, Cold Harbor, Virginia	Point Lookout, Maryland, transferred to Elmira Prison, NY, July 12, 1864	Exchanged October 29, 1864, at Venus Point, Savannah River, GA.
Smith, Peter W. Private	17	April 5, 1864, Fort Fisher, New Hanover County, North Carolina	Co. H, 36th Regiment, 2nd North Carolina Artillery	January 15, 1865, Fort Fisher, North Carolina	February 1, 1865, Elmira Prison Camp, New York	Died March 13, 1865 of Chronic Diarrhea, Grave No. 2432
Smith, Quintus M. Sergeant	18	October 31, 1861, Newton, North Carolina	Co. F, 38th North Carolina Infantry	May 6, 1864, Wilderness, Virginia	Point Lookout, Maryland, transferred to Elmira Prison, NY, August 14, 1864	Oath of Allegiance June 27, 1865
Smith, R. M. B. Private	Unk	January 20, 1862, Camp Hampton, South Carolina	Co. B, 4th South Carolina Cavalry	June 11, 1864, Trevilian Station, Louisa Court House, Virginia	Point Lookout, Maryland, transferred to Elmira Prison, NY, July 25, 1864	Died November 16, 1864 of Chronic Diarrhea. Grave No. 954

Name & Rank	Age	Enlisted	Regiment and State	Where Captured	Prison	Remarks
Smith, Randall H. Private	26	April 30, 1862, Lillington, Hartnett County, North Carolina	Co. C, 36th Regiment, 2nd North Carolina Artillery	January 15, 1865, Fort Fisher, North Carolina	February 1, 1865, Elmira Prison Camp, New York	Exchanged March 14, 1865 at Boulware's Wharf on the James River, Virginia
Smith, Richard C. Private	Unk	August 15, 1862, Richmond, Virginia	Co. C, 1st Maryland Cavalry	July 12, 1864, Near Washington, DC	Old Capital Prison, Washington, DC, transferred to Elmira Prison, NY, July 23, 1864	Exchanged March 10, 1865 at Boulware's Wharf on the James River, Virginia
Smith, Robert Private	Unk	July 7, 1861, Camp Moore, Louisiana	Co. D, 9th Louisiana Infantry	June 11, 1864, Wilderness, Virginia.	Old Capital Prison, Washington, DC, transferred to Elmira Prison, NY, July 23, 1864	Oath of Allegiance June 14, 1865
Smith, Robert Private	31	April 5, 1862, Elizabethtown, Bladen County, North Carolina	Co. H, 36th Regiment 2nd North Carolina Artillery	January 15, 1865, Fort Fisher, North Carolina	February 1, 1865, Elmira Prison Camp, New York	Died February 20, 1865 of Unknown Disease on Route to be Exchanged.
Smith, Robert Private	Unk	March 14, 1864, Orange County, Virginia	Co. H, 25th Virginia Infantry	May 5, 1864, Wilderness, Virginia	Point Lookout, Maryland, transferred to Elmira Prison, NY, August 17, 1864	Oath of Allegiance June 27, 1865
Smith, Robert J. Private	Unk	March 23, 1864, James Island, South Carolina	Co. F, 25th South Carolina Infantry	January 15, 1865, Fort Fisher, North Carolina	February 1, 1865, Elmira Prison Camp, New York	Died February 27, 1865 of Diarrhea, Grave No. 2159
Smith, Rueben Private	34	July 13, 1863, Camp Holmes, North Carolina	Co. H, 30th North Carolina Infantry	May 12, 1864, Near Spotsylvania Court House, Virginia	Point Lookout, Maryland, transferred to Elmira Prison, NY, August 14, 1864	Oath of Allegiance June 12, 1865
Smith, S. N. Private	Unk	June 20, 1861, Henderson, North Carolina	Co. D, 8th North Carolina Infantry	June 15, 1864, Petersburg, Virginia	Point Lookout, Maryland, transferred to Elmira Prison, NY, July 17, 1864	Died October 27, 1864 of Chronic Diarrhea, Grave No. 716
Smith, Samuel Private	23	May 16, 1861, Columbia, North Carolina	Co. A, 32nd North Carolina Infantry	May 10, 1864, Near Mine Run Spotsylvania, Virginia	Point Lookout, Maryland, transferred to Elmira Prison, NY, August 6, 1864	Oath of Allegiance May 15, 1865

Name & Rank	Age	Enlisted	Regiment and State	Where Captured	Prison	Remarks
Smith, Samuel A. Private	Unk	September 16, 1861, Monroe, Louisiana	Co. F, 2nd Louisiana Infantry	May 12, 1864, Spotsylvania Court House, Virginia	Point Lookout, Maryland, transferred to Elmira Prison, NY, August 17, 1864	Died September 24, 1864 of Chronic Diarrhea, Grave No. 366
Smith, Samuel C. Private	Unk	April 1, 1863, Gloucester Point, Virginia	Co. E, 26th North Carolina Infantry	June 17, 1864, Near Petersburg, Virginia	Point Lookout, Maryland, transferred to Elmira Prison, NY, July 30, 1864	Oath of Allegiance July 7, 1865
Smith, Simeon Private	25	March 6, 1863, Fort Caswell, Brunswick County, North Carolina	Co. E, 40th Regiment, 3rd North Carolina Artillery	January 15, 1865, Fort Fisher, North Carolina	February 1, 1865, Elmira Prison Camp, New York	Oath of Allegiance June 12, 1865
Smith, Stephen Allen Private	19	March 3, 1862, Wilmington, New Hanover County, North Carolina	Co. D, 36th Regiment, 2nd North Carolina Artillery	January 15, 1865, Fort Fisher, North Carolina	February 1, 1865, Elmira Prison Camp, New York	Died March 1, 1865 of Variola (Smallpox), Grave No. 2098
Smith, Stephen D. Private	Unk	July 9, 1861, Cherokee County, Georgia	Co. D, 14th Georgia Infantry	May 12, 1864, Spotsylvania Court House, Virginia	Point Lookout, Maryland, transferred to Elmira Prison, NY, July 30, 1864	Oath of Allegiance July 13, 1865
Smith, Thomas Private	Unk	Unknown	Co. B, 30th Virginia Infantry	July 15, 1864, Leasburg, Virginia	Old Capital Prison, Washington D. C. Transferred to Elmira Prison, NY, August 12, 1864	Died February 8, 1865 of Chronic Diarrhea, Grave No. 1935
Smith, Thomas Corporal	Unk	May 25, 1861, Floyd Court House, Virginia	Co. B, 42nd Virginia Infantry	May 12, 1864, Near Spotsylvania Court House, Virginia	Point Lookout, Maryland, transferred to Elmira Prison, NY, August 2, 1864	Died October 13, 1864 of Chronic Diarrhea, Grave No. 703
Smith, Thomas G. Private	36	July 15, 1862, Raleigh, North Carolina	Co. G, 15th North Carolina Infantry	June 2, 1864, Near Talapatomoy Creek, Cold Harbor, Hanover, Virginia	Point Lookout, Maryland, transferred to Elmira Prison, NY, July 12, 1864	Oath of Allegiance July 3, 1865
Smith, Thomas Gibson Private	20	March 6, 1863, Fort Caswell, Brunswick County, North Carolina	Co. E, 40th Regiment, 3rd North Carolina Artillery	January 15, 1865, Fort Fisher, North Carolina	February 1, 1865, Elmira Prison Camp, New York	Oath of Allegiance June 12, 1865

Name & Rank	Age	Enlisted	Regiment and State	Where Captured	Prison	Remarks
Smith, Thomas H. Private	21	July 18, 1861, Bay Point, South Carolina	Co. E, 11th South Carolina Infantry	June 16, 1864, Petersburg, Virginia	Point Lookout, Maryland, transferred to Elmira Prison, NY, July 25, 1864	Exchanged March 2, 1865 at Akins Landing on the James River, Virginia
Smith, Thomas M. Private	Unk	April 24, 1861, Mobile, Alabama	Co. K, 3rd Alabama Infantry	July 13, 1864, Near Washington, DC	Old Capital Prison, Washington, DC, transferred to Elmira Prison, NY, July 23, 1864	Exchanged March 14, 1865 at Boulware's Wharf on the James River, Virginia
Smith, Thomas M. Private	45	October 26, 1863, Fort Fisher, New Hanover County, North Carolina	Co. J, 36th Regiment, 2nd North Carolina Artillery	January 15, 1865, Fort Fisher, North Carolina	February 1, 1865, Elmira Prison Camp, New York	Oath of Allegiance June 30, 1865
Smith, Thomas R. Private	25	February 8, 1862, Lumberton, North Carolina	Co. A, 46th North Carolina Infantry	May 12, 1864, Near Spotsylvania, Virginia	Point Lookout, Maryland, transferred to Elmira Prison, NY, August 14, 1864	Escaped October 27, 1864 by Tunneling Under Fence.
Smith, W. B. Private	Unk	May 13, 1862, Savannah, Georgia	Co. E, 7th Georgia Cavalry	June 11, 1864, Trevilian Station, Louisa Court House, Virginia	Point Lookout, Maryland, transferred to Elmira Prison, NY, July 25, 1864	Transported for Exchange 10/11/64. Died 10/15/64 at US Army Hospital, Baltimore, MD.
Smith, W. H. Civilian	Unk	Unknown	Citizen of Louisiana	September 19, 1864, Tensan Parish, Louisiana	New Orleans, Louisiana, Transferred to Elmira Prison, New York, November 19, 1864	Exchanged February 13, 1865 at Boulware's wharf on the James River, Virginia
Smith, W. M. Private	Unk	March 10, 1863, White County, Georgia	Co. C, 24th Georgia Infantry	August 16, 1864, Front Royal, Virginia	Old Capital Prison, Washington, DC transferred to Elmira Prison, NY, August 29, 1864	Died April 12, 1865 of Variola (Smallpox), Grave No. 2683
Smith, W. M. Sergeant	24	April 15, 1863, Rockingham, Virginia	Co. C, 11th Virginia Cavalry	September 14, 1863, Near Culpepper, Virginia	Point Lookout, Maryland, transferred to Elmira Prison, NY, August 18, 1864	Exchanged October 29, 1864, at Venus Point, Savannah River, GA.

Name & Rank	Age	Enlisted	Regiment and State	Where Captured	Prison	Remarks
Smith, W. T. Sailor	Unk	Unknown	Confederate States Navy	April 6, 1865, Sailor's Creek, Virginia	Old Capital Prison, Washington D. C. Transferred to Elmira Prison, NY, May 2, 1865.	Oath of Allegiance June 21, 1865
Smith, W. T. Corporal	Unk	June 4, 1861, Montgomery, Alabama	Co. H, 10th Alabama Infantry	May 6, 1864, Wilderness, Virginia	Point Lookout, Maryland, transferred to Elmira Prison, NY, August 17, 1864	Died February 26, 1865 of Chronic Diarrhea, Grave No. 2294
Smith, W. T. Private	Unk	March 1, 1863, Franklin County, Georgia	Co. H, 24th Georgia Infantry	June 3, 1864, Gaines Mill Cold Harbor, Virginia	Point Lookout, Maryland, transferred to Elmira Prison, NY, July 12, 1864	Oath of Allegiance June 16, 1865
Smith, William Private	Unk	Unknown	Co. G, 7th Kentucky Mounted Infantry	June 30, 1864, Came into Lines at Mecklenberry County, Virginia	Point Lookout, Maryland, transferred to Elmira Prison, NY, July 23, 1864	Oath of Allegiance June 20, 1865
Smith, William Private	Unk	December 7, 1861, Camp Trousdale, Tennessee	Co. B, 44th Tennessee Infantry	June 17, 1864, Petersburg, Virginia	Point Lookout, Maryland, transferred to Elmira Prison, NY, July 30, 1864	Exchanged February 25, 1865 at Boulware's or Cox Wharf on the James River, Virginia
Smith, William Private	Unk	July 26, 1862, Virginia	Co. K, 1st Virginia Cavalry	October 2, 1864, Rockville, Maryland	Old Capital Prison, Washington, DC transferred to Elmira Prison, NY, August 27, 1864	Oath of Allegiance May 19, 1865
Smith, William Private	21	September 20, 1862, Leetown, Virginia	Co. F, 7th Virginia Cavalry	October 30, 1864, Hampshire County, Virginia	Old Capital Prison, Washington, DC, transferred to Elmira Prison, NY, December 17, 1864	Exchanged March 2, 1865 at Boulware's Wharf on the James River, Virginia

Name & Rank	Age	Enlisted	Regiment and State	Where Captured	Prison	Remarks
Smith, William Private	Unk	Unknown	Co. H, 22nd Virginia Cavalry	July 16, 1864, Loudoun County, Virginia	Old Capital Prison, Washington, DC, transferred to Elmira Prison, NY, July 23, 1864	Died January 31, 1865 of Pneumonia, Grave No. 1779
Smith, William Private	Unk	September 4, 1862, Richmond, Virginia	Co. E, 25th Battalion Virginia Infantry	July 12, 1864, Cox's Farm, Virginia	Point Lookout, Maryland, transferred to Elmira Prison, NY, August 6, 1864	Exchanged February 20, 1865 at Boulware's or Cox Wharf on the James River, Virginia
Smith, William B. Private	Unk	March 10, 1862, Henry County, Virginia	Co. G, 42nd Virginia Infantry	May 12, 1864, Near Spotsylvania Court House, Virginia	Point Lookout, Maryland, transferred to Elmira Prison, NY, August 6, 1864	Oath of Allegiance June 27, 1865
Smith, William D. Sergeant	Unk	February 16, 1862, Charleston, South Carolina	Co. J, 1st South Carolina Artillery	July 10, 1863, Morris Island, South Carolina	Point Lookout, Maryland, transferred to Elmira Prison, NY, August 18, 1864	Exchanged March 10, 1865 at Boulware's Wharf on the James River, Virginia
Smith, William D. Private	Unk	February 2, 1863, Whiteville, North Carolina	Co. G, 51st North Carolina Infantry	June 3, 1864, Gaines Mill Cold Harbor, Virginia	Point Lookout, Maryland, transferred to Elmira Prison, NY, July 9, 1864	Exchanged October 29, 1864, at Venus Point, Savannah River, GA.
Smith, William E. Private	18	February 12, 1864, Fort Fisher, New Hanover County, North Carolina	Co. C, 36th Regiment, 2nd North Carolina Artillery	January 15, 1865, Fort Fisher, North Carolina	February 1, 1865, Elmira Prison Camp, New York	Oath of Allegiance June 7, 1865
Smith, William F. Private	21	June 28, 1861, Abingdon, Virginia	Co. F, 48th Virginia Infantry	May 12, 1864, Spotsylvania Court House, Virginia	Point Lookout, Maryland, transferred to Elmira Prison, NY, August 2, 1864	Oath of Allegiance, June 27, 1865
Smith, William F. Private	Unk	Unknown	Co. B, 50th Virginia Infantry	May 12, 1864, Spotsylvania, Virginia	Point Lookout, Maryland, transferred to Elmira Prison, NY, July 23, 1864	Oath of Allegiance June 19, 1865

Name & Rank	Age	Enlisted	Regiment and State	Where Captured	Prison	Remarks
Smith, William H. Sergeant	Unk	August 21, 1862, Richmond, Virginia	Co. A, 2nd Battalion Maryland Infantry	May 3, 1864, Near Chesapeake Bay, Rockville, Maryland	Transferred August 28, 1864 from Baltimore, Maryland.	Exchanged February 25, 1865 at Boulware's or Cox Wharf on the James River, Virginia
Smith, William H. Private	18	December 4, 1862, Brunswick County, North Carolina	Co. F, 36th Regiment, 2nd North Carolina Artillery	January 15, 1865, Fort Fisher, North Carolina	February 1, 1865, Elmira Prison Camp, New York	Oath of Allegiance July 7, 1865
Smith, William H. Private	Unk	August 19, 1862, Mill Point, Pocahontas County, Virginia	Co. C, 17th Virginia Cavalry	July 14, 1864, Near Washington, DC	Old Capital Prison, Washington, DC, transferred to Elmira Prison, NY, July 23, 1864	Oath of Allegiance May 29, 1865
Smith, William Harden H. Private	21	February 1, 1862, Salisbury, North Carolina	Co. C, 42nd North Carolina Infantry	June 3, 1864, Gaines Mill Cold Harbor, Virginia	Point Lookout, Maryland, transferred to Elmira Prison, NY, July 12, 1864	Oath of Allegiance May 29, 1865
Smith, William M. Private	Unk	March 1, 1863, Wilmington, North Carolina	Co. F, 18th South Carolina Infantry	July 30, 1864, Petersburg, Virginia	Point Lookout, Maryland, transferred to Elmira Prison, NY, August 12, 1864	Exchanged October 29, 1864, at Venus Point, Savannah River, GA.
Smith, William R. Private	Unk	July 1, 1862, Columbus County, North Carolina	Co. H, 33rd North Carolina Infantry	May 12, 1864, Spotsylvania County Court House, Virginia	Point Lookout, Maryland, transferred to Elmira Prison, NY, August 14, 1864	Oath of Allegiance June 21, 1865
Smith, William T. Sergeant	Unk	June 2, 1861, Panne County, Virginia	Co. F, 15th Virginia Cavalry	November 14, 1863, Near Culpepper Court House, Virginia	Point Lookout, Maryland, transferred to Elmira Prison, NY, August 18, 1864	Exchanged March 10, 1865 at Boulware's Wharf on the James River, Virginia
Smith, Win Private	36	May 7, 1864, Union Court House, South Carolina	Co. B, 15th South Carolina Infantry	July 27, 1864, Petersburg, Virginia	Point Lookout, Maryland, transferred to Elmira Prison, NY, August 12, 1864	Oath of Allegiance June 19, 1865

Name & Rank	Age	Enlisted	Regiment and State	Where Captured	Prison	Remarks
Smither, Thomas E. Private	Unk	June 12, 1862, Camp Lewis, Virginia	Co. D, 9th Virginia Cavalry	June 1, 1864, Ashland, Virginia	Point Lookout, Maryland, transferred to Elmira Prison, NY, July 12, 1864	Exchanged March 14, 1865 at Boulware's Wharf on the James River, Virginia
Smitherman, Stephen C. Private	Unk	May 2, 1862, Bibb County, Alabama	Co. G, 44th Alabama Infantry	May 5, 1864, Wilderness, Virginia.	Old Capital Prison, Washington D. C. Transferred to Elmira Prison, NY, August 12, 1864	Exchanged February 20, 1865 at Boulware's or Cox Wharf on the James River, Virginia
Smithwick, William Hiram Private	21	January 23, 1862, Windsor, Bertie County, North Carolina	Co. C, 3rd Battalion North Carolina Light Artillery	January 15, 1865, Fort Fisher, North Carolina	February 1, 1865, Elmira Prison Camp, New York	Oath of Allegiance June 12, 1865
Smoke, A. E. Private	Unk	April 24, 1864, Orangeburg, South Carolina	Co. H, 25th South Carolina Infantry	January 15, 1865, Fort Fisher, North Carolina	February 1, 1865, Elmira Prison Camp, New York	Died February 21, 1865 of Diarrhea, Grave No. 2264
Smoke, David L. Private	22	April 18, 1861, Winchester, Virginia	Co. E, 2nd Virginia Infantry	May 25, 1864, North Anna River, Virginia	Point Lookout, Maryland, transferred to Elmira Prison, NY, July 12, 1864	Exchanged March 2, 1865 at Akins Landing on the James River, Virginia
Smoke, George A. Corporal	21	April 28, 1861, Tuskegee, Alabama	Co. B, 4th Alabama Infantry	May 6, 1864, Wilderness, Virginia	Point Lookout, Maryland, transferred to Elmira Prison, NY, August 17, 1864	Oath of Allegiance June 23, 1865
Smoke, Wiley Private	Unk	December 9, 1861, Camp Hampton, South Carolina	Co. H, 17th South Carolina Infantry	July 30, 1864, Petersburg, Virginia	Point Lookout, Maryland, transferred to Elmira Prison, NY, August 12, 1864	Exchanged October 29, 1864, at Venus Point, Savannah River, GA.
Smoot, Calvin Private	Unk	May 1, 1863, Charleston, South Carolina	Co. J, 18th South Carolina Infantry	July 30, 1864, Petersburg, Virginia	Point Lookout, Maryland, transferred to Elmira Prison, NY, August 12, 1864	Oath of Allegiance July 11, 1865
Smothers, A. J. Private	27	September 1, 1862, Raleigh, North Carolina	Co. K, 45th North Carolina Infantry	May 10, 1864, Spotsylvania Court House, Virginia	Point Lookout, Maryland, transferred to Elmira Prison, NY, August 6, 1864	Oath of Allegiance May 19, 1865

Name & Rank	Age	Enlisted	Regiment and State	Where Captured	Prison	Remarks
Smothers, Henry H. Private	Unk	February 2, 1863, Chesterfield District, South Carolina	Co. F, 26th South Carolina Infantry	July 30, 1864, Petersburg, Virginia	Point Lookout, Maryland, transferred to Elmira Prison, NY, August 12, 1864	Oath of Allegiance July 3, 1865
Smothers, Simeon Private	Unk	December 26, 1861, Chesterfield, South Carolina	Co. G, 21st South Carolina Infantry	January 15, 1865, Fort Fisher, North Carolina	February 1, 1865, Elmira Prison Camp, New York	Exchanged February 20, 1865 at Boulware's or Cox Wharf on the James River, Virginia
Smyer, John W. L. Private	Unk	October 7, 1863, Camp Vance, North Carolina	Co. K, 46th North Carolina Infantry	August 3, 1864, Petersburg, Virginia	Point Lookout, Maryland, transferred to Elmira Prison, NY, August 12, 1864	Died March 6, 1865 of Diarrhea, Grave No. 1963. Smyer, L. on Headstone.
Smyer, Silas B. Sergeant	25	April 27, 1861, Newton, North Carolina	Co. A, 12th North Carolina Infantry	March 25, 1865, Fort Stedman, VA. Shell Wound Right Thigh and Hand.	Old Capital Prison, Washington D. C. Transferred to Elmira Prison, NY, May 2, 1865.	Oath of Allegiance July 7, 1865
Snakenburg, William P. Private	18	June 12, 1861, New Orleans, Louisiana	Co. K, 14th Louisiana Infantry	May 12, 1864, Spotsylvania Court House, Virginia	Point Lookout, Maryland, transferred to Elmira Prison, NY, July 25, 1864	Exchanged February 25, 1865 at Boulware's or Cox Wharf on the James River, Virginia
Snavely, William F. Private	21	May 18, 1861, 7 Mile Ford, Virginia	Co. D, 48th Virginia Infantry	May 5, 1864, Wilderness, Virginia. Shell Wound Left Hip and Thorax.	Old Capital Prison, Washington D. C. Transferred to Elmira Prison, NY, August 12, 1864	Oath of Allegiance June 30, 1865
Snead, A. J. Private	25	June 17, 1861, Lewisburg, Virginia	Co. B, 26th Battalion, Virginia Infantry	June 3, 1864, Gaines Mill Cold Harbor, Virginia	Point Lookout, Maryland, transferred to Elmira Prison, NY, July 17, 1864	Exchanged March 2, 1865 at Akins Landing on the James River, Virginia

Name & Rank	Age	Enlisted	Regiment and State	Where Captured	Prison	Remarks
Snead, James N. Private	Unk	July 16, 1861, Lawrenceville, Georgia	Co. E, 3rd Georgia Sharp Shooters	August 16, 1864, Front Royal, Virginia	Old Capital Prison, Washington, DC transferred to Elmira Prison, NY, August 29, 1864	Died February 22, 1865 of Variola (Smallpox), Grave No. 2236
Snead, Jonathan Bonaparte Privat	30	April 30, 1862, Old Brunswick Town, North Carolina	3rd Co. G, 36th Regiment North Carolina, 2nd Artillery	January 15, 1865, Fort Fisher, North Carolina	February 1, 1865, Elmira Prison Camp, New York	Oath of Allegiance May 29, 1865
Snead, John B. Private	Unk	December 17, 1862, Richmond, Virginia	Co. A, 24th Virginia Cavalry	June 1, 1864, Hanover County, Virginia	Point Lookout, Maryland, transferred to Elmira Prison, NY, July 17,1864	Exchanged October 29, 1864, at Venus Point, Savannah River, GA.
Snead, John P. Private	Unk	January 2, 1864, Richmond, Virginia	Co. G, 24th Battalion Virginia Cavalry	June 13, 1864, Malvern Hill, Virginia	Point Lookout, Maryland, transferred to Elmira Prison, NY, July 30, 1864	Exchanged March 10, 1865 at Boulware's Wharf on the James River, Virginia
Snead, Samuel W. Private	Unk	August 22, 1861, Yates Lower Free School House, Virginia	Co. K, 13th Virginia Cavalry	July 7, 1864, Chuckatuck, Virginia	Point Lookout, Maryland, transferred to Elmira Prison, NY, August 6, 1864	Exchanged March 14, 1865 at Boulware's Wharf on the James River, Virginia
Snead, William P. Corporal	19	July 2, 1861, Bethel AM, Virginia	Co. F, 50th Virginia Infantry	May 5, 1864, Wilderness, Virginia. Gunshot Wound Right Thigh.	Old Capital Prison, Washington, DC, transferred to Elmira Prison, NY, December 17, 1864	Exchanged March 2, 1865 at Boulware's Wharf on the James River, Virginia
Snell, Swain S. Private	28	June 25, 1861, Plymouth, North Carolina	Co. G, 1st North Carolina Infantry	May 12, 1864, Spotsylvania, Virginia	Point Lookout Prison Camp, Maryland. Transferred to Elmira Prison Camp, NY, August 6, 1864	Died April 4, 1865 of Chronic Diarrhea, Grave. 2566
Snellgroves, B. L. Private	Unk	May 5, 1862, Pocotaligo, South Carolina	Co. F, 51st Georgia Infantry	June 1, 1864, Gaines Mill Cold Harbor, Virginia	Point Lookout, Maryland, transferred to Elmira Prison, NY, July 12, 1864	Oath of Allegiance June 14, 1865

Name & Rank	Age	Enlisted	Regiment and State	Where Captured	Prison	Remarks
Snellings, John H. Private	Unk	June 30, 1861, Camp Jackson, Virginia	Co. A, 4th Georgia Infantry	May 6, 1864, Wilderness, Virginia	Point Lookout, Maryland, transferred to Elmira Prison, NY, August 14, 1864	Exchanged February 25, 1865 at Boulware's or Cox Wharf on the James River, Virginia
Snellings, W. H. Private	Unk	September 1, 1862, Camp Mercer, Georgia	Co. D, 7th Georgia Cavalry	June 11, 1864, Trevilian Station, Louisa Court House, Virginia	Point Lookout, Maryland, transferred to Elmira Prison, NY, July 25, 1864	Exchanged February 20, 1865 at Boulware's or Cox Wharf on the James River, Virginia
Snider, John McC. Private	24	May 21, 1861, Brownsburg, Virginia	Co. G, 25th Virginia Infantry	May 5, 1864, Wilderness, Virginia	Point Lookout, Maryland, transferred to Elmira Prison, NY, August 17, 1864	Exchanged February 25, 1865 at Boulware's or Cox Wharf on the James River, Virginia
Snider, Robert B. Private	Unk	May 27, 1861, Marion, Virginia	Co. A, 8th Virginia Cavalry	July 16, 1864, Leesburg, Virginia	Old Capital Prison, Washington D. C. Transferred to Elmira Prison, NY, August 12, 1864	Oath of Allegiance June 23, 1865
Snider, Samuel E. Private	22	July 16, 1861, Blacksburg, Virginia	Co. L, 4th Virginia Infantry	May 12, 1864, Near Spotsylvania Court House, Virginia	Point Lookout, Maryland, transferred to Elmira Prison, NY, August 2, 1864	Exchanged March 2, 1865 at Akins Landing on the James River, Virginia
Snidon, Charles D. Corporal	21	April 17, 1861, Christiansburg, Virginia	Co. G, 4th Virginia Infantry	May 12, 1864, Spotsylvania Court House, Virginia	Point Lookout, Maryland, transferred to Elmira Prison, NY, August 2, 1864	Oath of Allegiance June 27, 1865
Sniper, William T. Sergeant	28	March 8, 1862, Tallahassee, Florida	Co. K, 5th Florida Infantry	May 12, 1864, Spotsylvania Court House, Virginia	Point Lookout, Maryland, transferred to Elmira Prison, NY, July 30, 1864	Oath of Allegiance June 23, 1865
Snipes, John Private	24	July 6, 1861, Goldsboro, North Carolina	Co. F, 10th Regiment, 1st North Carolina Artillery	January 15, 1865, Fort Fisher, North Carolina	February 1, 1865, Elmira Prison Camp, New York	Died February 20, 1865 of Pneumonia, Grave No. 2326. Headstone has Snepes.

Name & Rank	Age	Enlisted	Regiment and State	Where Captured	Prison	Remarks
Snipes, Sion Private	25	February 3, 1862, Elizabethtown, Bladen County, North Carolina	Co. E, 36th Regiment, 2nd North Carolina Artillery	January 15, 1865, Fort Fisher, North Carolina	February 1, 1865, Elmira Prison Camp, New York	Oath of Allegiance August 7, 1865
Snoddy, Crawford Private	Unk	May 4, 1864, Columbia, South Carolina	Co. C, 22nd South Carolina Infantry	June 18, 1864, Petersburg, Virginia	Point Lookout, Maryland, transferred to Elmira Prison, NY, July 25, 1864	Died October 28, 1864 of Chronic Diarrhea, Grave No. 727
Snow, Delaware Private	Unk	January 13, 1862, Charlottesville, Virginia	Co. D, 46th Virginia Infantry	June 17, 1864, Petersburg, Virginia	Point Lookout, Maryland, transferred to Elmira Prison, NY, July 30, 1864	Died September 19, 1864 of Diphtheria, Grave No. 516
Snyder, B. B. Private	Unk	Unknown	Co. H, 42nd Virginia Infantry	May 12, 1864, Spotsylvania Court House, Virginia	Point Lookout, Maryland, transferred to Elmira Prison, NY, August 2, 1864	Exchanged October 29, 1864, at Venus Point, Savannah River, GA.
Snyder, J. H. Civilian	Unk	Forsyth County, North Carolina	Citizen of North Carolina	April 21, 1864, Wilmington, North Carolina	Point Lookout, Maryland, transferred to Elmira Prison, NY, July 23, 1864	Died January 19, 1865 of Variola (Smallpox), Grave No. 1197
Snyder, William R. Private	21	July 8, 1862, Salem, Forsyth County, North Carolina	Co. G, 2nd Battalion North Carolina Infantry	May 10, 1864, Near Spotsylvania Court House, Virginia. Gunshot Wound.	Point Lookout, Maryland, transferred to Elmira Prison, NY, August 14, 1864	Oath of Allegiance May 13, 1865
Soloman, Thomas F. Private	23	February 1, 1862, Salisbury, North Carolina	Co. C, 42nd North Carolina Infantry	June 1, 1864, Gaines Farm Cold Harbor, Virginia	Point Lookout, Maryland, transferred to Elmira Prison, NY, July 12, 1864	Transferred 10/11/64 for Exchange. Died 10/20/64 of Chronic Diarrhea at Point Lookout, MD.
Solomon, Eugene M. Private	Unk	April 19, 1861, Norfolk, Virginia	Capt. Kevill's Battery, Richmond Howitzers, Virginia Artillery	July 7, 1864, Howlett's Farm, Virginia	Point Lookout, Maryland, transferred to Elmira Prison, NY, August 6, 1864	Oath of Allegiance May 13, 1865

Name & Rank	Age	Enlisted	Regiment and State	Where Captured	Prison	Remarks
Soots, Adam Private	Unk	May 9, 1863, Camp Holmes, Near Raleigh, North Carolina	Co. C, 3rd Battalion North Carolina Light Artillery	January 15, 1865, Fort Fisher, North Carolina	February 1, 1865, Elmira Prison Camp, New York	Died March 1, 1865 of Chronic Diarrhea, Grave No. 2097
Sorey, S. N. Private	Unk	May 10, 1861, Cape Henry Beach, Virginia	Co. K, 15th Virginia Cavalry	November 14, 1863, Near Culpepper Court House, Virginia	Point Lookout, Maryland, transferred to Elmira Prison, NY, August 18, 1864	Exchanged March 10, 1865 at Boulware's Wharf on the James River, Virginia
Sorrell, Robert A. Private	Unk	April 20, 1861, Alexandria, Virginia	Co. F, 6th Virginia Cavalry	July 17, 1863, Snickers Gap, Virginia	Point Lookout, Maryland, transferred to Elmira Prison, NY, August 18, 1864	Exchanged March 10, 1865 at Boulware's Wharf on the James River, Virginia
Souders, Fayette B. Private	23	April 18, 1861, Jefferson Court House, Virginia	Co. A, 2nd Virginia Infantry	May 12, 1864, Near Spotsylvania Court House, Virginia	Point Lookout, Maryland, transferred to Elmira Prison, NY, August 6, 1864	Exchanged March 14, 1865 at Boulware's Wharf on the James River, Virginia
South, C. Private	Unk	October 17, 1862, Sullivan County, Tennessee	Co. K, 63rd Tennessee Infantry	June 17, 1864, Petersburg, Virginia	Point Lookout, Maryland, transferred to Elmira Prison, NY, July 25, 1864	Died February 15, 1865 of Variola (Smallpox), Grave No. 2191
South, Samuel D. Private	Unk	Unknown	Co. E, 48th Virginia Infantry	May 12, 1864, Spotsylvania Court House, Virginia	Point Lookout, Maryland, transferred to Elmira Prison, NY, August 2, 1864	Oath of Allegiance, June 14, 1865
Southall, Henry Private	Unk	January 29, 1864, Wilcox, Alabama	Co. F, 1st Battalion Alabama Artillery	August 23, 1864, Fort Morgan, Alabama	Steam Press No. 4 New Orleans, Louisiana transferred to Elmira Prison, NY, October 8, 1864.	Oath of Allegiance June 21, 1865
Southall, James A. H. Private	Unk	Unknown	Co. A, 44th Battalion, Virginia Infantry	June 15, 1864, Near Petersburg, Virginia	Point Lookout, Maryland, transferred to Elmira Prison, NY, July 12, 1864	Oath of Allegiance May 29, 1865

Name & Rank	Age	Enlisted	Regiment and State	Where Captured	Prison	Remarks
Southard, Isaac W. Private	24	May 25, 1861, Madison Court House, Virginia	Co. D, 34th, Virginia Infantry	June 15, 1864, Near Petersburg, Virginia	Point Lookout, Maryland, transferred to Elmira Prison, NY, July 12, 1864	Oath of Allegiance June 16, 1865
Southard, Levi Private	35	March 18, 1862, Dobson, North Carolina	Co. A, 28th North Carolina Infantry	July 29, 1864, Gravel Hill, Petersburg, Virginia	Point Lookout, Maryland, transferred to Elmira Prison, NY, August 12, 1864	Died April 6, 1865 of Pneumonia, Grave No. 2638
Souther, Joshua Private	22	June 12, 1861, Wilkesboro, North Carolina	Co. C, 26th North Carolina Infantry	May 12, 1864, Spotsylvania Court House, Virginia	Point Lookout, Maryland, transferred to Elmira Prison, NY, July 30, 1864	Oath of Allegiance June 27, 1865
Southern, Leander Private	Unk	March 14, 1862, Newbern, Pulaski County, Virginia	Co. E, 24th Virginia Infantry	June 15, 1864, Near Petersburg, Virginia	Point Lookout, Maryland, transferred to Elmira Prison, NY, July 25, 1864	Oath of Allegiance June 14, 1865
Sowles, A. J. Private	24	April 24, 1861, Lee's, North Carolina	Co. C, 18th North Carolina Infantry	May 12, 1864, Spotsylvania Court House, Virginia	Point Lookout, Maryland, transferred to Elmira Prison, NY, August 12, 1864	Died 12/31/64 of Variola (Smallpox), Grave No. 1322. Name H. I. Soles on Headstone.
Sowles, Alexander Private	21	April 24, 1861, Lee's, North Carolina	Co. C, 18th North Carolina Infantry	May 12, 1864, Spotsylvania Court House, Virginia	Point Lookout, Maryland, transferred to Elmira Prison, NY, August 12, 1864	Died April 8, 1865 of Chronic Diarrhea, Grave No. 2644. Soles and 44th VA on Headstone.
Soza, Brilis Private	22	May 10, 1861, Camp Moore, Louisiana	Co. C, 5th Louisiana Infantry	May 12, 1864, Spotsylvania Court House, Virginia	Point Lookout, Maryland, transferred to Elmira Prison, NY, August 17, 1864	Oath of Allegiance May 12, 1865
Spangler, David Private	21	May 14, 1862, Zollicoffer, Sullivan County, Tennessee	Co. F, 63rd Tennessee Infantry	June 17, 1864, Petersburg, Virginia	Point Lookout, Maryland, transferred to Elmira Prison, NY, July 30, 1864	Exchanged March 10, 1865 at Boulware's Wharf on the James River, Virginia

Name & Rank	Age	Enlisted	Regiment and State	Where Captured	Prison	Remarks
Sparkman, J. H. Private	Unk	July 1, 1861, Hampshire, Tennessee	Co. G, Wheeler's 6th Tennessee Cavalry	May 17, 1863, Waverly, Tennessee	Point Lookout, Maryland, transferred to Elmira Prison, NY, August 18, 1864	Exchanged February 25, 1865 at Boulware's wharf on the James River, Virginia
Sparkman, William P. Private	32	March 10, 1862, Lumberton, North Carolina	Co. F, 51st North Carolina Infantry	June 1, 1864, Cold Harbor, Virginia	Point Lookout, Maryland, transferred to Elmira Prison, NY, July 12, 1864	Died October 13, 1864 of Chronic Diarrhea, Grave No. 701
Sparks, A. G. Private	Unk	Unknown	Co. J, 30th Louisiana Infantry	October 27, 1864, Bayou Grosstete, Point Coupee Parish, Louisiana	New Orleans, Louisiana transferred to Elmira November 19, 1864.	Exchanged February 25, 1865 at Boulware's or Cox Wharf on the James River, Virginia
Sparks, Charles B. Private	Unk	Unknown	Co. J, 2nd Louisiana Cavalry	October 27, 1864, Gross Bayou, Point Coupee Parish, Louisiana	New Orleans, Louisiana, Transferred to Elmira Prison, New York, November 19, 1864	Died January 1, 1865 of Typhoid-Pneumonia, Grave No. 1327
Sparks, Hugh Private	30	September 27, 1862, Raleigh, North Carolina	Co. C, 13th North Carolina Infantry	May 5, 1864, Wilderness, Virginia	Point Lookout, Maryland, transferred to Elmira Prison, NY, August 14, 1864	Died September 11, 1864 of Chronic Diarrhea, Grave No. 249
Sparks, Mathias A. Private	23	August 23, 1861, Camp Trousdale, Tennessee	Co. H, 23rd Tennessee Infantry	June 17, 1864, Petersburg, Virginia	Point Lookout, Maryland, transferred to Elmira Prison, NY, July 30, 1864	Oath of Allegiance May 29, 1865
Sparks, Thomas Private	Unk	August 24, 1861, Lawrenceville, Georgia	Co. F, 24th Georgia Infantry	June 1, 1864, Cold Harbor, Virginia	Point Lookout, Maryland, transferred to Elmira Prison, NY, July 12, 1864	Oath of Allegiance July 11, 1865
Sparks, Tilman Private	24	April 23, 1862, Hempstead, Texas	Co. B, Waller's Louisiana Cavalry	July 30, 1864, Concordia Parish, Louisiana	New Orleans, Louisiana, Transferred to Elmira Prison, New York, November 19, 1864	Oath of Allegiance June 14, 1865

Name & Rank	Age	Enlisted	Regiment and State	Where Captured	Prison	Remarks
Sparks, Welcome U. Private	Unk	March 1, 1862, Conyers, Georgia	Co. B, 35th Georgia Infantry	May 12, 1864, Spotsylvania Court House, Virginia	Point Lookout, Maryland, transferred to Elmira Prison, NY, August 12, 1864	Died November 10, 1864 of Pneumonia, Grave No. 787
Spaulding, Robert E. Private	Unk	December 31, 1861, Charlotte, Virginia	Co. B, 22nd Virginia Infantry	June 4, 1864, Gaines Farm, Cold Harbor, Virginia	Point Lookout, Maryland, transferred to Elmira Prison, NY, July 12, 1864	Oath of Allegiance June 27, 1865
Speake, Richard Private	Unk	April 27, 1861, Wetumpka, Alabama	Co. J, 3rd Alabama Infantry	May 12, 1864, Spotsylvania Court House, Virginia	Point Lookout, Maryland, transferred to Elmira Prison, NY, August 12, 1864	Oath of Allegiance June 16, 1865
Spears, Josiah W. Private	27	July 6, 1861, Salisbury, North Carolina	Co. K, 8th North Carolina Infantry	May 31, 1864, Cold Harbor, Virginia	Point Lookout, Maryland, transferred to Elmira Prison, NY, July 12, 1864	Exchanged 2/20/65. Died 3/12/65 at C. S. A. Hospital, Richmond, VA.
Spears, William Private	Unk	August 12, 1862, Statesville, North Carolina	Co. G, 37th North Carolina Infantry	July 29, 1864, Petersburg, Virginia	Point Lookout, Maryland, transferred to Elmira Prison, NY, August 12, 1864	Died May 31, 1865 of Chronic Diarrhea, Grave No. 2907
Speers, James B. Private	22	March 8, 1862, Mt. Lebanon, Louisiana	Co. C, 9th Louisiana Infantry	May 12, 1864, Spotsylvania Court House, Virginia	Point Lookout, Maryland, transferred to Elmira Prison, NY, August 17, 1864	Exchanged October 29, 1864, at Venus Point, Savannah River, GA.
Spell, David Private	18	April 10, 1863, Fort Fisher, New Hanover County, North Carolina	Co. C, 36th Regiment, 2nd North Carolina Artillery	January 15, 1865, Fort Fisher, North Carolina	February 1, 1865, Elmira Prison Camp, New York	Died March 24, 1865 of Chronic Diarrhea, Grave No. 2456
Spell, Eldred Sergeant	22	January 4, 1862, Waterboro, South Carolina	Co. J, 11th South Carolina Infantry	June 24, 1864, Petersburg, Virginia	Point Lookout, Maryland, transferred to Elmira Prison, NY, August 18, 1864	Exchanged March 14, 1865 at Boulware's Wharf on the James River, Virginia
Spell, Hardy Private	18	October 18, 1862, Fort Fisher, New Hanover County, North Carolina	Co. C, 36th Regiment, 2nd North Carolina Artillery	January 15, 1865, Fort Fisher, North Carolina	February 1, 1865, Elmira Prison Camp, New York	Died February 13, 1865 of Chronic Diarrhea, Grave No. 2044

Name & Rank	Age	Enlisted	Regiment and State	Where Captured	Prison	Remarks
Spellman, Dominick Sergeant	Unk	June 25, 1861, Charleston, South Carolina	Co. K, 1st South Carolina Infantry	July 29, 1864, Petersburg, Virginia	Point Lookout, Maryland, transferred to Elmira Prison, NY, August 12, 1864	Oath of Allegiance May 17, 1865
Spellman, Michael Private	Unk	May 1, 1863, Baton Rouge, Louisiana	Co. A, Miles' Legion Louisiana Cavalry	October 20, 1864, Lavinia, Louisiana	New Orleans, Louisiana transferred to Elmira November 19, 1864.	Nothing Further.
Spence, Abner Private	Unk	March 15, 1862, Norfolk County, Virginia	Co. J, 38th Virginia Infantry	August 3, 1864, Petersburg, Virginia	Point Lookout, Maryland, transferred to Elmira Prison, NY, August 12, 1864	Oath of Allegiance June 21, 1865
Spence, George W. Private	Unk	April 2, 1862, Mouth of Indian River, Virginia	Co. I, 29th Virginia Infantry	May 12, 1864, Petersburg, Virginia	Point Lookout, Maryland, transferred to Elmira Prison, NY, August 6, 1864	Oath of Allegiance June 21, 1865
Spence, James T. Private	Unk	Unknown	Co. E, 66th North Carolina Infantry	August 31, 1863, Big Black, Mississippi	Point Lookout, Maryland, transferred to Elmira Prison, NY, August 18, 1864	Exchanged March 10, 1865 at Boulware's wharf on the James River, Virginia
Spence, John A. Private	18	March 15, 1863, Fort Fisher, New Hanover County, North Carolina	Co. D, 36th Regiment, 2nd North Carolina Artillery	January 15, 1865, Fort Fisher, North Carolina	February 1, 1865, Elmira Prison Camp, New York	Died February 10, 1865 of Congestion of Lungs, Grave No. 2086
Spence, William Private	33	October 30, 1861, Harnett County, North Carolina	Co. I, 31st North Carolina Infantry	June 17, 1864, Petersburg, Virginia	Point Lookout, Maryland, transferred to Elmira Prison, NY, July 30, 1864	Oath of Allegiance July 3, 1865
Spencer, James Private	28	June 10, 1861, Selma, Alabama	Jeff Davis Alabama Artillery	May 5, 1864, Wilderness, Virginia	Point Lookout, Maryland, transferred to Elmira Prison, NY, August 17, 1864	Oath of Allegiance May 17, 1865
Spencer, James H. Private	Unk	June 7, 1861, New Market, Virginia	Co. H, 49th Virginia Infantry	May 30, 1864, Gaines Mill Cold Harbor, Virginia	Point Lookout, Maryland, transferred to Elmira Prison, NY, July 11, 1864	Oath of Allegiance June 30, 1865

Name & Rank	Age	Enlisted	Regiment and State	Where Captured	Prison	Remarks
Spencer, James J. Private	39	September 5, 1861, Patrick Court House, Virginia	Co. H, 58th Virginia Infantry	May 30, 1864 Mechanicsville, Virginia	Point Lookout, Maryland, transferred to Elmira Prison, NY, July 12, 1864	Died April 20, 1865 of Pneumonia, Grave No. 1382. Headstone has 28th VA.
Spencer, James M. Private	Unk	August 1, 1862, Highland County, Virginia	Co. E, 25th Virginia Infantry	May 15, 1864, Wilderness Spotsylvania, Virginia	Point Lookout, Maryland, transferred to Elmira Prison, NY, August 14, 1864	Oath of Allegiance June 14, 1865
Spencer, Jasper M. Private	Unk	August 12, 1861, Columbia, South Carolina	Co. G, 18th South Carolina Infantry	June 15, 1864, Near Petersburg, Virginia	Point Lookout, Maryland, transferred to Elmira Prison, NY, July 25, 1864	Oath of Allegiance June 19, 1865
Spencer, L. W. Private	22	May 3, 1863, Camp Millen, Florida	Co. G, 2nd Florida Cavalry	September 27, 1864, Marianna, Florida	New Orleans, Louisiana transferred to Elmira November 19, 1864.	Oath of Allegiance June 14, 1865
Spengler, George M. Sergeant	25	April 18, 1861, Strasburg, Virginia	Co. A, 10th Virginia Infantry	May 12, 1864, Spotsylvania Court House, Virginia	Point Lookout, Maryland, transferred to Elmira Prison, NY, August 2, 1864	Oath of Allegiance June 27, 1865
Spicer, George Washington Corporal	18	May 31, 1861, Raleigh, North Carolina	Co. B, 1st North Carolina Infantry	May 12, 1864, Near Spotsylvania Court House, Virginia	Point Lookout Prison, Maryland. Transferred to Elmira Prison Camp New York August 6, 1864.	Exchanged October 29, 1864, at Venus Point, Savannah River, GA.
Spiggle, Samuel Private	Unk	April 16, 1863, Rudes Hill, Virginia	Co. C, 2nd Virginia Infantry	May 12, 1864, Spotsylvania Court House, Virginia	Point Lookout, Maryland, transferred to Elmira Prison, NY, August 6, 1864	Exchanged October 29, 1864, at Venus Point, Savannah River, GA.
Spigner, Edward Private	Unk	April 11, 1862, Coles Island, South Carolina	Co. F, 25th South Carolina Infantry	January 15, 1865, Fort Fisher, North Carolina	February 1, 1865, Elmira Prison Camp, New York	Oath of Allegiance July 7, 1865

Name & Rank	Age	Enlisted	Regiment and State	Where Captured	Prison	Remarks
Spillman, William H. Private	21	April 5, 1862, East Bend, North Carolina	Co. F, 28th North Carolina Infantry	May 12, 1864, Spotsylvania County Court House, Virginia	Point Lookout, Maryland, transferred to Elmira Prison, NY, August 14, 1864	Oath of Allegiance June 21, 1865
Spitzer, Joseph E. Sergeant	Unk	April 16, 1862, Rudes Hill, Virginia	Co. C, 2nd Virginia Infantry	May 12, 1864, Near Spotsylvania Court House, Virginia	Point Lookout, Maryland, transferred to Elmira Prison, NY, August 6, 1864	Oath of Allegiance June 23, 1865
Spivey, Enoch Private	31	May 18, 1861, Lumberton, North Carolina	Co. D, 18th North Carolina Infantry	May 6, 1864, Wilderness, Virginia	Point Lookout, Maryland, transferred to Elmira Prison, NY, August 6, 1864	Exchanged March 14, 1865 at Boulware's Wharf on the James River, Virginia
Spivey, Josiah Private	Unk	Unknown	Co. F, 3rd North Carolina Infantry	May 6, 1864, Wilderness, Virginia	Point Lookout, Maryland, transferred to Elmira Prison, NY, July 25, 1864	Oath of Allegiance May 9, 1865
Spivey, William J. Private	17	April 28, 1864, Fort Fisher, New Hanover County, North Carolina	Co. F, 36th Regiment, 2nd North Carolina Artillery	January 15, 1865, Fort Fisher, North Carolina	February 1, 1865, Elmira Prison Camp, New York	Oath of Allegiance July 7, 1865
Spivey, Wright Private	Unk	July 1, 1862, Cleveland County, North Carolina	Co. H, 33rd North Carolina Infantry	May 12, 1864, Spotsylvania County Court House, Virginia	Point Lookout, Maryland, transferred to Elmira Prison, NY, August 14, 1864	Died January 23, 1865 of Variola (Smallpox), Grave No. 1593. Name William Spivry on Headstone.
Spoon, Henry M. Private	Unk	March 11, 1864, Raleigh, North Carolina	Co. E, 1st North Carolina Infantry	May 12, 1864, Spotsylvania Court House, Virginia	Point Lookout, Maryland, transferred to Elmira Prison, NY, August 6, 1864	Oath of Allegiance May 29, 1865
Spoon, Samuel Private	33	July 15, 1862, Raleigh, North Carolina	Co. E, 1st North Carolina Infantry	May 12, 1864, Spotsylvania Court House, Virginia	Point Lookout, Maryland, transferred to Elmira Prison, NY, August 6, 1864	Oath of Allegiance June 21, 1865

Name & Rank	Age	Enlisted	Regiment and State	Where Captured	Prison	Remarks
Spoon, William L. Private	30	July 15, 1862, Raleigh, North Carolina	Co. E, 1st North Carolina Infantry	May 12, 1864, Spotsylvania Court House, Virginia	Point Lookout, Maryland, transferred to Elmira Prison, NY, August 6, 1864	Oath of Allegiance May 15, 1865
Spotts, Jacob A. Private	Unk	April 25, 1861, Shepherdstown, Virginia	Co. H, 1st Virginia Cavalry	August 16, 1864, Front Royal, Virginia	Old Capital Prison, Washington, DC transferred to Elmira Prison, NY, August 29, 1864	Died December 28, 1864 of Chronic Diarrhea, Grave No. 1300
Spradley, C. L. Private	Unk	August 8, 1862, Pike County, Alabama	Co. F, 5th Alabama Infantry	August 10, 1864, Summit Point, Virginia	Old Capital Prison, Washington, DC transferred to Elmira Prison, NY, August 29, 1864	Oath of Allegiance June 30, 1865
Spratt, Charles Private	Unk	Unknown	Co. G, 7th North Carolina Infantry	April 2, 1865, Near Martinsburg, Virginia	Old Capital Prison, Washington D. C. Transferred to Elmira Prison, NY, May 2, 1865.	Oath of Allegiance June 12, 1865
Spriggs, John R. Sergeant	Unk	March 15, 1862, Lynchburg, Virginia	Co. D, 42nd Virginia Infantry	May 12, 1864, Near Spotsylvania Court House, Virginia	Point Lookout, Maryland, transferred to Elmira Prison, NY, August 2, 1864	Oath of Allegiance June 27, 1865
Spring, William Private	Unk	February 20, 1863, Albany, Georgia	Co. D, 64th Georgia Infantry	June 17, 1864, Petersburg, Virginia	Point Lookout, Maryland, transferred to Elmira Prison, NY, July 30, 1864	Died March 11, 1865 of Scorbutus (Scurvy), Grave No. 2428
Springs, Aaron Private	34	May 10, 1861, Bladen County, North Carolina	Co. H, 3rd North Carolina Infantry	May 12, 1864, Near Spotsylvania Court House, Virginia	Point Lookout, Maryland, transferred to Elmira Prison, NY, August 14, 1864	Died March 11, 1865 of Chronic Diarrhea, Grave No. 1841
Springs, William Vincent Private	Unk	April 7, 1864, Charleston, South Carolina	Co. A, 21st South Carolina Infantry	January 15, 1865, Fort Fisher, North Carolina	February 1, 1865, Elmira Prison Camp, New York	Died February 19, 1865 of Chronic Diarrhea, Grave No. 2340

Name & Rank	Age	Enlisted	Regiment and State	Where Captured	Prison	Remarks
Sprinkle, Mode Private	30	September 10, 1862, Raleigh, North Carolina	Co. I, 18th North Carolina Infantry	May 12, 1864, Spotsylvania Court House, Virginia	Point Lookout, Maryland, transferred to Elmira Prison, NY, August 6, 1864	Died October 5, 1864 of Chronic Diarrhea, Grave No. 607
Sprouse, Jacob M. Private	Unk	March 31, 1862, Allegheny, Virginia	Co. E, 31st Virginia Infantry	June 10, 1864, Spotsylvania Court House, Virginia	Point Lookout, Maryland, transferred to Elmira Prison, NY, July 23, 1864	Died December 30, 1864 of Variola (Smallpox), Grave No. 1310
Spruil, Friley J. Private	Unk	August 19, 1861, Leesburg, Virginia	Co. G, 18th Mississippi Infantry	May 8, 1864, Wilderness, Virginia	Point Lookout, Maryland, transferred to Elmira Prison, NY, August 14, 1864	Oath of Allegiance June 16, 1865
Spruill, T. J. Private	Unk	August 15, 1863, Pickensville, Alabama	Co. C, 41st Alabama Infantry	June 15, 1864, Petersburg, Virginia	Point Lookout, Maryland, transferred to Elmira Prison, NY, July 12, 1864	Oath of Allegiance June 16, 1865
Squires, Appleton Private	20	June 3, 1861, Washington, North Carolina	Co. E, 4th North Carolina Infantry	May 30, 1864 Mechanicsville, Virginia	Point Lookout, Maryland, transferred to Elmira Prison, NY, July 11,1864	Exchanged October 29, 1864, at Venus Point, Savannah River, GA.
Squires, John H. Musician Private	23	March 7, 1862, Bladen County, North Carolina	Co. B, 36th Regiment 2nd North Carolina Artillery	January 15, 1865, Fort Fisher, North Carolina	February 1, 1865, Elmira Prison Camp, New York	Exchanged March 2, 1865 at Akins Landing on the James River, Virginia
St. Sure, F. A. Private	Unk	July 17, 1861, Columbus, Tennessee	Co. A, Jackson's 1st Regiment, Tennessee Heavy Artillery	August 23, 1864, Fort Morgan, Alabama	New Orleans, Louisiana transferred to Elmira Prison, NY, December 4, 1864.	Exchanged February 25, 1865 at Boulware's or Cox Wharf on the James River, Virginia
Stack, W. H. Private	Unk	Unknown	Long's Battery No State	May 30, 1864, Hanover Junction, Virginia	Point Lookout, Maryland, transferred to Elmira Prison, NY, July 11,1864	Oath of Allegiance June 16, 1865

Name & Rank	Age	Enlisted	Regiment and State	Where Captured	Prison	Remarks
Stackhouse, John W. Private	Unk	May 21, 1863, Green Pond, Marion, South Carolina	Co. E, 4th South Carolina Cavalry	June 11, 1864, Trevilian Station, Louisa Court House, Virginia	Point Lookout, Maryland, transferred to Elmira Prison, NY, July 11,1864	Died September 19, 1864 of Chronic Diarrhea, Grave No. 520
Stacy, D. K. Private	Unk	February 15, 1863, Cokesbury, South Carolina	Co. F, Holcombe Legion, South Carolina	May 8, 1864, Jarrett's Depot, Virginia	Point Lookout, Maryland, transferred to Elmira Prison, NY, August 17, 1864	Exchanged February 20, 1865 at Boulware's or Cox Wharf on the James River, Virginia
Stacy, James F. Private	30	February 13, 1864, Johns Island, South Carolina	Co. F, 6th South Carolina Cavalry	August 23, 1864, Weldon, Railroad, VA. Gunshot Wound Left Hip, Severe.	Old Capital Prison, Washington D. C. Transferred to Elmira Prison, NY, March 27, 1865.	Oath of Allegiance June 21, 1865
Stacy, R. M. Private	Unk	December 18, 1861, Camp Hampton, South Carolina	Co. H, 18th South Carolina Infantry	July 30, 1864, Petersburg, Virginia	Point Lookout, Maryland, transferred to Elmira Prison, NY, August 12, 1864	Transferred for Exchange 10/11/64. Died 11/8/64 of Chronic Diarrhea at Point Lookout, MD.
Stacy, William R. Private	Unk	December 18, 1861, Camp Hampton, South Carolina	Co. H, 18th South Carolina Infantry	July 30, 1864, Petersburg, Virginia	Point Lookout, Maryland, transferred to Elmira Prison, NY, August 12, 1864	Died March 7, 1865 of Variola (Smallpox), Grave No. 2386
Stafford, J. B. Private	Unk	March 1, 1862, Rome, Georgia	Co. A, 8th Georgia Infantry	May 6, 1864, Wilderness, Virginia	Point Lookout, Maryland, transferred to Elmira Prison, NY, August 14, 1864	Exchanged March 2, 1865 at Akins Landing on the James River, Virginia
Stallings, Andrew J. Private	28	June 7, 1861, Wilson County, North Carolina	Co. B, 5th North Carolina Infantry	May 20, 1864, Spotsylvania Court House, Virginia	Point Lookout, Maryland, transferred to Elmira Prison, NY, July 3, 1864	Oath of Allegiance June 23, 1865
Stallings, John N. Private	37	July 13, 1861, Unionville, Tennessee	Co. F, 23rd Tennessee Infantry	June 17, 1864, Petersburg, Virginia	Point Lookout, Maryland, transferred to Elmira Prison, NY, July 30, 1864	Exchanged February 25, 1865 at Boulware's or Cox Wharf on the James River, Virginia

Name & Rank	Age	Enlisted	Regiment and State	Where Captured	Prison	Remarks
Stallings, John W. Private	16	May 1, 1863, Rockingham County, North Carolina	Co. G, 45th North Carolina Infantry	May 10, 1864, Spotsylvania Court House, Virginia	Point Lookout, Maryland, transferred to Elmira Prison, NY, August 6, 1864	Died April 17, 1865 of Variola (Smallpox), Grave No. 1351
Stallings, Octavius Private	20	May 4, 1861, Warrenton, North Carolina	Co. C, 12th North Carolina Infantry	May 20, 1864, Spotsylvania Court House, Virginia	Point Lookout, Maryland, transferred to Elmira Prison, NY, July 3, 1864	Died November 26, 1864 of Pneumonia, Grave No. 981
Stallings, Slade R. Private	20	April 22, 1861, Washington, North Carolina	Co. K, 10th Regiment, 1st North Carolina Artillery	January 15, 1865, Fort Fisher, North Carolina	February 1, 1865, Elmira Prison Camp, New York	Died March 10, 1865 of Pneumonia, Grave No. 1884
Stallings, William C. Corporal	Unk	August 30, 1862, Camp Randolph, Georgia	Co. B, 45th Georgia Infantry	May 6, 1864, Wilderness, Virginia	Point Lookout, Maryland, transferred to Elmira Prison, NY, August 14, 1864	Died January 29, 1865 of Variola (Smallpox), Grave No. 1807
Stallings, William W. Private	Unk	March 4, 1862, Forsyth, Georgia	Co. B, 45th Georgia Infantry	May 6, 1864, Wilderness, Virginia	Point Lookout, Maryland, transferred to Elmira Prison, NY, August 14, 1864	Exchanged February 20, 1865 at Boulware's or Cox Wharf on the James River, Virginia
Stallsworth, Joseph P. Private	Unk	May 11, 1861, Clinton, Alabama	Co. C, 11th Alabama Infantry	June 24, 1864, Petersburg, Virginia	Point Lookout, Maryland, transferred to Elmira Prison, NY, July 25, 1864	Oath of Allegiance May 29, 1865
Stalnacker, James H. Private	Unk	March 13, 1862, Tuscaloosa, Alabama	Co. A, 41st Alabama Infantry	May 16, 1864, Near Drury's Bluff, Virginia	Point Lookout, Maryland, transferred to Elmira Prison, NY, August 17, 1864	Oath of Allegiance June 30, 1865
Stalnaker, Benjamin F. Private	Unk	February 14, 1863, Jacksonboro, South Carolina	Co. H, 7th South Carolina Infantry	May 16, 1864, Near Drury's Bluff, Virginia	Point Lookout, Maryland, transferred to Elmira Prison, NY, August 17, 1864	Died October 9, 1864 of Chronic Diarrhea, Grave No. 585. Headstone has Stalnecked, 7th NC.

Name & Rank	Age	Enlisted	Regiment and State	Where Captured	Prison	Remarks
Stalnaker, Newton C.\n\nPrivate	Unk	May 31, 1861, Gilmer Court House, Virginia	Co. D, 31st Virginia Infantry	May 23, 1864, Hanover Junction, Virginia	Point Lookout, Maryland, transferred to Elmira Prison, NY, July 23, 1864	Oath of Allegiance May 29, 1865
Stalnaker, William W.\n\nPrivate	Unk	Unknown	Co. E, 19th Virginia Cavalry	July 15, 1864, Loudoun County, Virginia	Old Capital Prison, Washington, DC, transferred to Elmira Prison, NY, July 23, 1864	Exchanged October 29, 1864, at Venus Point, Savannah River, GA.
Stamp, James B.\n\nSergeant	Unk	April 27, 1861, Wetumpka, Alabama	Co. J, 3rd Alabama Infantry	May 12, 1864, Spotsylvania Court House, Virginia	Point Lookout, Maryland, transferred to Elmira Prison, NY, August 12, 1864	Exchanged March 14, 1865 at Boulware's Wharf on the James River, Virginia
Stanaland, Stephen B.\n\nPrivate	17	June 21, 1863, Fort Caswell, Brunswick County, North Carolina	Co. E, 40th Regiment, 3rd North Carolina Artillery	January 15, 1865, Fort Fisher, North Carolina	February 1, 1865, Elmira Prison Camp, New York	Oath of Allegiance July 26, 1865
Stancell, George R.\n\nPrivate	19	June 1, 1861, Lock's Creek, Cumberland County, North Carolina	Co. F, 24th North Carolina Infantry	June 17, 1864, Petersburg, Virginia	Point Lookout, Maryland, transferred to Elmira Prison, NY, July 25, 1864	Oath of Allegiance May 29, 1865
Standin, William H.\n\nPrivate	50	August 7, 1863, New Hanover County, North Carolina	Co. D, 13th Battalion North Carolina Light Artillery	January 15, 1865, Fort Fisher, North Carolina	February 1, 1865, Elmira Prison Camp, New York	Oath of Allegiance June 27, 1865
Standly, Wilbarn\n\nPrivate	Unk	June 29, 1861, Wytheville, Virginia	Co. B, 50th Virginia Infantry	May 12, 1864, Spotsylvania Court House, Virginia	Point Lookout, Maryland, transferred to Elmira Prison, NY, August 2, 1864	Oath of Allegiance June 27, 1865
Standly, William W.\n\nPrivate	Unk	June 29, 1861, Wytheville, Virginia	Co. B, 50th Virginia Infantry	May 12, 1864, Spotsylvania Court House, Virginia	Point Lookout, Maryland, transferred to Elmira Prison, NY, August 2, 1864	Oath of Allegiance June 27, 1865

Name & Rank	Age	Enlisted	Regiment and State	Where Captured	Prison	Remarks
Stanford, H. S. Private	Unk	August 24, 1861, Lawrenceville, Georgia	Co. F, 24th Georgia Infantry	August 16, 1864, Front Royal, Virginia	Old Capital Prison, Washington, DC transferred to Elmira Prison, NY, August 29, 1864	Exchanged March 2, 1865 at Akins Landing on the James River, Virginia
Stanley, H. S. Private	Unk	July 16, 1861, Lawrenceville, Georgia	Co. J, 16th Georgia Infantry	August 16, 1864, Front Royal, Virginia	Old Capital Prison, Washington, DC transferred to Elmira Prison, NY, August 29, 1864	Exchanged October 29, 1864, at Venus Point, Savannah River, GA.
Stanley, Jesse H. Private	30	July 16, 1862, Raleigh, North Carolina	Co. D, 5th North Carolina Infantry	May 12, 1864, Spotsylvania Court House, Virginia. Gunshot Wound Right Shoulder.	Old Capital Prison, Washington, DC transferred to Elmira Prison, NY, August 29, 1864	Exchanged October 29, 1864, at Venus Point, Savannah River, GA.
Stanley, John Private	Unk	Unknown	Co. H, 14th Louisiana Infantry	May 12, 1864, Spotsylvania Court House, Virginia	Point Lookout, Maryland, transferred to Elmira Prison, NY, July 25, 1864	Exchanged February 25, 1865 at Boulware's or Cox Wharf on the James River, Virginia
Stanley, Robert J. Private	Unk	March 20, 1862, Entrenched Camp, Virginia	Co. C, 6th Virginia Infantry	June 6, 1864, Cold Harbor, Virginia	Point Lookout, Maryland, transferred to Elmira Prison, NY, July 25, 1864	Oath of Allegiance May 29, 1865
Stansbury, Joseph Sergeant	Unk	April 9, 1863, Richmond, Virginia	Co. C, 2nd Battalion Maryland Cavalry	July 14, 1864, Near Washington, DC	Old Capital Prison, Washington, DC, transferred to Elmira Prison, NY, July 23, 1864	Oath of Allegiance May 17, 1865
Stansbury, Robert Private	37	June 10, 1861, Halifax County, North Carolina	Co. K, 1st North Carolina Infantry	May 12, 1864, Spotsylvania Court House, Virginia	Point Lookout, Maryland, transferred to Elmira Prison, NY, August 6, 1864	Oath of Allegiance June 9, 1865

Name & Rank	Age	Enlisted	Regiment and State	Where Captured	Prison	Remarks
Stanton, Benjamin F. Private	Unk	March 9, 1861, Prattville, Alabama	Co. E, 1st Battalion Alabama Artillery	August 23, 1864, Fort Morgan, Alabama	Steam Press No. 4 New Orleans, Louisiana transferred to Elmira Prison, NY, October 8, 1864.	Oath of Allegiance July 7, 1865
Staples, George W. Private	Unk	July 11, 1862, Lynchburg, Virginia	Co. I, 42nd Virginia Infantry	May 12, 1864, Near Spotsylvania Court House, Virginia	Point Lookout, Maryland, transferred to Elmira Prison, NY, August 6, 1864	Oath of Allegiance June 27, 1865
Starling, John Private	Unk	November 16, 1863, Raleigh, North Carolina	Co. C, 13th North Carolina Infantry	May 6, 1864, Wilderness, Virginia	Point Lookout, Maryland, transferred to Elmira Prison, NY, August 14, 1864	Oath of Allegiance May 29, 1865
Starling, Thomas Private	38	May 1, 1863, Fort Fisher, New Hanover County, North Carolina	Co. B, 36th Regiment, 2nd North Carolina Artillery	January 15, 1865, Fort Fisher, North Carolina	February 1, 1865, Elmira Prison Camp, New York	Oath of Allegiance July 19, 1865
Starnes, Ephraim Private	43	September 24, 1863, Union County, North Carolina	Co. H, 30th North Carolina Infantry	May 12, 1864, Near Spotsylvania Court House, Virginia	Point Lookout, Maryland, transferred to Elmira Prison, NY, August 14, 1864	Died January 12, 1865 of Congestion of the Brain, Grave No. 1488
Starnes, Jacob G. Sergeant	33	June 1, 1862, Camp Simons, South Carolina	Co. C, 17th South Carolina Infantry	July 30, 1864, Petersburg, Virginia	Point Lookout, Maryland, transferred to Elmira Prison, NY, August 12, 1864	Oath of Allegiance June 5, 1865
Starns, David A. Private	24	August 14, 1862, Statesville, North Carolina	Co. A, 18th North Carolina Infantry	May 12, 1864, Spotsylvania Court House, Virginia	Point Lookout, Maryland, transferred to Elmira Prison, NY, August 6, 1864	Died October 18, 1864 of Chronic Diarrhea, Grave No. 678
State, Frederick Private	35	June 22, 1861, New Orleans, Louisiana	Co. C, 14th Louisiana Infantry	May 5, 1864, Wilderness, Virginia. Gunshot Wound Left Thigh.	Old Capital Prison, Washington, DC, transferred to Elmira Prison, NY, July 23, 1864	Died September 17, 1864 of Chronic Diarrhea, Grave No. 164

Name & Rank	Age	Enlisted	Regiment and State	Where Captured	Prison	Remarks
Staten, William C. Corporal	25	September 15, 1862, Raleigh, North Carolina	Co. B, 31st North Carolina Infantry	June 1, 1864, Cold Harbor, Virginia	Point Lookout, Maryland, transferred to Elmira Prison, NY, July 12, 1864	Oath of Allegiance July 3, 1865
Staton, Andrew L. Private	30	August 15, 1861, Millner's Store, Amherst County, Virginia	Co. F, 58th Virginia Infantry	May 31, 1864 Mechanicsville, Virginia	Point Lookout, Maryland, transferred to Elmira Prison, NY, July 12, 1864	Oath of Allegiance June 19, 1865
Staton, John A. Private	Unk	August 30, 1861, Amherst County, Virginia	Co. F, 58th Virginia Infantry	May 31, 1864 Mechanicsville, Virginia	Point Lookout, Maryland, transferred to Elmira Prison, NY, July 12, 1864	Died November 27, 1864 of Chronic Diarrhea, Grave No. 896. Name Slaton on Headstone.
Staton, L. C. Private	Unk	April 18, 1862, Amherst, Virginia	Co. F, 50th Virginia Infantry	May 12, 1864, Spotsylvania Court House, Virginia	Point Lookout, Maryland, transferred to Elmira Prison, NY, August 2, 1864	Exchanged February 20, 1865 at Boulware's or Cox Wharf on the James River, Virginia
Steadham, William Private	25	August 15, 1862, Statesville, North Carolina	Co. K, 37th North Carolina Infantry	May 12, 1864, Spotsylvania, Virginia	Point Lookout, Maryland, transferred to Elmira Prison, NY, July 23, 1864	Died January 19, 1865 of Pneumonia, Grave No. 1200
Stean, Allan Private	Unk	September 13, 1864, Bennettsville, South Carolina	Co. F, 21st South Carolina Infantry	January 15, 1865, Fort Fisher, North Carolina	February 1, 1865, Elmira Prison Camp, New York	Died February 17, 1865 of Pneumonia, Grave No. 2221
Stedman, Stephen S. Sergeant	18	June 19, 1861, Three Creeks, Arkansas	Co. G, 3rd Arkansas Infantry	May 12, 1864, Spotsylvania Court House, Virginia	Point Lookout, Maryland, transferred to Elmira Prison, NY, August 12, 1864	Exchanged February 13, 1865 at Boulware's wharf on the James River, Virginia
Steedley, M. P. Private	Unk	Unknown	Co. F, 26th Louisiana Infantry	May 20, 1864, Spotsylvania Court House, Virginia	Point Lookout, Maryland, transferred to Elmira Prison, NY, July 3, 1864	Exchanged March 2, 1865 at Akins Landing on the James River, Virginia,

Name & Rank	Age	Enlisted	Regiment and State	Where Captured	Prison	Remarks
Steedman, John L. Private	Unk	April 23, 1861, Mobile, Alabama	Co. A, 3rd Alabama Infantry	May 12, 1864, Spotsylvania Court House, Virginia	Point Lookout, Maryland, transferred to Elmira Prison, NY, August 12, 1864	Exchanged March 2, 1865 at Akins Landing on the James River, Virginia
Steel, Abner B. Private	Unk	June 10, 1861, Cedar Falls, North Carolina	Co. M, 22nd North Carolina Infantry	May 24, 1864, Hanover Junction, Virginia	Point Lookout, Maryland, transferred to Elmira Prison, NY, July 11, 1864	Oath of Allegiance May 29, 1865
Steel, Robert Private	30	September 24, 1861, Union County, North Carolina	Co. E, 30th North Carolina Infantry	May 31, 1864 Old Church, Cold Harbor, Virginia	Point Lookout, Maryland, transferred to Elmira Prison, NY, July 12, 1864	Exchanged March 14, 1865 at Boulware's Wharf on the James River, Virginia
Steel, Stephen Private	17	March 4, 1862, Greensboro, North Carolina	Co. C, 45th North Carolina Infantry	July 12, 1864, Near Washington, DC	Old Capital Prison, Washington, DC, transferred to Elmira Prison, NY, July 23, 1864	Oath of Allegiance July 23, 1865
Steele, Dillard Private	43	March 8, 1862, Greensboro, North Carolina	Co. B, 45th North Carolina Infantry	May 10, 1864, Spotsylvania Court House, Virginia	Point Lookout, Maryland, transferred to Elmira Prison, NY, August 6, 1864	Exchanged February 20, 1865 at Boulware's or Cox Wharf on the James River, Virginia
Steele, James D. Private	27	June 25, 1861, Tallahatchie County, Mississippi	Co. F, 2nd Mississippi Infantry	May 8, 1864, Spotsylvania, Virginia. Gunshot Wound to Right Foot.	Old Capital Prison, Washington, DC, transferred to Elmira Prison, NY, July 23, 1864	Exchanged October 29, 1864, at Venus Point, Savannah River, GA.
Steele, John W. Civilian	Unk	Unknown	Citizen of Fairfax County, Virginia	December 18, 1863, Fairfax County, Virginia	Point Lookout, Maryland, transferred to Elmira Prison, NY, July 25, 1864	Exchanged March 10, 1865 at Boulware's Wharf on the James River, Virginia
Steell, W. G. Private	Unk	Unknown	Co. C, 1st North Carolina Cavalry	September 22, 1863, Near Madison Court House, Virginia	Point Lookout, Maryland, transferred to Elmira Prison, NY, August 18, 1864	Transferred For Exchange October 11, 1864 to Point Lookout Prison Camp, MD. No Further Information Available.

Name & Rank	Age	Enlisted	Regiment and State	Where Captured	Prison	Remarks
Steffey, John W. Private	20	July 2, 1861, Nickelsville, Scott County, Virginia	Co. E, 48th Virginia Infantry	May 12, 1864, Spotsylvania Court House, Virginia	Point Lookout, Maryland, transferred to Elmira Prison, NY, August 2, 1864	Oath of Allegiance June 19, 1865
Stegall, Ambrose M. Private	17	April 9, 1862, Monroe, North Carolina	Co. B, 43rd North Carolina Infantry	July 12, 1864, Near Washington, DC	Old Capital Prison, Washington, DC, transferred to Elmira Prison, NY, July 23, 1864	Oath of Allegiance May 29, 1865
Stein, John Civilian	Unk	Unknown	Citizen of Louisiana	September 19, 1864, Tensan Parish, Louisiana	New Orleans, Louisiana, Transferred to Elmira Prison, New York, November 19, 1864	Oath of Allegiance June 20, 1865
Steinmutz, Augustus Sergeant	25	June 4, 1861, Camp Moore, Louisiana	Co. G, 6th Louisiana Infantry	May 5, 1864, Wilderness, Virginia	Point Lookout, Maryland, transferred to Elmira Prison, NY, August 17, 1864	Exchanged February 25, 1865 at Boulware's or Cox Wharf on the James River, Virginia
Stephan, James E. Private	Unk	August 10, 1861, Richmond, Virginia	Co. C, 3rd Georgia Sharp Shooters	August 16, 1864, Front Royal, Virginia	Old Capital Prison, Washington, DC transferred to Elmira Prison, NY, August 29, 1864	Died March 14, 1865 of Diarrhea, Grave No. 2236
Stephens, Barnwell L. Sergeant	Unk	June 14, 1861, Valdosta, Georgia	Co. J, 12th Georgia Infantry	May 10, 1864, Spotsylvania Court House, Virginia	Point Lookout, Maryland, transferred to Elmira Prison, NY, July 25, 1864	Oath of Allegiance June 21, 1865
Stephens, James A. Private	Unk	July 7, 1861, McDonough, Georgia	Co. E, 53rd Georgia Infantry	May 24, 1864, South Anna, Virginia	Point Lookout Prison Camp, Maryland. Transferred to Elmira Prison, August 6, 1864	Died January 3, 1865 of Pneumonia, Grave No. 1346
Stephens, James E. Private	27	December 25, 1861, Bennettsville, South Carolina	Co. F, 21st South Carolina Infantry	January 15, 1865, Fort Fisher, North Carolina	February 1, 1865, Elmira Prison Camp, New York	Died February 23, 1865 of Pneumonia, Grave No. 2254. Headstone has E. Stevens.

Name & Rank	Age	Enlisted	Regiment and State	Where Captured	Prison	Remarks
Stephens, James G. Private	22	August 11, 1862, Merritt Bridge, Florida	Co. E, 2nd Battalion Florida Infantry	June 27, 1864, Near Petersburg, Florida	Point Lookout, Maryland, transferred to Elmira Prison, NY, July 25, 1864	Oath of Allegiance May 29, 1865
Stephens, James N. Private	Unk	September 30, 1861, Catawba, Virginia	Co. H, 26th Virginia Infantry	June 15, 1864, Near Petersburg, Virginia	Point Lookout, Maryland, transferred to Elmira Prison, NY, July 12,1864	Exchanged October 29, 1864, at Venus Point, Savannah River, GA.
Stephens, Jesse P. Private	Unk	December 10, 1861, Humboldt, Tennessee	Co. B, 1st Jackson's Tennessee Heavy Artillery	August 23, 1864, Fort Morgan, Alabama.	New Orleans, Louisiana transferred to Elmira Prison, NY, December 4, 1864.	Died February 15, 1865 of Chronic Diarrhea, Grave No. 2179
Stephens, John Private	Unk	April 15, 1864, Orange County, North Carolina	Co. G, 28th North Carolina Infantry	May 12, 1864, Spotsylvania County Court House, Virginia	Point Lookout, Maryland, transferred to Elmira Prison, NY, August 14, 1864	Exchanged March 10, 1865 at Boulware's Wharf on the James River, Virginia
Stephens, William H. Private	19	March 1, 1862, Raleigh, North Carolina	Co. C, 47th North Carolina Infantry	July 14, 1863, Falling Waters, Maryland	Point Lookout, Maryland, transferred to Elmira Prison, NY, August 18, 1864	Exchanged March 10, 1865 at Boulware's Wharf on the James River, Virginia
Stephenson, Benjamin T. Private	18	May 1, 1862, South Mills, North Carolina	Co. D, 32nd North Carolina Infantry	May 10, 1864, Near Mine Run Spotsylvania, Virginia	Point Lookout, Maryland, transferred to Elmira Prison, NY, August 6, 1864	Exchanged February 20, 1865 at Boulware's or Cox Wharf on the James River, Virginia
Stephenson, Bennett Private	19	July 15, 1862, Raleigh, North Carolina	Co. C, 5th North Carolina Infantry	May 12, 1864, Spotsylvania Court House, Virginia	Point Lookout, Maryland, transferred to Elmira Prison, NY, August 6, 1864	Died March 19, 1865 of Diarrhea, Grave No. 1563
Stephenson, John M. Sergeant	21	July 2, 1861, Wytheville, Virginia	Co. C, 50th Virginia Infantry	May 12, 1864 Spotsylvania Court House, Virginia	Point Lookout, Maryland, transferred to Elmira Prison, NY, August 2, 1864	Exchanged October 29, 1864, at Venus Point, Savannah River, GA.

Name & Rank	Age	Enlisted	Regiment and State	Where Captured	Prison	Remarks
Stepp, Fidella M. Private	35	March 18, 1862, Marion, North Carolina	Co. K, 22nd North Carolina Infantry	May 24, 1864, Hanover Junction, Virginia	Point Lookout, Maryland, transferred to Elmira Prison, NY, July 11, 1864	Exchanged October 29, 1864, at Venus Point, Savannah River, GA.
Stepp, Silas H. Private	Unk	April 27, 1863, Ashville, North Carolina	Co. C, 6th North Carolina Cavalry	June 22, 1864, Jackson Mill, North Carolina	Point Lookout, Maryland, transferred to Elmira Prison, NY, July 11, 1864	Died January 2, 1865 of Chronic Diarrhea and Pneumonia, Grave No. 1340
Sterbelt, Albert Civilian	Unk	East Louisiana	Citizen of Louisiana	October 7, 1864, Greenport, Louisiana,	New Orleans, Louisiana transferred to Elmira November 19, 1864.	Oath of Allegiance June 20, 1865
Sterling, Duncan J. Private	25	September 19, 1861, Fayetteville, North Carolina	Co. G, 33rd North Carolina Infantry	May 12, 1864, Spotsylvania County Court House, Virginia	Point Lookout, Maryland, transferred to Elmira Prison, NY, August 14, 1864	Died April 12, 1865 of Pneumonia, Grave No. 2686. Name D. J. Starling on Headstone.
Sterling, General P. Private	33	April 14, 1861, Newberry, South Carolina	Co. B, 3rd South Carolina Infantry	May 25, 1864, Hanover Junction, Virginia	Point Lookout, Maryland, transferred to Elmira Prison, NY, July 11, 1864	Died March 11, 1865 of Pneumonia, Grave No. 1836
Sterling, Thomas Private	38	May 1, 1863, Fort Fisher, North Carolina	Co. D, 36th Regiment, 2nd North Carolina Artillery	January 15, 1865, Fort Fisher, North Carolina	February 1, 1865, Elmira Prison Camp, New York	Oath of Allegiance July 19, 1865
Sterne, Moses Private	Unk	May 13, 1862, Thomaston, Georgia	Co. D, 13th Georgia Infantry	July 8, 1864, Harper's Ferry, Virginia	Old Capital Prison, Washington, DC, transferred to Elmira Prison, NY, July 23, 1864	Oath of Allegiance November 29, 1864. Early Release per Lincoln's Proclamation, 12/8/1863.
Sterrett, James A. Private	Unk	May 18, 1861, Sutton Valley, Virginia	Co. C, 25th Virginia Infantry	May 5, 1864, Wilderness, Virginia	Point Lookout, Maryland, transferred to Elmira Prison, NY, August 17, 1864	Exchanged February 25, 1865 at Boulware's or Cox Wharf on the James River, Virginia

Name & Rank	Age	Enlisted	Regiment and State	Where Captured	Prison	Remarks
Stevens, Arthur D. Private	Unk	March 4, 1863, Calhoun County, Georgia	Co. B, 51st Georgia Infantry	June 3, 1864, Gaines Farm Cold Harbor, Virginia	Point Lookout, Maryland, transferred to Elmira Prison, NY, July 12, 1864	Oath of Allegiance June 21, 1865
Stevens, Asbury W. Private	Unk	January 15, 1864, Macon, Georgia	Co. C, 64th Georgia Infantry	August 16, 1864, New Market, Virginia	Old Capital Prison, Washington, DC transferred to Elmira Prison, NY, August 27, 1864	Oath of Allegiance May 19, 1865
Stevens, Ballard P. Private	Unk	March 11, 1862, Newbern, Virginia	Co. C, 4th Virginia Infantry	May 12, 1864 Spotsylvania Court House, Virginia	Point Lookout, Maryland, transferred to Elmira Prison, NY, August 2, 1864	Oath of Allegiance June 27, 1865
Stevens, George M. Private	Unk	April 15, 1864, Richmond, Virginia	Co. E, 30th Virginia Sharp Shooters	July 14, 1864, Edward's Ferry, Virginia	Old Capital Prison, Washington, DC, transferred to Elmira Prison, NY, July 23, 1864	Exchanged March 2, 1865 at Akins Landing on the James River, Virginia
Stevens, James Private	Unk	June 6, 1861, Greenville, Butler County, Alabama	Co. G, 9th Alabama Infantry	May 6, 1864, Wilderness, Virginia	Point Lookout, Maryland, transferred to Elmira Prison, NY, August 17, 1864	Oath of Allegiance June 21, 1865
Stevens, James G. Private	Unk	August 10, 1861, Richmond, Virginia	Co. C, 3rd Battalion Georgia Sharp Shooters	August 16, 1864, Front Royal, Virginia	Old Capital Prison, Washington, DC. Transferred to Elmira Prison Camp, NY, August 29, 1864.	Died March 14, 1865 of Diarrhea, Grave No. 2434
Stevens, John B. Private	Unk	May 4, 1864, Petersburg, Virginia	Co. B, 3rd Archer's Battalion, Virginia Reserves Infantry	June 9, 1864, Petersburg, Virginia	Point Lookout, Maryland, transferred to Elmira Prison, NY, July 12,1864	Exchanged October 29, 1864, at Venus Point, Savannah River, GA.
Stevens, Joseph E. Private	33	February 5, 1862, Camp Stevens, North Carolina	Co. C, 18th North Carolina Infantry	May 12, 1864, Spotsylvania Court House, Virginia	Point Lookout, Maryland, transferred to Elmira Prison, NY, August 6, 1864	Died October 11, 1864 of Chronic Diarrhea, Grave No. 682

Name & Rank	Age	Enlisted	Regiment and State	Where Captured	Prison	Remarks
Stevens, Perry Private	Unk	August 16, 1863, Georgetown, South Carolina	Co. G, 27th South Carolina Infantry	June 24, 1864, Near Petersburg, Virginia	Point Lookout, Maryland, transferred to Elmira Prison, NY, August 18, 1864	Died February 19, 1865 of Unknown Causes, Grave No. 2341
Stevens, William Private	25	March 20, 1862, Danbury, North Carolina	Co. G, 53rd North Carolina Infantry	July 16, 1864, Rockville, Maryland	Old Capital Prison, Washington, DC, transferred to Elmira Prison, NY, July 23, 1864	Oath of Allegiance May 29, 1865
Stevens, William H. Private	26	December 9, 1861, Camp Trousdale, Tennessee	Co. G, 44th Tennessee Infantry	May 16, 1864, Near Drury's Bluff, Virginia	Point Lookout, Maryland, transferred to Elmira Prison, NY, August 17, 1864	Oath of Allegiance March 15, 1865. Early Release per Lincoln's Proclamation, 12/8/1863.
Stevens, William J. Private	Unk	March 1, 1863, Pulaski, Virginia	Co. E, 30th Virginia Sharp Shooters	July 14, 1864, Edward's Ferry, Virginia	Old Capital Prison, Washington, DC, transferred to Elmira Prison, NY, July 23, 1864	Oath of Allegiance May 29, 1865
Stevenson, Amos Private	39	February 25, 1863, Smithfield, North Carolina	Co. D, 31st North Carolina Infantry	June 1, 1864, Gaines Farm, Cold Harbor, Virginia	Point Lookout, Maryland, transferred to Elmira Prison, NY, July 12, 1864	Oath of Allegiance June 30, 1865
Stevenson, George Sergeant	28	June 7, 1861, Camp Moore, Louisiana	Co. D, 7th Louisiana Infantry	May 11, 1864, Spotsylvania Court House, Virginia	Point Lookout, Maryland, transferred to Elmira Prison, NY, August 17, 1864	Oath of Allegiance March 22, 1865. Early Release per Lincoln's Proclamation, 12/8/1863.
Stevenson, J. E. Private	Unk	December 28, 1861, Camp Hampton Legion, South Carolina	Co. F, Holcombe Legion, South Carolina	May 8, 1864, Jarrett's Depot, Virginia	Point Lookout, Maryland, transferred to Elmira Prison, NY, August 17, 1864	Died February 28, 1865 of Diarrhea, Grave No. 2138. Headstone has Stevenson.

Name & Rank	Age	Enlisted	Regiment and State	Where Captured	Prison	Remarks
Stevenson, Joseph C. Private	Unk	September 25, 1863, Camp Vance, North Carolina	Co. G, 37th North Carolina Infantry	July 29, 1864, Petersburg, Virginia	Point Lookout, Maryland, transferred to Elmira Prison, NY, August 12, 1864	Died August 27, 1864 of Chronic Diarrhea, Grave No. 103. Name Stephenson on Headstone.
Stevenson, William M. Private	31	March 25, 1863, Asheboro, North Carolina	Co. G, 40th Regiment, 3rd North Carolina Artillery	January 15, 1865, Fort Fisher, North Carolina	February 1, 1865, Elmira Prison Camp, New York	Oath of Allegiance May 29, 1865
Stewart, Andrew A. Private	18	March 22, 1862, Winston, North Carolina	Co. K, 45th North Carolina Infantry	May 20, 1864, Spotsylvania Court House, Virginia	Point Lookout, Maryland, transferred to Elmira Prison, NY, July 3, 1864	Exchanged October 29, 1864, at Venus Point, Savannah River, GA.
Stewart, Auguis Private	40	April 1, 1864, Camp Wyatt, New Hanover County, North Carolina	Co. D, 36th Regiment, 2nd North Carolina Artillery	January 15, 1865, Fort Fisher, North Carolina	February 1, 1865, Elmira Prison Camp, New York	Died March 14, 1865 of Pneumonia, Grave No. 1668
Stewart, Charles A. Musician Private	26	November 4, 1861, Sampson County, North Carolina	Co. A, 36th Regiment 2nd North Carolina Artillery	January 15, 1865, Fort Fisher, North Carolina	February 1, 1865, Elmira Prison Camp, New York	Died March 14, 1865 of Variola (Smallpox), Grave No. 1669
Stewart, Charles M. Private	Unk	December 11, 1861, Mississippi	Co. D, 2nd Virginia Infantry	July 16, 1864, Loudoun County, near Harper's Ferry, Maryland	July 23, 1864 Old Capital Prison, Washington DC. Transferred to Elmira July 23, 1864.	Oath of Allegiance August 26, 1864 per Lincoln. Early Release per Lincoln's Proclamation, 12/8/1863.
Stewart, Duncan J. Musician Private	25	October 20, 1863, Fort Caswell, Brunswick County, North Carolina	Co. D, 36th Regiment, 2nd North Carolina Artillery	January 15, 1865, Fort Fisher, North Carolina	February 1, 1865, Elmira Prison Camp, New York	Oath of Allegiance July 7, 1865
Stewart, Elijah L. Private	22	February 27, 1862, Reidsville, North Carolina	Co. G, 45th North Carolina Infantry	May 10, 1864, Spotsylvania Court House, Virginia	Point Lookout, Maryland, transferred to Elmira Prison, NY, August 6, 1864	Died November 11, 1864 of Chronic Diarrhea, Grave No. 824

Name & Rank	Age	Enlisted	Regiment and State	Where Captured	Prison	Remarks
Stewart, J. Franklin Private	21	March 19, 1862, Catawba County, North Carolina	Co. J, 49th North Carolina Infantry	May 16, 1864, Near Drury's Bluff, Virginia	Point Lookout, Maryland, transferred to Elmira Prison, NY, August 18, 1864	Exchanged October 29, 1864 at Venus Point, Savannah River, GA.
Stewart, J. J. Private	Unk	Unknown	Jeff Davis Alabama Artillery	May 5, 1864, Wilderness, Virginia	Point Lookout, Maryland, transferred to Elmira Prison, NY, August 17, 1864	Died February 17, 1865 of Variola (Smallpox), Grave No. 2224
Stewart, J. R. Private	Unk	Unknown	Captain Youngblood's Confederate States Signal Corps	October 12, 1864, Black River, Louisiana	New Orleans, Louisiana transferred to Elmira November 19, 1864.	Exchanged February 13, 1865 at Boulware's wharf on the James River, Virginia
Stewart, J. W. Private	Unk	Unknown	Co. B, 25th South Carolina Infantry	May 16, 1864, Near Drury's Bluff, Virginia	Point Lookout Prison Camp, Maryland. Transferred to Elmira Prison, August 18, 1864	Died April 24, 1865 of Unknown Disease, Grave No. 1410
Stewart, James Private	36	February 16, 1863, Johnsonville, North Carolina	Co. C, 35th North Carolina Infantry	June 17, 1864, Petersburg, Virginia	Point Lookout, Maryland, transferred to Elmira Prison, NY, July 30, 1864	Died October 5, 1864 of Pneumonia, Grave No. 641
Stewart, Jefferson W. Private	21	May 30, 1861, Webster, North Carolina	Co. B, 25th North Carolina Infantry	June 17, 1864, Petersburg, Virginia	Point Lookout, Maryland, transferred to Elmira Prison, NY, July 30, 1864	Died April 24, 1865 of Pneumonia, Grave No. 1440
Stewart, John Private	35	October 20, 1863, Fort Caswell, Brunswick County, North Carolina	Co. D, 36th Regiment, 2nd North Carolina Artillery	January 15, 1865, Fort Fisher, North Carolina	February 1, 1865, Elmira Prison Camp, New York	Died April 9, 1865 of Chronic Diarrhea, Grave No. 2610
Stewart, John A. Private	Unk	May 3, 1862, Mt. Polk, Alabama	Co. H, 48th Alabama Infantry	May 6, 1864, Wilderness, Virginia	Point Lookout, Maryland, transferred to Elmira Prison, NY, August 17, 1864	Exchanged March 14, 1865 at Boulware's Wharf on the James River, Virginia

Name & Rank	Age	Enlisted	Regiment and State	Where Captured	Prison	Remarks
Stewart, John A. Private	Unk	Unknown	Co. D, Battery Unknown, Virginia Light Artillery	July 16, 1864, Loudoun County, Virginia	Old Capital Prison, Washington, DC, transferred to Elmira Prison, NY, July 23, 1864	Oath of Allegiance May 15, 1865
Stewart, John M. Private	Unk	December 12, 1863, Weldon, North Carolina	Co. E, 56th North Carolina Infantry	May 14, 1864, Near Fort Darling, Virginia	Point Lookout Prison Camp, Maryland. Transferred to Elmira Prison, August 17, 1864	Died March 21, 1865 of Chronic Diarrhea, Grave No. 1547
Stewart, John W. Private	Unk	August 1, 1861, Lourina, Alabama	Co. K, 14th Alabama Infantry	May 31, 1864 Mechanicsville, Virginia	Point Lookout, Maryland, transferred to Elmira Prison, NY, July 11, 1864	Oath of Allegiance June 14, 1865
Stewart, Samuel C. Private	17	December 23, 1861, Georgetown, South Carolina	Co. B, 21st South Carolina Infantry	January 15, 1865, Fort Fisher, North Carolina	February 1, 1865, Elmira Prison Camp, New York	Died April 9, 1865 of Chronic Diarrhea, Grave No. 2555
Stewart, T. H. Corporal	Unk	August 21, 1862, Georgia	Co. F, 3rd Georgia Sharp Shooters	August 16, 1864, Front Royal, Virginia	Old Capital Prison, Washington, DC transferred to Elmira Prison, NY, August 29, 1864	Exchanged March 14, 1865 at Boulware's Wharf on the James River, Virginia
Stewart, W. D. Private	Unk	September 26, 1861, Camp Kirkpatrick, DeKalb County, Georgia	Co. K, 38th Georgia Infantry	May 20, 1864, Spotsylvania Court House, Virginia	Point Lookout, Maryland, transferred to Elmira Prison, NY, July 3, 1864	Died September 16, 1864 of Remittent Fever, Grave No. 173
Stewart, Wiley Private	18	March 14, 1862, Camp Leon, Florida	Co. A, 5th Florida Infantry	May 12, 1864, Spotsylvania Court House, Virginia	Point Lookout, Maryland, transferred to Elmira Prison, NY, August 12, 1864	Oath of Allegiance June 19, 1865
Stewart, William Corporal	Unk	October 1, 1861, Augusta, Georgia	Co. G, 38th Georgia Infantry	July 10, 1864, Maryland Heights, Maryland	Old Capital Prison, Washington, DC, transferred to Elmira Prison, NY, July 23, 1864	Oath of Allegiance May 29, 1865

Name & Rank	Age	Enlisted	Regiment and State	Where Captured	Prison	Remarks
Stewart, William Corporal	19	February 2, 1863, Wise County, Virginia	Co. A, 51st Virginia Infantry	May 30, 1864, Old Church, Cold Harbor, Virginia. Gunshot Wound Both Thighs.	Old Capital Prison, Washington, DC transferred to Elmira Prison, NY, August 29, 1864	Oath of Allegiance July 26, 1865
Stewart, William B. Private	Unk	August 31, 1863, Camp Randolph, Florida	Co. D, 64th Georgia Infantry	June 17, 1864, Petersburg, Virginia	Point Lookout, Maryland, transferred to Elmira Prison, NY, July 30, 1864	Died November 5, 1864 of Pneumonia, Grave No. 766
Stewart, William H. Private	Unk	March 12, 1862, Scott County, Virginia	Co. A, 48th Virginia Infantry	May 12, 1864 Spotsylvania Court House, Virginia	Point Lookout, Maryland, transferred to Elmira Prison, NY, August 2, 1864	Exchanged October 29, 1864, at Venus Point, Savannah River, GA.
Stiff, C.T. Private	Unk	August 11, 1862, Bedford County, Virginia	Co. G, 34th Virginia Infantry	June 15, 1864, Near Petersburg, Virginia	Point Lookout, Maryland, transferred to Elmira Prison, NY, July 12, 1864	Oath of Allegiance June 27, 1865
Stiff, John W. Private	Unk	March 25, 1863, Bedford County, Virginia	Co. G, 34th Virginia Infantry	June 15, 1864, Near Petersburg, Virginia	Point Lookout, Maryland, transferred to Elmira Prison, NY, July 12, 1864	Oath of Allegiance July 3, 1865
Stiff, P. H. Sergeant	Unk	June 12, 1861, Red Sulfur Springs, Virginia	Co. F, 26th Virginia Infantry	May 31, 1864, Chickahominy, Cold Harbor, Virginia	Point Lookout, Maryland, transferred to Elmira Prison, NY, July 12, 1864	Oath of Allegiance June 30, 1865
Stiff, Septimus Private	Unk	March 3, 1862, Bedford County, Virginia	Co. G, 34th Virginia Infantry	June 15, 1864, Near Petersburg, Virginia	Point Lookout, Maryland, transferred to Elmira Prison, NY, July 12, 1864	Oath of Allegiance July 3, 1865
Still, Benjamin Private	Unk	March 4, 1862, Monroe, Georgia	Co. C, 9th Georgia Infantry	October 14, 1864, Deep Bottom, Virginia. Gunshot Wound Left Knee.	Old Capital Prison, Washington, DC, transferred to Elmira Prison, NY, December 17, 1864	Exchanged February 13, 1865 at Boulware's Wharf on the James River, Virginia

Name & Rank	Age	Enlisted	Regiment and State	Where Captured	Prison	Remarks
Still, James T. Corporal	Unk	December 9, 1861, Camp Hampton, South Carolina	Co. H, 17th South Carolina Infantry	July 30, 1864, Petersburg, Virginia	Point Lookout, Maryland, transferred to Elmira Prison, NY, August 12, 1864	Died January 6, 1865 of Pneumonia, Grave No. 1234
Still, William M. Private	Unk	December 9, 1861, Camp Hampton, South Carolina	Co. H, 17th South Carolina Infantry	July 30, 1864, Petersburg, Virginia	Point Lookout, Maryland, transferred to Elmira Prison, NY, August 12, 1864	Exchanged October 29, 1864, at Venus Point, Savannah River, GA.
Stilwell, William Private	Unk	August 13, 1863, Tazewell County, Virginia	Co. J, 22nd Virginia Cavalry	July 15, 1864, Snickers' Gap, Virginia	Old Capital Prison, Washington D. C. Transferred to Elmira Prison, NY, August 12, 1864	Died November 16, 1864 of Chronic Diarrhea, Grave No. 959
Stinson, Elias D. Private	Unk	October 16, 1863, Montgomery, Alabama	Co. C, 1st Battalion Alabama Artillery	August 23, 1864, Fort Morgan, Alabama	New Orleans, Louisiana transferred to Elmira Prison, NY, December 4, 1864.	Died January 2, 1865 of Pneumonia, Grave No. 1341
Stinson, Henry M. Private	18	July 21, 1862, Chatham County, North Carolina	Co. J, 36th Regiment, 2nd North Carolina Artillery	January 15, 1865, Fort Fisher, North Carolina	February 1, 1865, Elmira Prison Camp, New York	Died May 17, 1865 of Jaundice, Grave No. 2956
Stinson, John Private	Unk	August 28, 1863, Fort Morgan, Alabama	Co. A, 1st Battalion Alabama Artillery	August 23, 1864, Fort Morgan, Alabama	New Orleans, Louisiana transferred to Elmira Prison, NY, December 4, 1864.	Died March 23, 1865 of Diarrhea, Grave No. 1511
Stinson, Joseph C. Private	Unk	November 14, 1863, Starlington, Butler County, Alabama	Co. E, 1st Battalion Alabama Artillery	August 23, 1864, Fort Morgan, Alabama	New Orleans, Louisiana transferred to Elmira Prison, NY, December 4, 1864.	Died December 22, 1864 of Rubeola (Measles), Grave No. 1091
Stinson, L. Private	Unk	November 14, 1863, Starlington, Butler County, Alabama	Co. A, 1st Battalion Alabama Artillery	August 23, 1864, Fort Morgan, Alabama	New Orleans, Louisiana transferred to Elmira December 5, 1864.	Died February 11, 1865 of Chronic Diarrhea, Grave No. 2058
Stockdall, Henry T. Private	Unk	August 2, 1861, Staunton, Virginia	Co. B, 52nd Virginia Infantry	May 30, 1864, Mechanicsville, Virginia	Point Lookout, Maryland, transferred to Elmira Prison, NY, July 9, 1864	Died August 18, 1864 of Chronic Diarrhea, Grave No. 118

Name & Rank	Age	Enlisted	Regiment and State	Where Captured	Prison	Remarks
Stockdall, William J. Private	Unk	August 2, 1861, Staunton, Virginia	Co. G, 52nd Virginia Infantry	May 20, 1864, Spotsylvania Court House, Virginia	Point Lookout, Maryland, transferred to Elmira Prison, NY, July 3, 1864	Died July 9, 1864 of Chronic Diarrhea, Grave No. 2854
Stockwell, Thomas Private	53	May 13, 1862, Camp Moore, Louisiana	Co. F, 3rd Louisiana Cavalry	October 9, 1864, Near Wilson's Ferry, Louisiana	New Orleans, Louisiana transferred to Elmira November 19, 1864.	Oath of Allegiance May 29, 1865
Stoffer, Napoleon B. Private	18	May 25, 1862, Salisbury, North Carolina	Co. D, 42nd North Carolina Infantry	June 2, 1864, Cold Harbor, Virginia	Transferred From Point Lookout Prison, MD, July 12, 1864. Train Never Arrived at Elmira Prison Camp, NY.	Died July 15, 1864 in Train Wreck at Shohola, Pennsylvania.
Stogner, Adam J. Private	Unk	May 8, 1862, Snow Hill, North Carolina	Co. D, 6th South Carolina Cavalry	June 11, 1864, Trevilian Station, Louisa Court House, Virginia	Point Lookout, Maryland, transferred to Elmira Prison, NY, July 25, 1864	Exchanged March 14, 1865 at Boulware's Wharf on the James River, Virginia
Stokely, Jacob Private	Unk	September 1. 1862, Cumberland Gap, Tennessee	Co. G, 17th Tennessee Infantry	June 17, 1864, Petersburg, Virginia	Point Lookout, Maryland, transferred to Elmira Prison, NY, July 30, 1864	Exchanged February 25, 1865 at Boulware's or Cox Wharf on the James River, Virginia
Stokes, B. B. Private	22	Unknown	Co. B, 1st Jackson's Tennessee Heavy Artillery	August 23, 1864, Fort Morgan, Alabama.	New Orleans, Louisiana transferred to Elmira Prison, NY, December 4, 1864.	Orders for Elmira, New York. Died 12/19/64 of Variola at US Army Hospital Fort Columbus, NY Harbor.
Stokes, James M. Private	Unk	May 11, 1861, New Orleans, Louisiana	Co. A, 2nd Louisiana Infantry	May 12, 1864, Spotsylvania Court House, Virginia	Point Lookout, Maryland, transferred to Elmira Prison, NY, August 17, 1864	Exchanged February 20, 1865 at Boulware's or Cox Wharf on the James River, Virginia
Stokes, James W. Private	21	March 29, 1862, Atlanta, Georgia	Co. G, Cobb's Legion Georgia	May 18, 1864, Kang George County, Virginia	Point Lookout, Maryland, transferred to Elmira Prison, NY, July 3, 1864	Exchanged October 29, 1864, at Venus Point, Savannah River, GA.

Name & Rank	Age	Enlisted	Regiment and State	Where Captured	Prison	Remarks
Stokes, Richard R. Private	Unk	June 17, 1861, Front Royal, Virginia	Co. D, 49th Virginia Infantry	May 30, 1864, Gaines Mill Cold Harbor, Virginia	Point Lookout, Maryland, transferred to Elmira Prison, NY, July 11, 1864	Oath of Allegiance June 30, 1865
Stokes, S. A. Private	Unk	Unknown	Co. C, 33rd North Carolina Infantry	May 6, 1864, Wilderness, Virginia	Point Lookout, Maryland, transferred to Elmira Prison, NY, August 14, 1864	Exchanged March 2, 1865 at Akins Landing on the James River, Virginia
Stokes, Thomas H. Private	Unk	July 1, 1862, Clinton, South Carolina	Co. J, 3rd South Carolina Infantry	May 24, 1864, Hanover Junction, Virginia	Point Lookout, Maryland, transferred to Elmira Prison, NY, July 12, 1864	Oath of Allegiance May 29, 1865
Stokes, W. E. Private	Unk	February 21, 1863, Pocotaligo, South Carolina	Co. J, 5th South Carolina Cavalry	June 11, 1864, Trevilian Station, Louisa Court House, Virginia	Point Lookout, Maryland, transferred to Elmira Prison, NY, July 25, 1864	Exchanged March 2, 1865 at Akins Landing on the James River, Virginia
Stokes, William F. Private	Unk	Unknown	Co. B, 1st Jackson's Tennessee Heavy Artillery	August 23, 1864, Fort Morgan, Alabama.	New Orleans, Louisiana transferred to Elmira Prison, NY, December 4, 1864.	Died March 12, 1865 of Chronic Diarrhea, Grave No. 1822
Stone, C. R. Corporal	Unk	Unknown	Confederate States Navy	September 12, 1863, Place Unknown	Point Lookout, Maryland, transferred to Elmira Prison, NY, August 18, 1864	Oath of Allegiance June 12, 1865
Stone, H. J. Private	Unk	March 3, 1864, Isle of Hope, Georgia	Co. G, 7th Georgia Cavalry	June 11, 1864, Trevilian Station, Louisa Court House, Virginia	Point Lookout, Maryland, transferred to Elmira Prison, NY, July 25, 1864	Oath of Allegiance June 16, 1865
Stone, Martin C. Corporal	Unk	April 17, 1861, Newbern, Virginia	Co. C, 4th Virginia Infantry	May 12, 1864 Spotsylvania Court House, Virginia	Point Lookout, Maryland, transferred to Elmira Prison, NY, August 2, 1864	Oath of Allegiance July 7, 1865

Name & Rank	Age	Enlisted	Regiment and State	Where Captured	Prison	Remarks
Stone, Norris Private	Unk	April 1, 1863, Richmond, Virginia	Co. E, 12th Virginia Cavalry	July 16, 1864, Poolesville, Maryland	Old Capital Prison, Washington, DC, transferred to Elmira Prison, NY, July 23, 1864	Oath of Allegiance May 15, 1865
Stone, W. H. Quarter Master Sergeant	Unk	Unknown	Co. A, Gober's Regiment Louisiana Cavalry	October 6, 1864, Clinton, Louisiana	New Orleans, Louisiana transferred to Elmira November 19, 1864.	Exchanged February 25, 1865 at Boulware's or Cox Wharf on the James River, Virginia
Stone, William Private	Unk	May 8, 1864, Spotsylvania County Court House, Virginia	Co. I, 13th North Carolina Infantry	August 3, 1864, Petersburg, Virginia	Point Lookout, Maryland, transferred to Elmira Prison, NY, August 12, 1864	Died September 10, 1864 of Chronic Diarrhea, Grave No. 255
Stone, William L. Sergeant	20	June 20, 1861, Christianville, Virginia	Co. C, 21st Virginia Infantry	May 12, 1864, Spotsylvania Court House, Virginia	Point Lookout, Maryland, transferred to Elmira Prison, NY, August 2, 1864	Oath of Allegiance June 23, 1865
Stone, William W. Private	Unk	April 1, 1861, Lacy's Store, Virginia	Co. B, 44th Virginia Infantry	May 12, 1864, Spotsylvania Court House, Virginia	Point Lookout, Maryland, transferred to Elmira Prison, NY, August 2, 1864	Oath of Allegiance June 27, 1865
Stonecypher, John H. Corporal	Unk	August 24, 1861, Habersham County, Georgia	Co. H, 24th Georgia Infantry	June 3, 1864, Gaines Mill Cold Harbor, Virginia	Point Lookout, Maryland, transferred to Elmira Prison, NY, July 12, 1864	Died September 25, 1864 of Typhoid Fever Grave No. 365
Stoner, John M. Private	Unk	October 23, 1863, N. Market, Virginia	Co. K, 12 Virginia Cavalry	October 11, 1863, Culpeper, Virginia	Old Capital Prison, Washington DC. Transferred to Elmira Prison Camp New York July 25, 1864.	Exchanged October 29, 1864, at Venus Point, Savannah River, GA.
Storgeal, J. Private	Unk	Unknown	Co. K, 23rd North Carolina Infantry	Unknown	Point Lookout Prison Camp, Maryland. Transferred to Elmira Prison, Unknown Date	Died January 22, 1865 of Unknown Disease, Grave No. 1578

Name & Rank	Age	Enlisted	Regiment and State	Where Captured	Prison	Remarks
Stork, John J. Private	20	August 15, 1861, Light Wood Knot Springs, Near Columbia, South Carolina	Co. A, 15th South Carolina Infantry	May 6, 1864, Near Mine Run Wilderness, Virginia	Point Lookout, Maryland, transferred to Elmira Prison, NY, August 17, 1864	Exchanged March 2, 1865 at Akins Landing on the James River, Virginia
Storm, Richard Private	28	August 6, 1862, Clifton, Virginia	Co. A, 9th Virginia Infantry	May 23, 1864, Chesterfield Station, Virginia	Point Lookout, Maryland, transferred to Elmira Prison, NY, July 23, 1864	Oath of Allegiance December 30, 1864. Early Release per Lincoln's Proclamation, 12/8/1863.
Story, B. F. Private	Unk	May 8, 1862, Augusta, Georgia	Co. A, 7th Georgia Cavalry	June 11, 1864, Trevilian Station, Louisa Court House, Virginia	Point Lookout, Maryland, transferred to Elmira Prison, NY, July 25, 1864	Died August 25, 1864 of Typhoid Fever, Grave No. 43
Story, William M. Corporal	Unk	March 10, 1862, Madison Court House, Virginia	Co. C, 4th Virginia Cavalry	August 16, 1864, Front Royal, Virginia	Old Capital Prison, Washington, DC transferred to Elmira Prison, NY, August 29, 1864	Oath of Allegiance June 30, 1865
Stout, J. R. Private	Unk	Unknown	Co. A, 1st Georgia Cavalry	May 31, 1864, Cold Harbor, Virginia	Point Lookout, Maryland, transferred to Elmira Prison, NY, July 12, 1864	Exchanged February 25, 1865 at Boulware's or Cox Wharf on the James River, Virginia
Stout, Lilburn Private	Unk	March 10, 1862, New Market, Virginia	Co. H, 5th Virginia Infantry	May 20, 1864, Spotsylvania Court House, Virginia	Point Lookout, Maryland, transferred to Elmira Prison, NY, July 3, 1864	Exchanged March 10, 1865 at Boulware's Wharf on the James River, Virginia
Stout, Michael Private	Unk	March 20, 1863, Frankford, Virginia	Co. K, 19th Virginia Cavalry	July 15, 1864, Loudoun County, Virginia	Old Capital Prison, Washington, DC, transferred to Elmira Prison, NY, July 23, 1864	Oath of Allegiance June 16, 1865

Name & Rank	Age	Enlisted	Regiment and State	Where Captured	Prison	Remarks
Stovall, Quincy Private	Unk	June 14, 1861, Elamville, Virginia	Co. D, 51st Virginia Infantry	July 16, 1864, Loudoun County, Virginia	Old Capital Prison, Washington, DC, transferred to Elmira Prison, NY, July 23, 1864	Oath of Allegiance May 29, 1865
Stovall, W. J. Private	Unk	September 10, 1861, Nashville, Tennessee	Co. A, Jackson's 1st Regiment, Tennessee Heavy Artillery	August 23, 1864, Fort Morgan, Alabama	New Orleans, Louisiana transferred to Elmira Prison, NY, December 4, 1864.	Exchanged February 25, 1865 at Boulware's or Cox Wharf on the James River, Virginia
Stowe, Harris Private	Unk	August 24, 1861, Homer, Georgia	Co. A, 24th Georgia Infantry	August 16, 1864, Front Royal, Virginia	Old Capital Prison, Washington, DC transferred to Elmira Prison, NY, August 29, 1864	Oath of Allegiance July 7, 1865
Stowe, Michael Private	Unk	August 24, 1861, Habersham County, Georgia	Co. H, 24th Georgia infantry	August 16, 1864, Front Royal, Virginia	Old Capital Prison, Washington, DC transferred to Elmira Prison, NY, August 29, 1864	Oath of Allegiance July 7, 1865
Stoy, Walter P. Private	19	March 14, 1862, Charleston, South Carolina	Co. E, 25th South Carolina Infantry	January 15, 1865, Fort Fisher, North Carolina	February 1, 1865, Elmira Prison Camp, New York	Oath of Allegiance August 7, 1865
Strange, John C. Corporal	Unk	August 13, 1863, Center Hill, Georgia	Co. B, 16th Georgia Infantry	June 3, 1864, Gaines Mill Cold Harbor, Virginia	Point Lookout, Maryland, transferred to Elmira Prison, NY, July 12, 1864	Oath of Allegiance July 7, 1865
Stratton, John J. Sergeant	Unk	April 19, 1862, Nelson County, Virginia	Co. F, 49th Virginia Infantry	May 30, 1864, Gaines Mill Cold Harbor, Virginia	Point Lookout, Maryland, transferred to Elmira Prison, NY, July 11, 1864	Oath of Allegiance June 30, 1865
Straughan, Thomas B. Private	23	April 15, 1861, Pittsboro, North Carolina	Co. J, 32nd North Carolina Infantry	June 10, 1864, Spotsylvania, Virginia	Point Lookout, Maryland, transferred to Elmira Prison, NY, July 25, 1864	Oath of Allegiance July 11, 1865

Name & Rank	Age	Enlisted	Regiment and State	Where Captured	Prison	Remarks
Straun, William W. Private	23	April 12, 1862, Union County, North Carolina	Co. J, 53rd North Carolina Infantry	May 20, 1864, Spotsylvania Court House, Virginia	Point Lookout, Maryland, transferred to Elmira Prison, NY, July 3, 1864	Exchanged March 2, 1865 at Akins Landing on the James River, Virginia
Strawbridge, W. John Private	Unk	March 7, 1863, Carrollson, Alabama	Co. C, 41th Alabama Infantry	May 16, 1864, Bermuda Hundred, Virginia	Point Lookout, Maryland, transferred to Elmira Prison, NY, July12, 1864	Died September 6, 1864 of Typhoid Pneumonia, Grave No. 245
Strawhorn, John T. Private	Unk	February 15, 1864, Sullivan's Island, South Carolina	Co. F, Holcombe Legion, South Carolina	May 8, 1864, Jarrett's Depot, Virginia	Point Lookout, Maryland, transferred to Elmira Prison, NY, August 17, 1864	Exchanged February 13, 1865 at Boulware's wharf on the James River, Virginia
Street, George W. Corporal	Unk	August 16, 1861, Hamburg, Edgefield District, South Carolina	Co. G, 1st South Carolina Infantry	July 29, 1864, Petersburg, Virginia	Point Lookout, Maryland, transferred to Elmira Prison, NY, August 12, 1864	Oath of Allegiance July 3, 1865
Street, James W. Private	Unk	Unknown	Co. B, 1st Louisiana Cavalry	October 3, 1864, East Baton Rouge, Louisiana	New Orleans, Louisiana transferred to Elmira November 19, 1864.	Exchanged February 20, 1865 at Boulware's wharf on the James River, Virginia
Stribling, William A. Corporal	Unk	July 4, 1861, Hamilton, Georgia	Co. K, 35th Georgia Infantry	May 5, 1864, Mine Run Wilderness, Virginia	Point Lookout, Maryland, transferred to Elmira Prison, NY, August 17, 1864	Oath of Allegiance June 30, 1865
Strickland, Alexander Private	18	March 12, 1862, Cerro Gordo, Columbus County, North Carolina	Co. E, 36th Regiment, 2nd North Carolina Artillery	January 15, 1865, Fort Fisher, North Carolina	February 1, 1865, Elmira Prison Camp, New York	Died February 18, 1865 of Chronic Diarrhea-Pneumonia, Grave No. 2216
Strickland, Alva Private	18	May 1, 1862, Wilmington, New Hanover County, North Carolina	Co. D, 36th Regiment, 2nd North Carolina Artillery	January 15, 1865, Fort Fisher, North Carolina	February 1, 1865, Elmira Prison Camp, New York	Died April 23, 1865 of Typhoid Fever, Grave No. 1402

Name & Rank	Age	Enlisted	Regiment and State	Where Captured	Prison	Remarks
Strickland, D. R. Private	21	March 3, 1862, Wilmington, North Carolina	Co. E, 30th North Carolina Infantry	May 12, 1864, Spotsylvania Court House, Virginia	Point Lookout, Maryland, transferred to Elmira Prison, NY, August 14, 1864	Oath of Allegiance June 27, 1865
Strickland, David Private	Unk	March 1, 1862, Cerro Gordo, Columbus County, North Carolina	Co. E, 36th Regiment, 2nd North Carolina Artillery	January 15, 1865, Fort Fisher, North Carolina	February 1, 1865, Elmira Prison Camp, New York	Oath of Allegiance July 7, 1865
Strickland, Martin Private	36	February 18, 1863, Sampson County, North Carolina	Co. A, 36th Regiment 2nd North Carolina Artillery	January 15, 1865, Fort Fisher, North Carolina	February 1, 1865, Elmira Prison Camp, New York	Died March 8, 1865 of Chronic Diarrhea, Grave No. 2602.
Strickland, Nathanial Private	19	March 7, 1862, Cerro Gordo, Columbus County, North Carolina	Co. E, 36th Regiment, 2nd North Carolina Artillery	January 15, 1865, Fort Fisher, North Carolina	February 1, 1865, Elmira Prison Camp, New York	Died March 12, 1865 of Pneumonia, Grave No. 1848
Strickland, Samuel Private	22	October 14, 1861, High House, Wake County, North Carolina	Co. H, 31st North Carolina Infantry	June 1, 1864, Gaines Mill Cold Harbor, Virginia	Point Lookout, Maryland, transferred to Elmira Prison, NY, July 12, 1864	Died August 4, 1864 Chronic Diarrhea, Grave No. 6
Strickland, Thomas J. Private	30	April 1, 1862, Cumberland County, North Carolina	Co. J, 51st North Carolina Infantry	June 1, 1864, Cold Harbor, Virginia	Transferred From Point Lookout Prison, MD, July 12, 1864. Train Never Arrived at Elmira Prison Camp, NY.	Died July 15, 1864 in Train Wreck at Shohola, Pennsylvania.
Strickland, William H. Private	36	February 9, 1862, Whiteville, Columbus County, North Carolina	Co. E, 36th Regiment, 2nd North Carolina Artillery	January 15, 1865, Fort Fisher, North Carolina	February 1, 1865, Elmira Prison Camp, New York	Exchanged March 14, 1865 at Boulware's Wharf on the James River, Virginia
Strickland, Y. I. Private	Unk	July 16, 1862, Raleigh, North Carolina	Co. D, 5th North Carolina Infantry	May 12, 1864, Spotsylvania Court House, Virginia	Point Lookout, Maryland, transferred to Elmira Prison, NY, August 6, 1864	Oath of Allegiance May 29, 1865
Stricklande, Henry Corporal	Unk	September 22, 1862, Waynesville, Georgia	Co. G, 7th Georgia Cavalry	June 11, 1864, Trevilian Station, Louisa Court House, Virginia	Point Lookout, Maryland, transferred to Elmira Prison, NY, July 25, 1864	Oath of Allegiance June 16, 1865

Name & Rank	Age	Enlisted	Regiment and State	Where Captured	Prison	Remarks
Stricklin, Jacob Private	18	March 11, 1862, Cerro Gordo, North Carolina	Co. E, 36th Regiment 2nd North Carolina Artillery	January 15, 1865, Fort Fisher, North Carolina	February 1, 1865, Elmira Prison Camp, New York	Died May 16, 1865 of Chronic Diarrhea, Grave No. 2959
Strider, James M. A. Sergeant	22	June 29, 1861, Montgomery, Randolph County, North Carolina	Co. H, 3rd North Carolina Infantry	May 12, 1864, Near Spotsylvania Court House, Virginia	Point Lookout, Maryland, transferred to Elmira Prison, NY, August 14, 1864	Died October 13, 1864 of Remittent Fever, Grave No. 565
Strider, Joel Private	27	March 7, 1862, Asheboro, North Carolina	Co. B, 52nd North Carolina Infantry	July 14, 1863, Falling Waters, Maryland	Point Lookout, Maryland, transferred to Elmira Prison, NY, August 18, 1864	Died September 20, 1864 of Chronic Diarrhea, Grave No. 507
Stringer, Alexander Private	Unk	September 23, 1861, Monroe, Louisiana	Co. F, 2nd Louisiana Infantry	November 8, 1863, Morton's Ford, Virginia	Old Capital Prison, Washington, DC transferred to Elmira Prison, NY, August 27, 1864	Exchanged February 25, 1865 at Boulware's or Cox Wharf on the James River, Virginia
Stringer, James B. Private	Unk	May 9, 1861, Camp Walker, New Orleans, Louisiana	Co. E, 2nd Louisiana Infantry	May 12, 1864, Spotsylvania Court House, Virginia	Point Lookout, Maryland, transferred to Elmira Prison, NY, August 17, 1864	Exchanged February 25, 1865 at Boulware's or Cox Wharf on the James River, Virginia
Stringer, William H. Private	23	May 22, 1861, Camp Moore, New Orleans, Louisiana	Co. E, 7th Louisiana Infantry	November 7, 1863, Rappahannock, Virginia	Point Lookout, Maryland, transferred to Elmira Prison, NY, August 18, 1864	Exchanged February 25, 1865 at Boulware's or Cox Wharf on the James River, Virginia
Stripling, A. C. Private	21	April 13, 1861, Spartanburg, South Carolina	Co. E, 3rd Battalion South Carolina Infantry	July 29, 1864, Petersburg, Virginia	Point Lookout, Maryland, transferred to Elmira Prison, NY, August 12, 1864	Oath of Allegiance June 19, 1865
Strock, Emery B. Private	Unk	April 13, 1864, James Island, South Carolina	Co. F, 25th South Carolina Infantry	January 15, 1865, Fort Fisher, North Carolina	February 1, 1865, Elmira Prison Camp, New York	Exchanged February 20, 1865. Died March 16, 1865 at Jackson Hospital, Richmond, VA

Name & Rank	Age	Enlisted	Regiment and State	Where Captured	Prison	Remarks
Stroh, G. Private	Unk	Unknown	Co. D, 1st South Carolina	May 24, 1864, Newton, Virginia	Point Lookout, Maryland, transferred to Elmira Prison, NY, July 12, 1864	Oath of Allegiance June 21, 1865
Stroman, Charles Private	Unk	April 11, 1862, Coles Island, South Carolina	Co. F, 25th South Carolina Infantry	January 15, 1865, Fort Fisher, North Carolina	February 1, 1865, Elmira Prison Camp, New York	Died May 10, 1865 of Variola (Smallpox), Grave No. 2788
Strong, Andrew Private	Unk	January 14, 1862, Camp Hampton, Columbia, South Carolina	Co. D, 17th South Carolina Infantry	July 30, 1864, Petersburg, Virginia	Point Lookout, Maryland, transferred to Elmira Prison, NY, August 12, 1864	Died October 30, 1864 of Typhoid Fever, Grave No. 732
Stroud, John W. Corporal	Unk	September 19, 1861, Randolph County, Alabama	Co. D, 13th Alabama Infantry	May 12, 1864, Spotsylvania Court House, Virginia	Point Lookout, Maryland, transferred to Elmira Prison, NY, August 2, 1864	Oath of Allegiance June 19, 1865
Stroup, David C. Private	26	July 6, 1863, Lincoln County, North Carolina	Co. H, 52nd North Carolina Infantry	May 12, 1864, Spotsylvania Court House, Virginia	Point Lookout, Maryland, transferred to Elmira Prison, NY, August 12, 1864	Exchanged February 20, 1865 at Boulware's or Cox Wharf on the James River, Virginia
Stroup, Joseph H. Private	30	July 30, 1861, Dallas, North Carolina	Co. B, 28th North Carolina Infantry	May 12, 1864, Spotsylvania, Virginia	Point Lookout, Maryland, transferred to Elmira Prison, NY, August 12, 1864	Exchanged October 29, 1864, at Venus Point, Savannah River, GA.
Stroup, M. A. Private	Unk	February 2, 1864, Camp Justice, South Carolina	Co. K, 18th South Carolina Infantry	July 30, 1864, Petersburg, Virginia	Point Lookout, Maryland, transferred to Elmira Prison, NY, August 12, 1864	Died December 9, 1864 of Pneumonia, Grave No. 1167.
Stroup, Moses Private	22	July 30, 1861, Dallas, Gaston County, North Carolina	Co. H, 28th North Carolina Infantry	May 12, 1864, Spotsylvania Court House, Virginia	Point Lookout, Maryland, transferred to Elmira Prison, NY, August 12, 1864	Oath of Allegiance June 19, 1865
Strow, William Private	Unk	April 30, 1864, Monroe Draft, Monroe, Virginia	Co. F, 26th Battalion Virginia Infantry	June 3, 1864, Gaines Farm Cold Harbor, Virginia	Point Lookout, Maryland, transferred to Elmira Prison, NY, July 12, 1864	Oath of Allegiance July 19, 1865

Name & Rank	Age	Enlisted	Regiment and State	Where Captured	Prison	Remarks
Stuart, Michael K. Private	Unk	June 9, 1861, Bibb County, Georgia	Co. H, 12th Georgia Infantry	May 10, 1864, Spotsylvania Court House, Virginia	Point Lookout, Maryland, transferred to Elmira Prison, NY, July 30, 1864	Died May 11, 1865 of Chronic Diarrhea, Grave No. 2741
Stuart, John W. Private	Unk	February 15, 1863, Princeton, Virginia	Co. D, 60th Virginia Infantry	August 17, 1864, Winchester, Virginia	Old Capital Prison, Washington, DC transferred to Elmira Prison, NY, August 29, 1864	Oath of Allegiance May 15, 1865
Stubbs, Albert M. Corporal	Unk	August 17, 1861, Gloucester Point, Virginia	Co. A, 26th Virginia Infantry	June 15, 1864, Near Petersburg, Virginia	Point Lookout, Maryland, transferred to Elmira Prison, NY, July 12, 1864	Exchanged March 14, 1865 at Boulware's Wharf on the James River, Virginia
Stubbs, D. D. Private	18	December 25, 1861, Bennettsville, South Carolina	Co. F, 21st South Carolina Infantry	January 15, 1865, Fort Fisher, North Carolina	February 1, 1865, Elmira Prison Camp, New York	Oath of Allegiance July 11, 1865
Stubbs, J. B. Private	Unk	March 1, 1863, Bennettsville, South Carolina	Co. G, 21st South Carolina Infantry	June 17, 1864, Petersburg, Virginia	Point Lookout, Maryland, transferred to Elmira Prison, NY, July 30, 1864	Exchanged March 3, 1865 on the James River, Virginia
Stubbs, James M. Private	19	April 20, 1861, Belle Roi., Virginia	Co. A, 26th Virginia Infantry	June 15, 1864, Near Petersburg, Virginia	Point Lookout, Maryland, transferred to Elmira Prison, NY, July 12, 1864	Exchanged March 14, 1865 at Boulware's Wharf on the James River, Virginia
Stubbs, Lawrence S. Corporal	18	April 20, 1861, Belle Roi., Virginia	Co. A, 26th Virginia Infantry	June 15, 1864, Near Petersburg, Virginia	Point Lookout, Maryland, transferred to Elmira Prison, NY, July 12, 1864	Oath of Allegiance July 3, 1865
Stubbs, Samuel F. Private	Unk	April 6, 1863, Bennettsville, South Carolina	Co. F, 21st South Carolina Infantry	January 15, 1865, Fort Fisher, North Carolina	February 1, 1865, Elmira Prison Camp, New York	Died February 11, 1865 of Typhoid-Pneumonia, Grave No. 2059
Stuckey, E. W. Private	28	January 1, 1862, Darlington District, South Carolina	Co. B, 21st South Carolina Infantry	June 24, 1864, Near Petersburg, Virginia	Point Lookout, Maryland, transferred to Elmira Prison, NY, August 18, 1864	Oath of Allegiance July 3, 1865

Name & Rank	Age	Enlisted	Regiment and State	Where Captured	Prison	Remarks
Stuckey, Jesse C. Private	23	February 14, 1862, Lillington, North Carolina	Co. H, 1st North Carolina Infantry	May 12, 1864, Spotsylvania Court House, Virginia	Point Lookout, Maryland, transferred to Elmira Prison, NY, August 6, 1864	Exchanged October 29, 1864, at Venus Point, Savannah River, GA.
Stukes, Alfred M. Private	Unk	January 29, 1863, Clarendon, South Carolina	Co. D, 4th South Carolina Cavalry	June 11, 1864, Trevilian Station, Louisa Court House, Virginia	Point Lookout, Maryland, transferred to Elmira Prison, NY, July 25, 1864	Died September 2, 1864 of Chronic Bronchitis, Grave No. 87
Stultz, Lafayette A. Private	Unk	June 22, 1861, Henry County, Virginia	Co. F, 42nd Virginia Infantry	May 12, 1864, Near Spotsylvania Court House, Virginia	Point Lookout, Maryland, transferred to Elmira Prison, NY, August 6, 1864	Died October 16, 1864 of Chronic Diarrhea, Grave No. 555. Regiment 24th Virginia on Headstone.
Stultz, Tyler C. Private	Unk	March 17, 1862, Henry County, Virginia	Co. F, 42nd Virginia Infantry	May 12, 1864, Near Spotsylvania Court House, Virginia	Point Lookout, Maryland, transferred to Elmira Prison, NY, August 6, 1864	Oath of Allegiance June 27, 1865
Stump, David Private	Unk	October 9, 1862, Tazewell County, Virginia	Co. J, 15th Virginia Cavalry	July 16, 1864, Loudoun County, Virginia	Old Capital Prison, Washington, DC, transferred to Elmira Prison, NY, July 23, 1864	Oath of Allegiance July 3, 1865
Stump, George T. Private	Unk	March 21, 1862, Floyd Court House, Virginia	Co. B, 42nd Virginia Infantry	May 12, 1864, Spotsylvania Court House, Virginia	Point Lookout, Maryland, transferred to Elmira Prison, NY, August 2, 1864	Died February 4, 1865 of Chronic Diarrhea, Grave No. 1888
Stump, James B. Sergeant	Unk	May 25, 1862, Floyd Court House, Virginia	Co. A, 42nd Virginia Infantry	May 12, 1864, Spotsylvania Court House, Virginia	Point Lookout, Maryland, transferred to Elmira Prison, NY, August 2, 1864	Oath of Allegiance June 19, 1865
Stunderfor, John N. Private	Unk	Unknown	Co. B, 15th Virginia Infantry	July 18, 1864, Snickers' Gap, Virginia	Old Capital Prison, Washington D. C. Transferred to Elmira Prison, NY, August 12, 1864	Oath of Allegiance July 3, 1865

Name & Rank	Age	Enlisted	Regiment and State	Where Captured	Prison	Remarks
Sturdivant, C. L. Private	Unk	May 4, 1864, Petersburg, Virginia	Co. A, 3rd Archer's Battalion, Virginia Reserves Infantry	June 9, 1864, Petersburg, Virginia	Point Lookout, Maryland, transferred to Elmira Prison, NY, July 12,1864	Exchanged October 29, 1864, at Venus Point, Savannah River, GA.
Sturdivant, Fabius Private	Unk	July 1, 1862, Raleigh, North Carolina	Co. I, 3rd North Carolina Cavalry	May 28, 1864, Hanover Junction, Virginia	Point Lookout, Maryland, transferred to Elmira Prison, NY, July 12,1864	Exchanged October 29, 1864, at Venus Point, Savannah River, GA.
Sturgeon, Hiram Private	Unk	August 15, 1864, Woodville, Mississippi	Co. E, Powers Mississippi Cavalry	October 8, 1864, A Woodville, Mississippi	New Orleans, Louisiana transferred to Elmira November 19, 1864.	Died April 5, 1865 of Pneumonia, Grave No. 2558. Headstone has 10th Battalion.
Sturgeon, Richard D. Private	Unk	July 14, 1862, Richland, South Carolina	Co. H, 7th Battalion South Carolina Infantry	May 16, 1864, Near Drury's Bluff, Virginia	Point Lookout, Maryland, transferred to Elmira Prison, NY, August 17, 1864	Died December 10, 1864 of Chronic Diarrhea, Grave No. 1055
Sturgill, James Private	Unk	December 25, 1863, Liberty Mills, Virginia	Co. B, 37th North Carolina Infantry	May 12, 1864, Spotsylvania Court House, Virginia	Point Lookout, Maryland, transferred to Elmira Prison, NY, August 12, 1864	Died March 19, 1865 of Pneumonia. No Grave in Woodlawn Cemetery, Elmira, NY.
Sturgill, Levi B. Private	24	September 15, 1861, Allegheny County, North Carolina	Co. K, 37th North Carolina Infantry	May 12, 1864, Spotsylvania Court House, Virginia	Point Lookout, Maryland, transferred to Elmira Prison, NY, August 12, 1864	Oath of Allegiance June 16, 1865
Sturkey, William Oscar Private	Unk	August 26, 1861, Camp Griffin, South Carolina	Co. B, Hampton Legion, South Carolina Infantry	June 14, 1864, St. Mary's Church, Virginia	Point Lookout, Maryland, transferred to Elmira Prison, NY, July 30, 1864	Oath of Allegiance July 3, 1865
Sturm, William G. Corporal	17	May 14, 1862, Zollicoffer, Tennessee	Co. F, 63rd Tennessee Infantry	June 17, 1864, Petersburg, Virginia	Point Lookout, Maryland, transferred to Elmira Prison, NY, July 30, 1864	Died October 10, 1864 of Pneumonia, Grave No. 677

Name & Rank	Age	Enlisted	Regiment and State	Where Captured	Prison	Remarks
Sturzenacker, Jacob

Private | Unk | March 24, 1864, Richmond, Virginia | Co. A, 6th Virginia Infantry | May 12, 1864, Spotsylvania Court House, Virginia | Point Lookout, Maryland, transferred to Elmira Prison, NY, July 25, 1864 | Oath of Allegiance May 29, 1865 |
| Stwin, Quinn

Private | 41 | Unknown | Co. D, Consolidated Crescent Louisiana Infantry | March 30, 1864, Near Pleasant Hill, Louisiana | New Orleans, Louisiana, Transferred to Elmira Prison, New York, November 19, 1864 | Oath of Allegiance May 29, 1865 |
| Styles, Nicholas

Corporal | Unk | March 13, 1863, Macon, Georgia | Co. B, 64th Georgia Infantry | June 17, 1864, Petersburg, Virginia | Point Lookout, Maryland, transferred to Elmira Prison, NY, July 25, 1864 | Oath of Allegiance May 20, 1865 |
| Sublett, T. C.

Private | Unk | February 10, 1864, Dublin, Virginia | Co. D, 5th Virginia Cavalry | May 11, 1864, Yellow Tavern, Hanover County, Virginia | Point Lookout, Maryland, transferred to Elmira Prison, NY, August 17, 1864 | Exchanged March 10, 1865 at Boulware's Wharf on the James River, Virginia |
| Sudduth, Albert O.

Private | 25 | April 24, 1861, Salem, Virginia | Co. H, 6th Virginia Cavalry | August 28, 1863, Farquire County, Virginia | Point Lookout, Maryland, transferred to Elmira Prison, NY, August 18, 1864 | Exchanged March 10, 1865 at Boulware's Wharf on the James River, Virginia |
| Sugart, William C.

Private | Unk | July 15, 1862, Raleigh, North Carolina | Co. D, 5th North Carolina Infantry | July 12, 1864, Near Washington, DC | Old Capital Prison, Washington, DC, transferred to Elmira Prison, NY, July 23, 1864 | Oath of Allegiance June 16, 1865 |
| Suggs, Isaiah Wilson

Private | 18 | February 25, 1864, Albemarle, North Carolina | Co. H, 14th North Carolina Infantry | May 12, 1864, Spotsylvania Court House, VA. Gunshot Wound Right Leg. Amputated Leg. | Old Capital Prison, Washington, DC transferred to Elmira Prison, NY, August 27, 1864 | Exchanged February 13, 1865 at Boulware's Wharf on the James River, Virginia |
| Suggs, James McKay

Private | 38 | December 18, 1862, Fort Anderson, Brunswick County, North Carolina | Co. H, 36th 2nd North Carolina Artillery | January 15, 1865, Fort Fisher, North Carolina | February 1, 1865, Elmira Prison Camp, New York | Died April 19, 1865 of Variola (Smallpox), Grave No. 1371 |

Name & Rank	Age	Enlisted	Regiment and State	Where Captured	Prison	Remarks
Suggs, John Private	Unk	January 24, 1864, Poplar Spring, Hall County, Georgia	Co. J, 24th Georgia infantry	August 16, 1864, Front Royal, Virginia	Old Capital Prison, Washington, DC transferred to Elmira Prison, NY, August 29, 1864	Oath of Allegiance July 7, 1865
Suit, William J. Private	40	August 17, 1863, Fort Branch, Martin County, North Carolina	Co. G, 40th Regiment, 3rd North Carolina Artillery	January 15, 1865, Fort Fisher, North Carolina	February 1, 1865, Elmira Prison Camp, New York	Exchanged February 20, 1865 at Boulware's or Cox Wharf on the James River, Virginia
Suit, William Riley Private	Unk	July 15, 1862, Camp Holmes, Raleigh, North Carolina	Co. D, 24th North Carolina Infantry	June 17, 1864, Petersburg, Virginia	Point Lookout, Maryland, transferred to Elmira Prison, NY, July 30, 1864	Oath of Allegiance July 7, 1865
Suiter, John W. Private	Unk	May 3, 1862, Bland County, Virginia	Co. D, 36th Virginia Infantry	July 8, 1864, Harper's Ferry, Virginia	Old Capital Prison, Washington, DC, transferred to Elmira Prison, NY, July 23, 1864	Died January 3, 1865 of Chronic Diarrhea, Grave No. 1506. Last Name Senter on Headstone.
Sullens, Andrew Private	23	June 20, 1861, Abingdon, Virginia	Co. B, 48th Virginia Infantry	May 12, 1864, Spotsylvania Court House, Virginia	Point Lookout, Maryland, transferred to Elmira Prison, NY, August 2, 1864	Died February 22, 1865 of Variola (Smallpox), Grave No. 2249
Sullivan, Adam Private	Unk	April 15, 1862, Wilmington, North Carolina	Co. C, 51st North Carolina Infantry	June 1, 1864, Cold Harbor, Virginia	Point Lookout, Maryland, transferred to Elmira Prison, NY, July 12, 1864	Transferred for Exchange 10/11/64. Died 10/18/64 of Consumption at Point Lookout, MD.
Sullivan, David Sergeant	Unk	February 18, 1864, In the Field, Virginia	Co. B, 41st Virginia Infantry	May 23, 1864, North Anna, Hanover Junction, Virginia	Point Lookout, Maryland, transferred to Elmira Prison, NY, July 25, 1864	Oath of Allegiance May 19, 1865
Sullivan, David C. Private	30	May 17, 1863, Camp Holmes, Raleigh, North Carolina	Co. D, 7th North Carolina Infantry	May 5, 1864, Wilderness, Virginia	Point Lookout, Maryland, transferred to Elmira Prison, NY, July 23, 1864	Oath of Allegiance May 29, 1865

Name & Rank	Age	Enlisted	Regiment and State	Where Captured	Prison	Remarks
Sullivan, Dennis L. Private	Unk	June 8, 1861, New Orleans, Louisiana	Co. K, 15th Louisiana Infantry	May 5, 1864, Wilderness, Virginia	Point Lookout, Maryland, transferred to Elmira Prison, NY, July 25, 1864	Exchanged February 13, 1865 at Boulware's wharf on the James River, Virginia
Sullivan, Ed Private	24	May 18, 1861, Greenville, Meriwether County, Georgia	Co. D, 8th Georgia Infantry	May 24, 1864, Hanover Junction, Virginia	Point Lookout, Maryland, transferred to Elmira Prison, NY, July 12, 1864	Oath of Allegiance June 14, 1865
Sullivan, Eugene Private	Unk	June 1, 1863, Coosa County, Alabama	Co. C, 61st Alabama Infantry	July 12, 1864, Near Washington, DC	Old Capital Prison, Washington, DC, transferred to Elmira Prison, NY, July 23, 1864	Oath of Allegiance May 15, 1865
Sullivan, John Private	Unk	November 16, 1863, Columbia, South Carolina	Co. H, 22nd South Carolina Infantry	July 30, 1864, Petersburg, Virginia	Point Lookout, Maryland, transferred to Elmira Prison, NY, August 12, 1864	Oath of Allegiance June 14, 1865
Sullivan, M. R. Private	Unk	July 2, 1863, Pocotaligo, South Carolina	Co. D, 4th South Carolina Cavalry	June 11, 1864, Trevilian Station, Louisa Court House, Virginia	Point Lookout, Maryland, transferred to Elmira Prison, NY, July 25, 1864	Transferred for Exchange 10/11/64. Died 11/19/64 of Chronic Diarrhea at US Army Hospital, Baltimore, MD.
Sullivan, Patrick Private	30	April 13, 1861, Wilmington, North Carolina	Co. A, 31st North Carolina Infantry	June 1, 1864, Gaines Farm, Virginia	Point Lookout, Maryland, transferred to Elmira Prison, NY, July 12, 1864	Exchanged October 29, 1864, at Venus Point, Savannah River, GA.
Sullivan, Richard T. Private	18	July 14, 1863, Fort Fisher, New Hanover County, North Carolina	Co. J, 36th Regiment, 2nd North Carolina Artillery	January 15, 1865, Fort Fisher, North Carolina	February 1, 1865, Elmira Prison Camp, New York	Died February 28, 1865 of Pneumonia, Grave No. 2144
Sullivan, Thomas Private	Unk	February 16, 1863, Atlanta, Georgia	Co. A, 64th Georgia Infantry	June 24, 1864, Petersburg, Virginia	Point Lookout, Maryland, transferred to Elmira Prison, NY, July 23, 1864	Oath of Allegiance May 17, 1865

Name & Rank	Age	Enlisted	Regiment and State	Where Captured	Prison	Remarks
Sullivan, W. J. Private	Unk	November 1, 1862, Charleston, South Carolina	Co. B, 27th South Carolina Infantry	June 24, 1864, Petersburg, Virginia	Point Lookout, Maryland, transferred to Elmira Prison, NY, July 23, 1864	Died March 4, 1865 of Diarrhea, Grave No. 1979
Sumerlin, Wily N. Private	Unk	March 20, 1864, Wilmington, North Carolina	Co. F, 10th Regiment, 1st North Carolina Artillery	January 15, 1865, Fort Fisher, North Carolina	February 1, 1865, Elmira Prison Camp, New York	Died March 20, 1865 of Diarrhea, Grave No. 1545
Summer, James B. Private	Unk	May 10, 1861, Grove Hill, Alabama	Co. J, 5th Alabama Infantry	May 12, 1864, Spotsylvania, Virginia	Old Capital Prison, Washington, DC, transferred to Elmira Prison, NY, July 23, 1864	Died April 4, 1865 of Chronic Diarrhea, Grave No. 2563
Summers, Caley A. Corporal	Unk	May 6, 1861, Grove Hill, Alabama	Co. I, 5th Alabama Infantry	May 20, 1864, Spotsylvania Court House, Virginia	Point Lookout, Maryland, transferred to Elmira Prison, NY, July 3, 1864	Exchanged March 10, 1865 at Boulware's Wharf on the James River, Virginia
Summers, John Private	Unk	June 21, 1863, Fetterman, Virginia	Co. A, 25th Virginia Infantry	May 5, 1864, Mine Run Wilderness, Virginia	Point Lookout, Maryland, transferred to Elmira Prison, NY, August 2, 1864	Died October 12, 1864 of Chronic Diarrhea, Grave No. 564
Summers, William Private	Unk	May 13, 1861, Fetterman, Virginia	Co. A, 25th Virginia Infantry	May 12, 1864, Spotsylvania Court House, Virginia	Point Lookout, Maryland, transferred to Elmira Prison, NY, August 2, 1864	Oath of Allegiance June 27, 1865
Summit, Heglar P. Private	21	September 2, 1861, Camp Fisher, North Carolina	Co. C, 28th North Carolina Infantry	May 12, 1864, Spotsylvania County Court House, Virginia	Point Lookout, Maryland, transferred to Elmira Prison, NY, August 14, 1864	Died November 16, 1864 of Chronic Diarrhea, Grave No. 960
Sumner, Aaron Private	Unk	May 25, 1862, Floyd Court House, Virginia	Co. B, 42nd Virginia Infantry	May 12, 1864, Spotsylvania Court House, Virginia	Point Lookout, Maryland, transferred to Elmira Prison, NY, August 2, 1864	Oath of Allegiance July 26, 1865
Sumner, J. J. Firemen	Unk	Unknown	Confederate States Navy	May 5, 1864, Albemarle Sound on Steamer CSS Bombshell	Point Lookout, Maryland, transferred to Elmira Prison, NY, August 17, 1864	Exchanged March 2, 1865 at Boulware's Wharf on the James River, Virginia

Name & Rank	Age	Enlisted	Regiment and State	Where Captured	Prison	Remarks
Sumner, Martin Private	26	June 17, 1861, Duplin County, North Carolina	Co. B, 3rd North Carolina Infantry	May 12, 1864, Near Spotsylvania Court House, Virginia	Point Lookout, Maryland, transferred to Elmira Prison, NY, August 14, 1864	Oath of Allegiance July 7, 1865
Sumner, Matthew Private	Unk	February 20, 1863, Albany, Georgia	Co. D, 64th Georgia Infantry	June 17, 1864, Petersburg, Virginia	Point Lookout, Maryland, transferred to Elmira Prison, NY, July 30, 1864	Died December 6, 1864 of Diarrhea, Grave No. 1017
Surrancy, Alfred H. Private	Unk	September 1, 1861, Reidsville, Tattnall County, Georgia	Co. B, 61st Georgia Infantry	May 12, 1864, Spotsylvania Court House, Virginia	Point Lookout, Maryland, transferred to Elmira Prison, NY, July 30, 1864	Oath of Allegiance June 30, 1865
Surratt, Josiah Private	16	March 25, 1862, Asheboro, North Carolina	Co. B, 52nd North Carolina Infantry	June 13, 1864, Near Gaines Mill, Virginia	Point Lookout, Maryland, transferred to Elmira Prison, NY, July 25, 1864	Oath of Allegiance May 19, 1865
Surrency, Samuel Private	Unk	September 1, 1861, Reidsville, Georgia	Co. K, 61st Georgia Infantry	July 6, 1864, Harper's Ferry, Virginia	Old Capital Prison, Washington, DC, transferred to Elmira Prison, NY, July 23, 1864	Exchanged February 20, 1865 at Boulware's or Cox Wharf on the James River, Virginia
Surrency, Wiley Private	Unk	January 17, 1864, Charlton County, Georgia	Co. G, 20th Battalion Georgia Cavalry	May 30, 1864, Old Church, Cold Harbor, Virginia	Point Lookout, Maryland, transferred to Elmira Prison, NY, July 12, 1864	Died March 30, 1865 of Pneumonia, Grave No. 2529
Suther, William F. Private	18	September 28, 1863, Concord, North Carolina	Co. A, 33rd North Carolina Infantry	May 6, 1864, Wilderness, Virginia	Point Lookout, Maryland, transferred to Elmira Prison, NY, August 14, 1864	Died October 13, 1864 of Typhoid-Pneumonia, Grave No. 705. Headstone has Name Suter.
Suther, William W. Private	Unk	April 4, 1862, Eatonton, Georgia	Co. G, 12th Georgia Infantry	May 10, 1864, Spotsylvania Court House, Virginia	Point Lookout, Maryland, transferred to Elmira Prison, NY, July 30, 1864	Oath of Allegiance June 19, 1865

Name & Rank	Age	Enlisted	Regiment and State	Where Captured	Prison	Remarks
Sutherland, John W. Private	Unk	July 1, 1861, Prince William County, Virginia	Co. B, 49th Virginia Infantry	November 26, 1864, Dumfries, Virginia	Old Capital Prison, Washington D. C. Transferred to Elmira Prison, NY, March 3, 1865.	Oath of Allegiance July 7, 1865
Suthers, James Private	Unk	February 2, 1863, Dublin, Virginia	Co. C, 51st Virginia Infantry	July 12, 1864, Near Washington, DC	Old Capital Prison, Washington, DC, transferred to Elmira Prison, NY, July 23, 1864	Died November 14, 1864 of Pleuro Pneumonia, Grave No. 800. Name Southers on Headstone.
Suttenfield, Thomas Private	Unk	Unknown	Co. A, 42nd Virginia Infantry	May 12, 1864, Spotsylvania Court House, Virginia	Point Lookout, Maryland, transferred to Elmira Prison, NY, August 2, 1864	Exchanged October 29, 1864, at Venus Point, Savannah River, GA.
Sutton, B. M. Private	Unk	June 17, 1863, Monticello, Florida	Co. K, 10th Florida Infantry	July 29, 1864, Petersburg, Virginia	Point Lookout, Maryland, transferred to Elmira Prison, NY, August 12, 1864	Died May 9, 1865 of Chronic Diarrhea, Grave No. 2783. Sutton, R. M. on Headstone.
Sutton, Bryan Private	Unk	January 3, 1863, Wilmington, North Carolina	Co. F, 10th Regiment, 1st North Carolina Artillery	January 15, 1865, Fort Fisher, North Carolina	February 1, 1865, Elmira Prison Camp, New York	Died March 6, 1865 of Pneumonia, Grave No. 2414
Sutton, John B. Private	40	July 23, 1861, Wilmington, North Carolina	Co. A, 18th North Carolina Infantry	May 12, 1864, Spotsylvania, Virginia	Point Lookout Prison Camp, Maryland. Transferred to Elmira Prison Camp, New York August 6, 1864	Died September 23, 1864 of Chronic Diarrhea, Grave No. 355
Sutton, John C. Private	18	June 10, 1863, Transferred from the Navy at Camp Holmes, near Raleigh, North Carolina	Co. G, 36th Regiment, 2nd North Carolina Artillery	January 15, 1865, Fort Fisher, North Carolina	February 1, 1865, Elmira Prison Camp, New York	Died April 16, 1865 of Pneumonia, Grave No. 2716
Sutton, Michael W. Private	17	March 5, 1862, Clinton, North Carolina	Co. B, 51st North Carolina Infantry	June 1, 1864, Cold Harbor, Virginia. Gunshot Wound of Back.	DeCamp General Hospital, David's Island New York Harbor.	Oath of Allegiance June 19, 1865

Name & Rank	Age	Enlisted	Regiment and State	Where Captured	Prison	Remarks
Sutton, Patterson F. Private	20	April 21, 1862, Guilford County, North Carolina	Co. A, 53rd North Carolina Infantry	June 10, 1864, Spotsylvania, Virginia	Point Lookout, Maryland, transferred to Elmira Prison, NY, July 25, 1864	Exchanged October 29, 1864, at Venus Point, Savannah River, GA.
Sutton, Sanford Sergeant	25	September 4, 1861, Camp Macon, North Carolina	Co. J, 8th North Carolina Infantry	June 1, 1864, Cold Harbor, Virginia	Point Lookout, Maryland, transferred to Elmira Prison, NY, July 12, 1864	Died January 4, 1865 of Chronic Diarrhea, Grave No. 1256
Sutton, Thomas E. Private	Unk	March 26, 1862, Dunnsville, Virginia	Co. C, 55th Virginia Infantry	June 3, 1864, Old Church, Cold Harbor, Virginia	Point Lookout, Maryland, transferred to Elmira Prison, NY, July 12, 1864	Oath of Allegiance July 3, 1865
Sutton, Thomas J. J. Private	31	July 18, 1861, Lumberton, North Carolina	Co. D, 18th North Carolina Infantry	May 6, 1864, Wilderness, Virginia	Point Lookout, Maryland, transferred to Elmira Prison, NY, August 6, 1864	Exchanged October 29, 1864, at Venus Point, Savannah River, GA.
Sutton, William B. Private	31	May 18, 1861, Lumberton, North Carolina	Co. D, 18th North Carolina Infantry	May 6, 1864, Wilderness, Virginia	Point Lookout, Maryland, transferred to Elmira Prison, NY, August 6, 1864	Exchanged October 29, 1864, at Venus Point, Savannah River, GA.
Sutton, William M. Private	28	July 23, 1862, North Carolina	Co. A, 3rd North Carolina Infantry	May 12, 1864, Near Spotsylvania County Court House, Virginia	Point Lookout, Maryland, transferred to Elmira Prison, NY, August 14, 1864	Oath of Allegiance June 21, 1865
Sutton, William S. Private	19	May 7, 1861, Asheville, North Carolina	Co. F, 16th North Carolina Infantry	May 10, 1864, Near Spotsylvania County Court House, Virginia	Point Lookout, Maryland, transferred to Elmira Prison, NY, August 14, 1864	Oath of Allegiance June 19, 1865
Swadley, James Private	Unk	May 18, 1861, Huntersville, Virginia	Co. I, 25th Virginia Infantry	May 12, 1864, Spotsylvania Court House, Virginia	Point Lookout, Maryland, transferred to Elmira Prison, NY, August 12, 1864	Died November 3, 1864 of Pneumonia, Grave No. 761

Name & Rank	Age	Enlisted	Regiment and State	Where Captured	Prison	Remarks
Swaim, Solomon D. Private	Unk	April 17, 1862, Yadkinville, North Carolina	Co. G, 44th North Carolina Infantry	May 12, 1864, Spotsylvania Court House, Virginia	Point Lookout, Maryland, transferred to Elmira Prison, NY, July 25, 1864	Died February 21, 1865 of Pneumonia, Grave No. 2304. Name Swann on Headstone.
Swain, William Private	40	July 23, 1861, Young's Crossroads, North Carolina	Co. D, 8th North Carolina Infantry	September 30, 1864, Chapman's Farm, Virginia	Old Capital Prison, Washington, DC, transferred to Elmira Prison, NY, December 17, 1864	Died January 9, 1865 of Pneumonia, Grave No. 1219
Swan, Henry Private	Unk	October 22, 1861, Camp Moore, Tennessee	Co. B, 1st Jackson's Tennessee Heavy Artillery	August 23, 1864, Fort Morgan, Alabama.	New Orleans, Louisiana transferred to Elmira Prison, NY, December 4, 1864.	Exchanged February 25, 1865 at Boulware's or Cox Wharf on the James River, Virginia
Swan, William D. Corporal	Unk	May 1, 1862, West View, Virginia	Co. B, 52nd Virginia Infantry	May 30, 1864, Mechanicsville, Virginia	Point Lookout, Maryland, transferred to Elmira Prison, NY, July 9, 1864	Oath of Allegiance June 14, 1865
Swank, T. W. Private	Unk	May 18, 1861, Rome, Georgia	Co. A, 8th Georgia Infantry	May 6, 1864, Wilderness, Virginia	Point Lookout, Maryland, transferred to Elmira Prison, NY, August 14, 1864	Oath of Allegiance May 29, 1865
Sweat, Andrew J. Private	Unk	March 1, 1862, Atlanta, Georgia	Co. F, 21st Georgia Infantry	July 16, 1864, Loudoun County, Virginia	Old Capital Prison, Washington, DC, transferred to Elmira Prison, NY, July 23, 1864	Died March 4, 1865 of Variola (Smallpox), Grave No. 1965. Name Swint on Headstone.
Sweat, Stephen S. Private	Unk	September 15, 1861, Florence, South Carolina	Co. C, 8th South Carolina Infantry	July 29, 1864, Petersburg, Virginia	Point Lookout, Maryland, transferred to Elmira Prison, NY, August 12, 1864	Exchanged February 20, 1865 at Boulware's or Cox Wharf on the James River, Virginia
Sweeney, Patrick Private	35	March 2, 1862, New Orleans, Louisiana	Co. G, 6th Louisiana Infantry	May 5, 1864, Wilderness, Virginia	Point Lookout, Maryland, transferred to Elmira Prison, NY, August 17, 1864	Oath of Allegiance May 19, 1865

Name & Rank	Age	Enlisted	Regiment and State	Where Captured	Prison	Remarks
Sweet, A. A. Private	Unk	Unknown	Co. B, 45th Georgia Infantry	May 6, 1864, Wilderness, Virginia	Point Lookout, Maryland, transferred to Elmira Prison, NY, August 14, 1864	Oath of Allegiance June 23, 1865
Sweet, Patrick H. Private	Unk	May 13, 1862, West Point, Virginia	Co. D, 53rd Virginia Infantry	May 30, 1864, King William County, Virginia	Point Lookout, Maryland, transferred to Elmira Prison, NY, July 12, 1864	Oath of Allegiance May 29, 1865
Swenney, D. H. Private	Unk	December 15, 1863, Bean Station, Tennessee	Co. B, 15th Alabama Infantry	May 6, 1864, Wilderness, Virginia	Point Lookout, Maryland, transferred to Elmira Prison, NY, August 17, 1864	Exchanged March 14, 1865 at Boulware's Wharf on the James River, Virginia
Swettman, Crawford Private	Unk	March 16, 1863, Atlanta, Georgia	Co. C, 64th Georgia Infantry	August 16, 1864, New Market, Virginia	Old Capital Prison, Washington, DC transferred to Elmira Prison, NY, August 27, 1864	Oath of Allegiance May 29, 1865
Swift, Worther T. Private	25	April 24, 1861, Frederick Hall, Virginia	Co. G, 23rd Virginia Infantry	May 12, 1864, Spotsylvania Court House, Virginia. Gunshot Wound Left Shoulder and Arm.	Old Capital Prison, Washington, DC transferred to Elmira Prison, NY, August 27, 1864	Exchanged March 2, 1865 at Akins Landing on the James River, Virginia
Swils, R. W. Private	Unk	Unknown	Co. B, 27th Mississippi Infantry	May 8, 1864, Wilderness, Virginia	Point Lookout, Maryland, transferred to Elmira Prison, NY, August 14, 1864	Oath of Allegiance June 16, 1865
Swimley, David M. Private	Unk	December 4, 1862, Guineas, Virginia	Co. D, 2nd Virginia Infantry	May 12, 1864, Near Spotsylvania Court House, Virginia	Point Lookout, Maryland, transferred to Elmira Prison, NY, August 6, 1864	Oath of Allegiance May 15, 1865
Swing, Kimsey Private	22	July 15, 1862, Raleigh, North Carolina	Co. E, 1st North Carolina Infantry	May 12, 1864, Spotsylvania Court House, Virginia	Point Lookout, Maryland, transferred to Elmira Prison, NY, August 6, 1864	Oath of Allegiance June 30, 1865

Name & Rank	Age	Enlisted	Regiment and State	Where Captured	Prison	Remarks
Swint, Andrew J. Private	Unk	February 13, 1863, Antioch, Georgia	Co. F, 21st Georgia Infantry	July 16, 1864, Loudoun County, Virginia	Old Capital Prison, Washington, DC, transferred to Elmira Prison, NY, July 23, 1864	Died March 4, 1865 of Variola (Smallpox), Grave No. 1965
Swint, John Private	Unk	February 13, 1863, Antioch, Georgia	Co. F, 21st Georgia Infantry	July 4, 1864, Harper's Ferry, Virginia	Old Capital Prison, Washington, DC, transferred to Elmira Prison, NY, July 23, 1864	Died January 18, 1865 of Chronic Diarrhea, Grave No. 1441
Swint, John G. Corporal	Unk	July 30, 1863, Chambers County, Alabama	Co. F, 61st Alabama Infantry	May 12, 1864, Spotsylvania Court House, Virginia	Point Lookout, Maryland, transferred to Elmira Prison, NY, July 30, 1864	Exchanged October 29, 1864, at Venus Point, Savannah River, GA.
Switzer, Barnes H. Private	Unk	March 5, 1861, Columbiana, Alabama	Co. C, 1st Battalion Alabama Artillery	August 23, 1864, Fort Morgan, Alabama	New Orleans, Louisiana transferred to Elmira Prison, NY, December 4, 1864.	Oath of Allegiance June 14, 1865
Sydenstricker John H. Corporal	Unk	July 9, 1861, Peterstown, Virginia	Co. D, 26th Battalion, Virginia Infantry	June 3, 1864, Gaines Farm Cold Harbor, Virginia	Point Lookout, Maryland, transferred to Elmira Prison, NY, July 17, 1864	Died February 6, 1864 of Variola (Smallpox) Grave No.1906
Sydnor, Dandridge Private	Unk	June 4, 1861, Warsaw, Virginia	Co. E, 40th Virginia Infantry	May 25, 1864, North Anna River, Virginia	Point Lookout, Maryland, transferred to Elmira Prison, NY, July 12, 1864	Exchanged February 20, 1865 at Boulware's or Cox Wharf on the James River, Virginia
Sykes, Edmund Private	28	May 1, 1862, Fort Fisher, New Hanover County, North Carolina	Co. C, 36th Regiment, 2nd North Carolina Artillery	January 15, 1865, Fort Fisher, North Carolina	February 1, 1865, Elmira Prison Camp, New York	Died March 3, 1865 of Chronic Diarrhea, Grave No. 1991
Sykes, Henry C. Private	20	September 2, 1861, Orange County, North Carolina	Co. G, 28th North Carolina Infantry	July 14, 1863, Falling Waters, Maryland	Point Lookout, Maryland, transferred to Elmira Prison, NY, August 18, 1864	Exchanged March 10, 1865. Died March 19, 1865 at Jackson Hospital, Richmond, VA.

Name & Rank	Age	Enlisted	Regiment and State	Where Captured	Prison	Remarks
Sykes, John F. Private	Unk	April 29, 1864, Jonesboro, Georgia	Co. D, 44th Georgia Infantry	July 16, 1864, Loudoun County, Virginia	Old Capital Prison, Washington, DC, transferred to Elmira Prison, NY, July 23, 1864	Oath of Allegiance June 17, 1865
Sylvester, William W. Private	Unk	May 5, 1862, Sumpter, Texas	Co. M, 1st Texas Infantry	May 22, 1864, North Anna, Virginia	Point Lookout, Maryland, transferred to Elmira Prison, NY, July 25, 1864	Oath of Allegiance June 14, 1865
Syphret, Obadiah J. Private	Unk	April 15, 1862, Orangeburg, South Carolina	Co. G, 25th South Carolina Infantry	January 15, 1865, Fort Fisher, North Carolina	February 1, 1865, Elmira Prison Camp, New York	Oath of Allegiance June 23, 1865
Szar, Andrew Private	20	July 31, 1861, New Orleans, Louisiana	1st Battalion Washington Artillery, Louisiana	June 22, 1864, Near Petersburg, Virginia	Point Lookout, Maryland, transferred to Elmira Prison, NY, July 25, 1864	Oath of Allegiance June 21, 1865

Name & Rank	Age	Enlisted	Regiment and State	Where Captured	Prison	Remarks
Tabler, Jesse Private	Unk	June 28, 1864, North Carolina	Co. K, 12th North Carolina Infantry	August 11, 1864, Winchester, Virginia	Old Capital Prison, Washington, DC transferred to Elmira Prison, NY, August 27, 1864	Died May 3, 1865 of Chronic Diarrhea, Grave No. 2752
Tabor, Andrew J. Private	Unk	July 9, 1861, Isabella, Worth County, Georgia	Co. 14th Georgia Infantry	May 12, 1864, Spotsylvania Court House, Virginia	Point Lookout, Maryland, transferred to Elmira Prison, NY, August 12, 1864	Oath of Allegiance June 23, 1865
Tabor, Jonathan D. Private	21	October 12, 1861, Camp Myers, Tennessee	Co. K, 25th Tennessee Infantry	May 16, 1864, Near Drury's Bluff, Virginia	Point Lookout, Maryland, transferred to Elmira Prison, NY, August 17, 1864	Exchanged February 25, 1865 at Boulware's or Cox Wharf on the James River, Virginia
Tabor, Thomas Private	45	January 8, 1863, Saluda, Virginia	Co. D, 24th Virginia Cavalry	May 13, 1864, Matthews County, Virginia	Point Lookout, Maryland, transferred to Elmira Prison, NY, July 23, 1864	Exchanged March 2, 1865 at Akins Landing on the James River, Virginia

Name & Rank	Age	Enlisted	Regiment and State	Where Captured	Prison	Remarks
Tackett, J. G. Private	24	July 15, 1862, South Grove, North Carolina	Co. H, 5th North Carolina Cavalry	May 20, 1864, Spotsylvania Court House, Virginia	Point Lookout, Maryland, transferred to Elmira Prison, NY, July 3, 1864	Died April 28, 1865 of Variola (Smallpox), Grave No. 2726
Tadlock, John W. Private	Unk	November 7, 1863, Raleigh, North Carolina	Co. B, 52nd North Carolina Infantry	May 12, 1864, Spotsylvania Court House, Virginia	Point Lookout, Maryland, transferred to Elmira Prison, NY, August 12, 1864	Oath of Allegiance May 29, 1865
Taff, Joseph D. Private	23	April 19, 1862, Riccoe's Bluff, Florida	Co. H, 5th Florida Infantry	May 12, 1864, Spotsylvania Court House, Virginia	Point Lookout, Maryland, transferred to Elmira Prison, NY, July 30, 1864	Transferred For Exchange October 11, 1864 to Point Lookout Prison Camp, MD. Died November 9, 1864 at Sea.
Taggart, R. A. Private	Unk	June 6, 1861, New Canton, Virginia	Co. C, 44th Virginia Infantry	May 12, 1864, Spotsylvania Court House, Virginia	Point Lookout, Maryland, transferred to Elmira Prison, NY, August 2,1864	Oath of Allegiance June 16, 1865
Talbert, Thomas J. Private	Unk	May 11, 1861, New Orleans, Louisiana	Co. A, 2nd Louisiana Infantry	May 20, 1864, Spotsylvania Court House, Virginia	Point Lookout, Maryland, transferred to Elmira Prison, NY, July 3, 1864	Transferred for Exchange 10/11/64. Died 10/21/64 at Point Lookout Prison Camp, MD.
Talley, Harley Private	22	August 5, 1861, Livingston, Overton County, Tennessee	Co. H, 25th Tennessee Infantry	May 16, 1864, Near Drury's Bluff, Virginia	Point Lookout, Maryland, transferred to Elmira Prison, NY, August 17, 1864	Died February 3, 1865 of Pneumonia, Grave No. 1746
Talley, Thomas G. Corporal	Unk	Unknown	Co. B, Hood's Battalion, Virginia Reserves	June 15, 1864, Petersburg, Virginia	Point Lookout, Maryland, transferred to Elmira Prison, NY, July 30, 1864	Transferred for Exchange 10/11/64. Died November 6, 1864 at Fort Monroe, VA.
Talley, William G. Private	18	October 7, 1862, Winchester, Virginia	Co. J, 12th Virginia Infantry	May 12, 1864, Spotsylvania Court House, Virginia. Gunshot Wound Right Thigh.	Old Capital Prison, Washington, DC transferred to Elmira Prison, NY, August 27, 1864	Died February 4, 1865 of General Debility, Grave No. 1899

Name & Rank	Age	Enlisted	Regiment and State	Where Captured	Prison	Remarks
Tallivast, Alex Private	Unk	January 15, 1863, Darlington, South Carolina	Co. B, 21st South Carolina Infantry	January 15, 1865, Fort Fisher, North Carolina	February 1, 1865, Elmira Prison Camp, New York	Died April 4, 1865 of Chronic Diarrhea, Grave No. 2556. Headstone has Tallavast, 20th South Carolina.
Tally, John W. R. Private	21	January 15, 1864, Selma, Alabama	Co. E, 1st Battalion Alabama Artillery	August 23, 1864, Fort Morgan, Alabama	Steam Press No. 4 New Orleans, Louisiana transferred to Elmira Prison, NY, October 8, 1864.	Exchanged 2/20/65. Died 2/28/65 Of Chronic Diarrhea at General Hospital Baltimore, MD
Tally, Stephen T. Private	Unk	May 28, 1861, Nashville, Tennessee	Co. C, 17th Tennessee Infantry	June 17, 1864, Petersburg, Virginia	Point Lookout, Maryland, transferred to Elmira Prison, NY, July 30, 1864	Oath of Allegiance April 1, 1865
Tally, Timothy A. Private	Unk	Unknown	Co. E, 1st Battalion Alabama Artillery	August 23, 1864, Fort Morgan, Alabama	Steam Press No. 4 New Orleans, Louisiana transferred to Elmira Prison, NY, October 8, 1864.	Died December 10, 1864 of Chronic Diarrhea, Grave No. 1043
Tally, William S. Private	25	March 6, 1863, Milton, North Carolina	Co. I, 45th North Carolina Infantry	May 10, 1864, Spotsylvania Court House, Virginia	Point Lookout, Maryland, transferred to Elmira Prison, NY, August 6, 1864	Oath of Allegiance June 12, 1865
Talton, A. J. Private	20	December 20, 1861, Chesterfield, South Carolina	Co. E, 21st South Carolina Infantry	January 15, 1865, Fort Fisher, North Carolina	February 1, 1865, Elmira Prison Camp, New York	Oath of Allegiance July 7, 1865
Tankersley, John Private	Unk	August 19, 1862, Chambers, Alabama	Co. F, 6th Alabama Infantry	May 20, 1864, Spotsylvania Court House, Virginia	Point Lookout, Maryland, transferred to Elmira Prison, NY, July 3, 1864	Died March 24, 1865 of Variola (Smallpox), Grave No. 2462
Tanner, Darius Private	30	September 4, 1862, Covington, Alabama	Co. C, 1st Battalion Alabama Artillery	August 23, 1864, Fort Morgan, Alabama	New Orleans, Louisiana transferred to Elmira Prison, NY, December 4, 1864.	Oath of Allegiance May 29, 1865

Name & Rank	Age	Enlisted	Regiment and State	Where Captured	Prison	Remarks
Tanner, George W. Private	18	October 28, 1861, Camp Hebert, Near Hampstead, Texas	Co. A, 12th Texas Cavalry	August 25, 1864, Bullets Bayou, Concordia Parish, Louisiana	New Orleans, Louisiana transferred to Elmira November 19, 1864.	Oath of Allegiance May 29, 1865
Tanner, Matthew Private	Unk	May 17, 1862, Orlando, Florida	Co. G, 8th Florida Infantry	May 6, 1864, Mine Run Wilderness, Virginia	Point Lookout, Maryland, transferred to Elmira Prison, NY, August 12, 1864	Exchanged October 29, 1864, at Venus Point, Savannah River, GA.
Tapscott, Samuel B. Private	24	April 30, 1861, Harper's Ferry, Virginia	Co. B, 2nd Virginia Infantry	May 12, 1864, Spotsylvania Court House, Virginia	Point Lookout, Maryland, transferred to Elmira Prison, NY, August 6, 1864	Transferred for Exchange 10/11/64. Died 11/3/64 of Unknown Causes at Fort Monroe, VA
Tarkington, Henry Z. Private	20	May 16, 1861, Columbia, North Carolina	Co. A, 32nd North Carolina Infantry	May 10, 1864, Near Mine Run Spotsylvania, Virginia	Point Lookout, Maryland, transferred to Elmira Prison, NY, August 6, 1864	Exchanged March 10, 1865 at Boulware's Wharf on the James River, Virginia
Tarpley, James W. Private	Unk	May 20, 1861, Nashville, Tennessee	Co. K, 7th Tennessee Infantry	May 2, 1864, Ely's Ford, Virginia	Point Lookout Prison Camp, Maryland. Transferred to Elmira Prison, August 17, 1864	Died January 13, 1865 of Typhoid-Pneumonia, Grave No. 1475. Headstone has R. Tarpley
Tarpley, R. B. 1st Sergeant	Unk	October 1, 1861, Nashville, Tennessee	Co. A, Jackson's 1st Regiment, Tennessee Heavy Artillery	August 23, 1864, Fort Morgan, Alabama	New Orleans, Louisiana transferred to Elmira Prison, NY, December 4, 1864.	Exchanged February 25, 1865 at Boulware's or Cox Wharf on the James River, Virginia
Tarras, P. H. Civilian	Unk	Unknown	Citizen of Louisiana	October 9, 1864, Kinssington, Louisiana	New Orleans, Louisiana transferred to Elmira November 19, 1864.	Oath of Allegiance December 15, 1864. Early Release per Lincoln's Proclamation, 12/8/1863.
Tart, Lee Sylvester Private	18	February 18, 1863, Fayetteville, North Carolina	Co. B, 56th North Carolina Infantry	June 18, 1864, Petersburg, Virginia	Point Lookout, Maryland, transferred to Elmira Prison, NY, July 30, 1864	Oath of Allegiance May 19, 1865

Name & Rank	Age	Enlisted	Regiment and State	Where Captured	Prison	Remarks
Tart, Samuel A. Private	Unk	August 30, 1862, Pike County, Alabama	Co. C, 6th Alabama Infantry	May 20, 1864, Spotsylvania Court House, Virginia	Point Lookout, Maryland, transferred to Elmira Prison, NY, July 3, 1864	Exchanged March 2, 1865 at Akins Landing on the James River, Virginia
Tate, George Corporal	24	July 22, 1861, Camp Moore, Louisiana	Co. D, 10th Louisiana Infantry	May 19, 1864, Spotsylvania, Virginia. Gunshot Wound Left Thigh and Right Hand.	Old Capital Prison, Washington, DC, transferred to Elmira Prison, NY, July 23, 1864	Exchanged February 25, 1865 at Boulware's or Cox Wharf on the James River, Virginia
Tate, James Private	39	May 4, 1861, Dobson, North Carolina	Co. A, 28th North Carolina Infantry	September 22, 1863, Near Liberty Mills, Near Madison Court House, Virginia	Point Lookout, Maryland, transferred to Elmira Prison, NY, August 18, 1864	Oath of Allegiance June 19, 1865. Refused to be Exchanged March 14, 1865.
Tate, James Private	Unk	July 19, 1861, Selma, Alabama	Co. C, 15th Virginia Cavalry	October 10, 1863, Rapidan River, Virginia	Point Lookout, Maryland, transferred to Elmira Prison, NY, July 25, 1864	Oath of Allegiance May 19, 1865
Tate, James B. Sergeant	Unk	January 1, 1862, Camp Hampton, Columbia, South Carolina	Co. H, 18th South Carolina Infantry	July 30, 1864, Petersburg, Virginia	Point Lookout, Maryland, transferred to Elmira Prison, NY, August 12, 1864	Exchanged October 29, 1864, at Venus Point, Savannah River, GA.
Tatman, H. Private	Unk	Unknown	Co. C, 18th Georgia Infantry	June 1, 1864, Cold Harbor, Virginia	Point Lookout, Maryland, transferred to Elmira Prison, NY, July 17, 1864	Transferred for Exchange October 11, 1864. No Further Information
Tatom, Alexander J. Private	30	December 12, 1862, Fort Anderson, Brunswick County, North Carolina	Co. H, 36th Regiment, 2nd North Carolina Artillery	January 15, 1865, Fort Fisher, North Carolina	February 1, 1865, Elmira Prison Camp, New York	Died March 13, 1865 of Variola (Smallpox), Grave No. 1832
Tatum, Charles J. Private	Unk	February 27, 1863, Camden, Arkansas	Co. E, 3rd Arkansas Infantry	May 12, 1864, Spotsylvania Court House, Virginia	Point Lookout, Maryland, transferred to Elmira Prison, NY, July 30, 1864	Exchanged February 25, 1865 at Boulware's or Cox Wharf on the James River, Virginia

Name & Rank	Age	Enlisted	Regiment and State	Where Captured	Prison	Remarks
Tatum, Silas E. Private	Unk	March 3, 1862, Dawson, Georgia	Co. N, 38th Georgia Infantry	July 12, 1864, Near Washington, DC	Old Capital Prison, Washington, DC, transferred to Elmira Prison, NY, July 23, 1864	Died May 20, 1865 of Pneumonia, Grave No. 2941
Taylor, A. J. Private	30	Unknown	Co. K, 40th Regiment, 3rd North Carolina Artillery	January 15, 1865, Fort Fisher, North Carolina	February 1, 1865, Elmira Prison Camp, New York	Died February 16, 1865 of Chronic Diarrhea, Grave No. 2208
Taylor, A. J. Corporal	Unk	July 26, 1861, Camp Jones, Virginia	Co. A, 1st Tennessee Infantry	July 14, 1863, Falling Waters, Virginia	Point Lookout, Maryland, transferred to Elmira Prison, NY, July 25, 1864	Died August 30, 1864 of Chronic Diarrhea. Grave No. 92
Taylor, Abram James Private	Unk	May 2, 1862, Cumberland County, North Carolina	Co. J, 51st North Carolina Infantry	June 1, 1864, Cold Harbor, Virginia	Point Lookout, Maryland, transferred to Elmira Prison, NY, July 12, 1864	Exchanged October 29, 1864, at Venus Point, Savannah River, GA.
Taylor, Albert Sergeant	Unk	October 13, 1861, Mobile, Alabama	Co. A, 21st Alabama Infantry	August 23, 1864, Fort Morgan, Alabama	Steam Press No. 4 New Orleans, Louisiana transferred to Elmira Prison, NY, October 8, 1864.	Oath of Allegiance June 21, 1865
Taylor, Alexander Private	Unk	August 1, 1863, Butler County, Alabama	Co. D, 61st Alabama Infantry	May 12, 1864, Spotsylvania, Virginia	Old Capital Prison, Washington, DC, transferred to Elmira Prison, NY, July 23, 1864	Died February 15, 1865 of Variola (Smallpox), Grave No. 2190
Taylor, Archibald B. Private	Unk	February 27, 1862, Monroe, Louisiana	Co. H, 12th Louisiana Infantry	May 16, 1863, Baker's Creek, Champion Hill, Mississippi	Point Lookout, Maryland, transferred to Elmira Prison, NY, August 18, 1864	Exchanged February 25, 1865 at Boulware's wharf on the James River, Virginia
Taylor, Blount Private	26	April 27, 1861, Snow Hill, North Carolina	Co. A, 3rd North Carolina Infantry	June 10, 1864, Spotsylvania Court House, Virginia	Point Lookout, Maryland, transferred to Elmira Prison, NY, July 25, 1864	Died July 4, 1865 of Variola (Smallpox), Grave No. 2835

Name & Rank	Age	Enlisted	Regiment and State	Where Captured	Prison	Remarks
Taylor, Cary Private	Unk	Unknown	Co. A, Captain Jones' Home Guard Florida	September 27, 1864, Marianna, Florida	New Orleans, Louisiana transferred to Elmira November 19, 1864.	Died December 27, 1864 of Variola (Smallpox), Grave No. 1301
Taylor, Charles A. Private	Unk	April 27, 1861, Oglethorpe, Macon County, Georgia	Co. J, 4th Georgia Infantry	May 10, 1864, Spotsylvania, Virginia. Gunshot Wound of Left Arm with Fracture of Humerus.	Old Capital Prison, Washington, DC, transferred to Elmira Prison, NY, December 17, 1864	Exchanged February 13, 1865 at Boulware's Wharf on the James River, Virginia
Taylor, Charles S. Private	Unk	July 2, 1861, Bethel Am., Virginia	Co. F, 50th Virginia Infantry	May 12, 1864, Spotsylvania Court House, Virginia	Point Lookout, Maryland, transferred to Elmira Prison, NY, August 2, 1864	Died March 4, 1865 of Diarrhea, Grave No. 1985. Headstone has 56th VA.
Taylor, Christopher Private	Unk	January 31, 1862, Allowed Gloucester Point, Virginia	Co. G, 22nd Battalion, Virginia Infantry	June 4, 1864, Cold Harbor, Virginia	Point Lookout, Maryland, transferred to Elmira Prison, NY, July 23, 1864	Oath of Allegiance May 29, 1865
Taylor, David C. Private	18	October 1, 1863, Sullivan's Island, South Carolina	Co. K, 8th North Carolina Infantry	June 1, 1864, Gaines Farm, Cold Harbor, Virginia	Point Lookout, Maryland, transferred to Elmira Prison, NY, July 12, 1864	Died December 4, 1864 of Chronic Diarrhea, Grave No. 879
Taylor, David D. Private	21	March 10, 1862, Cumberland County, North Carolina	Co. J, 51st North Carolina Infantry	June 1, 1864, Cold Harbor, Virginia	Point Lookout, Maryland, transferred to Elmira Prison, NY, July 12, 1864	Died March 4, 1865 of Typhoid Fever, Grave No. 2004
Taylor, David M. Sergeant	25	August 31, 1861, Lincolnton, North Carolina	Co. A, 34th North Carolina Infantry	May 6, 1864, Wilderness, Virginia	Point Lookout, Maryland, transferred to Elmira Prison, NY, August 14, 1864	Oath of Allegiance July 3, 1865
Taylor, G. W. Private	Unk	January 30, 1864, Wetumpka, Alabama	Co. F, 1st Battalion Alabama Artillery	August 23, 1864, Fort Morgan, Alabama	Steam Press No. 4 New Orleans, Louisiana transferred to Elmira Prison, NY, October 8, 1864.	Oath of Allegiance July 7, 1865

Name & Rank	Age	Enlisted	Regiment and State	Where Captured	Prison	Remarks
Taylor, George T. Sergeant	24	April 29, 1862, Tuscaloosa, Alabama	Co. A, 1st Battalion Alabama Artillery	August 23, 1864, Fort Morgan, Alabama	New Orleans, Louisiana transferred to Elmira Prison, NY, December 4, 1864.	Oath of Allegiance July 7, 1865
Taylor, Henderson B. Private	19	June 23, 1861, Camp Moore, Louisiana	Co. F, 8th Louisiana Infantry	June 2, 1864, Old Church, Cold Harbor, Virginia	Point Lookout, Maryland, transferred to Elmira Prison, NY, July 12, 1864	Exchanged February 25, 1865 at Boulware's or Cox Wharf on the James River, Virginia
Taylor, H. P. Private	Unk	June 30, 1862, Savannah, Georgia	Co. E, 7th Georgia Cavalry	June 11, 1864, Trevilian Station, Louisa Court House, Virginia	Point Lookout, Maryland, transferred to Elmira Prison, NY, July 12, 1864	Transferred for Exchange 10/11/64. Died 10/13/64 of Unknown Disease at US Army Hospital Baltimore, MD.
Taylor, Isaac J. Private	28	February 20, 1862, Fort Caswell, Brunswick County, North Carolina	Co. A, 36th Regiment, 2nd North Carolina Artillery	January 15, 1865, Fort Fisher, North Carolina	February 1, 1865, Elmira Prison Camp, New York	Died March 11, 1865 of Chronic Diarrhea, Grave No. 1861
Taylor, J. R. Private	Unk	Unknown	Co. F, 4th Virginia Cavalry	June 4, 1864, White Oak Swamp, Virginia	Point Lookout, Maryland, transferred to Elmira Prison, NY, July 12, 1864	Exchanged March 10, 1865 at Boulware's Wharf on the James River, Virginia
Taylor, Jacob Private	31	May 30, 1861, Weldon, North Carolina	Co. H, 5th North Carolina Infantry	May 10, 1864, Near Spotsylvania County Court House, Virginia	Point Lookout, Maryland, transferred to Elmira Prison, NY, August 14, 1864	Died October 1, 1864 of Erysipelas and Pneumonia, Grave No. 411
Taylor, James Post Ordinance Sergeant	Unk	Unknown	Captain Jackson's Co., 1st Tennessee Heavy Artillery	August 23, 1864, Fort Morgan, Alabama	New Orleans, Louisiana transferred to Elmira November 19, 1864.	Oath of Allegiance May 15, 1865
Taylor, James Private	Unk	May 1, 1862, White Sulfur Springs, Virginia	Co. C, 22nd Virginia Infantry	July 14, 1864, Frederick, Maryland	Old Capital Prison, Washington, DC, transferred to Elmira Prison, NY, July 23, 1864	Oath of Allegiance May 17, 1865

Name & Rank	Age	Enlisted	Regiment and State	Where Captured	Prison	Remarks
Taylor, James B. Private	Unk	April 4, 1862, Waynesville, Georgia	Co. A, 26th Georgia Infantry	May 6, 1864, Wilderness, Virginia	Point Lookout, Maryland, transferred to Elmira Prison, NY, August 14, 1864	Oath of Allegiance June 19, 1865
Taylor, James H. C. Private	20	April 27, 1861, Snow Hill, North Carolina	Co. A, 3rd North Carolina Infantry	May 12, 1864, Spotsylvania Court House, Virginia	Point Lookout, Maryland, transferred to Elmira Prison, NY, July 12, 1864	Oath of Allegiance June 12, 1865
Taylor, James R. Private	Unk	June 4, 1861, Salem, Virginia	Co. E, 42nd Virginia Infantry	May 12, 1864, Near Spotsylvania Court House, Virginia	Point Lookout, Maryland, transferred to Elmira Prison, NY, August 2, 1864	Oath of Allegiance June 30, 1865
Taylor, John Private	Unk	June 13, 1861, Lebanon, DeKalb County, Alabama	Co. E, 12th Alabama Infantry	July 14, 1864, Harper's Ferry, Virginia	Old Capital Prison, Washington, DC, transferred to Elmira Prison, NY, July 23, 1864	Oath of Allegiance May 17, 1865
Taylor, John R. Private	33	Unknown	Co. G, 19th Georgia Infantry	August 19, 1864, Weldon Railroad, Virginia. Gunshot Wound Right Thigh, Severe.	Old Capital Prison, Washington, DC, transferred to Elmira Prison, NY, December 17, 1864	Exchanged March 14, 1865 at Boulware's Wharf on the James River, Virginia
Taylor, Joseph D. Sergeant	28	June 24, 1861, Williamston, North Carolina	Co. H, 1st North Carolina Infantry	May 12, 1864, Spotsylvania Court House, Virginia	Point Lookout, Maryland, transferred to Elmira Prison, NY, August 6, 1864	Died March 24, 1865 of Variola (Smallpox), Grave No. 2446. Name John on Headstone.
Taylor, Joseph J. Sergeant	18	May 25, 1861, Wilson, North Carolina	Co. E, 7th North Carolina Infantry	May 6, 1864, Wilderness, Virginia	Point Lookout, Maryland, transferred to Elmira Prison, NY, August 14, 1864	Died September 29, 1864 of Typhoid Fever, Grave No. 429
Taylor, Joy S. Sergeant	Sgt	June 20, 1862, Greene County, North Carolina	Co. E, 3rd North Carolina Cavalry	May 31, 1864, Hanover Court House, Virginia	Point Lookout, Maryland, transferred to Elmira Prison, NY, July 6, 1864	Died December 25, 1864 of Pneumonia, Grave No. 1111

Name & Rank	Age	Enlisted	Regiment and State	Where Captured	Prison	Remarks
Taylor, Lockwood Alison Private	22	May 11, 1861, New Orleans, Louisiana	Co. D, 2nd Louisiana Infantry	May 12, 1864, Spotsylvania, Virginia	Old Capital Prison, Washington, DC, transferred to Elmira Prison, NY, July 23, 1864	Exchanged March 10, 1865 at Boulware's Wharf on the James River, Virginia
Taylor, Marshall Private	Unk	March 11, 1864, Liberty Mills, Virginia	Co. A, 37th North Carolina Infantry	May 12, 1864, Spotsylvania Court House, Virginia	Point Lookout, Maryland, transferred to Elmira Prison, NY, August 12, 1864	Died August 29, 1864 of Pneumonia, Grave No. 52
Taylor, Michael J. Private	Unk	March 4, 1862, Crawfordsville, Georgia	Co. D, 49th Georgia Infantry	May 6, 1864, Mine Run Wilderness, Virginia	Point Lookout, Maryland, transferred to Elmira Prison, NY, August 14, 1864	Exchanged October 29, 1864, at Venus Point, Savannah River, GA.
Taylor, Middleton E. Private	Unk	April 11, 1862, Coles Island, South Carolina	Co. F, 25th South Carolina Infantry	January 15, 1865, Fort Fisher, North Carolina	February 1, 1865, Elmira Prison Camp, New York	Exchanged February 20, 1865 at Boulware's or Cox Wharf on the James River, Virginia
Taylor, P. H. Private	Unk	April 11, 1862, Coles Island, South Carolina	Co. F, 25th South Carolina Infantry	January 15, 1865, Fort Fisher, North Carolina	February 1, 1865, Elmira Prison Camp, New York	Oath of Allegiance July 7, 1865
Taylor, Richard Private	30	November 6, 1861, Washington, North Carolina	Co. B, 61st North Carolina Infantry	June 16, 1864, Near Petersburg, Virginia	Point Lookout, Maryland, transferred to Elmira Prison, NY, July 12, 1864	Oath of Allegiance June 14, 1865
Taylor, Robert E. Private	Unk	February 19, 1862, Entrenched Camp, Virginia	Co. E, 6th Virginia Infantry	May 12, 1864, Spotsylvania Court House, Virginia	Point Lookout, Maryland, transferred to Elmira Prison, NY, August 6, 1864	Died September 19, 1864 of Chronic Diarrhea. No Grave in Woodlawn Cemetery.
Taylor, Robert M. Private	Unk	July 18, 1861, Urbanna, Virginia	Co. C, 55th Virginia Infantry	May 5, 1864, Wilderness, Virginia	Point Lookout, Maryland, transferred to Elmira Prison, NY, August 14, 1864	Exchanged March 10, 1865 at Boulware's Wharf on the James River, Virginia

Name & Rank	Age	Enlisted	Regiment and State	Where Captured	Prison	Remarks
Taylor, Rufus Private	22	August 27, 1863, Brandy Station, Virginia	Co. F, 7th Virginia Cavalry	September 14, 1863, Near Culpepper, Virginia	Point Lookout, Maryland, transferred to Elmira Prison, NY, August 18, 1864	Exchanged March 10, 1865 at Boulware's Wharf on the James River, Virginia
Taylor, S. L. Private	Unk	July 27, 1861, New Orleans, Louisiana	Co. A, 14th Louisiana Infantry	May 5, 1864, Wilderness, Virginia	Point Lookout, Maryland, transferred to Elmira Prison, NY, July 25, 1864	Exchanged February 25, 1865 at Boulware's or Cox Wharf on the James River, Virginia
Taylor, S. P. Private	Unk	November 22, 1863, Jasper, Alabama	Co. D, 8th Alabama Infantry	May 24, 1864, Hanover Junction, Virginia	Point Lookout, Maryland, transferred to Elmira Prison, NY, July 12, 1864	Died August 20, 1864 of Chronic Diarrhea, Grave No. 115
Taylor, Samuel W. Private	Unk	February 26, 1863, Atlanta, Georgia	Co. K, 64th Georgia Infantry	August 16, 1864, New Market, Virginia	Old Capital Prison, Washington, DC transferred to Elmira Prison, NY, August 27, 1864	Died November 12, 1864 of Chronic Diarrhea, Grave No. 820
Taylor, Theophilus E. Private	28	May 13, 1862, Goldsboro, North Carolina	Co. A, 3rd North Carolina Infantry	May 12, 1864, Near Spotsylvania Court House, Virginia	Point Lookout, Maryland, transferred to Elmira Prison, NY, August 14, 1864	Oath of Allegiance June 27, 1865
Taylor, W. C. Private	Unk	Unable to Find Soldier's Record	Co. A, 34th Texas Cavalry	August 25, 1864, Near Morganza, Louisiana	New Orleans, Louisiana transferred to Elmira November 19, 1864.	Died February 26, 1865 of Chronic Diarrhea, Grave No. 2295
Taylor, W. J. Private	18	July 17, 1861, Ranalesburg, North Carolina	Co. B 13th North Carolina Infantry	May 20, 1864, Spotsylvania Court House, Virginia	Point Lookout, Maryland, transferred to Elmira Prison, NY, July 3, 1864	Oath of Allegiance May 27, 1865
Taylor, William Private	Unk	Unknown	Co. B, 1st Jackson's Tennessee Heavy Artillery	August 23, 1864, Fort Morgan, Alabama.	New Orleans, Louisiana transferred to Elmira Prison, NY, December 4, 1864.	Oath of Allegiance May 15, 1865

Name & Rank	Age	Enlisted	Regiment and State	Where Captured	Prison	Remarks
Taylor, William Private	26	July 24, 1861, Pitt County, North Carolina	Co. G, 8th North Carolina Infantry	May 31, 1864, Cold Harbor, Virginia	Point Lookout, Maryland, transferred to Elmira Prison, NY, July 12, 1864	Died June 2, 1865 of Pneumonia Grave No. 2902
Taylor, William Private	Unk	May 1, 1863, Russell County, Virginia	Co. E, 21st Virginia Cavalry	October 11, 1864, New Market, Virginia	Old Capital Prison, Washington, DC, transferred to Elmira Prison, NY, December 17, 1864	Oath of Allegiance May 17, 1865
Taylor, William L. Private	44	February 14, 1864, Taylor Springs, Virginia	Co. K, 47th Virginia Infantry	May 6, 1864, Wilderness, Virginia	Point Lookout, Maryland, transferred to Elmira Prison, NY, July 23, 1864	Oath of Allegiance May 17, 1865
Taylor, William P. Private	Unk	June 4, 1861, Salem, Virginia	Co. E, 42nd Virginia Infantry	May 12, 1864, Near Spotsylvania Court House, Virginia	Point Lookout, Maryland, transferred to Elmira Prison, NY, August 2, 1864	Exchanged February 20, 1865 at Boulware's or Cox Wharf on the James River, Virginia
Taylor, William W. Private	Unk	February 1, 1863, Choctaw Bluff, Alabama	Co. A, 21st Alabama Infantry	August 23, 1864, Fort Morgan, Alabama	New Orleans, Louisiana. Transferred to Elmira Prison Camp, NY, October 8, 1864	Died March 10, 1865 of Diarrhea, Grave No. 1858
Taylor, Wilson J. Private	Unk	August 6, 1861, Bethlehem Church, Virginia	Co. E, 6th Virginia Infantry	July 30, 1864, Petersburg, Virginia	Point Lookout, Maryland, transferred to Elmira Prison, NY, August 12, 1864	Oath of Allegiance July 3, 1865
Taylor, Z. F. Private	Unk	May 17, 1862, Georgia	Co. F, 3rd Battalion Georgia Sharp Shooters	August 16, 1864, Front Royal, Virginia	Old Capital Prison, Washington, DC transferred to Elmira Prison, NY, August 29, 1864	Exchanged March 10, 1865 at Boulware's Wharf on the James River, Virginia
Teachey, William Private	17	March 15, 1862, Wilmington, North Carolina	Co. G, 51st North Carolina Infantry	June 3, 1864, Gaines Mill Cold Harbor, Virginia	Point Lookout, Maryland, transferred to Elmira Prison, NY, July 12, 1864	Died August 15, 1864 of Remittent Fever, Grave No. 23

Name & Rank	Age	Enlisted	Regiment and State	Where Captured	Prison	Remarks
Teaford, Jacob P. S. Corporal	Unk	July 6, 1861, Rich Mountain, Virginia	Co. H, 25th Virginia Infantry	May 5, 1864, Wilderness, Virginia	Point Lookout, Maryland, transferred to Elmira Prison, NY, August 14, 1864	Oath of Allegiance June 14, 1865
Teaford, John H. Private	Unk	July 6, 1861, Rich Mountain, Virginia	Co. F, 25th Virginia Infantry	May 5, 1864, Wilderness, Virginia	Point Lookout, Maryland, transferred to Elmira Prison, NY, August 17, 1864	Died September 25, 1864 of Chronic Diarrhea, Grave No. 362
Teague, Andrew J. Private	33	August 15, 1862, Statesville, North Carolina	Co. E, 37th North Carolina Infantry	May 12, 1864, Spotsylvania Court House, Virginia	Point Lookout, Maryland, transferred to Elmira Prison, NY, July 25, 1864	Died April 25, 1865 of Chronic Diarrhea, Grave No. 1420
Teague, M. M. Private	Unk	December 28, 1862, Talladega, Alabama	Jeff Davis Alabama Artillery	May 5, 1864, Wilderness, Virginia	Point Lookout, Maryland, transferred to Elmira Prison, NY, August 17, 1864	Oath of Allegiance May 29, 1865
Teague, O. S. Private	Unk	September 20, 1862, Randolph, Alabama	Jeff Davis Alabama Artillery	May 5, 1864, Wilderness, Virginia	Point Lookout, Maryland, transferred to Elmira Prison, NY, August 17, 1864	Died November 21, 1864 of Chronic Diarrhea, Grave No. 933
Teague, William C. Private	Unk	August 18, 1863, Laurens County Court House, South Carolina	Co. E, 6th South Carolina Cavalry	July 30, 1864, Lee's Mill, Petersburg, Virginia	Point Lookout, Maryland, transferred to Elmira Prison, NY, August 12, 1864	Died February 1, 1865 of Chronic Diarrhea, Grave No. 1769
Teal, W. G. Private	Unk	January 24, 1864, Chesterfield, South Carolina	Co. D, 21st South Carolina Infantry	January 15, 1865, Fort Fisher, North Carolina	February 1, 1865, Elmira Prison Camp, New York	Died April 8, 1865 of Pneumonia, Grave No. 2646. Headstone has G. W. Teel.
Teal, William E. Private	Unk	July 15, 1862, Raleigh, North Carolina	Co. A, 3rd North Carolina Infantry	May 12, 1864, Near Spotsylvania Court House, Virginia	Point Lookout, Maryland, transferred to Elmira Prison, NY, August 14, 1864	Exchanged October 29, 1864, at Venus Point, Savannah River, GA.

Name & Rank	Age	Enlisted	Regiment and State	Where Captured	Prison	Remarks
Templet, A. Private	Unk	Unknown	Co. A, Ogden's Battalion Louisiana Cavalry	September 17, 1864, Greenville Springs, Near East Baton Rouge, Louisiana	New Orleans, Louisiana transferred to Elmira November 19, 1864.	Exchanged February 25, 1865 at Boulware's or Cox Wharf on the James River, Virginia
Templeton, John C. Private	25	August 1, 1861, Waynesboro, Georgia	Co. E, Cobb's Legion Georgia	August 16, 1864, Front Royal, Virginia	Old Capital Prison, Washington, DC transferred to Elmira Prison, NY, August 29, 1864	Oath of Allegiance June 14, 1865
Templin, William J. Private	20	July 23, 1861, Selma, Alabama	Jeff Davis Alabama Artillery	May 5, 1864, Wilderness, Virginia	Point Lookout, Maryland, transferred to Elmira Prison, NY, August 17, 1864	Escaped October 27, 1864 by Tunneling Under Fence.
Terrell, John W. Private	24	July 15, 1861, Waynesboro, Virginia	Co. B, 52nd Virginia Infantry	May 29, 1864, Cold Harbor, Virginia. Gunshot Wound to Right Thigh.	Old Capital Prison, Washington, DC, transferred to Elmira Prison, NY, July 23, 1864	Exchanged February 20, 1865 at Boulware's or Cox Wharf on the James River, Virginia
Terrell, Solomon T. Private	Unk	Unknown	Co. B, 1st Jackson's Tennessee Heavy Artillery	August 23, 1864, Fort Morgan, Alabama.	New Orleans, Louisiana transferred to Elmira Prison, NY, December 4, 1864.	Exchanged February 13, 1865 at Boulware's wharf on the James River, Virginia
Terrell, William A. Private	20	August 20, 1862, Stevensburg, Virginia	Co. I, 3rd Virginia Cavalry	May 8, 1864, Spotsylvania, Virginia, Contusion Right Temple.	Old Capital Prison, Washington, DC, transferred to Elmira Prison, NY, July 23, 1864	Exchanged March 10, 1865 at Boulware's Wharf on the James River, Virginia
Terrell, William M. Sergeant	Unk	August 24, 1861, Habersham County, Georgia	Co. H, 24th Georgia Infantry	June 3, 1864, Gaines Mill Cold Harbor, Virginia	Point Lookout, Maryland, transferred to Elmira Prison, NY, July 12, 1864	Exchanged March 14, 1865 at Boulware's Wharf on the James River, Virginia
Terril, G. Calvin Private	Unk	April 18, 1861, Harrisonburg, Virginia	Co. D, 10th Virginia Infantry	May 12, 1864, Spotsylvania Court House, Virginia	Point Lookout, Maryland, transferred to Elmira Prison, NY, August 2, 1864	Oath of Allegiance June 27, 1865

Name & Rank	Age	Enlisted	Regiment and State	Where Captured	Prison	Remarks
Terrill, A. N. Private	Unk	February 13, 1863, Camp Prichard, South Carolina	Co. H, 4th South Carolina Cavalry	June 11, 1864, Trevilian Station, Louisa Court House, Virginia	Point Lookout, Maryland, transferred to Elmira Prison, NY, July 25, 1864	Exchanged March 14, 1865 at Boulware's Wharf on the James River, Virginia
Terry, Andrew P. Private	18	February 23, 1863, Livingston, Overton County, Tennessee	Co. J, 25th Tennessee Infantry	May 16, 1864, Near Drury's Bluff, Virginia	Point Lookout, Maryland, transferred to Elmira Prison, NY, August 17, 1864	Exchanged February 13, 1865 at Boulware's wharf on the James River, Virginia
Terry, Charles M. D. Corporal	23	May 25, 1861, Marshall County, Mississippi	Co. J, 19th Mississippi Infantry	May 15, 1864, Spotsylvania, Virginia. Gunshot Wound Left Thigh.	Old Capital Prison, Washington, DC, transferred to Elmira Prison, NY, July 23, 1864	Exchanged October 29, 1864, at Venus Point, Savannah River, GA.
Terry, E. S. Private	Unk	November 15, 1862, Shelbyville, Tennessee	Co. A, 17th Tennessee Infantry	June 17, 1864, Petersburg, Virginia	Point Lookout, Maryland, transferred to Elmira Prison, NY, July 30, 1864	Exchanged February 25, 1865 at Boulware's or Cox Wharf on the James River, Virginia
Terry, George W. Corporal	21	February 6, 1862, Williamsburg, South Carolina	Co. K, 25th South Carolina Infantry	January 15, 1865, Fort Fisher, North Carolina	February 1, 1865, Elmira Prison Camp, New York	Oath of Allegiance July 11, 1865
Terry, Horton Private	Unk	September 4, 1862, Covington, Alabama	Co. E, 1st Battalion Alabama Artillery	August 23, 1864, Fort Morgan, Alabama	Steam Press No. 4 New Orleans, Louisiana transferred to Elmira Prison, NY, October 8, 1864.	Died November 13, 1864 of Chronic Diarrhea, Grave No. 815
Terry, John C. Private	Unk	August 23, 1861, Camp Trousdale, Tennessee	Co. H, 23rd Tennessee Infantry	June 17, 1864, Petersburg, Virginia	Point Lookout, Maryland, transferred to Elmira Prison, NY, July 30, 1864	Exchanged February 13, 1865 at Boulware's wharf on the James River, Virginia
Terry, Joseph Private	Unk	March 10, 1862, Halifax, Virginia	Co. G, 6th Virginia Cavalry	May 11, 1864, Yellow Tavern, Hanover County, Virginia	Point Lookout, Maryland, transferred to Elmira Prison, NY, August 17, 1864	Exchanged March 10, 1865 at Boulware's Wharf on the James River, Virginia

Name & Rank	Age	Enlisted	Regiment and State	Where Captured	Prison	Remarks
Terry, Samuel B. Private	21	July 15, 1861, Lee County, Virginia	Co. G, 48th Virginia Infantry	June 10, 1864, Spotsylvania Court House, Virginia	Point Lookout, Maryland, transferred to Elmira Prison, NY, July 25, 1864	Oath of Allegiance July 11, 1865
Terry, Thomas D. Private	27	June 2, 1861, Corinth, Mississippi	Co. G, 6th Alabama Infantry	May 20, 1864, Spotsylvania Court House, Virginia	Point Lookout, Maryland, transferred to Elmira Prison, NY, July 3, 1864	Died February 14, 1865 of Pneumonia, Grave No. 2061
Tesh, James Corporal	21	March 20, 1862, Forsyth County, North Carolina	Co. D, 53rd North Carolina Infantry	May 20, 1864, Spotsylvania Court House, Virginia	Point Lookout, Maryland, transferred to Elmira Prison, NY, July 6, 1864	Oath of Allegiance May 29, 1865
Tesh, Jacob Private	19	May 8, 1861, Lexington, North Carolina	Co. A, 21st North Carolina Infantry	August 22, 1864, Charlestown, Virginia	Old Capital Prison, Washington, DC transferred to Elmira Prison, NY, August 29, 1864	Oath of Allegiance June 21, 1865
Tew, Alexander Private	Unk	May 9, 1862, New Hanover County, North Carolina	Co. I, 51st North Carolina Infantry	June 1, 1864, Cold Harbor, Virginia	Point Lookout, Maryland, transferred to Elmira Prison, NY, July 12, 1864	Died November 2, 1864 of Chronic Diarrhea, Grave No. 845
Tew, Daniel C. Private	16	April 7, 1862, Cumberland County, North Carolina	Co. I, 51st North Carolina Infantry	May 31, 1864, Cold Harbor, Virginia	Point Lookout, Maryland, transferred to Elmira Prison, NY, July 12, 1864	Oath of Allegiance June 21, 1865
Tew, Jackson Private	18	April 21, 1862, Cumberland County, North Carolina	Co. J, 51st North Carolina Infantry	June 1, 1864, Cold Harbor, Virginia	Point Lookout, Maryland, transferred to Elmira Prison, NY, July 12, 1864	Died October 28, 1864 of Pneumonia, Grave No. 722
Tew, James Martin Private	Unk	May 9, 1862, New Hanover County, North Carolina	Co. I, 51st North Carolina Infantry	June 1, 1864, Cold Harbor, Virginia	Point Lookout, Maryland, transferred to Elmira Prison, NY, July 12, 1864	Died December 2, 1864 of Rheumatism Cardilis, Grave No. 891

Name & Rank	Age	Enlisted	Regiment and State	Where Captured	Prison	Remarks
Tew, John R. Private	25	April 6, 1862, Cumberland County, North Carolina	Co. J, 51st North Carolina Infantry	June 1, 1864, Cold Harbor, Virginia	Point Lookout, Maryland, transferred to Elmira Prison, NY, July 12, 1864	Exchanged March 2, 1865 at Akins Landing on the James River, Virginia
Tew, Lemick J. Private	23	April 1, 1862, Cumberland County, North Carolina	Co. I, 51st North Carolina Infantry	June 1, 1864, Cold Harbor, Virginia	Point Lookout, Maryland, transferred to Elmira Prison, NY, July 12, 1864	Exchanged October 29, 1864, at Venus Point, Savannah River, GA.
Thacker, Elias A. Private	Unk	May 1, 1862, Richmond, Virginia	Sturdivant's Co. A, Virginia Light Artillery	June 15, 1864, Petersburg, Virginia	Point Lookout, Maryland, transferred to Elmira Prison, NY, July 12, 1864	Oath of Allegiance May 8, 1865
Thacker, James A. Sergeant	Unk	June 15, 1861, Buena Vista, Georgia	Co. K, 12th Georgia Infantry	May 10, 1864, Spotsylvania Court House, Virginia	Point Lookout, Maryland, transferred to Elmira Prison, NY, July 25, 1864	Oath of Allegiance June 27, 1865
Thacker, S. D. Private	Unk	January 1, 1863, Porter's Precinct, Virginia	Co. B, 15th Virginia Cavalry	September 14, 1863, Near Culpepper, Virginia	Point Lookout, Maryland, transferred to Elmira Prison, NY, August 18, 1864	Exchanged March 10, 1865 at Boulware's Wharf on the James River, Virginia
Thaggard, Amos Jerome Private	30	May 6, 1862, Elizabethtown, Bladen County, North Carolina	Co. K, 40th Regiment, 3rd North Carolina Artillery	January 15, 1865, Fort Fisher, North Carolina	February 1, 1865, Elmira Prison Camp, New York	Exchanged March 2, 1865 at Akins Landing on the James River, Virginia
Thaggard, James B. Private	35	March 15, 1863, Fort Fisher, Hanover County, North Carolina	Co. C, 36th Regiment, 2nd North Carolina Artillery	January 15, 1865, Fort Fisher, North Carolina	February 1, 1865, Elmira Prison Camp, New York	Oath of Allegiance June 12, 1865. Died June 27, 1865 of Diarrhea at US Army General Hospital, Fort Monroe, VA.
Thally, David J. Private	21	April 16, 1862, Old Brunswick Town, North Carolina	Co. G, 36th Regiment, 2nd North Carolina Artillery	January 15, 1865, Fort Fisher, North Carolina	February 1, 1865, Elmira Prison Camp, New York	Exchanged 2/20/65. Died 4/9/65 of Bronchitis at Confederate States Hospital, No. 11, Charlotte, NC

Name & Rank	Age	Enlisted	Regiment and State	Where Captured	Prison	Remarks
Tharp, Isaac T. Private	Unk	October 22, 1863, Wilmington, North Carolina	Co. K, 42nd North Carolina Infantry	June 3, 1864, Gaines Farm, Cold Harbor, Virginia	Point Lookout, Maryland, transferred to Elmira Prison, NY, July 12, 1864	Exchanged October 29, 1864, at Venus Point, Savannah River, GA.
Tharp, James Corporal	21	April 16, 1862, Old Brunswick Town, North Carolina	Co. A, 36th Regiment, 2nd North Carolina Artillery	January 15, 1865, Fort Fisher, North Carolina	February 1, 1865, Elmira Prison Camp, New York	Oath of Allegiance July 7, 1865
Thaxton, William R. Corporal	18	July 9, 1861, Jackson, Georgia	Co. J, 14th Georgia Infantry	May 12, 1864, Spotsylvania, Virginia. Gunshot Wound Face, Fracture Lower Jaw.	Old Capital Prison, Washington, DC, transferred to Elmira Prison, NY, December 17, 1864	Exchanged February 13, 1865 at Boulware's Wharf on the James River, Virginia
Thigpen, Bythel Private	26	June 11, 1861, Duplin County, North Carolina	Co. B, 3rd North Carolina Infantry	May 12, 1864, Near Spotsylvania Court House, Virginia	Point Lookout, Maryland, transferred to Elmira Prison, NY, August 14, 1864	Died April 19, 1865 of General Debility, Grave No. 1366
Thomas, A. M. Private	28	Unknown	Co. E, 37th Virginia Infantry	May 6, 1864, Wilderness, Virginia	Point Lookout, Maryland, transferred to Elmira Prison, NY, July 23, 1864	Oath of Allegiance March 15, 1864. Early Release per Lincoln's Proclamation, 12/8/1863.
Thomas, Charles W. Private	Unk	Unknown	Co. G, 25th North Carolina Infantry	May 12, 1864, Spotsylvania, Virginia	Old Capital Prison, Washington, DC, transferred to Elmira Prison, NY, July 23, 1864	Oath of Allegiance June 30, 1865
Thomas, David W. Private	Unk	March 10, 1862, Tomotley, South Carolina	Co. D, 14th South Carolina Infantry	July 29, 1864, Petersburg, Virginia	Point Lookout, Maryland, transferred to Elmira Prison, NY, August 12, 1864	Oath of Allegiance June 14, 1865
Thomas, George W. Private	Unk	April 14, 1864, Gordonsville, Georgia	Co. I, 16th Georgia Infantry	June 1, 1864, Gaines Farm, Virginia	Point Lookout, Maryland, transferred to Elmira Prison, NY, July 12, 1864	Exchanged October 29, 1864, at Venus Point, Savannah River, GA.

Name & Rank	Age	Enlisted	Regiment and State	Where Captured	Prison	Remarks
Thomas, George W. Private	21	June 20, 1861, Abingdon, Virginia	Co. B, 48th Virginia Infantry	June 10, 1864, Spotsylvania Court House, Virginia	Point Lookout, Maryland, transferred to Elmira Prison, NY, July 25, 1864	Oath of Allegiance July 11, 1865
Thomas, Hardy Private	Unk	February 12, 1864, Quitman County, Georgia	Co. F, 61st Georgia Infantry	May 12, 1864, Spotsylvania Court House, Virginia	Point Lookout, Maryland, transferred to Elmira Prison, NY, July 30, 1864	Oath of Allegiance July 7, 1865
Thomas, J. H. Private	Unk	January 24, 1864, Chesterfield, South Carolina	Co. D, 21st South Carolina Infantry	January 15, 1865, Fort Fisher, North Carolina	February 1, 1865, Elmira Prison Camp, New York	Oath of Allegiance July 7, 1865
Thomas, James Private	Unk	June 9, 1861, Camp Trousdale, Tennessee	Co. K, 17th Tennessee Infantry	June 17, 1864, Petersburg, Virginia	Point Lookout, Maryland, transferred to Elmira Prison, NY, July 30, 1864	Exchanged February 25, 1865 at Boulware's or Cox Wharf on the James River, Virginia
Thomas, James C. Private	Unk	February 10, 1864, Marianna, Florida	Co. A, 5th Battalion Florida Cavalry	September 23, 1864, Euchee Anna, Louisiana	New Orleans, Louisiana transferred to Elmira November 19, 1864.	Died December 7, 1864 of Chronic Diarrhea, Grave No. 1180
Thomas, James G. Private	Unk	June 11, 1861, Bledsoe's Store, Virginia	Co. K, 44th Virginia Infantry	May 12, 1864, Spotsylvania Court House, Virginia	Point Lookout, Maryland, transferred to Elmira Prison, NY, August 2, 1864	Oath of Allegiance June 27, 1865
Thomas, James W. Private	Unk	Unknown	Co. E, 21st Battalion Virginia Cavalry	July 12, 1864, Near Washington, DC	Old Capital Prison, Washington, DC, transferred to Elmira Prison, NY, July 23, 1864	Oath of Allegiance December 13, 1864. Early Release per Lincoln's Proclamation, 12/8/1863.
Thomas, Jonathan W. Private	Unk	Unknown	Co. A, 35th Battalion Virginia Cavalry	June 7, 1864, Drainville, Virginia	Old Capital Prison, Washington, DC, transferred to Elmira Prison, NY, July 23, 1864	Oath of Allegiance July 11, 1865

Name & Rank	Age	Enlisted	Regiment and State	Where Captured	Prison	Remarks
Thomas, Josiah H. Private	29	August 9, 1861, Whiteville, North Carolina	Co. C, 18th North Carolina Infantry	May 12, 1864, Spotsylvania Court House, Virginia	Point Lookout, Maryland, transferred to Elmira Prison, NY, August 6, 1864	Died March 6, 1865 of Variola (smallpox), Grave No. 2419
Thomas, Levin Private	Unk	Unknown	Co. B, 35th Battalion Virginia Cavalry	June 26, 1864, Leesburg, Virginia	Old Capital Prison, Washington, DC, transferred to Elmira Prison, NY, July 23, 1864	Oath of Allegiance June 14, 1865
Thomas, M. T. Private	Unk	Unknown	Co. H, 3rd North Carolina Infantry	May 8, 1864, Wilderness, Virginia	Point Lookout, Maryland, transferred to Elmira Prison, NY, August 14, 1864	Exchanged February 20, 1865 at Boulware's or Cox Wharf on the James River, Virginia
Thomas, Moses W. Private	23	July 13, 1861, Lincoln Factory, North Carolina	Co. D, 1st North Carolina Infantry	May 12, 1864, Spotsylvania Court House, Virginia	Point Lookout, Maryland, transferred to Elmira Prison, NY, August 6, 1864	Oath of Allegiance June 21, 1865
Thomas, Philip Private	Unk	March 17, 1862, Santee, South Carolina	Co. E, 5th South Carolina Cavalry	May 16, 1864, Near Drury's Bluff, Virginia	Point Lookout, Maryland, transferred to Elmira Prison, NY, July 25, 1864	Died October 1, 1864 of Typhoid Fever. Grave No. 421
Thomas, R. H. Private	Unk	Unknown	Co. G, 34th Virginia Infantry	June 15, 1864, Near Petersburg, Virginia	Point Lookout, Maryland, transferred to Elmira Prison, NY, July 25, 1864	Died June 13, 1865, Chronic Diarrhea, Grave No. 2882
Thomas, Richard Private	Unk	December 10, 1863, Ashepoo, South Carolina	Co. C, 11th South Carolina Infantry	May 16, 1864, Near Drury's Bluff, Virginia	Point Lookout, Maryland, transferred to Elmira Prison, NY, August 17, 1864	Exchanged March 2, 1865 at Akins Landing on the James River, Virginia
Thomas, Robert H. B. Corporal	Unk	March 4, 1863, Wake County, North Carolina	Co. D, 30th North Carolina Infantry	May 8, 1864, Wilderness, Virginia	Point Lookout, Maryland, transferred to Elmira Prison, NY, August 14, 1864	Died October 16, 1864 of Chronic Diarrhea, Grave No. 561

Name & Rank	Age	Enlisted	Regiment and State	Where Captured	Prison	Remarks
Thomas, Rol. M. Private	Unk	August 27, 1862, Salem, Virginia	Co. E, 18th South Carolina Infantry	July 30, 1864, Petersburg, Virginia	Point Lookout, Maryland, transferred to Elmira Prison, NY, August 12, 1864	Oath of Allegiance June 16, 1865
Thomas, Silas Private	Unk	March 7, 1862, Caroline County, Virginia	Co. K, 47th Virginia Infantry	May 5, 1864, Wilderness, Virginia	Point Lookout, Maryland, transferred to Elmira Prison, NY, July 23, 1864	Died November 25, 1864 of Chronic Diarrhea, Grave No. 912
Thomas, Thomas H. Corporal	22	September 15, 1862, Harnett County, North Carolina	Co. J, 31st North Carolina Infantry	June 1, 1864, Gaines Farm Cold Harbor, Virginia	Point Lookout, Maryland, transferred to Elmira Prison, NY, July 12, 1864	Exchanged March 2, 1865 at Akins Landing on the James River, Virginia
Thomas, W. Private	Unk	Unknown	Co. F, 5th North Carolina Infantry	June 3, 1864, Cold Harbor, Virginia	Point Lookout, Maryland, transferred to Elmira Prison, NY, July 12, 1864	Oath of Allegiance May 6, 1865
Thomas, W. Private	Unk	Unknown	Co. F, 13th South Carolina Infantry	Unknown	Unknown	Died March 17, 1865 of Unknown Disease, Grave No. 1717
Thomas, William Private	Unk	July 4, 1861, Calhoun, Gordon County, Georgia	Co. G, 21st Georgia Infantry	July 8, 1864, Harper's Ferry, Virginia	Old Capital Prison, Washington, DC, transferred to Elmira Prison, NY, July 23, 1864	Died February 4, 1865 of Chronic Diarrhea, Grave No. 1889
Thomas, William A. Private	Unk	June 8, 1861, Isbell's Store, Virginia	Co. D, 44th Virginia Infantry	May 12, 1864, Spotsylvania Court House, Virginia	Point Lookout, Maryland, transferred to Elmira Prison, NY, August 2, 1864	Oath of Allegiance June 16, 1865
Thomas, William H. Private	Unk	March 26, 1862, Camp Leon, Madison, Florida	Co. D, 5th Florida Infantry	May 12, 1864, Spotsylvania Court House, Virginia	Point Lookout, Maryland, transferred to Elmira Prison, NY, July 30, 1864	Oath of Allegiance June 19, 1865
Thomas, William J. Private	Unk	May 23, 1861, Coffee County, Alabama	Co. D, 12th Alabama Infantry	May 12, 1864, Spotsylvania Court House, Virginia	Point Lookout, Maryland, transferred to Elmira Prison, NY, August 17, 1864	Oath of Allegiance June 14, 1865

Name & Rank	Age	Enlisted	Regiment and State	Where Captured	Prison	Remarks
Thomas, William O. Private	Unk	June 11, 1861, Bledsoe's Store, Virginia	Co. K, 44th Virginia Infantry	May 12, 1864, Spotsylvania Court House, Virginia	Point Lookout, Maryland, transferred to Elmira Prison, NY, August 2, 1864	Exchanged March 14, 1865 at Boulware's Wharf on the James River, Virginia
Thomas, William R. Private	Unk	June 11, 1861, Bledsoe's Store, Virginia	Co. K, 44th Virginia Infantry	May 12, 1864, Spotsylvania Court House, Virginia	Point Lookout, Maryland, transferred to Elmira Prison, NY, August 2, 1864	Oath of Allegiance June 14, 1865
Thomason, James E. Private	Unk	May 20, 1862, Bedford County, Virginia	Co. J, 58th Virginia Infantry	May 20, 1864, Spotsylvania Court House, Virginia	Point Lookout, Maryland, transferred to Elmira Prison, NY, July 3, 1864	Oath of Allegiance June 30, 1865
Thomason, Presley Y. Private	24	July 15, 1862, Raleigh, North Carolina	Co. J, 3rd North Carolina Infantry	May 12, 1864, Near Spotsylvania County Court House, Virginia	Point Lookout, Maryland, transferred to Elmira Prison, NY, August 14, 1864	Oath of Allegiance June 27, 1865
Thomerson, John P. Private	Unk	July 15, 1861, Camp Pickens, Virginia	Co. D, 34th, Virginia Infantry	June 15, 1864, Near Petersburg, Virginia	Point Lookout, Maryland, transferred to Elmira Prison, NY, July 12, 1864	Died February 12, 1865 of Smallpox, Grave No. 2028
Thompson, A. Private	Unk	Unknown	Co. K, 2nd South Carolina Infantry	June 9, 1864, Petersburg, Virginia	Point Lookout, Maryland, transferred to Elmira Prison, NY, July 25, 1864	Oath of Allegiance May 19, 1865
Thompson, Andrew J. Private	Unk	January 1, 1864, Greenville, Alabama	Co. E, 1st Battalion Alabama Artillery	August 23, 1864, Fort Morgan, Alabama	Steam Press No. 4 New Orleans, Louisiana transferred to Elmira Prison, NY, October 8, 1864.	Died January 16, 1865 of Variola (Smallpox), Grave No. 1445
Thompson, Benjamin F. Private	24	April 18, 1861, Berryville, Virginia	Co. J, 2nd Virginia Infantry	August 17, 1864, Berryville, Virginia	Old Capital Prison, Washington, DC transferred to Elmira Prison, NY, August 29, 1864	Exchanged February 25, 1865 at Boulware's or Cox Wharf on the James River, Virginia

Name & Rank	Age	Enlisted	Regiment and State	Where Captured	Prison	Remarks
Thompson, D. V. Private	Unk	April 11, 1862, Coles Island, South Carolina	Co. F, 25th South Carolina Infantry	January 15, 1865, Fort Fisher, North Carolina	February 1, 1865, Elmira Prison Camp, New York	Oath of Allegiance July 11, 1865
Thompson, Edward D. Private	Unk	Date Unknown, Roberson County, North Carolina	Co. H, 36th Regiment, 2nd North Carolina Artillery	January 15, 1865, Fort Fisher, North Carolina	February 1, 1865, Elmira Prison Camp, New York	Oath of Allegiance July 11, 1865
Thompson, Francis M. Private	Unk	September 3, 1862, Butler County, Alabama	Co. E, 1st Battalion Alabama Artillery	August 23, 1864, Fort Morgan, Alabama	Steam Press No. 4 New Orleans, Louisiana transferred to Elmira Prison, NY, October 8, 1864.	Died October 25, 1864, Chronic Diarrhea, Grave No. 848
Thompson, George Private	24	September 5, 1862, Texas	Co. A, Baylor's Regiment Texas Cavalry	September 29, 1864, Near Mouth of the Red River, Texas	New Orleans, Louisiana transferred to Elmira November 19, 1864.	Oath of Allegiance May 19, 1865
Thompson, George Private	Unk	March 1, 1864, Kinston, North Carolina	Co. K, 57th North Carolina Infantry	July 8, 1864, Harper's Ferry, Virginia	Old Capital Prison, Washington, DC, transferred to Elmira Prison, NY, July 23, 1864	Oath of Allegiance May 29, 1865
Thompson, George W. Private	Unk	March 24, 1861, Eastville, Alabama	Co. E, 13th Alabama Infantry	May 12, 1864, Spotsylvania Court House, Virginia	Point Lookout, Maryland, transferred to Elmira Prison, NY, August 2, 1864	Oath of Allegiance May 15, 1865
Thompson, Hans Private	Unk	March 28, 1864, Mobile, Alabama	Co. E, 12th Alabama Infantry	July 8, 1864, Harper's Ferry, Virginia	Old Capital Prison, Washington, DC, transferred to Elmira Prison, NY, July 23, 1864	Died November 26, 1864 of Pleuro Pneumonia, Grave No. 905
Thompson, Henry Private	Unk	April 29, 1864, Columbia, South Carolina	Co. G, 23rd South Carolina Infantry	June 17, 1864, Petersburg, Virginia	Point Lookout, Maryland, transferred to Elmira Prison, NY, July 30, 1864	Died October 21, 1864 of Pneumonia, Grave No. 870

Name & Rank	Age	Enlisted	Regiment and State	Where Captured	Prison	Remarks
Thompson, J. Private	Unk	Unknown	Co. I, 5th Arsenal Battalion, Local Defense, Infantry	June 11, 1864, Chickahominy, Virginia	Point Lookout, Maryland, transferred to Elmira Prison, NY, July 23, 1864	Oath of Allegiance October 7, 1864. Early Release per Lincoln's Proclamation, 12/8/1863.
Thompson, J. A. Private	Unk	July 28, 1863, Tallapoosa County, Alabama	Co. G, 12th Alabama Infantry	July 12, 1864, Near Washington, DC	Old Capital Prison, Washington, DC, transferred to Elmira August 12, 1864	Died October 7, 1864 of Chronic Diarrhea, Grave No. 587
Thompson, J. C. Private	Unk	September 7, 1862, Charleston, South Carolina	Co. A, 27th South Carolina Infantry	June 24, 1864, Near Petersburg, Virginia	Point Lookout, Maryland, transferred to Elmira Prison, NY, August 18, 1864	Oath of Allegiance July 11, 1865
Thompson, J. J. Private	Unk	April 24, 1861, Richmond, Virginia	Captain Young's Battery Virginia Artillery	June 15, 1864, Petersburg, Virginia	Point Lookout, Maryland, transferred to Elmira Prison, NY, July 25, 1864	Exchanged February 20, 1865 at Boulware's or Cox Wharf on the James River, Virginia
Thompson, J. W. Private	Unk	Unknown	Co. K, 5th Florida Infantry	July 29, 1864, Deserted to Union Lines, Petersburg, Virginia	Point Lookout, Maryland, transferred to Elmira Prison, NY, August 12, 1864	Oath of Allegiance April 4, 1865. Early Release per Lincoln's Proclamation, 12/8/1863.
Thompson, James D. Private	23	August 30, 1861, Union County, North Carolina	Co. F, 40th Regiment, 3rd North Carolina Artillery	January 15, 1865, Fort Fisher, North Carolina	February 1, 1865, Elmira Prison Camp, New York	Oath of Allegiance July 11, 1865
Thompson, James H. Private	21	July 7, 1861, Camp Moore, Louisiana	Co. D, 9th Louisiana Infantry	May 12, 1864, Spotsylvania Court House, Virginia	Point Lookout, Maryland, transferred to Elmira Prison, NY, August 17, 1864	Oath of Allegiance June 14, 1865
Thompson, James M. Private	28	July 15, 1862, Alamance County, North Carolina	Co. B, 1st North Carolina Infantry	May 12, 1864, Spotsylvania Court House, Virginia	Point Lookout, Maryland, transferred to Elmira Prison, NY, August 6, 1864	Oath of Allegiance June 30, 1865

Name & Rank	Age	Enlisted	Regiment and State	Where Captured	Prison	Remarks
Thompson, Joel Private	Unk	February 11, 1862, Hiawassee, Georgia	Co. C, 24th Georgia Infantry	August 16, 1864, Front Royal, Virginia	Old Capital Prison, Washington, DC transferred to Elmira Prison, NY, August 29, 1864	Died March 29, 1865 of Pneumonia, Grave No. 2514
Thompson, John Private	Unk	September 7, 1862, Raleigh, North Carolina	Co. H, 18th North Carolina Infantry	May 12, 1864, Spotsylvania Court House, Virginia	Point Lookout, Maryland, transferred to Elmira Prison, NY, August 6, 1864	Exchanged October 29, 1864, at Venus Point, Savannah River, GA.
Thompson, John B. Sergeant	Unk	July 3, 1861, Peterstown, Virginia	Co. D, 26th Battalion, Virginia Infantry	June 3, 1864, Gaines Farm, Cold Harbor, Virginia	Point Lookout, Maryland, transferred to Elmira Prison, NY, July 17, 1864	Oath of Allegiance July 3, 1865
Thompson, John D. Private	17	March 4, 1862, Jackson, Georgia	Co. K, 45th Georgia Infantry	May 5, 1864, Wilderness, Virginia. Gunshot Wound Abdomen	Old Capital Prison, Washington, DC, transferred to Elmira Prison, NY, July 23, 1864	Died March 12, 1865 of Pneumonia, Grave No. 2425
Thompson, John Easy Private	30	February 28, 1862, Lumberton, North Carolina	Co. E, 51st North Carolina Infantry	June 1, 1864, Cold Harbor, Virginia	Point Lookout, Maryland, transferred to Elmira Prison, NY, July 12, 1864	Oath of Allegiance July 3, 1865
Thompson, John P. Major	Unk	Unknown	Staff, 12th Kentucky Cavalry	May 17, 1863, Owensboro, Kentucky	November 11, 1864, Old Capital Prison, Washington, DC. February 4, 1865 Elmira, Prison Camp, NY	Exchanged February 20, 1865 at Boulware's or Cox Wharf on the James River, Virginia
Thompson, John R. Private	Unk	May 18, 1861, Lisbon, Virginia	Co. C, 42nd Virginia Infantry	May 12, 1864, Spotsylvania Court House, Virginia	Point Lookout, Maryland, transferred to Elmira Prison, NY, August 2,1864	Died September 19, 1864 of Chronic Diarrhea, Grave No. 521. Headstone has 5th VA
Thompson, John W. Private	Unk	June 13, 1861, Camp McDonald, Georgia	Co. F, 18th Georgia Infantry	May 22, 1864, Spotsylvania, Virginia	Point Lookout, Maryland, transferred to Elmira Prison, NY, July 17, 1864	Oath of Allegiance June 14, 1865

Name & Rank	Age	Enlisted	Regiment and State	Where Captured	Prison	Remarks
Thompson, John W. Private	20	September 3, 1861, Mecklenburg County, North Carolina	Co. H, 35th North Carolina Infantry	June 17, 1864, Petersburg, Virginia	Point Lookout, Maryland, transferred to Elmira Prison, NY, July 30, 1864	Oath of Allegiance June 12, 1865
Thompson, Jones C. Private	Unk	Unknown	Co. J, 26th South Carolina Infantry	July 30, 1864, Petersburg, Virginia	Point Lookout, Maryland, transferred to Elmira Prison, NY, August 12, 1864	Died September 13, 1864 of Chronic Diarrhea, Grave No. 270
Thompson, Nathan Private	Unk	June 11, 1861, Camp McDonald, Georgia	Co. G, 18th Georgia Infantry	June 1, 1864, Cold Harbor, Virginia	Point Lookout, Maryland, transferred to Elmira Prison, NY, July 17, 1864	Oath of Allegiance June 21, 1865
Thompson, Nathan Private	Unk	August 2, 1861, Camp McDonald, Georgia	Co. G, 11th Georgia Infantry	June 1, 1864, Gaines Mill Cold Harbor, Virginia	Point Lookout, Maryland, transferred to Elmira Prison, NY, July 12, 1864	Oath of Allegiance June 21, 1865
Thompson, R. W. Private	Unk	September 1, 1861, Reidsville, Tattnall County, Georgia	Co. B, 61st Georgia Infantry	May 12, 1864, Spotsylvania Court House, Virginia	Point Lookout, Maryland, transferred to Elmira Prison, NY, July 30, 1864	Oath of Allegiance June 19, 1865
Thompson, Richard Private	21	July 5, 1861, Weldon, North Carolina	Co. K, 1st North Carolina Infantry	May 12, 1864, Spotsylvania Court House, Virginia	Point Lookout, Maryland, transferred to Elmira Prison, NY, August 6, 1864	Exchanged October 29, 1864, at Venus Point, Savannah River, GA.
Thompson, Rob S. Private	Unk	February 20, 1862, Acworth, Georgia	Co. A, 18th Georgia Infantry	June 1, 1864, Cold Harbor, Virginia	Point Lookout, Maryland, transferred to Elmira Prison, NY, July 17, 1864	Exchanged March 14, 1865 at Boulware's Wharf on the James River, Virginia
Thompson, Roberson J. Private	Unk	April 1, 1864, Randolph County, North Carolina	Co. L, 22nd North Carolina Infantry	May 27, 1864, Fredericks-burg, Virginia	Point Lookout, Maryland, transferred to Elmira Prison, NY, July 12, 1864	Oath of Allegiance December 29, 1864. Early Release per Lincoln's Proclamation, 12/8/1863.

Name & Rank	Age	Enlisted	Regiment and State	Where Captured	Prison	Remarks
Thompson, Samuel M. Private	17	Unknown	Co. ?, 12th Texas Cavalry	August 25, 1864, Bullets Bayou, Concordia Parish, Louisiana	New Orleans, Louisiana transferred to Elmira November 19, 1864.	Orders for Elmira Prison Camp but Died in Transit 12/16/64 of Chronic Diarrhea at U. S. Army Hospital Fort Columbus, NY.
Thompson, T. H. Private	Unk	May 17, 1862, Camp Pryor, Virginia	Co. K, 5th Virginia Cavalry	May 11, 1864, Yellow Tavern, Hanover County, Virginia	Point Lookout, Maryland, transferred to Elmira Prison, NY, July 12, 1864	Exchanged March 10, 1865 at Boulware's Wharf on the James River, Virginia
Thompson, Thomas Private	Unk	June 20, 1861, Abingdon, Virginia	Co. B, 48th Virginia Infantry	July 12, 1864, Near Washington, DC	Old Capital Prison, Washington, DC, transferred to Elmira Prison, NY, July 23, 1864	Oath of Allegiance May 17, 1865
Thompson, Thomas J. Private	Unk	September 3, 1862, Butler County, Alabama	Co. E, 1st Battalion Alabama Artillery	August 23, 1864, Fort Morgan, Alabama	Steam Press No. 4 New Orleans, Louisiana transferred to Elmira Prison, NY, October 8, 1864.	Died February 14, 1865 of Variola (Smallpox), Grave No. 2030
Thompson, Thomas P. Private	Unk	July 19, 1861, Montgomery, Alabama	Co. D, 13th Alabama Infantry	May 12, 1864, Spotsylvania Court House, Virginia	Point Lookout, Maryland, transferred to Elmira Prison, NY, August 2, 1864	Died December 16, 1864 of Pleuro Pneumonia, Grave No. 1062
Thompson, W. J. Private	Unk	May 28, 1861, Nashville, Tennessee	Co. H, 17th Tennessee Infantry	June 17, 1864, Petersburg, Virginia	Point Lookout, Maryland, transferred to Elmira Prison, NY, July 30, 1864	Oath of Allegiance May 19, 1865
Thompson, Wesley Private	18	August 17, 1863, Laurenburg, Richmond County, North Carolina	Co. F, 40th Regiment, 3rd North Carolina Artillery	January 15, 1865, Fort Fisher, North Carolina	February 1, 1865, Elmira Prison Camp, New York	Oath of Allegiance July 11, 1865

Name & Rank	Age	Enlisted	Regiment and State	Where Captured	Prison	Remarks
Thompson, William Private	22	June 5, 1861, Memphis, Tennessee	Co. D, 1st Jackson's Tennessee Heavy Artillery	August 23, 1864, Fort Morgan, Alabama.	New Orleans, Louisiana transferred to Elmira Prison, NY, December 4, 1864.	Oath of Allegiance May 29, 1865
Thompson, William A. Private	Unk	September 22, 1862, Waynesville, Georgia	Co. G, 7th Georgia Cavalry	June 11, 1864, Trevilian Station, Louisa Court House, Virginia	Point Lookout, Maryland, transferred to Elmira Prison, NY, July 25, 1864	Died November 20, 1864 of Chronic Diarrhea, Grave No. 944
Thompson, William E. Private	Unk	June 7, 1861, Richmond, Virginia	Co. C, 59th Virginia Infantry	May 8, 1864, Nottoway Bridge, Virginia	Point Lookout, Maryland, transferred to Elmira Prison, NY, August 17, 1864	Oath of Allegiance June 19, 1865
Thompson, William F. Private	Unk	Unknown	Co. B, 21st South Carolina Infantry	January 15, 1865, Fort Fisher, North Carolina	February 1, 1865, Elmira Prison Camp, New York	Died February 17, 1865 of Chronic Diarrhea, Grave No. 2230. Headstone has 24th SC.
Thompson, William H. Corporal	Unk	April 20, 1861, Lexington, Virginia	Co. H, 4th Virginia Infantry	May 12, 1864, Spotsylvania Court House, Virginia	Point Lookout, Maryland, transferred to Elmira Prison, NY, August 2, 1864	Exchanged March 10, 1865 at Boulware's Wharf on the James River, Virginia
Thompson, William M. Private	28	July 15, 1862, North Carolina	Co. G, 3rd North Carolina Infantry	May 12, 1864, Near Spotsylvania County Court House, Virginia	Point Lookout, Maryland, transferred to Elmira Prison, NY, August 14, 1864	Oath of Allegiance June 27, 1865
Thompson, William N. Private	Unk	Unknown	Co. B, 48th Virginia Infantry	May 12, 1864, Spotsylvania Court House, Virginia	Point Lookout, Maryland, transferred to Elmira Prison, NY, August 2, 1864	Died September 30, 1864 of Chronic Diarrhea, Grave No. 423
Thompson, William P. Private	20	July 15, 1862, Alamance County, North Carolina	Co. B, 1st North Carolina Infantry	May 12, 1864, Spotsylvania Court House, Virginia	Point Lookout, Maryland, transferred to Elmira Prison, NY, August 6, 1864	Oath of Allegiance June 30, 1865

Name & Rank	Age	Enlisted	Regiment and State	Where Captured	Prison	Remarks
Thompson, Willis A. Private	Unk	June 4, 1863, Fort Fisher, New Hanover County, North Carolina	Co. C, 36th Regiment, 2nd North Carolina Artillery	January 15, 1865, Fort Fisher, North Carolina	February 1, 1865, Elmira Prison Camp, New York	Oath of Allegiance June 12, 1865
Thomson, John W. Private	18	July 26, 1861, Camp Pickens, Anderson District, South Carolina	Co. A, 1st South Carolina Infantry	July 14, 1863, Falling Waters, Maryland	Point Lookout, Maryland, transferred to Elmira Prison, NY, August 18, 1864	Oath of Allegiance June 16, 1865
Thorn, John Private	Unk	Unknown	Co. B, 1st Jackson's Tennessee Heavy Artillery	August 23, 1864, Fort Morgan, Alabama.	New Orleans, Louisiana transferred to Elmira Prison, NY, December 4, 1864.	Exchanged February 25, 1865 at Boulware's or Cox Wharf on the James River, Virginia
Thornton, G. P. Private	Unk	May 9, 1861, New Orleans, Louisiana	Co. J, 2nd Louisiana Infantry	May 12, 1864, Spotsylvania Court House, Virginia	Point Lookout, Maryland, transferred to Elmira Prison, NY, August 17, 1864	Exchanged February 25, 1865 at Boulware's or Cox Wharf on the James River, Virginia
Thornton, George W. Private	18	July 8, 1861, Randolph, Alabama	Co. E, 5th Alabama Infantry	May 19, 1864, Spotsylvania Court House, Virginia	Old Capital Prison, Washington D. C. Transferred to Elmira Prison, NY, August 12, 1864	Oath of Allegiance May 12, 1865
Thornton, James Seaman	Unk	Unknown	Confederate States Steamer Bomb Shell	May 5, 1864, Albemarle Sound, North Carolina	Point Lookout, Maryland, transferred to Elmira Prison, NY, July 23, 1864	Oath of Allegiance April 15, 1865
Thornton, P. P. Private	Unk	Unknown	Co. F, 50th Virginia Infantry	May 12, 1864, Spotsylvania Court House, Virginia	Point Lookout, Maryland, transferred to Elmira Prison, NY, August 2, 1864	Oath of Allegiance June 21, 1865
Thornton, Richard A. Private	Unk	May 9, 1861, Ashland, Virginia	Co. G, 4th Virginia Cavalry	June 3, 1864, Near Talapatomoy Creek Cold Harbor, Virginia	Point Lookout, Maryland, transferred to Elmira Prison, NY, July 12, 1864	Oath of Allegiance July 7, 1865

Name & Rank	Age	Enlisted	Regiment and State	Where Captured	Prison	Remarks
Thornton, Robert Private	Unk	March 9, 1864, Dublin Depot, Virginia	Co. L, 26th Battalion Virginia Infantry	June 3, 1864, Gaines Farm Cold Harbor, Virginia	Point Lookout, Maryland, transferred to Elmira Prison, NY, July 17, 1864	Oath of Allegiance July 3, 1865
Thorp, Benjamin Private	18	January 1, 1863, Petersburg, Virginia	Co. K, 55th North Carolina Infantry	July 14, 1863, Falling Waters, Maryland	Point Lookout, Maryland, transferred to Elmira Prison, NY, August 18, 1864	Exchanged March 10, 1865 at Boulware's Wharf on the James River, Virginia
Threadgill, John W. Private	Unk	May 11, 1861, Clifton, Alabama	Co. J, 6th Alabama Infantry	July 16, 1864, Loudoun County, Virginia	Old Capital Prison, Washington, DC, transferred to Elmira Prison, NY, July 23, 1864	Oath of Allegiance July 7, 1865
Threat, Jeremiah Private	Unk	March 20, 1862, Lancaster, South Carolina	Co. H, 1st South Carolina Infantry	July 16, 1863, Battery Wagner, Morris Island, South Carolina	Point Lookout, Maryland, transferred to Elmira Prison, NY, August 18, 1864	Exchanged March 10, 1865 at Boulware's Wharf on the James River, Virginia
Thrift, Augustus Private	Unk	Unknown	Co. B, 1st Virginia Infantry	July 29, 1864, Petersburg, Virginia	Point Lookout, Maryland, transferred to Elmira Prison, NY, August 12, 1864	Oath of Allegiance May 17, 1865
Thrift, John W. Private	16	March 12, 1862, Randolph County, North Carolina	Co. L, 22nd North Carolina Infantry	May 23, 1864, North Anna River (Spotsylvania), Virginia	Point Lookout, Maryland, transferred to Elmira Prison, NY, July 12, 1864	Oath of Allegiance June 21, 1865
Throgmorton, James C. Private	Unk	July 1, 1861, Hampshire, Tennessee	Co. G, Wheeler's 6th Tennessee Cavalry	May 17, 1863, Waverly, Tennessee	Point Lookout, Maryland, transferred to Elmira Prison, NY, August 18, 1864	Exchanged February 25, 1865 at Boulware's wharf on the James River, Virginia
Thrower, Levi Private	Unk	November 18, 1863, Dale County, Alabama	Co. C, 61st Alabama Infantry	May 12, 1864, Spotsylvania Court House, Virginia	Point Lookout, Maryland, transferred to Elmira Prison, NY, July 30, 1864	Oath of Allegiance June 14, 1865

Name & Rank	Age	Enlisted	Regiment and State	Where Captured	Prison	Remarks
Thrower, William Private	23	July 15, 1862, Raleigh, North Carolina	Co. K, 1st North Carolina Infantry	May 12, 1864, Spotsylvania Court House, Virginia	Point Lookout, Maryland, transferred to Elmira Prison, NY, August 6, 1864	Exchanged October 29, 1864, at Venus Point, Savannah River, GA.
Thruston, James R. Sergeant	Unk	May 7, 1861, New Prospect, Virginia	Co. D, 26th Virginia Infantry	June 15, 1864, Near Petersburg, Virginia	Point Lookout, Maryland, transferred to Elmira Prison, NY, July 12,1864	Exchanged October 29, 1864, at Venus Point, Savannah River, GA.
Thurman, A. M. Private	Unk	February 5, 1862, Jefferson, Georgia	Co. C, 18th Georgia Infantry	June 1, 1864, Cold Harbor, Virginia	Point Lookout, Maryland, transferred to Elmira Prison, NY, July 17, 1864	Oath of Allegiance July 7, 1865
Thurman, Joseph C. Private	Unk	March 22, 1864, Decatur, Georgia	Co. E, 12th Georgia Infantry	May 6, 1864, Wilderness, Virginia	Point Lookout, Maryland, transferred to Elmira Prison, NY, July 25, 1864	Oath of Allegiance December 12, 1864. Early Release per Lincoln's Proclamation, 12/8/1863.
Thurman, N. S. Private	Unk	Unknown	Co. D, 44th Virginia Infantry	May 5, 1864, Orange Court House, Virginia	Point Lookout, Maryland, transferred to Elmira Prison, NY, August 2, 1864	Oath of Allegiance June 16, 1865
Thurman, Robert K. Private	Unk	July 24, 1861, J. Pasley's, Virginia	Co. F, 58th Virginia Infantry	May 20, 1864, Spotsylvania Court House, Virginia	Point Lookout, Maryland, transferred to Elmira Prison, NY, July 3, 1864	Oath of Allegiance June 30, 1865
Thurston, Benjamin F. Private	Unk	June 2, 1861, Little Plymouth, Virginia	Co. G, 26th Virginia Infantry	June 15, 1864, Petersburg, Virginia	Point Lookout, Maryland, transferred to Elmira Prison, NY, July 30, 1864	Died September 18, 1864 of Chronic Diarrhea, Grave No. 157
Thurston, J. W. Private	Unk	November 1, 1862, South Santee, South Carolina	Co. D, 4th South Carolina Cavalry	June 11, 1864, Trevilian Station, Louisa Court House, Virginia	Point Lookout, Maryland, transferred to Elmira Prison, NY, July 23, 1864	Died February 17, 1865 of Aneurisms of the Heart, Grave No. 2229

Name & Rank	Age	Enlisted	Regiment and State	Where Captured	Prison	Remarks
Thurston, Thomas H. Private	Unk	July 18, 1861, Urbanna, Virginia	Co. C, 55th Virginia Infantry	May 5, 1864, Wilderness, Virginia	Point Lookout, Maryland, transferred to Elmira Prison, NY, August 14, 1864	Exchanged March 2, 1865 at Akins Landing on the James River, Virginia
Thweatt, George C. Private	Unk	Unknown	Co. A, 44th Battalion Virginia Infantry	June 15, 1864, Near Petersburg, Virginia	Point Lookout, Maryland, transferred to Elmira Prison, NY, July 12, 1864	Exchanged February 25, 1865 at Boulware's or Cox Wharf on the James River, Virginia
Thweatt, James Private	Unk	July 8, 1861, Griffin, Georgia	Co. D, 13th Georgia Infantry	July 8, 1864, Boonesboro, Maryland	Old Capital Prison, Washington, DC, transferred to Elmira Prison, NY, July 23, 1864	Exchanged March 2, 1865 at Akins Landing on the James River, Virginia
Thweatt, Simon N. Private	Unk	November 5, 1862, Franklin, Tennessee	Co. J, 44th Tennessee Infantry	June 17, 1864, Petersburg, Virginia	Point Lookout, Maryland, transferred to Elmira Prison, NY, July 30, 1864	Died October 21, 1864 of Pneumonia, Grave No. 871. Name S. N. Thiveatt on Headstone.
Tibbetts, Charles Private	Unk	Unknown	Co. A, Ogden's Battalion Louisiana Cavalry	September 15, 1864, Near East Baton Rouge, Louisiana	New Orleans, Louisiana transferred to Elmira November 19, 1864.	Exchanged February 13, 1865 at Boulware's wharf on the James River, Virginia
Tibbs, Henry T. Private	Unk	Unknown	Co. E, 50th Virginia Infantry	May 12, 1864, Spotsylvania Court House, Virginia	Point Lookout, Maryland, transferred to Elmira Prison, NY, August 2, 1864	Exchanged October 29, 1864, at Venus Point, Savannah River, GA.
Tice, George W. Private	Unk	March 14, 1861, Skipperville, Alabama	Co. F, 1st Battalion Alabama Artillery	August 23, 1864, Fort Morgan, Alabama	Steam Press No. 4 New Orleans, Louisiana transferred to Elmira Prison, NY, October 8, 1864.	Died October 30, 1864 of Typhoid-Pneumonia, Grave. No. 743

Name & Rank	Age	Enlisted	Regiment and State	Where Captured	Prison	Remarks
Tidd, Wiley B. Private	Unk	February 24, 1862, Marion County, Georgia	Co. A, 27th Georgia Infantry	June 16, 1864, Petersburg, Virginia	Point Lookout, Maryland, transferred to Elmira Prison, NY, July 30, 1864	Died December 21, 1864 of Pneumonia, Grave No. 1080. Name William on Headstone.
Tidwell, Obadiah Sergeant	18	June 26, 1861, Atlanta, Georgia	Co. C, 21st Georgia Infantry	May 21, 1864, Spotsylvania Court House, Virginia	Point Lookout, Maryland, transferred to Elmira Prison, NY, July 23, 1864	Oath of Allegiance June 14, 1865
Tierney, Daniel Private	Unk	July 22, 1861, Camp Moore, Louisiana	Co. B, 10th Louisiana Infantry	May 12, 1864, Spotsylvania Court House, Virginia	Point Lookout, Maryland, transferred to Elmira Prison, NY, July 25, 1864	Exchanged February 25, 1865 at Boulware's or Cox Wharf on the James River, Virginia
Tifenbach, George T. Private	26	June 6, 1861, New Orleans, Louisiana	Co. C, 14th Louisiana Infantry	July 5, 1863, Gettysburg, Pennsylvania	Point Lookout, Maryland, transferred to Elmira Prison, NY, July 23, 1864	Oath of Allegiance May 19, 1865
Tiller, Marshall Private	Unk	March 18, 1862, Lexington, Georgia	Co. K, 6th Georgia Infantry	July 16, 1863, James Island, South Carolina	Point Lookout, Maryland, transferred to Elmira Prison, NY, August 18, 1864	Exchanged March 10, 1865 at Boulware's Wharf on the James River, Virginia
Tillett, Edward Private	Unk	September 5, 1862, Currituck County, North Carolina	Co. B, 8th North Carolina Infantry	June 1, 1864, Cold Harbor, Virginia	Point Lookout, Maryland, transferred to Elmira Prison, NY, July 15,1864	Oath of Allegiance July 3, 1865
Tillman, John E. C. 2nd Lieutenant	Unk	September 1, 1861, Eden Station, Georgia	Co. K, 61st Georgia Infantry	May 12, 1864, Spotsylvania Court House, Virginia	Point Lookout, Maryland, transferred to Elmira Prison, NY, July 30, 1864	Exchanged February 20, 1865 at Boulware's or Cox Wharf on the James River, Virginia
Tillman, John R. Private	25	October 28, 1863, Fort Fisher, New Hanover County, North Carolina	Co. J, 36th Regiment, 2nd North Carolina Artillery	January 15, 1865, Fort Fisher, North Carolina	February 1, 1865, Elmira Prison Camp, New York	Oath of Allegiance June 12, 1865

Name & Rank	Age	Enlisted	Regiment and State	Where Captured	Prison	Remarks
Tillman, Joshua A. Private	Unk	Unknown	Co. B, 1st Jackson's Tennessee Heavy Artillery	August 23, 1864, Fort Morgan, Alabama.	New Orleans, Louisiana transferred to Elmira Prison, NY, December 4, 1864.	Oath of Allegiance May 29, 1865
Tillman, Willis Private	Unk	October 13, 1861, Hall's Mill, Alabama	Co. B, 21st Alabama Infantry	August 23, 1860, Fort Morgan, Alabama	Steam Press No. 4, New Orleans, Louisiana transferred to Elmira Prison October 8, 1864.	Exchanged March 2, 1865 at Akins Landing on the James River, Virginia
Tilman, James W. Private	Unk	June 11, 1861, Bledsoe's, Fluvanna County, Virginia	Co. K, 44th Virginia Infantry	May 12, 1864, Spotsylvania Court House, Virginia	Point Lookout, Maryland, transferred to Elmira Prison, NY, July 25, 1864	Oath of Allegiance June 14, 1865
Timmany, James Private	Unk	July 27, 1861, New Orleans, Louisiana	Co. A, 14th Louisiana Infantry	May 5, 1864, Wilderness, Virginia	Point Lookout, Maryland, transferred to Elmira Prison, NY, July 23, 1864	Oath of Allegiance May 29, 1865
Timmons, John M. Private	Unk	October 14, 1863, Mount Pleasant, South Carolina	Co. I, 18th South Carolina Infantry	July 30, 1864, Petersburg, Virginia	Point Lookout, Maryland, transferred to Elmira Prison, NY, August 12, 1864	Died December 16, 1864 of Pneumonia, Grave No. 1270
Tindal, Emanuel Corporal	23	December 20, 1861, Camp Harllee, Britton's Neck, South Carolina	Co. J, 21st South Carolina Infantry	June 24, 1864, Petersburg, Virginia	Point Lookout, Maryland, transferred to Elmira Prison, NY, August 18, 1864	Oath of Allegiance July 11, 1865
Tindal, Roderick V. Private	25	September 25, 1861, Carricitos, Texas	Co. A, Yager's 1st Texas Cavalry	September 28, 1864, Simsport, Louisiana	New Orleans, Louisiana transferred to Elmira November 19, 1864.	Died December 5, 1864 of Pleuro Pneumonia, Grave No. 1015
Tindall, Calvin Private	19	October 31, 1862, Fort Fisher, Hanover County, North Carolina	Co. C, 36th Regiment, 2nd North Carolina Artillery	January 15, 1865, Fort Fisher, North Carolina	February 1, 1865, Elmira Prison Camp, New York	Died March 4, 1865 of Chronic Diarrhea, Grave No. 1992

Name & Rank	Age	Enlisted	Regiment and State	Where Captured	Prison	Remarks
Tindell, Miles S. Private	19	September 1, 1861, Sampson County, North Carolina	Co. A, 30th North Carolina Infantry	May 12, 1864, Near Spotsylvania Court House, Virginia	Point Lookout, Maryland, transferred to Elmira Prison, NY, August 14, 1864	Exchanged March 14, 1865 at Boulware's Wharf on the James River, Virginia
Tiner, James Private	44	March 19, 1862, Richmond County, North Carolina	Co. E, 52nd North Carolina Infantry	May 12, 1864, Spotsylvania Court House, Virginia	Point Lookout, Maryland, transferred to Elmira Prison, NY, August 12, 1864	Died March 13, 1865 of Pneumonia, Grave No. 1827
Tingle, Birney S. Private	21	May 10, 1861, Washington, North Carolina	Co. I, 3rd North Carolina Infantry	May 10, 1864, Spotsylvania County Court House, Virginia	Point Lookout, Maryland, transferred to Elmira Prison, NY, August 14, 1864	Oath of Allegiance June 27, 1865
Tingle, John W. Private	36	January 23, 1862, Craven County, North Carolina	Co. D, 40th Regiment, 3rd North Carolina Artillery	January 15, 1865, Fort Fisher, North Carolina	February 1, 1865, Elmira Prison Camp, New York	Exchanged February 20, 1865 at Boulware's or Cox Wharf on the James River, Virginia
Tinkler, Lawrence D. Private	Unk	July 14, 1862, Winnsboro, South Carolina	Co. H, 7th Battalion South Carolina Infantry	May 16, 1864, Near Drury's Bluff, Virginia	Point Lookout, Maryland, transferred to Elmira Prison, NY, August 17, 1864	Exchanged March 2, 1865 at Akins Landing on the James River, Virginia
Tinsbloom, John L. Private	Unk	November 1, 1861, Fort Lowry, Lowry Point, Virginia	Co. F, 55th Virginia Infantry	June 3, 1864, Old Church, Cold Harbor, Virginia	Point Lookout, Maryland, transferred to Elmira Prison, NY, July 12, 1864	Died December 14, 1864 of Pneumonia, Grave No. 1123
Tinsley, Augustine Wood Private	Unk	August 1, 1862, Madison Court House, Virginia	Co. C, 4th Virginia Cavalry	April 14, 1865, Farquier County, Virginia	Old Capital Prison, Washington D. C. Transferred to Elmira Prison, NY, May 2, 1865.	Oath of Allegiance July 3, 1865
Tinsly, John M. Corporal	Unk	June 17, 1861, Rocky Mount, Virginia	Co. K, 4th Virginia Infantry	May 12, 1864, Spotsylvania Court House, Virginia	Point Lookout, Maryland, transferred to Elmira Prison, NY, August 2, 1864	Oath of Allegiance June 27, 1865

Name & Rank	Age	Enlisted	Regiment and State	Where Captured	Prison	Remarks
Tippett, John H. Private	Unk	July 15, 1861, Leesburg, Virginia	Co. K, 6th Virginia Cavalry	July 15, 1864, Loudoun County, Virginia	Old Capital Prison, Washington, DC, transferred to Elmira Prison, NY, July 23, 1864	Oath of Allegiance June 15, 1865
Tippett, Lott W. Sergeant	34	May 13, 1861, Golden Place, Onslow County, North Carolina	Co. A, 3rd North Carolina Infantry	May 12, 1864, Near Spotsylvania Court House, Virginia	Point Lookout, Maryland, transferred to Elmira Prison, NY, August 14, 1864	Exchanged October 29, 1864, at Venus Point, Savannah River, GA.
Tippings, T. S. Private	Unk	November 27, 1861, Columbia, South Carolina	Co. F, 17th South Carolina Infantry	July 30, 1864, Petersburg, Virginia	Point Lookout, Maryland, transferred to Elmira Prison, NY, August 12, 1864	Died May 9, 1865 of Chronic Diarrhea, Grave No. 2779
Tipton, Charles G. Sergeant	Unk	Unknown	Co. A, 11th Florida Infantry	September 27, 1864, Marianna, Florida	New Orleans, Louisiana transferred to Elmira November 19, 1864.	Died December 9, 1864, of Pneumonia, Grave No. 1038
Tisdale, W. W. Private	Unk	April 12, 1862, Battery Island, South Carolina	Co. C, 25th South Carolina Infantry	January 15, 1865, Fort Fisher, North Carolina	February 1, 1865, Elmira Prison Camp, New York	Oath of Allegiance June 30, 1865
Tison, Cicero Sergeant	35	July 3, 1861, Atlanta, Georgia	Co. B, 11th Georgia Infantry	May 6, 1864, Mine Run, Wilderness, Virginia	Point Lookout, Maryland, transferred to Elmira Prison, NY, August 14, 1864	Exchanged March 2, 1865 at Akins Landing on the James River, Virginia
Tobias, John S. Private	Unk	February 1, 1864, Charleston, South Carolina	Co. J, 25th South Carolina Infantry	January 15, 1865, Fort Fisher, North Carolina	February 1, 1865, Elmira Prison Camp, New York	Died February 23, 1865 of Pneumonia, Grave No. 2244
Tobin, John Private	Unk	March 3, 1862, Luray, Virginia	Co. K, 10th Virginia Infantry	May 12, 1864, Spotsylvania Court House, Virginia	Point Lookout, Maryland, transferred to Elmira Prison, NY, August 2, 1864	Joined United States Army May 23-31, 1864.
Tobin, William Private	Unk	June 2, 1862, Luray, Virginia	Co. K, 10th Virginia Infantry	May 12, 1864, Spotsylvania Court House, Virginia	Point Lookout, Maryland, transferred to Elmira Prison, NY, August 2, 1864	Oath of Allegiance June 19, 1865

Name & Rank	Age	Enlisted	Regiment and State	Where Captured	Prison	Remarks
Todd, Bryant Private	25	June 1, 1861, T. L. Skinner, Edenton, North Carolina	Co. A, 1st North Carolina Infantry	May 5, 1864, Wilderness, Virginia	Point Lookout Prison Camp, Maryland. Transferred to Elmira Prison Camp, NY, August 6, 1864	Died April 7, 1865 of Chronic Diarrhea, Grave. 2652
Todd, Henry A. Sergeant	31	May 1, 1861, Nashville, North Carolina	Co. H, 32nd North Carolina Infantry	May 10, 1864, Near Mine Run, Virginia	Point Lookout, Maryland, transferred to Elmira Prison, NY, August 6, 1864	Oath of Allegiance June 21, 1865
Toffier, William A. Private	19	September 8, 1862, Camp Thompson, False River, Louisiana	Co. J, 2nd Louisiana Cavalry	August 10, 1864, Gross Bayou, Louisiana	New Orleans, Louisiana transferred to Elmira November 19, 1864.	Exchanged February 13, 1865 at Boulware's wharf on the James River, VA
Tolar, Robert M. Private	18	November 6, 1864, Bladen County, North Carolina	Co. B, 36th Regiment, 2nd North Carolina Artillery	January 15, 1865, Fort Fisher, North Carolina	February 1, 1865, Elmira Prison Camp, New York	Oath of Allegiance July 7t, 1865
Tolbert, Josiah P. Private	26	September 7, 1861, Albemarle, North Carolina	Co. K, 28th North Carolina Infantry	July 29, 1864, Petersburg, Virginia	Point Lookout, Maryland, transferred to Elmira Prison, NY, August 12, 1864	Oath of Allegiance July 3, 1865
Toliver, Jacob F. Private	30	September 15, 1861, Allegheny County, North Carolina	Co. K, 37th North Carolina Infantry	May 12, 1864, Spotsylvania, Virginia	Point Lookout, Maryland, transferred to Elmira Prison, NY, July 23, 1864	Exchanged October 29, 1864, at Venus Point, Savannah River, GA.
Toliver, Joseph Private	Unk	Unknown	Co. F, 6th Virginia Cavalry	August 14, 1864, Berryville, Virginia	Old Capital Prison, Washington, DC transferred to Elmira Prison, NY, August 29, 1864	Oath of Allegiance July 7, 1865
Toliver, Solomon Private	Unk	May 3, 1862, Gap Civil, Allegheny County, North Carolina	Co. J, 61st North Carolina Infantry	June 16, 1864, Petersburg, Virginia	Point Lookout, Maryland, transferred to Elmira Prison, NY, July 25, 1864	Died September 11, 1864 of Chronic Diarrhea, Grave No. 259

Name & Rank	Age	Enlisted	Regiment and State	Where Captured	Prison	Remarks
Tollerson, James Private	27	August 4, 1862, Brookhaven, Mississippi	Co. G, 13th Mississippi Infantry	July 2, 1863, Gettysburg, Pennsylvania	Point Lookout, Maryland, transferred to Elmira Prison, NY, July 25, 1864	Oath of Allegiance May 19, 1865
Tomberlin, Henry W. Private	Unk	March 4, 1864, Abbeville, Georgia	Co. E, 49th Georgia Infantry	May 6, 1864, Wilderness, Virginia	Point Lookout, Maryland, transferred to Elmira Prison, NY, July 12, 1864	Died October 1, 1864 of Typhoid Pneumonia, Grave No. 410
Tomblin, Derias B. Corporal	18	July 29, 1861, Livingston, Tennessee	Co. C, 25th Tennessee Infantry	May 16, 1864, Near Drury's Bluff, Virginia	Point Lookout, Maryland, transferred to Elmira Prison, NY, August 17, 1864	Exchanged February 25, 1865 at Boulware's or Cox Wharf on the James River, Virginia
Tomlinson, Jesse W. Private	Unk	September 27, 1862, Port Hudson, Louisiana	Co. J, 30th Louisiana Infantry	October 27, 1864, Bayou Grosstete, Point Coupee Parish, Louisiana	New Orleans, Louisiana transferred to Elmira November 19, 1864.	Exchanged February 25, 1865 at Boulware's or Cox Wharf on the James River, Virginia
Tomlinson, Joseph Private	Unk	March 29, 1862, Lewisburg, Virginia	Co. D, 26th Battalion Virginia Infantry	June 3, 1864, Cold Harbor, Virginia	Point Lookout, Maryland, transferred to Elmira Prison, NY, July 17, 1864	Died November 3, 1864 of Chronic Diarrhea, Grave No. 757
Tomlinson, Manson Private	Unk	April 20, 1861, Lexington, Virginia	Co. H, 4th Virginia Infantry	May 12, 1864, Spotsylvania Court House, Virginia	Point Lookout, Maryland, transferred to Elmira Prison, NY, August 2, 1864	Died September 19, 1864 of Chronic Diarrhea, Grave No. 502
Tompkins, Turner C. Sergeant	Unk	August 16, 1861, Hamburg, Edgefield District, South Carolina	Co. G, 1st South Carolina Infantry	May 23, 1864, North Anna, Virginia	Point Lookout, Maryland, transferred to Elmira Prison, NY, August 17, 1864	Oath of Allegiance July 3, 1865
Toney, Doctor F. Private	Unk	March 28, 1864, Atlanta, Georgia	Co. D, 44th Georgia Infantry	May 20, 1864, Spotsylvania Court House, Virginia	Point Lookout, Maryland, transferred to Elmira Prison, NY, July 3, 1864	Oath of Allegiance May 29, 1865

Name & Rank	Age	Enlisted	Regiment and State	Where Captured	Prison	Remarks
Toney, Marcus B. Private	Unk	Unknown	Co. C, 44th Virginia Infantry	May 12, 1864, Spotsylvania Court House, Virginia	Point Lookout, Maryland, transferred to Elmira Prison, NY, August 2,1864	Oath of Allegiance June 14, 1865
Toothman, Charles A. Sergeant	Unk	June 17, 1861, Lewisburg, Virginia	Co. G, 26th Battalion, Virginia Infantry	June 3, 1864, Gaines Farm, Cold Harbor, Virginia	Point Lookout, Maryland, transferred to Elmira Prison, NY, July 17, 1864	Oath of Allegiance July 3, 1865
Torrence, Robert S. Private	Unk	December 19, 1862, In Regiment, North Carolina	Co. H, 23rd North Carolina Infantry	May 12, 1864, Near Spotsylvania Court House, Virginia	Point Lookout, Maryland, transferred to Elmira Prison, NY, August 14, 1864	Oath of Allegiance June 27, 1865
Touchstone, Ben R. Private	Unk	February 21, 1863, Atlanta, Georgia	Co. N, 38th Georgia Infantry	August 12, 1864, Middletown, Virginia	Old Capital Prison, Washington, DC transferred to Elmira Prison, NY, August 29, 1864	Oath of Allegiance July 7, 1865
Towler, James R. Private	35	April 4, 1862, Eufaula, Alabama	Co. K, 15th Alabama Infantry	May 24, 1864, Bethel Church, North Anna, Virginia	Point Lookout Prison Camp, Maryland. Transferred to Elmira Prison, July 17, 1864	Died January 25, 1865 of Variola (Smallpox), Grave No. 1639
Townsend, C. N. Private	Unk	Unknown	Co. A, 1st Texas Infantry	May 24, 1864, North Anna, Virginia	Point Lookout, Maryland, transferred to Elmira Prison, NY, July 25, 1864	Oath of Allegiance May 19, 1865
Townsend, Isaac Private	Unk	August 13, 1861, New Orleans, Louisiana	Co. B, 7th Louisiana Infantry	May 11, 1864, Near Spotsylvania Court House, Virginia	Point Lookout, Maryland, transferred to Elmira Prison, NY, August 17, 1864	Exchanged February 25, 1865 at Boulware's or Cox Wharf on the James River, Virginia
Townsend, James S. Private	21	May 22, 1861, Wadesboro, North Carolina	Co. A, 23rd North Carolina Infantry	May 12, 1864, Near Spotsylvania Court House, Virginia	Point Lookout, Maryland, transferred to Elmira Prison, NY, August 14, 1864	Died March 21, 1865 of Diphtheria, Grave No. 1532

Name & Rank	Age	Enlisted	Regiment and State	Where Captured	Prison	Remarks
Townsend, John P. Private	32	February 12, 1862, Covington, Tennessee	Co. B, 1st Jackson's Tennessee Heavy Artillery	August 23, 1864, Fort Morgan, Alabama.	New Orleans, Louisiana transferred to Elmira Prison, NY, December 4, 1864.	Exchanged February 25, 1865 at Boulware's or Cox Wharf on the James River, Virginia
Trabue, Robert Woods Sergeant	Unk	September 7, 1861, Nashville, Tennessee	Co. A, Jackson's 1st Regiment, Tennessee Heavy Artillery	August 23, 1864, Fort Morgan, Alabama	New Orleans, Louisiana transferred to Elmira Prison, NY, December 4, 1864.	Exchanged February 25, 1865 at Boulware's or Cox Wharf on the James River, Virginia
Tracey, Nathan K. Private	30	June 19, 1861, Camp Moore, New Orleans, Louisiana	Co. A, 8th Louisiana Infantry	May 12, 1864, Spotsylvania Court House, Virginia	Point Lookout, Maryland, transferred to Elmira Prison, NY, August 17, 1864	Oath of Allegiance June 19, 1865
Tracy, James A. Private	Unk	September 11, 1863, Hillsboro, Virginia	Co. G, 31st Virginia Infantry	May 5, 1864, Mine Run Wilderness, Virginia	Point Lookout, Maryland, transferred to Elmira Prison, NY, August 2, 1864	Died April 26, 1865 of Chronic Diarrhea, Grave No. 1427
Trader, Leonard H. Corporal	Unk	July 18, 1861, Urbana, Virginia	Co. C, 55th Virginia Infantry	May 5, 1864, Wilderness, Virginia	Point Lookout, Maryland, transferred to Elmira Prison, NY, August 14, 1864	Exchanged March 14, 1865 at Boulware's Wharf on the James River, Virginia
Trail, Peter Private	Unk	May 1, 1862, Smyth County, Virginia	Co. E, 23rd Battalion Virginia Infantry	May 30, 1864, Old Church, Cold Harbor, VA. Gunshot Wound of Left Elbow. Amputated Left Arm.	Old Capital Prison, Washington, DC transferred to Elmira Prison, NY, August 27, 1864	Died December 8, 1864 of Chronic Diarrhea, Grave No. 1162
Trainer, John A. Private	25	September 28, 1861, Staunton, Virginia	Co. G, 5th Virginia Infantry	May 12, 1864, Spotsylvania Court House, Virginia	Point Lookout, Maryland, transferred to Elmira Prison, NY, July 3, 1864	Oath of Allegiance June 14, 1865
Trainer, Morgan B. Private	23	March 30, 1862, Camp Allegheny, Virginia	Co. F, 25th Virginia Infantry	May 5, 1864, Wilderness, Virginia	Point Lookout, Maryland, transferred to Elmira Prison, NY, August 17, 1864	Exchanged October 29, 1864, at Venus Point, Savannah River, GA.

Name & Rank	Age	Enlisted	Regiment and State	Where Captured	Prison	Remarks
Trainor, Michael Private	Unk	July 4, 1861, New Orleans, Louisiana	Co. II, 14th Louisiana Infantry	July 10, 1864, Frederick, Maryland	Old Capital Prison, Washington, DC, transferred to Elmira Prison, NY, July 23, 1864	Oath of Allegiance February 7, 1865
Trainum, Samuel Private	Unk	September 9, 1862, Butler County, Alabama	Co. F, 5th Alabama Infantry	May 5, 1864, Wilderness, Virginia	Point Lookout, Maryland, transferred to Elmira Prison, NY, August 12, 1864.	Oath of Allegiance June 14th 1865
Trammell, B. P. Corporal	Unk	April 14, 1861, Greenville, South Carolina	Co. H, 22nd South Carolina Infantry	July 30, 1864, Petersburg, Virginia	Point Lookout, Maryland, transferred to Elmira Prison, NY, August 12, 1864	Oath of Allegiance June 14, 1865
Traves, J. F. Private	Unk	June 2, 1861, Gloucester Point, Virginia	Co. A, 26th Virginia Infantry	June 15, 1864, Near Petersburg, Virginia	Point Lookout, Maryland, transferred to Elmira Prison, NY, July 12, 1864	Oath of Allegiance July 11, 1865
Trawick, Washington B. Private	19	July 10, 1861, Selma, Alabama	Jeff Davis Alabama Artillery	May 5, 1864, Wilderness, Virginia	Point Lookout, Maryland, transferred to Elmira Prison, NY, August 17, 1864	Escaped October 27, 1864 by Tunneling Under Fence.
Treadeway, Elijah S. Private	26	June 8, 1861, Marietta, Georgia	Co. G, 26th Mississippi Infantry	May 16, 1863, Baker's Creek, Champion Hill, Mississippi	Point Lookout, Maryland, transferred to Elmira Prison, NY, August 18, 1864	Died November 12, 1864 of Chronic Diarrhea, Grave No. 794
Treadwell, H. B. Private	Unk	March 13, 1862, Monroe, Georgia	Co. F, 16th Georgia Infantry	June 1, 1864, Gaines Farm, Virginia	Point Lookout, Maryland, transferred to Elmira Prison, NY, July 12, 1864	Died September 3, 1864 of Chronic Diarrhea, Grave No. 67
Trent, Roland H. Private	38	January 13, 1863, Campbell, Virginia	Co. C, 34th Virginia Infantry	October 27, 1864, Petersburg, Virginia. Gunshot Wound Back of Neck.	Old Capital Prison, Washington, DC, transferred to Elmira Prison, NY, December 17, 1864	Exchanged February 20, 1865. Died on the Route.

Name & Rank	Age	Enlisted	Regiment and State	Where Captured	Prison	Remarks
Trexler, Rufus Private	Unk	March 11, 1862, Salisbury, North Carolina	Co. B, 46th North Carolina Infantry	July 28, 1864, Malvern Hill, Virginia	Point Lookout, Maryland, transferred to Elmira Prison, NY, August 12, 1864	Oath of Allegiance May 29, 1865
Tribbetts, William Corporal	19	April 20, 1861, Lexington, Virginia	Co. H, 4th Virginia Infantry	May 12, 1864, Spotsylvania Court House, Virginia	Point Lookout, Maryland, transferred to Elmira Prison, NY, August 2, 1864	Oath of Allegiance June 27, 1865
Trice, George H. Private	Unk	December 18, 1861, King and Queen County, Virginia	Co. J, 26th North Carolina Infantry	June 17, 1864, Near Petersburg, Virginia	Point Lookout, Maryland, transferred to Elmira Prison, NY, July 30, 1864	Oath of Allegiance June 19, 1865
Trice, William Anderson Private	Unk	April 29, 1863, Richmond, Virginia	Co. E, 25th Battalion Virginia Infantry	July 12, 1864, Cox's Farm, Virginia	Point Lookout, Maryland, transferred to Elmira Prison, NY, August 6, 1864	Exchanged October 29, 1864, at Venus Point, Savannah River, GA.
Trigger, L. C. Private	Unk	September 15, 1863, Fredericksburg, Virginia	Co. E, 15th Virginia Cavalry	September 14, 1863, Near Culpepper, Virginia	Point Lookout, Maryland, transferred to Elmira Prison, NY, August 18, 1864	Transferred For Exchange 10/11/64 to Point Lookout Prison Camp, MD. Died 11/13/64 of Unknown Causes at Port Royal, SC
Trigloan, James H. Sergeant	22	September 25, 1861, Carucilos, Texas	Yager's 1st Texas Infantry	October 6, 1864, Near Hampton's Ferry, Louisiana	New Orleans, Louisiana transferred to Elmira November 19, 1864.	Exchanged March 10, 1865 at Boulware's Wharf on the James River, Virginia
Triplett, Franklin M. Private	24	September 14, 1861, Boone, North Carolina	Co. B, 37th North Carolina Infantry	May 12, 1864, Spotsylvania Court House, Virginia	Point Lookout, Maryland, transferred to Elmira Prison, NY, August 12, 1864	Exchanged March 2, 1865 at Akins Landing on the James River, Virginia
Tripp, Aaron W. Private	Unk	November 19, 1862, Estill Springs, Tennessee	Co. B, 44th Tennessee Infantry	June 17, 1864, Petersburg, Virginia	Point Lookout, Maryland, transferred to Elmira Prison, NY, July 30, 1864	Exchanged March 10, 1865 at Boulware's Wharf on the James River, Virginia

Name & Rank	Age	Enlisted	Regiment and State	Where Captured	Prison	Remarks
Tripp, Thomas H. Private	Unk	December 7, 1861, Camp Trousdale, Tennessee	Co. B, 44th Tennessee Infantry	June 17, 1864, Petersburg, Virginia	Point Lookout, Maryland, transferred to Elmira Prison, NY, July 30, 1864	Exchanged February 25, 1865 at Boulware's or Cox Wharf on the James River, Virginia
Trotter, William Private	Unk	May 25, 1862, Camp Moore, Louisiana	Co. E, 3rd Louisiana Cavalry	October 6, 1864, Clinton, Louisiana	New Orleans, Louisiana transferred to Elmira November 19, 1864.	Exchanged February 25, 1865 at Boulware's or Cox Wharf on the James River, Virginia
Trout, John M. Private	39	December 12, 1863, Dublin Depot, Virginia	Co. L, 26th Battalion Virginia Infantry	June 3, 1864, Gaines Farm Cold Harbor, Virginia	Point Lookout, Maryland, transferred to Elmira Prison, NY, July 17, 1864	Exchanged February 20, 1865 at Boulware's or Cox Wharf on the James River, Virginia
Trout, L. Private	Unk	June 11, 1862, Adam's Run, Tennessee	Co. A, Jackson's 1st Regiment, Tennessee Heavy Artillery	August 23, 1864, Fort Morgan, Alabama	New Orleans, Louisiana transferred to Elmira Prison, NY, December 4, 1864.	Exchanged February 25, 1865 at Boulware's or Cox Wharf on the James River, Virginia
Trout, William W. Private	Unk	June 11, 1862, Adam's Run, Tennessee	Co. A, Jackson's 1st Regiment, Tennessee Heavy Artillery	August 23, 1864, Fort Morgan, Alabama	New Orleans, Louisiana transferred to Elmira Prison, NY, December 4, 1864.	Oath of Allegiance March 8, 1865, Commissary General of Prisoners.
Troutman, Caleb M. Private	22	August 8, 1862, Raleigh, North Carolina	Co. B, 5th North Carolina Infantry	May 12, 1864, Spotsylvania Court House, Virginia	Point Lookout, Maryland, transferred to Elmira Prison, NY, August 6, 1864	Transferred for Exchange 10/11/64. Died 10/27/64 of Chronic Diarrhea at US Army Hospital, Baltimore, MD
Troutman, William H. Private	19	September 11, 1861, Mount Pleasant, North Carolina	Co. B, 8th North Carolina Infantry	May 31, 1864, Cold Harbor, Virginia	Point Lookout, Maryland, transferred to Elmira Prison, NY, July 12, 1864	Died April 21, 1865 of Chronic Diarrhea, Grave No. 1391

Name & Rank	Age	Enlisted	Regiment and State	Where Captured	Prison	Remarks
Trowbridge, Francis Private	Unk	Unknown	Co. E, 22nd Virginia Cavalry	July 17, 1864, Frederick, Maryland. Deserted to Union Lines.	Old Capital Prison, Washington D. C. Transferred to Elmira Prison, NY, August 12, 1864	Oath of Allegiance December 23, 1864. Early Release per Lincoln's Proclamation, 12/8/1863.
Troxle, William J. Private	Unk	February 12, 1863, Carter County, Tennessee	Co. B, 1st Jackson's Tennessee Heavy Artillery	August 23, 1864, Fort Morgan, Alabama.	New Orleans, Louisiana transferred to Elmira Prison, NY, December 4, 1864.	Died January 16, 1865 of Pneumonia, Grave No. 1451. Headstone has W. J. Troxel.
Troxler, Anderson Private	Unk	May 16, 1862, Camp Harris, Tennessee	Co. B, 17th Tennessee Infantry	June 17, 1864, Petersburg, Virginia	Point Lookout, Maryland, transferred to Elmira Prison, NY, July 30, 1864	Exchanged February 25, 1865 at Boulware's or Cox Wharf on the James River, Virginia
Troxler, William Private	Unk	March 3, 1864, Guilford County, North Carolina	Co. A, 53rd North Carolina Infantry	June 10, 1864, Spotsylvania, Virginia	Point Lookout, Maryland, transferred to Elmira Prison, NY, July 25, 1864	Died September 25, 1864 of Scorbutus (Scurvy). Grave No. 361
Troy, Thomas Private	27	June 19, 1861, New Orleans Louisiana,	Co. F, 14th Louisiana Infantry	May 12, 1864, Spotsylvania Court House, Virginia	Point Lookout, Maryland, transferred to Elmira Prison, NY, July 25, 1864	Oath of Allegiance May 17, 1865
Trugier, A. Civilian	Unk	Registered Enemy	Citizen of Louisiana	July 27, 1864, New Orleans, Louisiana	New Orleans, Louisiana transferred to Elmira November 19, 1864.	Oath of Allegiance June 20, 1865
Truitt, Lewis Private	28	April 23, 1862, Camp Mangum, North Carolina	Co. G, 45th North Carolina Infantry	May 10, 1864, Spotsylvania Court House, Virginia	Point Lookout, Maryland, transferred to Elmira Prison, NY, August 6, 1864	Oath of Allegiance June 12, 1865
Truitt, Thomas Private	18	July 13, 1863, Belle Isle, Virginia	Co. G, 45th North Carolina Infantry	May 10, 1864, Spotsylvania Court House, Virginia	Point Lookout, Maryland, transferred to Elmira Prison, NY, August 6, 1864	Exchanged February 20, 1865 at Boulware's or Cox Wharf on the James River, Virginia

Name & Rank	Age	Enlisted	Regiment and State	Where Captured	Prison	Remarks
Trull, Calvin Sergeant	Unk	May 5, 1862, Union County, North Carolina	Co. J, 53rd North Carolina Infantry	May 20, 1864, Spotsylvania Court House, Virginia	Point Lookout, Maryland, transferred to Elmira Prison, NY, July 6, 1864	Oath of Allegiance June 12, 1865
Truman, Joseph L. Private	Unk	July 30, 1863, Chambers County, Alabama	Co. F, 61st Alabama Infantry	May 12, 1864, Spotsylvania Court House, Virginia	Point Lookout, Maryland, transferred to Elmira Prison, NY, July 30, 1864	Exchanged October 29, 1864, at Venus Point, Savannah River, GA.
Truman, S. Private	Unk	Unknown	Co. E, 53rd Georgia Infantry	June 1, 1864, Gaines Mill Cold Harbor, Virginia	Point Lookout, Maryland, transferred to Elmira Prison, NY, July 17,1864	Oath of Allegiance May 19, 1865
Trussel, John W. Private	Unk	August 13, 1861, Camp Moore, Louisiana	Co. K, 12th Louisiana Infantry	May 16, 1863, Baker's Creek, Champion Hill, Mississippi	Point Lookout, Maryland, transferred to Elmira Prison, NY, August 18, 1864	Exchanged 2/25/65. Died 3/3/65 of Congestive Heart Failure at General Hospital No. 9, Richmond, Va.
Tuck, Edward J. Private	47	April 1, 1863, Kinston, North Carolina	Co. H, 24th North Carolina Infantry	June 17, 1864, Petersburg, Virginia	Point Lookout, Maryland, transferred to Elmira Prison, NY, July 30, 1864	Exchanged January 17, 1865 on the James River, Virginia
Tucker, A. G. Private	Unk	Unknown	2nd Class Virginia Militia	June 15, 1864, Petersburg, Virginia	Point Lookout, Maryland, transferred to Elmira Prison, NY, July 25, 1864	Exchanged March 10, 1865 at Boulware's Wharf on the James River, Virginia
Tucker, Alfred T. Private	Unk	May 15, 1862, Camp Davis, North Carolina	Co. K, 43rd North Carolina Infantry	May 16, 1864, Near Drury's Bluff, Virginia	Point Lookout, Maryland, transferred to Elmira Prison, NY, August 17, 1864	Oath of Allegiance June 12, 1865
Tucker, C. Private	Unk	Unknown	Co. A, Captain Norwood's Home Guard Florida	September 27, 1864, Marianna, Florida	New Orleans, Louisiana transferred to Elmira November 19, 1864.	No further Information Available

Name & Rank	Age	Enlisted	Regiment and State	Where Captured	Prison	Remarks
Tucker, Charles Private	Unk	Unknown	Co. A, 11th Florida Infantry	September 27, 1864, Marianna, Florida	Fort Columbus, New York Harbor. Transferred to Elmira Prison, November 20, 1864	Died December 11, 1864 of Chronic Diarrhea, Grave No. 1057
Tucker, George W. Private	37	September 16, 1862, Loundes, Alabama	Co. F, 1st Battalion Alabama Artillery	August 23, 1864, Fort Morgan, Louisiana	New Orleans, Louisiana transferred to Elmira November 19, 1864.	Died December 9, 1864 of Pneumonia, Grave No. 1175
Tucker, George W. S. Private	19	May 17, 1861, Garysburg, North Carolina	Co. F, 12th North Carolina Infantry	May 20, 1864, Spotsylvania Court House, Virginia	Point Lookout, Maryland, transferred to Elmira Prison, NY, July 3, 1864	Exchanged February 20, 1865 at Boulware's or Cox Wharf on the James River, Virginia
Tucker, J. M. Sergeant	Unk	July 19, 1861, Monroe, Georgia	Co. E, 16th Georgia Infantry	August 16, 1864, Front Royal, Virginia	Old Capital Prison, Washington, DC transferred to Elmira Prison, NY, August 29, 1864	Oath of Allegiance July 11, 1865
Tucker, James A. Private	Unk	January 14, 1862, Camp Walsh, South Carolina	Co. J, Holcombe Legion, South Carolina Infantry	May 7, 1864, Stony Creek, Virginia	Point Lookout, Maryland, transferred to Elmira Prison, NY, August 17, 1864	Exchanged February 20, 1865 at Boulware's or Cox Wharf on the James River, Virginia
Tucker, Kilba Private	28	February 15, 1862, Warsaw, North Carolina	Co. B, 51st North Carolina Infantry	June 15, 1864, Petersburg, Virginia	Point Lookout, Maryland, transferred to Elmira Prison, NY, July 12, 1864	Oath of Allegiance July 3, 1865
Tucker, L. D. Private	15	February 24, 1862, Camp Arrington, North Carolina	Co. H, 12th North Carolina Infantry	May 12, 1864, Near Spotsylvania, Virginia	Point Lookout, Maryland, transferred to Elmira Prison, NY, August 14, 1864	Oath of Allegiance June 23, 1865
Tucker, Matthew L. Private	21	August 30, 1861, Sangster's Crossroads, Fairfax, Virginia	Co. H, 6th Alabama Infantry	May 20, 1864, Spotsylvania Court House, Virginia	Point Lookout, Maryland, transferred to Elmira Prison, NY, July 3, 1864	Oath of Allegiance June 14, 1865

Name & Rank	Age	Enlisted	Regiment and State	Where Captured	Prison	Remarks
Tucker, Pinkney Private	40	October 14, 1863, Warrenton Court House, North Carolina	Co. J, 22nd North Carolina Infantry	May 24, 1864, Nelson's Ford, Virginia	Point Lookout, Maryland, transferred to Elmira Prison, NY, July 12, 1864	Oath of Allegiance June 14, 1865
Tucker, R. A. Private	Unk	October 30, 1863, Petersburg, Virginia	Co. F, 32nd Virginia Infantry	May 12, 1864, Henrico County, Virginia	Point Lookout, Maryland, transferred to Elmira Prison, NY, August 17, 1864	Exchanged October 29, 1864, at Venus Point, Savannah River, GA.
Tucker, William L. Private	18	August 28, 1861, Teachey's, North Carolina	Co. F, 30th North Carolina Infantry	May 20, 1864, Spotsylvania Court House, Virginia	Point Lookout, Maryland, transferred to Elmira Prison, NY, July 3, 1864	Exchanged February 13, 1865 at Boulware's wharf on the James River, Virginia
Tucker, William P. Corporal	24	July 7, 1861, Camp Moore, Louisiana	Co. E, 9th Louisiana Infantry	May 12, 1864, Spotsylvania Court House, Virginia	Point Lookout, Maryland, transferred to Elmira Prison, NY, August 17, 1864	Exchanged February 20, 1865 at Boulware's Wharf on the James River, Virginia
Tucker, Willis P. Private	24	May 13, 1865, Lynchburg, Virginia	Co. B, 2nd Virginia Cavalry	May 11, 1864, Near Beaver Dam Station, Virginia	Point Lookout, Maryland, transferred to Elmira Prison, NY, August 17, 1864	Exchanged March 10, 1865 at Boulware's Wharf on the James River, Virginia
Tuggle, Adam G. Private	Unk	September 24, 1861, Hall & Gwinett Counties, Georgia	Co. H, 35th Georgia Infantry	May 24, 1864, Hanover Junction, Virginia	Point Lookout, Maryland, transferred to Elmira Prison, NY, July 8, 1864	Oath of Allegiance June 16, 1865
Tuggle, Charles M. Private	Unk	March 18, 1863, Hog Mountain, Georgia	Co. H, 35th Georgia Infantry	May 24, 1864, Hanover Junction, Virginia	Point Lookout, Maryland, transferred to Elmira Prison, NY, July 11, 1864	Oath of Allegiance May 29, 1865
Tuggle, Manning J. Private	Unk	September 24, 1861, Hall & Gwinett Counties, Georgia	Co. H, 35th Georgia Infantry	May 24, 1864, Hanover Junction, Virginia	Point Lookout, Maryland, transferred to Elmira Prison, NY, July 11, 1864	Oath of Allegiance March 2, 1865. Early Release per Lincoln's Proclamation, 12/8/1863.

Name & Rank	Age	Enlisted	Regiment and State	Where Captured	Prison	Remarks
Tuggle, Nathanial Private	Unk	May 22, 1861, Spoon Creek, Virginia	Co. H, 42nd Virginia Infantry	May 12, 1864, Near Spotsylvania Court House, Virginia	Point Lookout, Maryland, transferred to Elmira Prison, NY, August 6, 1864	Oath of Allegiance June 27, 1865
Tulloch, James W. Private	Unk	August 10, 1863, Camp Lee, Virginia	Co. H, 22nd Battalion Virginia Infantry	May 5, 1864, Wilderness, Virginia	Point Lookout, Maryland, transferred to Elmira Prison, NY, August 14, 1864	Oath of Allegiance June 16, 1865
Tulloch, John J. Private	Unk	February 4, 1862, Goochland, Virginia	Co. H, 22nd Battalion Virginia Infantry	May 5, 1864, Wilderness, Virginia	Point Lookout, Maryland, transferred to Elmira Prison, NY, August 14, 1864	Died September 13, 1864 of Chronic Diarrhea, Grave No. 187. Name Tallah and 22nd NC on Headstone.
Tully, M. Private	29	October 1, 1862, Kanawha, Virginia	Co. H, 22nd Virginia Infantry	June 3, 1864, Gaines Farm Cold Harbor, Virginia	Point Lookout, Maryland, transferred to Elmira Prison, NY, July 12, 1864	Exchanged March 10, 1865 at Boulware's Wharf on the James River, Virginia
Tumage, L. Private	Unk	Unknown	Co. F, 21st South Carolina Infantry	January 15, 1865, Fort Fisher, North Carolina	February 1, 1865, Elmira Prison Camp, New York	Oath of Allegiance July 11, 1865
Tumber, C. B. Corporal	Unk	Unknown	Co. G, 2nd Virginia Infantry	May 20, 1864, Spotsylvania Court House, Virginia	Point Lookout, Maryland, transferred to Elmira Prison, NY, July 3, 1864	Exchanged February 13, 1865 at Boulware's wharf on the James River, Virginia
Tune, C. W. Sergeant	Unk	April 24, 1861, Richmond, Virginia	Captain Young's Battery Virginia Artillery	June 15, 1864, Petersburg, Virginia	Point Lookout, Maryland, transferred to Elmira Prison, NY, July 25, 1864	Oath of Allegiance July 3, 1865
Tune, Thomas Private	28	October 9, 1861, Enfield, Halifax County, North Carolina	Co. F, 36th Regiment, 2nd North Carolina Artillery	January 15, 1865, Fort Fisher, North Carolina	February 1, 1865, Elmira Prison Camp, New York	Died April 1, 1865 of Pneumonia, Grave No. 2574
Tune, W. S. Private	Unk	April 24, 1861, Richmond, Virginia	Captain Young's Battery Virginia Artillery	June 15, 1864, Petersburg, Virginia	Point Lookout, Maryland, transferred to Elmira Prison, NY, July 25, 1864	Died September 3, 1864 of Chronic Diarrhea, Grave No. 69

Name & Rank	Age	Enlisted	Regiment and State	Where Captured	Prison	Remarks
Tune, William Private	27	January 30, 1862, Newbern, Craven County, North Carolina	Co. F, 36th Regiment, 2nd North Carolina Artillery	January 15, 1865, Fort Fisher, North Carolina	February 1, 1865, Elmira Prison Camp, New York	Died March 31, 1865 of Variola (Smallpox), No Grave Found in Woodlawn Cemetery, NY
Tunstall, J. B. Private	18	June 11, 1862, Henderson, North Carolina	Co. G, 23rd North Carolina Infantry	May 9, 1864, Spotsylvania Court House, Virginia. Gunshot Wound Right Hip.	Old Capital Prison, Washington, DC transferred to Elmira Prison, NY, August 29, 1864	Oath of Allegiance June 19, 1865
Tunstall, Percy R. Sergeant	16	October 8, 1861, Hamilton, Martin County, North Carolina	Co. F, 31st North Carolina Infantry	June 1, 1864, Gaines Farm, Virginia	Point Lookout, Maryland, transferred to Elmira Prison, NY, July 12, 1864	Exchanged March 10, 1865 at Boulware's Wharf on the James River, Virginia
Turberville, A. H. Private	Unk	May 17, 1861, New Orleans, Louisiana	Captain Norwood's Co., Louisiana Cavalry	October 6, 1864, Lavinia, Louisiana	New Orleans, Louisiana transferred to Elmira November 19, 1864.	Exchanged February 25, 1865 at Boulware's or Cox Wharf on the James River, Virginia
Turkett, W. A. Private	Unk	April 1, 1863, Lineville, Alabama	Co. J, 14th Alabama Infantry	May 24, 1864, North Anna River (Spotslvania), Hanover Junction, Virginia	Point Lookout, Maryland, transferred to Elmira Prison, NY, July 11, 1864	Exchanged October 29, 1864, at Venus Point, Savannah River, GA.
Turley, Thomas B. Private	Unk	November 1, 1862, Raleigh County, Virginia	Co. A, 22nd Virginia Infantry	July 16, 1864, Poolesville, Maryland	Old Capital Prison, Washington, DC, transferred to Elmira Prison, NY, July 23, 1864	Oath of Allegiance May 29, 1865
Turnage, James Private	19	June 16, 1862, Greenville, North Carolina	Co. J, 44th North Carolina Infantry	May 31, 1864, Gaines Mill Cold Harbor, Virginia	Point Lookout, Maryland, transferred to Elmira Prison, NY, July 12, 1864	Oath of Allegiance May 29, 1865
Turner, Benjamin Sergeant	21	May 26, 1861, Heathsville, Virginia	Co. C, 40th Virginia Infantry	May 6, 1864, Wilderness, Virginia	Point Lookout, Maryland, transferred to Elmira Prison, NY, August 14, 1864	Oath of Allegiance June 23, 1865

Name & Rank	Age	Enlisted	Regiment and State	Where Captured	Prison	Remarks
Turner, David W. Private	24	March 29, 1862, Wilmington, North Carolina	Co. C, 51st North Carolina Infantry	June 1, 1864, Cold Harbor, Virginia	Point Lookout, Maryland, transferred to Elmira Prison, NY, July 12, 1864	Died January 12, 1865 of Pneumonia, Grave No. 1480
Turner, Edward W. Private	Unk	April 10, 1863, Charleston, South Carolina	Co. A, 51st North Carolina Infantry	June 1, 1864, Gaines Mill Cold Harbor, Virginia	Point Lookout, Maryland, transferred to Elmira Prison, NY, July 12, 1864	Exchanged February 20, 1865 at Boulware's or Cox Wharf on the James River, Virginia
Turner, Elisha Private	Unk	May 13, 1862, Savannah, Georgia	Co. E, 7th Georgia Cavalry	June 11, 1864, Louisa Court House, Trevilian Station, Virginia	Point Lookout, Maryland, transferred to Elmira Prison, NY, July 30, 1864	Died February 27, 1865 of Pleurisy, Grave No. 2153
Turner, James G. Private	Unk	January 14, 1864, Macon, Georgia	Co. C, 12th Georgia Infantry	July 12, 1864, Near Washington, DC	Old Capital Prison, Washington, DC, transferred to Elmira Prison, NY, July 23, 1864	Died January 21, 1865 of Pneumonia, Grave No. 1591
Turner, John Private	32	They eighth 1862, Wilmington, North Carolina	Co. H, 36th Regiment, 2nd North Carolina Artillery	January 15, 1865, Fort Fisher, North Carolina	Elmira Prison Camp, New York, February 1, 1865	Died March 8, 1865 of Pneumonia, Grave No. 2385
Turner, John E. Private	Unk	March 1, 1861, Mobile, Alabama	Co. A, 1st Battalion Alabama Artillery	August 23, 1864, Fort Morgan, Alabama	New Orleans, Louisiana transferred to Elmira Prison, NY, December 4, 1864.	Orders for Elmira, NY. Died in Transit 11/22/64 of Pneumonia at US Army Hospital Fort Columbus, NY Harbor
Turner, Joseph B. Private	Unk	January 14, 1862, Camp Walsh, South Carolina	Co. J, Holcombe Legion, South Carolina	May 7, 1864, Stony Creek, Virginia	Point Lookout, Maryland, transferred to Elmira Prison, NY, August 17, 1864	Exchanged February 20, 1865. Died March 13, 1865 of Chronic Diarrhea at Jackson Hospital, Richmond, VA

Name & Rank	Age	Enlisted	Regiment and State	Where Captured	Prison	Remarks
Turner, Lemuel L. Private	Unk	March 1, 1864, Raccoon Ford, Virginia	Co. D, 21st Georgia Infantry	May 12, 1864, Spotsylvania, Virginia. Gunshot Wound Left Shoulder.	Old Capital Prison, Washington, DC, transferred to Elmira Prison, NY, July 23, 1864	Exchanged March 2, 1865 at Akins Landing on the James River, Virginia
Turner, Martin L. Private	Unk	October 22, 1862, Near Winchester, Virginia	Co. D, 44th Virginia Infantry	May 12, 1864, Spotsylvania Court House, Virginia	Point Lookout, Maryland, transferred to Elmira Prison, NY, August 2, 1864	Died September 17, 1864 of Chronic Dysentery, Grave No. 308
Turner, Samuel Private	Unk	September 9, 1861, No. 2, C. Railroad, Eden Station, Georgia	Co. D, 61st Georgia Infantry	July 12, 1864, Near Washington, DC	Old Capital Prison, Washington, DC, transferred to Elmira Prison, NY, July 23, 1864	Oath of Allegiance June 14, 1865
Turner, Simon B. Private	Unk	May 6, 1862, Fair Play, Alabama	Co. K, 44th Alabama Infantry	July 29, 1864, Petersburg, Virginia	Point Lookout, Maryland, transferred to Elmira Prison, NY, August 12, 1864	Oath of Allegiance May 17, 1865
Turner, William H. Private	15	September 15, 1861, Auburn, Wake County, North Carolina	Co. D, 31st North Carolina Infantry	May 31, 1864, Cold Harbor, Virginia	Point Lookout, Maryland, transferred to Elmira Prison, NY, July 12, 1864	Died January 6, 1865 of Pleuritis, Grave No. 1241
Turner, William Wilson Private	Unk	March 31, 1862, Lynchburg, Virginia	Captain Shoemaker's Co., Virginia Horse Artillery	September 14, 1863, Near Culpepper, Virginia	Point Lookout, Maryland, transferred to Elmira Prison, NY, August 18, 1864	Exchanged March 10, 1865 at Boulware's Wharf on the James River, Virginia
Turnmire, David L. Private	Unk	February 15, 1864, Morganton, North Carolina	Co. B, 37th North Carolina Infantry	May 12, 1864, Spotsylvania Court House, Virginia	Point Lookout, Maryland, transferred to Elmira Prison, NY, August 12, 1864	Died September 15, 1864 of Chronic Diarrhea, Grave No. 279. Name Tunmire on Headstone.
Turnmire, Peter W. Private	27	September 14, 1861, Boone, North Carolina	Co. B, 37th North Carolina Infantry	May 12, 1864, Spotsylvania Court House, Virginia	Point Lookout, Maryland, transferred to Elmira Prison, NY, August 12, 1864	Oath of Allegiance June 16, 1865

Name & Rank	Age	Enlisted	Regiment and State	Where Captured	Prison	Remarks
Turpin, Archie B. Private	Unk	June 30, 1861, Gloucester Point, Virginia	Co. E, 5th Virginia Cavalry	May 28, 1864 Mechanics-ville, Virginia	Point Lookout, Maryland, transferred to Elmira Prison, NY, July 11, 1864	Oath of Allegiance May 13, 1865
Turpin, Thomas M. Private	Unk	March 3, 1862, Bedford County, Virginia	Co. G, 34th Virginia Infantry	June 15, 1864, Near Petersburg, Virginia	Point Lookout, Maryland, transferred to Elmira Prison, NY, July 12, 1864	Oath of Allegiance July 3, 1865
Turr, J. B. Private	Unk	Unknown	Co. K, 10th North Carolina Infantry	Unknown	Unknown	Died March 3, 1865 of Unknown Disease, Grave No. 2016
Tutarow, Thomas P. Private	18	September 3, 1862, Mocksville, North Carolina	Co. M, 7th Confederate Cavalry	May 7, 1864, Lyttleton, Virginia	Point Lookout, Maryland, transferred to Elmira Prison, NY, August 17, 1864	Died January 23, 1865 of Pneumonia, Grave No. 1603
Tuttle, David Private	Unk	February 13, 1861, Mobile, Alabama	Co. F, 1st Battalion Alabama Artillery	August 23, 1864, Fort Morgan, Alabama	Steam Press No. 4 New Orleans, Louisiana transferred to Elmira Prison, NY, October 8, 1864.	Died March 7, 1865 of Variola (Smallpox), Grave No. 2391
Tuttle, Jerome Private	Unk	March 19, 1863, Burton's Farm, Virginia	Co. G, 26th Virginia Infantry	June 15, 1864, Near Petersburg, Virginia	Point Lookout, Maryland, transferred to Elmira Prison, NY, July 12, 1864	Oath of Allegiance July 12, 1865
Tuttle, Martin Lee Private	Unk	April 8, 1864, Raleigh, North Carolina	Co. G, 2nd North Carolina Infantry	May 12, 1864, Spotsylvania, Virginia. Gunshot Wound Fracture Lower Jaw.	Old Capital Prison, Washington, DC, transferred to Elmira Prison, NY, December 17, 1864	Exchanged February 13, 1865 at Boulware's Wharf on the James River, Virginia
Twiddy, Uriah Private	21	May 16, 1861, Columbia, North Carolina	Co. A, 32nd North Carolina Infantry	May 10, 1864, Near Mine Run Spotsylvania, Virginia	Point Lookout, Maryland, transferred to Elmira Prison, NY, August 6, 1864	Died December 23, 1864 of Chronic Diarrhea, Grave No. 1097

Name & Rank	Age	Enlisted	Regiment and State	Where Captured	Prison	Remarks
Twiford, Henry V. Corporal	Unk	August 1, 1861, Princess Anne County, Virginia	Co. B, 6th Virginia Infantry	May 12, 1864, Near Spotsylvania Court House, Virginia	Point Lookout, Maryland, transferred to Elmira Prison, NY, August 6, 1864	Died September 19, 1864 of Chronic Diarrhea, Grave No. 319. Name Trifford on Headstone.
Tyler, James Private	31	January 25, 1862, Fort Caswell, Brunswick County, North Carolina	Co. A, 36th Regiment, 2nd North Carolina Artillery	January 15, 1865, Fort Fisher, North Carolina	February 1, 1865, Elmira Prison Camp, New York	Oath of Allegiance July 11, 1865
Tyler, Lucius A. Private	Unk	April 1, 1862, St. John, Hertford County, North Carolina	Co. C, 3rd Battalion North Carolina Light Artillery	January 15, 1865, Fort Fisher, North Carolina	February 1, 1865, Elmira Prison Camp, New York	Oath of Allegiance June 21, 1865
Tyner, William Private	39	March 10, 1862, Lumberton, North Carolina	Co. F, 51st North Carolina Infantry	June 1, 1864, Cold Harbor, Virginia	Transferred From Point Lookout Prison, MD, July 12, 1864. Train Never Arrived at Elmira Prison Camp, NY.	Died July 18, 1864 of Contusion, Grave No. 2853. Possibly from in Train Wreck at Shohola, PA.
Tyson, George W. Private	21	April 15, 1861, Pittsboro, North Carolina	Co. J, 32nd North Carolina Infantry	May 10, 1864, Wilderness, Virginia	Point Lookout, Maryland, transferred to Elmira Prison, NY, August 6, 1864	Died March 6, 1865 of Pneumonia, Grave No. 1962. Regiment 22nd NC on Headstone.
Tyson, Gideon A. Private	22	April 30, 1862, Wilmington, New Hanover County, North Carolina	Co. H, 36th Regiment, 2nd North Carolina Artillery	January 15, 1865, Fort Fisher, North Carolina	February 1, 1865, Elmira Prison Camp, New York	Oath of Allegiance July 7, 1865
Tysor, Thomas B. Corporal	24	April 15, 1861, Pittsboro, North Carolina	Co. J, 32nd North Carolina Infantry	July 13, 1864, Fort Stevens, DC. Gunshot Wound Left Elbow. Amputated Arm.	Old Capital Prison, Washington, DC transferred to Elmira Prison, NY, August 27, 1864	Exchanged March 2, 1865 at Akins Landing on the James River, Virginia

Name & Rank	Age	Enlisted	Regiment and State	Where Captured	Prison	Remarks
Tyus, Joseph M. Private	Unk	September 1, 1861, Sangster's Crossroads, Alabama	Co. G, 6th Alabama Infantry	May 5, 1864, Wilderness, Virginia	Point Lookout, Maryland, transferred to Elmira Prison, NY, August 17, 1864	Transferred For Exchange 10/11/64 to Point Lookout Prison Camp, MD. Died 10/26/64. Of Chronic Diarrhea at US Army Hospital Baltimore, MD
Tyus, Philip G. Private	40	August 11, 1862, Merritt Bridge, Florida	Co. E, 2nd Battalion Florida Infantry	June 25, 1864, Near Petersburg, Florida	Point Lookout, Maryland, transferred to Elmira Prison, NY, July 25, 1864	Oath of Allegiance May 21, 1865

Name & Rank	Age	Enlisted	Regiment and State	Where Captured	Prison	Remarks
Ulmer, G. L. Private	Unk	April 11, 1862, Coles Island, South Carolina	Co. F, 25th South Carolina Infantry	January 15, 1865, Fort Fisher, North Carolina	February 1, 1865, Elmira Prison Camp, New York	Oath of Allegiance July 11, 1865
Umbarger, James H. Private	Unk	December 22, 1863, Dublin, Virginia	Co. B, 4th Virginia Infantry	May 12, 1864, Spotsylvania Court House, Virginia	Point Lookout, Maryland, transferred to Elmira Prison, NY, August 2, 1864	Died September 14, 1864 of Pneumonia, Grave No. 285
Umbarger, Nathanial B. Private	Unk	February 16, 1863, Giles Court House, Virginia	Co. D, 30th Battalion Virginia Sharp Shooters	July 13, 1864, Near Washington, DC,	Old Capital Prison, Washington, DC, transferred to Elmira Prison, NY, July 23, 1864	Oath of Allegiance May 19, 1865
Underwood, Andrew J. Private	Unk	April 1, 1861, Lacy's Store, Virginia	Co. B, 44th Virginia Infantry	May 12, 1864, Spotsylvania Court House, Virginia	Point Lookout, Maryland, transferred to Elmira Prison, NY, August 2, 1864	Oath of Allegiance June 27, 1865
Underwood, Benjamin F. Private	Unk	March 4, 1862, Forsyth, Georgia	Co. B, 45th Georgia Infantry	May 6, 1864, Wilderness, Virginia	Point Lookout, Maryland, transferred to Elmira Prison, NY, August 14, 1864	Died February 17, 1865 of Chronic Diarrhea, Grave No. 2227

Name & Rank	Age	Enlisted	Regiment and State	Where Captured	Prison	Remarks
Underwood, Finis Private	Unk	December 7, 1862, Lebanon, Tennessee	Co. L, Jackson's 1st Regiment, Tennessee Heavy Artillery	August 23, 1864, Fort Morgan, Alabama	New Orleans, Louisiana transferred to Elmira Prison, NY, December 4, 1864.	Died January 28, 1865 of Typhoid Fever, Grave No. 1655
Underwood, Jesse Private	38	March 15, 1862, Floyd Court House, Virginia	Co. B, 42nd Virginia Infantry	May 12, 1864, Spotsylvania Court House, Virginia	Point Lookout Prison Camp, Maryland. Transferred to Elmira Prison, August 18, 1864	Died January 7, 1865 of Pneumonia, Grave No. 1231
Underwood, Jesse Private	Unk	July 4, 1861, Princeton, Virginia	Co. H, 60th Virginia Infantry	July 8, 1864, Harper's Ferry, Virginia	Old Capital Prison, Washington, DC, transferred to Elmira Prison, NY, July 23, 1864	Died February 4, 1865 of Variola (Smallpox), Grave No. 1742
Underwood, John Private	45	February 28, 1862, Graham, North Carolina	Co. D, 1st North Carolina Infantry	May 12, 1864, Spotsylvania Court House, Virginia	Point Lookout, Maryland, transferred to Elmira Prison, NY, August 6, 1864	Oath of Allegiance August 7, 1865
Underwood, Martin V. Private	21	November 13, 1861, Charleston, Tennessee	Co. J, 43rd Tennessee Infantry	May 17, 1863, Big Black, Mississippi	Point Lookout, Maryland, transferred to Elmira Prison, NY, July 23, 1864	Exchanged March 2, 1865 at Akins Landing on the James River, Virginia
Upchurch, James W. Sergeant	22	July 16, 1861, Forestville, North Carolina	Co. I, 1st North Carolina Infantry	May 12, 1864, Spotsylvania Court House, Virginia	Point Lookout, Maryland, transferred to Elmira Prison, NY, August 6, 1864	Exchanged February 20, 1865 at Boulware's or Cox Wharf on the James River, Virginia
Upshaw, James M. Sergeant	Unk	June 11, 1861, Camp McDonald, Georgia	Co. A, 3rd Battalion Georgia Sharp Shooters	August 16, 1864, Front Royal, Virginia	Old Capital Prison, Washington, DC transferred to Elmira Prison, NY, August 29, 1864	Exchanged March 10, 1865 at Boulware's Wharf on the James River, Virginia
Upton, Robert Private	Unk	August 20, 1862, Statesville, North Carolina	Co. F, 18th North Carolina Infantry	May 12, 1864, Spotsylvania Court House, Virginia	Point Lookout, Maryland, transferred to Elmira Prison, NY, August 6, 1864	Died April 3, 1865 of Dysentery, Grave No. 2570

Name & Rank	Age	Enlisted	Regiment and State	Where Captured	Prison	Remarks
Ursery, Richard Private	17	March 23, 1862, Union Parish, Louisiana	Co. A, 6th Louisiana Infantry	May 5, 1864, Wilderness, Virginia	Point Lookout, Maryland, transferred to Elmira Prison, NY, August 17, 1864	Exchanged February 13, 1865 at Boulware's wharf on the James River, Virginia
Usbornd, Hiram Private	Unk	May 6, 1861, Grove Hill, Alabama	Co. J, 5th Alabama Infantry	July 24, 1863, Manassas Gap, Virginia	Point Lookout, Maryland, transferred to Elmira Prison, NY, August 18,1864	Exchanged October 29, 1864, at Venus Point, Savannah River, GA.
Utley, Jasper T. Drummer Private	34	June 23, 1864, Orange County, North Carolina	Co. D, 1st Battalion North Carolina Heavy Artillery	January 15, 1865, Fort Fisher, North Carolina	February 1, 1865, Elmira Prison Camp, New York	Oath of Allegiance June 23, 1865
Uttback, James V. Private	Unk	May 1, 1863, Fetterman, Virginia	Co. A, 25th Virginia Infantry	May 5, 1864, Mine Run Wilderness, Virginia	Point Lookout, Maryland, transferred to Elmira Prison, NY, August 2, 1864	Exchanged October 29, 1864, at Venus Point, Savannah River, GA.

Name & Rank	Age	Enlisted	Regiment and State	Where Captured	Prison	Remarks
Vaden, Dodson Private	Unk	Unknown	Co. B, Hood's Battalion, Virginia Reserve Infantry	June 15, 1864, Petersburg, Virginia	Point Lookout, Maryland, transferred to Elmira Prison, NY, July 30, 1864	Exchange March 14, 1865 at Boulware's Wharf on the James River, Virginia
Van Buren, John H. Private	Unk	November 3, 1863, Camp Ransom, Virginia	Co. H, 26th Battalion Virginia Infantry	June 3, 1864, Gaines Mill, Cold Harbor, Virginia	Point Lookout, Maryland, transferred to Elmira Prison, NY, July 17,1864	Oath of Allegiance June 16, 1865
Vance, Henry Private	Unk	July 1, 1863, Pocahontas County, Virginia	Co. G, 19th Virginia Cavalry	July 16, 1864, Loudoun County, Virginia	Old Capital Prison, Washington, DC, transferred to Elmira Prison, NY, July 23, 1864	Oath of Allegiance June 14, 1865
Vandavin, V. Engineer	Unk	Unknown	Confederate States Navy	September 12, 1863, North Carolina	Point Lookout, Maryland, transferred to Elmira Prison, NY, July 15, 1864	No Additional Information

Name & Rank	Age	Enlisted	Regiment and State	Where Captured	Prison	Remarks
Vandiver, John B. Private	20	June 30, 1862, Abbeville, South Carolina	Co. H, 7th Battalion South Carolina Infantry	August 21, 1864, Weldon Railroad, Virginia. Gunshot Wound Left Thigh.	Old Capital Prison, Washington, DC, transferred to Elmira Prison, NY, December 17, 1864	Exchanged March 2, 1865 at Boulware's Wharf on the James River, Virginia
Van Horn, Arnold A. Private	Unk	September 3, 1861, Camp Butler, South Carolina	Co. I, 14th South Carolina Infantry	July 29, 1864, Petersburg, Virginia	Point Lookout, Maryland, transferred to Elmira Prison, NY, August 12, 1864	Exchanged October 29, 1864, at Venus Point, Savannah River, GA.
Van Horn, Joseph A. Private	24	May 10, 1861, Morganton, North Carolina	Co. E, 16th North Carolina Infantry	July 29, 1864, Petersburg, Virginia	Point Lookout, Maryland, transferred to Elmira Prison, NY, August 12, 1864	Died January 17, 1865 of Chronic Diarrhea, Grave No. 1438
Van Horn, Robert S. Private	24	April 28, 1861, Washington, Virginia	Co. B, 6th Virginia Cavalry	May 31, 1864, Cold Harbor, Virginia	Point Lookout, Maryland, transferred to Elmira Prison, NY, July 11, 1864	Exchanged October 29, 1864, at Venus Point, Savannah River, GA.
Vanlanding-ham, William T. Private	18	April 19, 1864, Lancaster Court House, South Carolina.	Co. H, 4th South Carolina Infantry	May 28, 1864, Old Church, Cold Harbor, VA. Gunshot Wound Left Thigh Severe. Amputated Left Leg.	Old Capital Prison, Washington, DC transferred to Elmira Prison, NY, August 27, 1864	Exchanged February 13, 1865 at Boulware's Wharf on the James River, Virginia
VanMeter, Edward P. Private	Unk	July 29, 1863, Brandy Station, Virginia	Co. F, 7th Virginia Cavalry	September 13, 1863, Near Culpepper Court House, Virginia	Point Lookout, Maryland, transferred to Elmira Prison, NY, August 18, 1864	Unable to Travel for March 10, 1865 Exchange. No Further Information
Vann, Chester R. Sergeant	32	March 29, 1862, Warsaw, North Carolina	Co. K, 51st North Carolina Infantry	June 1, 1864, Cold Harbor, Virginia	Point Lookout Prison Camp, Maryland. Transferred to Elmira Prison Camp July 17, 1864	Died October 29, 1864 of Pneumonia, Grave No. 729

Name & Rank	Age	Enlisted	Regiment and State	Where Captured	Prison	Remarks
VanPelt, Abraham C. Private	Unk	January 30, 1864, Greenville, Alabama	Co. F, 1st Battalion Alabama Artillery	August 23, 1864, Fort Morgan, Alabama	Steam Press No. 4 New Orleans, Louisiana transferred to Elmira Prison, NY, October 8, 1864.	Oath of Allegiance June 16, 1865
Varnadoe, Andrew J. Private	Unk	September 1, 1861, Reidsville, Georgia	Co. B, 61st Georgia Infantry	May 12, 1864, Spotsylvania Court House, Virginia	Point Lookout, Maryland, transferred to Elmira Prison, NY, July 25, 1864	Oath of Allegiance June 21, 1865
Vaughan, Alfred J. Private	Unk	April 21, 1861, Richmond, Virginia	Co. G, 1st Virginia Infantry	May 16, 1864, Near Drury's Bluff, Virginia	Point Lookout, Maryland, transferred to Elmira Prison, NY, July 17,1864	Oath of Allegiance June 27, 1865
Vaughan, Henry Private	Unk	June 21, 1861, Port Royal, Virginia	Co. E, 47th Virginia Infantry	June 3, 1864, Old Church, Cold Harbor, Virginia	Transferred From Point Lookout Prison, MD, July 12, 1864. Train Never Arrived at Elmira Prison Camp, NY.	Died July 15, 1864 in Train Wreck at Shohola, Pennsylvania.
Vaughan, Jasper N. Private	19	July 19, 1861, Camp Anderson, Tennessee	Co. F, 23rd Tennessee Infantry	June 17, 1864, Petersburg, Virginia	Point Lookout, Maryland, transferred to Elmira Prison, NY, July 30, 1864	Died February 5, 1865 of Pneumonia, Grave No. 1901
Vaughan, John W. Private	22	December 21, 1861, Nashville, Tennessee	Co. I, 44th Tennessee Infantry	June 17, 1864, Petersburg, Virginia	Point Lookout, Maryland, transferred to Elmira Prison, NY, July 30, 1864	Oath of Allegiance April 26, 1865. Early Release per Lincoln's Proclamation, 12/8/1863.
Vaughan, Richard H. Corporal	19	July 1, 1861, Murfreesboro, Tennessee	Co. E, 23rd Tennessee Infantry	June 17, 1864, Petersburg, Virginia	Point Lookout, Maryland, transferred to Elmira Prison, NY, July 30, 1864	Oath of Allegiance May 15, 1865
Vaughan, W. C. Private	Unk	Unknown	Co. F, 18th South Carolina Infantry	July 30, 1864, Petersburg, Virginia	Point Lookout, Maryland, transferred to Elmira Prison, NY, August 12, 1864	Oath of Allegiance July 3, 1865

Name & Rank	Age	Enlisted	Regiment and State	Where Captured	Prison	Remarks
Vaughan, William A. Private	Unk	February 12, 1863, Camp of Instruction, Virginia	Co. A, 4th Virginia Infantry	May 12, 1864, Spotsylvania Court House, Virginia	Point Lookout, Maryland, transferred to Elmira Prison, NY, July 25, 1864	Oath of Allegiance June 16, 1865
Vaughn, A. R. Corporal	Unk	November 7, 1861, Bethel, Virginia	Co. B, 3rd Virginia Cavalry	August 16, 1864, Front Royal, Virginia	Old Capital Prison, Washington, DC transferred to Elmira Prison, NY, August 29, 1864	Exchanged February 25, 1865 at Boulware's or Cox Wharf on the James River, Virginia
Vaughn, Abraham S. Private	Unk	March 20, 1862, Elk Creek, Virginia	Co. F, 4th Virginia Infantry	May 12, 1864, Spotsylvania Court House, Virginia	Point Lookout, Maryland, transferred to Elmira Prison, NY, August 2, 1864	Oath of Allegiance June 16, 1865
Vaughn, Q. C. Private	Unk	Unknown	Co. B, Hood's Battalion, Virginia Reserve Infantry	June 15, 1864, Petersburg, Virginia	Point Lookout, Maryland, transferred to Elmira Prison, NY, July 12,1864	Exchanged October 29, 1864, at Venus Point, Savannah River, GA.
Vaughn, Robert L. Private	Unk	March 1, 1863, Franklin County, Georgia	Co. H, 24th Georgia Infantry	August 16, 1864, Front Royal, Virginia	Old Capital Prison, Washington, DC. Transferred to Elmira Prison Camp, NY, August 29, 1864.	Died February 25, 1865 of Chronic Diarrhea, Grave No. 2290
Vaughn, William H. Private	20	June 8, 1861, Fayetteville, North Carolina	Co. D, 2nd North Carolina Cavalry	June 3, 1864, Near Talapatomoy Creek Cold Harbor, Virginia	Point Lookout, Maryland, transferred to Elmira Prison, NY, July 12, 1864	Oath of Allegiance June 21, 1865
Vaughn, William M. Private	18	February 25, 1862, Wadesboro, North Carolina	Co. K, 43rd North Carolina Infantry	May 16, 1864, Drury's Bluff, Virginia	Point Lookout, Maryland, transferred to Elmira Prison, NY, July 11, 1864	Exchanged March 14, 1865 at Boulware's Wharf on the James River, Virginia
Vaught, Larkin Corporal	Unk	August 25, 1861, Big Spring, Virginia	Co. J, 14th Tennessee Infantry	May 24, 1864, Hanover Junction, Virginia	Point Lookout, Maryland, transferred to Elmira Prison, NY, July 23, 1864	Oath of Allegiance May 29, 1865

Name & Rank	Age	Enlisted	Regiment and State	Where Captured	Prison	Remarks
Vause, Edward K. Private	22	June 10, 1861, Whiteville, North Carolina	Co. C, 18th North Carolina Infantry	May 12, 1864, Spotsylvania Court House, Virginia	Point Lookout, Maryland, transferred to Elmira Prison, NY, August 6, 1864	Exchanged October 29, 1864, at Venus Point, Savannah River, GA.
Veal, Joseph T. Private	17	Enlisted in November 1864.	Co. C, 3rd Battalion North Carolina Light Artillery	January 15, 1865, Fort Fisher, North Carolina	February 1, 1865, Elmira Prison Camp, New York	Exchanged February 20, 1865 at Boulware's or Cox Wharf on the James River, Virginia
Veitch, Isaac A. Private	Unk	May 25, 1861, Centreville, Virginia	Co. F, 6th Virginia Cavalry	May 12, 1864, Spotsylvania Court House, Virginia	Point Lookout, Maryland, transferred to Elmira Prison, NY, August 12, 1864	Oath of Allegiance July 11, 1865
Venable, David Private	Unk	April 1, 1862, Abingdon, Virginia	Co. F, 48th Virginia Infantry	May 12, 1864, Spotsylvania Court House, Virginia	Point Lookout, Maryland, transferred to Elmira Prison, NY, August 2, 1864	Oath of Allegiance, June 27, 1865
Venn, Frank H. Sergeant	23	May 25, 1861, Marshall County, Mississippi	Co. J, 19th Mississippi Infantry	May 22, 1864, North Anna, Virginia	Point Lookout, Maryland, transferred to Elmira Prison, NY, July 11, 1864	Oath of Allegiance June 14, 1865
Vest, John R. Private	Unk	May 18, 1861, Lisbon, Virginia	Co. C, 42nd Virginia Infantry	May 12, 1864, Spotsylvania Court House, Virginia	Point Lookout, Maryland, transferred to Elmira Prison, NY, August 2,1864	Oath of Allegiance June 19, 1865
Vest, Samuel Private	34	July 15, 1862, Forsyth County, North Carolina	Co. G, 33rd North Carolina Infantry	May 6, 1864, Wilderness, Virginia	Point Lookout, Maryland, transferred to Elmira Prison, NY, August 17, 1864	Died February 23, 1865 of Chronic Diarrhea, Grave No. 2245
Via, Wesley T. Corporal	Unk	May 21, 1861, Brownsburg, Virginia	Co. H, 25th Virginia Infantry	May 5, 1864, Wilderness, Virginia	Point Lookout, Maryland, transferred to Elmira Prison, NY, August 14, 1864	Oath of Allegiance June 19, 1865

Name & Rank	Age	Enlisted	Regiment and State	Where Captured	Prison	Remarks
Vicente, John H. Private	22	March 3, 1861, Baltimore, Virginia	Co. G, Butler's 1st South Carolina infantry	November 27, 1864, Charlotte, Virginia. Gunshot Wound of Arm.	Old Capital Prison, Washington, DC, transferred to Elmira Prison, NY, December 17, 1864	Oath of Allegiance June 23, 1865
Vick, Elisha Private	18	May 1, 1862, South Mills, North Carolina	Co. D, 32nd North Carolina Infantry	May 10, 1864, Near Mine Run Spotsylvania, Virginia	Point Lookout, Maryland, transferred to Elmira Prison, NY, August 6, 1864	Oath of Allegiance June 27, 1865
Vick, James Private	Unk	July 6, 1863, Camp Palmyra, Thomasville, Georgia	Co. E, 20th Battalion Georgia Cavalry	May 30, 1864, Cold Harbor, Virginia	Point Lookout, Maryland, transferred to Elmira Prison, NY, July 12, 1864	Exchanged October 29, 1864, at Venus Point, Savannah River, GA.
Vick, William H. Private	Unk	March 18, 1862, Marengo County, Alabama	Co. A, 43rd Alabama Infantry	June 17, 1864, Petersburg, Virginia	Point Lookout, Maryland, transferred to Elmira Prison, NY, July 30, 1864	Oath of Allegiance July 7, 1865
Vickers, James W. Private	Unk	March 14, 1862, Newbern, Virginia	Co. C, 4th Virginia Infantry	May 5, 1864, Wilderness, Virginia	Point Lookout, Maryland, transferred to Elmira Prison, NY, August 2, 1864	No Additional Information
Vickers, Joseph G. Private	19	September 2, 1861, Orange County Court House, North Carolina	Co. G, 28th North Carolina Infantry	May 6, 1864, Wilderness, Virginia	Point Lookout, Maryland, transferred to Elmira Prison, NY, August 14, 1864	Oath of Allegiance June 14, 1865
Vickery, Franklin Corporal	Unk	September 4, 1863, Butler County, Alabama	Co. D, 61st Alabama Infantry	May 12, 1864, Spotsylvania Court House, Virginia	Point Lookout, Maryland, transferred to Elmira Prison, NY, July 30, 1864	Oath of Allegiance July 11, 1865
Vickery, Miles A. Private	18	April 13, 1863, Camp Holmes, North Carolina	Co. F, 32nd North Carolina Infantry	May 10, 1864, Wilderness, Virginia	Point Lookout, Maryland, transferred to Elmira Prison, NY, August 6, 1864	Died November 15, 1864 of Pneumonia, Grave No. 798

Name & Rank	Age	Enlisted	Regiment and State	Where Captured	Prison	Remarks
Villepigue, C. L. Private	Unk	Unknown	Co. A, 7th Carolina Cavalry	May 7, 1864, Lyttleton, Virginia	Point Lookout, Maryland, transferred to Elmira Prison, NY, August 17, 1864	Died February 4, 1865 of Variola (Smallpox), Grave No. 1741
Vincent, J. B. Private	25	August 6, 1861, Petersburg, Virginia	Co. H, 2nd North Carolina Cavalry	September 22, 1863, Near Culpepper, Virginia	Point Lookout, Maryland, transferred to Elmira Prison, NY, August 18, 1864	Oath of Allegiance June 14, 1865
Vincent, James B. Private	29	June 20, 1861, Gander Hill, North Carolina	Co. D, 7th North Carolina Infantry	May 6, 1864, Wilderness, Virginia	Point Lookout, Maryland, transferred to Elmira Prison, NY, July 23, 1864	Oath of Allegiance May 13, 1865
Vincent, John Private	Unk	November 2, 1862, Newburg, Tennessee	Co. B, 3rd Tennessee Infantry	May 12, 1863, Raymond, Mississippi	Point Lookout, Maryland, transferred to Elmira Prison, NY, August 18, 1864	Exchanged February 25, 1865 at Boulware's wharf on the James River, Virginia
Vincent, William H. Private	Unk	May 17, 1861, Fairmont, Virginia	Co. A, 31st Virginia Infantry	May 12, 1864, Spotsylvania, Virginia	Point Lookout, Maryland, transferred to Elmira Prison, NY, July 23, 1864	Oath of Allegiance May 19, 1865
Vines, Chesley D. Private	Unk	May 29, 1863, Covington County, Alabama	Co. E, 61st Alabama Infantry	May 12, 1864, Spotsylvania Court House, Virginia	Point Lookout, Maryland, transferred to Elmira Prison, NY, July 3, 1864	Died March 20, 1865, Diarrhea, Grave No. 1575. Headstone has Vions.
Vines, Henry Private	18	April 30, 1862, Old Brunswick Town, North Carolina	Co. G, 36th Regiment, 2nd North Carolina Artillery	January 15, 1865, Fort Fisher, North Carolina	February 1, 1865, Elmira Prison Camp, New York	Oath of Allegiance July 20, 1865. Both Legs Amputated to Knees Because of Frostbite.
Vines, William Henry Private	Unk	September 3, 1862, Butler, Alabama	Co. F, 1st Battalion Alabama Artillery	August 23, 1864, Fort Morgan, Alabama	Steam Press No. 4 New Orleans, Louisiana transferred to Elmira Prison, NY, October 8, 1864.	Died December 2, 1864, of Pneumonia, Grave No. 1006

Name & Rank	Age	Enlisted	Regiment and State	Where Captured	Prison	Remarks
Vineyard, George W. Private	Unk	March 19, 1862, Scott County, Virginia	Co. H, 48th Virginia Infantry	May 12, 1864, Near Spotsylvania Court House, Virginia	Point Lookout, Maryland, transferred to Elmira Prison, NY, August 6, 1864	Oath of Allegiance June 27, 1865
Vineyard, William J. Private	20	March 19, 1862, Scott County, Virginia	Co. H, 48th Virginia Infantry	May 12, 1864, Near Spotsylvania Court House, Virginia	Point Lookout, Maryland, transferred to Elmira Prison, NY, August 6, 1864	Oath of Allegiance June 27, 1865
Vining, Elisha Private	Unk	June 15, 1861, Eatonton, Georgia	Co. G, 12th Georgia Infantry	May 10, 1864, Spotsylvania Court House, Virginia	Point Lookout, Maryland, transferred to Elmira Prison, NY, July 30, 1864	Oath of Allegiance June 21, 1865
Vinson, Daniel J. Private	Unk	June 8, 1863, Goldsboro, North Carolina	Co. F, 10th Regiment, 1st North Carolina Artillery	January 15, 1865, Fort Fisher, North Carolina	February 1, 1865, Elmira Prison Camp, New York	Died March 16, 1865 of Chronic Diarrhea, Grave No. 1701. Headstone has David J. Vinson.
Vinson, J. B. Private	Unk	September 12, 1862, Lowndes, Alabama	Co. F, 1st Battalion Alabama Artillery	August 23, 1864, Fort Morgan, Alabama	Steam Press No. 4 New Orleans, Louisiana transferred to Elmira Prison, NY, October 8, 1864.	Died November 29, 1864 of Chronic Diarrhea, Grave No. 986
Vinson, P. J. Private	Unk	September 12, 1862, Lowndes, Alabama	Co. F, 1st Battalion Alabama Artillery	August 23, 1864, Fort Morgan, Alabama	Steam Press No. 4 New Orleans, Louisiana transferred to Elmira Prison, NY, October 8, 1864.	Died January 5, 1865 of Chronic Diarrhea, Grave No. 1253
Vinson, Spiers D. Corporal	Unk	August 31, 1861, Reidsville, Georgia	Co. B, 61st Georgia Infantry	May 6, 1864, Wilderness, Virginia	Point Lookout, Maryland, transferred to Elmira Prison, NY, August 14, 1864	Oath of Allegiance May 17, 1865
Vinson, Uriah T. Private	Unk	September 12, 1863, Goldsboro, North Carolina	Co. F, 10th Regiment, 1st North Carolina Artillery	January 15, 1865, Fort Fisher, North Carolina	February 1, 1865, Elmira Prison Camp, New York	Died March 19, 1865 of Pneumonia, Grave No. 1581

Name & Rank	Age	Enlisted	Regiment and State	Where Captured	Prison	Remarks
Vinson, William J. Private	23	March 7, 1861, Autauga, Alabama	Co. E, 1st Battalion Alabama Artillery	August 23, 1864, Fort Morgan, Alabama	Steam Press No. 4 New Orleans, Louisiana transferred to Elmira Prison, NY, October 8, 1864.	Oath of Allegiance May 29, 1865
Vint, William Private	19	Unknown	Co. G, 18th Virginia Cavalry	August 10, 1864, Winchester, Virginia	Old Capital Prison, Washington, DC transferred to Elmira Prison, NY, August 29, 1864	Oath of Allegiance June 14, 1865
Vipperman, Emanuel J. Private	23	June 15, 1861, Washington County, Virginia	Co. D, 42nd Virginia Infantry	May 12, 1864, Spotsylvania Court House, Virginia	Point Lookout, Maryland, transferred to Elmira Prison, NY, August 6, 1864	Oath of Allegiance July 7, 1865
Vladimir, Samuel M. Private	Unk	April 10, 1862, Des Arc, Arkansas	Co. F, 3rd Battalion Missouri Cavalry	May 17, 1863, Big Black Bridge, Champion Hill, Mississippi	Point Lookout, Maryland, transferred to Elmira Prison, NY, August 18, 1864	Exchanged February 13, 1865 at Boulware's wharf on the James River, VA
Vocelle, Augustus Private	Unk	January 4, 1864, Charleston, South Carolina	Co. E, 25th South Carolina Infantry	January 15, 1865, Fort Fisher, North Carolina	February 1, 1865, Elmira Prison Camp, New York	Died March 21, 1865 of Pneumonia, Grave No. 1527
Voorhees, Abraham Private	21	March 16, 1861, Winchester, Virginia	Co. C, 2nd Virginia Infantry	May 12, 1864, Near Spotsylvania Court House, Virginia	Point Lookout, Maryland, transferred to Elmira Prison, NY, August 6, 1864	Exchanged October 29, 1864 at Venus Point, Savannah River, GA.
Voss, Albert G. Private	25	Unknown	Co. H, 2nd North Carolina Cavalry	April 1, 1865, Hatchers Run, Virginia. Saber Wound on Head.	Old Capital Prison, Washington D. C. Transferred to Elmira Prison, NY, May 2, 1865.	Oath of Allegiance July 7, 1865
Vuncannon, William Private	35	February 26, 1862, Jonesboro, North Carolina	Co. C, 3rd North Carolina Infantry	May 12, 1864, Near Spotsylvania County Court House, Virginia	Point Lookout, Maryland, transferred to Elmira Prison, NY, August 14, 1864	Died July 7, 1865 of Chronic Diarrhea, Grave No. 2842. Name Vancannon on Headstone.

Name & Rank	Age	Enlisted	Regiment and State	Where Captured	Prison	Remarks
Waddle, Hughston Sergeant	23	September 15, 1861, Allegheny County, North Carolina	Co. K, 37th North Carolina Infantry	July 29, 1864, Petersburg, Virginia	Point Lookout, Maryland, transferred to Elmira Prison, NY, August 12, 1864	Oath of Allegiance June 16, 1865
Wade, Allen A. Corporal	30	March 5, 1862, Summerville, North Carolina	Co. D, 3rd North Carolina Cavalry	May 14, 1864, Near Fort Darling, Virginia	Point Lookout, Maryland, transferred to Elmira Prison, NY, August 17, 1864	Died March 2, 1865 of Diarrhea, Grave No. 2010
Wade, F. S. Sergeant	Unk	Unknown	Captain McNally's Scouts Louisiana	July 21, 1864, Near Morganza, Louisiana	New Orleans, Louisiana transferred to Elmira November 19, 1864.	Exchanged February 25, 1865 at Boulware's or Cox Wharf on the James River, Virginia
Wade, Jacob Private	Unk	Unknown	Co. H, 50th Virginia Infantry	May 5, 1864, Wilderness, Virginia	Point Lookout, Maryland, transferred to Elmira Prison, NY, August 14, 1864	Oath of Allegiance June 27, 1865
Wade, James Private	Unk	Unknown	Co. A, 1st Louisiana Cavalry	October 6, 1864, Near Hampton's Ferry, Louisiana	New Orleans, Louisiana transferred to Elmira November 19, 1864.	Exchanged February 25, 1865 at Boulware's or Cox Wharf on the James River, Virginia
Wade, Moses T. Private	19	April 26, 1861, Townsville, North Carolina	Co. D, 12th North Carolina Infantry	July 14, 1863, Falling Waters, Maryland	Point Lookout, Maryland, transferred to Elmira Prison, NY, August 18, 1864	Exchanged March 10, 1865 at Boulware's Wharf on the James River, Virginia
Wade, William H. Private	19	July 23, 1861, Staunton, Virginia	Co. H, 52nd Virginia Infantry	May 30, 1864 Mechanics-ville, Virginia	Point Lookout, Maryland, transferred to Elmira Prison, NY, July 9, 1864	Oath of Allegiance June 30, 1865
Waggoner, Andrew J. Private	Unk	November 14, 1862, Estelle Springs, Tennessee	Co. B, 44th Tennessee Infantry	June 17, 1864, Petersburg, Virginia	Point Lookout, Maryland, transferred to Elmira Prison, NY, July 30, 1864	Died December 29, 1864 of Pneumonia, Grave No. 1314

Name & Rank	Age	Enlisted	Regiment and State	Where Captured	Prison	Remarks
Wagner, Jacob Private	Unk	June 12, 1861, New Orleans, Louisiana	Co. K, 14th Louisiana Infantry	May 12, 1864, Spotsylvania Court House, Virginia	Point Lookout, Maryland, transferred to Elmira Prison, NY, July 25, 1864	Exchanged March 10, 1865 at Boulware's Wharf on the James River, Virginia
Wagner, Joseph C. Private	Unk	February 16, 1864, Augusta, Georgia	Co. D, 15th Georgia, Infantry	June 4, 1864, Gaines Mill Cold Harbor, Virginia	Point Lookout, Maryland, transferred to Elmira Prison, NY, July 12, 1864	Exchanged March 2, 1865 at Akins Landing on the James River, Virginia
Wagner, Joseph Private	Unk	May 8, 1861, Charleston, Virginia	Co. A, 26th Battalion, Virginia Infantry	May 31, 1864, Chickahominy, Cold Harbor, Virginia	Point Lookout, Maryland, transferred to Elmira Prison, NY, July 12, 1864	Exchanged March 14, 1865 at Boulware's Wharf on the James River, Virginia
Wagoner, Charles L. Private	Unk	May 20, 1861, Camp Harris, Tennessee	Co. B, 44th Tennessee Infantry	June 17, 1864, Petersburg, Virginia	Point Lookout, Maryland, transferred to Elmira Prison, NY, July 30, 1864	Exchanged February 25, 1865 at Boulware's Wharf on the James River, Virginia
Wagoner, George H. Private	Unk	February 28, 1862, Greensboro, Georgia	Co. E, 3rd Battalion Georgia Sharp Shooters	August 16, 1864, Front Royal, Virginia	Old Capital Prison, Washington, DC transferred to Elmira Prison, NY, August 29, 1864	Oath of Allegiance July 7, 1865
Wagoner, Jacob W. Private	30	March 1, 1862, Kinston, North Carolina	Co. D, 33rd North Carolina Infantry	May 12, 1864, Near Spotsylvania Court House, Virginia	Point Lookout, Maryland, transferred to Elmira Prison, NY, August 14, 1864	Died January 5, 1865 of Chronic Diarrhea, Grave No. 1236. Name Wagner on Headstone.
Wagoner, James D.	Unk	July 1, 1863, Greensboro, Georgia	Co. E, 3rd Battalion Georgia Sharp Shooters	August 16, 1864, Front Royal, Virginia	Old Capital Prison, Washington, DC transferred to Elmira Prison, NY, August 29, 1864	Exchanged March 2, 1865 at Akins Landing on the James River, Virginia
Wainright, John Private	25	May 13, 1862, Goldsboro, North Carolina	Co. A, 3rd North Carolina Infantry	May 12, 1864, Near Spotsylvania Court House, Virginia	Point Lookout, Maryland, transferred to Elmira Prison, NY, August 14, 1864	Died November 18, 1864 of Remittent Fever, Grave No. 968

Name & Rank	Age	Enlisted	Regiment and State	Where Captured	Prison	Remarks
Wainright, John F. Private	23	April 17, 1861, Christiansburg, Virginia	Co. G, 4th Virginia Infantry	May 12, 1864, Spotsylvania Court House, Virginia	Point Lookout, Maryland, transferred to Elmira Prison, NY, August 2, 1864	Exchanged March 2, 1865 at Akins Landing on the James River, Virginia
Wainright, N. P. Private	Unk	August 4, 1862, Camp Moore, Louisiana	Co. H, 3rd Louisiana Cavalry	October 7, 1864, Camp Moore, Louisiana	New Orleans, Louisiana transferred to Elmira November 19, 1864.	Exchanged February 25, 1865 at Boulware's or Cox Wharf on the James River, Virginia
Wainscott, Ewing M. Private	28	December 5, 1861, Sac River, St. Clair County, Missouri	Co. B, 1st Missouri Cavalry	May 17, 1863, Big Black Bridge, Champion Hill, Mississippi	Point Lookout, Maryland, transferred to Elmira Prison, NY, August 18, 1864	Exchanged February 13, 1865 at Boulware's wharf on the James River, Virginia
Wainscott, Lewis A. Private	26	January 26, 1862, Springfield, Missouri	Co. B, 3rd Battalion Missouri Cavalry	May 17, 1863, Big Black Bridge, Champion Hill, Mississippi	Point Lookout, Maryland, transferred to Elmira Prison, NY, August 18, 1864	Exchanged October 29, 1864, at Venus Point, Savannah River, GA.
Walding, James A. Private	22	April 27, 1862, Pine Grove, Mississippi	Co. D, 2nd Mississippi Infantry	May 5, 1864, Wilderness, Virginia	Point Lookout, Maryland, transferred to Elmira Prison, NY, August 14, 1864	Oath of Allegiance June 21, 1865
Waldren, Moses Private	Unk	June 17, 1861, Rocky Mount, Virginia	Co. K, 42nd Virginia Infantry	May 12, 1864, Spotsylvania Court House, Virginia	Point Lookout, Maryland, transferred to Elmira Prison, NY, August 2, 1864	Oath of Allegiance June 27, 1865
Waldron, James C. Corporal	Unk	April 9, 1862, Lake City, Florida	Co. B, 5th Florida Infantry	May 12, 1864, Spotsylvania Court House, Virginia	Point Lookout, Maryland, transferred to Elmira Prison, NY, July 25, 1864	Oath of Allegiance June 14, 1865
Waldron, R. D. Private	Unk	September 22, 1862, Waynesville, Georgia	Co. G, 7th Georgia Cavalry	June 11, 1864, Trevilian Station, Louisa Court House, Virginia	Point Lookout, Maryland, transferred to Elmira Prison, NY, July 25, 1864	Oath of Allegiance July 7, 1865

Name & Rank	Age	Enlisted	Regiment and State	Where Captured	Prison	Remarks
Waldrop, David F. Private	33	May 9, 1861, Ashland, Virginia	Co. F, 4th Virginia Cavalry	June 11, 1864, Trevilian Station, Louisa Court House, Virginia	Point Lookout, Maryland, transferred to Elmira Prison, NY, July 25, 1864	Exchanged March 2, 1865 at Akins Landing on the James River, Virginia
Waldrop, R. J. Private	17	February 16, 1864, Richmond, Virginia	Co. E, 25th Battalion Virginia Infantry	July 12, 1864, Cox's Farm, Virginia	Point Lookout, Maryland, transferred to Elmira Prison, NY, August 6, 1864	Died October 5, 1864 of Chronic Diarrhea, Grave No. 643
Walker, A, A. Civilian, British Subject	Unk	Unknown	Citizen of Britain	October 7, 1864, Lavinia, Louisiana	New Orleans, Louisiana transferred to Elmira November 19, 1864.	Oath of Allegiance June 20, 1865
Walker, Alfred B. Private	18	May 10, 1862, Winston, North Carolina	Co. K, 52nd North Carolina Infantry	May 21, 1864, Spotsylvania Court House, Virginia	Point Lookout, Maryland, transferred to Elmira Prison, NY, July 25, 1864	Oath of Allegiance January 11, 1865. Early Release per Lincoln's Proclamation, 12/8/1863.
Walker, B. A. Private	Unk	February 28, 1862, Camp Walton, Florida	Co. D, 1st Florida Infantry	September 28, 1864, Near Vernon, Florida	New Orleans, Louisiana transferred to Elmira November 19, 1864.	Oath of Allegiance July 7, 1865
Walker, Benjamin F. Private	22	June 3, 1862, Richmond, Virginia	Co. B, 59th Virginia Infantry	June 17, 1864, Petersburg, Virginia. Gunshot Wound Right Foot.	Old Capital Prison, Washington, DC transferred to Elmira Prison, NY, August 27, 1864	Exchanged February 13, 1865 at Boulware's Wharf on the James River, Virginia
Walker, Buckley Private	29	July 16, 1862, Camp Holmes, Raleigh, North Carolina	Co. D, 24th North Carolina Infantry	June 17, 1864, Petersburg, Virginia	Point Lookout, Maryland, transferred to Elmira Prison, NY, July 30, 1864	Exchanged March 14, 1865 at Boulware's Wharf on the James River, Virginia
Walker, Charles Private	Unk	November 9, 1863, Mobile, Alabama	Co. E, 1st Battalion Alabama Artillery	August 23, 1864, Fort Morgan, Alabama	Steam Press No. 4 New Orleans, Louisiana transferred to Elmira Prison, NY, October 8, 1864.	Exchanged February 20, 1865 at Boulware's or Cox Wharf on the James River, Virginia

Name & Rank	Age	Enlisted	Regiment and State	Where Captured	Prison	Remarks
Walker, Charles Private	Unk	March 4, 1862, Pulaski County, Georgia	Co. K, 49th Georgia Infantry	May 6, 1864, Near Mine Run Wilderness, Virginia	Point Lookout, Maryland, transferred to Elmira Prison, NY, August 17, 1864	Transferred for Exchange 10/11/64. Died 10/16/64 of Unknown Causes at US Army Hospital, Baltimore, MD
Walker, David J. Private	18	September 7, 1863, Brunswick County, North Carolina	Co. G, 36th Regiment, 2nd North Carolina Artillery	January 15, 1865, Fort Fisher, North Carolina	February 1, 1865, Elmira Prison Camp, New York	Died March 21, 1865 of Chronic Diarrhea, Grave No. 1533
Walker, Elisha Private	19	February 22, 1862, Wrightsville, Georgia	Co. F, 14th Georgia Infantry	May 6, 1864, Wilderness, Virginia	Point Lookout, Maryland, transferred to Elmira Prison, NY, August 14, 1864	Died October 15, 1864 of Chronic Diarrhea, Grave No. 563
Walker, George M. Private	Unk	December 11, 1863, Petersburg, Virginia	2nd Signal Corp Confederate States of America	July 21, 1864, Pickett's Farm, Cunles Neck, Virginia	Point Lookout, Maryland, transferred to Elmira Prison, NY, August 18, 1864	Exchanged March 14, 1865 at Boulware's Wharf on the James River, Virginia
Walker, George W. Private	24	September 6, 1862, Statesville, North Carolina	Co. A, 23rd North Carolina Infantry	May 12, 1864, Near Spotsylvania Court House, Virginia	Point Lookout, Maryland, transferred to Elmira Prison, NY, August 14, 1864	Oath of Allegiance June 12, 1865
Walker, Green Private	Unk	March 4, 1862, Irwinville, Georgia	Co. F, 49th Georgia Infantry	May 12, 1864, Spotsylvania Court House, Virginia	Point Lookout, Maryland, transferred to Elmira Prison, NY, August 12, 1864	Died September 14, 1864 of Chronic Diarrhea, Grave No. 265
Walker, Green Private	36	March 15, 1862, Minden, Louisiana	Co. G, 8th Louisiana Infantry	May 9, 1864, Spotsylvania, Virginia. Gunshot Wound Right Fracture of Knee. Leg Amputated.	Old Capital Prison, Washington, DC, transferred to Elmira Prison, NY, December 17, 1864	Exchanged February 13, 1865 at Boulware's Wharf on the James River, Virginia
Walker, Henderson Private	19	October 17, 1861, High House, Wake County, North Carolina	Co. H, 31st North Carolina Infantry	June 1, 1864, Gaines Mill Cold Harbor, Virginia	Point Lookout, Maryland, transferred to Elmira Prison, NY, July 12, 1864	Oath of Allegiance July 3, 1865

Name & Rank	Age	Enlisted	Regiment and State	Where Captured	Prison	Remarks
Walker, Henry G. Sergeant	Unk	March 1, 1862, Salisbury, North Carolina	Co. D, 42nd North Carolina Infantry	June 1, 1864, Cold Harbor, Virginia	Point Lookout, Maryland, transferred to Elmira Prison, NY, July 12, 1864	Died January 1, 1865 of Pneumonia Grave No. 1324
Walker, Hezekiah H. Private	Unk	April 3, 1862, Saltville, Virginia	Co. F, 29th Virginia Infantry	June 2, 1864, Gaines Mill Cold Harbor, Virginia. Gunshot Wound of Lower Leg.	Old Capital Prison, Washington, DC, transferred to Elmira Prison, NY, July 23, 1864	Died December 10, 1864 of Pneumonia, Grave No. 1156
Walker, J. D. Private	Unk	August 14, 1861, Richmond, Virginia	Co. K, 16th Georgia Infantry	August 16, 1864, Front Royal, Virginia	Old Capital Prison, Washington, DC transferred to Elmira Prison, NY, August 29, 1864	Died March 13, 1865 of Variola (Smallpox), Grave No. 1829
Walker, J. L. Private	Unk	Unknown	Co. H, 26th Virginia Infantry	June 3, 1864, Gaines Mill, Cold Harbor, Virginia	Point Lookout, Maryland, transferred to Elmira Prison, NY, July 17,1864	Exchanged March 2, 1865 at Boulware's Wharf on the James River, Virginia
Walker, J. P. Private	Unk	August 7, 1862, Campbell, Virginia	Co. J, 2nd Virginia Cavalry	September 11, 1864, Fairfax Station, Virginia	Old Capital Prison, Washington, DC transferred to Elmira Prison, NY, August 27, 1864	Exchanged March 2, 1865 at Akins Landing on the James River, Virginia
Walker, James A. Private	20	April 28, 1862, Monticello, Florida	Co. G, 5th Florida Infantry	May 12, 1864, Spotsylvania Court House, Virginia	Point Lookout, Maryland, transferred to Elmira Prison, NY, July 30, 1864	Exchanged March 10, 1865 at Boulware's Wharf on the James River, Virginia
Walker, James S. Private	19	July 8, 1862, Dobson, North Carolina	Co. F, 23rd North Carolina Infantry	May 12, 1864, Near Spotsylvania, Virginia	Point Lookout, Maryland, transferred to Elmira Prison, NY, August 14, 1864	Died March 4, 1865 of Chronic Diarrhea, Grave No. 2003
Walker, Joel H. Private	56	October 1, 1861, Camp Mangum, Raleigh, North Carolina	Co. H, 31st North Carolina Infantry	June 1, 1864, Gaines Mill Cold Harbor, Virginia	Point Lookout, Maryland, transferred to Elmira Prison, NY, July 12, 1864	Died September 28, 1864 of Pneumonia Grave No. 442

Name & Rank	Age	Enlisted	Regiment and State	Where Captured	Prison	Remarks
Walker, John Private	Unk	September 22, 1862, Camp Fort, Georgia	Co. D, 7th Georgia Cavalry	June 11, 1864, Trevilian Station, Louisa Court House, Virginia	Point Lookout, Maryland, transferred to Elmira Prison, NY, July 25, 1864	Died January 30, 1865 of Chronic Bronchitis, Grave No. 1789
Walker, John Private	24	March 16, 1862, McDowell, North Carolina	Co. D, 49th North Carolina Infantry	June 2, 1864, Bermuda Hundred, Virginia	Point Lookout, Maryland, transferred to Elmira Prison, NY, July 12, 1864	Exchanged February 20, 1865 at Boulware's or Cox Wharf on the James River, Virginia
Walker, John A. Private	Unk	July 25, 1861, Delps Muster Grounds, Carroll County, Virginia	Co. C, 29th Virginia Infantry	June 3, 1864, Chickahominy, Cold Harbor, Virginia	Point Lookout, Maryland, transferred to Elmira Prison, NY, July 12, 1864	Oath of Allegiance July 3, 1865
Walker, John B. Private	24	December 17, 1861, Camp on Sac River, Missouri	Co. C, 1st Missouri Cavalry	May 17, 1863, Big Black Bridge, Champion Hill, Mississippi	Point Lookout, Maryland, transferred to Elmira Prison, NY, August 18, 1864	Exchanged February 25, 1865 at Boulware's or Cox Wharf on the James River, Virginia
Walker, John F. Private	Unk	May 21, 1861, Brownsburg, Virginia	Co. H, 25th Virginia Infantry	May 5, 1864, Wilderness, Virginia	Point Lookout, Maryland, transferred to Elmira Prison, NY, August 17, 1864	Died October 7, 1864 of Chronic Diarrhea, Grave No. 582
Walker, John L. Private	Unk	August 29, 1863, White Sulfur Springs, Virginia	Co. H, 26th Battalion, Virginia Infantry	June 3, 1864, Gaines Mill Cold Harbor, Virginia	Point Lookout, Maryland, transferred to Elmira Prison, NY, July 17, 1864	Exchanged March 2, 1865 at Akins Landing on the James River, Virginia
Walker, John W. Private	Unk	July 18, 1863, Camp Cobb, Georgia	Co. B, 64th Georgia Infantry	June 17, 1864, Petersburg, Virginia	Point Lookout, Maryland, transferred to Elmira Prison, NY, July 30, 1864	Died December 17, 1864 of Pneumonia, Grave No. 1273.
Walker, Johnathan Private	23	March 16, 1862, McDowell, North Carolina	Co. D, 49th North Carolina Infantry	June 2, 1864, Bermuda Hundred, Virginia	Point Lookout, Maryland, transferred to Elmira Prison, NY, July 12, 1864	Exchanged February 20, 1865 at Boulware's or Cox Wharf on the James River, Virginia

Name & Rank	Age	Enlisted	Regiment and State	Where Captured	Prison	Remarks
Walker, L. D. Private	Unk	February 9, 1864, Montgomery, Alabama	Co. A, 1st Battalion Alabama Artillery	August 23, 1864, Fort Morgan, Alabama.	New Orleans, Louisiana transferred to Elmira Prison, NY, December 4, 1864.	Died January 14, 1865, Pneumonia, Grave No. 1460
Walker, Milton S. Private	20	August 10, 1861, Camp Butler, South Carolina	Co. D, 14th South Carolina Infantry	July 29, 1864, Petersburg, Virginia	Point Lookout, Maryland, transferred to Elmira Prison, NY, August 12, 1864	Oath of Allegiance July 11, 1865
Walker, P. A. Private	Unk	Unknown	Co. A, 26th Virginia Infantry	June 15, 1864, Near Petersburg, Virginia	Point Lookout, Maryland, transferred to Elmira Prison, NY, July 12, 1864	Oath of Allegiance July 3, 1865
Walker, W. C. Private	Unk	April 23, 1863, Fort Morgan, Alabama	Co. F, 1st Battalion Alabama Artillery	August 23, 1864, Fort Morgan, Alabama	Steam Press No. 4 New Orleans, Louisiana transferred to Elmira Prison, NY, October 8, 1864.	Died March 20, 1865 of Intermittent Fever, Grave No. 1567
Walker, William Private	17	October 17, 1861, High House, Wake County, North Carolina	Co. H, 31st North Carolina Infantry	June 1, 1864, Gaines Mill Cold Harbor, Virginia	Point Lookout, Maryland, transferred to Elmira Prison, NY, July 12, 1864	Oath of Allegiance July 3, 1865
Walker, William A. Private	26	August 27, 1861, Jefferson County, North Carolina	Co. A, 37th North Carolina Infantry	May 12, 1864, Near Spotsylvania Court House, Virginia	Point Lookout, Maryland, transferred to Elmira Prison, NY, August 14, 1864	Exchanged October 29, 1864, at Venus Point, Savannah River, GA.
Walker, William F. Private	Unk	Unknown	Co. K, Holcombe Legion, South Carolina Infantry	May 7, 1864, Stony Creek, Virginia	Point Lookout, Maryland, transferred to Elmira Prison, NY, August 17, 1864	Died April 19, 1865 of Chronic Diarrhea, Grave No. 1373
Walker, William F. Private	Unk	February 28, 1862, Goldsboro, North Carolina	Co. C, 52nd North Carolina Infantry	May 22, 1864, Near Hatteras Mills, Edenton, North Carolina	Point Lookout, Maryland, transferred to Elmira Prison, NY, July 23, 1864	Transferred for Exchange 10/11/64. Died 1/27/65 of Chronic Diarrhea at Point Lookout, MD.

Name & Rank	Age	Enlisted	Regiment and State	Where Captured	Prison	Remarks
Walker, William J. Private	Unk	July 8, 1862, Hillsboro, North Carolina	Co. F, 33rd North Carolina Infantry	May 6, 1864, Wilderness, Virginia	Old Capital Prison, Washington D. C. Transferred to Elmira Prison, NY, July 14, 1864	Oath of Allegiance June 19, 1865
Walker, William M. Sergeant	Unk	November 20, 1862, McMinnville, Tennessee	Co. D, 44th Tennessee Infantry	June 17, 1864, Petersburg, Virginia	Point Lookout, Maryland, transferred to Elmira Prison, NY, July 30, 1864	Oath of Allegiance May 29, 1865
Walkup, Thomas Private	Unk	January 1, 1863, Lewisburg, Virginia	Co. G, 26th Battalion, Virginia Infantry	May 31, 1864, Chickahominy, Cold Harbor, Virginia	Point Lookout, Maryland, transferred to Elmira Prison, NY, July 12, 1864	Oath of Allegiance May 29, 1865
Wall, Andrew J. Private	19	June 5, 1861, Dobson, North Carolina	Co. H, 21st North Carolina Infantry	July 8, 1864, Harper's Ferry, Virginia	Point Lookout, Maryland, transferred to Elmira Prison, NY, July 23, 1864	Oath of Allegiance July 3, 1865
Wall, George W. Private	33	July 25, 1863, Danbury, North Carolina	Co. I, 21st North Carolina Infantry	July 8, 1864, Harper's Ferry, Virginia	Point Lookout, Maryland, transferred to Elmira Prison, NY, July 23, 1864	Exchanged February 20, 1865 at Boulware's or Cox Wharf on the James River, Virginia
Wall, J. C. Private	18	May 20, 1863, Wilmington, North Carolina	Co. B, 31st North Carolina Infantry	June 1, 1864, Cold Harbor, Virginia	Point Lookout, Maryland, transferred to Elmira Prison, NY, July 12, 1864	Exchanged October 29, 1864, at Venus Point, Savannah River, GA.
Wall, John Sergeant	Unk	August 24, 1861, Atlanta, Georgia	Co. E, 3rd Battalion Georgia Sharp Shooters	August 16, 1864, Front Royal, Virginia	Old Capital Prison, Washington, DC transferred to Elmira Prison, NY, August 29, 1864	Oath of Allegiance May 29, 1865
Wall, John R. Private	Unk	September 20, 1863, Clayton, North Carolina	Co. C, 24th North Carolina Infantry	June 17, 1864, Petersburg, Virginia	Point Lookout, Maryland, transferred to Elmira Prison, NY, July 30, 1864	Died September 20, 1864 of Chronic Diarrhea, Grave No. 343

Name & Rank	Age	Enlisted	Regiment and State	Where Captured	Prison	Remarks
Wall, Mial Private	41	August 17, 1863, Fort Branch, Martin County, North Carolina	Co. G, 40th Regiment, 3rd North Carolina Heavy Artillery	January 15, 1865, Fort Fisher, North Carolina	February 1, 1865, Elmira Prison Camp, New York	Oath of Allegiance June 12, 1865
Wall, Milton D. C. Private	Unk	August 24, 1861, Clayton, Georgia	Co. E, 24th Georgia Infantry	August 16, 1864, Front Royal, Virginia	Old Capital Prison, Washington, DC transferred to Elmira Prison, NY, August 29, 1864	Died November 23, 1864 of Pneumonia, Grave No. 925
Wall, Samuel D. Private	19	March 15, 1862, Woodville, Mississippi	Co. K, 16th Mississippi Infantry	August 21, 1864, Weldon Railroad, Virginia. Gunshot Wound Groin.	Old Capital Prison, Washington, DC, transferred to Elmira Prison, NY, December 17, 1864	Exchanged February 20, 1865 at Boulware's or Cox Wharf on the James River, Virginia
Wallace, Albert S. Private	Unk	June 8, 1861, Amelia County Court House, Virginia	Co. H, 44th Virginia Infantry	May 12, 1864, Spotsylvania Court House, Virginia	Point Lookout, Maryland, transferred to Elmira Prison, NY, August 2, 1864	Died October 8, 1864 of Pneumonia, Grave No. 656
Wallace, Daniel Private	Unk	November 21, 1863, Camden, Alabama	Co. A, 1st Battalion Alabama Artillery	August 23, 1864, Fort Morgan, Alabama	New Orleans, Louisiana transferred to Elmira Prison, NY, December 4, 1864.	Died March 5, 1865 of Typhoid-Pneumonia, Grave No. 1973
Wallace, Henry W. Private	48	May 15, 1862, Fort St. Philip, Brunswick County, North Carolina	Co. G, 36th Regiment, 2nd North Carolina Artillery	January 15, 1865, Fort Fisher, North Carolina	February 1, 1865, Elmira Prison Camp, New York	Died February 18, 1865 of Pneumonia, Grave No. 2359
Wallace, James S. Private	Unk	August 20, 1862, Richmond, Virginia	Co. E, 25th Battalion Virginia Infantry	July 12, 1864, Cox's Farm, Virginia	Point Lookout, Maryland, transferred to Elmira Prison, NY, August 6, 1864	Oath of Allegiance June 16, 1865
Wallace, Joseph G. Private	Unk	April 16, 1864, Camp Vance, North Carolina	Co. F, 37th North Carolina Infantry	July 29, 1864, Petersburg, Virginia	Point Lookout, Maryland, transferred to Elmira Prison, NY, August 12, 1864	Exchanged October 29, 1864, at Venus Point, Savannah River, GA.

Name & Rank	Age	Enlisted	Regiment and State	Where Captured	Prison	Remarks
Wallace, Robert Private	Unk	September 9, 1863, Macon, Georgia	Co. K, 12th Georgia Infantry	May 10, 1864, Spotsylvania Court House, Virginia	Point Lookout, Maryland, transferred to Elmira Prison, NY, July 25, 1864	Exchanged February 13, 1865 at Boulware's wharf on the James River, Virginia
Wallace, Rufus Private	27	September 12, 1861, Carthage, North Carolina	Co. C, 35th North Carolina Infantry	June 17, 1864, Petersburg, Virginia	Point Lookout, Maryland, transferred to Elmira Prison, NY, July 30, 1864	Died September 30, 1864 of Pneumonia, Grave No. 397. First Name Robert on Headstone.
Wallace, Wilson Private	Unk	April 28, 1862, Camp Pillow, South Carolina	Co. J, 17th South Carolina Infantry	July 30, 1864, Petersburg, Virginia	Point Lookout, Maryland, transferred to Elmira Prison, NY, August 12, 1864	Oath of Allegiance June 19, 1865
Wallen, Elisha Private	Unk	May 25, 1864, Camp Vance, North Carolina	Co. I, 34th North Carolina Infantry	June 22, 1864, Near Petersburg, Virginia	Point Lookout, Maryland, transferred to Elmira Prison, NY, July 23, 1864	Died October 22, 1864 of Pneumonia, Grave No. 867. Name Whallen on Headstone.
Waller, John W. Private	27	April 5, 1862, Knoxville, Tennessee	Co. G, 63rd Tennessee Infantry	June 17, 1864, Near Petersburg, Virginia	Point Lookout, Maryland, transferred to Elmira Prison, NY, July 30, 1864	Exchanged February 25, 1865 at Boulware's or Cox Wharf on the James River, Virginia
Waller, Thomas H. Private	Unk	March 1, 1862, Catawba, Virginia	Co. H, 3rd Virginia Cavalry	August 16, 1864, Front Royal, Virginia	Old Capital Prison, Washington, DC transferred to Elmira Prison, NY, August 29, 1864	Exchanged February 20, 1865 at Boulware's or Cox Wharf on the James River, Virginia
Walling, J. A. Private	Unk	April 11, 1862, Coles Island, South Carolina	Co. F, 25th South Carolina Infantry	January 15, 1865, Fort Fisher, North Carolina	February 1, 1865, Elmira Prison Camp, New York	Oath of Allegiance July 7, 1865
Wallis, J. J. Sergeant	Unk	July 17, 1861, Center Hill, Georgia	Co. B, 16th Georgia Infantry	August 16, 1864, Front Royal, Virginia	Old Capital Prison, Washington, DC transferred to Elmira Prison, NY, August 29, 1864	Oath of Allegiance July 21, 1865

Name & Rank	Age	Enlisted	Regiment and State	Where Captured	Prison	Remarks
Wallis, S. W. Private	Unk	May 9, 1861, New Orleans, Louisiana	Co. K, 2nd Louisiana Infantry	May 12, 1864, Spotsylvania Court House, Virginia	Point Lookout, Maryland, transferred to Elmira Prison, NY, August 17, 1864	Exchanged February 25, 1865 at Boulware's or Cox Wharf on the James River, Virginia
Walls, Adly Private	33	January 1, 1862, Pfafftown, North Carolina	Co. C, 33rd North Carolina Infantry	May 12, 1864, Near Spotsylvania Court House, Virginia	Point Lookout, Maryland, transferred to Elmira Prison, NY, August 14, 1864	Oath of Allegiance June 30, 1865
Walls, James D. Sergeant	Unk	August 15. 1861, Cumberland Gap, Tennessee	Co. D, 17th Tennessee Infantry	June 17, 1864, Petersburg, Virginia	Point Lookout, Maryland, transferred to Elmira Prison, NY, July 30, 1864	Exchanged February 13, 1865 at Boulware's wharf on the James River, Virginia
Walraven, Elijah Private	Unk	February 21, 1862, Acworth, Georgia	Co. E, 3rd Battalion Georgia Sharp Shooters	August 16, 1864, Front Royal, Virginia	Old Capital Prison, Washington, DC transferred to Elmira Prison, NY, August 29, 1864	Oath of Allegiance July 7, 1865
Walsh, Augustin, Private	29	June 7, 1861, Camp Moore, Louisiana	Co. B, 7th Louisiana Infantry	May 11, 1864, Near Spotsylvania Court House, Virginia	Point Lookout, Maryland, transferred to Elmira Prison, NY, August 17, 1864	Exchanged March 10, 1865 at Boulware's wharf on the James River, Virginia
Walsh, Harvey Private	Unk	March 23, 1863, Wilkes County, North Carolina	Co. I, 53rd North Carolina Infantry	July 12, 1864, Near Washington, DC,	Point Lookout, Maryland, transferred to Elmira Prison, NY, July 23, 1864	Died April 18, 1865 of Pneumonia, Grave No. 1348
Walsh, James Private	Unk	October 1, 1861, Little Rock, Arkansas	Co. B, Jackson's 1st Regiment, Tennessee Heavy Artillery	August 23, 1864, Fort Morgan, Alabama	New Orleans, Louisiana transferred to Elmira Prison, NY, December 4, 1864.	Oath of Allegiance May 29, 1865
Walsh, Murphy S. Private	Unk	Unknown	Co. G, 1st North Carolina Infantry	Unknown	Unknown	Died January 26, 1865 of Unknown Disease, Grave No. 1627

Name & Rank	Age	Enlisted	Regiment and State	Where Captured	Prison	Remarks
Walsh, William Corporal	Unk	March 20, 1863, Wilkes County, North Carolina	Co. K, 53rd North Carolina Infantry	July 12, 1864, Near Washington, DC,	Point Lookout, Maryland, transferred to Elmira Prison, NY, July 23, 1864	Died September 24, 1864 of Chronic Diarrhea, Grave No. 464
Walston, Jarrett Private	19	July 15, 1862, Raleigh, North Carolina	Co. K, 1st North Carolina Infantry	May 12, 1864, Spotsylvania Court House, Virginia	Point Lookout, Maryland, transferred to Elmira Prison, NY, August 6, 1864	Died March 15, 1865 of Pneumonia, Grave No. 1681
Walt, C. Private	Unk	April 1, 1864, Bat Tracy, Tennessee	Co. A, Jackson's 1st Regiment, Tennessee Heavy Artillery	August 23, 1864, Fort Morgan, Alabama	New Orleans, Louisiana transferred to Elmira Prison, NY, December 4, 1864.	Exchanged February 13, 1865 at Boulware's wharf on the James River, Virginia
Walter, Allison E. Private	18	May 1, 1861, Fort Johnson, North Carolina	Co. B, 20th North Carolina Infantry	May 12, 1864, Near Spotsylvania Court House, Virginia	Point Lookout, Maryland, transferred to Elmira Prison, NY, August 14, 1864	Exchanged March 2, 1865 at Akins Landing on the James River, Virginia
Walter, Frederick Private	Unk	October 15, 1861, Fort Henry, Tennessee	Co. B, 1st Jackson's Tennessee Heavy Artillery	August 23, 1864, Fort Morgan, Alabama.	New Orleans, Louisiana transferred to Elmira Prison, NY, December 4, 1864.	Exchanged February 25, 1865 at Boulware's or Cox Wharf on the James River, Virginia
Walter, M. A. Sergeant	Unk	July 7, 1862, Concord, North Carolina	Co. F, 57th North Carolina Infantry	August 22, 1864, Charlestown, Virginia	Old Capital Prison, Washington, DC transferred to Elmira Prison, NY, August 29, 1864	Oath of Allegiance June 21, 1865
Walters, A. M. Private	Unk	Unknown	Co. D, 7th Louisiana Infantry	Unknown	Unknown	Died February 20, 1865 of Unknown Disease, Grave. 2315
Walters, John H. Private	Unk	March 15, 1862, Culpepper Court House, Virginia	Co. B, 13th Virginia Infantry	July 5, 1863, Gettysburg, Pennsylvania	Point Lookout, Maryland, transferred to Elmira Prison, NY, July 25, 1864	Exchanged October 29, 1864, at Venus Point, Savannah River, GA.

Name & Rank	Age	Enlisted	Regiment and State	Where Captured	Prison	Remarks
Walters, John M. Private	Unk	March 26, 1864, Camp Holmes, North Carolina	Co. H, 13th North Carolina Infantry	May 6, 1864, Wilderness, Virginia	Point Lookout, Maryland, transferred to Elmira Prison, NY, July 25, 1864	Oath of Allegiance May 29, 1865
Walthall, Silas L. Private	23	April 17, 1861, Christiansburg, Virginia	Co. G, 4th Virginia Infantry	May 12, 1864, Spotsylvania Court House, Virginia	Point Lookout, Maryland, transferred to Elmira Prison, NY, August 2, 1864	Oath of Allegiance June 16, 1865
Waltham, Elisha E. Private	19	May 16, 1862, Camp McIntosh, North Carolina	Co. K, 3rd North Carolina Infantry	May 12, 1864, Near Spotsylvania County Court House, Virginia	Point Lookout, Maryland, transferred to Elmira Prison, NY, August 14, 1864	Exchanged February 20, 1865 at Boulware's or Cox Wharf on the James River, Virginia
Waltham, John D. Private	21	May 16, 1862, Camp McIntosh, North Carolina	Co. K, 3rd North Carolina Infantry	May 12, 1864, Near Spotsylvania County Court House, Virginia	Point Lookout, Maryland, transferred to Elmira Prison, NY, August 14, 1864	Oath of Allegiance June 21, 1865
Waltham, Seth Private	29	May 31, 1861, Middle Sound, North Carolina	Co. E, 1st North Carolina Infantry	May 12, 1864, Spotsylvania Court House, Virginia	Point Lookout, Maryland, transferred to Elmira Prison, NY, August 6, 1864	Oath of Allegiance June 30, 1865
Walton, John Private	Unk	August 15, 1863, Halifax Court House, Virginia	Co. C, 59th Virginia Infantry	June 17, 1864, Petersburg, Virginia	Point Lookout, Maryland, transferred to Elmira Prison, NY, July 30, 1864	Exchanged 3/14/65. Died 4/6/65 at Chimborazo Hospital, Richmond, VA.
Walton, Samuel L. Private	Unk	February 24, 1862, Thompson's Store, Columbia County, Arkansas	Co. D, 12th Battalion, Arkansas Sharpshooters	May 16, 1863, Big Black, Champion Hill, Mississippi	Point Lookout, Maryland, transferred to Elmira Prison, NY, August 18, 1864	Exchanged February 20, 1865 at Boulware's or Cox Wharf on the James River, Virginia
Walton, Tilman M. Private	Unk	January 22, 1864, Orange County Court House, North Carolina	Co. B, 22nd North Carolina Infantry	May 6, 1864, Wilderness, Virginia	Point Lookout, Maryland, transferred to Elmira Prison, NY, August 14, 1864	Died November 5, 1864 of Pneumonia, Grave No. 765

Name & Rank	Age	Enlisted	Regiment and State	Where Captured	Prison	Remarks
Walton, Wiley Private	24	Unknown	Co. D, 50th Georgia Infantry	May 12, 1864, Spotsylvania, Virginia. Gunshot Wound Shoulder and Thigh.	Old Capital Prison, Washington, DC, transferred to Elmira Prison, NY, July 23, 1864	Exchanged October 29, 1864, at Venus Point, Savannah River, GA.
Walton, William Private	19	March 24, 1862, Marion, North Carolina	Co. B, 22nd North Carolina Infantry	May 6, 1864, Wilderness, Virginia	Point Lookout, Maryland, transferred to Elmira Prison, NY, August 14, 1864	Oath of Allegiance June 27, 1865
Wamack, John E. Private	Unk	April 7, 1862, Petersburg, Virginia	Co. F, 13th Virginia Cavalry	July 29, 1864, Petersburg, Virginia	Point Lookout, Maryland, transferred to Elmira Prison, NY, August 12, 1864	Oath of Allegiance June 16, 1865
Wammock, K. Thomas Private	22	June 12, 1861, Halifax County, North Carolina	Co. K, 1st North Carolina Infantry	May 12, 1864, Spotsylvania Court House, Virginia	Point Lookout, Maryland, transferred to Elmira Prison, NY, August 6, 1864	Oath of Allegiance June 12, 1865
Warbriton, Martin Van Buren Private	Unk	February 19, 1862, Richmond, Virginia	Capt. A. R. Courtney's Battery, Virginia Light Artillery	July 4, 1864, Major Allen's Farm, Virginia	Point Lookout, Maryland, transferred to Elmira Prison, NY, August 6, 1864	Died April 11, 1865 of Chronic Diarrhea, Grave No. 2687
Ward, A. J. Private	Unk	Unknown	Co. G, 27th South Carolina Infantry	June 24, 1864, Near Petersburg, Virginia	Point Lookout, Maryland, transferred to Elmira Prison, NY, August 18, 1864	Died October 2, 1864 of Chronic Diarrhea, Grave No. 416
Ward, Alfred C. Private	35	February 28, 1862, Greensboro, North Carolina	Co. B, 45th North Carolina Infantry	May 10, 1864, Spotsylvania Court House, Virginia	Point Lookout, Maryland, transferred to Elmira Prison, NY, August 6, 1864	Died January 22, 1865 of Variola (Smallpox), Grave No. 1597
Ward, Charles Private	30	June 7, 1861, Camp Moore, Louisiana	Co. C, 7th Louisiana Infantry	May 11, 1864, Near Spotsylvania Court House, Virginia	Point Lookout, Maryland, transferred to Elmira Prison, NY, August 17, 1864	Exchanged February 25, 1865 at Boulware's or Cox Wharf on the James River, Virginia

Name & Rank	Age	Enlisted	Regiment and State	Where Captured	Prison	Remarks
Ward, Enoch C. Private	Unk	April 3, 1862, Saltville, Virginia	Co. F, 29th, Virginia Infantry	June 1, 1864, Gaines Mill Cold Harbor, Virginia	Point Lookout, Maryland, transferred to Elmira Prison, NY, July 12, 1864	Oath of Allegiance June 19, 1865
Ward, Hardy Private	Unk	March 13, 1861, Prattville, Alabama	Co. E, 1st Battalion Alabama Artillery	August 23, 1864, Fort Morgan, Alabama	New Orleans, Louisiana transferred to Elmira Prison, NY, December 4, 1864.	Died December 25, 1864 of Variola (Smallpox), Grave No. 1291
Ward, James M. Private	17	May 6, 1862, Fort St. Philip, Brunswick County, North Carolina	Co. C, 36th Regiment, 2nd North Carolina Artillery	January 15, 1865, Fort Fisher, North Carolina	Elmira Prison Camp, New York, February 1, 1865	Died March 17, 1865 of Diarrhea, Grave No. 1556
Ward, James M. Private	Unk	April 5, 1864, Camp Vance, Raleigh, North Carolina	Co. I, 57th North Carolina Infantry	July 12, 1864, Near Washington, DC,	Old Capital Prison, Washington, DC, transferred to Elmira Prison, NY, July 23, 1864	Died August 27, 1864 of Typhoid Fever, Grave No. 104
Ward, James W. Private	Unk	March 11, 1861, Wetumpka, Alabama	Co. E, 1st Battalion Alabama Artillery	August 23, 1864, Fort Morgan, Alabama	Steam Press No. 4 New Orleans, Louisiana transferred to Elmira Prison, NY, October 8, 1864.	Died January 11, 1865 of Chronic Diarrhea, Grave No. 1492
Ward, Joel Reaves Private	18	April 16, 1862, Old Brunswick Town, North Carolina	Co. G, 36th Regiment, 2nd North Carolina Artillery	January 15, 1865, Fort Fisher, North Carolina	February 1, 1865, Elmira Prison Camp, New York	Exchanged March 14, 1865 at Boulware's Wharf on the James River, Virginia
Ward, John W. Private	Unk	July 11, 1862, Lynchburg, Virginia	Co. I, 42nd Virginia Infantry	May 12, 1864, Near Spotsylvania Court House, Virginia	Point Lookout, Maryland, transferred to Elmira Prison, NY, August 6, 1864	Exchanged October 29, 1864, at Venus Point, Savannah River, GA.
Ward, Jonathan M. Private	Unk	July 27, 1861, Wyhteville, Virginia	Co. A, 50th Virginia Infantry	May 12, 1864, Spotsylvania Court House, Virginia	Point Lookout, Maryland, transferred to Elmira Prison, NY, August 2, 1864	Oath of Allegiance June 19, 1865

Name & Rank	Age	Enlisted	Regiment and State	Where Captured	Prison	Remarks
Ward, Joseph Private	24	June 4, 1861, Camp Moore, Louisiana	Co. F, 6th Louisiana Infantry	May 5, 1864, Wilderness, Virginia	Point Lookout, Maryland, transferred to Elmira Prison, NY, August 17, 1864	Exchanged October 29, 1864, at Venus Point, Savannah River, GA.
Ward, Joseph W. Private	39	November 1, 1861, Fort Ellis, Near Newbern, Craven County, North Carolina	Co. F, 36th Regiment, 2nd North Carolina Artillery	January 15, 1865, Fort Fisher, North Carolina	February 1, 1865, Elmira Prison Camp, New York	Exchanged February 20, 1865 at Boulware's or Cox Wharf on the James River, Virginia
Ward, Lawrence M. Private	28	July 21, 1863, Raleigh, North Carolina	Co. F, 24th North Carolina Infantry	June 17, 1864, Petersburg, Virginia	Point Lookout Prison Camp, Maryland. Transferred to Elmira Prison, July 30, 1864	Died December 10, 1864 of Congestion of the Brain, Grave No. 1044
Ward, Lorenzo Dow Private	30	May 1, 1862, Jefferson, North Carolina	Co. A, 37th North Carolina Infantry	May 12, 1864, Spotsylvania, Virginia. Gunshot Wound Left Side of Face.	Old Capital Prison, Washington, DC, transferred to Elmira Prison, NY, July 23, 1864	Died May 10, 1865 of Chronic Diarrhea, Grave No. 2784
Ward, McDaniel D. Private	20	April 24, 1861, Whiteville, Columbus County, North Carolina	Co K, 20th North Carolina Infantry	May 12, 1864, Near Spotsylvania Court House, Virginia	Point Lookout, Maryland, transferred to Elmira Prison, NY, August 14, 1864	Oath of Allegiance June 27, 1865
Ward, Melvin C. Private	Unk	July 27, 1861, Wyhteville, Virginia	Co. A, 50th Virginia Infantry	May 12, 1864, Spotsylvania Court House, Virginia	Point Lookout, Maryland, transferred to Elmira Prison, NY, August 2, 1864	Died February 22, 1865 of Typhoid Fever, Grave No. 2240
Ward, Oran W. Private	19	February 1, 1864, Randolph County, North Carolina	Co. F, 24th North Carolina Infantry	June 17, 1864, Petersburg, Virginia	Point Lookout, Maryland, transferred to Elmira Prison, NY, July 30, 1864	Died December 24, 1864 of Pneumonia, Grave No. 1093
Ward, Robert H. Private	Unk	October 13, 1861, Mobile, Alabama	Co. A, 21st Alabama Infantry	August 23, 1864 Fort Morgan, Alabama	New Orleans, Louisiana. Transferred to Elmira Prison Camp October 8, 1864	Oath of Allegiance June 14, 1865

Name & Rank	Age	Enlisted	Regiment and State	Where Captured	Prison	Remarks
Ward, Samuel Private	Unk	February 25, 1861, Abbeville, Alabama	Co. A, 1st Battalion Alabama Artillery	August 23, 1864, Fort Morgan, Alabama	New Orleans, Louisiana transferred to Elmira Prison, NY, December 4, 1864.	Oath of Allegiance May 15, 1865
Ward, Solomon R. Private	19	April 16, 1862, Old Brunswick Town, North Carolina	Co. G, 36th Regiment, 2nd North Carolina Artillery	January 15, 1865, Fort Fisher, North Carolina	February 1, 1865, Elmira Prison Camp, New York	Exchanged March 14, 1865 at Boulware's Wharf on the James River, Virginia
Ward, T. Private	Unk	Unknown	Co. B, 3rd Alabama Infantry	May 12, 1864, Spotsylvania Court House, Virginia	Point Lookout, Maryland, transferred to Elmira Prison, NY, August 12, 1864	Exchanged March 10, 1865 at Boulware's Wharf on the James River, Virginia
Ward, William H. Sergeant	21	April 20, 1861, Lynnhaven Beach, Princess Court House, Virginia	Co. D, 15th Virginia Cavalry	September 14, 1863, Dumpries, Near Culpepper, Virginia	Point Lookout, Maryland, transferred to Elmira Prison, NY, August 18, 1864	Exchanged March 10, 1865 at Boulware's Wharf on the James River, Virginia
Ward, William J. Private	26	December 20, 1861, Orange County, North Carolina	Co. G, 28th North Carolina Infantry	May 12, 1864, Near Spotsylvania Court House, Virginia	Point Lookout, Maryland, transferred to Elmira Prison, NY, August 14, 1864	Died October 6, 1864 of Chronic Diarrhea, Grave No. 597
Warden, James D. Private	Unk	July 11, 1861, Washington Point, Virginia	Co. A, 61st Virginia Infantry	May 24, 1864 Mechanics-ville, Virginia	Point Lookout, Maryland, transferred to Elmira Prison, NY, July 12, 1864	Oath of Allegiance July 19, 1865
Wardrope, Aaron J. Private	25	April 29, 1861, Marshall, North Carolina	Co. H, 16th North Carolina Infantry	May 6, 1864, Mine Run, Wilderness, Virginia	Point Lookout, Maryland, transferred to Elmira Prison, NY, August 14, 1864	Oath of Allegiance June 23, 1865
Ware, James B. Private	18	April 23, 1861, Gloucester Court House, Virginia	Co. A, 26th Virginia Infantry	June 15, 1864, Near Petersburg, Virginia	Point Lookout, Maryland, transferred to Elmira Prison, NY, July 12, 1864	Oath of Allegiance July 3, 1865
Ware, John H. Private	20	June 1, 1864, New Hanover County, North Carolina	Co. D, 13th Battalion North Carolina Light Artillery	January 15, 1865, Fort Fisher, North Carolina	February 1, 1865, Elmira Prison Camp, New York	Exchanged March 2, 1865 at Akins Landing on the James River, Virginia

Name & Rank	Age	Enlisted	Regiment and State	Where Captured	Prison	Remarks
Ware, Joseph P. H. Private	Unk	May 24, 1861, Urbanna, Virginia	Co. H, 55th Virginia Infantry	May 5, 1864, Wilderness, Virginia	Point Lookout, Maryland, transferred to Elmira Prison, NY, August 14, 1864	Exchanged October 29, 1864 at Venus Point, Savannah River, GA.
Ware, Robert R. Private	Unk	November 13, 1861, Savannah, Georgia	Co. E, 31st Georgia Infantry	July 18, 1864, Snickers' Gap, Virginia	Old Capital Prison, Washington D. C. Transferred to Elmira Prison, NY, July 12, 1864	Oath of Allegiance June 30, 1865
Ware, William T. Private	Unk	May 21, 1861, Valley Head, Virginia	Co. I, 25th Virginia Infantry	May 12, 1864, Spotsylvania Court House, Virginia	Point Lookout, Maryland, transferred to Elmira Prison, NY, August 12, 1864	Oath of Allegiance May 19, 1865
Ware, William W. Private	Unk	June 22, 1861, Richmond, Virginia	Co. C, 46th Virginia Infantry	June 16, 1864, Petersburg, Virginia	Point Lookout, Maryland, transferred to Elmira Prison, NY, July 25, 1864	Oath of Allegiance June 21, 1865
Warfield, William Civilian	Unk	Unknown	Virginia Citizen	May 3, 1864, Came in Union Lines at West Point, Virginia	Point Lookout, Maryland, transferred to Elmira Prison, NY, July 23, 1864	Oath of Allegiance December 1, 1864. Early Release per Lincoln's Proclamation, 12/8/1863.
Warmack, L. H. Private	Unk	December 9, 1861, Camp Trousdale, Tennessee	Co. K, 44th Tennessee Infantry	June 17, 1864, Petersburg, Virginia	Point Lookout, Maryland, transferred to Elmira Prison, NY, July 30, 1864	Died April 9, 1865 of Chronic Diarrhea, Grave No. 2625. Name Womack on Headstone.
Warmington, James Private	22	July 30, 1861, Salisbury, North Carolina	Co. K, 8th North Carolina Infantry	June 1, 1864, Gaines Farm, Cold Harbor, Virginia	Point Lookout, Maryland, transferred to Elmira Prison, NY, July 12, 1864	Died March 17, 1865 of Variola (Smallpox), Grave No. 1706
Warner, H. W. Private	27	September 3, 1862, Mocksville, North Carolina	Co. G, 7th Confederate Cavalry	May 7, 1864, Cypress Bridge, Virginia	Point Lookout, Maryland, transferred to Elmira Prison, NY, August 17, 1864	Oath of Allegiance June 23, 1865

Name & Rank	Age	Enlisted	Regiment and State	Where Captured	Prison	Remarks
Warner, Henry Private	20	February 25, 1862, Hardeeville, South Carolina	Co. J, 11th South Carolina Infantry	May 16, 1864, Near Drury's Bluff, Virginia	Point Lookout, Maryland, transferred to Elmira Prison, NY, July 25, 1864	Oath of Allegiance May 29, 1865
Warren, B. F. Private	Unk	October 1, 1862, Leetown, Virginia	Co. C, 5th Virginia Cavalry	June 11, 1864, Louisa Court House, Trevilian Station, Virginia	Point Lookout, Maryland, transferred to Elmira Prison, NY, July 30, 1864	Died January 29, 1865 of Variola (Smallpox), Grave No. 1808
Warren, Bluford E. Private	Unk	July 2, 1861, Bethel Am., Virginia	Co. F, 50th Virginia Infantry	May 12, 1864, Spotsylvania Court House, Virginia	Point Lookout, Maryland, transferred to Elmira Prison, NY, August 2, 1864	Died February 2, 1865 of Variola (Smallpox), Grave No. 1753
Warren, Burris F. Private	Unk	October 1, 1862, Lee Town, Virginia	Co. C, 5th Virginia Cavalry	June 11, 1864, Trevilian Station, Louisa Court House, Virginia	Point Lookout, Maryland, transferred to Elmira Prison, NY, July 25, 1864	Died January 29, 1865 of Variola (Smallpox), Grave No. 1808
Warren, G. S. Private	Unk	August 30, 1861, Waterboro, South Carolina	Co. J, 11th South Carolina Infantry	June 24, 1864, Petersburg, Virginia	Point Lookout, Maryland, transferred to Elmira Prison, NY, August 18, 1864	Transferred For Exchange 10/11/64 to Point Lookout Prison Camp, MD. Died 12/11/64 of Chronic Diarrhea at US Army Hospital Baltimore, MD.
Warren, Hiram Private	29	March 1, 1862, Reidsville, North Carolina	Co. H, 45th North Carolina Infantry	May 20, 1864, Spotsylvania Court House, Virginia	Point Lookout, Maryland, transferred to Elmira Prison, NY, July 3, 1864	Exchanged October 29, 1864, at Venus Point, Savannah River, GA.
Warren, J. Q. Private	30	April 27, 1861, Newton, North Carolina	Co. A, 12th North Carolina Infantry	July 12, 1864, Near Washington, DC,	Point Lookout, Maryland, transferred to Elmira Prison, NY, July 23, 1864	Oath of Allegiance July 7, 1865
Warren, James C. Private	25	April 4, 1862, Sampson County, North Carolina	Co. I, 51st North Carolina Infantry	May 31, 1864, Cold Harbor, Virginia	Point Lookout, Maryland, transferred to Elmira Prison, NY, July 12, 1864	Exchanged March 14, 1865 at Boulware's Wharf on the James River, Virginia

Name & Rank	Age	Enlisted	Regiment and State	Where Captured	Prison	Remarks
Warren, James D. Corporal	21	August 16, 1861, Luka, Mississippi	Co. G, 26th Mississippi Infantry	May 5, 1864, Wilderness, Virginia	Point Lookout, Maryland, transferred to Elmira Prison, NY, August 14, 1864	Exchanged 3/2/65, Died 3/15/65 at Howard's Grove Hospital, Richmond, VA
Warren, Jesse A. Private	Unk	December 24, 1863, Petersburg, Virginia	Signal Corps, Confederate States Army	July 6, 1864, Surrey County, Virginia	Point Lookout, Maryland, transferred to Elmira Prison, NY, August 6, 1864	Oath of Allegiance September 30, 1864. Early Release per Lincoln's Proclamation, 12/8/1863.
Warren, Lafayette L. Private	21	April 13, 1863, Camp Holmes, North Carolina	Co. F, 32nd North Carolina Infantry	May 10, 1864, Wilderness, Virginia	Point Lookout, Maryland, transferred to Elmira Prison, NY, August 6, 1864	Died February 20, 1865 of Chronic Diarrhea, Grave No. 2339
Warren, Lewis E. Private	Unk	May 20, 1861, Jonesboro, Clayton County, Georgia	Co. E, 10th Georgia Infantry	May 6, 1864, Near Mine Run Wilderness, Virginia	Point Lookout, Maryland, transferred to Elmira Prison, NY, August 17, 1864	Transferred to US Service April 24, 1865
Warren, William H. Private	41	September 30, 1861, Beaufort County, North Carolina	Co. C, 40th Regiment, 3rd North Carolina Artillery	January 15, 1865, Fort Fisher, North Carolina	February 1, 1865, Elmira Prison Camp, New York	Exchanged March 2, 1865 at Akins Landing on the James River, Virginia
Warren, William H. Private	28	March 13, 1862, Danville, Virginia	Co. C, 5th Virginia Cavalry	June 11, 1864, Louisa Court House, Trevilian Station, Virginia	Point Lookout, Maryland, transferred to Elmira Prison, NY, July 30, 1864	Oath of Allegiance May 29, 1865
Warrick, William Private	Unk	October 28, 1863, Goldsboro, North Carolina	Co. F, 10th Regiment, 1st North Carolina Artillery	January 15, 1865, Fort Fisher, North Carolina	February 1, 1865, Elmira Prison Camp, New York	Died February 26, 1865 of Variola (Smallpox), Grave No. 2147
Warrick, William R. Private	Unk	April 27, 1862, Crumps, Virginia	Co. C, 8th Virginia Cavalry	July 16, 1864, Loudoun County, Virginia	Old Capital Prison, Washington, DC, transferred to Elmira Prison, NY, July 23, 1864	Died May 22, 1865 of Chronic Diarrhea, Grave No. 2934

Name & Rank	Age	Enlisted	Regiment and State	Where Captured	Prison	Remarks
Warrin, H. E. Corporal	19	May 6, 1862, Knoxville, Tennessee	Co. G, 63rd Tennessee Infantry	June 17, 1864, Near Petersburg, Virginia	Point Lookout, Maryland, transferred to Elmira Prison, NY, July 30, 1864	Exchanged February 25, 1865 at Boulware's or Cox Wharf on the James River, Virginia
Warring, Robert Civilian	Unk	Caroline County, Virginia	Citizen of Virginia	May 21, 1864, Caroline County, Virginia	Point Lookout, Maryland, transferred to Elmira Prison, NY, July 23, 1864	Died September 22, 1864 of Chronic Diarrhea, Grave No. 480
Warwick, Joseph Private	Unk	March 13, 1862, Greenville, Alabama	Co. J, 59th Alabama Infantry	June 17, 1864, Petersburg, Virginia	Point Lookout, Maryland, transferred to Elmira Prison, NY, July 30, 1864	Transferred For Exchange 10/11/64 to Point Lookout Prison Camp, MD. Died 10/31/64 at Fort Monroe, VA.
Wash, Thomas N. Private	Unk	June 8, 1861, Isbell's Store, Virginia	Co. D, 44th Virginia Infantry	May 12, 1864, Spotsylvania Court House, Virginia	Point Lookout, Maryland, transferred to Elmira Prison, NY, August 2, 1864	Oath of Allegiance June 14, 1865
Washam, Ison Private	Unk	August 2, 1862, Talladega, Alabama	Co. G, 12th Alabama Infantry	July 11, 1864, Frederick, Maryland	Point Lookout, Maryland, transferred to Elmira Prison, NY, July 23, 1864	Oath of Allegiance June 19, 1865
Washington, George Sergeant	Unk	March 20, 1861, Montgomery, Alabama	Co. E, 1st Battalion Alabama Artillery	August 23, 1864, Fort Morgan, Alabama	Steam Press No. 4 New Orleans, Louisiana transferred to Elmira Prison, NY, October 8, 1864.	Exchanged March 2, 1865 at Akins Landing on the James River, Virginia
Waters, A. V. Private	Unk	September 20, 1862, Savannah, Georgia	Co. A, 7th Georgia Cavalry	June 11, 1864, Trevilian Station, Louisa Court House, Virginia	Point Lookout, Maryland, transferred to Elmira Prison, NY, July 25, 1864	Died September 17, 1864 of Typhoid Fever, Grave No. 172
Waters, B. F. Private	Unk	December 9, 1863, Georgetown, Georgia	Co. B, 7th Georgia Cavalry	June 11, 1864, Trevilian Station, Louisa Court House, Virginia	Point Lookout, Maryland, transferred to Elmira Prison, NY, July 25, 1864	Exchanged October 29, 1864, at Venus Point, Savannah River, GA.

Name & Rank	Age	Enlisted	Regiment and State	Where Captured	Prison	Remarks
Waters, Francis E. Sergeant	Unk	August 30, 1862, Calhoun, Georgia	Co. F, 49th Virginia Infantry	May 6, 1864, Mine Run Wilderness, Virginia	Point Lookout, Maryland, transferred to Elmira Prison, NY, July 23, 1864	Oath of Allegiance December 29, 1864. Early Release per Lincoln's Proclamation, 12/8/1863.
Waters, James C. Private	28	April 22, 1861, Washington, North Carolina	Co. K, 10th Regiment, 1st North Carolina Artillery	January 15, 1865, Fort Fisher, North Carolina	February 1, 1865, Elmira Prison Camp, New York	Exchanged February 20, 1865 at Boulware's or Cox Wharf on the James River, Virginia
Waters, James O. Private	18	August 20, 1862, Statesville, North Carolina	Co. F, 18th North Carolina Infantry	May 12, 1864, Spotsylvania Court House, Virginia	Point Lookout, Maryland, transferred to Elmira Prison, NY, August 6, 1864	Exchanged March 2, 1865 at Akins Landing on the James River, Virginia
Waters, Joseph Private	Unk	April 21, 1861, Harrisonburg, Virginia	Co. B, 10th Virginia Infantry	May 12, 1864, Spotsylvania Court House, Virginia	Point Lookout, Maryland, transferred to Elmira Prison, NY, August 2, 1864	Oath of Allegiance June 14, 1865
Waters, T. W. Sergeant	Unk	July 1, 1861, Marietta, Georgia	Co. F, 3rd Battalion Georgia Sharp Shooters	August 16, 1864, Front Royal, Virginia	Old Capital Prison, Washington, DC transferred to Elmira Prison, NY, August 29, 1864	Died April 17, 1865 of Pneumonia, Grave No. 1364
Watkins, Charles Private	Unk	July 1, 1862, Richmond, Virginia	Co. E, 5th Virginia Cavalry	May 11, 1864, Yellow Tavern, Hanover County, Virginia	Point Lookout, Maryland, transferred to Elmira Prison, NY, August 17, 1864	Oath of Allegiance June 19, 1865
Watkins, Clinton Private	23	July 26, 1861, Forestville, North Carolina	Co. J, 1st North Carolina Infantry	May 12, 1864, Spotsylvania Court House, Virginia	Point Lookout, Maryland, transferred to Elmira Prison, NY, August 6, 1864	Oath of Allegiance June 27, 1865
Watkins, James M. Private	17	March 15, 1863, Fredericks-burg, Virginia	Co. C, 14th North Carolina Infantry	May 30, 1864, Todd's Farm, Mechanics-ville, Virginia	Point Lookout, Maryland, transferred to Elmira Prison, NY, July 25, 1864	Died August 26, 1864 of Rubeola (Measles), Grave No. 108

Name & Rank	Age	Enlisted	Regiment and State	Where Captured	Prison	Remarks
Watkins, James R. Private	35	February 12, 1862, Warrenton, North Carolina	Co. G, 43rd North Carolina Infantry	July 13, 1864, Silver Springs, Fort Stevens, Washington, DC. Gunshot Wound Left Knee and Thigh. Leg Amputated.	Old Capital Prison, Washington, DC transferred to Elmira Prison, NY, August 27, 1864	Exchanged February 25, 1865 at Boulware's or Cox Wharf on the James River, Virginia
Watkins, Jeremiah Private	Unk	April 1, 1863, Pocahontas County, Virginia	Co. C, 19th Virginia Cavalry	July 10, 1864, Germantown, Maryland	Old Capital Prison, Washington, DC, transferred to Elmira Prison, NY, July 23, 1864	Oath of Allegiance May 29, 1865
Watkins, John T. Private	Unk	March 4, 1862, Burke County, Georgia	Co. B, 48th Georgia Infantry	May 24, 1864, Spotsylvania Court House, Virginia	Point Lookout, Maryland, transferred to Elmira Prison, NY, July 11, 1864	Exchanged February 20, 1865 at Boulware's or Cox Wharf on the James River, Virginia
Watkins, Uriah P. Private	Unk	May 15, 1862, Camp Davis, Wilmington, North Carolina	Co. K, 11th North Carolina Infantry	July 14, 1863, Falling Waters, Maryland	Point Lookout, Maryland, transferred to Elmira Prison, NY, July 25, 1864	Exchanged October 29, 1864, at Venus Point, Savannah River, GA.
Watkins, William B. Private	Unk	May 24, 1861, Urbana, Virginia	Co. H, 55th Virginia Infantry	May 6, 1864, Wilderness, Virginia	Point Lookout Prison Camp, Maryland. Transferred to Elmira Prison Camp, New York August 14, 1864	Died September 13, 1864 of congestive Remit and Fever, Grave No. 185
Watson, Alexander Private	21	May 16, 1862, Boxville, Georgia	Co. K, 61st Georgia Infantry	May 12, 1864, Spotsylvania Court House, Virginia	Point Lookout, Maryland, transferred to Elmira Prison, NY, July 30, 1864	Oath of Allegiance June 30, 1865
Watson, Allen Private	Unk	June 11, 1861, Drayton, Georgia	Co. F, 12th Georgia Infantry	May 10, 1864, Spotsylvania Court House, Virginia	Point Lookout, Maryland, transferred to Elmira Prison, NY, July 25, 1864	Oath of Allegiance June 21, 1865

Name & Rank	Age	Enlisted	Regiment and State	Where Captured	Prison	Remarks
Watson, Archibald Private	Unk	Unknown	Co. E, 1st Battalion Alabama Artillery	August 23, 1864, Fort Morgan, Alabama	Steam Press No. 4 New Orleans, Louisiana transferred to Elmira Prison, NY, October 8, 1864.	Oath of Allegiance May 29, 1865
Watson, Asa Private	Unk	Unknown	Co. F, 3rd Louisiana Cavalry	October 6, 1864, Clinton, Louisiana	New Orleans, Louisiana transferred to Elmira November 19, 1864.	Exchanged February 25, 1865 at Boulware's or Cox Wharf on the James River, Virginia
Watson, Charles L. Private	21	April 1, 1862, Camp Brazos, Texas	Co. D, 10th Texas Infantry	July 19, 1864, Rodney, Mississippi	New Orleans, Louisiana transferred to Elmira November 19, 1864.	Exchanged March 14, 1865 at Boulware's Wharf on the James River, Virginia
Watson, Daniel Private	22	Unknown Date, Union County, North Carolina	Co. F, 40th Regiment, 3rd North Carolina Artillery	January 15, 1865, Fort Fisher, North Carolina	February 1, 1865, Elmira Prison Camp, New York	Exchanged March 2, 1865 at Akins Landing on the James River, Virginia
Watson, Jacob Private	19	April 8, 1862, Mt. Jackson, Virginia	Co. E, 11th Virginia Cavalry	May 19, 1863, Near Strasburg, Virginia	November 11, 1864, Old Capital Prison, Washington, DC. February 4, 1865 Elmira, Prison Camp, NY.	Exchanged March 2, 1865 at Akins Landing on the James River, Virginia
Watson, Jacob H. Private	Unk	August 5, 1861, Danielsville, Georgia	Co. C, 16th Georgia Infantry	June 1, 1864, Gaines Farm, Virginia	Point Lookout, Maryland, transferred to Elmira Prison, NY, July 12, 1864	Exchanged February 13, 1865 at Boulware's wharf on the James River, Virginia
Watson, John H. Private	19	October 19, 1861, Elizabethtown, Bladen County, North Carolina	Co. G, 36th Regiment, 2nd North Carolina Artillery	January 15, 1865, Fort Fisher, North Carolina	February 1, 1865, Elmira Prison Camp, New York	Oath of Allegiance August 7, 1865
Watson, Nathanial S. Private	18	September 5, 1861, Redcap Springs, Robeson County, North Carolina	Co. F, 40th Regiment, 3rd North Carolina Artillery	January 15, 1865, Fort Fisher, North Carolina	February 1, 1865, Elmira Prison Camp, New York	Died March 18, 1865 of Pneumonia, Grave No. 1722

Name & Rank	Age	Enlisted	Regiment and State	Where Captured	Prison	Remarks
Watson, Samuel D. Sergeant	20	March 10, 1862, Lumberton, North Carolina	Co. E, 51st North Carolina Infantry	June 1, 1864, Cold Harbor, Virginia	Transferred From Point Lookout Prison, MD, July 12, 1864. Train Never Arrived at Elmira Prison Camp, NY.	Died July 15, 1864 in Train Wreck at Shohola, Pennsylvania.
Watson, Simeon Private	29	May 21, 1861, Camp Cheatham, Tennessee	Co. F, 3rd Tennessee Infantry	May 12, 1863, Raymond, Mississippi	Point Lookout, Maryland, transferred to Elmira Prison, NY, August 18, 1864	Oath of Allegiance April 11, 1865
Watson, W. H. H. Sergeant	Unk	July 13, 1861, Hartwell, Georgia	Co. C, 16th Georgia Infantry	August 16, 1864, Front Royal, Virginia	Old Capital Prison, Washington, DC transferred to Elmira Prison, NY, August 29, 1864	Oath of Allegiance July 7, 1865
Watson, William Private	32	November 20, 1863, Camp Holmes, North Carolina	Co. F, 22nd North Carolina Infantry	May 6, 1864, Wilderness, Virginia	Point Lookout, Maryland, transferred to Elmira Prison, NY, August 14, 1864	Oath of Allegiance June 27, 1865
Watson, William H. Private	21	March 24, 1862, Forsyth County, North Carolina	Co. D, 53rd North Carolina Infantry	May 20, 1864, Spotsylvania Court House, Virginia	Point Lookout, Maryland, transferred to Elmira Prison, NY, July 3, 1864	Oath of Allegiance May 17, 1865
Watson, William L. Private	Unk	July 11, 1863, Coosa County, Alabama	Co. J, 61st Alabama Infantry	May 24, 1864, North Anna, Virginia	Point Lookout, Maryland, transferred to Elmira Prison, NY, July 11, 1864	Died February 27, 1865 of Smallpox, Grave No. 2141
Watts, J. R. Private	Unk	June 11, 1861, Georgia	Co. F, 3rd Battalion Georgia Sharp Shooters	August 16, 1864, Front Royal, Virginia	Old Capital Prison, Washington, DC transferred to Elmira Prison, NY, August 29, 1864	Oath of Allegiance July 7, 1865

Name & Rank	Age	Enlisted	Regiment and State	Where Captured	Prison	Remarks
Watts, Richard A. Private	22	May 10, 1861, Lynchburg, Virginia	Captain Shoemaker's Horse Artillery, Virginia	September 13, 1863, Near Culpepper Court House, Virginia	Point Lookout, Maryland, transferred to Elmira Prison, NY, August 18, 1864	Exchanged February 25, 1865 at Boulware's or Cox Wharf on the James River, Virginia
Watts, Thomas Private	Unk	February 24, 1863, Port Hudson, Louisiana	Co. B, 1st Jackson's Tennessee Heavy Artillery	August 23, 1864, Fort Morgan, Alabama.	New Orleans, Louisiana transferred to Elmira Prison, NY, December 4, 1864.	Oath of Allegiance May 29, 1865
Way, David A. Corporal	25	April 11, 1862, Coles Island, South Carolina	Co. F, 25th South Carolina Infantry	August 20, 1864, Weldon Railroad, VA. Gunshot Wound Both Thighs, Severe.	Old Capital Prison, Washington, DC, transferred to Elmira Prison, NY, December 17, 1864	Exchanged February 20, 1865 at Boulware's or Cox Wharf on the James River, Virginia
Way, George M. T. Private	Unk	October 1, 1861, Augusta, Georgia	Co. G, 38th Georgia Infantry	May 20, 1864, Spotsylvania Court House, Virginia	Point Lookout, Maryland, transferred to Elmira Prison, NY, July 3, 1864	Died July 25, 1864 of Chronic Diarrhea, Grave No. 2850
Way, George W. Private	Unk	March 19, 1862, Waterboro, South Carolina	Co. J, 11th South Carolina Infantry	June 24, 1864, Near Petersburg, Virginia	Point Lookout, Maryland, transferred to Elmira Prison, NY, August 18, 1864	Exchanged October 29, 1864, at Venus Point, Savannah River, GA.
Way, W. B. Private	Unk	April 11, 1862, Coles Island, South Carolina	Co. F, 25th South Carolina Infantry	January 15, 1865, Fort Fisher, North Carolina	February 1, 1865, Elmira Prison Camp, New York	Oath of Allegiance July 26, 1865
Weakley, Minor Private	19	May 21, 1861, Madison County Court House, Virginia	Co. D, 34th Virginia Infantry	June 17, 1864, Petersburg, Virginia	Point Lookout, Maryland, transferred to Elmira Prison, NY, July 30, 1864	Exchanged February 13, 1865 at Boulware's wharf on the James River, Virginia
Weatherby, George Private	Unk	Unknown	Co. J, 38th Georgia Infantry	June 1, 1864, Bowling Green, Virginia	Point Lookout, Maryland, transferred to Elmira Prison, NY, July 12, 1864	Died September 25, 1864 of Chronic Diarrhea, Grave No. 368. Name Weatherbite on Headstone.

Name & Rank	Age	Enlisted	Regiment and State	Where Captured	Prison	Remarks
Weatherly, W. H. Private	Unk	December 9, 1861, Camp Polk, Tennessee	Co. A, Jackson's 1st Regiment, Tennessee Heavy Artillery	August 23, 1864, Fort Morgan, Alabama	New Orleans, Louisiana transferred to Elmira Prison, NY, December 4, 1864.	Exchanged March 14, 1865 at Boulware's Wharf on the James River, Virginia
Weatherman, Bartholomew W. Private	20	August 13, 1861, Yadkinville, North Carolina	Co. I, 28th North Carolina Infantry	July 29, 1864, Petersburg, Virginia	Point Lookout, Maryland, transferred to Elmira Prison, NY, August 12, 1864	Died December 12, 1864 of Pneumonia, Grave No. 1139
Weaver, Charles W. Private	28	May 18, 1861, Huntersville, Virginia	Co. I, 25th Virginia Infantry	May 12, 1864, Spotsylvania Court House, Virginia	Point Lookout, Maryland, transferred to Elmira Prison, NY, August 12, 1864	Exchanged October 29, 1864, at Venus Point, Savannah River, GA.
Weaver, E. Civilian	Unk	Unknown	Citizen of Guilford County, North Carolina	April 21, 1864, Wilmington, North Carolina	Point Lookout, Maryland, transferred to Elmira Prison, NY, July 25, 1864	Died September 20, 1864 of Chronic Diarrhea. Grave No. 506
Weaver, Henry C. Private	Unk	Unknown	Co. J, 14th North Carolina Infantry	May 20, 1864, Spotsylvania Court House, Virginia	Point Lookout, Maryland, transferred to Elmira Prison, NY, July 3, 1864	Exchanged February 13, 1865 at Boulware's wharf on the James River, Virginia
Weaver, John R. Private	21	June 22, 1862, Richmond, Virginia	Co. K, 21st Virginia Infantry	May 12, 1864, Spotsylvania Court House, Virginia	Point Lookout, Maryland, transferred to Elmira Prison, NY, August 2, 1864	Died September 5, 1864 of Pneumonia, Grave No. 241
Weaver, John T. Private	21	September 2, 1861, Orange County, North Carolina	Co. G, 28th North Carolina Infantry	July 29, 1864, Petersburg, Virginia	Point Lookout, Maryland, transferred to Elmira Prison, NY, August 12, 1864	Oath of Allegiance June 19, 1865
Weaver, Peter Private	Unk	March 4, 1862, Homersville, Georgia	Co. G, 50th Georgia Infantry	June 1, 1864, Gaines Mill Cold Harbor, Virginia	Point Lookout, Maryland, transferred to Elmira Prison, NY, July 12, 1864	Oath of Allegiance May 19, 1865

Name & Rank	Age	Enlisted	Regiment and State	Where Captured	Prison	Remarks
Weaver, Robert Private	Unk	Unknown	Co. H, 6th Virginia Cavalry	August 18, 1863, Marcum Station, Virginia	Point Lookout, Maryland, transferred to Elmira Prison, NY, August 18, 1864	Exchanged March 14, 1865 at Boulware's Wharf on the James River, Virginia
Weaver, Robert L. Private	Unk	May 18, 1861, Huntersville, Virginia	Co. I, 25th Virginia Infantry	May 12, 1864, Spotsylvania Court House, Virginia	Point Lookout, Maryland, transferred to Elmira Prison, NY, August 12, 1864	Oath of Allegiance June 19, 1865
Weaver, Thomas Private	Unk	October 1, 1861, High Point, North Carolina	Co. E, 18th North Carolina Infantry	May 12, 1864, Spotsylvania Court House, Virginia	Point Lookout, Maryland, transferred to Elmira Prison, NY, August 6, 1864	Exchanged March 2, 1865 at Akins Landing on the James River, Virginia
Weaver, William H. Private	Unk	September 9, 1862, Butler County, Alabama	Co. F, 5th Alabama Infantry	May 5, 1864, Wilderness, Virginia	Point Lookout Prison Camp, Maryland. Transferred to Elmira Prison Camp, New York August 17, 1864	Died September 15, 1864 of Typhoid Fever, Grave No. 293
Webb, Alvis C. Private	26	February 27, 1862, Reidsville, North Carolina	Co. E, 45th North Carolina Infantry	May 10, 1864, Spotsylvania Court House, Virginia	Point Lookout, Maryland, transferred to Elmira Prison, NY, August 6, 1864	Died January 8, 1865 of Pneumonia, Grave No. 1226
Webb, Atlas L. Private	30	March 19, 1862, Richmond County, North Carolina	Co. E, 52nd North Carolina Infantry	July 14, 1863, Falling Waters, Maryland	Point Lookout, Maryland, transferred to Elmira Prison, NY, August 18, 1864	Died February 9, 1865 of Chronic Diarrhea, Grave No. 1950. Headstone has Elias S. Webb.
Webb, David F. Private	21	March 21, 1862, Union County, North Carolina	Co. I, 53rd North Carolina Infantry	July 12, 1864, Near Washington, DC,	Old Capital Prison, Washington, DC, transferred to Elmira Prison, NY, July 23, 1864	Exchanged February 20, 1865 at Boulware's or Cox Wharf on the James River, Virginia
Webb, Henry Private	35	June 22, 1861, Wytheville, Virginia	Co. H, 50th Virginia Infantry	May 12, 1864, Spotsylvania Court House, Virginia	Point Lookout, Maryland, transferred to Elmira Prison, NY, August 2, 1864	Exchanged October 29, 1864, at Venus Point, Savannah River, GA.

Name & Rank	Age	Enlisted	Regiment and State	Where Captured	Prison	Remarks
Webb, John L. Private	21	March 17, 1862, Richmond County, North Carolina	Co. E, 52nd North Carolina Infantry	May 12, 1864, Spotsylvania Court House, Virginia	Point Lookout, Maryland, transferred to Elmira Prison, NY, August 12, 1864	Exchanged February 20, 1865 at Boulware's or Cox Wharf on the James River, Virginia
Webb, L. T. Sergeant	Unk	September 7, 1861, Nashville, Tennessee	Co. A, Jackson's 1st Regiment, Tennessee Heavy Artillery	August 23, 1864, Fort Morgan, Alabama	New Orleans, Louisiana transferred to Elmira Prison, NY, December 4, 1864.	Exchanged March 10, 1865 at Boulware's Wharf on the James River, Virginia
Webb, Martin Private	18	May 19, 1864, Appomattox, Virginia	Co. B, 46th Virginia Infantry	June 18, 1864, Petersburg, Virginia. Gunshot Wound Both Thighs, Severe.	Old Capital Prison, Washington, DC, transferred to Elmira Prison, NY, December 17, 1864	Exchanged February 13, 1865 at Boulware's Wharf on the James River, Virginia
Webb, Nathanial Private	40	November 11, 1861, Camp Potomac, Virginia	Co. F, 2nd North Carolina Infantry	May 20, 1864, Spotsylvania Court House, Virginia	Point Lookout, Maryland, transferred to Elmira Prison, NY, July 3, 1864	Died October 2, 1864 of Scorbutus (Scurvy), Grave No. 628
Webb, Nelson R. Private	45	September 15, 1862, Raleigh, North Carolina	Co. E, 31st North Carolina Infantry	June 1, 1864, Gaines Farm, Virginia	Point Lookout, Maryland, transferred to Elmira Prison, NY, July 12, 1864	Exchanged March 2, 1865 at Akins Landing on the James River, Virginia
Webb, Robert W. Ordinance Sergeant	23	April 1, 1862, Windsor, North Carolina	Field and Staff, 32nd North Carolina Infantry	May 10, 1864, Wilderness, Virginia	Point Lookout, Maryland, transferred to Elmira Prison, NY, August 6, 1864	Exchanged February 25, 1865 at Boulware's or Cox Wharf on the James River, Virginia
Webb, Theo R. Private	Unk	June 12, 1861, Red Sulfur Springs, Virginia	Co. F, 26th Battalion, Virginia Infantry	June 3, 1864, Gaines Farm, Cold Harbor, Virginia	Point Lookout, Maryland, transferred to Elmira Prison, NY, July 17, 1864	Oath of Allegiance July 11, 1865
Webb, Theodore R. Private	Unk	June 12, 1861, Red Sulfur Springs, Virginia	Co. F, 26th Battalion, Virginia Infantry	June 3, 1864, Gaines Farm Cold Harbor, Virginia	Point Lookout, Maryland, transferred to Elmira Prison, NY, July 17, 1864	Oath of Allegiance July 11, 1865

Name & Rank	Age	Enlisted	Regiment and State	Where Captured	Prison	Remarks
Webb, Thomas B. Private	19	April 30, 1864, Monroe Draft, Monroe, Virginia	Co. F, 26th Battalion, Virginia Infantry	June 3, 1864, Gaines Farm Cold Harbor, Virginia	Point Lookout, Maryland, transferred to Elmira Prison, NY, July 17, 1864	Exchanged February 20, 1865 at Boulware's or Cox Wharf on the James River, Virginia
Webb, W. A. Private	Unk	December 23, 1863, Decatur, Georgia	Co. C, 7th Georgia Cavalry	June 11, 1864, Trevilian Station, Louisa Court House, Virginia	Point Lookout, Maryland, transferred to Elmira Prison, NY, July 25, 1864	Died September 14, 1864 of Chronic Diarrhea, Grave No. 283.
Webb, William H. Private	Unk	June 12, 1861, Red Sulfur Springs, Virginia	Co. F, 26th Battalion, Virginia Infantry	May 31, 1864, Chickahominy, Cold Harbor, Virginia	Point Lookout, Maryland, transferred to Elmira Prison, NY, July 12, 1864	Died December 9, 1864 of Chronic Diarrhea, Grave No. 1165
Webber, Charles S. Corporal	28	May 28, 1861, Corinth, Mississippi	Co. D, 17th Mississippi Infantry	May 8, 1864, Spotsylvania, Virginia	Point Lookout, Maryland, transferred to Elmira Prison, NY, August 17, 1864	Oath of Allegiance May 17, 1865
Webber, Rueben Nicholas Private	23	June 7, 1861, Camp Moore, Louisiana	Co. D, 7th Louisiana Infantry	May 11, 1864, Spotsylvania Court House, Virginia	Point Lookout, Maryland, transferred to Elmira Prison, NY, August 17, 1864	Oath of Allegiance May 17, 1865
Webster, John F. Private	Unk	July 25, 1863, Raleigh, North Carolina	Co. A, 21st North Carolina Infantry	August 22, 1864, Charlestown, Virginia	Old Capital Prison, Washington, DC transferred to Elmira Prison, NY, August 29, 1864	Oath of Allegiance May 29, 1865
Webster, Robert H. Private	Unk	Unknown	Co. H, 17th Tennessee Infantry	June 17, 1864, Petersburg, Virginia	Point Lookout, Maryland, transferred to Elmira Prison, NY, July 30, 1864	Exchanged February 13, 1865 at Boulware's wharf on the James River, Virginia
Webster, Thomas M. Private	Unk	September 2, 1861, Camp Darlington, Virginia	Co. G, 8th South Carolina Infantry	July 2, 1863, Gettysburg, Pennsylvania	Point Lookout, Maryland, transferred to Elmira Prison, NY, August 18, 1864	Exchanged October 29, 1864 at Venus Point, Savannah River, GA.

Name & Rank	Age	Enlisted	Regiment and State	Where Captured	Prison	Remarks
Weeks, Albert Civilian	Unk	Unknown	Citizen of Prince William County, Virginia	November 28, 1863, Prince William County, Virginia	Point Lookout, Maryland, transferred to Elmira Prison, NY, July 25, 1864	Exchanged March 10, 1865 at Boulware's Wharf on the James River, Virginia
Weeks, Ben C. Private	Unk	September 18, 1862, Camp Wyatt, North Carolina	Co. C, 5th North Carolina Cavalry	September 22, 1863, Near Madison Court House, Virginia	Point Lookout, Maryland, transferred to Elmira Prison, NY, August 18, 1864	Exchanged February 20, 1865 at Boulware's or Cox Wharf on the James River, Virginia
Weeks, Joshua H. Private	Unk	March 4, 1862, Telfar County, Georgia	Co. K, 49th Georgia Infantry	May 24, 1864, Hanover Junction, Virginia	Point Lookout, Maryland, transferred to Elmira Prison, NY, July 12, 1864	Died September 15, 1864 of Remittent Fever, Grave No. 289. First Name William on Headstone.
Weeks, Samuel L. Private	UnK	May 11, 1861, New Orleans, Louisiana	Co. H, 2nd Louisiana Infantry	May 12, 1864, Wilderness Spotsylvania, Virginia	Point Lookout, Maryland, transferred to Elmira Prison, NY, August 17, 1864	Exchanged February 25, 1865 at Boulware's or Cox Wharf on the James River, Virginia
Weeks, Silas W. Private	Unk	July 1, 1862, Edgecombe County, North Carolina	Co. E, 33rd North Carolina Infantry	May 12, 1864, Spotsylvania Court House, Virginia	Point Lookout, Maryland, transferred to Elmira Prison, NY, July 3, 1864	Oath of Allegiance June 23, 1865
Weeman, R. E. Firemen	Unk	Unknown	Confederate States Navy	May 5, 1864, Albemarle Sound on Steamer CSS Bombshell	Point Lookout, Maryland, transferred to Elmira Prison, NY, August 17, 1864	Oath of Allegiance June 21, 1865
Weibler, John Private	21	June 11, 1861, New Orleans, Louisiana	Co. K, 14th Louisiana Infantry	May 12, 1864, Spotsylvania Court House, Virginia	Point Lookout, Maryland, transferred to Elmira Prison, NY, July 28, 1864.	Exchanged February 13, 1865 at Boulware's wharf on the James River, Virginia

Name & Rank	Age	Enlisted	Regiment and State	Where Captured	Prison	Remarks
Weicking, Frederick Private	18	August 27, 1861, Charleston, South Carolina	Co. L, McCreary's 1st South Carolina Infantry	July 29, 1864, Petersburg, Virginia	Point Lookout Prison Camp, Maryland. Transferred to Elmira Prison Camp, New York August 12, 1864	Died October 1, 1864 of Chronic Diarrhea, Grave No. 415
Weigle, George Private	Unk	September 19, 1863, Augusta, Georgia	Co. A, 7th Georgia Cavalry	June 11, 1864, Trevilian Station, Louisa Court House, Virginia	Point Lookout, Maryland, transferred to Elmira Prison, NY, July 28, 1864	Oath of Allegiance June 21, 1865
Weiss, Silas M. Private	Unk	April 1, 1862, Place Unknown	Co. D, 50th Virginia Infantry	May 20, 1864, Spotsylvania Court House, Virginia	Point Lookout, Maryland, transferred to Elmira Prison, NY, July 3, 1864	Oath of Allegiance June 30, 1865
Welch, C. Private	Unk	Unknown	Co. F, 61st Georgia Infantry	May 12, 1864, Spotsylvania Court House, Virginia	Point Lookout, Maryland, transferred to Elmira Prison, NY, July 30, 1864	Transferred For Exchange October 11, 1864 to Point Lookout Prison Camp, MD. No Further Information
Welch, Ed S. Private	19	April 26, 1862, Jonesboro, Tennessee	Co. D, 63rd Tennessee Infantry	June 17, 1864, Petersburg, Virginia	Point Lookout, Maryland, transferred to Elmira Prison, NY, July 30, 1864	Exchanged March 10, 1865 at Boulware's Wharf on the James River, Virginia
Welch, J. R. Private	Unk	May 28, 1861, Nashville, Tennessee	Co. H, 17th Tennessee Infantry	June 17, 1864, Petersburg, Virginia	Point Lookout, Maryland, transferred to Elmira Prison, NY, July 30, 1864	Exchanged February 13, 1865 at Boulware's wharf on the James River, Virginia
Welch, James T. Private	Unk	September 5, 1862, Coffee County, Alabama	Co. F, 1st Battalion Alabama Artillery	August 23, 1864, Fort Morgan, Alabama	Steam Press No. 4 New Orleans, Louisiana transferred to Elmira Prison, NY, October 8, 1864.	Died November 16, 1864 of Chronic Diarrhea, Grave No. 958

Name & Rank	Age	Enlisted	Regiment and State	Where Captured	Prison	Remarks
Welch, John Private	19	March 26, 1863, Chatham County, North Carolina	Co. G, 40th Regiment, 3rd North Carolina Heavy Artillery	January 15, 1865, Fort Fisher, North Carolina	February 1, 1865, Elmira Prison Camp, New York	Died March 22, 1865 of Pneumonia, Grave No. 1524
Welch, John Sergeant	Unk	July 28, 1861, Bristol, Tennessee	Co. C, 17th Tennessee Infantry	June 17, 1864, Petersburg, Virginia	Point Lookout, Maryland, transferred to Elmira Prison, NY, July 30, 1864	Exchanged February 13, 1865 at Boulware's wharf on the James River, Virginia
Welch, John F. Private	Unk	March 26, 1861, Columbiana, Alabama	Co. C, 1st Battalion Alabama Artillery	August 23, 1864, Fort Morgan, Alabama	New Orleans, Louisiana transferred to Elmira Prison, NY, December 4, 1864.	Died December 21, 1864 of Variola (Smallpox), Grave No. 1796
Welch, Robert A. Private	Unk	August 5, 1861, Monterey, Virginia	Co. H, 25th Virginia Infantry	May 20, 1864, Spotsylvania Court House, Virginia	Point Lookout, Maryland, transferred to Elmira Prison, NY, July 3, 1864	Oath of Allegiance May 13, 1865
Welch, W. A. Private	Unk	June 12, 1862, Camp McDonald, Georgia	Co. H, 18th Georgia Infantry	June 1, 1864, Cold Harbor, Virginia	Point Lookout, Maryland, transferred to Elmira Prison, NY, July 17, 1864	Oath of Allegiance July 7, 1865
Welch, William H. Private	Unk	September 5, 1862, Coffee County, Alabama	Co. F, 1st Battalion Alabama Artillery	August 23, 1864, Fort Morgan, Alabama	Steam Press No. 4 New Orleans, Louisiana transferred to Elmira Prison, NY, October 8, 1864.	Died May 1, 1865 of Acute Rheumatism, Grave No. 2737
Welchel, Alexander S. Private	Unk	February 21, 1862, Gainesville, Georgia	Co. A, 11th Georgia Infantry	May 24, 1864, Hanover Junction, Virginia	Point Lookout, Maryland, transferred to Elmira Prison, NY, August 12, 1864	Oath of Allegiance July 7, 1865
Weldon, F. M. Private	Unk	April 9, 1862, Loachapoka, Tallapoosa County, Alabama	Co. C, 47th Alabama Infantry	May 6, 1864, Wilderness, Virginia	Point Lookout, Maryland, transferred to Elmira Prison, NY, August 17, 1864	Oath of Allegiance June 14, 1865

Name & Rank	Age	Enlisted	Regiment and State	Where Captured	Prison	Remarks
Welles, Willis Benjamin Private	Unk	July 30, 1861, Livingston, Tennessee	Co. J, 25th Tennessee Infantry	June 17, 1864, Near Petersburg, Virginia	Point Lookout, Maryland, transferred to Elmira Prison, NY, July 30, 1864	Exchanged February 25, 1865 at Boulware's or Cox Wharf on the James River, Virginia
Wellon, D. Sergeant	Unk	Unknown	Co. G, 25th Virginia Infantry	May 5, 1864, Wilderness, Virginia	Point Lookout, Maryland, transferred to Elmira Prison, NY, August 17, 1864	Exchanged March 14, 1865 at Boulware's Wharf on the James River, Virginia
Wellons, James H. Private	19	July 15, 1862, Raleigh, North Carolina	Co. C, 5th North Carolina Infantry	May 12, 1864, Spotsylvania Court House, Virginia	Point Lookout, Maryland, transferred to Elmira Prison, NY, August 6, 1864	Died April 4, 1865 of Variola (Smallpox), Grave No. 2550. Name Williams on Headstone.
Wellons, William F. Private	Unk	February 20, 1863, Albany, Georgia	Co. D, 64th Georgia Infantry	June 17, 1864, Petersburg, Virginia	Point Lookout, Maryland, transferred to Elmira Prison, NY, July 30, 1864	Died February 8, 1865 of Typhoid-Pneumonia, Grave No. 1933
Wells, Alfred M. Private	Unk	Unknown	Co. G, 36th Regiment, 2nd North Carolina Artillery	January 15, 1865, Fort Fisher, North Carolina	February 1, 1865, Elmira Prison Camp, New York	Exchanged 2/20/65. Died 3/5/65 of Variola (Smallpox) at US Army Hospital, Bermuda Hundred, VA
Wells, Christopher C. Private	Unk	March 31, 1864, Camp of 52nd Regiment, Virginia	Co. E, 52nd Virginia Infantry	May 20, 1864, Spotsylvania Court House, Virginia	Point Lookout, Maryland, transferred to Elmira Prison, NY, July 3, 1864	Exchanged October 29, 1864, at Venus Point, Savannah River, GA.
Wells, David Private	41	August 18, 1863, Wilson, Wilson County, North Carolina	Co. D, 40th Regiment, 3rd North Carolina Artillery	January 15, 1865, Fort Fisher, North Carolina	February 1, 1865, Elmira Prison Camp, New York	Exchanged March 14, 1865 at Boulware's Wharf on the James River, Virginia
Wells, H. Private	Unk	Unknown	Co. B, Hood's Battalion, Virginia Reserves	June 15, 1864, Petersburg, Virginia	Point Lookout, Maryland, transferred to Elmira Prison, NY, July 30, 1864	Exchanged October 29, 1864, at Venus Point, Savannah River, GA.

Name & Rank	Age	Enlisted	Regiment and State	Where Captured	Prison	Remarks
Wells, Jacob Private	Unk	August 23, 1863, Fort Caswell, Brunswick County, North Carolina	Co. D, 36th Regiment, 2nd North Carolina Artillery	January 15, 1865, Fort Fisher, North Carolina	February 1, 1865, Elmira Prison Camp, New York	Died February 15, 1865 of Pneumonia, Grave No. 2171
Wells, John F. Private	Unk	July 18, 1861, Camp Cheatham, Tennessee	Co. E, 3rd Tennessee Infantry	May 12, 1863, Raymond, Mississippi	Point Lookout, Maryland, transferred to Elmira Prison, NY, August 18, 1864	Oath of Allegiance May 21, 1865
Wells, Latuna L. Private	Unk	June 7, 1861, Richmond, Virginia	Co. C, 59th Virginia Infantry	May 8, 1864, Nottoway Bridge, Virginia	Point Lookout, Maryland, transferred to Elmira Prison, NY, August 17, 1864	Died September 28, 1864 of Chronic Diarrhea, Grave No. 441. Headstone has Lee S. Wells.
Wells, Lucien Private	30	May 5, 1862, Jackson, Mississippi	Co. E, 18th Mississippi Infantry	May 8, 1864, Wilderness, Virginia	Point Lookout, Maryland, transferred to Elmira Prison, NY, August 14, 1864	Exchanged February 20, 1865 at Boulware's or Cox Wharf on the James River, Virginia
Wells, Peter W. Private	39	May 5, 1864, Petersburg, Virginia	Co. B, Hood's Battalion, Virginia Reserves	June 15, 1864, Petersburg, Virginia	Point Lookout, Maryland, transferred to Elmira Prison, NY, July 30, 1864	Oath of Allegiance May 29, 1865
Wells, William S. Private	Unk	August 12, 1861, Resaca, Georgia	Co. G, 28th Georgia Infantry	August 19, 1864, Weldon Railroad, Virginia. Gunshot Wound Right Leg, Severe.	Old Capital Prison, Washington D. C. Transferred to Elmira Prison, NY, March 27, 1865.	Oath of Allegiance July 11, 1865
Welsh, James Private	19	February 26, 1862, New Orleans, Louisiana	Co. G, 7th Louisiana Infantry	May 12, 1864, Near Spotsylvania Court House, Virginia	Point Lookout, Maryland, transferred to Elmira Prison, NY, August 17, 1864	Exchanged February 13, 1865 at Boulware's wharf on the James River, Virginia
Welsh, Thomas Private	Unk	Unknown	Dodd's Louisiana Cavalry	October 6, 1864, Clinton, Louisiana	New Orleans, Louisiana transferred to Elmira November 19, 1864.	Oath of Allegiance May 29, 1865

Name & Rank	Age	Enlisted	Regiment and State	Where Captured	Prison	Remarks
Welsh, William H. Private	Unk	March 4, 1862, Mobile, Alabama	Co. A, 21st Alabama Infantry	August 25, 1864, Fort Morgan, Louisiana	New Orleans, Louisiana transferred to Elmira November 19, 1864.	Oath of Allegiance May 19, 1865
Welton, James S. Private	Unk	October 10, 1862, Rippon, Virginia	Co. F, 7th Virginia Cavalry	September 13, 1863, Near Culpepper, Virginia	Point Lookout, Maryland, transferred to Elmira Prison, NY, August 18, 1864	Exchanged March 10, 1865 at Boulware's Wharf on the James River, Virginia
Wescoat, St. J. D. Private	19	May 13, 1862, Charleston, South Carolina	Co. H, 25th South Carolina Infantry	January 15, 1865, Fort Fisher, North Carolina	February 1, 1865, Elmira Prison Camp, New York	Exchanged February 20, 1865 at Boulware's or Cox Wharf on the James River, Virginia
Wesson, William C. Corporal	35	October 1, 1861, Shelby, North Carolina	Co. A, 34th North Carolina Infantry	July 14, 1863, Falling Waters, Maryland	Point Lookout, Maryland, transferred to Elmira Prison, NY, August 18, 1864	Exchanged March 14, 1865 at Boulware's Wharf on the James River, Virginia
West, Alexander Private	25	July 8, 1862, Oxford, North Carolina	Co. J, 23rd North Carolina Infantry	May 12, 1864, Near Spotsylvania Court House, Virginia	Point Lookout, Maryland, transferred to Elmira Prison, NY, August 14, 1864	Died October 17, 1864 of Chronic Diarrhea, Grave No. 550
West, Arthur M. Private	17	October 19, 1861, Elizabethtown, Bladen County, North Carolina	Co. J, 36th Regiment, 2nd North Carolina Artillery	January 15, 1865, Fort Fisher, North Carolina	February 1, 1865, Elmira Prison Camp, New York	Oath of Allegiance June 12, 1865
West, George W. Private	16	August 1, 1864, Fort Fisher, New Hanover County, North Carolina	Co. H, 36th Regiment, 2nd North Carolina Artillery	January 15, 1865, Fort Fisher, North Carolina	February 1, 1865, Elmira Prison Camp, New York	Oath of Allegiance June 12, 1865
West, James J. Private	Unk	March 1, 1864, Frederick, Virginia	Co. K, 23rd Virginia Cavalry	February 1, 1865, Shenandoah Springs, Blue Ridge, Virginia	Old Capital Prison, Washington D. C. Transferred to Elmira Prison, NY, March 3, 1865.	Oath of Allegiance June 30, 1865

Name & Rank	Age	Enlisted	Regiment and State	Where Captured	Prison	Remarks
West, James M. Private	Unk	April 29, 1862, Cedar Bluff, Alabama	Co. H, 48th Alabama Infantry	May 6, 1864, Wilderness, Virginia	Point Lookout, Maryland, transferred to Elmira Prison, NY, August 17, 1864	Died March 28, 1865 of Chronic Diarrhea, Grave No. 2492
West, James T. Private	Unk	March 25, 1862, Fredericks-burg, Virginia	Co. C, 38th Read's Battalion, Virginia Light Artillery	June 3, 1864, Gaines Farm, Cold Harbor, Virginia	Point Lookout, Maryland, transferred to Elmira Prison, NY, July 17, 1864	Oath of Allegiance June 27, 1865
West, John Private	Unk	March 3, 1862, Bedford County, Virginia	Co. G, 34th Virginia Infantry	June 15, 1864, Near Petersburg, Virginia	Point Lookout, Maryland, transferred to Elmira Prison, NY, July 12, 1864	Died October 22, 1864 of Diphtheria, Grave No. 872
West, John E. Private	18	April 5, 1862, Smithfield, North Carolina	Co. E, 24th North Carolina Infantry	May 16, 1864, Near Drury's Bluff, Virginia	Point Lookout, Maryland, transferred to Elmira Prison, NY, August 18, 1864	Oath of Allegiance June 12, 1865
West, John W. Private	24	May 26, 1861, New Orleans, Louisiana	Co. J, 8th Louisiana Infantry	May 12, 1864, Spotsylvania Court House, Virginia	Point Lookout, Maryland, transferred to Elmira Prison, NY, August 17, 1864	Exchanged March 10, 1865 at Boulware's wharf on the James River, Virginia
West, Joseph Private	Unk	January 14, 1862, Camp Walsh, South Carolina	Co. J, Holcombe Legion, South Carolina Infantry	May 7, 1864, Stony Creek, Virginia	Point Lookout, Maryland, transferred to Elmira Prison, NY, August 17, 1864	Died February 3, 1865 of Variola (Smallpox), Grave No. 1954. Headstone has James.
West, Robert Private	23	July 8, 1862, Oxford County, North Carolina	Co. J, 23rd North Carolina Infantry	May 12, 1864, Near Spotsylvania, Virginia	Point Lookout, Maryland, transferred to Elmira Prison, NY, August 14, 1864	Exchanged October 29, 1864, at Venus Point, Savannah River, GA.
West, W. F. Private	Unk	March 16, 1864, Richmond, Virginia	Co. B, 15th Virginia Cavalry	May 11, 1864, Near Ashland, Virginia	Point Lookout, Maryland, transferred to Elmira Prison, NY, August 17, 1864. Ward 9	Died March 2, 1865 of Pneumonia, Grave No. 2024

Name & Rank	Age	Enlisted	Regiment and State	Where Captured	Prison	Remarks
West, Washington Private	Unk	March 3, 1862, Bedford County, Virginia	Co. G, 34th Virginia Infantry	June 15, 1864, Near Petersburg, Virginia	Point Lookout, Maryland, transferred to Elmira Prison, NY, July 12, 1864	Died December 9, 1864 of Chronic Diarrhea and Pneumonia, Grave No. 1173
West, William J. Private	Unk	August 13, 1861, Camp Moore, Louisiana	Co. K, 12th Louisiana Infantry	May 16, 1863, Baker's Creek, Champion Hill, Mississippi	Point Lookout, Maryland, transferred to Elmira Prison, NY, August 18, 1864	Exchanged February 25, 1865 at Boulware's wharf on the James River, Virginia
West, William J. Private	21	October 19, 1861, Elizabethtown, Bladen County, North Carolina	Co. J, 36th Regiment, 2nd North Carolina Artillery	January 15, 1865, Fort Fisher, North Carolina	February 1, 1865, Elmira Prison Camp, New York	Died April 9, 1865 of Acute Dysentery, Grave No. 2614
West, Witfield Private	Unk	March 3, 1862, Bedford County, Virginia	Co. G, 34th Virginia Infantry	June 15, 1864, Near Petersburg, Virginia	Point Lookout, Maryland, transferred to Elmira Prison, NY, July 12, 1864	Exchanged March 14, 1865 at Boulware's Wharf on the James River, Virginia
Westbrook, Jesse E. Private	25	May 14, 1862, Magnolia, North Carolina	Co. A, 43rd North Carolina Infantry	July 14, 1864, Near Washington, DC	Old Capital Prison, Washington, DC transferred to Elmira Prison, NY, August 29, 1864	Oath of Allegiance June 19, 1865
Westbrook, William M. Private	Unk	Unknown	Co. F, 3rd Louisiana Cavalry	August 25, 1864, Near Clinton, Louisiana	New Orleans, Louisiana transferred to Elmira November 19, 1864.	Died March 10, 1865 of Diarrhea, Grave No. 1867
Westbrook, Y. J. Private	Unk	July 16, 1862, Raleigh, North Carolina	Co. D, 5th North Carolina Infantry	May 12, 1864, Spotsylvania Court House, Virginia	Point Lookout, Maryland, transferred to Elmira Prison, NY, August 6, 1864	Transferred for Exchange 10/11/64. Died 10/19/64 of Unknown Causes at Point Lookout, MD.
Westcoat, George W. Private	40	September 5, 1863, Fort Holmes, New Hanover County, North Carolina	Co. G, 36th Regiment, 2nd North Carolina Artillery	January 15, 1865, Fort Fisher, North Carolina. Wounded	February 1, 1865, Elmira Prison Camp, New York	Exchanged March 2, 1865 at Akins Landing on the James River, Virginia

Name & Rank	Age	Enlisted	Regiment and State	Where Captured	Prison	Remarks
Westfall, Asberry P. Private	30	October 1, 1862, Reedyville, Virginia	Co. G, 60th Virginia Infantry	July 20, 1864, Berryville, Virginia	Old Capital Prison, Washington D. C. Transferred to Elmira Prison, NY, July 12, 1864	Oath of Allegiance May 29, 1865
Westmoreland, James J. Private	Unk	August 24, 1861, Atlanta, Georgia	Co. E, 3rd Battalion Georgia Sharp Shooters	August 16, 1864, Front Royal, Virginia	Old Capital Prison, Washington, DC transferred to Elmira Prison, NY, August 29, 1864	Oath of Allegiance June 21, 1865
Westmoreland, Jesse G. Private	Unk	January 14, 1862, Camp Walsh, South Carolina	Co. J, Holcombe Legion, South Carolina Infantry	May 7, 1864, Stony Creek, Virginia	Point Lookout, Maryland, transferred to Elmira Prison, NY, August 17, 1864	Died December 10, 1864 of Chronic Diarrhea, Grave No. 1040
Westmoreland, John M. Private	25	August 15, 1861, Pfafftown, North Carolina	Co. J, 33rd North Carolina Infantry	May 6, 1864, Wilderness, Virginia	Old Capital Prison, Washington D. C. Transferred to Elmira Prison, NY, July 14, 1864	Exchanged March 14, 1865 at Boulware's Wharf on the James River, Virginia
Weston, Isaac Private	Unk	Unknown	Co. B, 50th Virginia Infantry	May 12, 1864, Spotsylvania Court House, Virginia	Point Lookout, Maryland, transferred to Elmira Prison, NY, August 2, 1864	Oath of Allegiance May 17, 1865
Weston, Richard Private	28	May 13, 1862, Onslow County, North Carolina	Co. E, 3rd North Carolina Infantry	May 12, 1864, Near Spotsylvania Court House, Virginia	Point Lookout, Maryland, transferred to Elmira Prison, NY, August 14, 1864	Died September 23, 1864 of Remittent Fever and Erysipelas, Grave No. 477
Westray, Richard Private	24	May 31, 1861, Nashville, North Carolina	Co. H, 32nd North Carolina Infantry	May 10, 1864, Near Mine Run Spotsylvania, Virginia	Point Lookout, Maryland, transferred to Elmira Prison, NY, August 6, 1864	Died June 7, 1865 of Chronic Diarrhea, Grave No. 2890
Wetherington, Abner M. Private	26	May 27, 1861, Cone Creek, Near Newbern, North Carolina	Co. F, 2nd North Carolina Infantry	July 27, 1864, Cone Creek, Near Newbern, North Carolina	Point Lookout, Maryland, transferred to Elmira Prison, NY, August 18, 1864	Oath of Allegiance May 19, 1865

Name & Rank	Age	Enlisted	Regiment and State	Where Captured	Prison	Remarks
Wetherington, James G. Private	Unk	July 10, 1862, Snow Hill, North Carolina	Co. F, 66th North Carolina Infantry	June 3, 1864, Cold Harbor, Virginia	Point Lookout, Maryland, transferred to Elmira Prison, NY, July 17,1864	Oath of Allegiance July 3, 1865
Whaley, Braddock Private	37	April 1, 1862, Magnolia, North Carolina	Co. C, 51st North Carolina Infantry	June 1, 1864, Cold Harbor, Virginia	Point Lookout, Maryland, transferred to Elmira Prison, NY, July 12, 1864	Oath of Allegiance July 3, 1865
Whalin, W. P. Private	Unk	March 1, 1864, Hanover Junction, Virginia	2nd Battalion Maryland Artillery	May 11, 1864, Yellow Tavern, Hanover County, Virginia	Point Lookout, Maryland, transferred to Elmira Prison, NY, August 17, 1864	Oath of Allegiance June 19, 1865
Whatley, Benjamin F. Sergeant	Unk	September 20, 1861, Monroe, Louisiana	Co. H, 2nd Louisiana Infantry	May 12, 1864, Wilderness Spotsylvania, Virginia	Point Lookout, Maryland, transferred to Elmira Prison, NY, August 17, 1864	Exchanged March 10, 1865 at Boulware's Wharf on the James River, Virginia
Whatley, J. C. Private	Unk	August 1, 1862, Alexandria, Alabama	Co. D, 10th Alabama Infantry	May 12, 1864, Spotsylvania Court House, Virginia	Point Lookout, Maryland, transferred to Elmira Prison, NY, August 17, 1864	Exchanged October 29, 1864, at Venus Point, Savannah River, GA.
Wheat, N. F. Private	Unk	August 2, 1861, Richmond, Virginia	Co. D, 1st Virginia Infantry	May 16, 1864, Near Drury's Bluff, Virginia	Point Lookout, Maryland, transferred to Elmira Prison, NY, August 17, 1864	Oath of Allegiance March 10, 1865 Early Release per Lincoln's Proclamation, 12/8/1863.
Wheatley, J. B. Private	Unk	Unknown	Co. F, 12th Texas Cavalry	August 26, 1864, Bullits Bayou, Concordia, Louisiana	New Orleans, Louisiana transferred to Elmira November 19, 1864.	Exchanged March 2, 1865 at Akins Landing on the James River, Virginia
Wheelan, John Sergeant	30	June 19, 1861, New Orleans, Louisiana	Co. F, 14th Louisiana Infantry	May 12, 1864, Spotsylvania Court House, Virginia	Point Lookout, Maryland, transferred to Elmira Prison, NY, July 25, 1864	Exchanged March 14, 1865 at Boulware's Wharf on the James River, Virginia

Name & Rank	Age	Enlisted	Regiment and State	Where Captured	Prison	Remarks
Wheelan, Thomas Sergeant	Unk	July 22, 1861, Camp Moore, Louisiana	Co. B, 10th Louisiana Infantry	May 5, 1864, Wilderness, Virginia	Point Lookout, Maryland, transferred to Elmira Prison, NY, July 25, 1864	Oath of Allegiance May 19, 1865
Wheeler, Albert Private	Unk	February 29, 1864, Richmond, Virginia	2nd Battery Maryland Artillery	July 12, 1864, Near Washington, DC,	Point Lookout, Maryland, transferred to Elmira Prison, NY, July 23, 1864	Oath of Allegiance May 29, 1865
Wheeler, Jacob E. Private	Unk	July 23, 1861, Staunton, Virginia	Co. H, 52nd Virginia Infantry	May 30, 1864 Mechanics-ville, Virginia	Point Lookout, Maryland, transferred to Elmira Prison, NY, July 9, 1864	Died October 5, 1864 of Chronic Diarrhea, Grave No. 603. First Name James on Headstone.
Wheeler, James T. Private	Unk	August 24, 1861, Hiawassee, Georgia	Co. D, 24th Georgia Infantry	August 16, 1864, Front Royal, Virginia	Old Capital Prison, Washington, DC transferred to Elmira Prison, NY, August 29, 1864	Died March 25, 1865 of Pneumonia, Grave No. 2457
Wheeler, James Y. Private	22	February 27, 1862, Reidsville, North Carolina	Co. E, 45th North Carolina Infantry	May 10, 1864, Spotsylvania Court House, Virginia	Point Lookout, Maryland, transferred to Elmira Prison, NY, August 6, 1864	Exchanged October 29, 1864, at Venus Point, Savannah River, GA.
Wheeler, Jesse Private	24	September 15, 1861, Auburn, North Carolina	Co. D, 31st North Carolina Infantry	June 1, 1864, Gaines Farm, Cold Harbor, Virginia	Point Lookout, Maryland, transferred to Elmira Prison, NY, July 12, 1864	Oath of Allegiance May 19, 1865
Wheeler, Joseph H. Private	33	July 6, 1861, Jackson, North Carolina	Co. H, 2nd North Carolina Cavalry	September 22, 1863, Near Culpepper, Virginia	Point Lookout, Maryland, transferred to Elmira Prison, NY, August 18, 1864	Exchanged March 10, 1865 at Boulware's Wharf on the James River, Virginia
Wheeler, Josiah Private	Unk	May 31, 1861, Mobile, Alabama	Co. A, 3rd Alabama Infantry	June 1, 1864, Gaines Farm, Cold Harbor, Virginia	Point Lookout, Maryland, transferred to Elmira Prison, NY, July 17, 1864	Oath of Allegiance August 11, 1864. Early Release per Lincoln's Proclamation, 12/8/1863.

Name & Rank	Age	Enlisted	Regiment and State	Where Captured	Prison	Remarks
Wheeler, Leven M. Private	20	February 27, 1862, Reidsville, North Carolina	Co. E, 45th North Carolina Infantry	May 10, 1864, Spotsylvania Court House, Virginia	Point Lookout, Maryland, transferred to Elmira Prison, NY, August 6, 1864	Oath of Allegiance June 12, 1865
Wheeler, Owen Private	40	February 26, 1862, Fayetteville, Cumberland County, North Carolina	Co. D, 36th Regiment, 2nd North Carolina Artillery	January 15, 1865, Fort Fisher, North Carolina	February 1, 1865, Elmira Prison Camp, New York	Died May 3, 1865 of Pneumonia, Grave No. 2748
Wheeler, Reese H. Sergeant	Unk	May 22, 1861, Rose Hill, Virginia	Co. E, 37th Virginia Infantry	May 12, 1864, Spotsylvania Court House, Virginia	Point Lookout, Maryland, transferred to Elmira Prison, NY, August 2, 1864	Oath of Allegiance June 27, 1865
Wheeler, Simeon Private	Unk	October 13, 1861, Hall's Mill, Alabama	Co. A, 21st Alabama Infantry	August 23, 1864, Fort Morgan, Alabama	Steam Press No. 4 New Orleans, Louisiana transferred to Elmira Prison, NY, October 8, 1864.	Oath of Allegiance May 29, 1865
Wheelis, William C. Private	Unk	January 24, 1864, Mobile, Alabama	Co. E, 1st Battalion Alabama Artillery	August 23, 1864, Fort Morgan, Alabama	Steam Press No. 4 New Orleans, Louisiana transferred to Elmira Prison, NY, October 8, 1864.	Exchanged February 13, 1865 at Boulware's wharf on the James River, Virginia
Whelan, Rody Private	Unk	April 7, 1862, Charleston, South Carolina	Co. H, 27th South Carolina Infantry	June 18, 1864, Petersburg, Virginia	Point Lookout, Maryland, transferred to Elmira Prison, NY, July 25, 1864	Died October 5, 1864 of Chronic Diarrhea. Grave No. 598
Whetstine, David Private	Unk	May 23, 1862, Lincolnton, Lincoln County, North Carolina	Co. B, 23rd North Carolina Infantry	May 20, 1864, Spotsylvania Court House, Virginia	Point Lookout, Maryland, transferred to Elmira Prison, NY, July 3, 1864	Exchanged October 29, 1864, at Venus Point, Savannah River, GA.
Whetstone, J. D. Private	Unk	March 1, 1862, Audaugaville, Alabama	Co. G, 6th Alabama Infantry	May 14, 1864, Spotsylvania Court House, Virginia	Point Lookout, Maryland, transferred to Elmira Prison, NY, August 17, 1864	Oath of Allegiance June 27, 1865

Name & Rank	Age	Enlisted	Regiment and State	Where Captured	Prison	Remarks
Whichard, Joseph J. Private	20	September 14, 1861, Pitt County, North Carolina	Co. G, 8th North Carolina Infantry	June 2, 1864, Cold Harbor, Virginia. Gunshot Wound of Right Groin.	DeCamp General Hospital, David's Island New York Harbor.	Oath of Allegiance June 30, 1865
Whicker, S. E. Private	26	July 4, 1862, Winston, North Carolina	Co. D, 57th North Carolina Infantry	May 23, 1864, North Anna, Virginia	Point Lookout, Maryland, transferred to Elmira Prison, NY, July 25, 1864	Died September 14, 1864 of Chronic Diarrhea, Grave No. 286
Whishenant, Alberto B. Private	35	June 15, 1861, Concorde, North Carolina	Co. A, 20th North Carolina Infantry	March 25, 1865, Fort Fisher, Virginia. Shell Contusion of Right Hip and Back.	Old Capital Prison, Washington D. C. Transferred to Elmira Prison, NY, May 12, 1865.	Oath of Allegiance June 12, 1865
Whisman, James M. Private	Unk	July 27, 1861, Wyhteville, Virginia	Co. A, 50th Virginia Infantry	May 12, 1864, Spotsylvania Court House, Virginia	Point Lookout, Maryland, transferred to Elmira Prison, NY, August 2, 1864	Died January 12, 1865 of Pneumonia, Grave No. 1479
Whitaker, B. F. Private	Unk	April 28, 1862, Camp Pillow, South Carolina	Co. F, 17th South Carolina Infantry	July 30, 1864, Petersburg, Virginia	Point Lookout, Maryland, transferred to Elmira Prison, NY, August 12, 1864	Died September 11, 1864 of Chronic Diarrhea, Grave No. 251
Whitaker, John H. Sergeant	20	July 25, 1861, Tullahoma, Tennessee	Co. K, 25th Tennessee Infantry	June 17, 1864, Petersburg, Virginia	Point Lookout, Maryland, transferred to Elmira Prison, NY, July 23, 1864	Exchanged February 25, 1865 at Boulware's or Cox Wharf on the James River, Virginia
Whitaker, Levi Private	20	September 13, 1861, Dobson, Surrey County, North Carolina	Co. F, 2nd Battalion, North Carolina Infantry	May 20, 1864, Spotsylvania Court House, Virginia	Point Lookout, Maryland, transferred to Elmira Prison, NY, July 3, 1864	Oath of Allegiance May 17, 1865
Whitaker, William G. Private	19	September 1, 1862, Milledgeville, Georgia	Co. H, 4th Georgia Infantry	July 12, 1864, Near Washington, DC. Gunshot Wound Right Leg.	Old Capital Prison, Washington, DC transferred to Elmira Prison, NY, August 27, 1864	Exchanged March 10, 1865 at Boulware's Wharf on the James River, Virginia

Name & Rank	Age	Enlisted	Regiment and State	Where Captured	Prison	Remarks
White, A. J. Private	Unk	Unknown	Co. B, 21st Virginia Cavalry	July 16, 1864, Snicker's Gap, Loudoun County, Virginia	Old Capital Prison, Washington, DC, transferred to Elmira Prison, NY, July 23, 1864	Died January 13, 1865 of Disease of the Heart, Grave No. 1478
White, Ambrose Private	26	June 16, 1862, Livingston, Louisiana	Wingfield's 3rd Louisiana Cavalry	September 12, 1864, Greenville Springs, Near East Baton Rouge, Louisiana	New Orleans, Louisiana transferred to Elmira November 19, 1864.	No Further Information Available.
White, B. F. Private	Unk	January 30, 1864, Greensboro, North Carolina	Co. K, 45th North Carolina Infantry	July 12, 1864, Near Washington, DC,	Old Capital Prison, Washington, DC, transferred to Elmira Prison, NY, July 23, 1864	Exchanged October 29, 1864, at Venus Point, Savannah River, GA.
White, Benjamin F. Private	Unk	December 21, 1861, Nashville, Tennessee	Co. I, 44th Tennessee Infantry	June 17, 1864, Petersburg, Virginia	Point Lookout, Maryland, transferred to Elmira Prison, NY, July 30, 1864	Exchanged February 25, 1865 at Boulware's or Cox Wharf on the James River, Virginia
White, Calvin Private	Unk	May 10, 1864, Wilmington, North Carolina	Co. K, 18th South Carolina Infantry	July 30, 1864, Petersburg, Virginia	Point Lookout, Maryland, transferred to Elmira Prison, NY, August 12, 1864	Died September 1, 1864 of Chronic Diarrhea, Grave No. 89
White, E. F. Private	Unk	July 4, 1862, Mecklenburg County, North Carolina	Co. H, 35th North Carolina Infantry	June 17, 1864, Petersburg, Virginia	Point Lookout, Maryland, transferred to Elmira Prison, NY, July 30, 1864	Oath of Allegiance February 13, 1865. Early Release per Lincoln's Proclamation, 12/8/1863.
White, Eli Private	23	Unknown	Co. K, 40th Regiment, 3rd North Carolina Artillery	January 15, 1865, Fort Fisher, North Carolina	February 1, 1865, Elmira Prison Camp, New York	Died April 23, 1865 of Pneumonia, Grave No. 1401
White, Evans Civilian	Unk	Unknown	Citizen of Louisiana	August 26, 1864, Near Clinton, Louisiana	New Orleans, Louisiana transferred to Elmira November 19, 1864.	Exchanged March 10, 1865 at Boulware's Wharf on the James River, Virginia

Name & Rank	Age	Enlisted	Regiment and State	Where Captured	Prison	Remarks
White, Friley Sergeant	Unk	January 28, 1862, Columbia, North Carolina	Co. G, 1st North Carolina Infantry	May 12, 1864, Wilderness Spotsylvania, Virginia	Point Lookout, Maryland, transferred to Elmira Prison, NY, August 6, 1864	Oath of Allegiance June 12, 1865
White, Garnett Private	Unk	March 1, 1862, Camp Bartow, Georgia	Co. H, 38th Georgia Infantry	July 16, 1864, Snicker's Gap, Loudoun County, Virginia	Old Capital Prison, Washington, DC, transferred to Elmira Prison, NY, July 23, 1864	Died July 27, 1865 of Unknown Disease, Grave No. 2859
White, George B. Private	23	May 20, 1862, Estellville, Virginia	Co. D, 37th Virginia Infantry	May 12, 1864, Spotsylvania Court House, Virginia. Gunshot Wound Right Arm and Side.	Old Capital Prison, Washington, DC transferred to Elmira Prison, NY, August 29, 1864	Exchanged February 20, 1865 at Boulware's or Cox Wharf on the James River, Virginia
White, George W. Private	Unk	June 10, 1861, Morgan, Georgia	Co. D, 12th Georgia Infantry	May 10, 1864, Spotsylvania Court House, Virginia	Point Lookout, Maryland, transferred to Elmira Prison, NY, July 30, 1864	Died January 9, 1865 of Chronic Diarrhea, Grave No. 1211
White, Hardy Private	17	Unknown	Co. G, 36th Regiment, 2nd North Carolina Artillery	January 15, 1865, Fort Fisher, North Carolina	February 1, 1865, Elmira Prison Camp, New York	Exchanged March 14, 1865 at Boulware's Wharf on the James River, Virginia
White, Henry Private	Unk	Unknown	Co. B, 12th Georgia Infantry	July 16, 1864, Loudoun County, Virginia	Old Capital Prison, Washington, DC, transferred to Elmira Prison, NY, July 23, 1864	Exchanged February 20, 1865 at Boulware's or Cox Wharf on the James River, Virginia
White, Henry A. Private	Unk	September 23, 1861, Atlanta, Georgia	Co. K, 35th Georgia Infantry	May 23, 1864, North Anna, Virginia	Point Lookout, Maryland, transferred to Elmira Prison, NY, July 12, 1864	Oath of Allegiance June 19, 1865
White, Henry B. Private	18	June 9, 1861, Camp Moore, Louisiana	Co. J, 15th Louisiana Infantry	May 20, 1864, Spotsylvania Court House, Virginia	Point Lookout, Maryland, transferred to Elmira Prison, NY, July 3, 1864	Exchanged February 13, 1865 at Boulware's Wharf on the James River, Virginia

Name & Rank	Age	Enlisted	Regiment and State	Where Captured	Prison	Remarks
White, Henry H. Private	Unk	June 17, 1861, Lewisburg, Virginia	Co. G, 26th Battalion, Virginia Infantry	June 3, 1864, Gaines Farm, Cold Harbor, Virginia	Point Lookout, Maryland, transferred to Elmira Prison, NY, July 17, 1864	Exchanged March 2, 1865 at Akins Landing on the James River, Virginia
White, Hugh Sergeant	Unk	January 14, 1862, Camp Hampton, Columbia, South Carolina	Co. D, 17th South Carolina Infantry	July 30, 1864, Petersburg, Virginia	Point Lookout, Maryland, transferred to Elmira Prison, NY, August 12, 1864	Oath of Allegiance June 30, 1865
White, J. B. Private	42	January 1, 1862, Camp Harlee, Georgetown, South Carolina	Co. I, 25th South Carolina Infantry	January 15, 1865, Fort Fisher, North Carolina	February 1, 1865, Elmira Prison Camp, New York	Oath of Allegiance June 23, 1865
White, James M. Private	60	July 13, 1861, Jacksonville, Florida	Co. B, 2nd Florida Infantry	May 12, 1864, Spotsylvania Court House, Virginia	Point Lookout, Maryland, transferred to Elmira Prison, NY, August 12, 1864	Oath of Allegiance June 19, 1865
White, James M. Private	Unk	March 15, 1862, Washington County, Virginia	Co. J, 48th Virginia Infantry	May 12, 1864, Spotsylvania Court House, Virginia	Point Lookout, Maryland, transferred to Elmira Prison, NY, August 2, 1864	Oath of Allegiance June 16, 1865
White, James S. Private	Unk	August 27, 1862 Jefferson County, Alabama	Co. A, 21st Alabama Infantry	August 23, 1864 Fort Morgan, Alabama	New Orleans, Louisiana. Transferred to Elmira Prison Camp October 8, 1864	Exchanged March 2, 1865. Died March 7, 1865 of Chronic Diarrhea at Wayside Hospital #9, Richmond, VA
White, Jerry M. Private	Unk	January 1, 1862, Georgetown, South Carolina	Co. K, 21st South Carolina Infantry	January 15, 1865, Fort Fisher, North Carolina	February 1, 1865, Elmira Prison Camp, New York	Exchanged March 2, 1865 at Akins Landing on the James River, Virginia
White, John Private	Unk	March 13, 1863, Frankford, Virginia	Co. E, 19th Virginia Cavalry	July 15, 1864, Loudoun County, Virginia	Old Capital Prison, Washington, DC, transferred to Elmira Prison, NY, July 23, 1864	Exchanged February 13, 1865 at Boulware's wharf on the James River, Virginia

Name & Rank	Age	Enlisted	Regiment and State	Where Captured	Prison	Remarks
White, John A. Corporal	18	June 22, 1861, Wilmington, North Carolina	Co. F, 3rd North Carolina Infantry	May 12, 1864, Near Spotsylvania Court House, Virginia	Point Lookout, Maryland, transferred to Elmira Prison, NY, August 14, 1864	Oath of Allegiance May 29, 1865
White, John H. Private	Unk	March 15, 1862, Washington County, Virginia	Co. J, 48th Virginia Infantry	May 12, 1864, Spotsylvania Court House, Virginia	Point Lookout, Maryland, transferred to Elmira Prison, NY, August 2, 1864	Oath of Allegiance June 16, 1865
White, John W. Sergeant	Unk	July 20, 1861, Gloucester Point, Virginia	Co. B, 26th Virginia Infantry	June 15, 1864, Near Petersburg, Virginia	Point Lookout, Maryland, transferred to Elmira Prison, NY, July 12,1864	Transferred for Exchange 10/11/1864. Died 10/22/64 of Unknown Causes at Point Lookout, MD.
White, Joseph M. Private	19	May 26, 1861, Baldwyn, Mississippi	Co. K, 19th Mississippi Infantry	May 9, 1864, Spotsylvania, Virginia	Old Capital Prison, Washington, DC, transferred to Elmira Prison, NY, December 17, 1864	Oath of Allegiance June 27, 1865
White, M. A. Private	Unk	Unknown	Co. A, Gober's Regiment Louisiana Cavalry	August 25, 1864, Near Clinton, Louisiana	New Orleans, Louisiana transferred to Elmira November 19, 1864.	Exchanged February 25, 1865 at Boulware's or Cox Wharf on the James River, Virginia
White, Peter Corporal	Unk	August 4, 1862, Dallas, Georgia	Co. C, 7th Georgia Infantry	May 6, 1864, Near Mine Run Wilderness, Virginia	Point Lookout, Maryland, transferred to Elmira Prison, NY, August 17, 1864	Died December 23, 1864 of Pneumonia, Grave No. 1099
White, Robert Private	Unk	Unknown	Co. B, Davis Battalion Virginia Cavalry	July 16, 1864, Snicker's Gap, Loudoun County, Virginia	Old Capital Prison, Washington, DC, transferred to Elmira Prison, NY, July 23, 1864	Died March 17, 1865 of Chronic Diarrhea, Grave No. 1698

Name & Rank	Age	Enlisted	Regiment and State	Where Captured	Prison	Remarks
White, Robert Private	19	February 15, 1862, Edenton, North Carolina	Co. F, 11th North Carolina Infantry	July 14, 1863, Falling Waters, Maryland	Old Capital Prison, Washington, DC, transferred to Elmira Prison, NY, August 18, 1864	Exchanged March 10, 1865 at Boulware's Wharf on the James River, Virginia
White, Robert E. Private	Unk	March 17, 1864, Macon, Georgia	Co. K, 35th Georgia Infantry	May 24, 1864, Hanover Junction, Virginia	Point Lookout, Maryland, transferred to Elmira Prison, NY, July 11, 1864	Exchanged February 20, 1865 at Boulware's or Cox Wharf on the James River, Virginia
White, S. B. Private	Unk	October 15, 1861, Fort Henry, Tennessee	Co. D, 1st Jackson's Tennessee Heavy Artillery	August 23, 1864, Fort Morgan, Alabama.	New Orleans, Louisiana transferred to Elmira Prison, NY, December 4, 1864.	Exchanged February 25, 1865 at Boulware's or Cox Wharf on the James River, Virginia
White, Samuel Easter Sergeant	Unk	June 6, 1861, New Canton, Virginia	Co. C, 44th Virginia Infantry	May 12, 1864, Spotsylvania Court House, Virginia	Point Lookout, Maryland, transferred to Elmira Prison, NY, August 2, 1864	Oath of Allegiance June 16, 1865
White, Swan Private	Unk	January 15, 1864, Dobson, North Carolina	Co. G, 28th North Carolina Infantry	May 12, 1864, Near Spotsylvania Court House, Virginia	Point Lookout, Maryland, transferred to Elmira Prison, NY, August 14, 1864	Oath of Allegiance May 29, 1865
White, T. T. Private	Unk	May 20, 1861, Hamburg, Arkansas	Co. K, 3rd Arkansas Infantry	May 12, 1864, Spotsylvania Court House, Virginia	Point Lookout, Maryland, transferred to Elmira Prison, NY, July 30, 1864	Exchanged February 13, 1865 at Boulware's wharf on the James River, Virginia
White, Thomas John Private	19	March 24, 1862, Lewisburg, Virginia	Co. E, 26th Battalion, Virginia Infantry	June 3, 1864, Gaines Farm, Cold Harbor, Virginia	Point Lookout, Maryland, transferred to Elmira Prison, NY, July 17, 1864	Died January 12, 1865 of Pluero. Pneumonia, Grave No. 1486

Name & Rank	Age	Enlisted	Regiment and State	Where Captured	Prison	Remarks
White, William Private	42	July 30, 1862, Petersburg, Virginia	Co. E, 45th North Carolina Infantry	May 10, 1864, Spotsylvania Court House, Virginia	Point Lookout, Maryland, transferred to Elmira Prison, NY, August 6, 1864	Exchanged 2/13/65. Died 2/27/65 of Unknown Causes at General Hospital No. 9, Richmond, VA.
White, William B. Private	Unk	March 4, 1863, Greenville, Alabama	Co. J, 59th Alabama Infantry	June 17, 1864, Petersburg, Virginia	Point Lookout, Maryland, transferred to Elmira Prison, NY, July 30, 1864	Died March 19, 1865 of Chronic Diarrhea, Grave No. 1721
White, William C. Private	Unk	May 15, 1862, Camp Pritchard, South Carolina	Co. K, Phillips Legion, Georgia	June 1, 1864, Gaines Farm, Virginia	Point Lookout, Maryland, transferred to Elmira Prison, NY, July 12, 1864	Died November 19, 1864, Chronic Diarrhea, Grave No. 508
White, William H. Sergeant	21	April 29, 1861, Meadsville, Virginia	Co. H, 14th Virginia Infantry	May 10, 1864, Near Petersburg, Virginia	Point Lookout, Maryland, transferred to Elmira Prison, NY, August 17, 1864	Exchanged March 2, 1865 at Akins Landing on the James River, Virginia
White, William J. Private	Unk	March 1, 1864, Unionville, South Carolina	Co. B, 18th South Carolina Infantry	July 30, 1864, Petersburg, Virginia	Point Lookout, Maryland, transferred to Elmira Prison, NY, August 12, 1864	Died October 5, 1864 of Chronic Diarrhea, Grave No. 608
White, William R. Corporal	25	January 1, 1862, Camp Harlee, Georgetown, South Carolina	Co. I, 25th South Carolina Infantry	January 15, 1865, Fort Fisher, North Carolina	February 1, 1865, Elmira Prison Camp, New York	Oath of Allegiance June 27, 1865
White, William S. Private	17	August 6, 1863, Pocahontas County, Virginia	Co. A, 20th Virginia Cavalry	July 13, 1864, Rockville, Maryland	Old Capital Prison, Washington, DC, transferred to Elmira Prison, NY, July 23, 1864	Died October 2, 1864 of Typhoid Fever, Grave No. 422
White, William S. Private	Unk	July 2, 1861, Bethel Am., Virginia	Co. F, 50th Virginia Infantry	May 12, 1864, Spotsylvania Court House, Virginia	Point Lookout, Maryland, transferred to Elmira Prison, NY, August 2, 1864	Died September 20, 1864 of Typhoid Fever, Grave No. 508

Name & Rank	Age	Enlisted	Regiment and State	Where Captured	Prison	Remarks
White, William W. Private	31	March 25, 1862, Grahamville, South Carolina	Co. K, 4th South Carolina Cavalry	May 28, 1864, Hanover County, Virginia. Gunshot Wound Right Leg Below Knee.	Old Capital Prison, Washington D. C. Transferred to Elmira Prison, NY, July 12, 1864	Exchanged February 25, 1865 at Boulware's or Cox Wharf on the James River, Virginia
White, William Watkins Private	Unk	February 26, 1862, Sewell's Point, Virginia	Co. A, 41st Virginia Infantry	May 24, 1864, North Anna, Virginia	Point Lookout, Maryland, transferred to Elmira Prison, NY, July 12,1864	Exchanged October 29, 1864, at Venus Point, Savannah River, GA.
Whiteby, J. A. Private	Unk	August 20, 1862, Calhoun, Georgia	Co. F, 24th Georgia Infantry	June 1, 1864, Cold Harbor, Virginia	Point Lookout, Maryland, transferred to Elmira Prison, NY, July 12, 1864	Oath of Allegiance June 16, 1865
Whitefield, S. J. Sergeant	Unk	February 10, 1862, Duplin County, North Carolina	Co. B, 3rd North Carolina Infantry	May 12, 1864, Near Spotsylvania Court House, Virginia	Point Lookout, Maryland, transferred to Elmira Prison, NY, August 14, 1864	Exchanged March 14, 1865 at Boulware's Wharf on the James River, Virginia
Whitehead, Eli Private	22	January 1, 1862, Near Newbern, Craven County, North Carolina	Co. G, 36th Regiment, 2nd North Carolina Artillery	January 15, 1865, Fort Fisher, North Carolina	February 1, 1865, Elmira Prison Camp, New York	Died April 10, 1865 of Chronic Diarrhea, Grave No. 2665
Whitehead, Henry B. Corporal	Unk	July 18, 1861, Grand Junction, Tennessee	Co. A, Jackson's 1st Regiment, Tennessee Heavy Artillery	August 23, 1864, Fort Morgan, Alabama	New Orleans, Louisiana transferred to Elmira Prison, NY, December 4, 1864.	No Further Information Available.
Whitehead, John O. Private	Unk	September 27, 1863, Orange County Court House, Virginia	Co. A, Jeff Davis Legion Mississippi Cavalry	June 11, 1864, Trevilian Station, Louisa Court House, Virginia	Point Lookout, Maryland, transferred to Elmira Prison, NY, July 25, 1864	Transferred For Exchange October 11, 1864 to Point Lookout Prison Camp, MD. No Further Information
Whitehearst, William R. Private	20	May 30, 1861, Camden County, North Carolina	Co. B, 32nd North Carolina Infantry	May 10, 1864, Near Mine Run Spotsylvania, Virginia	Point Lookout, Maryland, transferred to Elmira Prison, NY, August 6, 1864	Died April 2, 1865 of Diarrhea, Grave No. 2577

Name & Rank	Age	Enlisted	Regiment and State	Where Captured	Prison	Remarks
Whiteheart, Willis Private	Unk	September 29, 1863, Raleigh, North Carolina	Co. G, 13th North Carolina Infantry	May 9, 1864, Beaver Dam Station, Virginia	Point Lookout, Maryland, transferred to Elmira Prison, NY, July 25, 1864	Died September 13, 1864 of Chronic Diarrhea, Grave No. 266
Whitehurst, David W. Sergeant	30	April 22, 1861, Washington Point, Virginia	Co. F, 41st Virginia Infantry	July 20, 1864, Petersburg, Virginia. Deserted to Union Lines.	Old Capital Prison, Washington D. C. Transferred to Elmira Prison, NY, August 12, 1864	Oath of Allegiance October 18, 1864. Early Release per Lincoln's Proclamation, 12/8/1863.
Whitehurst, Robert W. Private	Unk	April 1, 1862, Ocean View, Virginia	Co. C, 15th Virginia Infantry	May 11, 1864, Near Mechanicsville, Virginia	Point Lookout, Maryland, transferred to Elmira Prison, NY, August 17, 1864	Exchanged March 2, 1865 at Akins Landing on the James River, Virginia
Whitenack, William H. Corporal	Unk	May 25, 1862, Floyd Court House, Virginia	Co. B, 42nd Virginia Infantry	May 5, 1864, Near Wilderness Tavern, Virginia	Point Lookout, Maryland, transferred to Elmira Prison, NY, August 2, 1864	Oath of Allegiance May 17, 1865
Whitener, Newton Private	Unk	March 10, 1863, Newton, North Carolina	Co. F, 23rd North Carolina Infantry	May 12, 1864, Near Spotsylvania, Virginia	Point Lookout, Maryland, transferred to Elmira Prison, NY, August 14, 1864	Exchanged February 20, 1865 at Boulware's or Cox Wharf on the James River, Virginia
Whitesell, Daniel R. Private	17	April 2, 1863, Skinker's Neck, North Carolina	Co. E, 1st North Carolina Infantry	May 12, 1864, Spotsylvania Court House, Virginia	Point Lookout, Maryland, transferred to Elmira Prison, NY, August 6, 1864	Oath of Allegiance June 30, 1865
Whitesell, George G. Private	20	July 15, 1862, Alamance County, North Carolina	Co. E, 1st North Carolina Infantry	May 12, 1864, Spotsylvania Court House, Virginia	Point Lookout, Maryland, transferred to Elmira Prison, NY, August 6, 1864	Exchanged October 29, 1864, at Venus Point, Savannah River, GA.
Whitesides, James D. Sergeant	Unk	February 25, 1861, Selma, Alabama	Co. C, 1st Battalion Alabama Artillery	August 23, 1864, Fort Morgan, Alabama	New Orleans, Louisiana transferred to Elmira Prison, NY, December 4, 1864.	Oath of Allegiance July 7, 1865

Name & Rank	Age	Enlisted	Regiment and State	Where Captured	Prison	Remarks
Whitesides, James J. Private	Unk	August 12, 1862, Statesville, North Carolina	Co. H, 37th North Carolina Infantry	May 12, 1864, Spotsylvania Court House, Virginia	Point Lookout, Maryland, transferred to Elmira Prison, NY, August 12, 1864	Oath of Allegiance June 23, 1865
Whitesides, William P. Sergeant	Unk	February 25, 1861, Selma, Alabama	Co. C, 1st Battalion Alabama Artillery	August 23, 1864, Fort Morgan, Alabama	New Orleans, Louisiana transferred to Elmira Prison, NY, December 4, 1864.	Oath of Allegiance June 21, 1865
Whitfield, Benjamin Private	25	March 8, 1862, Monticello, Florida	Co. G, 5th Florida Infantry	June 22, 1864, Near Petersburg, Virginia	Point Lookout, Maryland, transferred to Elmira Prison, NY, August 12, 1864	Oath of Allegiance June 14, 1865
Whitfield, Benjamin F. Private	17	July 22, 1861, Goldsboro, North Carolina	Co. H, 1st North Carolina Cavalry	September 13, 1863, Kelly's Ford, Near Culpepper, Virginia	Point Lookout, Maryland, transferred to Elmira Prison, NY, August 18, 1864	Exchanged February 25, 1865 at Boulware's or Cox Wharf on the James River, Virginia
Whitfield, George V. Private	31	March 1, 1861, Nashville, North Carolina	Co. H, 32nd North Carolina Infantry	May 10, 1864, Near Mine Run Spotsylvania, Virginia	Point Lookout, Maryland, transferred to Elmira Prison, NY, August 6, 1864	Transferred for Exchange 10/11/64. Died 10/22/64 of Unknown Causes at Point Lookout, MD.
Whitfield, J. A. Corporal	Unk	July 29, 1861, Lineville, Talladega County, Alabama	Co. J, 14th Alabama Infantry	May 24, 1864, Hanover Junction, Virginia	Point Lookout, Maryland, transferred to Elmira Prison, NY, July 11, 1864	Exchanged March 14, 1865 at Boulware's Wharf on the James River, Virginia
Whitford, Christopher C. Private	Unk	October 15, 1861, Fort Henry, Tennessee	Co. B, 1st Jackson's Tennessee Heavy Artillery	August 23, 1864, Fort Morgan, Alabama.	New Orleans, Louisiana transferred to Elmira Prison, NY, December 4, 1864.	Exchanged February 25, 1865 at Boulware's or Cox Wharf on the James River, Virginia
Whithers, James E. Private	20	April 20, 1861, Lexington, Virginia	Co. H, 4th Virginia Infantry	May 18, 1864, Spotsylvania Court House, Virginia	Point Lookout, Maryland, transferred to Elmira Prison, NY, July 3, 1864	Exchanged March 2, 1865 at Akins Landing on the James River, Virginia

Name & Rank	Age	Enlisted	Regiment and State	Where Captured	Prison	Remarks
Whiting, William N. Private	23	March 21, 1861, Craney Island, Virginia	Co. G, 6th Virginia Infantry	July 30, 1864, Petersburg, Virginia	Point Lookout, Maryland, transferred to Elmira Prison, NY, August 12, 1864	Exchanged March 2, 1865 at Akins Landing on the James River, Virginia
Whitlock, Charles A. Sergeant Major	20	March 8, 1862, Madison, Florida	Co. E, 5th Florida Infantry	May 12, 1864, Spotsylvania Court House, Virginia	Point Lookout, Maryland, transferred to Elmira Prison, NY, July 30, 1864	Exchanged March 2, 1865 at Akins Landing on the James River, Virginia
Whitlock, James B. Private	Unk	January 30, 1863, Richmond, Virginia	Co. E, 25th Battalion Virginia Infantry	July 12, 1864, Cox's Farm, Virginia	Point Lookout, Maryland, transferred to Elmira Prison, NY, August 6, 1864	Oath of Allegiance July 3, 1865
Whitmine, A. J. Sergeant	Unk	Unknown	Co. J, 4th Virginia Infantry	May 12, 1864, Spotsylvania Court House, Virginia	Point Lookout, Maryland, transferred to Elmira Prison, NY, July 3, 1864	Oath of Allegiance June 14, 1865
Whitmire, John Private	Unk	Unknown	Co. H, 1st North Carolina Cavalry	September 13, 1863, Kelly's Ford, Near Culpepper, Virginia	Point Lookout, Maryland, transferred to Elmira Prison, NY, August 18, 1864	Exchanged March 10, 1865 at Boulware's Wharf on the James River, Virginia
Whitmore, Adam J. Sergeant	Unk	Unknown	Co. I, 4th Virginia Infantry	May 12, 1864, Spotsylvania Court House, Virginia	Point Lookout, Maryland, transferred to Elmira Prison, NY, August 6, 1864	Oath of Allegiance June 14, 1865
Whitmore, David H. Private	Unk	May 21, 1861, Brownsburg, Virginia	Co. H, 25th Virginia Infantry	May 5, 1864, Wilderness, Virginia	Point Lookout, Maryland, transferred to Elmira Prison, NY, August 17, 1864	Died October 18, 1864 of Chronic Diarrhea, Grave No. 545. Headstone has Whitemore.
Whitmore, John B. Private	29	March 15, 1862, Camp Allegheny, Virginia	Co. H, 25th Virginia Infantry	May 5, 1864, Wilderness, Virginia	Point Lookout, Maryland, transferred to Elmira Prison, NY, August 17, 1864	Exchanged March 2, 1865 at Akins Landing on the James River, Virginia

Name & Rank	Age	Enlisted	Regiment and State	Where Captured	Prison	Remarks
Whitney, Samuel E. Private	Unk	March 7, 1862, Pine Creek, Texas	Co. D, Alexander's Texas Cavalry	September 19, 1864, Tenan Parish, Louisiana	New Orleans, Louisiana transferred to Elmira November 19, 1864.	Exchanged March 14, 1865 at Boulware's Wharf on the James River, Virginia
Whittaker, Byrd Private	Unk	July 4, 1861, Princeton, Virginia	Co. H, 50th Virginia Infantry	July 8, 1864, Rockville, Maryland	Point Lookout, Maryland, transferred to Elmira Prison, NY, July 23, 1864	Died April 23, 1865 of Chronic Diarrhea, Grave No. 1404
Whittaker, E. B. Corporal	Unk	September 5, 1862, Russell, Alabama	Co. A, 1st Alabama Artillery	August 23, 1864, Fort Morgan, Alabama.	New Orleans, Louisiana transferred to Elmira Prison, NY, December 4, 1864.	Died February 19, 1865 of Chronic Diarrhea, Grave No. 2344
Whitten, A. Private	18	May 1, 1863, Coosawhatchie, South Carolina	Co. G, 27th South Carolina Infantry	June 24, 1864, Near Petersburg, Virginia	Point Lookout, Maryland, transferred to Elmira Prison, NY, August 17, 1864	Exchanged March 14, 1865 at Boulware's Wharf on the James River, Virginia
Whitten, Francis M. Private	Unk	May 9, 1861, New Orleans, Louisiana	Co. H, 2nd Louisiana Infantry	May 5, 1864, Wilderness, Virginia	Point Lookout, Maryland, transferred to Elmira Prison, NY, August 17, 1864	Exchanged February 13, 1865 at Boulware's wharf on the James River, Virginia
Whitten, Henry P. Private	20	December 13, 1861, Columbia, South Carolina	Co. C, 18th South Carolina Infantry	July 30, 1864, Battle of the Crater, Petersburg, Virginia	Point Lookout, Maryland, transferred to Elmira Prison, NY, August 12, 1864	Oath of Allegiance July 3, 1865
Whitten, Horace J. B. Private	Unk	June 21, 1861, Camp Jackson, West Point, Georgia	Co. D, 4th Georgia Infantry	July 16, 1864, Loudoun County, Virginia	Old Capital Prison, Washington, DC, transferred to Elmira Prison, NY, July 23, 1864	Died October 2, 1864 of Chronic Diarrhea, Grave No. 618
Whitten, M. B. Private	Unk	January 17, 1862, Anderson, South Carolina	Co. G, 27th South Carolina Infantry	June 24, 1864, Near Petersburg, Virginia	Point Lookout, Maryland, transferred to Elmira Prison, NY, August 17, 1864	Oath of Allegiance July 11, 1865

Name & Rank	Age	Enlisted	Regiment and State	Where Captured	Prison	Remarks
Whittimore, James M. Private	23	February 27, 1862, Reidsville, North Carolina	Co. E, 45th North Carolina Infantry	May 10, 1864, Spotsylvania Court House, Virginia	Point Lookout, Maryland, transferred to Elmira Prison, NY, August 6, 1864	Exchanged March 10, 1865 at Boulware's Wharf on the James River, Virginia
Whittington, S. E. Private	20	October 1, 1862, Raleigh, North Carolina	Co. J, 32nd North Carolina Infantry	May 10, 1864, Wilderness, Virginia	Point Lookout, Maryland, transferred to Elmira Prison, NY, August 6, 1864	Died October 23, 1864 of Chronic Diarrhea, Grave No. 866
Whittle, S. W. Private	Unk	May 14, 1862, Perry, Georgia	Co. H, 45th Georgia Infantry	May 6, 1864, Wilderness, Virginia	Point Lookout, Maryland, transferred to Elmira Prison, NY, August 14, 1864	Exchanged February 13, 1865 at Boulware's wharf on the James River, Virginia
Whittman, Jacob Private	22	March 11, 1862, New Orleans, Louisiana	Co. F, 5th Louisiana Infantry	May 12, 1864, Spotsylvania Court House, Virginia	Point Lookout, Maryland, transferred to Elmira Prison, NY, August 17, 1864	Oath of Allegiance May 15, 1865
Whitton, A. E. Private	Unk	Unknown	Co. C, 42nd Virginia Cavalry	September 13, 1863, Near Culpepper, Virginia	Point Lookout, Maryland, transferred to Elmira Prison, NY, August 18, 1864	Exchanged March 10, 1865 at Boulware's Wharf on the James River, Virginia
Whitworth, Robert George Private	25	May 23, 1862, Lincolnton, Lincoln County, North Carolina	Co. B, 23rd North Carolina Infantry	May 20, 1864, Spotsylvania Court House, Virginia	Point Lookout, Maryland, transferred to Elmira Prison, NY, July 12, 1864	Oath of Allegiance May 17, 1865
Wickline, David H. Private	Unk	October 7, 1863, Lewisburg, Virginia	Co. E, 26th Battalion, Virginia Infantry	May 30, 1864, Cold Harbor, Virginia	Point Lookout, Maryland, transferred to Elmira Prison, NY, July 12, 1864	Died February 22, 1865 of Chronic Diarrhea, Grave No. 2300
Wickline, Joseph S. Corporal	Unk	August 16, 1862, Union, Virginia	Co. E, 26th Battalion, Virginia Infantry	May 30, 1864, Cold Harbor, Virginia	Point Lookout, Maryland, transferred to Elmira Prison, NY, July 12, 1864	Exchanged March 14, 1865 at Boulware's Wharf on the James River, Virginia

Name & Rank	Age	Enlisted	Regiment and State	Where Captured	Prison	Remarks
Wicks, James A. Corporal	26	June 19, 1861, New Orleans, Louisiana	Co. E, 8th Louisiana Infantry	May 5, 1864, Wilderness, Virginia	Point Lookout, Maryland, transferred to Elmira Prison, NY, August 14, 1864	Exchanged February 13, 1865 at Boulware's wharf on the James River, Virginia
Wier, John E. Sergeant	18	April 18, 1861, Millwood, Virginia	Co. B, 2nd Virginia Infantry	May 12, 1864, Spotsylvania Court House, Virginia	Point Lookout, Maryland, transferred to Elmira Prison, NY, August 6, 1864	Exchanged March 2, 1865 at Akins Landing on the James River, Virginia
Wiggington, Jackson Andrew Private	Unk	March 1, 1864, Frederick, Virginia	Co. K, 23rd Virginia Cavalry	March 1, 1864, Frederick, Virginia	November 11, 1864, Old Capital Prison, Washington, DC. February 4, 1865 Elmira, Prison Camp, NY.	Oath of Allegiance July 7, 1865
Wiggington, Robert A. Private	21	July 20, 1861, Camp Pickens, Anderson District South Carolina	Co. A, Orr's Rifles, 1st South Carolina Infantry	July 14, 1863, Falling Waters, Maryland	Point Lookout, Maryland, transferred to Elmira Prison, NY, July 12, 1864	Died December 24, 1864 of Pneumonia, Grave No. 1095
Wiggins, Baker Private	Unk	March 23, 1862, Marion, South Carolina	Co. B, Orr's South Carolina Infantry	July 28, 1864, Malvern Hill, VA. Gunshot Wound Fracture of Fibula of Left Leg.	Old Capital Prison, Washington, DC, transferred to Elmira Prison, NY, December 17, 1864	Exchanged February 13, 1865. Died May 11, 1865 of Phthisis Pulmonalis.
Wiggins, James M. Corporal	21	March 8, 1862, Camp Bartow, Georgia	Co. K, 38th Georgia Infantry	May 6, 1864, Near Mine Run Wilderness, Virginia	Point Lookout, Maryland, transferred to Elmira Prison, NY, August 17, 1864	Oath of Allegiance June 23, 1865
Wiggins, James P. Private	Unk	May 20, 1862, Camp Harris, Tennessee	Co. D, 17th Tennessee Infantry	June 17, 1864, Petersburg, Virginia	Point Lookout, Maryland, transferred to Elmira Prison, NY, July 30, 1864	Exchanged February 25, 1865 at Boulware's or Cox Wharf on the James River, Virginia
Wiggins, John Private	Unk	Unknown	Co. G, 6th North Carolina Infantry	May 30, 1864, Old Church, Cold Harbor, Virginia	Point Lookout, Maryland, transferred to Elmira Prison, NY, July 11, 1864	Exchanged March 14, 1865 at Boulware's Wharf on the James River, Virginia

Name & Rank	Age	Enlisted	Regiment and State	Where Captured	Prison	Remarks
Wiggins, John C. Private	Unk	June 15, 1861, Macon, Georgia	Co. C, 12th Georgia Infantry	May 10, 1864, Spotsylvania Court House, Virginia	Point Lookout, Maryland, transferred to Elmira Prison, NY, July 30, 1864	Oath of Allegiance May 29, 1865
Wiggins, John C. Private	Unk	July 15, 1862, Raleigh, North Carolina	Co. G, 3rd North Carolina Infantry	May 12, 1864, Near Spotsylvania, Virginia	Point Lookout, Maryland, transferred to Elmira Prison, NY, July 23, 1864	Died November 15, 1864 of Chronic Diarrhea, Grave No. 952
Wiggins, Leonard E. Private	Unk	March 1, 1863, Columbus County, North Carolina	Co. K, 20th North Carolina Infantry	July 12, 1864, Near Washington, DC	Old Capital Prison, Washington, DC. Elmira Prison Camp, NY, July 25, 1864	Died February 2, 1865 of Typhoid Fever, Grave No. 1917
Wiggs, Haywood Private	24	February 25, 1862, Wadesboro, North Carolina	Co. K, 43rd North Carolina Infantry	July 11, 1864, Fort Stevens, DC. Gunshot Wound of Left Leg.	Old Capital Prison, Washington, DC. Transferred to Elmira Prison Camp, NY, March 3, 1865.	Died April 8, 1865 of Variola (Smallpox), Grave No. 2652
Wiggs, Henry Private	18	July 24, 1861, Goldsboro, North Carolina	Co. F, 10th Regiment, 1st North Carolina Artillery	January 15, 1865, Fort Fisher, North Carolina	February 1, 1865, Elmira Prison Camp, New York	Oath of Allegiance July 11, 1865
Wilaby, Solomon C. Private	25	March 4, 1862, Zebulon, Pike County, Georgia	Co. H, 44th Georgia Infantry	May 12, 1864, Spotsylvania, Virginia	Old Capital Prison, Washington, DC, transferred to Elmira Prison, NY, July 23, 1864	Died October 7, 1864 of Chronic Diarrhea, Grave No. 589
Wilborn, James C. Private	Unk	April 3, 1862, Athens, Georgia	Co. H, Cobb's Legion Georgia Infantry	June 11, 1864, Trevilian Station, Louisa Court House, Virginia	Point Lookout, Maryland, transferred to Elmira Prison, NY, July 25, 1864	Oath of Allegiance June 21, 1865
Wilburn, John Private	17	May 22, 1861, New Orleans, Louisiana	Co. E, 7th Louisiana Infantry	May 12, 1864, Near Spotsylvania Court House, Virginia	Point Lookout, Maryland, transferred to Elmira Prison, NY, August 17, 1864	Exchanged February 13, 1865 at Boulware's wharf on the James River, Virginia

Name & Rank	Age	Enlisted	Regiment and State	Where Captured	Prison	Remarks
Wilcox, John W. Corporal	Unk	September 22, 1862, Waynesville, Georgia	Co. G, 7th Georgia Cavalry	June 11, 1864, Trevilian Station, Louisa Court House, Virginia	Point Lookout, Maryland, transferred to Elmira Prison, NY, July 25, 1864	Oath of Allegiance June 23, 1865
Wilcox, R. B. Private	Unk	Unknown	Co. B, 39th Virginia Militia, Infantry	June 15, 1864, Petersburg, Virginia	Point Lookout, Maryland, transferred to Elmira Prison, NY, July 12,1864	Exchanged October 29, 1864, at Venus Point, Savannah River, GA.
Wilcox, Redden Private	16	February 28, 1862, Lumberton, North Carolina	Co. E, 51st North Carolina Infantry	June 1, 1864, Cold Harbor, Virginia	Point Lookout, Maryland, transferred to Elmira Prison, NY, July 12, 1864	Died November 28, 1864 of Pleuro Pneumonia, Grave No. 989
Wilder, Benjamin K. Private	41	March 11, 1862, Gourdins Depot, Williamsburg, South Carolina	Co. K, 25th South Carolina Infantry	January 15, 1865, Fort Fisher, North Carolina	February 1, 1865, Elmira Prison Camp, New York	Died March 16, 1865 of Pneumonia, Grave No. 1693
Wilder, George C. Private	26	July 23, 1862, North Carolina	Co. G, 3rd North Carolina Infantry	May 12, 1864, Near Spotsylvania County Court House, Virginia	Point Lookout, Maryland, transferred to Elmira Prison, NY, August 14, 1864	Exchanged March 14, 1865 at Boulware's Wharf on the James River, Virginia
Wilder, J. C. Private	20	September 15, 1862, Camp Mangum, North Carolina	Co. D, 31st North Carolina Infantry	May 31, 1864, Cold Harbor, Virginia	Point Lookout, Maryland, transferred to Elmira Prison, NY, July 12, 1864	Exchanged October 29, 1864, at Venus Point, Savannah River, GA.
Wilder, James T. Private	Unk	April 28, 1861, Albany, Georgia	Co. E, 4th Georgia Infantry	May 10, 1864, Spotsylvania, Virginia. Gunshot Wound Right Thigh.	Old Capital Prison, Washington, DC, transferred to Elmira Prison, NY, July 23, 1864	Exchanged March 10, 1865 at Boulware's Wharf on the James River, Virginia
Wilder, L. Private	Unk	March 10, 1863, James Island, South Carolina	Co. K, 25th South Carolina Infantry	January 15, 1865, Fort Fisher, North Carolina	February 1, 1865, Elmira Prison Camp, New York	Died April 2, 1865 of Intermittent Fever, Grave No. 2575
Wilder, Troy L. Private	36	March 1, 1861, Nashville, North Carolina	Co. H, 32nd North Carolina Infantry	May 10, 1864, Near Mine Run Spotsylvania, Virginia	Point Lookout, Maryland, transferred to Elmira Prison, NY, August 6, 1864	Exchanged October 29, 1864, at Venus Point, Savannah River, GA.

Name & Rank	Age	Enlisted	Regiment and State	Where Captured	Prison	Remarks
Wileman, Robert L. Corporal	Unk	March 19, 1862, McMinnville, Tennessee	Co. K, 44th Tennessee Infantry	June 17, 1864, Petersburg, Virginia	Point Lookout, Maryland, transferred to Elmira Prison, NY, July 30, 1864	Oath of Allegiance May 29, 1865
Wiles, H. Private	Unk	Unknown	Co. A, 3rd Georgia Cavalry	June 1, 1864, White House, Virginia	Point Lookout, Maryland, transferred to Elmira Prison, NY, July 12, 1864	Exchanged March 14, 1865 at Boulware's Wharf on the James River, Virginia
Wiles, William Private	Unk	April 11, 1862, Coles Island, South Carolina	Co. F, 25th South Carolina Infantry	January 15, 1865, Fort Fisher, North Carolina	February 1, 1865, Elmira Prison Camp, New York	Died May 11, 1865 of Acute Diarrhea, Grave No. 2795
Wiley, Thomas W. Private	Unk	June 12, 1861, Farmville, Virginia	Co. G, 44th Virginia Infantry	July 12, 1864, Near Washington, DC,	Point Lookout, Maryland, transferred to Elmira Prison, NY, July 23, 1864	Oath of Allegiance May 17, 1865
Wiley, William H. Sergeant	Unk	June 3, 1863, Saltville, Virginia	Co. B, 21st Virginia Cavalry	July 3, 1864, Leestown, Virginia	Point Lookout, Maryland, transferred to Elmira Prison, NY, July 23, 1864	Oath of Allegiance June 14, 1865
Wilford, Richard Private	Unk	Unknown	Co. A, North Carolina Home Guards	May 2, 1864, Harper's Ferry, Virginia	Old Capital Prison, Washington, DC, transferred to Elmira July 25, 1864	Oath of Allegiance May 29, 1865
Wilhelm, Jesse Private	40	June 28, 1861, Salisbury, North Carolina	Co. I, 32nd North Carolina Infantry	May 12, 1864, Spotsylvania Court House, Virginia	Point Lookout, Maryland, transferred to Elmira Prison, NY, August 6, 1864	Oath of Allegiance May 29, 1865
Wilhoit, Gomalian O. Sergeant	22	May 15, 1862, Salisbury, North Carolina	Co. C, 42nd North Carolina Infantry	June 3, 1864, Cold Harbor, Virginia	Point Lookout, Maryland, transferred to Elmira Prison, NY, July 12, 1864	Oath of Allegiance July 3, 1865
Wilkerson, Henry F. Private	21	September 10, 1863, Chaffin's Farm, Virginia	Co. F, 46th Virginia Infantry	June 17, 1864, Near Petersburg, Virginia	Point Lookout, Maryland, transferred to Elmira Prison, NY, July 25, 1864	Oath of Allegiance April 1, 1865

Name & Rank	Age	Enlisted	Regiment and State	Where Captured	Prison	Remarks
Wilkerson, John W. Private	25	August 24, 1862, Richmond, Virginia	Co. F, 46th Virginia Infantry	June 17, 1864, Petersburg, Virginia	Point Lookout, Maryland, transferred to Elmira Prison, NY, July 23, 1864	Oath of Allegiance April 1, 1865
Wilkerson, Samuel Private	20	May 31, 1861, Raleigh, North Carolina	Co. B, 1st North Carolina Infantry	May 12, 1864, Spotsylvania Court House, Virginia	Point Lookout, Maryland, transferred to Elmira Prison, NY, August 6, 1864	Died January 30, 1865 of Chronic Diarrhea, Grave No. 1813. 18th Regiment on Headstone.
Wilkes, John O. Private	Unk	May 9, 1862, Reidsville, Georgia	Co. H, 61st Georgia Infantry	May 12, 1864, Spotsylvania Court House, Virginia	Point Lookout, Maryland, transferred to Elmira Prison, NY, July 30, 1864	Exchanged March 10, 1865 at Boulware's Wharf on the James River, Virginia
Wilkes, Joseph T. Private	Unk	January 1, 1862, Camp Harlee, Chesterfield, South Carolina	Co. D, 21st South Carolina Infantry	January 15, 1865, Fort Fisher, North Carolina	February 1, 1865, Elmira Prison Camp, New York	Exchanged March 2, 1865 at Akins Landing on the James River, Virginia
Wilkins, John T. Corporal	Unk	April 19, 1861, Harrisonburg, Virginia	Co. B, 10th Virginia Infantry	May 12, 1864, Spotsylvania Court House, Virginia	Point Lookout, Maryland, transferred to Elmira Prison, NY, August 2, 1864	Exchanged February 20, 1865 at Boulware's or Cox Wharf on the James River, Virginia
Wilkins, Nathaniel Private	31	May 19, 1861, Princess Anne County, Virginia	Co. F, 6th Virginia Infantry	May 12, 1864, Near Spotsylvania Court House, Virginia	Point Lookout, Maryland, transferred to Elmira Prison, NY, August 6, 1864	Oath of Allegiance May 29, 1865
Wilkins, P. P. Private	Unk	Unknown	Co. A, 26th Virginia Infantry	June 3, 1864, Gaines Mill Cold Harbor, Virginia	Point Lookout, Maryland, transferred to Elmira Prison, NY, July 17,1864	Exchanged October 29, 1864, at Venus Point, Savannah River, GA.
Wilkins, S. S. Private	Unk	Unknown	Co. C, 51st North Carolina Infantry	Unknown	Point Lookout Prison Camp, MD. Transferred to Elmira Prison Camp NY Date Unknown	Died August 1, 1864 of Unknown Disease, Grave No. 145

Name & Rank	Age	Enlisted	Regiment and State	Where Captured	Prison	Remarks
Wilkins, Thomas J. Private	25	August 1, 1861, Camp Jones, Mississippi	Co. E, 11th Mississippi Infantry	August 18, 1864, Petersburg, Virginia. Gunshot Wound Left Leg.	Old Capital Prison, Washington, DC, transferred to Elmira Prison, NY, December 17, 1864	Exchanged February 13, 1865 at Boulware's Wharf on the James River, Virginia
Wilkinson, James Private	Unk	October 20, 1862, Marion Court House, South Carolina	Co. D, 25th South Carolina Infantry	January 15, 1865, Fort Fisher, North Carolina	February 1, 1865, Elmira Prison Camp, New York	Oath of Allegiance July 7, 1865
Wilkinson, William Private	Unk	October 19, 1861, Richmond, Virginia	Co. E, 59th Virginia Infantry	May 7, 1864, Nottoway Bridge, Virginia	Point Lookout, Maryland, transferred to Elmira Prison, NY, August 17, 1864	Transferred For Exchange 10/11/64 to Point Lookout Prison Camp, MD. Died 11/6/64 of Chronic Diarrhea
Wilkinson, William H. Private	30	October 10, 1862, Newton, North Carolina	Co. E, 32nd North Carolina Infantry	May 10, 1864, Wilderness, Virginia	Point Lookout, Maryland, transferred to Elmira Prison, NY, August 6, 1864	Died February 16, 1865 of Pneumonia, Grave No. 2211
Wilks, H. D. Private	Unk	Unknown	Co. D, 13th Battalion North Carolina Light Artillery	January 15, 1865, Fort Fisher, North Carolina	February 1, 1865, Elmira Prison Camp, New York	Exchanged February 20, 1865 at Boulware's or Cox Wharf on the James River, Virginia
Willard, Christopher Sergeant	32	November 18, 1861, Columbia, South Carolina	Co. A, 18th South Carolina Infantry	July 30, 1864, Petersburg, Virginia	Fort Columbus, NY Harbor, transferred to Elmira December 4, 1864.	Oath of Allegiance July 11, 1865
Willard, John P. Private	Unk	September 20, 1862, Charleston, Virginia	Co. A, 26th Battalion, Virginia Infantry	June 3, 1864, Gaines Mill Cold Harbor, Virginia	Point Lookout, Maryland, transferred to Elmira Prison, NY, July 17, 1864	Oath of Allegiance May 29, 1865
Willborn, Thomas W. Private	28	April 1, 1864, Person County, North Carolina	Co. H, 24th North Carolina Infantry	June 17, 1864, Petersburg, Virginia	Point Lookout, Maryland, transferred to Elmira Prison, NY, July 30, 1864	Oath of Allegiance May 29, 1865

Name & Rank	Age	Enlisted	Regiment and State	Where Captured	Prison	Remarks
Willet, William Private	Unk	Unknown	Co. B, 1st Jackson's Tennessee Heavy Artillery	August 23, 1864, Fort Morgan, Alabama.	New Orleans, Louisiana transferred to Elmira Prison, NY, December 4, 1864.	Oath of Allegiance May 29, 1865
Willets, Benjamin B. Privat	18	July 20, 1862, Fort St. Philip, Brunswick County, North Carolina	Co. G, 36th Regiment North Carolina, 2nd Artillery	January 15, 1865, Fort Fisher, North Carolina.	February 1, 1865, Elmira Prison Camp, New York	Oath of Allegiance July 11, 1865
Willets, Jacob L. Private	22	April 16, 1862, Old Brunswick Town, Brunswick County, North Carolina	Co. G, 36th Regiment North Carolina, 2nd Artillery	January 15, 1865, Fort Fisher, North Carolina. Wounded.	February 1, 1865, Elmira Prison Camp, New York	Died Of Chronic Diarrhea April 14, 1865. Grave No. 2707
Willets, John J. Private	21	April 16, 1862, Old Brunswick Town, North Carolina	Co. G, 36th Regiment, 2nd North Carolina Artillery	January 15, 1865, Fort Fisher, North Carolina.	February 1, 1865, Elmira Prison Camp, New York	Died May 7, 1865 of Pneumonia, Grave No. 2770
Willets, William J. Private	26	April 16, 1862, Old Brunswick Town, North Carolina	Co. G, 36th Regiment, 2nd North Carolina Artillery	January 15, 1865, Fort Fisher, North Carolina. Wounded	February 1, 1865, Elmira Prison Camp, New York	Died March 4, 1865 of Pneumonia, Grave No. 1977
Willhight, Henry Y. Private	25	May 20, 1861, Louisburg, North Carolina	Co. K, 32nd North Carolina Infantry	May 10, 1864, Near Mine Run Spotsylvania, Virginia	Point Lookout, Maryland, transferred to Elmira Prison, NY, August 6, 1864	Oath of Allegiance June 27, 1865
William, Washington A. Private	Unk	March 15, 1864, Camp Vance, North Carolina	Co. F, 22nd North Carolina Infantry	May 6, 1864, Wilderness, Virginia. Gunshot Wound Left Heel.	Old Capital Prison, Washington, DC, transferred to Elmira Prison, NY, July 23, 1864	Oath of Allegiance May 29, 1865
Williams, A. H. Private	37	January 1, 1862, Camp Harlee, Chesterfield, South Carolina	Co. D, 21st South Carolina Infantry	January 15, 1865, Fort Fisher, North Carolina	February 1, 1865, Elmira Prison Camp, New York	Died April 20, 1865 of Acute Diarrhea, Grave No. 1379. Headstone has A. W. Williams
Williams, A. S. Private	26	May 9, 1861, Rutherford, North Carolina	Co. E, 16th North Carolina Infantry	May 6, 1864, Wilderness, Virginia	Point Lookout, Maryland, transferred to Elmira Prison, NY, August 14, 1864	Oath of Allegiance June 30, 1865

Name & Rank	Age	Enlisted	Regiment and State	Where Captured	Prison	Remarks
Williams, Alex Private	Unk	March 29, 1862, Lewisburg, Virginia	Co. D, 26th Battalion Virginia Infantry	June 3, 1864, Cold Harbor, Virginia	Point Lookout, Maryland, transferred to Elmira Prison, NY, July 12, 1864	Died September 6, 1864, of Gastro-Enteritis Grave No. 244
Williams, Amos Private	38	March 7, 1862, Wilmington, New Hanover County, North Carolina	Co. E, 36th Regiment, 2nd North Carolina Artillery	January 15, 1865, Fort Fisher, North Carolina	February 1, 1865, Elmira Prison Camp, New York	Died February 20, 1865 on Route to be Exchanged.
Williams, Anderson Private	18	July 16, 1861, Forestville, North Carolina	Co. J, 1st North Carolina Infantry	May 12, 1864, Wilderness Spotsylvania, Virginia	Point Lookout, Maryland, transferred to Elmira Prison, NY, August 6, 1864	Oath of Allegiance June 12, 1865
Williams, Andrew J. Private	30	June 25, 1861, Russell, Virginia	Co. K, 48th Virginia Infantry	May 12, 1864, Spotsylvania Court House, Virginia	Point Lookout, Maryland, transferred to Elmira Prison, NY, August 2, 1864	Oath of Allegiance June 22, 1865
Williams, Andrew T. Private	22	February 16, 1863, Bladen County, North Carolina	Co. B, 36th Regiment, 2nd North Carolina Artillery	January 15, 1865, Fort Fisher, North Carolina	February 1, 1865, Elmira Prison Camp, New York	Oath of Allegiance July 11, 1865
Williams, Anthony M. Private	Unk	May 14, 1861, White Sulfur Springs, Virginia	Co. G, 11th Virginia Cavalry	September 22, 1863, Near Culpepper, Virginia	Point Lookout, Maryland, transferred to Elmira Prison, NY, August 18, 1864	Died January 6, 1865 of Chronic Diarrhea, Grave No. 1230
Williams, Ashley D. Sergeant	25	May 28, 1861, Meherrin, Virginia	Co. K, 21st Virginia Infantry	May 12, 1864, Spotsylvania Court House, Virginia	Point Lookout, Maryland, transferred to Elmira Prison, NY, August 2, 1864	Exchanged October 29, 1864, at Venus Point, Savannah River, GA.
Williams, B. Private	Unk	December 16, 1862, Macon, Georgia	Captain Slaten's Battery, Georgia Artillery	June 17, 1864, Petersburg, Virginia	Point Lookout, Maryland, transferred to Elmira Prison, NY, July 30, 1864	Died January 11, 1865 of Variola (Smallpox), Grave No. 1213
Williams, Benjamin F. Private	Unk	June 18, 1861, Randolph County, North Carolina	Co. L, 22nd North Carolina Infantry	May 23, 1864, Hanover Junction, Virginia	Point Lookout, Maryland, transferred to Elmira Prison, NY, July 23, 1864	Oath of Allegiance May 29, 1865

Name & Rank	Age	Enlisted	Regiment and State	Where Captured	Prison	Remarks
Williams, Benjamin J. Private	26	February 15, 1862, Conyers, Georgia	Co. B, 18th Georgia Infantry	June 1, 1864, Cold Harbor, Virginia	Point Lookout, Maryland, transferred to Elmira Prison, NY, July 17, 1864	Oath of Allegiance June 21, 1865
Williams, Boling W. Private	Unk	April 27, 1861, Tuskegee, Alabama	Co. C, 3rd Alabama Infantry	July 16, 1864, Loudoun County, Virginia	Old Capital Prison, Washington, DC, transferred to Elmira Prison, NY, July 23, 1864	Exchanged October 29, 1864, at Venus Point, Savannah River, GA.
Williams, Brice F. Private	26	May 13, 1862, Onslow County, North Carolina	Co. E, 3rd North Carolina Infantry	May 12, 1864, Near Spotsylvania Court House, Virginia	Point Lookout, Maryland, transferred to Elmira Prison, NY, August 14, 1864	Exchanged March 14, 1865 at Boulware's Wharf on the James River, Virginia
Williams, Bryce Corporal	23	June 11, 1861, Wilmington, North Carolina	Co. E, 1st North Carolina Infantry	May 12, 1864, Spotsylvania Court House, Virginia	Point Lookout, Maryland, transferred to Elmira Prison, NY, August 6, 1864	Oath of Allegiance May 19, 1865
Williams, Charles M. Private	Unk	August 27, 1862 Jefferson County, Alabama	Co. A, 21st Alabama Infantry	August 23, 1864, Fort Morgan, Alabama	New Orleans, Louisiana. Transferred to Elmira Prison Camp October 8, 1864	Oath of Allegiance June 21, 1865
Williams, Charles O. Private	30	August 27, 1861, Union County, North Carolina	Co. E, 40th Regiment, 3rd North Carolina Artillery	January 15, 1865, Fort Fisher, North Carolina	February 1, 1865, Elmira Prison Camp, New York	Exchanged March 2, 1865 at Akins Landing on the James River, Virginia
Williams, Daniel Private	Unk	August 10, 1863, Chambers County, Alabama	Co. F, 61st Alabama Infantry	May 12, 1864, Spotsylvania Court House, Virginia	Point Lookout, Maryland, transferred to Elmira Prison, NY, July 30, 1864	Exchanged February 25, 1865 at Boulware's or Cox Wharf on the James River, Virginia
Williams, Daniel M. Private	Unk	March 1, 1862, Smithville, Brunswick County, North Carolina	Co. G, 3rd North Carolina Infantry	May 12, 1864, Near Spotsylvania Court House, Virginia	Point Lookout, Maryland, transferred to Elmira Prison, NY, August 14, 1864	Exchanged March 2, 1865 at Akins Landing on the James River, Virginia

Name & Rank	Age	Enlisted	Regiment and State	Where Captured	Prison	Remarks
Williams, Daniel M. Corporal	20	April 26, 1861, Mocksville, North Carolina	Co. F, 13th North Carolina Infantry	May 6, 1864, Wilderness, Virginia	Point Lookout, Maryland, transferred to Elmira Prison, NY, August 14, 1864	Exchanged February 20, 1865 at Boulware's or Cox Wharf on the James River, Virginia
Williams, Daniel W. Private	Unk	April 17, 1861, Christiansburg, Virginia	Co. G, 4th Virginia Infantry	May 12, 1864, Spotsylvania Court House, Virginia	Point Lookout, Maryland, transferred to Elmira Prison, NY, August 2, 1864	Exchanged March 10, 1865 at Boulware's Wharf on the James River, Virginia
Williams, David F. Private	18	January 27, 1864, LaGrange, Georgia	Co. B, 60th Georgia Infantry	May 12, 1864, Spotsylvania, Virginia. Gunshot Wound Right Thigh and Abdomen.	Old Capital Prison, Washington, DC, transferred to Elmira Prison, NY, July 23, 1864	Exchanged February 20, 1865 at Boulware's or Cox Wharf on the James River, Virginia
Williams, Edward Private	Unk	November 4, 1864, Fort Holmes, New Hanover County, North Carolina	Co. E, 40th Regiment, 3rd North Carolina Artillery	January 15, 1865, Fort Fisher, North Carolina	February 1, 1865, Elmira Prison Camp, New York	Exchanged March 14, 1865 at Boulware's Wharf on the James River, Virginia
Williams, George W. Private	22	July 25, 1861, Tullahoma, Tennessee	Co. K, 25th Tennessee Infantry	May 16, 1864, Near Drury's Bluff, Virginia	Point Lookout, Maryland, transferred to Elmira Prison, NY, August 17, 1864	Exchanged February 25, 1865 at Boulware's or Cox Wharf on the James River, Virginia
Williams, Gilbert Private	Unk	May 15, 1864, Snow Hill, North Carolina	Co. A, 18th North Carolina Infantry	July 29, 1864, Petersburg, Virginia	Point Lookout, Maryland, transferred to Elmira Prison, NY, August 12, 1864	Died December 3, 1864 of Pneumonia, Grave No. 888
Williams, Giles B. Corporal	Unk	April 30, 1862, Camp Holmes, New Hanover County, North Carolina	Co. E, 51st North Carolina Infantry	June 1, 1864, Cold Harbor, Virginia	Point Lookout, Maryland, transferred to Elmira Prison, NY, July 12, 1864	Oath of Allegiance July 3, 1865
Williams, Harrison Private	Unk	July 12, 1861, Buchanan, Georgia	Co. A, 35th Georgia Infantry	May 6, 1864, Wilderness, Virginia	Point Lookout, Maryland, transferred to Elmira Prison, NY, August 14, 1864	Died November 7, 1864 of Chronic Diarrhea, Grave No. 768

Name & Rank	Age	Enlisted	Regiment and State	Where Captured	Prison	Remarks
Williams, Harry C. Sergeant	Unk	July 2, 1861, Bethel Am., Virginia	Co. F, 50th Virginia Infantry	May 12, 1864, Spotsylvania Court House, Virginia	Point Lookout, Maryland, transferred to Elmira Prison, NY, August 2, 1864	Exchanged February 20, 1865 at Boulware's or Cox Wharf on the James River, Virginia
Williams, Henry J. Sergeant	22	June 24, 1861, Plymouth, North Carolina	Co. G, 1st North Carolina Infantry	May 12, 1864, Wilderness Spotsylvania, Virginia	Point Lookout, Maryland, transferred to Elmira Prison, NY, August 6, 1864	Oath of Allegiance June 12, 1865
Williams, Hill Sergeant	25	January 31, 1861, Onslow County, North Carolina	Co. F, 3rd North Carolina Infantry	May 12, 1864, Near Spotsylvania Court House, Virginia	Point Lookout, Maryland, transferred to Elmira Prison, NY, August 14, 1864	Exchanged March 14, 1865 at Boulware's Wharf on the James River, Virginia
Williams, Isaac Private	Unk	Unknown	Co. H, 11th North Carolina Infantry	May 30, 1864 Mechanics-ville, Virginia	Point Lookout, Maryland, transferred to Elmira Prison, NY, July 11, 1864	Exchanged March 2, 1865 at Akins Landing on the James River, Virginia
Williams, Isaac W. Private	22	March 5, 1863, Fort Caswell, Brunswick County, North Carolina	Co. E, 40th Regiment, 3rd North Carolina Artillery	January 15, 1865, Fort Fisher, North Carolina	February 1, 1865, Elmira Prison Camp, New York	Exchanged 2/20/65. Died 3/12/65 of Chronic Diarrhea at Confederate States Army Hospital, Richmond, VA
Williams, J. Private	Unk	Unknown	Co. F, 21st South Carolina Infantry	January 15, 1865, Fort Fisher, North Carolina	February 1, 1865, Elmira Prison Camp, New York	Oath of Allegiance July 11, 1865
Williams, J. G. Private	Unk	June 15, 1862, Marion, South Carolina	Co. J, 21st South Carolina Infantry	June 24, 1864, Near Petersburg, Virginia	Point Lookout, Maryland, transferred to Elmira Prison, NY, August 18, 1864	Exchanged March 14, 1865 at Boulware's Wharf on the James River, Virginia
Williams, J. H. Private	20	Unknown	Co. E, 40th Regiment, 3rd North Carolina Artillery	January 15, 1865, Fort Fisher, North Carolina	February 1, 1865, Elmira Prison Camp, New York	Died April 3, 1865 of Chronic Diarrhea, Grave No. 2550

Name & Rank	Age	Enlisted	Regiment and State	Where Captured	Prison	Remarks
Williams, J. L. Private	Unk	December 27, 1861, Yorkville, South Carolina	Co. C, 17th South Carolina Infantry	July 30, 1864, Petersburg, Virginia	Point Lookout, Maryland, transferred to Elmira Prison, NY, August 12, 1864	Oath of Allegiance July 3, 1865
Williams, J. M. Sergeant	Unk	April 15, 1861, Livingston, Alabama	Co. G, 5th Alabama Infantry	May 5, 1864, Wilderness, Virginia	Point Lookout, Maryland, transferred to Elmira Prison, NY, August 17, 1864	Oath of Allegiance June 19, 1865
Williams, J. M. Civilian	Unk	Unknown	Citizen of North Carolina	January 15, 1865, Fort Fisher, North Carolina	February 1, 1865, Elmira Prison Camp, New York	Exchanged March 14, 1865 at Boulware's Wharf on the James River, Virginia
Williams, J. R. Private	Unk	May 2, 1864, Marianna, Florida	Co. C, 1st Reserves Florida Infantry	September 27, 1864, Marianna, Florida	New Orleans, Louisiana transferred to Elmira November 19, 1864.	Died March 13, 1865 of Variola (Smallpox), Grave No. 1833. Headstone has Virginia.
Williams, J. R. Private	Unk	Unknown	Co. K, 1st Texas Cavalry	August 8, 1864, Williamsport, Louisiana	New Orleans, Louisiana transferred to Elmira November 19, 1864.	Exchanged March 14, 1865 at Boulware's Wharf on the James River, Virginia
Williams, James Private	41	March 5, 1862, Carroll County, Virginia	Co. F, 29th Virginia Infantry	May 30, 1864, Cold Harbor, Virginia. Gunshot Wound Left Arm.	Point Lookout, Maryland, transferred to Elmira Prison, NY, July 23, 1864	Died January 18, 1865 of Variola (Smallpox), Grave No. 1210
Williams, James A. Private	Unk	March 27, 1864, Petersburg, Virginia	Co. B, 31st North Carolina Infantry	June 1, 1864, Cold Harbor, Virginia	Point Lookout, Maryland, transferred to Elmira Prison, NY, July 12, 1864	Died September 17, 1864 of Jaundice and Chronic Diarrhea, Grave No. 150
Williams, James D. Private	Unk	January 15, 1864, Selma, Alabama	Co. E, 1st Battalion Alabama Artillery	August 23, 1864, Fort Morgan, Alabama	Steam Press No. 4 New Orleans, Louisiana transferred to Elmira Prison, NY, October 8, 1864.	Exchanged March 2, 1865 at Akins Landing on the James River, Virginia

Name & Rank	Age	Enlisted	Regiment and State	Where Captured	Prison	Remarks
Williams, James F. Corporal	23	July 9, 1861, Murfreesboro, North Carolina	Co. F, 1st North Carolina Infantry	May 12, 1864, Wilderness Spotsylvania, Virginia	Point Lookout, Maryland, transferred to Elmira Prison, NY, August 6, 1864	Oath of Allegiance May 13, 1865
Williams, James H. Private	26	May 6, 1862, Forsyth, Monroe County, Georgia	Co. K, 53rd Georgia Infantry	June 1, 1864, Cold Harbor, Virginia	Transferred From Point Lookout Prison, MD, July 12, 1864. Train Never Arrived at Elmira Prison Camp, NY.	Died July 15, 1864 in Train Wreck at Shohola, Pennsylvania.
Williams, James H. Private	32	July 12, 1862, Davidson College, North Carolina	Co. K, 56th North Carolina Infantry	March 25, 1865, Petersburg, Virginia. Gunshot Wound Left Forearm.	Old Capital Prison, Washington D. C. Transferred to Elmira Prison, NY, May 12, 1865.	Oath of Allegiance July 3, 1865
Williams, James J. Private	21	July 25, 1861, Tullahoma, Tennessee	Co. K, 25th Tennessee Infantry	May 16, 1864, Near Drury's Bluff, Virginia	Point Lookout, Maryland, transferred to Elmira Prison, NY, August 17, 1864	Exchanged February 25, 1865 at Boulware's or Cox Wharf on the James River, Virginia
Williams, James R. Private	22	May 13, 1862, Onslow County, North Carolina	Co. E, 3rd North Carolina Infantry	May 12, 1864, Near Spotsylvania Court House, Virginia	Point Lookout, Maryland, transferred to Elmira Prison, NY, August 14, 1864	Oath of Allegiance June 27, 1865
Williams, James W. Private	32	March 2, 1862, McCollum's Schoolhouse, Reidsville, North Carolina	Co. E, 45th North Carolina Infantry	May 10, 1864, Spotsylvania Court House, Virginia	Point Lookout, Maryland, transferred to Elmira Prison, NY, August 6, 1864	Died January 19, 1865 of Chronic Diarrhea, Grave No. 1206
Williams, James W. Private	18	February 27, 1862, Reidsville, North Carolina	Co. G, 45th North Carolina Infantry	May 10, 1864, Spotsylvania Court House, Virginia	Point Lookout, Maryland, transferred to Elmira Prison, NY, August 6, 1864	Died October 29, 1864 of Chronic Diarrhea, Grave No. 728
Williams, Joel Private	34	February 9, 1863, Clinton, Sampson County, North Carolina	Co. D, 36th Regiment, 2nd North Carolina Artillery	January 15, 1865, Fort Fisher, North Carolina	February 1, 1865, Elmira Prison Camp, New York	Died March 4, 1865 of Pneumonia, Grave No. 1972

Name & Rank	Age	Enlisted	Regiment and State	Where Captured	Prison	Remarks
Williams, John Private	Unk	Unknown	Co. A, 2nd Battalion North Carolina Infantry	May 10, 1864, Near Spotsylvania County Court House, Virginia	Point Lookout, Maryland, transferred to Elmira Prison, NY, August 14, 1864	Died October 28, 1864 of Chronic Diarrhea, Grave No. 725
Williams, John Sergeant	24	February 24, 1862, Wadesboro, North Carolina	Co. H, 43rd North Carolina Infantry	July 12, 1864, Near Washington, DC,	Old Capital Prison, Washington, DC, transferred to Elmira Prison, NY, July 23, 1864	Oath of Allegiance May 29, 1865
Williams, John Private	Unk	October 27, 1862, Richmond County, North Carolina	Co. C, 53rd North Carolina Infantry	July 12, 1864, Near Washington, DC,	Old Capital Prison, Washington, DC, transferred to Elmira Prison, NY, July 23, 1864	Oath of Allegiance June 12, 1865
Williams, John Private	Unk	April 4, 1862, Bennettsville, South Carolina	Co. F, 21st South Carolina Infantry	June 17, 1864, Petersburg, Virginia	Point Lookout, Maryland, transferred to Elmira Prison, NY, July 30, 1864	Oath of Allegiance July 11, 1865 Also Captured January 15, 1865 at Fort Fisher, NC.
Williams, John A. Private	Unk	April 8, 1863, Troy, Alabama	Co. F, 1st Battalion Alabama Artillery	August 23, 1864, Fort Morgan, Alabama	Steam Press No. 4 New Orleans, Louisiana transferred to Elmira Prison, NY, October 8, 1864.	Died April 22, 1865 of Pneumonia, Grave No. 1396
Williams, John J. Private	22	Unknown	Co. D, 1st Virginia Cavalry	July 27, 1864, Lovettsville, Virginia	Old Capital Prison, Washington D. C. Transferred to Elmira Prison, NY, July 12, 1864	Oath of Allegiance April 4, 1865. Early Release per Lincoln's Proclamation, 12/8/1863.
Williams, John W. No. 1 Private	Unk	April 3, 1861, Mobile, Alabama	Co. F, 1st Battalion Alabama Artillery	August 23, 1864, Fort Morgan, Alabama	Steam Press No. 4 New Orleans, Louisiana transferred to Elmira Prison, NY, October 8, 1864.	Exchanged March 2, 1865 at Akins Landing on the James River, Virginia

Name & Rank	Age	Enlisted	Regiment and State	Where Captured	Prison	Remarks
Williams, John W. No. 2 Private	Unk	April 8, 1862, Greenville, Alabama	Co. F, 1st Battalion Alabama Artillery	August 23, 1864, Fort Morgan, Alabama	Steam Press No. 4 New Orleans, Louisiana transferred to Elmira Prison, NY, October 8, 1864.	Oath of Allegiance May 29, 1865
Williams, John W. Private	Unk	May 18, 1864, Fort Holmes, New Hanover County, North Carolina	Co. K, 40th Regiment, 3rd North Carolina Artillery	January 15, 1865, Fort Fisher, North Carolina	February 1, 1865, Elmira Prison Camp, New York	Died March 18, 1864 of Typhoid Fever, Grave No. 2458
Williams, Joseph Private	Unk	June 12, 1861, Harpers Ferry, Virginia	Co. E, 10th Virginia Infantry	May 12, 1864, Spotsylvania Court House, Virginia	Point Lookout, Maryland, transferred to Elmira Prison, NY, August 2, 1864	Oath of Allegiance June 16, 1865
Williams, Joseph T. Private	25	June 27, 1861, Colerain, North Carolina	Co. F, 5th North Carolina Infantry	May 12, 1864, Spotsylvania Court House, Virginia	Point Lookout, Maryland, transferred to Elmira Prison, NY, August 6, 1864	Oath of Allegiance May 29, 1865
Williams, Josephus M. Corporal	Unk	June 2, 1861, Centerville, Virginia	Co. C, 26th North Carolina Infantry	June 17, 1864, Near Petersburg, Virginia	Point Lookout, Maryland, transferred to Elmira Prison, NY, July 30, 1864	Exchanged March 14, 1865 at Boulware's Wharf on the James River, Virginia
Williams, Josiah B. Private	40	June 5, 1861, Memphis, Tennessee	Co. A, Jackson's 1st Regiment, Tennessee Heavy Artillery	August 23, 1864, Fort Morgan, Alabama	New Orleans, Louisiana transferred to Elmira Prison, NY, December 4, 1864.	Exchanged February 25, 1865 at Boulware's or Cox Wharf on the James River, Virginia
Williams, Junis Corporal	Unk	October 13, 1861, Mobile, Alabama	Co. A, 21st Alabama Infantry	August 23, 1864, Fort Morgan, Alabama	Steam Press No. 4, New Orleans, Louisiana transferred to Elmira Prison, NY, October 8, 1864.	Oath of Allegiance June 14, 1865
Williams, L. Private	Unk	Unknown	Co. A, 60th North Carolina Infantry	June 2, 1864, Near Talapatomoy Creek Cold Harbor, Virginia	Point Lookout, Maryland, transferred to Elmira Prison, NY, July 12, 1864	Exchanged March 14, 1865 at Boulware's Wharf on the James River, Virginia

Name & Rank	Age	Enlisted	Regiment and State	Where Captured	Prison	Remarks
Williams, Martain Blaney Corporal	18	August 30, 1861, Bug Hill, North Carolina	Co. C, 18th North Carolina Infantry	May 12, 1864, Spotsylvania Court House, Virginia	Point Lookout, Maryland, transferred to Elmira Prison, NY, August 6, 1864	Oath of Allegiance June 21, 1865
Williams, Nathan W. Private	22	October 5, 1862, Drury's Bluff, Virginia	Co. E, 45th North Carolina Infantry	May 10, 1864, Spotsylvania Court House, Virginia	Point Lookout, Maryland, transferred to Elmira Prison, NY, August 6, 1864	Oath of Allegiance June 12, 1865
Williams, Richard Private	36	February 9, 1863, Clinton, Sampson County, North Carolina	Co. C, 36th Regiment, 2nd North Carolina Artillery	January 15, 1865, Fort Fisher, North Carolina	February 1, 1865, Elmira Prison Camp, New York	Exchanged March 2, 1865 at Akins Landing on the James River, Virginia
Williams, Robert Sailor	Unk	Unknown	Confederate States Navy	January 15, 1865, Fort Fisher, North Carolina.	February 1, 1865, Elmira Prison Camp, New York	Oath of Allegiance May 29, 1865
Williams, Rufus Sergeant	Unk	July 3, 1861, Peterstown, Virginia	Co. D, 26th Battalion Virginia Infantry	June 3, 1864, Cold Harbor, Virginia	Point Lookout, Maryland, transferred to Elmira Prison, NY, July 12, 1864	Died October 19, 1864 of Chronic Diarrhea Grave No. 536
Williams, Sampson Private	Unk	December 29, 1861, Monticello, Florida	Co. A, 5th Florida Infantry	May 12, 1864, Spotsylvania Court House, Virginia	Point Lookout, Maryland, transferred to Elmira Prison, NY, August 12, 1864	Oath of Allegiance June 23, 1865
Williams, Samuel Private	24	November 7, 1862, Raleigh North Carolina	Co. B, 52nd North Carolina Infantry	May 25, 1864, Spotsylvania Court House, Virginia	Point Lookout, Maryland, transferred to Elmira Prison, NY, July 12, 1864	Died August 20, 1864, Chronic Diarrhea, Grave No. 113
Williams, Samuel Private	Unk	Unknown	19th Battalion Virginia Heavy Artillery	August 1, 1864, Harper's Ferry, Virginia	Old Capital Prison, Washington D. C. Transferred to Elmira Prison, NY, July 12, 1864	Oath of Allegiance May 15, 1865

Name & Rank	Age	Enlisted	Regiment and State	Where Captured	Prison	Remarks
Williams, Stephen H. Private	Unk	Unknown	Co. E, 50th Virginia Infantry	May 12, 1864, Spotsylvania Court House, Virginia	Point Lookout, Maryland, transferred to Elmira Prison, NY, August 2, 1864	Transferred for Exchange 10/11/1864. Exchanged at Venus Point, Savannah River, GA, 11/15/1864
Williams, Thomas H. Sergeant	Unk	May 10, 1862, Meriwether County, Georgia	Co. A, 60th Georgia Infantry	May 20, 1864, Spotsylvania Court House, Virginia	Point Lookout, Maryland, transferred to Elmira Prison, NY, July 3, 1864	Died September 26, 1864 of Remittent Fever, Grave No. 451
Williams, W. W. Private	Unk	October 4, 1861, Randolph, Alabama	Co. E, 1st Battalion Alabama Artillery	August 23, 1864, Fort Morgan, Alabama	Steam Press No. 4 New Orleans, Louisiana transferred to Elmira Prison, NY, October 8, 1864.	Died October 24, 1864 of Chronic Diarrhea, Grave No. 709
Williams, W. W. Sergeant	Unk	August 22, 1861, Milliston, Barnwell District, South Carolina	Co. A, 1st South Carolina Infantry	May 23, 1864, North Anna, Virginia	Point Lookout, Maryland, transferred to Elmira Prison, NY, August 17, 1864	Exchanged March 2, 1865 at Akins Landing on the James River, Virginia
Williams, Weldon Private	50	June 4, 1861, Camp Moore, Louisiana	Co. D, 6th Louisiana Infantry	May 5, 1864, Mine Run, Wilderness, Virginia	Point Lookout Prison Camp, Maryland. Transferred to Elmira Prison, NY, August 17, 1864	Died February 4, 1865 of Pneumonia, Grave No. 1886
Williams, William Corporal	Unk	March 8, 1862, Columbia County, Arkansas	Co. K, 19th Arkansas Infantry	May 17, 1863, Big Black River, Mississippi	Point Lookout, Maryland, transferred to Elmira Prison, NY, August 18, 1864	Exchanged February 13, 1865 at Boulware's Wharf on the James River, Virginia
Williams, William Private	Unk	October 2, 1863, Mocksville, North Carolina	Co. M, 7th Confederate Cavalry	May 7, 1864, Littleton, Virginia	Point Lookout, Maryland, transferred to Elmira Prison, NY, July 25, 1864	Died October 1, 1864 of Chronic Diarrhea. Grave No. 409

Name & Rank	Age	Enlisted	Regiment and State	Where Captured	Prison	Remarks
Williams, William Private	Unk	Unknown	Co. E, 20th Georgia Infantry	July 4, 1864, Petersburg, Virginia	Old Capital Prison, Washington, DC, transferred to Elmira Prison, NY, July 23, 1864	Oath of Allegiance April 21, 1865
Williams, William B. Sergeant	Unk	June 25, 1861, Wytheville, Virginia	Co. I, 50th Virginia Infantry	May 12, 1864 Spotsylvania Court House, Virginia	Point Lookout, Maryland, transferred to Elmira Prison, NY, August 2, 1864	Died May 10, 1865 of Variola (Smallpox), Grave No. 2787
Williams, William D. Private	18	June 10, 1862, Robeson County, North Carolina	Co. E, 40th Regiment, 3rd North Carolina Artillery	January 15, 1865, Fort Fisher, North Carolina	February 1, 1865, Elmira Prison Camp, New York	Oath of Allegiance July 11, 1865
Williams, William J. Private	22	August 16, 1861, Luka, Mississippi	Co. G, 26th Mississippi Infantry	May 8, 1864, Wilderness, Virginia	Point Lookout, Maryland, transferred to Elmira Prison, NY, August 14, 1864	Oath of Allegiance June 14, 1865
Williams, William W. Private	Unk	October 4, 1861, Randolph, Alabama	Co. C, 1st Battalion Alabama Artillery	August 23, 1864, Fort Morgan, Alabama	Steam Press No. 4 New Orleans, Louisiana transferred to Elmira Prison, NY, October 8, 1864.	Died October 24, 1864 of Chronic Diarrhea, Grave No. 709
Williams, William W. Sergeant	Unk	August 22, 1861, Barnwell District, South Carolina	Co. A, 1st South Carolina Infantry	May 23, 1864, North Anna, Virginia	Point Lookout, Maryland, transferred to Elmira Prison, NY, August 17, 1864	Exchanged March 2, 1865 at Akins Landing on the James River, Virginia
Williams, Wilson Private	40	July 24, 1861, Newland, North Carolina	Co. A, 8th North Carolina Infantry	June 1, 1864, Cold Harbor, Virginia	Point Lookout, Maryland, transferred to Elmira Prison, NY, July 12, 1864	Exchanged 2/20/65. Died 3/8/65 of Typhoid Fever at Jackson Hospital, Richmond, VA.
Williamson, Abraham Sergeant	29	May 31, 1861, Middle Sound, North Carolina	Co. E, 1st North Carolina Infantry	May 12, 1864, Spotsylvania Court House, Virginia	Point Lookout, Maryland, transferred to Elmira Prison, NY, August 6, 1864	Oath of Allegiance June 19, 1865

Name & Rank	Age	Enlisted	Regiment and State	Where Captured	Prison	Remarks
Williamson, Dallas M. Private	18	March 7, 1862, Wilmington, New Hanover County, North Carolina	Co. E, 36th Regiment, 2nd North Carolina Artillery	January 15, 1865, Fort Fisher, North Carolina	February 1, 1865, Elmira Prison Camp, New York	Oath of Allegiance July 11, 1865
Williamson, Daniel S. Private	30	May 8, 1862, Fort Caswell, Brunswick County, North Carolina	Co. E, 36th Regiment, 2nd North Carolina Artillery	January 15, 1865, Fort Fisher, North Carolina	February 1, 1865, Elmira Prison Camp, New York	Died March 14, 1865 of Chronic Diarrhea, Grave No. 1674
Williamson, Eli Private	18	February 14, 1863, Wilson County, North Carolina	Co. A, 55th North Carolina Infantry	May 9, 1864, Near Spotsylvania County Court House, Virginia	Point Lookout, Maryland, transferred to Elmira Prison, NY, August 14, 1864	Exchanged March 2, 1865 at Boulware's Wharf on the James River, Virginia
Williamson, Elton Private	29	February 25, 1862, Washington Point, Virginia	Co. E, 61st Virginia Infantry	August 18, 1864, Weldon Railroad, Virginia. Gunshot Wound Both Thighs.	Old Capital Prison, Washington, DC, transferred to Elmira Prison, NY, December 17, 1864	Exchanged March 2, 1865 at Boulware's Wharf on the James River, Virginia
Williamson, Hosea W. Private	20	March 1, 1862, Wilmington, North Carolina	Co. E, 36th Regiment, 2nd North Carolina Artillery	January 15, 1865, Fort Fisher, North Carolina	February 1, 1865, Elmira Prison Camp, New York	Oath of Allegiance July 11, 1865
Williamson, James Private	23	September 1, 1861, Sampson County, North Carolina	Co. A, 30th North Carolina Infantry	May 12, 1864, Near Spotsylvania Court House, Virginia	Point Lookout, Maryland, transferred to Elmira Prison, NY, August 14, 1864	Oath of Allegiance June 23, 1865
Williamson, James Private	42	August 20, 1863, Whiteville, Columbus County, North Carolina	Co. E, 36th Regiment, 2nd North Carolina Artillery	January 15, 1865, Fort Fisher, North Carolina	February 1, 1865, Elmira Prison Camp, New York	Died April 11, 1865 of Pneumonia, Grave No. 2692
Williamson, James Wilde Sergeant	27	March 18, 1862, Darlington, South Carolina	Co. B, 21st South Carolina Infantry	January 15, 1865, Fort Fisher, North Carolina	February 1, 1865, Elmira Prison Camp, New York	Died March 16, 1865 of Pneumonia, Grave No. 1690
Williamson, John Private	Unk	Unknown	Co. E, 20th Georgia Infantry	July 4, 1864, Petersburg, Virginia	Old Capital Prison, Washington, DC, transferred to Elmira Prison, NY, July 23, 1864	Oath of Allegiance May 19, 1865

Name & Rank	Age	Enlisted	Regiment and State	Where Captured	Prison	Remarks
Williamson, Joseph J. M. V. B. Private	22	April 24, 1861, Big Hill, Columbus County, North Carolina	Co. C, 18th North Carolina Infantry	May 12, 1864, Spotsylvania Court House, Virginia	Point Lookout, Maryland, transferred to Elmira Prison, NY, August 6, 1864	Oath of Allegiance June 30, 1865
Williamson, Joseph W. Private	34	July 16, 1862, Fort Caswell, Brunswick County, North Carolina	Co. E, 36th Regiment, 2nd North Carolina Artillery	January 15, 1865, Fort Fisher, North Carolina	February 1, 1865, Elmira Prison Camp, New York	Died June 21, 1865 of Chronic Diarrhea, Grave No. 2813. Headstone has Joshua.
Williamson, Joshua Robert Private	17	March 1, 1862, Cerro Gordo, Columbus County, North Carolina	Co. E, 36th Regiment, 2nd North Carolina Artillery	January 15, 1865, Fort Fisher, North Carolina	February 1, 1865, Elmira Prison Camp, New York	Died February 15, 1865 of Congestion of Lungs, Grave No. 2183
Williamson, R. M. Private	Unk	July 2, 1862, Savannah, Georgia	Co. B, 7th Georgia Cavalry	June 11, 1864, Trevilian Station, Louisa Court House, Virginia	Point Lookout, Maryland, transferred to Elmira Prison, NY, July 25, 1864	Died December 31, 1864 of Pneumonia, Grave No. 1326
Williamson, Thomas F. Private	19	April 24, 1861, Philadelphia, Mississippi	Co. D, 11th Mississippi Infantry	May 30, 1864, Cold Harbor, Virginia	Point Lookout, Maryland, transferred to Elmira Prison, NY, July 11, 1864	Exchanged February 20, 1865 at Boulware's or Cox Wharf on the James River, Virginia
Williamson, W. S. Private	Unk	March 22, 1861, Selma, Alabama	Co. C, 1st Battalion Alabama Artillery	August 23, 1864, Fort Morgan, Alabama	New Orleans, Louisiana transferred to Elmira Prison, NY, December 4, 1864.	Oath of Allegiance July 7, 1865
Williamson, Walker Private	Unk	November 4, 1862, Christiansburg, Virginia	Co. G, 4th Virginia Infantry	May 12, 1864, Spotsylvania Court House, Virginia	Point Lookout, Maryland, transferred to Elmira Prison, NY, August 2, 1864	Died October 10, 1864 of Chronic Diarrhea, Grave No. 670
Williford, Henry J. Private	Unk	July 18, 1862, Cumberland County, North Carolina	Co. C, 3rd North Carolina Infantry	May 12, 1864, Near Spotsylvania County Court House, Virginia	Point Lookout, Maryland, transferred to Elmira Prison, NY, August 14, 1864	Exchanged March 2, 1865 at Akins Landing on the James River, Virginia

Name & Rank	Age	Enlisted	Regiment and State	Where Captured	Prison	Remarks
Williford, Richard Private	37	April 4, 1862, Mingo, North Carolina	Co. K, 51st North Carolina Infantry	June 1, 1864, Cold Harbor, Virginia	Point Lookout, Maryland, transferred to Elmira Prison, NY, July 17,1864	Exchanged February 20, 1865 at Boulware's or Cox Wharf on the James River, Virginia
Williford, Sion Private	21	February 25, 1862, Fayetteville, North Carolina	Co. C, 3rd North Carolina Infantry	May 12, 1864, Near Spotsylvania County Court House, Virginia	Point Lookout, Maryland, transferred to Elmira Prison, NY, August 14, 1864	Oath of Allegiance June 19, 1865
Willis, Amell Private	Unk	March 14, 1862, Newbern, Virginia	Co. C, 4th Virginia Infantry	May 5, 1864, Wilderness, Virginia	Point Lookout, Maryland, transferred to Elmira Prison, NY, August 2, 1864	Transferred for Exchange 10/11/64. Died 11/6/64 at Fort Monroe, VA.
Willis, Cass Private	16	April 24, 1863, Fort Fisher, New Hanover County, North Carolina	Co. H, 36th Regiment, 2nd North Carolina Artillery	January 15, 1865, Fort Fisher, North Carolina	February 1, 1865, Elmira Prison Camp, New York	Oath of Allegiance June 12, 1865
Willis, Charles T. Private	Unk	July 1, 1862, Wilmington, North Carolina	Co. K, 10th Regiment, 1st North Carolina Artillery	January 15, 1865, Fort Fisher, North Carolina	February 1, 1865, Elmira Prison Camp, New York	Oath of Allegiance June 16, 1865
Willis, Henry D. Private	Unk	July 25, 1862, Washington County, Virginia	Co. F, 30th Battalion Virginia Sharpshooters	July 12, 1864, Frederick, Maryland	Old Capital Prison, Washington DC. Transferred to Elmira Prison Camp, NY July 25, 1864.	Died August 20, 1864 of Rubeola (Measles), Grave No. 112
Willis, J. V. Private	32	April 6, 1862, Bartow County, Georgia	Co. K, 18th Georgia Infantry	June 1, 1864, Cold Harbor, Virginia	Point Lookout, Maryland, transferred to Elmira Prison, NY, July 17,1864	Oath of Allegiance June 16, 1865
Willis, James L. Corporal	22	July 3, 1861, Atlanta, Georgia	Co. B, 11th Georgia Infantry	May 6, 1864, Mine Run, Wilderness, Virginia	Point Lookout, Maryland, transferred to Elmira Prison, NY, August 14, 1864	Oath of Allegiance June 14, 1865
Willis, John S. Sergeant	38	January 6, 1862, Elizabethtown, Bladen County, North Carolina	Co. J, 36th Regiment, 2nd North Carolina Artillery	January 15, 1865, Fort Fisher, North Carolina	February 1, 1865, Elmira Prison Camp, New York	Oath of Allegiance June 12, 1865

Name & Rank	Age	Enlisted	Regiment and State	Where Captured	Prison	Remarks
Willis, William N. Private	18	August 19, 1861, Fort Fisher, New Hanover County, North Carolina	Co. H, 36th Regiment, 2nd North Carolina Artillery	January 15, 1865, Fort Fisher, North Carolina. Wounded	February 1, 1865, Elmira Prison Camp, New York	Oath of Allegiance June 12, 1865
Willis, William S. Private	Unk	July 25, 1862, Washington County, Virginia	Co. F, 30th Virginia Sharp Shooters	July 12, 1864, Frederick, Maryland	Old Capital Prison, Washington, DC, transferred to Elmira Prison, NY, July 23, 1864	Died August 20, 1864 of Rubeola (Measles), Grave No. 112
Willoughby, Ruel Private	22	September 16, 1861, Pitt County, North Carolina	Co. G, 8th North Carolina Infantry	May 31, 1864, Cold Harbor, Virginia	Point Lookout, Maryland, transferred to Elmira Prison, NY, July 12, 1864	Exchanged March 2, 1865 at Akins Landing on the James River, Virginia
Willowghby, Michael A. Private	Unk	July 26, 1861, Brockville, Randolph County, Alabama	Co. K, 13th Alabama Infantry	May 12, 1864, Spotsylvania Court House, Virginia	Point Lookout, Maryland, transferred to Elmira Prison, NY, July 30, 1864	Exchanged February 20, 1865 at Boulware's or Cox Wharf on the James River, Virginia
Wills, Armstead E. Private	Unk	January 13, 1863, Crab Bottom, Virginia	Co. H, 44th Virginia Infantry	May 12, 1864, Spotsylvania Court House, Virginia	Point Lookout, Maryland, transferred to Elmira Prison, NY, August 2, 1864	Exchanged October 29, 1864, at Venus Point, Savannah River, GA.
Wills, Thomas B. Private	Unk	April 29, 1861, Suffolk, Virginia	Co. A, 19th Battalion Virginia Infantry	May 6, 1864, Fearnsville, Wilderness, Virginia	Point Lookout, Maryland, transferred to Elmira Prison, NY, August 17, 1864	Exchanged March 2, 1865 at Akins Landing on the James River, Virginia
Wilman, John Private	Unk	October 15, 1861, Fort Henry, Tennessee	Co. B, 1st Jackson's Tennessee Heavy Artillery	August 23, 1864, Fort Morgan, Alabama.	New Orleans, Louisiana transferred to Elmira Prison, NY, December 4, 1864.	Exchanged February 25, 1865 at Boulware's or Cox Wharf on the James River, Virginia
Wilmoth, W. R. Private	Unk	October 1, 1863, Dobson, Virginia	Co. C, 21st North Carolina Infantry	August 22, 1864, Charlestown, Virginia	Old Capital Prison, Washington, DC transferred to Elmira Prison, NY, August 29, 1864	Oath of Allegiance June 21, 1865

Name & Rank	Age	Enlisted	Regiment and State	Where Captured	Prison	Remarks
Wilson, A. J. Private	21	Unknown	Co. J, 48th North Carolina Infantry	May 24, 1864 Mechanics-ville, Virginia	Point Lookout, Maryland, transferred to Elmira Prison, NY, July 9, 1864	Oath of Allegiance June 16, 1865
Wilson, Alex M. Private	Unk	Unknown	Co. A, 37th Virginia Infantry	July 12, 1864, Near Washington, DC,	Point Lookout, Maryland, transferred to Elmira Prison, NY, July 23, 1864	Oath of Allegiance July 3, 1865
Wilson, Alexander Private	34	January 28, 1864, Camp Lee, Virginia	Co. A, 9th Virginia Infantry	May 23, 1864, Chesterfield Station, Virginia	Point Lookout, Maryland, transferred to Elmira Prison, NY, July 23, 1864	Oath of Allegiance November 22, 1864. Early Release per Lincoln's Proclamation, 12/8/1863.
Wilson, Andrew J. Sergeant	Unk	May 14, 1861, Franklin, Virginia	Co. E, 25th Virginia Infantry	May 12, 1864, Spotsylvania Court House, Virginia	Point Lookout, Maryland, transferred to Elmira Prison, NY, August 12, 1864	Oath of Allegiance July 11, 1865
Wilson, Burrell Private	16	Unknown	Co. E, 36th Regiment, 2nd North Carolina Artillery	January 15, 1865, Fort Fisher, North Carolina. Wounded	February 1, 1865, Elmira Prison Camp, New York	Exchanged March 2, 1865 at Akins Landing on the James River, Virginia
Wilson, Cary D. Private	Unk	May 25, 1862, Floyd Court House, Virginia	Co. B, 42nd Virginia Infantry	May 12, 1864, Spotsylvania Court House, Virginia	Point Lookout, Maryland, transferred to Elmira Prison, NY, August 2, 1864	Died September 23, 1864 of Pneumonia, Grave No. 476. Headstone has First Name Gray.
Wilson, Charles W. Private	Unk	March 30, 1862, Camp Allegheny, Virginia	Co. F, 25th Virginia Infantry	May 5, 1864, Wilderness, Virginia	Point Lookout, Maryland, transferred to Elmira Prison, NY, August 17, 1864	Exchanged February 13, 1865 at Boulware's wharf on the James River, Virginia
Wilson, D. Private	16	Unknown	Co. D, 13th Battalion North Carolina Light Artillery	January 15, 1865, Fort Fisher, North Carolina	February 1, 1865, Elmira Prison Camp, New York	Oath of Allegiance June 23, 1865

Name & Rank	Age	Enlisted	Regiment and State	Where Captured	Prison	Remarks
Wilson, D. C. Private	Unk	Unknown	Co. F, 3rd Louisiana Cavalry	August 25, 1864, Near Clinton, Louisiana	New Orleans, Louisiana transferred to Elmira November 19, 1864.	Exchanged February 13, 1865 at Boulware's wharf on the James River, Virginia
Wilson, Daniel C. Private	Unk	March 10, 1862, Chatham County, North Carolina	Co. E, 3rd North Carolina Cavalry	May 27, 1864, Hanover, Virginia	Point Lookout, Maryland, transferred to Elmira Prison, NY, July 12, 1864	Died March 22, 1965 of Pneumonia, Grave No. 2440
Wilson, David B. Private	21	May 27, 1861, Staunton, Virginia	Co. D, 25th Virginia Infantry	May 12, 1864, Near Spotsylvania Court House, Virginia	Point Lookout, Maryland, transferred to Elmira Prison, NY, August 2, 1864	Exchanged February 20, 1865 at Boulware's or Cox Wharf on the James River, Virginia
Wilson, Enoch C. Private	Unk	July 24, 1861, Union, Virginia	Co. A, 6th Virginia Cavalry	December 9, 1863, Loudoun County, Virginia	Point Lookout, Maryland, transferred to Elmira Prison, NY, August 17, 1864	Oath of Allegiance June 21, 1865
Wilson, Frank Private	Unk	February 24, 1862, Jacksonville, Alabama	Co. G, 10th Alabama Infantry	May 6, 1864, Wilderness, Virginia	Point Lookout, Maryland, transferred to Elmira Prison, NY, August 17, 1864	Died February 25, 1865 of Chronic Diarrhea, Grave No. 2278
Wilson, G. T. Private	Unk	August 1, 1861, Louina, Alabama	Co. K, 14th Alabama Infantry	July 29, 1864, Petersburg, Virginia	Point Lookout, Maryland, transferred to Elmira Prison, NY, August 12, 1864	Oath of Allegiance May 15, 1865
Wilson, George Private	Unk	March 10, 1862, Winchester, Virginia	Co. B, 11th Virginia Cavalry	September 13, 1863, Near Culpepper, Virginia	Point Lookout, Maryland, transferred to Elmira Prison, NY, August 18, 1864	Died April 7, 1865 of Variola (Smallpox), Grave No. 2650
Wilson, Harvey J. Private	Unk	July 16, 1861, Christiansburg, Virginia	Co. G, 4th Virginia Infantry	May 12, 1864, Spotsylvania Court House, Virginia	Point Lookout, Maryland, transferred to Elmira Prison, NY, August 2, 1864	Oath of Allegiance June 27, 1865

Name & Rank	Age	Enlisted	Regiment and State	Where Captured	Prison	Remarks
Wilson, Henry N. Private	25	August 14, 1861, Newton, North Carolina	Co. B, 32nd North Carolina Infantry	May 10, 1864, Wilderness, Virginia	Point Lookout, Maryland, transferred to Elmira Prison, NY, August 6, 1864	Oath of Allegiance June 30, 1865
Wilson, Isaac W. Private	Unk	May 15, 1862, Camp Harris, Tennessee	Co. C, 17th Tennessee Infantry	June 17, 1864, Petersburg, Virginia	Point Lookout, Maryland, transferred to Elmira Prison, NY, July 30, 1864	Exchanged February 13, 1865 at Boulware's wharf on the James River, Virginia
Wilson, James B. Sergeant	Unk	May 1, 1862, Adams Run, South Carolina	Co. K, Holcombe Legion, South Carolina Infantry	May 7, 1864, Stony Creek, Virginia	Point Lookout, Maryland, transferred to Elmira Prison, NY, August 17, 1864	Died January 23, 1865 of Chronic Diarrhea, Grave No. 1609
Wilson, James H. Private	Unk	July 24, 1861, J. Pasley's, Virginia	Co. E, 58th Virginia Infantry	May 20, 1864, Spotsylvania Court House, Virginia	Point Lookout, Maryland, transferred to Elmira Prison, NY, July 3, 1864	Oath of Allegiance June 19, 1865
Wilson, John Private	26	May 7, 1861, New Orleans, Louisiana	Co. K, 5th Louisiana Infantry	May 5, 1864, Wilderness, Virginia	Point Lookout, Maryland, transferred to Elmira Prison, NY, August 17, 1864	Exchanged February 13, 1865 at Boulware's wharf on the James River, Virginia
Wilson, John Private	35	Unknown	Co. G, 1st South Carolina Infantry	August 21, 1864, Weldon Railroad, Virginia	Old Capital Prison, Washington D. C. Transferred to Elmira Prison, NY, May 12, 1865.	Oath of Allegiance July 11, 1865
Wilson, John Berry Private	29	April 20, 1861, Lexington, Virginia	Co. H, 4th Virginia Infantry	May 12, 1864, Spotsylvania Court House, Virginia	Point Lookout, Maryland, transferred to Elmira Prison, NY, August 2, 1864	Exchanged February 20, 1865 at Boulware's or Cox Wharf on the James River, Virginia
Wilson, John G. Corporal	Unk	March 4, 1862, Suffolk, Virginia	Co. E, 3rd Battalion Georgia Sharp Shooters	August 16, 1864, Front Royal, Virginia	Old Capital Prison, Washington, DC transferred to Elmira Prison, NY, August 29, 1864	Oath of Allegiance May 29, 1865

Name & Rank	Age	Enlisted	Regiment and State	Where Captured	Prison	Remarks
Wilson, John H. Private	20	February 18, 1863, Sampson County, North Carolina	Co. E, 36th Regiment, 2nd North Carolina Artillery	January 15, 1865, Fort Fisher, North Carolina	February 1, 1865, Elmira Prison Camp, New York	Exchanged March 2, 1865 at Akins Landing on the James River, Virginia
Wilson, John H. Private	18	April 18, 1861, Blacksburg, Virginia	Co. E, 4th Virginia Infantry	May 12, 1864, Near Spotsylvania Court House, Virginia	Point Lookout, Maryland, transferred to Elmira Prison, NY, August 2, 1864	Exchanged October 29, 1864, at Venus Point, Savannah River, GA.
Wilson, John W. Private	Unk	Unknown	Co. C, 6th Virginia Cavalry	July 20, 1864, Fauquier County, Virginia	Old Capital Prison, Washington D. C. Transferred to Elmira Prison, NY, July 12, 1864	Exchanged March 10, 1865 at Boulware's Wharf on the James River, Virginia
Wilson, Joseph L. Private	21	May 29, 1861, Charlotte, North Carolina	Co. G, 6th North Carolina Infantry	July 17, 1864, Frederick, Maryland	Old Capital Prison, Washington D. C. Transferred to Elmira Prison, NY, July 12, 1864	Oath of Allegiance May 13, 1865
Wilson, Joseph S. Private	27	December 5, 1862, Drury's Bluff, Virginia	Co. H, 45th North Carolina Infantry	May 20, 1864, Spotsylvania Court House, Virginia	Point Lookout, Maryland, transferred to Elmira Prison, NY, July 3, 1864	Exchanged March 14, 1865 at Boulware's Wharf on the James River, Virginia
Wilson, Lucian W. Private	18	January 6, 1864, Fort Caswell, Brunswick County, North Carolina	Co. D, 36th Regiment, 2nd North Carolina Artillery	January 15, 1865, Fort Fisher, North Carolina	February 1, 1865, Elmira Prison Camp, New York	Died April 3, 1865 of Chronic Diarrhea, Grave No. 2565
Wilson, M. J. Corporal	Unk	March 30, 1862, York County, Virginia	Co. G, 3rd Virginia Cavalry	May 9, 1864, Spotsylvania Court House, Virginia	Point Lookout, Maryland, transferred to Elmira Prison, NY, August 17, 1864	Exchanged March 2, 1865 at Akins Landing on the James River, Virginia
Wilson, Obadiah Corporal	Unk	July 15, 1863, Gilmer County, Virginia	Co. E, 19th Virginia Cavalry	July 15, 1864, Loudoun County, Virginia	Point Lookout, Maryland, transferred to Elmira Prison, NY, July 23, 1864	Died March 23, 1865 of Variola (Smallpox), Grave No. 2447

Name & Rank	Age	Enlisted	Regiment and State	Where Captured	Prison	Remarks
Wilson, R. A. Private	Unk	Unknown	Co. E, 22nd North Carolina Infantry	June 11, 1864, Turkey Hill, Cold Harbor, Virginia	Point Lookout, Maryland, transferred to Elmira Prison, NY, July 25, 1864	Oath of Allegiance May 21, 1865
Wilson, Richard Private	Unk	July 27, 1861, Wytheville, Virginia	Co. A, 50th Virginia Infantry	May 12, 1864, Spotsylvania Court House, Virginia	Point Lookout, Maryland, transferred to Elmira Prison, NY, August 2, 1864	Exchanged October 29, 1864, at Venus Point, Savannah River, GA.
Wilson, Richard R. Private	Unk	Unknown	Co. A, 1st Maryland Cavalry	July 10, 1864, Frederick, Maryland	Point Lookout, Maryland, transferred to Elmira Prison, NY, July 23, 1864	Died February 11, 1865 of Variola (Smallpox), Grave No. 2082
Wilson, Robert H. Private	Unk	May 22, 1861, Warsaw, Virginia	Co. B, 40th Virginia Infantry	July 14, 1863, Falling Waters, Maryland	Point Lookout, Maryland, transferred to Elmira Prison, NY, August 18, 1864	Exchanged February 25, 1865 at Boulware's or Cox Wharf on the James River, Virginia
Wilson, Robert Lee Private	18	March 30, 1863, Mecklenburg County, North Carolina	Co. H, 35th North Carolina Infantry	June 17, 1864, Petersburg, Virginia	Point Lookout, Maryland, transferred to Elmira Prison, NY, July 30, 1864	Died February 4, 1865 of Chronic Diarrhea, Grave No. 1891
Wilson, Samuel W. Private	19	May 15, 1862, Charlotte, North Carolina	Co. B, 53rd North Carolina Infantry	July 12, 1864, Near Washington, DC. Gunshot Wound Left Thigh.	Old Capital Prison, Washington, DC transferred to Elmira Prison, NY, August 27, 1864	Exchanged March 14, 1865 at Boulware's Wharf on the James River, Virginia
Wilson, Thomas A. Private	24	July 7, 1861, Camp Moore, Louisiana	Co. D, 9th Louisiana Infantry	July 18, 1864, Shenandoah River, Virginia	Old Capital Prison, Washington D. C. Transferred to Elmira Prison, NY, July 12, 1864	Exchanged March 10, 1865 at Boulware's Wharf on the James River, Virginia
Wilson, Thomas B. Corporal	Unk	May 18, 1861, Sutton, Virginia	Co. C, 25th Virginia Infantry	May 12, 1864, Near Spotsylvania Court House, Virginia	Point Lookout, Maryland, transferred to Elmira Prison, NY, August 2, 1864	Oath of Allegiance June 27, 1865

Name & Rank	Age	Enlisted	Regiment and State	Where Captured	Prison	Remarks
Wilson, W. C. Private	Unk	March 18, 1862, Pee Dee Bridge, South Carolina	Co. K, 21st South Carolina Infantry	May 16, 1864, Near Drury's Bluff, Virginia	Point Lookout, Maryland, transferred to Elmira Prison, NY, August 17, 1864	Died March 24, 1865 of Intermittent Fever, Grave No. 2450
Wilson, W. David Private	23	January 14, 1862, Columbia, South Carolina	Co. B, 7th Battalion South Carolina	August 21, 1864, Weldon Railroad, Near Petersburg, Virginia. Contusion Left Foot.	Old Capital Prison, Washington, DC transferred to Elmira Prison, NY, August 27, 1864	Died December 9, 1864 of Chronic Diarrhea, Grave No.1036. Headstone has Daniel Wilson.
Wilson, William A. Private	Unk	September 25, 1862, Kanawha, Virginia	Co. H, 22nd Virginia Infantry	June 3, 1864, Gaines Farm Cold Harbor, Virginia	Point Lookout, Maryland, transferred to Elmira Prison, NY, July 12, 1864	Oath of Allegiance June 16, 1865
Wilson, William E. Private	Unk	January 10, 1862, Columbia, South Carolina	Co. C, 22nd South Carolina Infantry	July 30, 1864, Petersburg, Virginia	Point Lookout, Maryland, transferred to Elmira Prison, NY, August 12, 1864	Transferred for Exchange 10/11/64. Died 11/11/64 of Chronic Diarrhea at US Army Hospital Baltimore, MD
Wilson, William H. Corporal	Unk	June 11, 1861, Hevener's Store, Virginia	Co. F, 25th Virginia Infantry	May 5, 1864, Wilderness, Virginia	Point Lookout, Maryland, transferred to Elmira Prison, NY, August 14, 1864	Oath of Allegiance June 23, 1865
Wilson, William M. Private	25	April 22, 1861, Shelby, North Carolina	Co. E, 12th North Carolina Infantry	May 6, 1864, Wilderness, Virginia	Point Lookout, Maryland, transferred to Elmira Prison, NY, August 14, 1864	Oath of Allegiance June 21, 1865
Wilson, Willis Private	Unk	Unknown	Co. D, Richardson's Battalion Confederate Light Artillery	July 2, 1864, Near Richmond, James River, Virginia	Point Lookout, Maryland, transferred to Elmira Prison, NY, July 26,1864	Oath of Allegiance May 19, 1865
Wilson, Zorobable Private	22	June 4, 1861, St. Paul's, Floral, North Carolina	Co. G, 24th North Carolina Infantry	June 17, 1864, Near Petersburg, Virginia	Point Lookout, Maryland, transferred to Elmira Prison, NY, July 30, 1864	Died September 15, 1864 of Chronic Diarrhea, Grave No. 300

Name & Rank	Age	Enlisted	Regiment and State	Where Captured	Prison	Remarks
Wimer, Emanuel Private	Unk	May 18, 1861, Franklin, Virginia	Co. K, 25th Virginia Infantry	May 5, 1864, Mine Run, Wilderness, Virginia	Point Lookout, Maryland, transferred to Elmira Prison, NY, August 2, 1864	Oath of Allegiance June 14, 1865
Winchell, William H. Private	Unk	April 13, 1864, Tuskegee, Alabama	Co. H, 61st Alabama Infantry	August 12, 1864, Winchester, Virginia	Old Capital Prison, Washington, DC transferred to Elmira Prison, NY, August 29, 1864	Oath of Allegiance July 7, 1865
Wine, George P. Private	21	June 24, 1861, Beverly, Virginia	Co. G, 25th Virginia Infantry	May 5, 1864, Wilderness, Virginia	Point Lookout, Maryland, transferred to Elmira Prison, NY, August 17, 1864	Exchanged March 2, 1865 at Akins Landing on the James River, Virginia
Winecoff. John M. Private	28	June 26, 1863, Camp, North Carolina	Co. A, 52nd North Carolina Infantry	May 12, 1864, Spotsylvania Court House, Virginia	Point Lookout, Maryland, transferred to Elmira Prison, NY, July 30, 1864	Exchanged October 29, 1864, at Venus Point, Savannah River, GA.
Winders, William D. Private	23	May 10, 1862, Fort Johnson, North Carolina	Co. E, 20th North Carolina Infantry	May 20, 1864, Spotsylvania Court House, Virginia	Point Lookout, Maryland, transferred to Elmira Prison, NY, July 3, 1864	Exchanged October 29, 1864, at Venus Point, Savannah River, GA.
Windham, D. D. Private	28	July 16, 1862, Raleigh, North Carolina	Co. D, 5th North Carolina Infantry	May 12, 1864, Spotsylvania Court House, Virginia	Point Lookout, Maryland, transferred to Elmira Prison, NY, August 6, 1864	Oath of Allegiance June 30, 1865
Windham, John Private	18	April 20, 1862, Gourdin's Dept., South Carolina	Co. K, 25th South Carolina Volunteers	January 15, 1865, Fort Fisher, North Carolina	January 30, 1865, Elmira Prison Camp, New York	Exchanged February 20, 1865 at Boulware's or Cox Wharf on the James River, Virginia
Windon, James T. Sergeant	28	May 9, 1861, New Orleans, Louisiana	Co. F, 2nd Louisiana Infantry	May 12, 1864, Wilderness Spotsylvania, Virginia	Point Lookout, Maryland, transferred to Elmira Prison, NY, August 17, 1864	Exchanged February 25, 1865 at Boulware's or Cox Wharf on the James River, Virginia

Name & Rank	Age	Enlisted	Regiment and State	Where Captured	Prison	Remarks
Windsor, Luther E. Private	Unk	July 17, 1861, Davis House, Virginia	Co. A, 4th Virginia Cavalry	June 7, 1864, Prince William County, Virginia	Old Capital Prison, Washington, DC, transferred to Elmira Prison, NY, July 23, 1864	Oath of Allegiance June 5, 1865
Winfree, Adicus Private	Unk	June 18, 1861, Richmond, Virginia	Co. H, 44th Virginia Infantry	May 12, 1864, Spotsylvania Court House, Virginia	Point Lookout, Maryland, transferred to Elmira Prison, NY, August 2, 1864	Exchanged March 10, 1865 at Boulware's Wharf on the James River, Virginia
Wingard, Job F. Private	Unk	February 23, 1863, Pocotaligo, South Carolina	Co. F, 5th South Carolina Cavalry	June 11, 1864, Trevilian Station, Louisa Court House, Virginia	Point Lookout, Maryland, transferred to Elmira Prison, NY, July 25, 1864	Exchanged March 10, 1865 at Boulware's Wharf on the James River, Virginia
Wingate, T. J. Private	17	May 16, 1862, Callahan, Florida	Co. K, 2nd Florida Cavalry	September 12, 1863, Big Black, Mississippi	Point Lookout, Maryland, transferred to Elmira Prison, NY, August 18, 1864	Died September 26, 1864 of Pneumonia, Grave No. 379
Wingate, W. H. Private	Unk	September 22, 1862, Waynesville, Georgia	Co. G, 7th Georgia Cavalry	June 11, 1864, Trevilian Station, Louisa Court House, Virginia	Point Lookout, Maryland, transferred to Elmira Prison, NY, July 25, 1864	Transferred for Exchange 10/11/64. Died 10/21/64 of Chronic Diarrhea at Point Lookout, MD.
Wingfield, W. W. Sergeant	30	March 22, 1862, Porter's Precinct, Virginia	Co. B, 15th Virginia Cavalry	May 11, 1864, Near Ashland, Virginia	Point Lookout, Maryland, transferred to Elmira Prison, NY, August 17, 1864	Exchanged October 29, 1864, at Venus Point, Savannah River, GA.
Wingo, E. E. Private	Unk	May 1, 1864, Amelia County, Virginia	Co. G, 1st Virginia Cavalry	May 12, 1864, Spotsylvania Court House, Virginia	Point Lookout, Maryland, transferred to Elmira Prison, NY, August 12, 1864	Exchanged October 29, 1864, at Venus Point, Savannah River, GA.
Winhall, Hiram Private	25	April 19, 1861, Norfolk City, Virginia	Co. H, 6th Virginia Infantry	May 12, 1864, Near Spotsylvania Court House	Point Lookout, Maryland, transferred to Elmira Prison, NY, July 23, 1864	Oath of Allegiance May 13, 1865

Name & Rank	Age	Enlisted	Regiment and State	Where Captured	Prison	Remarks
Winkle, Jacob Private	33	July 19, 1862, Jonesboro, Tennessee	Co. K, 63rd Tennessee Infantry	June 17, 1864, Petersburg, Virginia	Point Lookout, Maryland, transferred to Elmira Prison, NY, July 30, 1864	Exchanged February 25, 1865 at Boulware's or Cox Wharf on the James River, Virginia
Winkler, Abraham Private	37	March 10, 1864, Hancock County, Tennessee	Co. D, 7th Tennessee Infantry	May 12, 1864, Spotsylvania Court House, Virginia	Point Lookout, Maryland, transferred to Elmira Prison, NY, July 23, 1864	Died March 5, 1865 of Diarrhea, Grave No. 2410
Winklet, Anthony W. Private	Unk	March 3, 1862, Saint Landry Parish, Louisiana	Co. C, 6th Louisiana Infantry	May 5, 1864, Wilderness, Virginia	Point Lookout, Maryland, transferred to Elmira Prison, NY, August 17, 1864	Died February 15, 1865 of Variola (Smallpox), Grave No. 2165. Name Winkler on Headstone.
Winn, Barney B. Private	18	June 24, 1862, Coosawhatchie, South Carolina	Co. E, 11th South Carolina Infantry	June 16, 1864, Petersburg, Virginia	Point Lookout, Maryland, transferred to Elmira Prison, NY, July 25, 1864	Oath of Allegiance May 29, 1865
Winn, H. Private	Unk	Unknown	Co. D, McCreary's 1st South Carolina Infantry	May 24, 1864, Newton, Virginia	Point Lookout, Maryland, transferred to Elmira Prison, NY, July 12, 1864	Died September 29, 1864 of Chronic Diarrhea, Grave No. 424
Winn, R. G. Corporal	Unk	February 28, 1862, Louisburg, North Carolina	Co. D, 8th North Carolina Infantry	May 31, 1864, Cold Harbor, Virginia	Point Lookout, Maryland, transferred to Elmira Prison, NY, July 12, 1864	Exchanged March 10, 1865 at Boulware's Wharf on the James River, Virginia
Winn, Richard C. Private	24	July 18, 1861, Bay Point, South Carolina	Co. E, 11th South Carolina Infantry	June 16, 1864, Petersburg, Virginia	Point Lookout, Maryland, transferred to Elmira Prison, NY, July 25, 1864	Exchanged March 2, 1865 at Akins Landing on the James River, Virginia
Winn, Thomas Sailor	Unk	Unknown	Confederate States Navy	January 15, 1865, Fort Fisher, North Carolina.	February 1, 1865, Elmira Prison Camp, New York	Oath of Allegiance May 29, 1865

Name & Rank	Age	Enlisted	Regiment and State	Where Captured	Prison	Remarks
Winn, William Private	Unk	Unknown	Co. A, Captain Norwood's Home Guard Florida	September 27, 1864, Marianna, Florida	New Orleans, Louisiana. Had Received Orders to Be Transferred to Elmira November 19, 1864.	Died December 21, 1864 of Chronic Diarrhea at Fort Columbus, New York Harbor.
Winner, Marks W. Private	Unk	May 17, 1861, New Orleans, Louisiana	Co. B, 3rd Louisiana Infantry	May 20, 1863, Synder's Bluff, Virginia	Point Lookout, Maryland, transferred to Elmira Prison, NY, August 18, 1864	Exchanged February 13, 1865 at Boulware's Wharf on the James River, Virginia
Winstead, Elijah Private	18	June 4, 1861, Wilson, North Carolina	Co. G, 5th North Carolina Infantry	May 12, 1864, Spotsylvania Court House, Virginia	Point Lookout, Maryland, transferred to Elmira Prison, NY, August 6, 1864	Oath of Allegiance June 27, 1865
Winstead, Ferrol F. Private	Unk	March 1, 1862, Heathsville, Virginia	Co. C, 40th Virginia Infantry	May 5, 1864, Wilderness, Virginia	Point Lookout, Maryland, transferred to Elmira Prison, NY, August 14, 1864	Oath of Allegiance June 27, 1865
Winstead, James F. Corporal	18	September 25, 1861, Camp Branch, Roxboro, North Carolina	Co. E, 35th North Carolina Infantry	June 17, 1864, Petersburg, Virginia	Point Lookout, Maryland, transferred to Elmira Prison, NY, July 30, 1864	Exchanged October 29, 1864, at Venus Point, Savannah River, GA.
Winstead, William T. Private	Unk	March 15, 1864, Nash County, North Carolina	Co. D, 47th North Carolina Infantry	May 24, 1864, Hanover Junction, Virginia	Point Lookout, Maryland, transferred to Elmira Prison, NY, July 11, 1864	Exchanged March 14, 1865 at Boulware's Wharf on the James River, Virginia
Winston, Andrew J. Sergeant	Unk	June 18, 1861, Richmond, Virginia	Co. G, 44th Virginia Infantry	May 12, 1864, Spotsylvania Court House, Virginia	Point Lookout, Maryland, transferred to Elmira Prison, NY, August 12, 1864	Oath of Allegiance June 16, 1865
Winston, James H. Private	Unk	Unknown	Co. B, 20th Alexander's Louisiana Infantry	September 2, 1864, Near Natchez, Mississippi	New Orleans, Louisiana transferred to Elmira November 19, 1864.	Died December 17, 1864 of Pneumonia and Chronic Diarrhea, Grave No. 1278

Name & Rank	Age	Enlisted	Regiment and State	Where Captured	Prison	Remarks
Wintermoyer, Thomas M. Private	27	April 23, 1861, Harper's Ferry, Virginia	Co. B, 2nd Virginia Infantry	May 12, 1864, Near Spotsylvania Court House, Virginia	Point Lookout, Maryland, transferred to Elmira Prison, NY, August 6, 1864	Exchanged October 29, 1864, at Venus Point, Savannah River, GA.
Winters, George Private	18	September 10, 1861, Nash County, North Carolina	Co. J, 30th North Carolina Infantry	May 18, 1864, Spotsylvania Court House, Virginia	Point Lookout, Maryland, transferred to Elmira Prison, NY, July 3, 1864	Oath of Allegiance June 30, 1865
Wirich, George W. Private	Unk	Unknown	Co. C, 51st Virginia Infantry	July 31, 1864, Sharpsburg, Virginia	Old Capital Prison, Washington, DC. Transferred to Elmira Prison Camp, NY, August 12, 1865	Died February 2, 1865 of Variola (Smallpox), Grave No. 1765. Name Myrick on Headstone.
Wise, Randolph Private	21	November 12, 1863, Randolph County, Virginia	Co. C, 20th Virginia Cavalry	July 11, 1864, Craigsville, Maryland	Old Capital Prison, Washington, DC, transferred to Elmira Prison, NY, July 23, 1864	Exchanged March 14, 1865 at Boulware's Wharf on the James River, Virginia
Wise, V. F. Private	Unk	November 5, 1863, James Island, South Carolina	Co. F, 25th South Carolina Infantry	January 15, 1865, Fort Fisher, North Carolina	February 1, 1865, Elmira Prison Camp, New York	Exchanged February 20, 1865 at Boulware's or Cox Wharf on the James River, Virginia
Wise, William Private	Unk	Unknown	Co. B, 14th Tennessee Infantry	Unknown	Unknown	Died November 4, 1864 of Unknown Disease, Grave No. 839
Wise, William F. Private	29	May 22, 1862, Lincolnton, Lincoln County, North Carolina	Co. D, 1st North Carolina Infantry	May 12, 1864, Spotsylvania Court House, Virginia	Point Lookout, Maryland, transferred to Elmira Prison, NY, August 6, 1864	Oath of Allegiance June 21, 1865
Wiseman, George Washington Private	Unk	August 1, 1861, Staunton, Virginia	Co. H, 25th Virginia Infantry	May 5, 1864, Wilderness, Virginia	Point Lookout, Maryland, transferred to Elmira Prison, NY, August 17, 1864	Transferred for Exchange February 20, 1865. Died on Boat, Date and Causes Unknown

Name & Rank	Age	Enlisted	Regiment and State	Where Captured	Prison	Remarks
Wiseman, H. H. Private	28	February 16, 1862, Covington, Tennessee	Co. C, 1st Jackson's Tennessee Heavy Artillery	August 23, 1864, Fort Morgan, Alabama.	New Orleans, Louisiana transferred to Elmira Prison, NY, December 4, 1864.	Exchanged February 13, 1865 at Boulware's wharf on the James River, Virginia
Wiseman, Jeremiah G. Private	29	September 26, 1863, Coffee County, Alabama	Co. H, 6th Alabama Infantry	July 12, 1864, Near Washington, DC. Gunshot Wound Fracture Left Leg.	Old Capital Prison, Washington, DC transferred to Elmira Prison, NY, August 27, 1864	Died June 23, 1865 of Pneumonia, Grave No. 2819
Wiseman, W. R. Private	Unk	May 16, 1861, Alisona, Tennessee	Co. A, 17th Tennessee Infantry	June 17, 1864, Petersburg, Virginia	Point Lookout, Maryland, transferred to Elmira Prison, NY, July 30, 1864	Exchanged February 13, 1865 at Boulware's wharf on the James River, Virginia
Wiseman, William F. Private	24	April 17, 1861, Augusta County, Virginia	Co. D, 5th Virginia Infantry	June 3, 1864, Gaines Farm Cold Harbor, Virginia	Point Lookout, Maryland, transferred to Elmira Prison, NY, July 12, 1864	Oath of Allegiance July 3, 1865
Wisenbaker, J. F. Private	Unk	May 18, 1862, Savannah, Georgia	Co. B, 7th Georgia Cavalry	June 11, 1864, Trevilian Station, Louisa Court House, Virginia	Point Lookout, Maryland, transferred to Elmira Prison, NY, July 25, 1864	Oath of Allegiance June 30, 1865
Wisher, Joseph A. Private	Unk	December 27, 1861, Yorkville, South Carolina	Co. C, 17th South Carolina Infantry	July 30, 1864, Petersburg, Virginia	Point Lookout, Maryland, transferred to Elmira Prison, NY, August 12, 1864	Died May 18, 1865 of Pneumonia, Grave No. 2948
Witherington, Benjamin R. Private	Unk	August 5, 1861, Pitt County, North Carolina	Co. G, 8th North Carolina Infantry	May 31, 1864, Cold Harbor, Virginia	Point Lookout, Maryland, transferred to Elmira Prison, NY, July 12, 1864	Oath of Allegiance June 30, 1865
Witherington, J. G. Private	Unk	January 28, 1862, Pitt County, North Carolina	Co. F, 66th North Carolina Infantry	June 3, 1864, Gaines Mill Cold Harbor, Virginia	Point Lookout, Maryland, transferred to Elmira Prison, NY, July 12, 1864	Oath of Allegiance July 3, 1865

Name & Rank	Age	Enlisted	Regiment and State	Where Captured	Prison	Remarks
Withers, H. J. Private	Unk	May 9, 1861, New Orleans, Louisiana	Co. D, 2nd Louisiana Infantry	May 12, 1864, Spotsylvania Court House, Virginia	Point Lookout, Maryland, transferred to Elmira Prison, NY, August 17, 1864	Supposed to be Exchanged February 13, 1865. Unable to travel. No Further Information
Withers, James D. Private	Unk	Unknown	Co. I, 1st North Carolina Infantry	May 12, 1864, Spotsylvania Court House, Virginia	Point Lookout, Maryland, transferred to Elmira Prison, NY, August 6, 1864	Died September 26, 1864 of Typhoid Fever, Grave No. 371
Witherspoon, Lucius L. Private	17	February 1, 1862, Newbern, North Carolina	Co. D, 1st North Carolina Infantry	May 12, 1864, Spotsylvania Court House, Virginia	Point Lookout, Maryland, transferred to Elmira Prison, NY, August 6, 1864	Oath of Allegiance July 3, 1865
Witherspoon, Sidney L. Private	29	April 1, 1862, Goldsboro, North Carolina	Co. D, 1st North Carolina Infantry	May 12, 1864, Spotsylvania Court House, Virginia	Point Lookout, Maryland, transferred to Elmira Prison, NY, August 6, 1864	Exchanged October 29, 1864, at Venus Point, Savannah River, GA.
Withrow, James W. Private	21	September 12, 1863, Orange County Court House, Virginia	Co. H, 25th Virginia Infantry	May 5, 1864, Wilderness, Virginia	Point Lookout, Maryland, transferred to Elmira Prison, NY, August 17, 1864	Died February 25, 1865 of Chronic Diarrhea, Grave No. 2274
Witt, John W. Private	Unk	March 1, 1863, Liberty, Virginia	Co. C, 42nd Virginia Infantry	May 12, 1864, Spotsylvania Court House, Virginia	Point Lookout, Maryland, transferred to Elmira Prison, NY, August 2,1864	Exchanged March 14, 1865 at Boulware's Wharf on the James River, Virginia
Witt, William A. Private	Unk	May 31, 1861, Yellow Branch, Virginia	Co. D, 42nd Virginia Infantry	May 12, 1864, Near Spotsylvania Court House, Virginia	Point Lookout, Maryland, transferred to Elmira Prison, NY, August 6, 1864	Oath of Allegiance July 3, 1865
Wofford, Thomas C. Private	30	August 27, 1861, Spartanburg, South Carolina	Co. F, 13th South Carolina Infantry	July 29, 1864, Petersburg, Virginia	Point Lookout, Maryland, transferred to Elmira Prison, NY, August 12, 1864	Died March 17, 1865 of Pneumonia, Grave No. 1712

Name & Rank	Age	Enlisted	Regiment and State	Where Captured	Prison	Remarks
Wolf, Charles B. Private	Unk	Unknown	Co. E, 50th Virginia Infantry	May 12, 1864, Spotsylvania Court House, Virginia	Point Lookout, Maryland, transferred to Elmira Prison, NY, August 2, 1864	Died September 11, 1864 of Chronic Diarrhea, Grave No. 256. Name Woolfe on Headstone.
Wolf, D. W. Private	Unk	Unknown	Co. G, 25th South Carolina Infantry	January 15, 1865, Fort Fisher, North Carolina	February 1, 1865, Elmira Prison Camp, New York	Died March 1, 1865 of Diarrhea, Grave No. 2100
Wolf, Hillard E. Private	Unk	April 29, 1862, Macon, Georgia	Co. J, 61st Georgia Infantry	July 12, 1864, Near Washington, DC,	Old Capital Prison, Washington, DC, transferred to Elmira Prison, NY, July 23, 1864	Oath of Allegiance May 17, 1865
Wolf, J. A. Corporal	Unk	April 24, 1864, Orangeburg, South Carolina	Co. H, 25th South Carolina Infantry	January 15, 1865, Fort Fisher, North Carolina	February 1, 1865, Elmira Prison Camp, New York	Oath of Allegiance July 7, 1865
Wolf, J. H. Sergeant	Unk	June 17, 1861, Conrad's Store, Virginia	Co. I, 10th Virginia Infantry	May 12, 1864, Spotsylvania Court House, Virginia	Point Lookout, Maryland, transferred to Elmira Prison, NY, August 2, 1864	Exchanged March 2, 1865 at Akins Landing on the James River, Virginia
Wolfe, Andrew J. Private	25	July 30, 1861, Marion, Virginia	Co. D, 4th Virginia Infantry	May 12, 1864, Spotsylvania, Virginia. Gunshot Wound Left Shoulder.	Old Capital Prison, Washington, DC, transferred to Elmira Prison, NY, July 23, 1864	Oath of Allegiance June 30, 1865
Wolfe, Charles J. Private	Unk	June 15, 1861, Columbus, Georgia	Co. E, 12th Georgia Infantry	May 10, 1864, Spotsylvania Court House, Virginia	Point Lookout, Maryland, transferred to Elmira Prison, NY, July 30, 1864	Exchanged October 29, 1864, at Venus Point, Savannah River, GA.
Wolfe, James S. Private	Unk	May 9, 1861, Camp Jackson, Virginia	Co. E, 50th Virginia Infantry	May 12, 1864, Spotsylvania Court House, Virginia	Point Lookout, Maryland, transferred to Elmira Prison, NY, August 2, 1864	Exchanged at Venus Point, Savannah River, GA, 11/15/1864
Wolfe, William M. Private	Unk	May 20, 1862, Estelleville, Virginia	Co. C, 37th Virginia Infantry	May 12, 1864, Spotsylvania Court House, Virginia	Point Lookout, Maryland, transferred to Elmira Prison, NY, August 2, 1864	Oath of Allegiance June 27, 1865

Name & Rank	Age	Enlisted	Regiment and State	Where Captured	Prison	Remarks
Wolfenberger, Robert Sergeant	29	March 17, 1862, Allegheny, Virginia	Co. G, 31st Virginia Infantry	March 25, 1865, Fort Stedman, VA. Gunshot Wound of Face.	Old Capital Prison, Washington D. C. Transferred to Elmira Prison, NY, May 12, 1865.	Oath of Allegiance July 7, 1865
Wolfrey, Benjamin George Private	Unk	March 10, 1862, Orange County, Virginia	Co. C, 7th Virginia Infantry	June 11, 1864, Spotsylvania Court House, Virginia	Point Lookout, Maryland, transferred to Elmira Prison, NY, July 25, 1864	Exchanged October 29, 1864, at Venus Point, Savannah River, GA.
Wolfrey, James H. Private	Unk	April 18, 1861, Harrisonburg, Virginia	Co. B, 10th Virginia Infantry	May 12, 1864, Spotsylvania Court House, Virginia	Point Lookout, Maryland, transferred to Elmira Prison, NY, August 2, 1864	Exchanged February 13, 1865 at Boulware's wharf on the James River, Virginia
Wolfrey, Jerry M. Private	Unk	March 10, 1862, Orange County, Virginia	Co. C, 7th Virginia Infantry	June 11, 1864, Spotsylvania Court House, Virginia	Point Lookout, Maryland, transferred to Elmira Prison, NY, July 25, 1864	Exchanged October 29, 1864, at Venus Point, Savannah River, GA.
Womack, J. Private	Unk	June 9, 1862, Charleston, South Carolina	Co. D, 5th South Carolina Cavalry	June 11, 1864, Trevilian Station, Louisa Court House, Virginia	Point Lookout, Maryland, transferred to Elmira Prison, NY, July 25, 1864	Escaped October 27, 1864 by Tunneling Under Fence.
Womble, Albert Private	Unk	February 11, 1863, Raleigh, North Carolina	Co. I, 3rd North Carolina Cavalry	May 27, 1864, Hanover Junction, Virginia	Point Lookout, Maryland, transferred to Elmira Prison, NY, July 11, 1864	Died March 15, 1865 of Pneumonia, Grave No. 1663. Name Wamble and 41st NC on Headstone.
Womble, Henry J. Private	Unk	Unknown	Co. J, 3rd North Carolina Cavalry	May 27, 1864, Pamunkey River, Virginia	Point Lookout, Maryland, transferred to Elmira Prison, NY, July 12, 1864	Exchanged February 13, 1865 at Boulware's wharf on the James River, Virginia
Womble, William Private	20	April 15, 1861, Pittsboro, North Carolina	Co. I, 32nd North Carolina Infantry	May 10, 1864, Wilderness, Virginia	Point Lookout, Maryland, transferred to Elmira Prison, NY, August 6, 1864	Oath of Allegiance June 14, 1865

Name & Rank	Age	Enlisted	Regiment and State	Where Captured	Prison	Remarks
Wood, A. F. Private	Unk	July 29, 1861, Lineville, Talladega County, Alabama	Co. J, 14th Alabama Infantry	May 24, 1864, Near Anderson's Station, Hanover Junction, Virginia	Point Lookout, Maryland, transferred to Elmira Prison, NY, July 11, 1864	Oath of Allegiance June 18, 1865
Wood, Andrew J. Private	Unk	August 24, 1861, Hiawassee, Georgia	Co. D, 24th Georgia Infantry	June 1, 1864, Cold Harbor, Virginia	Point Lookout, Maryland, transferred to Elmira Prison, NY, July 12, 1864	Oath of Allegiance July 7, 061865
Wood, Benjamin F. Private	Unk	August 16, 1861, Gadsden, Alabama	Co. B, 4th Alabama Cavalry	July 27, 1863, Shelbyville, Tennessee	Point Lookout, Maryland, transferred to Elmira Prison, NY, August 17, 1864	Oath of Allegiance June 19, 1865
Wood, Benjamin N. Corporal	Unk	June 2, 1861, Luray, Virginia	Co. K, 10th Virginia Infantry	May 12, 1864, Spotsylvania Court House, Virginia	Point Lookout, Maryland, transferred to Elmira Prison, NY, August 2, 1864	Oath of Allegiance June 27, 1865
Wood, Britton Private	23	July 15, 1862, Raleigh, North Carolina	Co. K, 1st North Carolina Infantry	May 18, 1864, Spotsylvania Court House, Virginia	Point Lookout, Maryland, transferred to Elmira Prison, NY, July 3, 1864	Exchanged March 14, 1865 at Boulware's Wharf on the James River, Virginia
Wood, Caleb Private	18	March 14, 1862, Lincoln County, North Carolina	Co. D, 1st North Carolina Infantry	May 12, 1864, Spotsylvania Court House, Virginia	Point Lookout, Maryland, transferred to Elmira Prison, NY, August 6, 1864	Oath of Allegiance June 30, 1865
Wood, Drury B. Private	Unk	March 17, 1862, Woodstock, Virginia	Co. G, 6th Virginia Cavalry	May 11, 1864, Yellow Tavern, Hanover County, Virginia	Point Lookout, Maryland, transferred to Elmira Prison, NY, August 17, 1864	Oath of Allegiance June 14, 1865
Wood, E. M. Private	Unk	September 5, 1862, Coffee County, Alabama	Co. F, 1st Battalion Alabama Artillery	August 23, 1864, Fort Morgan, Alabama	Steam Press No. 4 New Orleans, Louisiana transferred to Elmira Prison, NY, October 8, 1864.	Died January 26, 1865 of Variola (Smallpox), Grave No. 1641

Name & Rank	Age	Enlisted	Regiment and State	Where Captured	Prison	Remarks
Wood, Edmond B. Private	Unk	July 11, 1861, Lynchburg, Virginia	Co. I, 42nd Virginia Infantry	May 12, 1864, Spotsylvania Court House, Virginia	Point Lookout, Maryland, transferred to Elmira Prison, NY, August 12, 1864	Oath of Allegiance May 29, 1865
Wood, Furney Private	18	May 14, 1862, Fayetteville, North Carolina	Co. B, 56th North Carolina Infantry	June 18, 1864, Petersburg, Virginia	Point Lookout, Maryland, transferred to Elmira Prison, NY, July 30, 1864	Died November 4, 1864 of Typhoid-Pneumonia, Grave No. 840
Wood, George W. Private	Unk	March 17, 1862, Luray, Page County, Virginia	Co. K, 10th Virginia Infantry	May 20, 1864, Spotsylvania Court House, Virginia	Point Lookout, Maryland, transferred to Elmira Prison, NY, July 3, 1864	Oath of Allegiance June 30, 1865
Wood, J. Private	Unk	Unknown	Co. B, 45th Georgia Infantry	May 6, 1864, Wilderness, Virginia	Point Lookout, Maryland, transferred to Elmira Prison, NY, August 14, 1864	Oath of Allegiance June 14, 1865
Wood, J. R. Private	Unk	May 27, 1861, Fayetteville, Georgia	Co. J, 10th Georgia Infantry	July 27, 1864, Petersburg, Virginia	Point Lookout, Maryland, transferred to Elmira Prison, NY, August 12, 1864	Oath of Allegiance May 15, 1865
Wood, John Private	Unk	June 15, 1861, Washington County, Virginia	Co. F, 48th Virginia Infantry	July 12, 1864, Near Washington, DC,	Point Lookout, Maryland, transferred to Elmira Prison, NY, July 23, 1864	Oath of Allegiance May 17, 1865
Wood, John R. B. Private	Unk	March 15, 1864, Louisa County, Virginia	Capt. Carrington's Battery, Cutshaw's Battalion, Virginia Light Artillery	July 4, 1864, Major Allen's Farm, Virginia	Point Lookout, Maryland, transferred to Elmira Prison, NY, August 6, 1864	Oath of Allegiance July 3, 1865
Wood, Joseph P. Private	22	June 6, 1861, Person County, North Carolina	Co. H, 24th North Carolina Infantry	June 17, 1864, Petersburg, Virginia	Point Lookout, Maryland, transferred to Elmira Prison, NY, July 30, 1864	Oath of Allegiance May 29, 1865

Name & Rank	Age	Enlisted	Regiment and State	Where Captured	Prison	Remarks
Wood, L. A. Private	Unk	Unknown	Co. B, 2nd North Carolina Infantry	July 31, 1864, Near Washington, DC	Old Capital Prison, Washington, DC transferred to Elmira Prison, NY, August 29, 1864	Oath of Allegiance June 30, 1865
Wood, Manning A. Private	Unk	January 10, 1862, Columbia, South Carolina	Co. C, 22nd South Carolina Infantry	May 6, 1864, Newbern, North Carolina	Point Lookout, Maryland, transferred to Elmira Prison, NY, August 17, 1864	Died December 26, 1864 of Typhoid-Pneumonia, Grave No. 1289
Wood, Miles Private	Unk	August 19, 1862, Coffee County, Alabama	Co. E, 1st Battalion Alabama Artillery	August 23, 1864, Fort Morgan, Alabama	Steam Press No. 4 New Orleans, Louisiana transferred to Elmira Prison, NY, October 8, 1864.	Died February 21, 1865 of Diarrhea, Grave No. 2296
Wood, O. P. Sergeant	Unk	December 17, 1863, Columbia, South Carolina	Co. C, 22nd South Carolina Infantry	July 30, 1864, Petersburg, Virginia	Point Lookout, Maryland, transferred to Elmira Prison, NY, August 12, 1864	Exchanged March 14, 1865 at Boulware's Wharf on the James River, Virginia
Wood, R. M. Sergeant	Unk	April 28, 1862, Georgia	Co. F, 3rd Battalion Georgia Sharp Shooters	August 16, 1864, Front Royal, Virginia	Old Capital Prison, Washington, DC transferred to Elmira Prison, NY, August 29, 1864	Oath of Allegiance July 19, 1865
Wood, S. L. Private	41	August 5, 1862, Richmond, Virginia	Co. K, 24th Georgia Infantry	August 16, 1864, Front Royal, Virginia	Old Capital Prison, Washington, D. C., Transferred to Elmira August 29, 1864	Exchanged February 20, 1865 at Boulware's or Cox Wharf on the James River, Virginia
Wood, W. H. Private	38	March 22, 1862, Porter's Precinct, Virginia	Co. B, 15th Virginia Infantry	May 12, 1864, Near Mechanics-ville, Virginia	Point Lookout, Maryland, transferred to Elmira Prison, NY, August 17, 1864	Died May 23, 1865 of Variola (Smallpox), Grave No. 2927

Name & Rank	Age	Enlisted	Regiment and State	Where Captured	Prison	Remarks
Wood, William C. C. Private	Unk	June 2, 1862, Luray, Virginia	Co. K, 10th Virginia Infantry	May 12, 1864, Spotsylvania Court House, Virginia	Point Lookout, Maryland, transferred to Elmira Prison, NY, August 2, 1864	Oath of Allegiance May 29, 1865
Wood, William F. Private	Unk	September 5, 1862, Coffee County, Alabama	Co. F, 1st Battalion Alabama Artillery	August 23, 1864, Fort Morgan, Alabama	Steam Press No. 4 New Orleans, Louisiana transferred to Elmira Prison, NY, October 8, 1864.	Died October 24, 1864 of Typhoid Fever, Grave No. 712
Wood, William H. Private	Unk	July 1, 1861, Prince William County, Virginia	Co. B, 49th Virginia Infantry	May 30, 1864, Chickahominy, Cold Harbor, Virginia	Point Lookout, Maryland, transferred to Elmira Prison, NY, July 11, 1864	Exchanged March 14, 1865 at Boulware's Wharf on the James River, Virginia
Wood, William R. Sergeant	Unk	June 4, 1861, Camp Moore, Louisiana	Co. A, 6th Louisiana Infantry	May 4, 1864, Near Spotsylvania Wilderness, Virginia	Point Lookout, Maryland, transferred to Elmira Prison, NY, August 17, 1864	Exchanged February 25, 1865 at Boulware's or Cox Wharf on the James River, Virginia
Wood, William T. Private	17	March 14, 1862, Wilmington, North Carolina	Co. A, 51st North Carolina Infantry	June 1, 1864, Gaines Mill Cold Harbor, Virginia	Point Lookout, Maryland, transferred to Elmira Prison, NY, July 12, 1864	Exchanged October 29, 1864, at Venus Point, Savannah River, GA.
Wood, William W. Private	Unk	April 1, 1864, Kinston, North Carolina	Co. C, 38th Battalion Virginia Light Artillery	June 3, 1864, Gains Farm, Cold Harbor, Virginia	Point Lookout, Maryland, transferred to Elmira Prison, NY, July 17, 1864	Exchanged March 10, 1865 at Boulware's wharf on the James River, Virginia
Woodall, J. W. Private	Unk	August 21, 1861, Clarksville, Georgia	Co. E, 16th Georgia Infantry	August 16, 1864, Front Royal, Virginia	Old Capital Prison, Washington, DC transferred to Elmira Prison, NY, August 29, 1864	Exchanged October 29, 1864, at Venus Point, Savannah River, GA.
Woodall, Jesse A. Sergeant	Unk	June 21, 1861, Camp McDonald, Georgia	Co. D, 18th Georgia Infantry	June 1, 1864, Cold Harbor, Virginia	Point Lookout, Maryland, transferred to Elmira Prison, NY, July 17, 1864	Oath of Allegiance June 14, 1865

Name & Rank	Age	Enlisted	Regiment and State	Where Captured	Prison	Remarks
Woodall, Samuel Private	Unk	May 22, 1861, Spoon Creek, Virginia	Co. H, 42nd Virginia Infantry	May 12, 1864, Near Spotsylvania Court House, Virginia	Point Lookout, Maryland, transferred to Elmira Prison, NY, August 6, 1864	Died November 26, 1864 of Chronic Diarrhea, Grave No. 975
Woodall, William W. Private	Unk	December 18, 1863, Mortous Ford, Virginia	Co. D, 42nd Virginia Infantry	May 12, 1864, Near Spotsylvania Court House, Virginia	Point Lookout, Maryland, transferred to Elmira Prison, NY, August 6, 1864	Oath of Allegiance June 14, 1865
Woodcock, John J. Private	21	May 17, 1861, Lower Black River District, North Carolina	Co. E, 18th North Carolina Infantry	May 12, 1864, Spotsylvania Court House, Virginia	Point Lookout, Maryland, transferred to Elmira Prison, NY, August 6, 1864	Oath of Allegiance June 30, 1865
Woodell, Enoch Corporal	19	November 20, 1861, Asheboro, North Carolina	Co. F, 2nd Battalion, North Carolina Infantry	May 20, 1864, Spotsylvania Court House, Virginia	Point Lookout, Maryland, transferred to Elmira Prison, NY, July 3, 1864	Exchanged October 29, 1864, at Venus Point, Savannah River, GA.
Woodham, John A. Private	Unk	August 15, 1862, Dale County, Alabama	Co. G, 15th Alabama Infantry	May 6, 1864, Wilderness, Virginia	Point Lookout, Maryland, transferred to Elmira Prison, NY, August 17, 1864	Died June 4, 1865 of Chronic Diarrhea, Grave No. 2897. Headstone has Initials I. A.
Woodland, James H. Private	21	April 20, 1861, Belle Roi., Virginia	Co. A, 26th Virginia Infantry	June 15, 1864, Near Petersburg, Virginia	Point Lookout, Maryland, transferred to Elmira Prison, NY, July 12, 1864	Died February 23, 1865 of Smallpox, Grave No. 2263
Woodord, Abram Private	18	June 20, 1861, Abingdon, Virginia	Co. B, 48th Virginia Infantry	May 12, 1864, Spotsylvania Court House, Virginia	Point Lookout, Maryland, transferred to Elmira Prison, NY, August 2, 1864	Died March 25, 1865 of Variola (Smallpox), Grave No. 2463
Woodring, Colla L. Private	22	December 31, 1861, Springfield, Missouri	Co. G, 1st Missouri Cavalry	May 17, 1863, Big Black Bridge, Champion Hill, Mississippi	Point Lookout, Maryland, transferred to Elmira Prison, NY, August 18, 1864	Exchanged February 13, 1865 at Boulware's wharf on the James River, Virginia

Name & Rank	Age	Enlisted	Regiment and State	Where Captured	Prison	Remarks
Woodruff, David C. Sergeant	24	May 31, 1861, Raleigh, North Carolina	Co. B, 1st North Carolina Infantry	May 12, 1864, Spotsylvania Court House, Virginia	Point Lookout, Maryland, transferred to Elmira Prison, NY, August 6, 1864	Oath of Allegiance June 21, 1865
Woodruff, J. A. Private	Unk	May 28, 1861, Meherrin, Virginia	Co. K, 21st Virginia Infantry	May 12, 1864, Spotsylvania Court House, Virginia	Point Lookout, Maryland, transferred to Elmira Prison, NY, August 2, 1864	Exchanged 3/2/65. Died 3/21/65 of Pleuro Pneumonia & Diarrhea at Hospital No. 9, Richmond, VA.
Woods, Charles W. Sergeant	Unk	September 6, 1862, Lewisburg, Virginia	Co. A, 26th Battalion, Virginia Infantry	June 3, 1864, Gaines Farm, Cold Harbor, Virginia	Point Lookout, Maryland, transferred to Elmira Prison, NY, July 17, 1864	Exchanged February 13, 1865 at Boulware's wharf on the James River, Virginia
Woods, David B. Private	Unk	June 11, 1861, Hevener's Store, Virginia	Co. F, 25th Virginia Infantry	May 31, 1864, Old Church, Cold Harbor, Virginia	Point Lookout, Maryland, transferred to Elmira Prison, NY, July 11, 1864	Died December 28, 1864 of Smallpox, Grave No. 1302
Woods, John H. Private	19	February 8, 1863, Kinston, North Carolina	Co. A, 2nd Battalion North Carolina Infantry	May 10, 1864, Near Spotsylvania County Court House, Virginia	Point Lookout, Maryland, transferred to Elmira Prison, NY, August 14, 1864	Oath of Allegiance June 27, 1865
Woods, John H. Corporal	Unk	July 2, 1861, Bethel Am., Virginia	Co. F, 50th Virginia Infantry	May 12, 1864, Spotsylvania Court House, Virginia	Point Lookout, Maryland, transferred to Elmira Prison, NY, August 2, 1864	Oath of Allegiance June 14, 1865
Woods, John J. Private	Unk	February 6, 1864, Grove Hill, Alabama	Co. C, 1st Battalion Alabama Artillery	August 23, 1864, Fort Morgan, Alabama	New Orleans, Louisiana transferred to Elmira Prison, NY, December 4, 1864.	Oath of Allegiance June 16, 1865
Woods, John R. Private	Unk	October 1, 1861, Augusta, Georgia	Co. C, 38th Georgia Infantry	May 20, 1864, Spotsylvania Court House, Virginia	Point Lookout, Maryland, transferred to Elmira Prison, NY, July 3, 1864	Died February 17, 1865 of Typhoid Fever, Grave No. 7

Name & Rank	Age	Enlisted	Regiment and State	Where Captured	Prison	Remarks
Woods, Joseph G. Private	32	June 17, 1861, Rocky Mount, Virginia	Co. K, 42nd Virginia Infantry	May 12, 1864, Spotsylvania Court House, Virginia	Point Lookout, Maryland, transferred to Elmira Prison, NY, August 2, 1864	Exchanged 2/20/65. Died 3/1/65 of Chronic Diarrhea at US Army Hospital Baltimore, MD
Woods, William J. Corporal	Unk	June 15, 1861, Macon County, Georgia	Co. A, 12th Georgia Infantry	May 6, 1864, Wilderness, Virginia	Point Lookout, Maryland, transferred to Elmira Prison, NY, August 14, 1864	Oath of Allegiance June 19, 1865
Woods, William W. Private	Unk	April 1, 1864, Kinston, North Carolina	Co. C, 38th Read's Battalion, Virginia Light Artillery	June 3, 1864, Gaines Farm, Cold Harbor, Virginia	Point Lookout, Maryland, transferred to Elmira Prison, NY, July 17, 1864	Exchanged March 10, 1865 at Boulware's Wharf on the James River, Virginia
Woodside, Isaiah W. Private	Unk	June 28, 1862, Huttansville, Virginia	Co. A, 25th Virginia Infantry	May 5, 1864, Wilderness, Virginia	Point Lookout, Maryland, transferred to Elmira Prison, NY, July 23, 1864	Died December 17, 1864 of Chronic Diarrhea, Grave No. 1284
Woodson, Ezra L. Private	Unk	May 27, 1861, Buckhannon, Virginia	Co. B, 25th Virginia Infantry	May 12, 1864, Spotsylvania Court House, Virginia	Point Lookout, Maryland, transferred to Elmira Prison, NY, July 30, 1864	Oath of Allegiance June 23, 1865
Woodson, James M. Private	26	May 27, 1861, Buckhannon, Virginia	Co. B, 25th Virginia Infantry	May 6, 1864, Wilderness, Virginia	Point Lookout, Maryland, transferred to Elmira Prison, NY, July 23, 1864	Exchanged March 2, 1865 at Akins Landing on the James River, Virginia
Woodson, M. R. Private	27	May 2, 1862, Guineas, Virginia	Co. J, 5th Virginia Cavalry	May 11, 1864, Yellow Tavern, Hanover County, Virginia	Point Lookout, Maryland, transferred to Elmira Prison, NY, August 17, 1864	Exchanged October 29, 1864, at Venus Point, Savannah River, GA.
Woodson, Walter N. Private	Unk	March 1, 1864, Floyd Court House, Virginia	Co. G, 21st Virginia Cavalry	July 10, 1864, Frederick, Maryland	Point Lookout, Maryland, transferred to Elmira Prison, NY, July 23, 1864	Exchanged February 13, 1865 at Boulware's Wharf on the James River, Virginia

Name & Rank	Age	Enlisted	Regiment and State	Where Captured	Prison	Remarks
Woodson, William T. Private	18	February 28, 1862, Camp Pickens, Stanardsville, Virginia	Co. D, 34th Virginia Infantry	June 15, 1864, Near Petersburg, Virginia	Point Lookout, Maryland, transferred to Elmira Prison, NY, July 23, 1864	Oath of Allegiance June 19, 1865
ʹWoodward, A. Private	Unk	Unknown	Co. C, 15th Virginia Cavalry	June 1, 1864, Potomac River, Virginia	Old Capital Prison, Washington, DC, transferred to Elmira Prison, NY, July 23, 1864	Died November 26, 1864 of Chronic Diarrhea, Grave No. 976
Woodward, John A. Private	19	April 5, 1864, Fort Fisher, New Hanover County, North Carolina	Co. H, 36th Regiment, 2nd North Carolina Artillery	January 15, 1865, Fort Fisher, North Carolina	February 1, 1865, Elmira Prison Camp, New York	Died February 7, 1865 of Pneumonia, Grave No. 1927
Woodward, Stephen M. Private	19	May 18, 1861, Edenton, North Carolina	Co. A, 1st North Carolina Infantry	May 12, 1864, Wilderness Spotsylvania, Virginia	Point Lookout, Maryland, transferred to Elmira Prison, NY, August 6, 1864	Oath of Allegiance June 12, 1865
Woodward, T. J. Private	Unk	April 5, 1862, Charleston, South Carolina	Co. G, 27th South Carolina Infantry	June 24, 1864, Near Petersburg, Virginia	Point Lookout, Maryland, transferred to Elmira Prison, NY, August 18, 1864	Died September 19, 1864 of Chronic Diarrhea, Grave No. 501
Woody, Francis M. Private	Unk	April 1, 1864, Person County, North Carolina	Co. H, 24th North Carolina Infantry	June 17, 1864, Petersburg, Virginia	Point Lookout, Maryland, transferred to Elmira Prison, NY, July 30, 1864	Oath of Allegiance May 29, 1865
Woody, Parkison C. S. Private	Unk	September 7, 1863, Warren County, Virginia	Co. D, 23rd Virginia Cavalry	July 30, 1864, Charlestown, Virginia	Old Capital Prison, Washington D. C. Transferred to Elmira Prison, NY, July 12, 1864	Oath of Allegiance July 7, 1865
Woody, R. L. Corporal	35	March 22, 1862, Porter's Precinct, Virginia	Co. B, 15th Virginia Cavalry	May 11, 1864, Near Ashland, Virginia	Point Lookout, Maryland, transferred to Elmira Prison, NY, August 17, 1864. Ward 9	Died April 28, 1865 of Pneumonia, Grave No. 2727

Name & Rank	Age	Enlisted	Regiment and State	Where Captured	Prison	Remarks
Woody, Rueben J. Private	Unk	June 6, 1861, Person County, North Carolina	Co. H, 24th North Carolina Infantry	June 17, 1864, Petersburg, Virginia	Point Lookout, Maryland, transferred to Elmira Prison, NY, July 30, 1864	Exchanged March 14, 1865 at Boulware's Wharf on the James River, Virginia
Woody, Wiley Private	Unk	July 1, 1863, Martinsburg, Virginia	Co. E, 6th Virginia Cavalry	September 13, 1863, Near Culpepper, Virginia	Point Lookout, Maryland, transferred to Elmira Prison, NY, August 18, 1864	Exchanged March 14, 1865 at Boulware's Wharf on the James River, Virginia
Woolbright, Randle Private	18	December 3, 1862, Murfreesboro, Tennessee	Co. K, 25th Tennessee Infantry	June 17, 1864, Petersburg, Virginia	Point Lookout, Maryland, transferred to Elmira Prison, NY, July 23, 1864	Oath of Allegiance July 11, 1865
Woolen, Samuel T. Private	22	February 27, 1862, Reidsville, North Carolina	Co. E, 45th North Carolina Infantry	May 10, 1864, Spotsylvania Court House, Virginia	Point Lookout, Maryland, transferred to Elmira Prison, NY, August 6, 1864	Transferred for Exchange 10/11/64. Died 10/31/64 of Chronic Diarrhea at US Army Hospital, Baltimore, MD.
Woolfe, Henry J. Private	Unk	October 24, 1861, Camp Wayne, Georgia	Co. G, 61st Georgia Infantry	May 12, 1864, Spotsylvania Court House, Virginia	Point Lookout, Maryland, transferred to Elmira Prison, NY, July 30, 1864	Exchanged February 20, 1865 at Boulware's or Cox Wharf on the James River, Virginia
Woolwine, John E. Private	Unk	April 29, 1862, White Sulfur Springs, Virginia	Co. F, 26th Battalion, Virginia Infantry	June 3, 1864, Gaines Mill Cold Harbor, Virginia	Point Lookout, Maryland, transferred to Elmira Prison, NY, July 17, 1864	Oath of Allegiance May 29, 1865
Wooton, James E. Private	Unk	May 4, 1862, Pickens County, Alabama	Co. K, 41st Alabama Infantry	May 16, 1864, Near Drury's Bluff, Virginia	Point Lookout, Maryland, transferred to Elmira Prison, NY, August 17, 1864	Oath of Allegiance June 27, 1865
Wootten, Daniel T. Private	18	April 18, 1861, Warrenton, North Carolina	Co. F, 12th North Carolina Infantry	May 12, 1864, Near Spotsylvania, Virginia	Point Lookout, Maryland, transferred to Elmira Prison, NY, August 14, 1864	Oath of Allegiance June 21, 1865

Name & Rank	Age	Enlisted	Regiment and State	Where Captured	Prison	Remarks
Worick, Manley Private	Unk	Unknown	Co. H, 12th North Carolina Infantry	July 31, 1864, Sharpsburg, Maryland	Old Capital Prison, Washington, DC transferred to Elmira Prison, NY, August 29, 1864	Transferred to A. A. P. M. G. February 27, 1865. No Further Information
Workman, Jacob L. Private	24	August 20, 1862, Statesville, North Carolina	Co. K, 23rd North Carolina Infantry	May 12, 1864, Near Spotsylvania Court House, Virginia	Point Lookout, Maryland, transferred to Elmira Prison, NY, August 14, 1864	Died January 22, 1865 of Variola (Smallpox), Grave No. 1589. James, 12th NC on Headstone.
Workman, Sidney Private	18	September 17, 1861, Orange County, North Carolina	Co. G, 28th North Carolina Infantry	May 12, 1864, Near Spotsylvania Court House, Virginia	Point Lookout, Maryland, transferred to Elmira Prison, NY, August 14, 1864	Died February 1, 1865 of Variola (Smallpox), Grave No. 1756
Worley, Charles S. Private	Unk	August 13, 1861, Camp Moore, Louisiana	Co. C, 12th Louisiana Infantry	May 16, 1863, Baker's Creek, Champion Hill, Mississippi	Point Lookout, Maryland, transferred to Elmira Prison, NY, August 18, 1864	Exchanged February 25, 1865 at Boulware's wharf on the James River, Virginia
Worley, Columbus L. Private	22	March 14, 1863, Gainesville, Alabama	Co. A, 5th Battalion Alabama Infantry	July 1, 1863, Gettysburg, Pennsylvania. Gunshot Wound Right Ankle.	Point Lookout, Maryland, transferred to Elmira Prison Camp, New York, July 23, 1864.	Oath of Allegiance May 17, 1865
Worley, Mirada D. Sergeant	Unk	May 15, 1861, Montgomery, Alabama	Co. D, 6th Alabama Infantry	May 20, 1864, Spotsylvania Court House, Virginia	Point Lookout, Maryland, transferred to Elmira Prison, NY, July 3, 1864	Oath of Allegiance June 30, 1865
Worley, Patrick B. Private	Unk	January 20, 1862, Kenansville, Duplin County, North Carolina	Co. B, 3rd North Carolina Infantry	May 12, 1864, Near Spotsylvania Court House, Virginia	Point Lookout, Maryland, transferred to Elmira Prison, NY, August 14, 1864	Exchanged February 13, 1865 at Boulware's wharf on the James River, Virginia

Name & Rank	Age	Enlisted	Regiment and State	Where Captured	Prison	Remarks
Worley, Thomas Private	Unk	August 24, 1861, Clayton, Georgia	Co. E, 24th Georgia Infantry	July 29, 1864, Near Petersburg, Virginia	Point Lookout, Maryland, transferred to Elmira Prison, NY, August 12, 1864	Oath of Allegiance June 21, 1865
Wornack, William H. Private	32	August 16, 1862, Lincoln, North Carolina	Co. K, 5th North Carolina Cavalry	May 1, 1861, Ashland Station, Virginia	Point Lookout, Maryland, transferred to Elmira Prison, NY, July 12, 1864	Died April 21, 1865 of Chronic Diarrhea, Grave No. 1387
Worrell, Aaron Private	Unk	Unknown	Co. I, 50th Virginia Infantry	May 12, 1864, Spotsylvania Court House, Virginia	Point Lookout, Maryland, transferred to Elmira Prison, NY, August 2, 1864	Died March 16, 1865 of Chronic Diarrhea, Grave No. 1682
Worrell, Ervin Private	Unk	February 15, 1863, Wilmington, North Carolina	Co. F, 10th Regiment, 1st North Carolina Artillery	January 15, 1865, Fort Fisher, North Carolina	February 1, 1865, Elmira Prison Camp, New York	Died February 9, 1865 of Pneumonia, Grave No. 1947
Worrell, Jesse Private	Unk	Unknown	Co. I, 50th Virginia Infantry	May 12, 1864, Spotsylvania Court House, Virginia	Point Lookout, Maryland, transferred to Elmira Prison, NY, August 2, 1864	Exchanged October 29, 1864, at Venus Point, Savannah River, GA.
Worrell, John Private	Unk	October 15, 1863, Goldsboro, North Carolina	Co. F, 10th Regiment, 1st North Carolina Artillery	February 11, 1865, Near Fort Fisher, North Carolina	January 30, 1865, Elmira Prison Camp, New York.	Died March 11, 1865 of Pneumonia, Grave No. 1843
Worseley, William H. H. Private	Unk	July 1, 1862, Edgecombe County, North Carolina	Co. E, 33rd North Carolina Infantry	July 14, 1863, Falling Waters, Maryland	Point Lookout, Maryland, transferred to Elmira Prison, NY, August 18, 1864	Died November 6, 1864 of Chronic Diarrhea, Grave No. 771. Headstone has W. H. Woosley.
Worsham, Alex Private	Unk	Unknown	Co. D, 1st Louisiana Cavalry	August 25, 1864, Near Clinton, Louisiana	New Orleans, Louisiana transferred to Elmira November 19, 1864.	Exchanged February 13, 1865 at Boulware's Wharf on the James River, Virginia
Worsham, J. R. Private	Unk	June 10, 1861, Ridgeville, South Carolina	Co. I, 25th South Carolina Infantry	January 15, 1865, Fort Fisher, North Carolina	January 30, 1865, Elmira Prison Camp, New York.	Died February 24, 1865 Pneumonia, Grave No. 2241

Name & Rank	Age	Enlisted	Regiment and State	Where Captured	Prison	Remarks
Worsham, John Private	17	March 11, 1862, Gourdins Depot, Williamsburg, South Carolina	Co. I, 25th South Carolina Infantry	January 15, 1865, Fort Fisher, North Carolina	February 1, 1865, Elmira Prison Camp, New York	Exchanged February 20, 1865 at Boulware's or Cox Wharf on the James River, Virginia
Worsham, Robert A. Private	Unk	April 25, 1862, Euharlee, Georgia	Co. H, 60th Georgia Infantry	September 19, 1864, Cedar Creek, Virginia	Old Capital Prison, Washington, DC, transferred to Elmira Prison, NY, December 17, 1864	Died April 8, 1865 of Chronic Diarrhea, Grave No. 2624
Worthing, W. A. Private	Unk	May 9, 1861, Ashland, Virginia	Co. G, 4th Virginia Cavalry	August 16, 1864, Front Royal, Virginia	Old Capital Prison, Washington, DC transferred to Elmira Prison, NY, August 29, 1864	Died February 13, 1865 of Variola (Smallpox), Grave No. 2038. Headstone has Wortham.
Worthington, Caleb Private	23	August 20, 1861, Pitt County, North Carolina	Co. G, 8th North Carolina Infantry	May 31, 1864, Cold Harbor, Virginia	Point Lookout, Maryland, transferred to Elmira Prison, NY, July 12, 1864	Exchanged March 14, 1865 at Boulware's Wharf on the James River, Virginia
Worthington, Craven A. Private	Unk	May 1, 1862, Lumpkin, Georgia	Co. E, 31st Georgia Infantry	July 18, 1864, Snickers' Gap, Virginia	Old Capital Prison, Washington D. C. Transferred to Elmira Prison, NY, July 12, 1864	Exchanged March 10, 1865 at Boulware's Wharf on the James River, Virginia
Worthy, T. C. Sergeant	Unk	January 20, 1862, Camp Hampton, South Carolina	Co. B, 4th South Carolina Cavalry	May 30, 1864, Old Church, Cold Harbor, Virginia	Point Lookout, Maryland, transferred to Elmira Prison, NY, July 12, 1864	Exchanged March 2, 1865 at Akins Landing on the James River, Virginia
Wray, Beverly C. Sergeant	Unk	June 17, 1861, Rocky Mount, Virginia	Co. K, 42nd Virginia Infantry	May 12, 1864, Spotsylvania Court House, Virginia	Point Lookout, Maryland, transferred to Elmira Prison, NY, August 2, 1864	Oath of Allegiance June 23, 1865

Name & Rank	Age	Enlisted	Regiment and State	Where Captured	Prison	Remarks
Wray, Robert M. Private	21	February 27, 1862, Reidsville, North Carolina	Co. E, 45th North Carolina Infantry	May 10, 1864, Spotsylvania Court House, Virginia	Point Lookout Prison Camp, Maryland. Transferred to Elmira Prison Camp, NY, August 6, 1864	Died May 19, 1865 of Pneumonia, Grave No. 2951. Headstone has R. M. Ray
Wren, Thomas N. Private	Unk	December 27, 1861, Camp Lee, Charleston, South Carolina	Co. A, 17th South Carolina Infantry	July 30, 1864, Petersburg, Virginia	Point Lookout, Maryland, transferred to Elmira Prison, NY, August 12, 1864	Died November 18, 1864 of Chronic Diarrhea, Grave No. 963. Headstone has Regiment 61st SC.
Wrenn, Albert W. Private	Unk	May 25, 1861, Fairfax County, Virginia	Co. E, 6th Virginia Cavalry	August 3, 1864, Burke's Station, Virginia	Old Capital Prison, Washington D. C. Transferred to Elmira Prison, NY, July 12, 1864	Exchanged March 10, 1865 at Boulware's Wharf on the James River, Virginia
Wrenn, James J. Civilian	Unk	Unknown	Citizen of Dinwitty County, Virginia	June 24, 1864, Dinwitty County, Virginia	Point Lookout, Maryland, transferred to Elmira Prison, NY, July 25, 1864	Died September 17, 1864 of Chronic Diarrhea, Grave No. 167
Wrenn, Lafayette Private	Unk	May 1, 1864, Taylorsville, North Carolina	Co. B, 12th North Carolina Infantry	May 10, 1864, Spotsylvania Court House, Virginia. Gunshot Wound Left Thigh.	Old Capital Prison, Washington, DC transferred to Elmira Prison, NY, August 29, 1864	Exchanged October 29, 1864, at Venus Point, Savannah River, GA.
Wrenn, William Private	Unk	May 9, 1864, Greenville, North Carolina	Co. E, 35th North Carolina Infantry	June 17, 1864, Petersburg, Virginia	Point Lookout, Maryland, transferred to Elmira Prison, NY, July 30, 1864	Died October 2, 1864 of Pneumonia, Grave No. 626
Wright, Andrew J. Private	Unk	May 20, 1861, Rocky Mount, Virginia	Co. K, 42nd Virginia Infantry	May 12, 1864, Spotsylvania Court House, Virginia	Point Lookout, Maryland, transferred to Elmira Prison, NY, August 2, 1864	Exchanged February 20, 1865 at Boulware's or Cox Wharf on the James River, Virginia

Name & Rank	Age	Enlisted	Regiment and State	Where Captured	Prison	Remarks
Wright, Cary W. Private	Unk	May 26, 1861, Williamsburg, Virginia	Co. F, 32nd Virginia Infantry	June 28, 1864, Petersburg, Virginia	Point Lookout, Maryland, transferred to Elmira Prison, NY, July 23, 1864	Oath of Allegiance April 18, 1865
Wright, Charles A. Private	23	December 5, 1861, Sac River, St. Clair County, Missouri	Co. G, 1st Missouri Cavalry	May 17, 1863, Big Black Bridge, Champion Hill, Mississippi	Point Lookout, Maryland, transferred to Elmira Prison, NY, August 18, 1864	Exchanged February 13, 1865 at Boulware's wharf on the James River, Virginia
Wright, D. A. Private	Unk	January 12, 1861, Newberry, South Carolina	Co. B, 1st South Carolina Infantry	July 14, 1863, Falling Waters, Maryland	Point Lookout, Maryland, transferred to Elmira Prison, NY, August 18, 1864	Exchanged February 25, 1865 at Boulware's or Cox Wharf on the James River, Virginia
Wright, David F. Sergeant	Unk	August 1, 1863, Montgomery County, Alabama	Co. B, 61st Alabama Infantry	May 12, 1864, Spotsylvania Court House, Virginia	Point Lookout, Maryland, transferred to Elmira Prison, NY, July 30, 1864	Died October 18, 1864 of Chronic Diarrhea, Grave No. 542
Wright, E. C. Private	Unk	July 14, 1862, Chester, South Carolina	Co. H, 7th Battalion South Carolina Infantry	May 16, 1864, Near Drury's Bluff, Virginia	Point Lookout, Maryland, transferred to Elmira Prison, NY, August 17, 1864	Transferred For Exchange 10/11/64 to Point Lookout Prison, MD. Died 10/28/64 of Chronic Diarrhea.
Wright, Emanual Sam Sergeant	18	April 26, 1861, Columbus County, North Carolina	Co. D, 20th North Carolina Infantry	May 12, 1864, Near Spotsylvania Court House, Virginia	Point Lookout Prison, Maryland. Transferred to Elmira Prison Camp New York August 14, 1864.	Exchanged October 29, 1864, at Venus Point, Savannah River, GA.
Wright, Henry Private	44	August 2, 1861, Bowling Green, Virginia	Co. G, 47th Virginia Infantry	May 31, 1864, Port Royal, Virginia	Point Lookout, Maryland, transferred to Elmira Prison, NY, July 12, 1864	Died March 30, 1865 of Typhoid Fever, Grave No. 2530
Wright, Hezekiah J. Private	Unk	April 27, 1861, Wetumpka, Alabama	Co. J, 3rd Alabama Infantry	May 12, 1864, Spotsylvania Court House, Virginia	Point Lookout, Maryland, transferred to Elmira Prison, NY, August 12, 1864	Exchanged March 14, 1865 at Boulware's Wharf on the James River, Virginia

Name & Rank	Age	Enlisted	Regiment and State	Where Captured	Prison	Remarks
Wright, J. J. Private	Unk	September 13, 1861, Whitesville, Georgia	Co. E, 61st Georgia Infantry	May 12, 1864, Spotsylvania Court House, Virginia	Point Lookout, Maryland, transferred to Elmira Prison, NY, July 30, 1864	Oath of Allegiance June 30, 1865
Wright, J. P. Private	Unk	February 19, 1864, Greenville, South Carolina	Co. H, 22nd South Carolina Infantry	July 30, 1864, Petersburg, Virginia	Point Lookout, Maryland, transferred to Elmira Prison, NY, August 12, 1864	Died April 9, 1865 of Variola (Smallpox), Grave No. 2611
Wright, James D. Private	Unk	January 18, 1864, Brunswick County, North Carolina	Co. F, 36th Regiment, 2nd North Carolina Artillery	January 15, 1865, Fort Fisher, North Carolina	February 1, 1865, Elmira Prison Camp, New York	Exchanged February 20, 1865. Died May 28, 1865 of Variola (Smallpox) at Jackson Hospital, Richmond, VA.
Wright, James D. Sergeant	Unk	March 24, 1862, Camp Gist, South Carolina	Co. B, 27th South Carolina Infantry	June 24, 1864, Near Petersburg, Virginia	Point Lookout, Maryland, transferred to Elmira Prison, NY, August 18, 1864	Exchanged November 15, 1864. Died March 14, 1865 of Unknown Causes at Fayetteville Hospital No. 6, NC.
Wright, James L. Private	Unk	April 10, 1864, Camp Holmes, Near Raleigh, North Carolina	Co. K, 10th Regiment, 1st North Carolina Artillery	January 15, 1865, Fort Fisher, North Carolina	February 1, 1865, Elmira Prison Camp, New York	Died April 18, 1865 of Variola (Smallpox), Grave No. 1365
Wright, James M. Private	Unk	January 1, 1862, Camp Hampton, Columbia, South Carolina	Co. H, 18th South Carolina Infantry	July 30, 1864, Petersburg, Virginia	Point Lookout, Maryland, transferred to Elmira Prison, NY, August 12, 1864	Died October 20, 1864 of Chronic Diarrhea, Grave No. 525
Wright, James O. Private	19	June 26, 1861, Camp McDonald, Georgia	Co. A, Phillips Legion, Georgia	August 16, 1864, Front Royal, Virginia	Old Capital Prison, Washington, DC transferred to Elmira Prison, NY, August 29, 1864	Oath of Allegiance June 21, 1865
Wright, John F. Private	Unk	Unknown	Co. H, 45th Georgia Infantry	May 6, 1864, Wilderness, Virginia	Point Lookout, Maryland, transferred to Elmira Prison, NY, August 14, 1864	Exchanged March 2, 1865 at Akins Landing on the James River, Virginia

Name & Rank	Age	Enlisted	Regiment and State	Where Captured	Prison	Remarks
Wright, John R. Private	28	August 12, 1863, East Tennessee	Co. D, 14th Tennessee Infantry	May 5, 1864, Wilderness, Virginia	Point Lookout, Maryland, transferred to Elmira Prison, NY, July 23, 1864	Oath of Allegiance December 24, 1864. Early Release per Lincoln's Proclamation, 12/8/1863.
Wright, John T. Private	Unk	June 20, 1861, Lynnhaven Beach, Virginia	Co. J, 15th Virginia Infantry	May 12, 1864, Near Ashland, Virginia	Point Lookout, Maryland, transferred to Elmira Prison, NY, August 17, 1864	Oath of Allegiance June 19, 1865
Wright, Patrick Henry Private	Unk	March 26, 1862, Camp Pryor, Virginia	Co. G, 13th Virginia Cavalry	June 17, 1864, Surry County, Virginia	Point Lookout, Maryland, transferred to Elmira Prison, NY, July 30, 1864	Oath of Allegiance June 16, 1865
Wright, Richard J. Sergeant	22	April 28, 1861, New Orleans, Louisiana	Co. A, 1st Louisiana Infantry	May 5, 1864, Wilderness, Virginia	Point Lookout, Maryland, transferred to Elmira Prison, NY, August 17, 1864	Exchanged February 25, 1865 at Boulware's or Cox Wharf on the James River, Virginia
Wright, Silas M. Private	18	April 19, 1862, Cleveland County, North Carolina	Co. F, 55th North Carolina Infantry	May 6, 1864, Wilderness, Virginia	Point Lookout, Maryland, transferred to Elmira Prison, NY, July 25, 1864	Oath of Allegiance May 29, 1865
Wright, William Private	37	July 1, 1863, Raleigh, North Carolina	Co. F, 6th North Carolina Infantry	November 7, 1863, Rappahannock, Virginia	Point Lookout, Maryland, transferred to Elmira Prison, NY, July 25, 1864	Died September 20, 1864 of Chronic Diarrhea, Grave No. 326
Wright, William A. Private	40	September 6, 1861, Camp Kirkpatrick, Georgia	Co. K, 38th Georgia Infantry	June 1, 1864, Cold Harbor, Virginia	Point Lookout, Maryland, transferred to Elmira Prison, NY, July 15, 1864	Oath of Allegiance June 16, 1865
Wright, William F. Private	21	Unknown	Co. B, 1st Jackson's Tennessee Heavy Artillery	August 23, 1864, Fort Morgan, Alabama.	New Orleans, Louisiana transferred to Elmira Prison, NY, December 4, 1864.	Died December 17, 1864 of Chronic Bronchitis, Grave No. 1282

Name & Rank	Age	Enlisted	Regiment and State	Where Captured	Prison	Remarks
Wright, William M. Private	41	July 24, 1861, Salisbury, North Carolina	Co. K, 8th North Carolina Infantry	May 31, 1864, Cold Harbor, Virginia	Point Lookout, Maryland, transferred to Elmira Prison, NY, July 12, 1864	Exchanged March 14, 1865 at Boulware's Wharf on the James River, Virginia
Wright, William P. Private	Unk	July 11, 1862, Lynchburg, Virginia	Co. I, 42nd Virginia Infantry	May 12, 1864, Near Spotsylvania Court House, Virginia	Point Lookout, Maryland, transferred to Elmira Prison, NY, August 6, 1864	Exchanged October 29, 1864, at Venus Point, Savannah River, GA.
Wriley, William T. Private	26	February 28, 1862, Conyers, Georgia	Co. B, 35th Georgia Infantry	May 6, 1864, Wilderness, Virginia	Point Lookout, Maryland, transferred to Elmira Prison, NY, August 14, 1864	Exchanged February 20, 1865 at Boulware's or Cox Wharf on the James River, Virginia
Wring, Isaac E. Private	Unk	January 15, 1864, Camp Holmes, North Carolina	Co. D, 18th North Carolina Infantry	May 12, 1864, Spotsylvania Court House, Virginia	Point Lookout, Maryland, transferred to Elmira Prison, NY, August 6, 1864	Oath of Allegiance May 19, 1865
Wroten, William S. Private	23	April 20, 1861, Belle Roi, Virginia	Co. A, 26th Virginia Infantry	June 15, 1864, Near Petersburg, Virginia	Point Lookout, Maryland, transferred to Elmira Prison, NY, July 12, 1864	Oath of Allegiance July 3, 1865
Wyant, David W. Corporal	Unk	April 18, 1861, McGaheysville, Virginia	Co. E, 10th Virginia Infantry	May 12, 1864, Spotsylvania Court House, Virginia	Point Lookout, Maryland, transferred to Elmira Prison, NY, August 2, 1864	Oath of Allegiance June 16, 1865
Wyant, Isaac Corporal	Unk	April 18, 1861, McGaheysville, Virginia	Co. E, 10th Virginia Infantry	May 12, 1864, Spotsylvania Court House, Virginia	Point Lookout, Maryland, transferred to Elmira Prison, NY, August 2, 1864	Exchanged October 29, 1864 at Venus Point, Savannah River, GA.
Wyatt, James I. Private	22	July 22, 1861, Salisbury, North Carolina	Co. K, 8th North Carolina Infantry	June 1, 1864, Gaines Farm, Cold Harbor, Virginia	Point Lookout, Maryland, transferred to Elmira Prison, NY, July 12, 1864	Exchanged 2/20/65. Died 3/27/65 of Debility at Jackson Hospital, Richmond, VA.

Name & Rank	Age	Enlisted	Regiment and State	Where Captured	Prison	Remarks
Wyatt, John W. Private	Unk	January 11, 1863, Henry County, Virginia	Co. F, 42nd Virginia Infantry	May 12, 1864, Near Spotsylvania Court House, Virginia	Point Lookout, Maryland, transferred to Elmira Prison, NY, August 6, 1864	Died September 15, 1864 of Chronic Diarrhea, Grave No. 277
Wyatt, William Private	Unk	September 17, 1862, Chaffin's Farm, Virginia	Co. G, 26th Virginia Infantry	June 15, 1864, Petersburg, Virginia	Point Lookout, Maryland, transferred to Elmira Prison, NY, July 30, 1864	Died October 24, 1864 of Typhoid Fever, Grave No. 857
Wyatt, William M. Corporal	20	March 11, 1862, Spring Garden, Rockingham County, North Carolina	Co. G, 45th North Carolina Infantry	May 10, 1864, Spotsylvania Court House, Virginia	Point Lookout, Maryland, transferred to Elmira Prison, NY, August 6, 1864	Oath of Allegiance May 13, 1865
Wylie, Thomas S. Corporal	Unk	March 19, 1862, Camp Pillow, South Carolina	Co. D, 17th South Carolina Infantry	July 30, 1864, Petersburg, Virginia	Point Lookout, Maryland, transferred to Elmira Prison, NY, August 12, 1864	Died November 30, 1864 of Chronic Diarrhea, Grave No. 994
Wyman, Levi Sergeant	20	May 24, 1861, Corinth, Mississippi	Co. D, 18th Mississippi Infantry	May 8, 1864, Wilderness, Virginia	Point Lookout, Maryland, transferred to Elmira Prison, NY, July 25, 1864	Oath of Allegiance January 21, 1865
Wymberly, W. A. Private	Unk	August 23, 1861, Camp Trousdale, Tennessee	Co. H, 23rd Tennessee Infantry	June 17, 1864, Petersburg, Virginia	Point Lookout, Maryland, transferred to Elmira Prison, NY, July 30, 1864	Exchanged February 13, 1865 at Boulware's wharf on the James River, Virginia
Wyndham, P. M. Private	Unk	April 8, 1862, Louisa Court House, Virginia	Co. I, 25th South Carolina Infantry	January 15, 1865, Fort Fisher, North Carolina	February 1, 1865, Elmira Prison Camp, New York	Oath of Allegiance July 11, 1865
Wynn, Peter F. Private	Unk	May 15, 1861, Germantown, Tennessee	Co. B, 1st Jackson's Tennessee Heavy Artillery	August 23, 1864, Fort Morgan, Alabama.	New Orleans, Louisiana transferred to Elmira Prison, NY, December 4, 1864.	Exchanged February 13, 1865 at Boulware's wharf on the James River, Virginia
Wynn, Thomas D. Private	22	June 24, 1861, Williamston, North Carolina	Co. H, 1st North Carolina Infantry	May 12, 1864, Spotsylvania Court House, Virginia	Point Lookout, Maryland, transferred to Elmira Prison, NY, August 6, 1864	Died April 7, 1865 of Pneumonia, Grave No. 2640

Name & Rank	Age	Enlisted	Regiment and State	Where Captured	Prison	Remarks
Wynn, Thomas L. Private	Unk	August 6, 1861, Camp Pulaski, Louisiana	Co. G, 15th Louisiana Infantry	May 12, 1864, Spotsylvania Court House, Virginia	Point Lookout, Maryland, transferred to Elmira Prison, NY, July 25, 1864	Exchanged February 13, 1865 at Boulware's wharf on the James River, Virginia
Wyrick, Calvin G. Private	Unk	March 18, 1863, Greensboro, North Carolina	Co. B, 45th North Carolina Infantry	May 10, 1864, Spotsylvania Court House, Virginia	Point Lookout, Maryland, transferred to Elmira Prison, NY, August 6, 1864	Exchanged 2/20/65 on the James River, Virginia. Died 3/21/65 of Variola (Smallpox).
Wyrick, J. Private	Unk	July 20, 1861, Wytheville, Virginia	Co. C, 51st Virginia Infantry	July 10, 1864, Frederick, Maryland	Point Lookout, Maryland, transferred to Elmira Prison, NY, July 23, 1864	Oath of Allegiance June 21, 1865
Wyrick, Laban V. Private	Unk	October 2, 1863, Sullivan's Island, South Carolina	Co. H, 7th Battalion South Carolina Infantry	May 16, 1864, Near Drury's Bluff, Virginia	Point Lookout, Maryland, transferred to Elmira Prison, NY, August 17, 1864	Oath of Allegiance June 27, 1865
Wyrick, Milton W. Private	19	February 27, 1862, Greensboro, North Carolina	Co. B, 45th North Carolina Infantry	May 10, 1864, Spotsylvania Court House, Virginia	Point Lookout, Maryland, transferred to Elmira Prison, NY, August 6, 1864	Oath of Allegiance June 12, 1865
Wysong, Lafayette R. Private	Unk	March 20, 1862, Elk Creek, Virginia	Co. F, 4th Virginia Infantry	May 12, 1864, Spotsylvania Court House, Virginia	Point Lookout, Maryland, transferred to Elmira Prison, NY, August 2, 1864	Exchanged October 29, 1864, at Venus Point, Savannah River, GA.

Name & Rank	Age	Enlisted	Regiment and State	Where Captured	Prison	Remarks
Yager, James Private	Unk	February 18, 1862, Scottsville, Alabama	Co. C, 1st Battalion Alabama Artillery	August 23, 1864, Fort Morgan, Alabama	New Orleans, Louisiana transferred to Elmira Prison, NY, December 4, 1864.	Oath of Allegiance June 16, 1865
Yancy, George G. Private	Unk	June 6, 1861, New Canton, Virginia	Co. C, 44th Virginia Infantry	May 12, 1864, Spotsylvania Court House, Virginia	Point Lookout, Maryland, transferred to Elmira Prison, NY, August 2,1864	Exchanged October 29, 1864, at Venus Point, Savannah River, GA.

Name & Rank	Age	Enlisted	Regiment and State	Where Captured	Prison	Remarks
Yarboro, Moses C. Private	23	December 20, 1861, Cheraw, South Carolina	Co. D, 21st South Carolina Infantry	January 15, 1865, Fort Fisher, North Carolina	February 1, 1865, Elmira Prison Camp, New York	Oath of Allegiance July 26, 1865
Yarborough, Christopher C. Private	Unk	March 19, 1861, Wetumpka, Alabama	Co. E, 1st Battalion Alabama Artillery	August 23, 1864, Fort Morgan, Alabama	Steam Press No. 4 New Orleans, Louisiana transferred to Elmira Prison, NY, October 8, 1864.	Oath of Allegiance June 16, 1865
Yarborough, H. Private	Unk	Unknown	Co. B, 11th Battalion Louisiana Infantry	September 18, 1864, Durham Springs, Louisiana	New Orleans, Louisiana transferred to Elmira November 19, 1864.	Died March 10, 1865 of Diarrhea, Grave No. 1866. Headstone has 10th Battalion.
Yarborough, Joshua T. Private	Unk	February 28, 1864, Augusta, Georgia	Co. A, 21st Georgia Infantry	July 9, 1864, Frederick, Maryland	Old Capital Prison, Washington, DC transferred to Elmira Prison, NY, August 27, 1864	Exchanged February 20, 1865 at Boulware's or Cox Wharf on the James River, Virginia
Yarborough, T. L. Private	Unk	May 19, 1862, Darlington, South Carolina	Co. B, 21st South Carolina Infantry	January 15, 1865, Fort Fisher, North Carolina	February 1, 1865, Elmira Prison Camp, New York	Died April 28, 1865 of Pneumonia, Grave No. 2728. Headstone has T. Y., 21st SC Artillery
Yarbrough, Elijah M. Private	Unk	September 6, 1861, Eastville, Alabama	Co. E, 13th Alabama Infantry	May 12, 1864, Spotsylvania Court House, Virginia	Point Lookout, Maryland, transferred to Elmira Prison, NY, August 2, 1864	Died July 17, 1865 of Unknown Disease, Elmira, NY. Grave No. 2871
Yarbrough, Robert B. Private	Unk	August 3, 1862, Notasulga, Alabama	Co. L, 6th Alabama Infantry	May 5, 1864, Wilderness, Virginia	Point Lookout, Maryland, transferred to Elmira Prison, NY, August 17,1864	Oath of Allegiance May 12, 1865
Yarley, James C. Private	30	January 4, 1862, Walterboro, South Carolina	Co. J, 11th South Carolina Infantry	June 24, 1864, Near Petersburg, Virginia	Point Lookout, Maryland, transferred to Elmira Prison, NY, August 18, 1864	Exchanged March 14, 1865 at Boulware's Wharf on the James River, Virginia

Name & Rank	Age	Enlisted	Regiment and State	Where Captured	Prison	Remarks
Yates, Daniel F. Private	18	July 8, 1862, Greensboro, North Carolina	Co. H, 1st North Carolina Infantry	May 12, 1864, Wilderness Spotsylvania, Virginia	Point Lookout, Maryland, transferred to Elmira Prison, NY, August 6, 1864	Died April 3, 1865 of Variola (smallpox), Grave No. 2559
Yates, George W. Private	Unk	June 22, 1861, Wytheville, Virginia	Co. K, 50th Virginia Infantry	May 6, 1864, Wilderness, Virginia	Point Lookout, Maryland, transferred to Elmira Prison, NY, August 14, 1864	Oath of Allegiance June 19, 1865
Yates, Harrison Private	22	September 15, 1862, Camp Mangum, Raleigh, North Carolina	Co. B, 31st North Carolina Infantry	June 1, 1864, Cold Harbor, Virginia	Point Lookout, Maryland, transferred to Elmira Prison, NY, July 12, 1864	Exchanged October 29, 1864, at Venus Point, Savannah River, GA.
Yates, J. D. Corporal	Unk	March 8, 1862, Clarksburg, Virginia	Co. J, 55th Virginia Infantry	May 5, 1864, Wilderness, Virginia	Point Lookout, Maryland, transferred to Elmira Prison, NY, August 14, 1864	Exchanged February 13, 1865 at Boulware's wharf on the James River, Virginia
Yates, Wiley Private	38	September 7, 1861, Quitman County, Georgia	Co. C, 61st Georgia Infantry	May 12, 1864, Spotsylvania Court House, Virginia	Point Lookout, Maryland, transferred to Elmira Prison, NY, July 30, 1864	Exchanged February 20, 1865 at Boulware's or Cox Wharf on the James River, Virginia
Yaun, Garrett Private	Unk	March 16, 1862, Autuaga County, Alabama	Co. B, 59th Alabama Infantry	May 16, 1864, Petersburg, Bermuda Hundred, Virginia	Point Lookout, Maryland, transferred to Elmira Prison, NY, July 12, 1864	Oath of Allegiance June 16, 1865
Yearout, John Private	23	April 17, 1861, Christiansburg, Virginia	Co. G, 4th Virginia Infantry	May 12, 1864, Spotsylvania Court House, Virginia	Point Lookout, Maryland, transferred to Elmira Prison, NY, August 2, 1864	Oath of Allegiance August 7, 1865
Yeonge, Joseph S. Private	Unk	January 20, 1862, Camp Hampton, South Carolina	Co. B, 4th South Carolina Cavalry	June 11, 1864, Trevilian Station, Louisa Court House, Virginia	Point Lookout, Maryland, transferred to Elmira Prison, NY, July 25, 1864	Exchanged February 20, 1865 at Boulware's or Cox Wharf on the James River, Virginia

Name & Rank	Age	Enlisted	Regiment and State	Where Captured	Prison	Remarks
Yerby, James Private	38	July 15, 1862, Raleigh, North Carolina	Co. J, 3rd North Carolina Infantry	May 10, 1864, Near Spotsylvania County Court House, Virginia	Point Lookout, Maryland, transferred to Elmira Prison, NY, August 14, 1864	Exchanged February 13, 1865 at Boulware's wharf on the James River, Virginia
Yoder, Alfred Marcus Private	18	September 1, 1861, Newton, North Carolina	Co. B, 23rd North Carolina Infantry	May 12, 1864, Spotsylvania Court House, Virginia	Point Lookout, Maryland, transferred to Elmira Prison, NY, August 14, 1864	Exchanged October 29, 1864, at Venus Point, Savannah River, GA.
Yopp, Robert W. Private	35	May 13, 1861, Golden Place, Onslow County, North Carolina	Co. A, 3rd North Carolina Infantry	May 12, 1864, Near Spotsylvania County Court House, Virginia	Point Lookout, Maryland, transferred to Elmira Prison, NY, August 14, 1864	Exchanged March 2, 1865 at Akins Landing on the James River, Virginia
York, Eli Private	Unk	March 8, 1864, Guilford County, North Carolina	Co. A, 53rd North Carolina Infantry	May 20, 1864, Near Spotsylvania Court House, Virginia	Point Lookout, Maryland, transferred to Elmira Prison, NY, July 23, 1864	Died September 16, 1864 of Chronic Diarrhea, Grave No. 306
Young, A. J. Private	Unk	January 8, 1862, Camp Hampton, South Carolina	Co. K, 18th South Carolina Infantry	July 30, 1864, Petersburg, Virginia	Point Lookout, Maryland, transferred to Elmira Prison, NY, August 12, 1864	Exchanged October 29, 1864, at Venus Point, Savannah River, GA.
Young, Alfred B. Private	23	March 3, 1862, Saint Landry Parish, Louisiana	Co. C, 6th Louisiana Infantry	May 5, 1864, Wilderness, Virginia	Point Lookout, Maryland, transferred to Elmira Prison, NY, August 17, 1864	Exchanged March 10, 1865 at Boulware's Wharf on the James River, Virginia
Young, Edwin J. Private	Unk	June 12, 1861, Red Sulfur Springs, Virginia	Co. F, 26th Battalion, Virginia Infantry	June 3, 1864, Gaines Farm, Cold Harbor, Virginia	Point Lookout, Maryland, transferred to Elmira Prison, NY, July 17, 1864	Oath of Allegiance July 3, 1865
Young, Emory F. Private, Hospital Steward	Unk	September 8, 1862, Camp Clifton, Virginia	Co. D, 47th Virginia Infantry	September 22, 1863, Near Madison Court House, Virginia	Old Capital Prison, Washington D. C. Transferred to Elmira Prison, NY, August 18,1864	Exchanged October 29, 1864, at Venus Point, Savannah River, GA.

Name & Rank	Age	Enlisted	Regiment and State	Where Captured	Prison	Remarks
Young, Ezekiel Private	20	July 15, 1862, Raleigh, North Carolina	Co. G, 1st North Carolina Infantry	May 12, 1864, Wilderness Spotsylvania, Virginia	Point Lookout, Maryland, transferred to Elmira Prison, NY, August 6, 1864	Oath of Allegiance June 12, 1865
Young, Furney G. Private	27	May 8, 1862, Murfreesboro, North Carolina	Co. A, 24th North Carolina Infantry	June 17, 1864, Petersburg, Virginia	Point Lookout, Maryland, transferred to Elmira Prison, NY, July 30, 1864	Exchanged March 14, 1865 at Boulware's Wharf on the James River, Virginia
Young, George W. Private	Unk	December 29, 1863, Montgomery, Alabama	Co. E, 1st Battalion Alabama Artillery	August 23, 1864, Fort Morgan, Alabama	Steam Press No. 4 New Orleans, Louisiana transferred to Elmira Prison, NY, October 8, 1864.	Oath of Allegiance July 7, 1865
Young, Harrison Private	21	April 27, 1864, Richmond, Virginia	Co. D, 14th Virginia Infantry	Jarrett Station, Danville Railroad, Near Richmond, Virginia	Point Lookout, Maryland, transferred to Elmira Prison, NY, July 23, 1864	Died September 17, 1864 of Chronic Diarrhea and Scurvy, Grave No. 163
Young, J. H. Private	Unk	Unknown	Co. C, 25th South Carolina Infantry	January 15, 1865, Fort Fisher, North Carolina	February 1, 1865, Elmira Prison Camp, New York	Exchanged March 2, 1865 at Akins Landing on the James River, Virginia
Young, James A. B. Private	20	July 20, 1861, Camp Pickens, Anderson District, South Carolina	Co. G, 1st South Carolina Infantry	July 14, 1863, Falling Waters, Maryland	Point Lookout, Maryland, transferred to Elmira Prison, NY, August 14, 1864	Died August 15, 1864 of Solus of the Calf Muscle, Grave No. 28
Young, James M. Private	Unk	December 29, 1863, Montgomery, Alabama	Co. E, 1st Battalion Alabama Artillery	August 23, 1864, Fort Morgan, Alabama	Steam Press No. 4 New Orleans, Louisiana transferred to Elmira Prison, NY, October 8, 1864.	Died April 5, 1865 of Pneumonia, Grave No. 2543
Young, John B. Sergeant	Unk	August 19, 1861, Amite City, Louisiana	Co. H, 15th Louisiana Infantry	May 12, 1864, Spotsylvania Court House, Virginia	Point Lookout, Maryland, transferred to Elmira Prison, NY, July 25, 1864	Exchanged March 10, 1865 at Boulware's Wharf on the James River, Virginia

Name & Rank	Age	Enlisted	Regiment and State	Where Captured	Prison	Remarks
Young, John M. Private	Unk	June 6, 1861, New Orleans, Louisiana	Co. B, 14th Louisiana Infantry	May 12, 1864, Spotsylvania Court House, Virginia	Point Lookout, Maryland, transferred to Elmira Prison, NY, July 25, 1864	Exchanged February 13, 1865 at Boulware's wharf on the James River, Virginia
Young, Joseph J. Private	26	July 15, 1862, Raleigh, North Carolina	Co. J, 1st North Carolina Infantry	May 12, 1864, Spotsylvania Court House, Virginia	Point Lookout, Maryland, transferred to Elmira Prison, NY, August 6, 1864	Exchanged October 29, 1864, at Venus Point, Savannah River, GA.
Young, Lenard A. Private	26	May 20, 1861, Louisburg, North Carolina	Co. K, 32nd North Carolina Infantry	May 10, 1864, Near Mine Run Spotsylvania, Virginia	Point Lookout, Maryland, transferred to Elmira Prison, NY, August 6, 1864	Oath of Allegiance June 27, 1865
Young, Martin A. Private	Unk	April 13, 1863, Hendersonville, North Carolina	Co. D, 6th North Carolina Cavalry	June 22, 1864, Jackson's Mills, Near Kinston, North Carolina	Point Lookout, Maryland, transferred to Elmira Prison, NY, July 23, 1864	Died March 1, 1865 of Diarrhea, Grave No. 1994
Young, Preston B. Private	Unk	June 12, 1861, Red Sulfur Springs, Virginia	Co. F, 26th Battalion, Virginia Infantry	June 3, 1864, Gaines Farm, Cold Harbor, Virginia	Point Lookout, Maryland, transferred to Elmira Prison, NY, July 17, 1864	Oath of Allegiance July 3, 1865
Young, Robert J. Sergeant	34	February 27, 1862, Reidsville, North Carolina	Co. E, 45th North Carolina Infantry	May 10, 1864, Spotsylvania Court House, Virginia	Point Lookout, Maryland, transferred to Elmira Prison, NY, August 6, 1864	Exchanged March 10, 1865 at Boulware's Wharf on the James River, Virginia
Young, Thomas A. Private	Unk	December 28, 1861, Georgetown, South Carolina	Co. K, 21st South Carolina Infantry	July 10, 1863, Morris Island, South Carolina	Point Lookout, Maryland, transferred to Elmira Prison, NY, August 18, 1864	Exchanged October 29, 1864, at Venus Point, Savannah River, GA.
Young, Thomas B. Private	23	April 18, 1861, Jefferson Court House, Virginia	Co. A, 2nd Virginia Infantry	May 12, 1864, Near Spotsylvania Court House, Virginia	Point Lookout, Maryland, transferred to Elmira Prison, NY, August 6, 1864	Exchanged March 2, 1865 at Akins Landing on the James River, Virginia

Name & Rank	Age	Enlisted	Regiment and State	Where Captured	Prison	Remarks
Young, Wesley M. Private	21	May 9, 1862, Camp McIntosh, North Carolina	Co. J, 1st North Carolina Infantry	May 12, 1864, Wilderness Spotsylvania, Virginia	Point Lookout, Maryland, transferred to Elmira Prison, NY, August 6, 1864	Oath of Allegiance June 12, 1865
Young, William Franklin Corporal	23	July 15, 1862, Wake County, North Carolina	Co. H, 3rd North Carolina Infantry	May 12, 1864, Spotsylvania Court House, Virginia	Point Lookout, Maryland, transferred to Elmira Prison, NY, August 2, 1864	Died April 24, 1865 of Chronic Diarrhea, Grave No. 1406
Young, William H. Sergeant	32	April 25, 1862, Pee Dee Bridge, South Carolina	Co. K, 21st South Carolina Infantry	August 21, 1864, Weldon Railroad, Near Petersburg, Virginia. Gunshot Wound Left Leg.	DeCamp General Hospital, David's Island New York Harbor.	Exchanged March 14, 1865 at Boulware's Wharf on the James River, Virginia
Youngblood, Adam J. Private	Unk	May 18, 1862, Savannah, Georgia	Co. B, 7th Georgia Cavalry	June 11, 1864, Trevilian Station, Louisa Court House, Virginia	Point Lookout, Maryland, transferred to Elmira Prison, NY, July 25, 1864	Exchanged March 2, 1865 at Akins Landing on the James River, Virginia
Youngblood, Ira A. Private	18	August 10, 1861, Camp Butler, South Carolina	Co. D, D, 14th South Carolina Infantry	May 24, 1864, Wilderness, Virginia	Point Lookout, Maryland, transferred to Elmira Prison, NY, August 17, 1864	Died March 8, 1865 of Pneumonia, Grave No. 2368. Name S. A. Youngblood on Headstone.
Youngblood, John L. Private	Unk	August 23, 1862, Pike County, Alabama	Co. D, 5th Alabama Infantry	May 5, 1864, Wilderness, Virginia	Point Lookout, Maryland, transferred to Elmira Prison, NY, August 17, 1864	Exchanged October 29, 1864, at Venus Point, Savannah River, GA.
Youngblood, Nathanial M. Private	Unk	March 27, 1861, Elyton, Alabama	Co. C, 1st Battalion Alabama Artillery	August 23, 1864, Fort Morgan, Alabama	New Orleans, Louisiana transferred to Elmira Prison, NY, December 4, 1864.	Died December 28, 1865 of Variola (Smallpox), Grave No. 2132
Younger, William Private	33	March 5, 1862, Yanceyville, North Carolina	Co. J, 45th North Carolina Infantry	May 10, 1864, Spotsylvania Court House, Virginia	Point Lookout, Maryland, transferred to Elmira Prison, NY, August 6, 1864	Died January 25, 1865 of Peritonitis, Grave No. 1617

Name & Rank	Age	Enlisted	Regiment and State	Where Captured	Prison	Remarks
Zedaker, John Private	Unk	April 15, 1862, Charleston, South Carolina	Co. B, 18th South Carolina Infantry	July 30, 1864, Battle of the Crater, Petersburg, Virginia	Point Lookout, Maryland, transferred to Elmira Prison, NY, August 12, 1864	Oath of Allegiance May 17, 1865
Zehe, John H. Private	Unk	February 10, 1864, Bluffton, South Carolina	Co. E, 11th South Carolina Infantry	June 16, 1864, Petersburg, Virginia	Point Lookout, Maryland, transferred to Elmira Prison, NY, July 25, 1864	Died October 24, 1864 of Chronic Diarrhea, Grave No. 856
Zekiel, Aaron Private	Unk	July 1, 1862, Orangeburg, South Carolina	Co. G, 27th South Carolina Infantry	June 24, 1864, Near Petersburg, Virginia	Point Lookout, Maryland, transferred to Elmira Prison, NY, August 18, 1864	Exchanged March 14, 1865 at Boulware's Wharf on the James River, Virginia
Zell, James A. Private	22	March 1, 1862, Berryville, Virginia	Co. F, 7th Virginia Cavalry	September 14, 1863, Near Culpepper, Virginia	Point Lookout, Maryland, transferred to Elmira Prison, NY, August 18, 1864	Exchanged March 10, 1865 at Boulware's Wharf on the James River, Virginia
Zerr, George H. Private	Unk	June 6, 1861, New Orleans, Louisiana	Co. C, 14th Louisiana Infantry	May 12, 1864, Spotsylvania Court House, Virginia	Point Lookout, Maryland, transferred to Elmira Prison, NY, July 25, 1864	Exchanged February 13, 1865 at Boulware's wharf on the James River, Virginia
Zimbro, Robert Corporal	18	July 23, 1861, Staunton, Virginia	Co. H, 52nd Virginia Infantry	May 30, 1864, Mechanics-ville, Virginia	Point Lookout, Maryland, transferred to Elmira Prison, NY, July 9, 1864	Oath of Allegiance May 15, 1865
Zirkle, John E. Private	Unk	September 6, 1862, Pulaski, Georgia	Co. E, 30th Battalion Georgia Sharp Shooters	August 13, 1864, Winchester, Virginia	Old Capital Prison, Washington, DC transferred to Elmira Prison, NY, August 27, 1864	Oath of Allegiance May 15, 1865
Zollers, R. D. Sergeant	Unk	February 27, 1862, Charleston, South Carolina	Co. D, 5th South Carolina Cavalry	June 11, 1864, Trevilian Station, Louisa Court House, Virginia	Point Lookout, Maryland, transferred to Elmira Prison, NY, July 25, 1864	Exchanged October 29, 1864, at Venus Point, Savannah River, GA.

Name & Rank	Age	Enlisted	Regiment and State	Where Captured	Prison	Remarks
Unknown	Unk	Unknown	Unknown	Unknown	Unknown	Grave No. 1558
Unknown	Unk	Unknown	Unknown	Unknown	Unknown	Grave No. 1814
Unknown	Unk	Unknown	Unknown	Unknown	Unknown	Grave No. 2026
Unknown	Unk	Unknown	Unknown	Unknown	Unknown	Grave No. 2049
Unknown	Unk	Unknown	Unknown	Unknown	Unknown	Grave No. 2481
Unknown	Unk	Unknown	Unknown	Unknown	Unknown	Grave No. 2482
Unknown	Unk	Unknown	Unknown	Unknown	Unknown	Grave No. 2860

Deadly Civil War Diseases

All prison officials were either consciously or unconsciously guilty of promoting disease; whether this was due to overcrowding, which led to water pollution, or merely ignoring sick prisoners until they were too ill to save. Either way, they shared responsibility for the alarming number of deadly diseases in their prison.

The deadliest diseases that preyed upon the Elmira prisoners listed according to severity were: chronic diarrhea, pneumonia, variola (smallpox), and typhoid fever.[1]

After the war former prisoner William R. Greer wrote about the medical situation in Elmira, "In spite of all hygienic precautions, including an enforced vaccination, illness and mortality steadily increased. Pneumonia, typhoid, and smallpox simply raged even in the wards. The hospitals, being inadequate to meet the situation, the daily death rate of smallpox alone was registered as forty cases. Finally, I became ill, partly from exposure to the intense cold and from insufficient and improper food. I lay in my bunk without medical attention and was gradually sinking from sheer weakness and exhaustion."

Former prisoner Walter D. Addison wrote about the horrors of 19th century vaccinations in *The Southern Historical Collection of the North Carolina* at Chapel Hill. "The courageous manner in which men were vaccinated excelled anything I have ever witnessed even surpassing the acts of savages. The modus operandi was to assemble the men in long lines with coats off and arms bared; then the butchering began by illiterate and irresponsible men. They would take hold of a thick piece of flesh, dip a lancet into the diluted virus, and then thrust it entirely through the pinched-up flesh. The spurious virus soon produced such fearfully disastrous results that it became necessary to construct gangrene hospitals, from which arose a dreadful stench. Scores died from the effects; others losing arms. I have seen the sickening effects of their villainous vaccinations. There are many who can verify the above."[2]

Diarrhea

Chronic diarrhea was the leading cause of death at all military prisons during the Civil War. Diarrhea is a bacterial disease with severe abdominal discomfort, cramping and causes frequent, violent defecation which produces a liquid stool. The stools often contain mucus and may be blood streaked. The chronic diarrhea patient is likely to be anemic and suffering from malnutrition. One of the harmful effects of diarrhea is severe depletion of body fluids leading to an electrolyte imbalance. Electrolytes are essential minerals in your body that are necessary for nerve and muscle function and other critical processes. Potassium supply is especially depleted by diarrhea. Ignorant of germs, men in prison shared eating utensils which helped this disease to spread. During the Civil War diarrhea was treated with astringents, tonics and stimulants. Diarrhea claimed 1,454 lives making it number one on the list of Elmira's most deadly diseases.[3]

Reverend I. W. K. Handy, of the Presbyterian Church of Virginia, remembers what a difficult time men who suffered with chronic diarrhea had. "Sick men, perfectly emaciated from diarrhea, have been obliged to stagger through their quarters to the outhouse on the bank of the river, with filth streaming upon their legs; and then, unable to help themselves, they have fallen upon the pathway, and have been found dead in the morning. Barefooted, bareheaded and ragged men, tottering with disease, have been left to suffer long for the necessary clothing or medicines, which might have been abundantly supplied."[4]

"I was in the hospital myself a month with (diarrhea). Weakness and starvation had caused me to lose my sight, consequently often times when wandering some distance from our ward spots appeared before my eyes that I was dependent upon some kind comrade to lead me home. The blindness left me as I grew stronger. Others suffered the same way. Many times, a poor fellow staggered along until his old shaky legs fail to support him, and then he staggered until he was on his feet again with a ghastly smile trying to bear it bravely. It was touching to see the poor, ragged gaunt, half famished, much abused, noble fellows trying to be cheerful through it all."

Former prisoner Anthony M. Keiley wrote that diarrhea was so common that the disease affected everyone. "Visited all my comrades today, and, with one exception, found them all suffering like myself from exhausting diarrhea, induced by the poisonous water."[5]

Dysentery

Many prisoners died of chronic dysentery, but not at the alarming rate of diarrhea. Dysentery is a bacterial infection whose symptoms are intestinal inflammation especially that of the colon, abdominal pain and cramping, a high fever, chills, and frequent foul-smelling stools often containing blood and mucus. Quite often there is straining to evacuate the bowels and the stools are accompanied by a fluid discharge. Although commonly confused with diarrhea, this disease is caused by a different type of bacteria. Dysentery was spread by malnourished prisoners who shared eating utensils and water. Dysentery claimed 13 lives making it number 10 on the list of Elmira's most deadly diseases.[6]

Erysipelas

Erysipelas is a bacterial infection in the upper layer of the skin that normally only affects the legs or the face. It is a highly contagious disease that can cause death if left untreated. Also known as St. Anthony's fire, erysipelas is a disease which produces a fever, reddened, bumpy texture to the skin plus a fiery red rash with raised edges that can easily be distinguished from the skin around it. More severe infections can result in vesicles or pox-like marks on the infected areas. The symptoms include stinging and itching lesions, inflammation of the skin, vomiting, fever, headache and sore throat and sometimes complete prostration can occur. Erysipelas infections can enter the skin through minor trauma, such as a bruise, ulcer, burn, wound, or incision. Erysipelas claimed 14 lives making it number 9 on the list of Elmira's most deadly diseases.

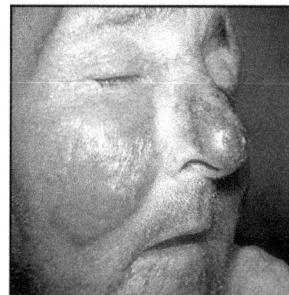

Facial Erysipelas on cheeks and nose.

Intermittent Fever

Intermittent fever has recurring elevated temperatures separated by intervals during which the temperature is normal at least once during a 24-hour period. A variation of intermittent fever is alternate day fever, which can occur in patients with malaria.

Typical symptoms include a high fever of 105°, headache, tiredness, fatigue and chills. In acute cases these symptoms become chronic, intensify, and result in death. Intermittent fever claimed the lives of 10 men making it the 11th most deadly disease at Elmira.[7]

Measles

Measles, also known as Rubeola, is a highly contagious, viral disease that produces a distinctive, three to five-day rash, 103° to 104° fever and swollen lymph nodes. It usually begins as flat red spots that appear on the face at the hairline and spread downward to the neck, trunk, arms, legs, and feet. Small, raised bumps may also appear on top of the flat red spots. The spots may become joined together as they spread from the head to the rest of the body. Often considered to be an early childhood disease it usually infected the younger soldiers and could possibly be deadly. This disease is caused by the rubella virus and is transmitted through contact with blood, urine, stools, or infected persons. Twenty prisoners died with measles making it number 8th on the list of Elmira's most deadly diseases.[8]

Pneumonia

Pneumonia is a severe bacterial infection of the lungs which often impairs gas exchange. This disease is characterized by a persistent cough, sharp chest pain, shortness of breath, blood-streaked or brownish sputum and a high fever. Pulse and respiration increase to almost twice their normal rates. Pneumonia frequently , one out of four victims. Often this illness got worse because of the poor prison diet. Due to the water pollution at the prison camp pneumonia has become closely linked to chronic diarrhea which robbed the victim of further nutrition. Pneumonia is closely linked to Typhoid fever and a description of this disease is found under Typhoid/Pneumonia. Pneumonia claimed 828 lives making it number two on the list of Elmira's most deadly diseases.[9]

Civil War soldiers were under tremendous stress when they got captured and went North to prison because they were constantly worried about what would become of them and their families. The men heard many horror stories from other soldiers who had were in prison and it was understandable the new men were frightened. A prisoner's ability to fight disease was weakened by stress, worry, a poor diet, inadequate water, clothing and shelter. Given all these sources for disease it was now possible for a simple cold to develop into pneumonia.

Remittent Fever

Elevated body temperature showing fluctuation each day, but never falling to normal. Fifty-one prisoners died of remittent fever making it the 5th most deadly disease at Elmira.[10]

Scurvy

Hundreds of years ago sailors at sea were commonly affected by a disease that attacked the gums and teeth. Doctors quickly diagnosed the problem as a lack of fresh fruit and vegetables containing vitamin C. By the time of the American Civil War scurvy was a well-known disease which could be easily prevented with a proper diet. There was absolutely no reason for the appearance of this disease in civil war prisons. The existence of scurvy was due to a callous disregard by prison officials for a prisoner's nutritional needs. Scurvy claimed 33 lives making the 7th on the list of Elmira's most deadly diseases.

A person suffering from scurvy has a serious lack of vitamin C in his system which is essential for the production of collagen, a substance that binds teeth and bones. Symptoms include weakness, swollen and bleeding gums, loose teeth, poor wound healing, black and blue spots on the skin and depression.[11]

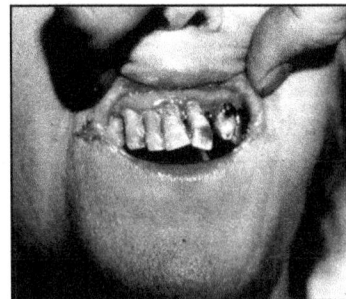

Scurvy victim suffering from bleeding, receding gums and loose teeth.

All prison officials were either consciously or unconsciously guilty of promoting disease; whether this was due to overcrowding, which led to water pollution, or merely ignoring sick prisoners until they were too ill to save. Either way, they shared responsibility for diseases in their prison. Scurvy, however, is unlike other diseases since it can be traced directly to prisoner's diet. Colonel William Hoffman, the Commissary General of Prisoners, insisted on controlling every aspect of a prisoner's life; whether it was shelter, clothing or diet. This being the case, the men's food was his responsibility. Hoffman could not plead ignorance of scurvy because he had been warned many times by prison commandants and surgeons about the presence of the disease.

Trying to combat scurvy the Federals added vinegar to the prisoner's diet. Since vinegar was made from fermented apple juice the liquid contained some vitamin C.

Former prisoner Luther Hopkins remembers the vinegar on his meals. "The dinners consisted of a tin cup of soup (generally bean or other vegetable), a small piece of meat on a tin plate, on which a little vinegar was poured to prevent scurvy."[12]

Another prisoner, Private Malachi Bowden remembers the Yankee antidote for scurvy. "They (prison officials) did allow us to draw a copious supply of vinegar. I ate this with my diet, and drank it with water, hoping that it might help to keep down the disease."[13]

Smallpox

Smallpox, also known as variola, is a highly contagious disease that is so severe 75% of the individuals who become infected do not survive. An over-crowded prison environment where the men have a poor diet and live in filthy conditions is a breeding ground for deadly diseases such as smallpox. Since the smallpox virus can live on clothing and blankets for up to 18 months, it spread with a vengeance inside the prison.[14]

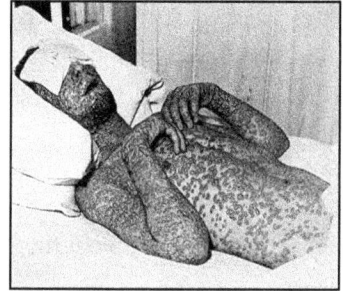
Smallpox victim

All though Smallpox cases were introduced to Elmira Prison camp in November 1864 most of the cases occurred in 1865. During this eight-month period smallpox claimed 381 lives at the prison making it the 3rd most deadly disease at Elmira prison camp. During this time many of the soldier's records never listed a cause of death. It is probable that many of these deaths were caused by smallpox.

Typhoid Fever

Typhoid fever is a bacterial disease, often referred to as remittent fever. Its symptoms includes abdominal tenderness headache, sweating, cough, high fever of 104°, bloody stool, confusion delirium and severe fatigue or weakness. Typhoid fever bacteria are deposited in water or food by a human carrier and then spread to other people in the area. Victims can develop a fever that may reach 105° and have a severe headache while lying exhausted with half-closed eyes in what is known as the typhoid state. Periods of chills and sweating may occur with a loss of appetite.

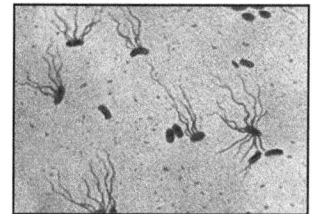
Typhoid Fever bacteria

Victims often become carriers and pass the bacteria to others through their urine and feces. Where sanitation is poor the organisms may enter the water supply.[15]

The victim's Typhoid fever can be closely linked to pneumonia and a description of this disease is located below. Twelve percent of typhoid fever victims die from the disease.

One hundred ninety-three prisoners died of typhoid fever making this the 4th deadly disease at El-mira.

Typhoid-Pneumonia

This condition occurs when a prisoner is already being ill with typhoid fever, and then develops pneumonia because of his weakened state. This not only complicates his diagnosis, but generally leads to his health deteriorating rapidly and usually resulting in death. Forty-eight prisoners died of typhoid-pneumonia making it the 6th deadly disease at Elmira.[16]

Civil War Medical Terminology

Disease	Description
Abcpsia	Blindness
Abscessus	A swollen, inflamed area of the body where pus gathers.
Acute	Severe
Aegrotantem	Illness, sickness
Ague	Recurring fever and chills of malaria.
Ambustio	A burn or scald
Anaemic	Suffering from anemia. Pale and sickly looking.
Anasarca	Generalized edema or dropsy. Medical condition characterized by widespread swelling of the skin due to a discharge of fluid usually caused by liver failure.
Anchylosis	A stiffening of the joints.
Aphonia	A loss of voice due to biological or psychological causes.
Apoplexy	Paralysis due to stroke. A stroke occurs when there is poor blood flow to the brain, usually caused by a blood clot, causing tissue to die.
Anasarca	A medical condition characterized by widespread swelling of the skin due to effusion of fluid in extremities is usually caused liver failure as well as severe malnutrition or protein deficiency.
Ascites	Accumulation of serous fluid in the abdominal cavity
Bad Blood	Syphilis
Bilious Fever	A term applied to certain intestinal and malarial fevers. Medical diagnosis thought to arise from stomach bile and accompanied by a fever and strong diarrhea. This may be caused by a liver disorder.
Black Death	Bubonic plague
Bloody Flux	Bloody stools caused by dysentery.
Brain Fever	Meningitis or typhus
Bright's Disease	Kidney disease

Camp Fever	Typhus is often referred to as camp fever because of the abundance of lice found in camp. Also see: Typhoid-Pneumonia
Catarrh	Inflammation of mucous membrane most commonly in the throat and nose, accompanied by an increased secretion mucous, sometimes accompanied by fever, or, rarely cerebral hemorrhage.
Cephalalgia	Headache
Cerebritis	Infection of the brain.
Cerebro Spinal Meningitis	Cerebro Spinal Meningitis is an inflammation of the membranes of both the brain and spinal cord.
Chilblain	Swelling of the extremities caused by exposure to cold.
Chin Cough	Whooping Cough
Chorea	Disease of the nervous system which is characterized by jerky, involuntary movements.
Chronic	Lasting three months or more.
Chronic Diarrhea	Chronic diarrhea is the condition of having at least three loose or liquid bowel movements each day and has lasted for at least four weeks. It can result in dehydration due to fluid loss. Signs of dehydration often begin with loss of the normal stretchiness of the skin and changes in personality. This can progress to decreased urination, loss of skin color, a fast heart rate, and a decrease in responsiveness as it becomes more severe. This disease is caused by the consumption of contaminated food and water which transmit bacteria and parasites to your body. Prisons with large populations and unsanitary conditions can lead to potentially deadly, large-scale epidemics of the disease.
Colica	Acute abdominal pains caused by abnormal condition of the bowel.
Congestion	An excessive accumulation of blood or other fluid in a body part or blood vessel. In congestive fever the internal organs become gorged with blood.
Congestiva	Excessive accumulation of blood in parts of the body.
Congestive	Relating to or affected by an abnormal collection of blood or other fluid Example: "congestive heart disease"
Congestive Chill	Indicating an unnatural accumulation of blood in some part of the body: as, a congestive chill.

Congestion of the Brain	This disease consists of an accumulation of blood in the cerebral tissue. It is caused by any impediment to the return of blood from the brain, such as a tumor of the neck, smallpox, heart disease or an injury such as a fall where the victim has a contusion of his head. This disease is the same as inflammation of the brain.
Congestive Fever	Malaria
Congestion of the Lungs	Pneumonia
Congestive Chills	Malaria with diarrhea
Conjunctivitis	Inflammation of the eye or eyelid.
Consecutiva	Unrelated illness following another.
Consumption	Tuberculosis. Consumption typically attacks the lungs but can also affect other parts of the body. It is spread through the air when people who have an active TB infection cough, or sneeze transmit respiratory fluids through the air. The classic symptoms of active TB infection are a chronic cough with blood-tinged sputum, fever, night sweats, and weight loss.
Continua	Without interruption.
Continued Fever	See Typhoid-Pneumonia.
Contusion	A bruise or injury where the skin is not broken.
Cramp Colic	Appendicitis
Crop Sickness	Overextended stomach
Croup	Laryngitis, diphtheria, or strep throat
Cystitis	Inflammation of the bladder.
Debilitas	Abnormal weakness or feebleness. The state of being unable to care for self.
Debility	Abnormal weakness or feebleness. The state of being unable to care for self.
Delirium Tremens	Hallucinations & seizures due to alcohol withdrawal.

Diarrhea, Chronic	Chronic diarrhea is the condition of having at least three loose or liquid bowel movements each day and this condition lasts for at least four weeks. It can result in dehydration due to fluid loss. Signs of dehydration often begin with loss of the normal stretchiness of the skin and changes in personality. This can progress to decreased urination, loss of skin color, a fast heart rate, and a decrease in responsiveness as it becomes more severe. This disease is caused by the consumption of contaminated food and water which transmit bacteria and parasites to your body. Prisons with large populations and unsanitary conditions can lead to potentially deadly large-scale epidemics of the disease.
Diphtheria	Contagious disease of the throat.
Dropsy of the Brain	Encephalitis, disease with acute onset of fever, headache, confusion, and sometimes seizures.
Dropsy	Edema, an abnormal accumulation of fluid in the tissue spaces, cavities, or joint capsules of the body, causing swelling of the area.
Dysentery	Inflammation of intestinal membrane
Encephalitis	Swelling of the brain
Enteritis	Inflammation of the bowels
Eruptive Diseases	Diseases that share like characteristics such as fever and eruptive blisters of the skin. These include Diphtheria, measles, Variola (Smallpox) and Typhoid Fever
Erysipelas	An acute infectious rash usually on any of the legs and toes, face, arms, and fingers characterized by inflammation of the skin. It appears as a red, swollen, warm, hardened, and painful rash similar in consistency to an orange peel. Symptoms include a fever, headache, fatigue, and chills.
Febris	Fever
Flux	Discharge of fluid from the body especially when excessive or abnormal: as in diarrhea.
Galloping Consumption	Pulmonary Tuberculosis
Gangrene	Gangrene is a potentially life-threatening condition that arises when a considerable mass of body tissue dies. This may occur after an injury or infection or poor blood circulation. Prisoners often develop gangrene after becoming frost bitten due to freezing weather.

Gangrene Oris	Also referred to as cancrum oris. Infection of the mouth or genitals brought on by malnutrition, poor hygiene, unsafe drinking water and recent illness. Mouth develops ulcers which can degrade the bones in the face. The disease is associated with high mortality.
Gastroenteritis	Gastroenteritis is a condition that causes irritation and inflammation of the stomach and intestines.
Glandular Fever	Mononucleosis. A sore throat where the patient's tonsils become swollen and develop a whitish-yellow covering. The lymph nodes in the neck are frequently swollen and painful.
Green Sickness	Anemia. Disease of the blood characterized by weakness, or fatigue, general malaise, and sometimes poor concentration.
Gripe	Influenza
Hemophthis	Spitting of blood.
Hemorrhia	Heavy Bleeding.
Herpes	An inflammatory virus disease of the skin or mucous membranes.
Hospital Fever	Commonly called Typhoid Fever. Also see Typhoid-Pneumonia.
Hospital Gangrene	An antiquated medical term that refers to a time in medicine where wound infection and pus were considered a normal part of wound healing. Civil War surgeons welcomed the sight of pus because it was believed at the time that patients must pass thru this stage of wound healing to restore health. Very often hospital gangrene was fatal because the patients were usually kept in crowded, unsanitary hospitals.
Hydrocephalus	Medical condition in which there is an abnormal accumulation of cerebrospinal fluid in the brain. This causes increased intracranial pressure inside the skull. Also known as water on the brain.
Hydrothorax	An abnormal amount of watery fluid in the cavity around the lungs.
Incised Wound	A clean cut, as by a sharp instrument.
Inflammation of the Brain	This disease consists of an accumulation of blood in the cerebral tissue. It is caused by any impediment to the return of blood from the brain, such as a tumor of the neck, smallpox, heart disease or an injury such as a fall where the victim has a contusion of his head. This disease is the same as congestion of the brain. May be due to encephalitis.
Inflammation of Lungs	Pneumonia

Inflammation of Pleura	An inflammation of the pleura, or pleurisy, which is the moist, double-layered membrane that surrounds the lung and lines the rib cage. The condition can make breathing extremely painful.
Intermittent	Stopping and starting, usually referring to Intermittent Fever.
Intermittent Fever	A malarial fever in which feverish periods lasting a few hours then alternate with periods in which the temperature is normal.
Intussusception of Bowel	Intussusception of bowel is a medical condition in which a part of the intestine has invaginated, or folded into itself creating a pocket, resulting in an obstruction.
Jail Fever	Typhus is a bacterial disease spread by lice or fleas. It is characterized Abdominal pain, headache, red rash, and high fever.
Jaundice	Yellowing of the skin due to liver dysfunction.
Lithiasis	Abnormal concretion, usually composed of mineral salts, occurring within the human body.
Lock Jaw	Tetanus. Prolonged muscle spasms that affect the jaw, chest, neck, back and abdominal muscles. Mortality rates reported vary from 48% to 73%.
Lumbago	Back Ache
Lung Fever	Pneumonia
Lung Sickness	Tuberculosis
Malaria	Malaria is a mosquito-borne infectious disease.
Malarial Fever	Fever caused by Malaria. Also known as intermittent or remittent fever where symptom-free periods can occur. These periods can be anywhere from a day to several days. The fever begins again followed by an intermittent period.
Mania	Insanity
Miasma	Poisonous vapors thought to infect the air.
Morbi Cutis	A skin disease
Moribund	Approaching death; About to die.
Morsal	Gangrene
Mortis	Death

Myelitis	Inflammation of the spine.
Myocarditits	Inflammation of the heart muscles.
Necrosis	Decay of bones or tissue, usually skin.
Nephritis	Inflammation of the kidneys.
Neuralgia	A stabbing, burning, and often quite severe pain that occurs along a damaged nerve.
Nostalgia	Disease marked by homesickness, melancholia and loss of appetite.
Ophthalmia	Relating to the eyes.
Orchitis	An inflammation of one or both testicles, most commonly associated with the virus that causes mumps.
Otalgia	Earache
Otilga	Earache
Palsy	Paralysis or loss of muscle control.
Pericariditis	Inflammation of the heart.
Paronychia	A painful, pus-producing inflammation at the end of a toe or finger
Parotitis	Mumps
Paroxysm	Convulsion
Peritoneum	The peritoneum is the serous membrane that forms the lining of the abdominal cavity.
Phlegmon	Inflammation, especially of the connective tissues, leading to ulceration or abscess.
Phrenic Nerve Congestion	The phrenic nerve is a nerve that originates in the neck (C3-C5) and passes down between the lung and heart to reach the diaphragm. It is important for breathing, as it passes motor information to the diaphragm and receives sensory information from it. There are two phrenic nerves, a left and a right one. When either of the nerves becomes swollen or inflamed the patient will have difficulty breathing.
Phrenitis	Inflammation of the brain
Phthisis	Consumption, Tuberculosis

Phthisis Pulmonalis	A wasting away of the body or any part as in tuberculosis or consumption.
Pleurisy	An inflammation of the pleura, which is the moist, double-layered membrane that surrounds the lung and lines the rib cage. The condition can make breathing extremely painful.
Pleuritis	Pleurisy, inflammation of the lining of the pleural cavity surrounding the lungs. Characterized by a sharp, stabbing pain in the chest that gets worse with deep breathing, coughing, sneezing, or laughing.
Pneumonia	Inflammatory condition of the lung affecting primarily the microscopic air sacs known as alveoli. This disease is usually caused by infection with viruses or bacteria.
Podagra	Gout
Pott's Disease	Tuberculosis of the spinal vertebrae.
Pox	Syphilis
Pulmonalis	Relating to the heart.
Putrid Fever	Typhus, so called from the decomposing and offensive state of the discharges and diseased textures of the body.
Purpura	Purpura is the appearance of red or purple discolorations on the skin that do not blanch on applying pressure. They are caused by bleeding underneath the skin.
Pyaemia	Widespread abscesses caused by pus-forming organisms in the blood.
Qyotidiana	A fever occurring or returning daily.
Remittent Fever	A fever that drops but does not altogether disappear. May be a misdiagnosis of typhoid fever.
Renal Affliction	Where the kidneys fail to filter waste products from the blood.
Rickets	Disease of the skeletal system.
Rheumatic Pericarditis	Inflammation and swelling of the pericardium (fibrous sac surrounding the heart) that occurs as a complication in people with rheumatism.
Rheumatism	Condition characterized by inflammation or pain in muscles, joints.
Rubeola	Measles
Scarlet Fever	Disease characterized by a red rash and sore.

Scorbutus	Also known as scurvy.
Screws	Rheumatism
Scrofula	Tuberculosis of the neck lymph nodes or lymphatic glands.
Scurvy	Scurvy is a disease resulting from a deficiency of vitamin C, or ascorbic acid, which is required for the synthesis of collagen in humans. Early symptoms of scurvy are malaise and lethargy, followed by formation of spots on the skin, poor wound healing, spongy gums, and bleeding from the mucous membranes. As scurvy advances, there can be accumulation of pus in wounds, loss of teeth, jaundice, fever, neuropathy and death.
Ship's Fever	Typhus
Softening of the Brain	Sudden impairment of neurological function, especially that resulting from a cerebral hemorrhage; a stroke.
Smallpox	Smallpox is a disease which is spread by close contact with the sores or respiratory droplets of an infected person. Since it is a viral disease smallpox first exhibits symptoms similar to influenza and the common cold. People with the disease have a fever of at least 101°, muscle pain, headache and severe fatigue. Since the digestive tract is often involved, nausea and vomiting and back ache often occur. A few days later, flat, red spots appear first on your face, hands and forearms, and later your trunk. Within a day or two, many of the lesions turn into small blisters filled with a clear fluid, which then turns into pus. Scabs begin to form eight to nine days later and eventually fall off, leaving deep, pitted scars. Since the smallpox virus can live on clothing and blankets for up to 18 months, it spreads with a vengeance inside the prison environment. This highly contagious disease is so severe 75% of the individuals who become infected to not survive.
Spotted Fever	Typhus, cerebrospinal meningitis fever.
St. Vitus Dance	Nervous twitches, chorea
Syncope	Fainting, losing consciousness indicating a more serious illness.
Tetanus	An infectious, often-fatal disease caused by a specific bacterium that enters the body through wounds.
Typhoid Fever	Typhoid fever, also known simply as typhoid, is a bacterial infection due to Salmonella typhi which causes symptoms. Symptoms include a high fever, weakness, abdominal pain, and headaches. This disease is caused by the consumption of food and water contaminated with the salmonella bacteria. Typhoid Fever is also known as hospital fever. *Medical and Surgical History of the Civil War, Volume V, Page 71*
Typhus	A bacterial infection that comes from lice or fleas on rats.

Typhoid-Pneumonia	Hybrid fever resulting from the combined influence of Typhoid Fever and Pneumonia. Also known as Typho-Malarial Fever and sometimes called Bilious Pneumonia, Camp Fever, Hospital Fever, Nervous Fever and Continued Fever. *Medical and Surgical History of the Civil War, Volume V, Page 71, 75-76.*
Typhus	Disease transmitted especially by body lice and is marked by high fever, stupor alternating with delirium, intense headache, and a dark red rash.
Variola	Smallpox
Venesection	Bleeding
Vulnus Incisum	Relating to a wound caused by a cut.
Vulnus Punctum	Relating to a wound caused by a puncture.
Vulnus Sclopeticum	Relating to a wound, typically a gunshot wound.
Vulnus	Relating to a wound.
Whitlow	Paronychia. A painful, pus-producing inflammation at the end of a toe or finger.
Winter Fever	Pneumonia
Yellow Jack	Yellow Fever

Elmira Prison Camp Monthly Returns

July 1864 to July 1865

Figures taken from Series II, Volume 8, Prisoners of War, pages 997-1003

Elmira Prison Camp	On Hand	Joined	Total	Exchange	Died	Escaped	Oath of Allegiance	Sick	Citizens
July 1864	0	4,424	4,424	0	11	2	0	177	48
August 1864	4,411	5,195	9,606	0	115	0	10	394	47
September 1864	9,480	0	9,480	0	385	0	13	563	47
October 1864	9,082	359	9,441	1,264	276	11	12	640	46
November 1864	7,878	380	8,258	0	207	1	23	666	78
December 1864	8,027	374	8,401	0	269	2	30	758	75
January 1865	8,100	502	8,602	0	285	0	20	1,015	69
February 1865	8,295	701	8,996	1,491	426	0	33	1,398	71
March 1865	7,046	56	7,102	1,518	491	0	39	823	56
April 1865	5,054	1	5,055	0	267	1	33	647	35
May 1865	4,754	131	4,885	0	131	0	1,144	509	34
June 1865	3,610	0	3,610	0	54	0	2,509	218	34
July 1865	1,047	0	1,047	0	16	0	889	0	0

Total Prisoners 12,121

Total Deaths Reported 2,933

Confederate Prisoners Who Died at Elmira Prison Camp and Have No Grave in Woodlawn, Cemetery, New York

	Name & Rank	Enlisted	Regiment And State	Where Captured	Prison	Remarks
1.	Austin, J. E. Private	July 16, Raleigh, North Carolina	Co. D, 5th North Carolina Infantry	May 5, 18, 1864 Spotsylvania Court House, Virginia	Point Lookout, Maryland, transferred to Elmira Prison, NY, July 6, 1864	Died March 19, 1865 of Variola (Smallpox). No Grave in Woodlawn National Cemetery.
	Bullard, John Isom Private	March 7, 1862, Cerro Gordo, Columbus County, North Carolina	Co. F, 36th Regiment 2nd North Carolina Artillery	January 15, 1865, Fort Fisher, North Carolina	February 1, 1865, Elmira Prison Camp, New York	Died February 27, 1865 of Pneumonia, No Grave Found in Woodlawn National Cemetery.
2.	Chambers, Rueben P. Corporal	March 18, 1862, Homer, Georgia	Co. A, 24th Georgia Infantry	August 16, 1864, Front Royal, Virginia	Old Capital Prison, Washington, DC transferred to Elmira Prison, NY, August 29, 1864	Died May 19, 1865 of Variola ((Smallpox). No Grave in Woodlawn National Cemetery.
3.	Clemmons, George M. Private	February 6, 1863, Fort Caswell, North Carolina	Co. G, 36th Regiment, 2nd North Carolina Artillery	January 15, 1865, Fort Fisher, North Carolina	January 30, 1865, Elmira Prison Camp, New York.	Died April 24, 1865 of Pneumonia. No Grave Found in Woodlawn National Cemetery.
4.	Cook, Joel Private	May 2, 1862, Jonesboro, Tennessee	Co. K, 63rd Tennessee Infantry	June 17, 1864, Petersburg, Virginia	Point Lookout, Maryland, transferred to Elmira Prison, NY, July 30, 1864	Died April 17, 1865 of Chronic Dysentery. No Grave Found in Woodlawn National Cemetery.
5.	Cruse, Rufus J. Sergeant	July 13, 1861, Salisbury, North Carolina	Co. K, 8th North Carolina Infantry	June 1, 1864, Gaines Farm, Cold Harbor, Virginia	Point Lookout, Maryland, transferred to Elmira Prison, NY, July 17, 1864	Died April 29, 1865 of Chronic Diarrhea. No Grave Found in Woodlawn National Cemetery.
	Darden Paul Private	September 1, 1864, Murfreesboro, Hertford County, North Carolina	Co. C, 3rd Battalion, North Carolina Light Artillery	January 15, 1865, Fort Fisher, North Carolina	February 1, 1865, Elmira Prison Camp, New York	Died of Pneumonia April 2, 1865. No Grave in Woodlawn National Cemetery.

	Name & Rank	Enlisted	Regiment And State	Where Captured	Prison	Remarks
6.	Early, Moses Citizen	Unknown	North Carolina Citizen	January 15, 1865, Fort Fisher, North Carolina	Elmira Prison Camp, New York, January 30, 1865	Died of Chronic Diarrhea February 12, 1865. Grave Not Found at Woodlawn Cemetery.
7.	Ezzel, Alexander H. Private	July 23, 1862, North Carolina	Co. G, 3rd North Carolina Infantry	May 12, 1864, Near Spotsylvania, Virginia	Point Lookout, Maryland, transferred to Elmira Prison, NY, August 14, 1864	Died May 23, 1865 of Chronic Diarrhea. No Grave Found in Woodlawn National Cemetery.
8.	Farmer, J. Private	Unknown	Co. H, 36th Regiment, 2nd North Carolina Artillery	January 15, 1865, Fort Fisher, North Carolina	Elmira Prison Camp, February 1, 1865	Died March 8, 1865 of Pneumonia. No Grave Found in Woodlawn National Cemetery.
9.	Foster, John B. Private	February 7, 1862, Gloucester Point, Virginia	Co. B, 26th Virginia Infantry	June 15, 1864, Near Petersburg, Virginia	Point Lookout, Maryland, transferred to Elmira Prison, NY, July 12, 1864	Died December 7, 1864 of Pneumonia. No Grave Found in Woodlawn National Cemetery.
10.	Furr, John B. Private	March 24, 1864, Wilmington, North Carolina	Co. K, 1st North Carolina Artillery	January 15, 1865, Fort Fisher, North Carolina	January 30, 1865, Elmira Prison Camp, New York	Died March 3, 1865 of Variola (Smallpox). No Grave Found in Woodlawn National Cemetery.
11.	Gordon, William J. Private	September 11, 1862, Calhoun, Georgia	Co. B, 24th Georgia Infantry	August 16, 1864, Front Royal, Virginia	Old Capital Prison, Washington, DC transferred to Elmira Prison, NY, August 29, 1864	Oath of Allegiance May 15, 1865. Died June 5, 1865 of Chronic Diarrhea. No Grave Found in Woodlawn National Cemetery.
12.	Hamington, J. L. Private	Unknown	Co. H, 13th North Carolina Cavalry	May 20, 1864, Spotsylvania Court House, Virginia	Point Lookout, Maryland, transferred to Elmira Prison, NY, July 6, 1864	Died February 7, 1865 of Smallpox. No Grave in Woodlawn National Cemetery.

	Name & Rank	Enlisted	Regiment And State	Where Captured	Prison	Remarks
	Herrell, J. G. Citizen	Unknown	North Carolina Citizen, Unknown	January 15, 1865, Fort Fisher, North Carolina	January 31, 1865, Elmira Prison, NY	Died of Variola (Smallpox) 4/18/1865, Grave Not at Woodlawn Cemetery
13.	Hoard, James Private	June 25, 1861, Plymouth, North Carolina	Co. H, 1st North Carolina Infantry	May 12, 1864, Spotsylvania, Virginia	Point Lookout, Maryland, transferred to Elmira Prison, NY, August 6, 1864	Died March 28, 1865 of Pneumonia. No Grave Found in Woodlawn National Cemetery.
14.	Gordon, William J. Private	September 11, 1862, Calhoun, Georgia	Co. B, 24th Georgia Infantry	August 16, 1864, Front Royal, Virginia	Old Capital Prison, Washington, DC transferred to Elmira Prison, NY, August 29, 1864	Died June 5, 1865 of Chronic Diarrhea. No Grave in Woodlawn National Cemetery.
15.	Ladd, T. M. Private	Unknown	Conscript	Unknown	Point Lookout, Maryland, transferred to Elmira Prison, NY, July 17,1864	Died February 14, 1865 of Chronic Diarrhea. No Grave at Woodlawn National Cemetery. Information from Elmira Prison Morning Report February 15, 1865.
16.	McCall, O. P. Private	Unknown	Co. H, 48th Georgia Infantry	May 6, 1864, Wilderness, Virginia	Point Lookout, Maryland, transferred to Elmira Prison, NY, August 14, 1864	Died March 13, 1865 of Chronic Diarrhea. No Grave in Woodlawn National Cemetery.
17.	McWatters, Ansil Private	January 14, 1862, Camp Hampton, South Carolina	Co. D, 17th South Carolina Infantry	July 30, 1864, Near Petersburg, Virginia	Point Lookout, Maryland, transferred to Elmira Prison, NY, August 12, 1864	Died February 20, 1865 of Variola (Smallpox). No Grave Found in Woodlawn National Cemetery.
18.	O'Brien, M. J. Private	April 30, 1861, Camp Moore, New Orleans, Louisiana	Co. H, 5th Louisiana Infantry	November 7, 1863, Rappahannock, Virginia	Point Lookout, Maryland, transferred to Elmira Prison, NY, July 12,1864	Died Unknown Month and Date 1865 of Unknown Disease. No Grave in Woodlawn National Cemetery.

	Name & Rank	Enlisted	Regiment And State	Where Captured	Prison	Remarks
19.	Parmer, John N. Private	May 21, 1863, Montgomery, Alabama	Co. A, 61st Alabama Infantry	May 12, 1864, Spotsylvania Court House, Virginia	Point Lookout, Maryland, transferred to Elmira Prison, NY, July 30, 1864	Died March 16, 1865 of Diarrhea. No Grave in Woodlawn National Cemetery.
20.	Price, Irvin Private	April 12, 1864, Raleigh, North Carolina	Co. E, 7th North Carolina Infantry	May 6, 1864, Wilderness, Virginia	Point Lookout, Maryland, transferred to Elmira Prison, NY, August 14, 1864	Died October 12, 1864 of Chronic Diarrhea. No Grave Found in Woodlawn National Cemetery.
21.	Quesenberry John Private	Unknown	Co. C, 50th Virginia Infantry	May 12, 1864, Spotsylvania Court House, Virginia	Point Lookout, Maryland, transferred to Elmira Prison, NY, August 2, 1864	Died February 13, 1865 of Chronic Diarrhea. No Grave Found in Woodlawn National Cemetery.
22.	Rivers, Jacob J. Private	June 10, 1861, Morgan, Georgia	Co. D, 12th Georgia Infantry	May 10, 1864, Spotsylvania Court House, Virginia	Point Lookout, Maryland, transferred to Elmira Prison, NY, July 30, 1864	Died March 22, 1865 of Variola (Smallpox). No Grave in Woodlawn National Cemetery.
23.	Sartin, Aaron H. Sergeant	December 9, 1861, Camp Trousdale, Tennessee	Co. K, 44th Tennessee Infantry	June 17, 1864, Petersburg, Virginia	Point Lookout, Maryland, transferred to Elmira Prison, NY, July 30, 1864	Died July 18, 1865 of Unknown Disease. No Grave Found in Woodlawn National Cemetery.
24.	Saussy, G. Nowlan Private	September 17, 1861, Savannah, Georgia	Co. F, Jeff Davis Legion	September 22, 1863, Near Madison Court House, Virginia	Point Lookout, Maryland, transferred to Elmira Prison, NY, August 18, 1864	Died February 25, 1865 of Variola (Smallpox). No Grave in Woodlawn National Cemetery.
25.	Sturgill, James Private	December 25, 1863, Liberty Mills, Virginia	Co. B, 37th North Carolina Infantry	May 12, 1864, Spotsylvania, Virginia	Point Lookout, Maryland, transferred to Elmira Prison, NY, August 12, 1864	Died March 19, 1865 of Pneumonia. No Grave Found in Woodlawn National Cemetery.

	Name & Rank	Enlisted	Regiment And State	Where Captured	Prison	Remarks
26.	Taylor, Robert E. Private	February 19, 1862, Entrenched Camp, Virginia	Co. E, 6th Virginia Infantry	May 12, 1864, Spotsylvania Court House, Virginia	Point Lookout, Maryland, transferred to Elmira Prison, NY, August 6, 1864	Died September 19, 1864 of Chronic Diarrhea. No Grave Found in Woodlawn National Cemetery.
27.	Tune, William Private	January 30, 1862, Newbern, Craven County, North Carolina	Co. F, 36th Regiment, 2nd North Carolina Artillery	January 15, 1865, Fort Fisher, North Carolina	February 1, 1865, Elmira Prison Camp, New York	Died March 31, 1865 of Variola (Smallpox), No Grave Found in Woodlawn Cemetery, NY

Soldiers that the author found in the Elmira arrival records but could not find in the Regimental Confederate soldier's records.

Name & Rank	Age	Enlisted	Regiment and State	Where Captured	Prison	Remarks
Allen, J. W. Private	Unk	Unable to Find Soldier's Regimental Records	Co. A, 1st Alabama Artillery	August 23, 1864, Fort Morgan, Alabama.	New Orleans, Louisiana transferred to Elmira Prison, NY, December 4, 1864.	Oath of Allegiance June 14, 1865
Barker, H. Private	Unk	Unable to Find Soldier's Regimental Records	Co. H, Thomas's Legion, No State	August 11, 1864, Winchester, Virginia	Point Lookout, Maryland, transferred to Elmira Prison, NY, August 29, 1864	Exchanged February 20, 1865 at Boulware's or Cox Wharf on the James River, Virginia
Bell, Elijah Private	Unk	Unable to Find Soldier's Regimental Record	Co. C, 3rd Virginia Cavalry	August 16, 1864, Front Royal, Virginia	Point Lookout, Maryland, transferred to Elmira Prison, NY, August 29, 1864	Exchanged March 14, 1865 at Boulware's Wharf on the James River, Virginia
Bims, J. Private	Unk	Unable to Find Soldier's Regimental Record	Co. ?, 24th Georgia Infantry	August 16, 1864, Front Royal, Virginia	Point Lookout, Maryland, transferred to Elmira Prison, NY, August 29, 1864	Oath of Allegiance June 27, 1865
Brannon, A. Y. F. Private	Unk	Unable to Find Soldier's Regimental Record	Co. A, 12th Battalion, Georgia infantry	August 8, 1864, Shepherdstown, Maryland	Point Lookout, Maryland, transferred to Elmira Prison, NY, August 18, 1864	Oath of Allegiance July 7, 1865
Brown, ? Private	Unk	Unable to Find Soldier's Regimental Record	Co. E, 7th Virginia Cavalry	October 31, 1864, Warren County, Virginia	Old Capital Prison, Washington, DC, transferred to Elmira Prison, NY, December 17, 1864	Died April ?, 1865 of Unknown Disease, Grave No. Unknown
Brown, W. Private	Unk	Unable to Find Soldier's Regimental Record	Co. D, 1st South Carolina R.	July 14, 1863, Falling Waters, Maryland	Point Lookout, Maryland, transferred to Elmira Prison, NY, August 18, 1864	Exchanged March 2, 1865 at Akins Landing on the James River, Virginia

Name & Rank	Age	Enlisted	Regiment and State	Where Captured	Prison	Remarks
Collier, J. Private	Unk	Unable to Find Soldier's Regimental Record	Co. A, 8th Texas Infantry	March 21, 1864, Natchitoches. Virginia	Old Capital Prison, Washington, DC transferred to Elmira Prison, NY, August 27, 1864	Oath of Allegiance May 21, 1865
Collins, C. P. Private	Unk	Unable to Find Soldier's Regimental Record	Cameron's Battalion Louisiana	September 13, 1864, Tensan Parish, Louisiana	New Orleans, Louisiana, Transferred to Fort Columbus, NY Harbor Transferred to Elmira Prison November 5, 1864	Exchanged February 25, 1865 at Boulware's or Cox Wharf on the James River, Virginia
Coweey, J. W. Private	Unk	Unable to Find Soldier's Regimental Record	Co. C, 1st Battalion Louisiana Infantry	October 6, 1864, Near Hampton's Ferry, Louisiana	New Orleans, Louisiana transferred to Elmira November 19, 1864.	Exchanged February 25, 1865 at Boulware's or Cox Wharf on the James River, Virginia
Craig, D. L. Private	Unk	Unable to Find Soldier's Regimental Record	Co. A, West Arkansas Battalion	September 19, 1864, Near Morganza, Louisiana	New Orleans, Louisiana, Transferred to Fort Columbus, NY Harbor Transferred to Elmira November 5, 1864	Oath of Allegiance December 29, 1864. Early Release per Lincoln's Proclamation, 12/8/1863.
Daly, B. N. Private	Unk	Unable to Find Soldier's Regimental Record	Co. H, Gober's Louisiana Cavalry	September 25, 1864, Near Morganza, Louisiana	New Orleans, Louisiana, Transferred to Fort Columbus, NY Harbor. Transferred to Elmira November 5, 1864	Oath of Allegiance July 7, 1865
Dodson, J. P. Private	Unk	Unable to Find Soldier's Regimental Record	Co. H, 15th Texas Infantry	August 19, 1864, Tensan Parish, Louisiana	New Orleans, Louisiana, Transferred to Fort Columbus, NY Harbor Transferred to Elmira November 5, 1864	Oath of Allegiance June 23, 1865

Name & Rank	Age	Enlisted	Regiment and State	Where Captured	Prison	Remarks
Dormick, Frederick Private	Unk	Unable to Find Soldier's Regimental Record	Captain Slayton's Macon Light Artillery, Georgia	July 15, 1864, Petersburg, Virginia	Old Capital Prison, Washington, DC transferred to Elmira Prison, NY, August 27, 1864	Exchanged February 25, 1865 at Boulware's or Cox Wharf on the James River, Virginia
Dullie, J. Private	Unk	Unable to Find Soldier's Regimental Record	Co. C, 4th Texas infantry	April 23, 1864, Cane River, Louisiana	New Orleans, Louisiana, Transferred to Elmira Prison, New York, November 19, 1864	Oath of Allegiance May 17, 1865
Grimes, G. W. Private	Unk	Unable to Find Soldier's Regimental Record	Co. A, Georgia Legion Infantry	June 6, 1864, Gaines Farms, Cold Harbor, Virginia	Point Lookout, Maryland, transferred to Elmira Prison, New York, July 17, 1864	Oath of Allegiance May 19, 1865
Flynn, J. B. Sergeant	Unk	Unable to Find Soldier's Regimental Record	Co. F, Powers Mississippi Regiment	August 25, 1864, Near Clinton, Louisiana	New Orleans, Louisiana, Transferred to Elmira Prison, New York, November 19, 1864	Exchanged February 25, 1865 at Boulware's or Cox Wharf on the James River, Virginia
H?, W. A. Private	Unk	Unable to Find Soldier's Regimental Record	Co. B, 24th Georgia Infantry	August 16, 1864, Front Royal, Virginia	Old Capital Prison, Washington, DC transferred to Elmira Prison, NY, August 29, 1864	Oath of Allegiance May 17, 1865
Hanna, John Private	Unk	Unable to Find Soldier's Regimental Record	Co. C, 7th State Not Legible	May 12, 1863, Raymond, Mississippi	Point Lookout, Maryland, transferred to Elmira Prison, NY, August 18, 1864	Exchanged March 14, 1865 at Boulware's Wharf on the James River, Virginia
Harris, G. P. Private	Unk	Unable to Find Soldier's Regimental Record	Fennog Battery State Unknown	October 6, 1864, Clinton, Louisiana	New Orleans, Louisiana transferred to Elmira November 19, 1864.	Exchanged February 25, 1865 at Boulware's or Cox Wharf on the James River, Virginia

Name & Rank	Age	Enlisted	Regiment and State	Where Captured	Prison	Remarks
Hartland, K. T. Private	Unk	Unable to Find Soldier's Regimental Record	Co. B, 16th Georgia Infantry	August 16, 1864, Front Royal, Virginia	Point Lookout, Maryland, transferred to Elmira Prison, NY, August 29, 1864	Exchanged March 14, 1865 at Boulware's Wharf on the James River, Virginia
Harwood, B. Private	Unk	Unable to Find Soldier's Regimental Record	Co. H, 30th Virginia Infantry	May 26, 1864, Port Royal, South Carolina	Point Lookout, Maryland, transferred to Elmira Prison New York, July 17, 1864	Transferred for exchange October 11, 1864. No Additional Information.
Hoggins, O. Private	Unk	Unable to Find Soldier's Regimental Record	Co. F, 6th Virginia Cavalry	September 14, 1863, Near Culpepper, Virginia	Point Lookout, Maryland, transferred to Elmira Prison, NY, August 18, 1864	Exchanged March 10, 1865 at Boulware's Wharf on the James River, Virginia
Kassler, John H. Private	Unk	Unable to Find Soldier's Regimental Record	Co. G, 11th Virginia Cavalry	August 19, 1864, Montgomery County, Virginia	Old Capital Prison, Washington, DC transferred to Elmira Prison, NY, August 29, 1864	Exchanged March 14, 1865 at Boulware's Wharf on the James River, Virginia
King, C. Private	Unk	Unable to Find Soldier's Regimental Record	Co. A, ? Cavalry	August 21, 1864, Grand Gal?, Louisiana	New Orleans, Louisiana, Transferred to Elmira Prison, New York, November 19, 1864	Exchanged February 13, 1865 at Boulware's wharf on the James River, Virginia
Knowlton, John W. Private	Unk	Unable to Find Soldier's Regimental Record	Co. E, 44th Georgia Infantry	July 12, 1864, Near Warrenton, Virginia	Old Capital Prison, Washington, DC transferred to Elmira Prison, NY, August 27, 1864	Exchanged February 13, 1865 at Boulware's wharf on the James River, Virginia
Lawrence, F. J. Private	Unk	Unable to Find Soldier's Regimental Record	King's Battery Louisiana Artillery	August 8, 1864, Tensan Parish, Louisiana	New Orleans, Louisiana, Transferred to Elmira Prison, New York, November 19, 1864	Exchanged February 20, 1865 at Boulware's or Cox Wharf on the James River, Virginia
Lynden-striker, J. H. Corporal	Unk	Unable to Find Soldier's Regimental Record	Co. J, 24th South Carolina Infantry	June 25, 1864, Near Petersburg Virginia	Unknown	Transferred for Exchange October 11, 1864. No Further Information.

Name & Rank	Age	Enlisted	Regiment and State	Where Captured	Prison	Remarks
Malfrass, T. D. Private	Unk	Unable to Find Soldier's Regimental Record	Co. E, 18th North Carolina Infantry	May 12, 1864, Spotsylvania, Virginia	Point Lookout, Maryland, transferred to Elmira Prison, New York, July 12, 1864	No Information Found.
Mastiller, W. W. Private	Unk	Unable to Find Soldier's Regimental Record	Co. C, 4th Virginia Cavalry	August 22, 1863, Prince William County, Virginia	Point Lookout, Maryland, transferred to Elmira Prison, NY, August 18, 1864	Transferred for Exchange October 11, 1864. Nothing Further.
Morgan, J. Private	Unk	Unable to Find Soldier's Regimental Record	Captain Guyol's Co. Louisiana Artillery	August 25, 1864, Near Clinton, Louisiana	New Orleans, Louisiana, Transferred to Elmira Prison, New York, November 19, 1864	Exchanged February 13, 1865 at Boulware's wharf on the James River, Virginia
Nicholas, W. L. Private	Unk	Unable to Find Soldier's Regimental Record	Regiment Not Legible. Virginia Cavalry	September 13, 1863, Near Culpepper Court House, Virginia	Point Lookout, Maryland, transferred to Elmira Prison, NY, August 18, 1864	Oath of Allegiance June 9, 1865
Palmer, J. A. Private	Unk	Unable to Find Soldier's Regimental Record	Co. G, 16th North Carolina Infantry	August 16, 1864, Front Royal, Virginia	Old Capital Prison, Washington, DC transferred to Elmira Prison, NY, August 29, 1864	Exchanged March 14, 1865 at Boulware's Wharf on the James River, Virginia
Penn, G. A. Private	Unk	Unable to Find Soldier's Regimental Record	Co. F, Powers Louisiana Regiment	August 25, 1864, Near Clinton, Louisiana	New Orleans, Louisiana, Transferred to Elmira Prison, New York, November 19, 1864	Exchanged February 25, 1865 at Boulware's or Cox Wharf on the James River, Virginia
Peters, J. H. Private	Unk	Unable to Find Soldier's Regimental Record	Co. A, 12th North Carolina Cavalry	September 14, 1863, Near Culpepper Court House, Virginia	Point Lookout, Maryland, transferred to Elmira Prison, NY, August 18, 1864	Exchanged March 10, 1865 at Boulware's Wharf on the James River, Virginia
Pine, William Private	Unk	Unable to Find Soldier's Regimental Record	Co. J, 18th Virginia Infantry	August 19, 1864, Point of Rocks, Maryland	Old Capital Prison, Washington, DC transferred to Elmira Prison, NY, August 27, 1864	Oath of Allegiance May 13, 1865

Name & Rank	Age	Enlisted	Regiment and State	Where Captured	Prison	Remarks
Regan, S. Private	Unk	Unable to Find Soldier's Regimental Record	Co. K, 13th Georgia Cavalry	May 5, 1864, Hanover Court House, Virginia	Point Lookout, Maryland, transferred to Elmira Prison, New York, July 17, 1864	Unknown
Reynolds, S. L. Private	Unk	Unable to Find Soldier's Regimental Record	Co. E, 26th Virginia Infantry	June 3, 1864, Gaines Farm, Cold Harbor, Virginia	Point Lookout, Maryland, transferred to Elmira Prison, New York, July 17, 1864	Unknown
Rice, J. F. Private	Unk	Unable to Find Soldier's Regimental Record	Co. E, 34th Texas Cavalry	August 25, 1864, Near Morganza, Louisiana	New Orleans, Louisiana, Transferred to Elmira Prison, New York, November 19, 1864	Oath of Allegiance June 19, 1865
Ruels, J. W. Private	Unk	Unable to Find Soldier's Regimental Record	Co. E, 31st North Carolina Infantry	June 1, 1864, Gaines Mill, Cold Harbor, Virginia	Transferred from Point Lookout Prison, Maryland, July 12, 1864. Train Never Arrived at Elmira Prison, New York.	Died July 15, 1864 in Train Wreck at Shohola, Pennsylvania.
Saitam, G. Private	Unk	Unable to Find Soldier's Regimental Record	Co. C, 3rd Battalion Georgia Infantry	August 16, 1864, Front Royal, Virginia	Old Capital Prison, Washington, DC transferred to Elmira Prison, NY, August 27, 1864	Exchanged March 14, 1865 at Boulware's Wharf on the James River, Virginia
Sanders, T. C. Private	Unk	Unable to Find Soldier's Regimental Record	Co. C, 7th Alabama Infantry	April 20, 1864, Milton, Louisiana	New Orleans, Louisiana, Transferred to Elmira Prison, New York, November 19, 1864	Died February 16, 1865 of Variola (Smallpox), Grave No. 2200. Headstone has Saunders.
Slaughter, S. H. Private	Unk	Unable to Find Soldier's Regimental Record	Co. K, 1st Texas Cavalry	August 6, 1864, Williamsport, Louisiana	New Orleans, Louisiana, Transferred to Elmira Prison, New York, November 19, 1864	Oath of Allegiance June 19, 1865

Name & Rank	Age	Enlisted	Regiment and State	Where Captured	Prison	Remarks
Smatley, G. C. Private	Unk	Unable to Find Soldier's Regimental Record	Co. C, Georgia Legion Infantry	June 1, 1864, Cold Harbor, Virginia	Transferred from Point Lookout Prison, Maryland, July 12, 1864. Train Never Arrived at Elmira Prison Camp, NY	Died July 15, 1864 in Train Wreck at Shohola, Pennsylvania
Smith, T. H. Private	Unk	Unable to Find Soldier's Regimental Record	Co. A, West Battery Louisiana Artillery	September 30, 1864, Near Morganza, Louisiana	New Orleans, Louisiana, Transferred to Elmira Prison, New York, November 19, 1864	Exchanged February 13, 1865 at Boulware's wharf on the James River, Virginia
Whitfield, B. Private	Unk	Unable to Find Soldier's Regimental Record	Stuart's Virginia Artillery	September 14, 1863, Kelly's Ford, Near Culpepper, Virginia	Point Lookout, Maryland, transferred to Elmira Prison, NY, August 18, 1864	Exchanged February 25, 1865 at Boulware's or Cox Wharf on the James River, Virginia
Wilson, E. J. Private	Unk	Unable to Find Soldier's Regimental Record	Co. K, 16th Virginia Infantry	August 16, 1864, Front Royal, Virginia	Old Capital Prison, Washington, DC transferred to Elmira Prison, NY, August 29, 1864	Exchanged March 2, 1865 at Akins Landing on the James River, Virginia

Elmira Prison's Confederate Soldiers Who Died During Exchange

Soldiers Listed by Exchange Date

Name	Enlisted	Regiment. State	Where Captured	Prison	Remarks
Exchange October 11, 1864					
Adams, Joshua J, Private	March 27, 1862, Surrey County, North Carolina	Co. J, 53rd North Carolina Infantry	July 13, 1864, Near Washington, DC,	Old Capital Prison, Washington, DC, transferred to Elmira July 23, 1864	Transferred for Exchange October 11, 1864, Died October 26, 1864 of Chronic Diarrhea at Point Lookout, Maryland
Allen, John A. Private	July 3, 1861, White Sulfur Springs, Virginia	Co. G, 22nd Virginia Infantry	June 3, 1864, Gaines Mill, Cold Harbor, Virginia	Point Lookout, Maryland, transferred to Elmira Prison, NY, July 17,1864	Transferred for Exchange October 11, 1864. Died October 17, 1864 of Unknown Disease at US Army Hospital, Baltimore, Maryland.
Brigman, John Private	September 16, 1863, Union County, North Carolina	Co. E, 30th North Carolina Infantry	May 31, 1864, Old Church, Virginia	Point Lookout, Maryland, transferred to Elmira Prison, NY, July 8, 1864	Transferred for Exchange October 11, 1864, Died October 24, 1864 of Chronic Diarrhea at Point Lookout, Maryland
Chewning, Booker P. Private	March 2, 1863, Centreville, Virginia	Co. F, 26th Battalion, Virginia Infantry	June 3, 1864, Gaines Farm, Cold Harbor, Virginia	Point Lookout, Maryland, transferred to Elmira Prison, NY, July 12, 1864	Transferred for Exchange October 11, 1864, Died of Unknown Causes October 13th at U. S. Army Hospital in Baltimore, Maryland
Davidson, William R. D. Private	July 8, 1861, Bristol, Tennessee	Co. F, 37th North Carolina Infantry	May 12, 1864, Spotsylvania, Virginia, Gunshot Wound Left Thigh	Old Capital Prison, Washington, DC, transferred to Elmira July 23, 1864	Transferred for Exchange October 11, 1864, Died October 27, 1864 of Typhoid Fever at Point Lookout, Maryland
Doughtie, Thomas Private	September 15, 1862, Camp Mangum, Raleigh, North Carolina	Co. B, 31st North Carolina Infantry	May 31, 1864, Cold Harbor, Virginia	Point Lookout, Maryland, transferred to Elmira Prison, NY, July 12, 1864	Transferred for Exchange October 11, 1864, Died October 20, 1864 of Chronic Diarrhea at Point Lookout, MD,

Name	Enlisted	Regiment. State	Where Captured	Prison	Remarks
Fletcher, John C. Sergeant	September 22, 1862, Waynesville, Georgia	Co. G, 7th Georgia Cavalry	June 11, 1864, Travillian Station, Louisa Court House, Virginia	Point Lookout, Maryland, transferred to Elmira Prison, NY, July 25, 1864	Transferred for Exchange October 11, 1864. Died October 20, 1864 of Unknown Disease at Point Lookout Prison, Maryland.
Giles, William Private	June 1, 1861, Lock's Creek, North Carolina	Co. E, 8th North Carolina Infantry	May 31, 1864, Cold Harbor, Virginia	Point Lookout, Maryland, transferred to Elmira Prison, NY, July 12, 1864	Transferred for Exchange October 11, 1864. Hospitalized Baltimore U. S. Army Hospital, MD, Died April 29, 1865, of Debility
Gilpin, John Private	August 8, 1863, Tazewell County, Virginia	Co. B, 22nd Virginia Cavalry	July 16, 1864, Loudon County, Virginia	Old Capital Prison, Washington, DC, Transferred to Elmira July 23, 1864	Transferred for exchange October 11, 1864, Died October 13, 1864 at US Army General Hospital, Baltimore, Maryland
Gordon, James M. Sergeant	September 19, 1861, Kittrells, North Carolina	Co. J, 2nd North Carolina Cavalry	September 16, 1863, Culpepper, Virginia	Old Capital Prison, Washington, DC, transferred to Elmira July 23, 1864	Transferred for Exchange October 11, 1864. Died October 25, 1864 of Chronic Diarrhea Point Lookout, Maryland.
Johnson, John W. Private	May 21, 1863, Camp Instruction, Virginia	Co. I, 26th Battalion, Virginia Infantry	June 3, 1864, Gaines Mill, Cold Harbor, Virginia	Point Lookout, Maryland, transferred to Elmira Prison, NY, July 17, 1864	Transferred for Exchange October 11, 1864, Died in Steamship Northern Light
Lester, John H. Private	April 15, 1864, Macon County, Georgia	Co. J, 7th Georgia Cavalry	June 11, 1864, Travillian Station, Louisa Court House, Virginia	Point Lookout, Maryland, transferred to Elmira Prison, NY, July 25, 1864	Transferred for Exchange October 11, 1864. Died October 26, 1864 of Chronic Diarrhea at Point Lookout Prison, Maryland

Name	Enlisted	Regiment. State	Where Captured	Prison	Remarks
Lively, Joseph A. Private	September 4, 1863, Camp Sam Jones, Virginia	Co. H, 26th Battalion, Virginia Infantry	June 3, 1864, Gaines Farm, Cold Harbor, Virginia	Point Lookout, Maryland, transferred to Elmira Prison, NY, July 17, 1864	Transferred for Exchange October 11, 1864, Died October 19, 1864 at U. S. Army General West Hospital, Baltimore, Maryland
McDonald, Franklin M. Private	April 23, 1864, Petersburg, Virginia	Co. F, 51st North Carolina Infantry	June 1, 1864, Cold Harbor, Virginia	Point Lookout, Maryland, transferred to Elmira Prison, NY, July 12, 1864	Transferred for Exchange October 11, 1864 at Akins Landing on the James River, Virginia, Died October 27, 1864 of Chronic Diarrhea at Point Lookout, MD
McDonald, John C. Private	June 1, 1864, Tazewell County, Virginia	Co. J, 16th Virginia Infantry	July 10, 1864, Frederick, Maryland	Old Capital Prison, Washington, DC, transferred to Elmira July 23, 1864	Transferred for Exchange October 11, 1864. Died Point Lookout November 23, 1864 of Chronic Diarrhea.
McGrady, John W. Private	June 1, 1864, Carroll, Virginia	Co. F, 25th Virginia Cavalry	July 6, 1864, Harper's Ferry, Virginia	Old Capital Prison, Washington, DC, transferred to Elmira July 23, 1864	Transferred for Exchange October 11, 1864. Died October 27, 1864 of Chronic Diarrhea at Point Lookout Prison, Maryland
Miller, Robert J. Private	February 15, 1862, Warsaw, North Carolina	Co. B, 51st North Carolina Infantry	June 1, 1864, Cold Harbor, Virginia	Point Lookout, Maryland, transferred to Elmira Prison, NY, July 12, 1864	Transferred for Exchange October 11, 1864. Died October 23, 1864 of Chronic Diarrhea at Point Lookout, MD
Moody, Samuel S. Private	September 22, 1862, Waynesville, Georgia	Co. G, 7th Georgia Cavalry	June 11, 1864, Travillian Station, Louisa Court House, Virginia	Point Lookout, Maryland, transferred to Elmira Prison, NY, July 25, 1864	Transferred for Exchange October 29, 1864. Died October 26, 1864 of Chronic Diarrhea at Point Lookout Prison, Maryland.

Name	Enlisted	Regiment. State	Where Captured	Prison	Remarks
Moore, James A. Sergeant	May 12, 1862, Camp Holmes, North Carolina	Co. A, 51st North Carolina Infantry	June 1, 1864, Gaines Mill, Virginia	Point Lookout, Maryland, transferred to Elmira Prison, NY, July 12, 1864	Transferred for Exchange October 11, 1864, Died October 31, 1864 of Unknown Causes at Fort Monroe, Virginia
Myers, Evan Thomas Private	April 16, 1862, Near Mount Jackson, Virginia	Co. I, 2nd Virginia Infantry	May 24, 1864, South Anna, Virginia	Point Lookout, Maryland, transferred to Elmira Prison, NY, July 9, 1864	Transferred for Exchange October 11, 1864, Died November 3, 1864 at Fort Monroe of Unknown Causes.
Patterson, John E. Private	March 9, 1863, Fayetteville, North Carolina	Co. E, 8th North Carolina Infantry	May 31, 1864, Cold Harbor, Virginia	Point Lookout, Maryland, transferred to Elmira Prison, NY, July 12,1864	Transferred for Exchange October 11, 1864. Died October 30, 1864 of Unknown Disease at Fort Monroe, Virginia.
Phillips, Levi W. Private	September 16, 1861, Meriwether County, Georgia	Co. A, 60th Georgia Infantry	May 20, 1864, Spotsylvania Court House, Virginia	Point Lookout, Maryland, transferred to Elmira Prison, NY, July 3, 1864	Transferred for Exchange October 11, 1864, Died October 22, 1864 at Point Lookout, Maryland
Pitman, Isham Private	May 5, 1862, Camp Holmes, New Hanover, North Carolina	Co. E, 51st North Carolina Infantry	June 1, 1864, Cold Harbor, Virginia	Point Lookout, Maryland, transferred to Elmira Prison, NY, July 12, 1864	Transferred for Exchange October 11, 1864 at Akins Landing on the James River, Virginia, Died November 2, 1864 at Fort Monroe, Virginia
Rice, Thomas C. Private	July 27, 1861, Big Island, Virginia	Co. C, 58th Virginia Infantry	May 20, 1864, Spotsylvania Court House, Virginia	Point Lookout, Maryland, transferred to Elmira Prison, NY, July 3, 1864	Transferred for Exchange October 11, 1864. Died November 2, 1864 of Chronic Diarrhea at US Army Hospital, Baltimore, Maryland
Roberts, Stephen Private	May 19, 1862, Fredrickburg, Virginia	Co. E, 16th Georgia Infantry	June 1, 1864, Cold Harbor, Virginia	Point Lookout, Maryland, transferred to Elmira Prison, NY, July 12, 1864	Transferred for Exchange October 11, 1864, Died October 22, 1864, of Unknown Disease

Name	Enlisted	Regiment. State	Where Captured	Prison	Remarks
Shaw, John A. Private	March 5, 1862, Lumber Bridge, North Carolina	Co. D, 51st North Carolina Infantry	June 16, 1864, Near Petersburg, Near Bermuda Hundred, Virginia	Point Lookout, Maryland, transferred to Elmira Prison, NY, July 12, 1864	Transferred for Exchange October 11, 1864. Died October 14, 1864 of Unknown Causes, U. S. Army General Hospital, Baltimore, MD
Soloman, Thomas F. Private	February 1, 1862, Salisbury, North Carolina	Co. C, 42nd North Carolina Infantry	June 1, 1864, Gaines Farm, Cold Harbor, Virginia	Point Lookout, Maryland, transferred to Elmira Prison, NY, July 12, 1864	Transferred October 11, 1864 for Exchange, Died October 20, 1864 of Chronic Diarrhea at Point Lookout, Maryland
Sullivan, Adam Private	April 15, 1862, Wilmington, North Carolina	Co. C, 51st North Carolina Infantry	June 1, 1864, Cold Harbor, Virginia	Point Lookout, Maryland, transferred to Elmira Prison, NY, July 12, 1864	Transferred for Exchange October 11, 1864. Died October 18, 1864 of Consumption at Point Lookout, Maryland
Talbert, Thomas J. Private	May 11, 1861, New Orleans, Louisiana	Co. A, 2nd Louisiana Infantry	May 20, 1864, Spotsylvania Court House, Virginia	Point Lookout, Maryland, transferred to Elmira Prison, NY, July 3, 1864	Exchanged October 11, 1864, Died October 21, 1864 of Unknown Disease at Point Lookout Prison Camp, Maryland
Walker, William F. Private	February 28, 1862, Goldsboro, North Carolina	Co. C, 52nd North Carolina Infantry	May 22, 1864, Near Hatteras Mills, Edenton, North Carolina	Point Lookout, Maryland, transferred to Elmira Prison, NY, July 23, 1864	Transferred for Exchange October 11, 1864. Died January 27, 1865 of Chronic Diarrhea at Point Lookout Prison Camp, Maryland
Wingate, W. H. Private	September 22, 1862, Waynesville, Georgia	Co. G, 7th Georgia Cavalry	June 11, 1864, Travillian Station, Louisa Court House, Virginia	Point Lookout, Maryland, transferred to Elmira Prison, NY, July 25, 1864	Transferred for Exchange October 11, 1864. Died October 21, 1864 of Chronic Diarrhea at Point Lookout Prison Camp, Maryland
Exchange February 13, 1865					

Name	Enlisted	Regiment. State	Where Captured	Prison	Remarks
Martin, Simeon Private	September 21, 1863, Lewisburg, Virginia	Co. A, 26th Battalion, Virginia Infantry	June 3, 1864, Gaines Farm, Cold Harbor, Virginia	Point Lookout, Maryland, transferred to Elmira Prison, NY, July 12, 1864	Exchanged February 13, 1865. Died March 10, 1865 of Chronic Diarrhea at Chimborazo Hospital No. 2, Richmond, Virginia
Parker, Joseph Private	June 28, 1862, Poplar Springs, Hall County, Georgia	Co. J, 24th Georgia Infantry	June 1, 1864, Cold Harbor, Virginia	Point Lookout, Maryland, transferred to Elmira Prison, NY, July 1 I 2, 1864	Exchanged February 13, 1865. Died March 8, 1865 of Rheumatism at Jackson Hospital, Richmond, Virginia
Price, Eli P. Private	July 5, 1861, Halifax County, North Carolina	Co. J, 8th North Carolina Infantry	June 1, 1864, Cold Harbor, Virginia	Point Lookout, Maryland, transferred to Elmira Prison, NY, July 12, 1864	Exchanged February 13, 1865. Died March 3, 1865 at Howard's Grove General Hospital, Richmond, Virginia
Exchange February 20, 1865					
Barwick, George W. Private	Charleston, SC, 5/18/1862	Co. I, 25th South Carolina Infantry	January 15, 1865, Fort Fisher, North Carolina	January 30, 1865, Elmira Prison Camp, New York	Exchanged 2/20/1865 On James River, VA, Died 3/10/1865 from Debility & Frostbite at Howard's Grove General Hospital, Richmond, VA
Bonnet, D. D. Private	March 1, 1864, Columbia, South Carolina	Co. D, 25th South Carolina Infantry	January 15, 1865, Fort Fisher, North Carolina	Elmira Prison Camp January 30, 1865	Exchanged February 20, 1865. Died March 7, 1865 of Chronic Diarrhea at Hospital No. 9, Richmond, VA
Bray, D. C. K. Private	March 5, 1862 Wilmington, North Carolina	Co. D, 40th Regiment, 3rd North Carolina Heavy Artillery	January 15, 1865, Fort Fisher, North Carolina	February 1, 1865, Elmira Prison Camp, New York	Exchanged February 20, 1865. Died March 6, 1865 of Chronic Diarrhea at General Hospital, Richmond, Virginia.

Name	Enlisted	Regiment. State	Where Captured	Prison	Remarks
Buie, William N. Sergeant	Wilmington, New Hanover County NC, 11/5/1861,	3rd Co. B, 36th Regiment North Carolina, 2nd Artillery	January 15, 1865, Fort Fisher, North Carolina	January 30, 1865, Elmira Prison Camp, New York	Exchanged on the James River, VA, 2/20/1865, Died of Variola (smallpox), 4/27/1865, Marine USA Hospital, Baltimore, MD
Caler, J. E. Private	April 12, 1862, Battery Island, South Carolina	Co. C, 25th South Carolina Infantry	January 15, 1865, Fort Fisher, North Carolina	January 30, 1865, Elmira Prison Camp, New York	Died on the Route to be Exchanged February 20, 1865
Cannon, Archibald Private	New Hanover County, NC, 2/27/1862,	2nd Co. D, 36th Regiment North Carolina, 2nd Artillery	January 15, 1865, Fort Fisher, North Carolina	February 1, 1865, Elmira Prison Camp, New York	Exchanged on the James River, VA, 2/20/1865, Admitted Howard Grove Hospital, Richmond, VA, 3/11/1865, Died of Pneumonia, 3/11/1865
Chambers, James G. Private	October 4, 1864, Wilmington, North Carolina	Co. K, 10th Regiment, 1st North Carolina Artillery	January 15, 1865, Fort Fisher, North Carolina	January 31, 1865, Elmira Prison Camp, NY	Died on the Route to be Exchanged February 20, 1865.
Clayton, William W. Private	Coles Island, SC, 4/11/1862	Co. F, 25th South Carolina Infantry	January 15, 1865, Fort Fisher, North Carolina	January 30, 1865, Elmira Prison Camp, New York	Exchanged 2/20/1865, Died Chronic Diarrhea 3/26/1865, USA General Hospital, Baltimore, MD
Crawley, Hider D. Private	February 18, 1862, Newbern, North Carolina	Co. F, 36th Regiment, 2nd North Carolina Artillery	January 15, 1865, Fort Fisher, North Carolina. Wounded	February 1, 1865, Elmira Prison Camp, New York	Died on Route to be Exchanged February 20, 1865.
Crumpler, Micajah H. Private	July 23, 1863, New Hanover County, North Carolina	Co. G, 40th Regiment, 3rd North Carolina Artillery	January 15, 1865, Fort Fisher, North Carolina	February 1, 1865, Elmira Prison Camp, New York	Transferred for Exchange February 20, 1865. Died February 21, 1865 of Unknown Disease on Route to be Exchanged.
Dillard, S.H. Private	September 1, 1864, Sampson County, North Carolina	Co. D, 1st Battalion North Carolina Heavy Artillery	January 15, 1865, Fort Fisher, North Carolina. Wounded.	February 1, 1865, Elmira Prison Camp, New York	Exchanged February 20, 1865. Died March 8, 1865 of Typhoid Fever at CSA Hospital, Richmond, VA.

Name	Enlisted	Regiment. State	Where Captured	Prison	Remarks
Ethridge, Ransom Private	August 19, 1863, Brunswick County, North Carolina	Co. F, 36th Regiment 2nd North Carolina Artillery	January 15, 1865, Fort Fisher, North Carolina	February 1, 1865, Elmira Prison Camp, New York	Exchanged February 20, 1865. Died April 6, 1865 of Chronic Diarrhea, at Jackson Hospital, Richmond, Virginia
Gallaher, John Private	February 11, 1863, Abingdon, Virginia	Co. L, 26th Battalion Virginia Infantry	June 3, 1864, Gaines Farm, Cold Harbor, Virginia	Point Lookout, Maryland, transferred to Elmira Prison, NY, July 12, 1864	Exchanged February 20, 1865. Died March 12, 1865 of Phthisis Pulmonalis at Chimborazo Hospital No.2, Richmond, VA
Garner, William J. Private	January 25, 1864, James Island, South Carolina	Co. C, 25th South Carolina Infantry	January 15, 1865, Fort Fisher, North Carolina	January 30, 1865 Elmira Prison Camp, New York	Exchanged February 20, 1865. Died Of Unknown Disease 3/9/1865 In Howard's Grove Hospital, Richmond, VA
Gregg, W. W. Private	August 31, 1863, Marion, South Carolina	Co. J, 21st South Carolina Infantry	January 15, 1865, Fort Fisher, North Carolina	January 30, 1865, Elmira Prison Camp, New York	Exchanged February 20, 1865. Died March 3, 1865 of Unknown Causes, Brought from Flag Of Truce Boat Dead.
Hodges, Elihue S. Private	January 1, 1862, Camp Harlee, Georgetown, South Carolina	Co. I, 25th South Carolina Infantry	January 15, 1865, Fort Fisher, North Carolina	January 30, 1865, Elmira Prison Camp, New York	Exchanged February 20, 1865. Died March 4, 1865 at Richmond Wayside Hospital #9, VA.
Holden, Richard W. Private	August 24, 1863, Fort Caswell, Brunswick County, North Carolina	Co. G, 36th Regiment 2nd North Carolina Artillery	January 15, 1865, Fort Fisher, North Carolina	Elmira Prison Camp February 1, 1865. Gunshot Wound Right Breast.	Exchanged February 20, 1865. Died March 12, 1865 of Variola (Smallpox) at Howard Grove Hospital, Richmond, Virginia.

Name	Enlisted	Regiment. State	Where Captured	Prison	Remarks
Joyner, James H. Private	May 16, 1862, Fort St. Philip, Brunswick County, North Carolina	Co. G, 36th Regiment 2nd North Carolina Artillery	January 15, 1865, Fort Fisher, North Carolina	Elmira Prison Camp February 1, 1865	Exchanged February 20, 1865. Died March 20, 1865 of Unknown Disease at Pettigrew Hospital, Raleigh, North Carolina
Kite, Andrew J. Private	June 1, 1861, Luray, Page County, Virginia	Co. H, 33rd Virginia Infantry	July 8, 1864, Harper's Ferry, Virginia	Old Capital Prison, Washington, DC, transferred to Elmira July 23, 1864	Exchanged February 20, 1865. Died March 7, 1865 of Chronic Diarrhea at Chimborazo Hospital No. 2, Richmond, Virginia
Lewis, Alexander J. Private	April 16, 1862, Fort St. Philips, North Carolina	Co. G, 36th Regiment North Carolina Artillery	January 15, 1865, Fort Fisher, North Carolina	February 1, 1865, Elmira Prison Camp, New York	Exchanged February 20, 1865. Died March 20, 1865 of Pneumonia at General Hospital No. 8, Raleigh, North Carolina
Long, Lillington D. Private	February 3, 1862, Elizabethtown, Bladen County, North Carolina	Co. J, 36th Regiment North Carolina Artillery	January 15, 1865, Fort Fisher, North Carolina	February 1, 1865, Elmira Prison Camp, New York	Exchanged February 20, 1865. Died April 2, 1865 of Unknown Disease at Howard's Grove Hospital, Richmond, Virginia.
McDuffie, Henry F. Private	July 16, 1862, Fort St. Philips, North Carolina	Co. K, 40th Regiment, 3rd North Carolina Artillery	January 15, 1865, Fort Fisher, North Carolina	Elmira Prison Camp February 1, 1865	Died February 20, 1865 of Unknown Disease on Boat to be Exchanged.
McLean, Weston G. Sergeant	February 28, 1862, Lumberton, North Carolina	Co. E, 51st North Carolina Infantry	June 1, 1864, Cold Harbor, Virginia	Point Lookout, Maryland, transferred to Elmira Prison, NY, July 12, 1864	Exchanged February 20, 1865. Died March 12, 1865 of Chronic Diarrhea at Jackson Hospital, Richmond, Virginia
McMillan, Daniel Private	August 12, 1864, Fort Caswell, Brunswick County, North Carolina	Co. C, 3rd Battalion North Carolina Light Artillery	January 15, 1865, Fort Fisher, North Carolina	February 1, 1865, Elmira Prison Camp, New York	Exchanged February 20, 1865. Died of Unknown Disease on Route to be Exchanged.

Name	Enlisted	Regiment. State	Where Captured	Prison	Remarks
Mercer, Absalum Private	May 5, 1864, Fort Caswell, Brunswick County, North Carolina	Co. A, 36th 2nd North Carolina Artillery	January 15, 1865, Fort Fisher, North Carolina	February 1, 1865, Elmira Prison Camp, New York	Died February 20, 1865 of Unknown Disease on Route to be Exchanged.
Mints, Stephen Private	April 16, 1862, Old Brunswick, North Carolina	Co. G, 36th 2nd North Carolina Artillery	January 15, 1865, Fort Fisher, North Carolina	February 1, 1865, Elmira Prison Camp, New York	Exchanged February 20, 1865. Died March 20, 1865 of Unknown Disease at Howard Grove Hospital, Richmond, Virginia
Murphy, James W. Private	June 25, 1863, Fort Johnson, North Carolina	Co. G, 40th Regiment, 3rd North Carolina Artillery	January 15, 1865, Fort Fisher, North Carolina	Elmira Prison Camp February 1, 1865	Exchanged February 20, 1865. Died March 16, 1865 of Chronic Diarrhea at Jackson Hospital, Richmond, Virginia
Prevatt, Henry C. Private	May 1, 1862, Camp Holmes, New Hanover, North Carolina	Co. E, 51st North Carolina Infantry	June 1, 1864, Cold Harbor, Virginia	Point Lookout, Maryland, transferred to Elmira Prison, NY, July 12, 1864	Exchanged February 20, 1865. Died March 27, 1865 at Howard's Grove General Hospital, Richmond, Virginia
Smith, Robert Private	April 5, 1862, Elizabethtown, Bladen County, North Carolina	Co. H, 36th Regiment 2nd North Carolina Artillery	January 15, 1865, Fort Fisher, North Carolina	February 1, 1865, Elmira Prison Camp, New York	Died February 20, 1865 of Unknown Disease on Route to be Exchanged.
Spears, Josiah W. Private	July 6, 1861, Salisbury, North Carolina	Co. K, 8th North Carolina Infantry	May 31, 1864, Cold Harbor, Virginia	Point Lookout, Maryland, transferred to Elmira Prison, NY, July 12, 1864	Transferred for Exchange February 20, 1865. Died March 12, 1865, at C. S. A. Hospital, Richmond, Virginia
Strock, Emery B. Private	April 13, 1864, James Island, South Carolina	Co. F, 25th South Carolina Infantry	January 15, 1865, Fort Fisher, North Carolina	January 30, 1865, Elmira Prison Camp, New York,	Exchanged February 20, 1865. Died March 16, 1865 at Jackson Hospital, Richmond, Virginia.

Name	Enlisted	Regiment. State	Where Captured	Prison	Remarks
Thally, David J. Private	April 16, 1862, Old Brunswick Town, North Carolina	Co. G, 36th Regiment, 2nd North Carolina Artillery	January 15, 1865, Fort Fisher, North Carolina	February 1, 1865, Elmira Prison Camp, New York	Exchanged February 20, 1865. Died April 9, 1865 of Bronchitis at Confederate States Hospital, No. 11, Charlotte, North Carolina
Wells, Alfred M. Private	Unknown	Co. G, 36th Regiment, 2nd North Carolina Artillery	January 15, 1865, Fort Fisher, North Carolina	February 1, 1865, Elmira Prison Camp, New York	Exchanged February 20, 1865. Died March 5, 1865 of Variola (Smallpox) at US Army Hospital, Bermuda Hundred, Virginia
Williams, Amos Private	March 7, 1862, Wilmington, New Hanover County, North Carolina	Co. E, 36th Regiment, 2nd North Carolina Artillery	January 15, 1865, Fort Fisher, North Carolina	February 1, 1865, Elmira Prison Camp, New York	Died February 20, 1865 on Route to be Exchanged.
Williams, Isaac W. Private	March 5, 1863, Fort Caswell, Brunswick County, North Carolina	Co. E, 40th Regiment, 3rd North Carolina Artillery	January 15, 1865, Fort Fisher, North Carolina. Wounded	February 1, 1865, Elmira Prison Camp, New York	Exchanged February 20, 1865. Died March 12, 1865 of Chronic Diarrhea at Confederate States Army Hospital, Richmond, Virginia.
Williams, Wilson Private	July 24, 1861, Newland, North Carolina	Co. A, 8th North Carolina Infantry	June 1, 1864, Cold Harbor, Virginia	Point Lookout, Maryland, transferred to Elmira Prison, NY, July 12, 1864	Exchanged February 20, 1865. Died March 8, 1865 of Typhoid Fever at Jackson Hospital, Richmond, Virginia
Wright, James D. Private	January 18, 1864, Brunswick County, North Carolina	Co. F, 36th Regiment, 2nd North Carolina Artillery	January 15, 1865, Fort Fisher, North Carolina	February 1, 1865, Elmira Prison Camp, New York	Exchanged February 20, 1865. Died May 28, 1865 of Variola (Smallpox) at Jackson Hospital, Richmond, Virginia.

Name	Enlisted	Regiment. State	Where Captured	Prison	Remarks
Wyatt, James I. Private	July 22, 1861, Salisbury, North Carolina	Co. K, 8th North Carolina Infantry	June 1, 1864, Gaines Farm, Cold Harbor, Virginia	Point Lookout, Maryland, transferred to Elmira Prison, NY, July 12, 1864	Exchanged February 20, 1865. Died March 27, 1865 of Debility at Jackson General Hospital, Richmond, Virginia
Exchange March 2, 1865					
Burroughs, Thomas J. Private	July 18, 1861, Camp Pickens, Stanardsville, Virginia	Co. D, 34th, Virginia Infantry	June 15, 1864, Near Petersburg, Virginia	Point Lookout, Maryland, transferred to Elmira Prison, NY, July 12, 1864	Transferred for Exchange March 2, 1865, Died of Scurvy March 16, 1865 at Chimborazo Hospital #2, Richmond, Virginia
Campbell, William A. Private	Wilmington, New Hanover County, NC, 11/5/1861, Mustered in at Wilmington, Volunteer	3rd Co. B, 36th Regiment North Carolina, 2nd Artillery	January 15, 1865, Fort Fisher, North Carolina	February 1, 1865, Elmira Prison Camp, New York	Exchanged on the James River, VA, March 2, 1865, Admitted Hospital, Richmond, VA, Died 3/9/1865 Cause Unknown
Ford, John H. Private	March 15, 1864, Fort Fisher, New Hanover, North Carolina	Co. G, 36th Regiment, 2nd North Carolina Artillery	January 15, 1865, Fort Fisher, North Carolina	Elmira Prison Camp February 1, 1865	Exchanged March 2, 1865. Died May 2, 1865 of Typhoid Fever at Jackson Hospital Richmond, Virginia
Godwin, Joel G. Private	May 1, 1862, Fayetteville, Georgia	Co. C, 53rd Georgia Infantry	June 1, 1864, Gaines Mill, Cold Harbor, Virginia	Point Lookout, Maryland, transferred to Elmira Prison, NY, July 17, 1864	Transferred for Exchange March 2, 1865, Died May 3, 1865 at Jackson Hospital, Richmond, Virginia
Grady, Lewis H. Private	July 13, 1863, Duplin County, North Carolina	Co. G, 40th Regiment, 3rd North Carolina Artillery	January 15, 1865, Fort Fisher, North Carolina	Elmira Prison Camp February 1, 1865	Exchanged March 2, 1865. Died March 15, 1865 of Pneumonia at Jackson Hospital, Richmond, Virginia.

Name	Enlisted	Regiment. State	Where Captured	Prison	Remarks
Grub, Absalom Private	October 15, 1862, Raleigh, North Carolina	Co. K, 42nd North Carolina Infantry	June 3, 1864, Gaines Mill, Cold Harbor, Virginia	Point Lookout, Maryland, transferred to Elmira Prison, NY, July 17, 1864	Transferred for Exchange March 2, 1865, Died April 5, 1865 of Debility at Jackson Hospital, Richmond, Virginia
Jackson, Alfred Webb Private	October 25, 1863, Fort Fisher, North Carolina	Co. E, 36th Regiment 2nd North Carolina Artillery	January 15, 1865, Fort Fisher, North Carolina	Elmira Prison Camp February 1, 1865	Exchanged March 2, 1865. Died March 24, 1865 of Chronic Diarrhea at Way Station Hospital No. 1, Weldon, North Carolina.
Johnson, William F. Private	October 28, 1861, Wilmington, North Carolina	Co. E, 36th Regiment 2nd North Carolina Artillery	January 15, 1865, Fort Fisher, North Carolina	Elmira Prison Camp February 1, 1865	Exchanged March 2, 1865. Died March 9, 1865 of Chronic Diarrhea at Moore Hospital, Richmond, Virginia
Kerr, William D. Sergeant	May 2, 1862, Camp Morgan, North Carolina	Co. A, 51st North Carolina Infantry	June 1, 1864, Gaines Mill, Virginia	Point Lookout, Maryland, transferred to Elmira Prison, NY, July 12, 1864	Exchanged March 2, 1865. Died March 17, 1865 of Debilitas at Jackson Hospital, Richmond, Virginia
Legrand, Julius C. Private	March 8, 1864, Fort Fisher, North Carolina	Co. J, 36th Regiment North Carolina Artillery	January 15, 1865, Fort Fisher, North Carolina	February 1, 1865, Elmira Prison Camp, New York	Exchanged March 2, 1865. Died March 10, 1865 of Chronic Diarrhea-Typhoid Fever at Wayside Hospital No. 9, Richmond, Virginia.
Love, Thomas J. Serfgeant	September 19, 1861, Red Springs, Robeson County, North Carolina	Co. E, 40th Regiment, 3rd North Carolina Artillery	January 15, 1865, Fort Fisher, North Carolina	February 1, 1865, Elmira Prison Camp, New York	Exchange March 2, 1865. Died March 15, 1865 of Chronic Diarrhea at General Hospital No. 8, Raleigh, North Carolina
Marsh, Neill Private	September 20, 1863, Cumberland County, North Carolina	Co. B, 36th 2nd North Carolina Artillery	January 15, 1865, Fort Fisher, North Carolina	February 1, 1865, Elmira Prison Camp, New York	Exchanged March 2, 1865. Died March 19, 1865 of Typhoid-Pneumonia at Pettigrew Hospital, Raleigh, North Carolina.

Name	Enlisted	Regiment. State	Where Captured	Prison	Remarks
McMasters, Wesley W. Private	May 25, 1863, Asheboro, North Carolina	Co. G, 40th Regiment, 3rd North Carolina Artillery	January 15, 1865, Fort Fisher, North Carolina	January 30, 1865, Elmira Prison Camp, New York.	Exchanged 3/2/1865, Died of Remittent Fever 3/18/1865 At Jackson Hospital, Richmond, VA, Buried in Hollywood Cemetery, VA
Moore, James Private	October 6, 1863, Dobson, North Carolina	Co. C, 21st North Carolina Infantry	July 10, 1864, Harper's Ferry, Virginia	Old Capital Prison, Washington, DC, transferred to Elmira July 23, 1864	Exchanged March 2, 1865. Died April 15, 1865 of Typhoid Fever at Jackson Hospital, Richmond, VA. Buried at Hollywood Cemetery, VA
Owens, Thomas S. Private	June 7, 1861, Middle Sound, New Hanover County, North Carolina	Co. E, 1st North Carolina Infantry	May 12, 1864, Near Spotsylvania Court House, Virginia	Point Lookout Prison, Maryland. Transferred to Elmira Prison Camp New York August 6, 1864.	Exchanged March 2, 1865. Died April 19, 1865 of Typhoid Fever at Jackson Hospital, Richmond, Virginia.
Pattishall, Z. G. Private	April 6, 1863, Chatham County, North Carolina	Co. E, 8th North Carolina Infantry	June 1, 1864, Gaines Mill, Cold Harbor, Virginia	Point Lookout, Maryland, transferred to Elmira Prison, NY, July 17,1864	Exchanged March 2, 1865. Died March 15, 1865 of Unknown Disease at Jackson Hospital, Richmond, Virginia
Perdue, William Private	April 22, 1863, Fort Johnson, Smithville, North Carolina	Co. G, 40th Regiment, 3rd North Carolina Artillery	January 15, 1865, Fort Fisher, North Carolina	January 30, 1865, Elmira Prison Camp, New York,	Exchanged March 2, 1865. Died April 5, 1865 of Chronic Diarrhea at Pettigrew Hospital, No. 13, Raleigh, North Carolina.
Perry, Wiley N. Private	January 28, 1862, Bladen County, North Carolina	Co. B, 36th Regiment, 2nd North Carolina Artillery	January 15, 1865, Fort Fisher, North Carolina	February 1, 1865, Elmira Prison Camp, New York	Exchanged March 2, 1865. Died March 15, 1865 of Typhoid Fever at Moore Hospital, Richmond, Virginia

Name	Enlisted	Regiment. State	Where Captured	Prison	Remarks
Powell, Warren T. Private	September 24, 1861, Roberson County, North Carolina	Co. E, 40th 3rd Regiment North Carolina Artillery	January 15, 1865, Fort Fisher, North Carolina	February 1, 1865, Elmira Prison Camp, New York	Exchanged March 2, 1865. Died April 24, 1865 of Chronic Diarrhea at Jackson Hospital, Richmond, Virginia
Ray, John P. Private	April 8, 1864, Madison, Florida	Co. 8th Florida Infantry	May 25, 1864, North Anna River, Virginia	Point Lookout, Maryland, transferred to Elmira Prison, NY, July 9, 1864	Exchanged March 2, 1865. Died October 13, 1864 of Unknown Disease at USA General Hospital, Baltimore, MD
Reece, Alfred C. Private	October 6, 1861, Milton County, Georgia	Co. D, 38th Georgia Infantry	May 20, 1864, Spotsylvania Court House, Virginia	Point Lookout, Maryland, transferred to Elmira Prison, NY, July 3, 1864	Exchanged March 2, 1865. March 11, 1865 of Chronic Diarrhea at Wayside Hospital No. 9, Richmond, Virginia
Shuler, F. P. H. Private	April 11, 1862, Coles Island, South Carolina	Co. F, 25th South Carolina Infantry	January 15, 1865, Fort Fisher, North Carolina	January 30, 1865, Elmira Prison Camp, New York,	Exchanged March 2, 1865. Died April 7, 1865 at Jackson Hospital, Richmond, Virginia.
White, James S. Private	August 27, 1862 Jefferson County, Alabama	Co. A, 21st Alabama Infantry	August 23, 1864 Fort Morgan, Alabama	New Orleans, Louisiana. Transferred to Elmira October 8, 1864	Exchanged March 2, 1865. Died March 7, 1865 of Chronic Diarrhea at Wayside Hospital #9, Richmond, Virginia.
Exchange March 14, 1865					
Davis, Edward W. Private	Fort St. Philip, Brunswick County, NC, 7/7/1862,	2nd Co. K, 40th Regiment, 3rd North Carolina Light Artillery	January 15, 1865, Fort Fisher, North Carolina	January 30, 1865, Elmira Prison Camp, New York	Exchanged 3/14/1865, Died of Consumption 5/17/1865, Richmond, Jackson Hospital, VA. Buried Hollywood Cemetery, VA

Name	Enlisted	Regiment. State	Where Captured	Prison	Remarks
Nugent, James Private	July 15, 1863, Mobile, Alabama	Co. F, 6th Louisiana Infantry	July 8, 1864, Harper's Ferry, Virginia	Old Capital Prison, Washington, DC, transferred to Elmira July 23, 1864	Exchanged March 14, 1865. Died May 17, 1865 at Shreveport General Hospital, Louisiana
Barrett, Franklin Private	April 27, 1861, Cleveland County, North Carolina	Co. C, 15th North Carolina Infantry	June 2, 1864, Near Talapatomoy Creek, Old Church, Virginia	Point Lookout, Maryland, transferred to Elmira Prison, NY, July 17, 1864	Exchanged March 14, 1865, Hospitalized for Pneumonia & Scurvy, March 19, 1865, Jackson Hospital, Richmond, Virginia
Edwards, Fern D. Private	September 4, 1861, Columbus, Georgia	Co. A, 31st Georgia Infantry	May 12, 1864, Spotsylvania, Virginia	Old Capital Prison, Washington D. C. Transferred to Elmira Prison, NY, August 28, 1864	Exchanged March 14, 1865. Died March 27, 1865 of Pneumonia at Wayside General Hospital No. 9, Richmond, Virginia
Grantham, John Q. Private	December 11, 1864, Fort Holmes, Brunswick County, North Carolina	Co. E, 40th Regiment, 3rd North Carolina Artillery	January 15, 1865, Fort Fisher, North Carolina	February 1, 1865, Elmira Prison Camp, New York	Exchanged March 14, 1865. Died April 5, 1865 of Typhoid Fever at Jackson Hospital, Richmond, Virginia
Hewitt, Allen Private	April 25, 1864, Decatur, Georgia	Co. E, 12th Georgia Infantry	July 12, 1864, Near Washington, DC	Old Capital Prison, Washington, DC, transferred to Elmira July 23, 1864	Exchanged March 14, 1865. Died March 12, 1865 of Intermittent Fever at Jackson Hospital Richmond, Virginia
Hodges, John H. Private	September 1, 1863, Robison County, North Carolina	Co. B, 36th Regiment 2nd North Carolina Artillery	January 15, 1865, Fort Fisher, North Carolina	Elmira Prison Camp February 1, 1865	Exchanged March 14, 1865. Died March 27, 1865 of Chronic Diarrhea at CSA Way Hospital, Greensboro, NC
Legrand, Hosmar Private	September 14, 1863, Fort Fisher, North Carolina	Co. J, 36th Regiment North Carolina Artillery	January 15, 1865, Fort Fisher, North Carolina	February 1, 1865, Elmira Prison Camp, New York	Transferred for Exchange. Died March 8, 1865 of Chronic Diarrhea-Typhoid Fever on Steamer to be Exchanged.

Name	Enlisted	Regiment. State	Where Captured	Prison	Remarks
Rawls, Joseph A. Private	August 3, 1864 at St. Johns, North Carolina	Co. C, 3rd Battalion North Carolina Light Artillery	January 15, 1865, Fort Fisher, North Carolina	February 1, 1865, Elmira Prison Camp, New York	Exchanged March 14, 1865. Died March 31, 1865 at Jackson Hospital, Richmond, VA
Sikes, Lucian Private	May 12, 1862, Fort Fisher, New Hanover County, North Carolina	Co. J, 36th Regiment, 2nd North Carolina Artillery	January 15, 1865, Fort Fisher, North Carolina	February 1, 1865, Elmira Prison Camp, New York	Exchange March 14, 1865. Died April 7, 1865 of Debility at Jackson Hospital, Richmond, Virginia

Died Shortly After Taking the Oath of Allegiance

Name & Rank	Enlisted	Regiment and State	Where Captured	Prison	Remarks
McEwen, Archibald Daniel Corporal	May 6, 1862, Elizabethtown, Bladen County, North Carolina	Co. K, 40th Regiment, 3rd North Carolina Artillery	January 15, 1865, Fort Fisher, North Carolina	February 1, 1865, Elmira Prison Camp, New York	Oath of Allegiance June 12, 1865. Died June 19, 1865 of Chronic Diarrhea at Manchester, Virginia
Thaggard, James B. Private	March 15, 1863, Fort Fisher, New Hanover County, North Carolina	Co. C, 36th Regiment North Carolina, 2nd Artillery	January 15, 1865, Fort Fisher, North Carolina	February 1, 1865, Elmira Prison Camp, New York	Oath of Allegiance June 12, 1865. Died of Chronic Diarrhea June 27, 1865 at USA Hospital in City Point, Virginia.
Thally, David J. Private	April 16, 1862, Old Brunswick Town, North Carolina	Co. G, 36th Regiment, 2nd North Carolina Artillery	January 15, 1865, Fort Fisher, North Carolina	February 1, 1865, Elmira Prison Camp, New York	Exchanged 2/20/65. Died 4/9/65 of Bronchitis at Confederate States Hospital, No. 11, Charlotte, NC

Confederate Prisoners Who Died in the Shohola, PA, Train Wreck

The Confederate Soldiers On This List Were Being Transferred on July 12, 1864, From Point Lookout Prison Camp, MD, To Elmira Prison Camp, NY, When the Train Crashed. There Were Many Discrepancies Found On The Monument In Woodlawn National Cemetery Which Prompted Me To Make This List. Two Men With Injuries Were Added Because They Later Died at Elmira Due to Their Injuries They Received In The Wreck. One Man Was Added To This List Because He Was Missing From the Woodlawn Cemetery Monument.

List Compiled by Richard H. Triebe

1.	Adams, Joseph Private	Unk	May 25, 1863, Camp Holmes, North Carolina	Co. A, 51st North Carolina Infantry	June 1, 1864, Cold Harbor, Virginia	Transferred From Point Lookout Prison, MD, July 12, 1864. Train Never Arrived at Elmira Prison Camp, NY.	Died July 15, 1864, in Train Accident at Shohola, Pennsylvania.
2.	Baker, Jesse E. Private	Unk	May 1, 1862, Nichol's Depot, South Carolina	Co. F, 51st North Carolina Infantry	June 1, 1864, Cold Harbor, Virginia	Transferred From Point Lookout Prison, MD, July 12, 1864. Train Never Arrived at Elmira Prison Camp, NY.	Died July 15, 1864, in Train Accident at Shohola, Pennsylvania.
3.	Baxley, John W. Private	Unk	March 11, 1863, Charleston, South Carolina	Co. E, 31st North Carolina Infantry	June 1, 1864, Gaines Farm, Cold Harbor, Virginia	Transferred From Point Lookout Prison, MD, July 12, 1864. Train Never Arrived at Elmira Prison Camp, NY.	Died July 15, 1864, in Train Accident at Shohola, Pennsylvania.
4.	Bessent, James H. Corporal	Unk	March 9, 1863, James Island, South Carolina	Co. G, 51st North Carolina Infantry	June 3, 1864, Gaines Mill, Cold Harbor, Virginia	Transferred From Point Lookout Prison, MD, July 12, 1864. Train Never Arrived at Elmira Prison Camp, NY.	Died July 15, 1864, in Train Accident at Shohola, Pennsylvania.
5.	Biggs, Resden Private Name on Monument Spelled Briggs	23	September 6, 1861, Lumberton, North Carolina	Co. A, 31st North Carolina Infantry	June 1, 1864, Gaines Farm, Cold Harbor, Virginia	Transferred From Point Lookout Prison, MD, July 12, 1864. Train Never Arrived at Elmira Prison Camp, NY.	Died July 15, 1864, in Train Accident at Shohola, Pennsylvania.

6.	Bird, John S. Private	Unk	November 25, 1862, Floyd Court House, Virginia	Co. I, 26th Battalion Virginia Infantry	June 3, 1864, Gaines Farm, Cold Harbor, Virginia	Transferred From Point Lookout Prison, MD, July 12, 1864. Train Never Arrived at Elmira Prison Camp, NY.	Died July 15, 1864, in Train Accident at Shohola, Pennsylvania.
7.	Bowers, William Private	Unk	August 8, 1862, Davidson County, North Carolina	Co. B, 48th North Carolina Infantry	June 3, 1864, Near Talapatomoy Creek, Cold Harbor, Virginia	Transferred From Point Lookout Prison, MD, July 12, 1864. Train Never Arrived at Elmira Prison Camp, NY.	Died July 15, 1864, in Train Accident at Shohola, Pennsylvania.
8.	Bright, John W. Private	Unk	April 30, 1864, Lewisburg, Virginia	Co. A, 26th Battalion, Virginia Infantry	June 3, 1864, Gaines Mill, Cold Harbor, Virginia	Transferred From Point Lookout Prison, MD, July 12, 1864. Train Never Arrived at Elmira Prison Camp, NY.	Died July 15, 1864, in Train Accident at Shohola, Pennsylvania.
9.	Bryant, Travis Private First Name on Monument Spelled Travers	Unk	March 5, 1862, Cumberland County, North Carolina	Co. J, 51st North Carolina Infantry	June 1, 1864, Cold Harbor, Virginia	Transferred From Point Lookout Prison, MD, July 12, 1864. Train Never Arrived at Elmira Prison Camp, NY.	Died July 15, 1864, in Train Accident at Shohola, Pennsylvania.
10.	Calahan, C. Private Name on Monument Spelled Callehan	Unk	Unknown	Co. C, 10th Virginia Cavalry	June 3, 1864, Gaines Farm, Cold Harbor, Virginia	Transferred From Point Lookout Prison, MD, July 12, 1864. Train Never Arrived at Elmira Prison Camp, NY.	Died July 15, 1864, in Train Accident at Shohola, Pennsylvania.
11.	Campbell, John Private	25	June 19, 1861, Camp Moore, Tangipaho, Louisiana	Co. D, 8th Louisiana Infantry	May 12, 1864, Spotsylvania Court House, Virginia	Transferred From Point Lookout Prison, MD, July 12, 1864. Train Never Arrived at Elmira Prison Camp, NY.	Died July 15, 1864, in Train Wreck at Shohola, Pa. Grave No. 2852. Headstone has 3rd Regiment

12.	Carroll, John W. Private Last Name on Monument Spelled Cary	25	April 4, 1862, Cumberland County, North Carolina	Co. I, 51st North Carolina Infantry	June 1, 1864, Cold Harbor, Virginia	Point Lookout, Maryland, transferred to Elmira Prison, NY July 17,1864	Died July 15, 1864, in Train Accident at Shohola, Pennsylvania.
13.	Davis, John D. Private	18	March 27, 1862, Cumberland County, North Carolina	Co. J, 51st North Carolina Infantry	June 1, 1864, Cold Harbor, Virginia	Transferred From Point Lookout Prison, MD, July 12, 1864. Train Never Arrived at Elmira Prison Camp, NY.	Died July 15, 1864, in Train Accident at Shohola, Pennsylvania.
14.	Deaver, Nathan H. Private Last Name on Monument Spelled Dever	Unk	April 11, 1862, Cumberland County, North Carolina	Co. I, 51st North Carolina Infantry	June 1, 1864, Cold Harbor, Virginia	Transferred From Point Lookout Prison, MD, July 12, 1864. Train Never Arrived at Elmira Prison Camp, NY.	Died July 15, 1864, in Train Accident at Shohola, Pennsylvania.
15.	Fuller, Byam Private	Unk	March 1, 1862, Franklin County, Georgia	Co. H, 24th Georgia Infantry	June 3, 1864, Gaines Mill, Cold Harbor, Virginia	Transferred From Point Lookout Prison, MD, July 12, 1864. Train Never Arrived at Elmira Prison Camp, NY.	Died July 15, 1864, in Train Accident at Shohola, Pennsylvania.
16.	Gatton, William F. Private	Unk	Unknown	Co. B, 35th Battalion Virginia Cavalry	June 3, 1864, Gaines Mill, Virginia	Transferred From Point Lookout Prison, MD, July 12, 1864. Train Never Arrived at Elmira Prison Camp, NY.	Died July 15, 1864, in Train Accident at Shohola, Pennsylvania.
17.	Green, Henry Private	Unk	September 17, 1862, Clifton, Virginia	Co. A, 9th Virginia Infantry	June 12, 1864, Cold Harbor, Virginia	Transferred From Point Lookout Prison, MD, July 12, 1864. Train Never Arrived at Elmira Prison Camp, NY.	Died July 15, 1864, in Train Accident at Shohola, Pennsylvania.

18.	Ham, William B. Sergeant	20	August 24, 1861, Kingsbury, North Carolina	Co. E, 8th North Carolina Infantry	June 1, 1864, Gaines Mill, Cold Harbor, Virginia	Transferred From Point Lookout Prison, MD, July 12, 1864. Train Never Arrived at Elmira Prison Camp, NY.	Died July 15, 1864, in Train Accident at Shohola, Pennsylvania.
19.	Hardison, James J. Private	Unk	March 1, 1862, Cumberland County, North Carolina	Co. I, 51st North Carolina Infantry	June 1, 1864, Cold Harbor, Virginia	Transferred From Point Lookout Prison, MD, July 12, 1864. Train Never Arrived at Elmira Prison Camp, NY.	Died July 15, 1864, in Train Accident at Shohola, Pennsylvania.
20.	Hatch, J. S. Private	Unk	May 5, 1862, Zebulon, Georgia	Co. H, 53rd Georgia Infantry	June 1, 1864, Gaines Mill, Cold Harbor, Virginia	Transferred From Point Lookout Prison, MD, July 12, 1864. Train Never Arrived at Elmira Prison Camp, NY.	Died July 15, 1864, in Train Accident at Shohola, Pennsylvania.
21.	Haynes, Robert P. Sergeant	Unk	May 1, 1862, White Sulfur Springs, Virginia	Co. H, 26th Battalion Virginia Infantry	June 3, 1864, Gaines Mill, Cold Harbor, Virginia	Transferred From Point Lookout Prison, MD, July 12, 1864. Train Never Arrived at Elmira Prison Camp, NY.	Died July 15, 1864, in Train Accident at Shohola, Pennsylvania.
22.	Jackson, William M. Private	Unk	May 1, 1862, Fayetteville, Georgia	Co. C, 53rd Georgia Infantry	June 1, 1864, Gaines Mill, Cold Harbor, Virginia	Transferred From Point Lookout Prison, MD, July 12, 1864. Train Never Arrived at Elmira Prison Camp, NY.	Died July 15, 1864, in Train Accident at Shohola, Pennsylvania.
23.	Johnson, John D. Private This Man is Missing From the Monument.	24	September 15, 1862, Camp Mangum, Raleigh, North Carolina	Co. B, 31st North Carolina Infantry	June 1, 1864, Cold Harbor, Virginia	Transferred From Point Lookout Prison, MD, July 12, 1864. Train Never Arrived at Elmira Prison Camp, NY.	Died From Wounds July 18, 1864, in Train Accident at Shohola, Pennsylvania.

24.	Jones, William Apcatesby Private	Unk	Unknown	Co. H, 26th Battalion Virginia Infantry Battalion number on Monument is 22nd VA	June 3, 1864, Gaines Farm, Cold Harbor, Virginia	Transferred From Point Lookout Prison, MD, July 12, 1864. Train Never Arrived at Elmira Prison Camp, NY.	Died July 15, 1864, in Train Accident at Shohola, Pennsylvania.
25.	Joyner, Archer Private Name on Monument Spelled Joiner	Unk	March 1, 1862, Suffolk, Virginia	Co. C, 13th Virginia Cavalry	June 1, 1864, Ashland, Cold Harbor, Virginia	Transferred From Point Lookout Prison, MD, July 12, 1864. Train Never Arrived at Elmira Prison Camp, NY.	Died July 15, 1864, in Train Accident at Shohola, Pennsylvania.
26.	Lamkin, T. C. Private Name on Monument Spelled Samkins	Unk	August 4, 1863, Columbia County, Georgia	Co. C, 20th Battalion Georgia Cavalry	June 1, 1864, Gaines Farm, Cold Harbor, Virginia	Transferred From Point Lookout Prison, MD, July 12, 1864. Train Never Arrived at Elmira Prison Camp, NY.	Died July 15, 1864, in Train Accident at Shohola, Pennsylvania. Conflicting Account Also Says Prisoner Was Received at Elmira July 17, 1864. There Is No Release in Solder's Record So It Is Likely He Died In Train Wreck.
27.	Lee, William Private Name on Monument Spelled Lee, S. W.	Unk	February 7, 1863, Sampson County, North Carolina	Co. K, 51st North Carolina Infantry Regiment on Monument is 8th NC	June 1, 1864, Cold Harbor, Virginia	Transferred From Point Lookout Prison, MD, July 12, 1864. Train Never Arrived at Elmira Prison Camp, NY.	Died July 15, 1864, in Train Accident at Shohola, Pennsylvania.
28.	Manning, Wallace Private	34	October 8, 1861, Martin County, North Carolina	Co. F, 31st North Carolina Infantry	June 1, 1864, Gaines Mill, Cold Harbor, Virginia	Transferred From Point Lookout Prison, MD, July 12, 1864. Train Never Arrived at Elmira Prison Camp, NY.	Died July 15, 1864, in Train Accident at Shohola, Pennsylvania.

29.	McCarquedale, Malcolm Private Name on Monument Spelled McCorquadale	Unk	May 23. 1863, Cumberland County, North Carolina	Co. I, 51st North Carolina Infantry	June 1, 1864, Cold Harbor, Virginia	Transferred From Point Lookout Prison, MD, July 12, 1864. Train Never Arrived at Elmira Prison Camp, NY.	Died July 15, 1864, in Train Accident at Shohola, Pennsylvania.
30.	McCurry, T. W. Private Name on Monument Spelled McCurvey	Unk	Unknown	Co. A, 16th Georgia Infantry	June 1, 1864, Gaines Farm Cold Harbor, Virginia	Transferred From Point Lookout Prison, MD, July 12, 1864. Train Never Arrived at Elmira Prison Camp, NY.	Died July 15, 1864, in Train Accident at Shohola, Pennsylvania.
31.	McQuage, Alexander Private Name on Monument Spelled McQuaque	18	February 27, 1863, Hansen County, North Carolina	Co. B, 31st North Carolina Infantry	June 1, 1864, Cold Harbor, Virginia	Transferred From Point Lookout Prison, MD, July 12, 1864. Train Never Arrived at Elmira Prison Camp, NY.	Died July 15, 1864, in Train Accident at Shohola, Pennsylvania.
32.	Mitchell, Joseph Private	Unk	November 24, 1862, Richmond, Virginia	Co. B, 24th Virginia Cavalry Regiment on Monument is 42nd VA	May 4, 1864, Gloucester Point, Virginia	Transferred From Point Lookout Prison, MD, July 12, 1864. Train Never Arrived at Elmira Prison Camp, NY.	Died July 15, 1864, in Train Accident at Shohola, Pennsylvania.
33.	Monroe, Duncan Private Name on Monument Spelled Munroe	38	April 9, 1862, Cumberland County, North Carolina	Co. I, 51st North Carolina Infantry	June 1, 1864, Cold Harbor, Virginia	Transferred From Point Lookout Prison, MD, July 12, 1864. Train Never Arrived at Elmira Prison Camp, NY.	Died July 15, 1864, in Train Accident at Shohola, Pennsylvania.

34.	Nunnery, William Private	Unk	May 3, 1862, Cumberland County, North Carolina	Co. J, 51st North Carolina Infantry	June 1, 1864, Cold Harbor, Virginia	Transferred From Point Lookout Prison, MD, July 12, 1864. Train Never Arrived at Elmira Prison Camp, NY.	Died July 15, 1864, in Train Accident at Shohola, Pennsylvania. Conflicting Account Also Says Prisoner Was Received at Elmira July 17, 1864. There Is No Release in Solder's Record So It Is Likely He Died In Train Wreck.
35.	Parks, Creed J. Private Name on Monument Spelled Parks, J. C.	Unk	May 8, 1861, Kanawha Court House, Virginia	Co. H, 22nd Virginia Infantry	June 3, 1864, Gaines Farm Cold Harbor, Virginia	Transferred From Point Lookout Prison, MD, July 12, 1864. Train Never Arrived at Elmira Prison Camp, NY.	Died July 15, 1864, in Train Accident at Shohola, Pennsylvania.
36.	Patrick, John M. Private Name on Monument Spelled Patrick, J. N.	Unk	July 10, 1862, Kanawha, Virginia	Co. H, 22nd Virginia Infantry Regiment on Monument is 28th VA	June 3, 1864, Gaines Farm, Cold Harbor, Virginia	Transferred From Point Lookout Prison, MD, July 12, 1864. Train Never Arrived at Elmira Prison Camp, NY.	Died July 15, 1864, in Train Accident at Shohola, Pennsylvania.
37.	Perks, John L. Private Name on Monument Spelled Peiks	Unk	June 21, 1861, Port Royal, Virginia	Co. E, 47th Virginia Infantry	May 28, 1864, Central Point Virginia	Transferred From Point Lookout Prison, MD, July 12, 1864. Train Never Arrived at Elmira Prison Camp, NY.	Died July 15, 1864, in Train Accident at Shohola, Pennsylvania.
38.	Pitchford, Robert D. Private	22	August 8, 1862, Camp Beauregard, North Carolina	Co. E, 1st North Carolina Cavalry	June 1, 1864, Near Talapatomy Creek, Cold Harbor, Virginia	Transferred From Point Lookout Prison, MD, July 12, 1864. Train Never Arrived at Elmira Prison Camp, NY.	Died July 15, 1864, in Train Accident at Shohola, Pennsylvania.

39.	Pope, Doctor W. Private	Unk	April 26, 1862, Cumberland County, North Carolina	Co. J, 51st North Carolina Infantry	June 1, 1864, Cold Harbor, Virginia	Transferred From Point Lookout Prison, MD, July 12, 1864. Train Never Arrived at Elmira Prison Camp, NY.	Died July 15, 1864, in Train Accident at Shohola, Pennsylvania.
40.	Reaser, Philip Private	Unk	March 29, 1862, Lewisburg, Virginia	Co. D, 26th Battalion Virginia Infantry	June 3, 1864, Cold Harbor, Virginia	Transferred From Point Lookout Prison, MD, July 12, 1864. Train Never Arrived at Elmira Prison Camp, NY.	Died July 15, 1864, in Train Accident at Shohola, Pennsylvania.
41.	Revill, Henry Private Name on Monument Spelled Rules, J. W.	21	September 6, 1861, Lumberton, North Carolina	Co. E, 31st North Carolina Infantry	June 3, 1864, Gaines Farm Cold Harbor, Virginia	Transferred From Point Lookout Prison, MD, July 12, 1864. Train Never Arrived at Elmira Prison Camp, NY.	Died July 15, 1864, in Train Accident at Shohola, Pennsylvania.
42.	Sandford, James F. Private	20	February 22, 1862, Granville County, North Carolina	Co. A, 44th North Carolina Infantry	June 1, 1864, Shady Grove Church, Cold Harbor, Virginia	Transferred From Point Lookout Prison, MD, July 12, 1864. Train Never Arrived at Elmira Prison Camp, NY.	Died July 15, 1864, in Train Accident at Shohola, Pennsylvania.
43.	Sapp, F. W. Private Name on Monument Spelled Sapt	Unk	March 14, 1864, Raleigh, North Carolina	Co. A, 2nd North Carolina Cavalry 22nd Regiment on Monument	June 1, 1864, Hanover Court House, Cold Harbor, Virginia	Transferred From Point Lookout Prison, MD, July 12, 1864. Train Never Arrived at Elmira Prison Camp, NY.	Died July 15, 1864, in Train Accident at Shohola, Pennsylvania.
44.	Seago, Patrick H. Private	21	September 15, 1862, Camp Mangum, Raleigh, North Carolina	Co. B, 31st North Carolina Infantry	June 1, 1864, Cold Harbor, Virginia	Transferred From Point Lookout Prison, MD, July 12, 1864. Train Never Arrived at Elmira Prison Camp, NY.	Died July 15, 1864, in Train Accident at Shohola, Pennsylvania.

45.	Senter, Caleb O. Private Name on Monument Spelled Center	32	March 25, 1862, Sharon Station, Lincoln County, North Carolina	Co. H, 52nd North Carolina Infantry	June 2, 1864, Near Talapatomoy Creek, Cold Harbor, Virginia	Transferred From Point Lookout Prison, MD, July 12, 1864. Train Never Arrived at Elmira Prison Camp, NY.	Died July 15, 1864, in Train Accident at Shohola, Pennsylvania.
46.	Smalley, G. T. Private Name on Monument Spelled Smatley	Unk	March 16, 1863, Virginia	Co. C, Phillips Legion Georgia Infantry	June 1, 1864, Gaines Farm, Cold Harbor, Virginia	Transferred From Point Lookout Prison, MD, July 12, 1864. Train Never Arrived at Elmira Prison Camp, NY.	Died July 15, 1864, in Train Accident at Shohola, Pennsylvania.
47.	Stoffer, Napoleon B. Private Name on Monument Spelled Stauffer	18	May 25, 1862, Salisbury, North Carolina	Co. D, 42nd North Carolina Infantry	June 2, 1864, Cold Harbor, Virginia	Transferred From Point Lookout Prison, MD, July 12, 1864. Train Never Arrived at Elmira Prison Camp, NY.	Died July 15, 1864, in Train Accident at Shohola, Pennsylvania.
48.	Strickland, Thomas J. Private	30	April 1, 1862, Cumberland County, North Carolina	Co. J, 51st North Carolina Infantry	June 1, 1864, Cold Harbor, Virginia	Transferred From Point Lookout Prison, MD, July 12, 1864. Train Never Arrived at Elmira Prison Camp, NY.	Died July 15, 1864, in Train Accident at Shohola, Pennsylvania.
49.	Tyner, William Private Name Not On Monument	39	March 10, 1862, Lumberton, North Carolina	Co. F, 51st North Carolina Infantry	June 1, 1864, Cold Harbor, Virginia	Transferred From Point Lookout Prison, MD, July 12, 1864. Train Never Arrived at Elmira Prison Camp, NY.	Died July 17, 1864, from Contusion Suffered in Train Accident at Shohola, Pennsylvania.
50.	Vaughan, Henry Private	Unk	June 21, 1861, Port Royal, Virginia	Co. E, 47th Virginia Infantry	June 3, 1864, Old Church, Cold Harbor, Virginia	Transferred From Point Lookout Prison, MD, July 12, 1864. Train Never Arrived at Elmira Prison Camp, NY.	Died July 15, 1864, in Train Accident at Shohola, Pennsylvania.

51.	Watson, Samuel D. Sergeant	20	March 10, 1862, Lumberton, North Carolina	Co. E, 51st North Carolina Infantry	June 1, 1864, Cold Harbor, Virginia	Transferred From Point Lookout Prison, MD, July 12, 1864. Train Never Arrived at Elmira Prison Camp, NY.	Died July 15, 1864, in Train Accident at Shohola, Pennsylvania.
52.	Williams, James H. Private	26	May 6, 1862, Forsyth, Monroe County, Georgia	Co. K, 53rd Georgia Infantry	June 1, 1864, Cold Harbor, Virginia	Transferred From Point Lookout Prison, MD, July 12, 1864. Train Never Arrived at Elmira Prison Camp, NY.	Died July 15, 1864, in Train Accident at Shohola, Pennsylvania.
53.	Ruels, J. W. Private	Unk	Unable to Find Soldier's Regimental Record	Co. E, 31st North Carolina Infantry	June 1, 1864, Gaines Mill, Cold Harbor, Virginia	Transferred from Point Lookout Prison, Maryland, July 12, 1864. Train Never Arrived at Elmira Prison, New York.	Died July 15, 1864, in Train Accident at Shohola, Pennsylvania.
54.	Smatley, G. C. Private	Unk	Unable to Find Soldier's Regimental Record	Co. C, Georgia Legion Infantry	June 1, 1864, Cold Harbor, Virginia	Transferred from Point Lookout Prison, Maryland, July 12, 1864. Train Never Arrived at Elmira Prison Camp, NY	Died July 15, 1864, in Train Accident at Shohola, Pennsylvania.
	Cain, N. Private Name on Monument Not Found in Records.	Unk	Unknown	Pegram's Battery Virginia Light Artillery	Unknown	Unknown	Died July 15, 1864, in Train Accident at Shohola, Pennsylvania.
	Sancford, W. B. Private Name on Monument Not Found in Records.	Unk	Unknown	Co. K, 18th Georgia Cavalry	Unknown	Unknown	Died July 15, 1864, in Train Accident at Shohola, Pennsylvania.

Monthly Number of Prisoners Who Died At Elmira Prison Camp

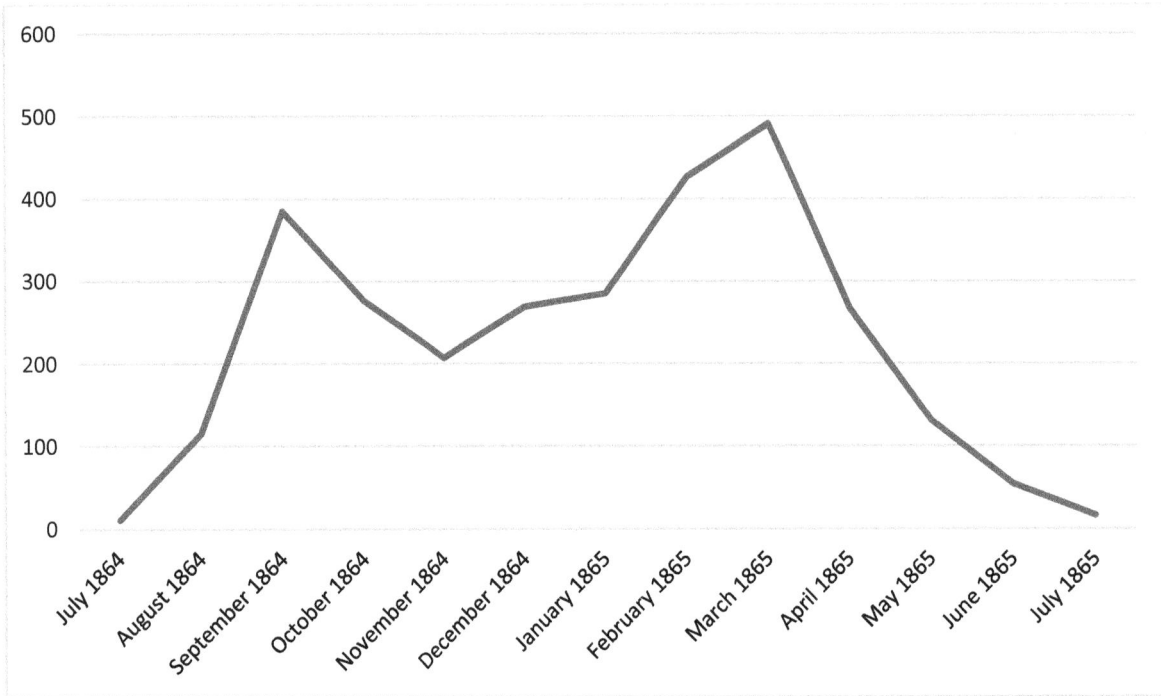

Monthly Deaths of Prisoners Who Were Sick

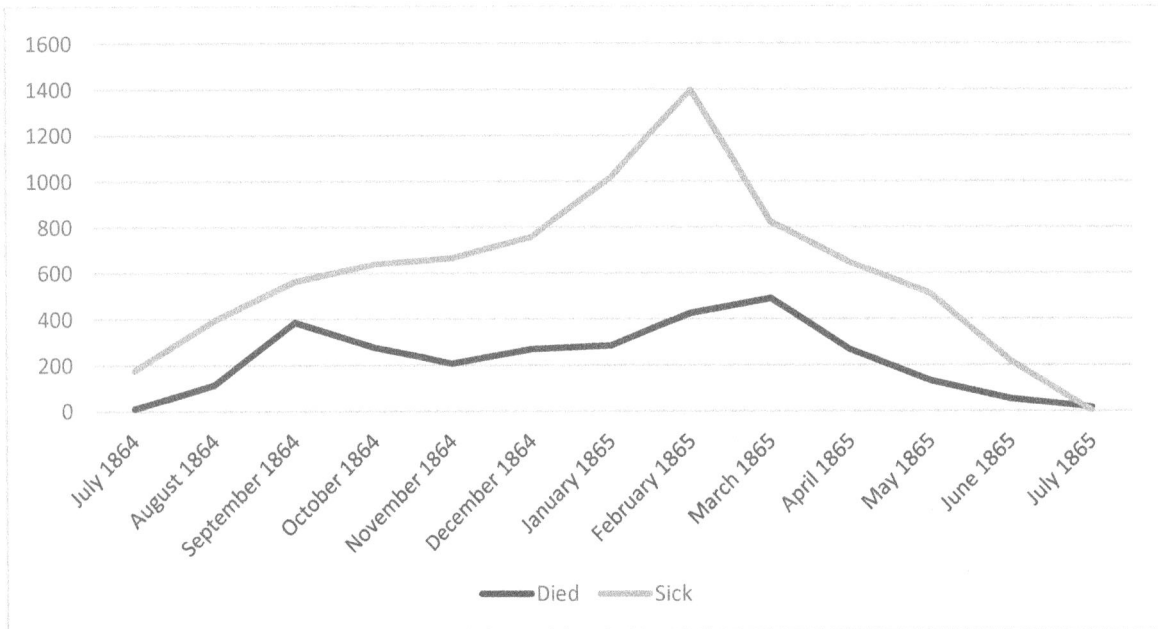

Notes

Elmira Prison Camp Roster, Volume III:

1. *The Medical and Surgical History of the War of the Rebellion, (1861-65), Prepared in Accordance Acts of Congress, Under the Direction of Surgeon General Joseph K. Barnes, United States Army,* Washington Government Printing Office, 1870, Also source from medical history.

2. Addison, Walter D., *Recollections of a Confederate Soldier of the Prison-Pens of Point Lookout, Maryland, and Elmira, New York,* pages 4-5;

3. *The Medical and Surgical History of the War of the Rebellion,* Volume III, page 37; *The Medical and Surgical History of the War of the Rebellion,* Washington: Government Printing Office, 1879; Miller-Keane, *Encyclopedia & Dictionary of Medicine, Nursing, & Allied Heath, Fifth Edition,* Page 420; Miller-Keane, *Encyclopedia & Dictionary of Medicine, Nursing, & Allied Heath, Fifth Edition,* W. B. Saunders Company, Philadelphia, PA, 1992;

4. Handy, Reverend I. W. K., *Southern Historical Society Papers,* Volume 1, April 1876, page 271;

5. King, John A., *My Experience in the Confederate Army and In Northern Prisons,* page 37; Keiley Anthony M., *In Vinculis Or, The Prisoner Of War,* page 86;

6. *The Medical and Surgical History of the War of the Rebellion,* Volume III, page 37; *The Medical and Surgical History of the War of the Rebellion,* Washington: Government Printing Office, 1879; Miller-Keane, *Encyclopedia & Dictionary of Medicine, Nursing, & Allied Heath, Fifth Edition,* Page 457; Miller-Keane, *Encyclopedia & Dictionary of Medicine, Nursing, & Allied Heath, Fifth Edition,* W. B. Saunders Company, Philadelphia, PA, 1992;

7. Miller-Keane, *Encyclopedia & Dictionary of Medicine, Nursing, & Allied Heath, Fifth Edition,* Pages 551-553; Miller-Keane, *Encyclopedia & Dictionary of Medicine, Nursing, & Allied Heath, Fifth Edition,* W. B. Saunders Company, Philadelphia, PA, 1992;

8. Miller-Keane, *Encyclopedia & Dictionary of Medicine, Nursing, & Allied Heath, Fifth Edition,* Page 890; Miller-Keane, *Encyclopedia & Dictionary of Medicine, Nursing, & Allied Heath, Fifth Edition,* W. B. Saunders Company, Philadelphia, PA, 1992; *The Medical and Surgical History of the War of the Rebellion,* Washington: Government Printing Office, 1879;

9. *The Medical and Surgical History of the War of the Rebellion,* Volume VI, pages 751-752; *The Medical and Surgical History of the War of the Rebellion,* Washington: Government Printing Office, 1879; Miller-Keane, *Encyclopedia & Dictionary of Medicine, Nursing, & Allied Heath, Fifth Edition,* Page 1,344; Miller-Keane, *Encyclopedia & Dictionary of Medicine, Nursing, & Allied Heath, Fifth Edition,* W. B. Saunders Company, Philadelphia, PA, 1992;

10. *The Medical and Surgical History of the War of the Rebellion,* Volume VI, page 553; *The Medical and Surgical History of the War of the Rebellion,* Washington: Government Printing Office, 1879; Miller-Keane, *Encyclopedia & Dictionary of Medicine, Nursing, & Allied Heath, Fifth Edition,* Page 1,344; Miller-Keane, *Encyclopedia & Dictionary of Medicine, Nursing, & Allied Heath, Fifth Edition,* W. B. Saunders Company, Philadelphia, PA, 1992;

11. Miller-Keane, *Encyclopedia & Dictionary of Medicine, Nursing, & Allied Heath, Fifth Edition,* Page 1,344; Miller-Keane, *Encyclopedia & Dictionary of Medicine, Nursing, & Allied Heath, Fifth Edition,* W. B. Saunders Company, Philadelphia, PA, 1992;

12. Hopkins, Luther, *Prison life at Point Lookout,* page 88;

13. Bowden, the Reverend Malachi, *My Life as a Yankee Captive,* page 97;

14. Rose, Minnie Bowen, Editorial Director, *Diseases, Nursing Reference Library,* page 391; Rose, Minnie Bowen, Editorial Director, *Diseases, Nursing Reference Library,* pages 669-670;

15. Miller-Keane, *Encyclopedia & Dictionary of Medicine, Nursing, & Allied Heath, Fifth Edition,* Page 1,545, W. B. Saunders Company, Philadelphia, PA, 1992;

16. *The Medical and Surgical History of the War of the Rebellion, (1861-65), Prepared in Accordance Acts of Congress, Under the Direction of Surgeon General Joseph K. Barnes, United States Army,* Washington Government Printing Office, 1870.

Bibliography

Articles and Periodicals:

Bowden, the Reverend Malachi, *My Life as a Yankee Captive.* Published in the Atlanta Journal and Constitution Magazine.

Byrne, Thomas E., *"Elmira's Civil War Prison Camp: 1864-1865," Chemung Historical Journal, volume 10, No. 1, (September1964)*: page 1287,

Davis, Thaddeus C., *Confederate Veteran* Magazine, February 1899, page 65;

Ewan, R.B., *Reminiscences of Prison Life at Elmira, N.Y.,* January 1908;

Huffman, James, *Prisoner of War, Atlantic Magazine* 163, no. 4, April 1939;

Jones, James P., *A Rebel's Diary of Elmira Prison Camp, Chemung Historical Journal* 20, no. 3, March 1975;

Sherrill, Miles, *A Soldier's Story: Prison Life and Other Incidents,* University of North Carolina at Chapel Hill, 1998;

Stamp, James B., *Ten Months Experience in Northern Prisons, Alabama Historical Quarterly 18,* pages 486-498;

Taylor, G.T., *Prison Experience in Elmira, N.Y., Confederate Veteran* Magazine 20, no. 7, July 1912;

The Treatment of Prisoners during the War Between the States, Southern Historical Society Papers 1, no. 3, March 1876;

The Treatment of Prisoners during the War, Southern Historical Society Papers 1, no. 4, April 1876;

Turner, Henry M. *Civil War Times Illustrated,* 31 (October/November, 1980);

Wade, F.S., *Getting Out of Prison, Confederate Veteran* magazine 34, no. 10, October 1926;

Ward, John Shirley, *Responsibility for the Death of Prisoners, Confederate Veteran* magazine 4, no. 1, January 1896;

Wyeth, John Allan, *Cold Cheer at Camp Morton, Century Magazine* 41 no. 6 (April 1891) 848;

Books:

Benson, Berry, Susan W. Benson, ed., *Berry Benson's Civil War Book: Memoirs of a Confederate Scout and Sharpshooter,* Athens, Ga.: University of Georgia Press, 1962;

Diagnostic and Statistical Manual of Mental Disorders, 5th Edition, *Arlington: American Psychiatric Publishing, pages 160–168,* American Psychiatric Publishing, May 27, 2013;

Gray, Michael P., *The Business of Captivity: Elmira and It's Civil War Prison,* The Kent State University Press, 2001;

Hampson, Helen (Wyeth), My Great-Great Grandfather Was a Prisoner of War . . . Libby Prison, 2002;

Heartsill, W. W., *Fourteen Hundred and 91 Days in the Confederate Army,* Edited by Bell Irvin Wiley, Broadfoot Publishing Co., Wilmington North Carolina, 1987.

Holmes, Clay W., *The Elmira Prison Camp: A History of the Military Prison at Elmira, N.Y. July 6, 1864, to July 10, 1865.* New York: Knickerbocker Press, 1912;

Hopkins, Luther, *Prison life at Point Lookout.*

Horigan, Michael, *Elmira: Death Camp of the North,* Stackpole Books, 2002;

Huffman, James, *Ups and Downs of a Confederate Soldier,* New York: William E. Rudge's Sons, 1940;

Keiley, Anthony M., *In Vinculis; or, The Prisoner of War: Being The Experience Of A Rebel In Two Federal Pens,* Blelock & Co., No. 19 Beekman Street, New York, 1866;

King, John A., *My Experience in the Confederate Army, and in Northern Prisons,* Roanoke, West Virginia, Stonewall Jackson Chapter No. 1333, United Daughters of the Confederacy, Clarksburg, West Virginia, 1917;

Leon, Louis, *Diary of a Tarheel Confederate Prisoner,* Charlotte, N.C.: Stone, 1913;

Malone,Whatley Pierson Jr., *The Diary of Bartlett Yancy Malone,* Published by the University of Chapel Hill, 1919.

Manarin, Louis H. and Weymouth T. Jordan, eds., *North Carolina Troops1861-1865: A Roster,* 13 volumes, Raleigh, North Carolina: Division of Archives and History, 1966-1993;

Miller-Keane, *Encyclopedia & Dictionary of Medicine, Nursing, & Allied Heath, Fifth Edition,* W. B. Saunders Company, Philadelphia.

Opie, John N., *A Rebel Cavalryman with Lee, Stuart, and Jackson,* Morningside Press, Chicago: W.B. Conkey, 1899.

Ottman, Walter H., *A History of the City of Elmira, New York;*

Pickenpaugh, Roger, *Captives In Gray,* The University of Alabama Press, 2009;

Speer, Lonnie R., *Portals To Hell: Military Prisons of the Civil War,* Stackpole Books, 1997;

Speer, Lonnie R., *War of Vengeance: Acts of Retaliation against Civil War POWs,* Stackpole Books, 2002;

Toney, Marcus B., *The Privations of a Private,* Nashville and Dallas: M.E. Church, South, Smith and Lamar, 1907;

Towner, Ausburn, *Our County and Its People - A History of the Valley and County of Chemung From the Closing years of the Eighteenth Century,* D. Mason & Publishers, 1892;

Watkins, Sam R., *Co. Aytch, Maury Grays, First Tennessee Regiment or, A Side Show to the Big Show,* Chattanooga, Tennessee, Times Printing Company, 1900;

Wilkeson, Frank, *Turned Inside Out: Recollections of a Private Soldier in the Army of the Potomac,* New York and London: G.P. Putnam's Sons, 1887;

Williamson, James J., *Prison Life in the Old Capital and Reminiscences of the Civil War,* West Orange, New Jersey, 1911.

Manuscripts:

Greer, William R. Papers, *Recollections of a Private Soldier of the Army of the Confederate States,* Manuscript Department, William R. Perkins Library, Duke University, North Carolina

Papers:

Sanger, Eugene F., *Eugene F. Sanger Papers, Records of the Office of the Adjutant General, Regimental Correspondence, 1861-1865,* Maine State Archives. College of William and Mary, William Lamb Collection;

Official Publications:

Confederate States of America, Congress, *Joint Select Committee to Investigate the Condition and Treatment of Prisoners of War,* March, 1865;

The Medical and Surgical History of the War of the Rebellion, (1861-65), Prepared in Accordance Acts of Congress, Under the Direction of Surgeon General Joseph K. Barnes, United States Army, Washington Government Printing Office, 1870, Volumes I, III, VI.

North Carolina Troops 1861-1865, 22 Volumes, Broadfoot Publishing, edited by Louis H. Marin, and Numerous authors.

War of the Rebellion Official Records of the Union and Confederate Armies, Series II, Volumes IV, VII, XXVI. Washington, D.C., Government Printing Office, 1870.

Confederate States of America, Congress, *Joint Select Committee to Investigate the Condition and Treatment of Prisoners of War,* March, 1865;

Newspapers:

Daily National Intelligencer, Washington, D. C.,
Elmira Daily Advertiser,
Elmira Daily Gazette,
New York Times,
New York Tribune,

Index

A

Addison, Walter D.
 remembers the cruel vaccinations the prisoners had to endure, 465

B

blankets, 468
Bowden, Malachi
 Yankee's supplied vinegar with meals to fight scurvy, 468

C

chronic diarrhea
 describes disease, 465
Confederate prisoner I. W. K. Handy
 recalls chronic diarrhea, 465
Confederate prisoner Luther Hopkins
 recalls vinegar added to diet, 468
Confederate prisoner Malachi Bowden
 recalls vinegar added to diet, 468

D

diarrhea, 465
 disease described, 465
diet
 how it affected prison's health, 467
diseases common to Point Lookout, 465
dysentery
 disease described, 466

E

erysipelas
 disease described, 466

F

Fort Fisher, 5

G

Greenlee, John P.
 photograph of Greenlee, 467

H

Handy, I. W. K.
 describes the prisoner with diarrhea, 465

Hoffman, Union Colonel William
 insisted on complete contol, 467
 responsibility for scurvy, 467
Hopkins, Luther
 recalls using vinegar to fight scurvy, 468

K

Keiley, Anthony M.
 recalls how everyone became sick with diarrhea, 466

L

lice, 475, 479

P

poor diet
 how it affected prison's health, 467

S

Sanger, Major Eugene F., 511
scurvy
 disease described, 467
 symptoms, 467
Scurvy
 photograph of scurvy victim, 465, 467
Sisters of Charity
 photograph of Sister, 465
smallpox
 disease described, 468
smallpox tent, 468
stress
 how it affected the prisoner's health, 467
suffering at Point Lookout, 466, 467

T

tent
 smallpox, 468
typhoid fever
 disease described, 468
 symptoms, 468

V

vaccination, 465
vaccinations, 465
vinegar
 used to combat scurvy, 468

W

Walter D. Addison
recalls vaccinations, 465

worry
how it affected prison's health, 467

www.ingramcontent.com/pod-product-compliance
Lightning Source LLC
Chambersburg PA
CBHW062019090426
42811CB00005B/899